Russia, the USSR, and Eastern Europe

Russia, the USSR, and Eastern Europe

A Bibliographic Guide to
English Language Publications,
1964-1974

Compiled by
Stephan M. Horak

Edited by
Rosemary Neiswender

1978

Libraries Unlimited, Inc.
Littleton, Colorado

LIBRARIES UNLIMITED, INC.
P.O. Box 263
Littleton, Colorado 80160

––––––––––––––––––––––––––––––

Library of Congress Cataloging in Publication Data

Horak, Stephan M   1920-
    Russia, the USSR, and Eastern Europe.

    Includes index.
    1. Europe, Eastern--Bibliography.
I. Neiswender, Rosemary. II. Title.
Z2483.H54   [DJK9]   016.947   77-20696
ISBN 0-87287-178-9

TABLE OF CONTENTS

PART I
GENERAL AND INTERRELATED THEMES

PART II
RUSSIAN EMPIRE PRIOR TO 1917 AND USSR;
NON-RUSSIAN REPUBLICS; JEWS

PART III
EASTERN EUROPE
(INCLUDING THE GDR AND THE BALKAN PENINSULA)

Chapter 11—Individual Countries (cont'd)

Chapter 11—Individual Countries (cont'd)

To

Christine,

Julie and Arkady

INTRODUCTION

Although guides to the increasing volume of studies in English relating to the Soviet Union and Eastern Europe are available through a number of excellent indexes and bibliographies, no comprehensive survey has appeared since Paul Horecky's *Russia and the Soviet Union: A Bibliographic Guide to Western Publications* (1965) and his companion volumes to *East Central Europe* (1969) and *Southeastern Europe* (1969). The present compilation is designed to update selective bibliographic coverage of these areas in the social sciences and humanities by bringing together an annotated listing of significant titles published from 1964 to 1974. Although initially intended as a revision of the compiler's *Junior Slavica*, a bibliography of basic English-language publications in the social sciences (Libraries Unlimited, 1968), coverage has been broadened to include titles in literature, linguistics, and the fine arts. Entries are accompanied by critical annotations, excerpted (and in some cases adapted) from reviews published in major U.S. and British Slavic journals. In instances where no published reviews were found, annotations have been supplied by the compiler. Full bibliographic citations are given for quoted reviews; a list of journal abbreviations precedes the text.

The bibliography comprises three major divisions: Part I covers general works on the USSR, Eastern Europe, and communism; Part II deals with more specific topics concerning Russia to 1917, the Soviet Union, the non-Russian Soviet republics, and Jews in the USSR; and Part III covers Eastern Europe, including the Balkans. East Germany, Hungary, Rumania, and Albania, though non-Slavic, are included for geographic and political reasons, but the historical Byzantine Empire and Greece are excluded, save for a few titles of importance. Only monographic publications are listed, since journal articles and dissertations are well documented in standard indexes.

The index includes authors, compilers, editors, and translators. Numbering refers to entries, not pages. To preserve uniformity, the Library of Congress transliteration system has been used throughout, except where variant forms are more commonly employed.

Because of its concentration on basic titles, augmented by authoritative critical reviews, the present work should serve as a useful tool for a wide audience, including students, researchers, librarians, and the general reader with interests in the Slavic area.

The completion of this updated bibliography has been dependent on several outside factors which deserve my grateful acknowledgment. Above all, I am deeply indebted to the editor of the *Slavic Review*, Professor James R. Millar, for his consent to quote from reviews published in that journal. More than half the annotations were taken from the *Slavic Review*, assuring a high standard not only in the selection of titles but in the quality of the reviews. I am no less indebted to the editors of the *Canadian Slavonic Papers, Russian Review, East European Quarterly, Slavic and East European Journal*, and *Slavonic and East European Review*, in whose respective pages about one-third of the annotations originated. Less frequently consulted journals and my own contributions have supplied the remaining entries.

My gratitude is also extended to the Faculty Research Council of Eastern Illinois University for their contribution of financial aid to cover part of the technical expenses incurred during the preparation of the manuscript. Libraries Unlimited, Inc., and particularly its president, Dr. Bohdan S. Wynar, deserve my special thanks for most valuable advice. Furthermore, my appreciation goes to the University of Illinois Library and its staff, and to Professor Ralph T. Fisher, Jr., Director of the University's Russian and East European Center, whose initiative has produced one of the largest collections of Slavica in this country, thus assisting me in carrying out this endeavor. Finally, to my wife Mary Luise, who put the raw material into a readable manuscript, should go a share of my gratitude. Indeed, this work testifies to the fact that the final product is the sum of many contributions fused by the author.

Stephan M. Horak
January 1976

ABBREVIATIONS OF
PERIODICALS CONSULTED

AHR	*The American Historical Review*
CASS	*Canadian-American Slavic Studies*
CSP	*Canadian Slavonic Papers*
ECE	*East Central Europe*
EEQ	*East European Quarterly*
HSN	*Hungarian Studies Newsletter*
History, RNB	*History: Reviews of New Books*
JBS	*Journal of Baltic Studies*
JMH	*The Journal of Modern History*
Lit.	*Lituanus: The Lithuanian Quarterly*
NP	*Nationalities Papers*
PR	*The Polish Review*
RR	*The Russian Review*
SEEJ	*The Slavic and East European Journal*
SEER	*The Slavonic and East European Review*
SJA	*Soviet Jewish Affairs*
SR	*Slavic Review*
SS	*Soviet Studies*
UQ	*The Ukrainian Quarterly*
R	Reviewer

PART I

GENERAL AND INTERRELATED THEMES

Chapter 1

General Reference Works

1. **The American Bibliography of Slavic and East European Studies**
   (1957–). Published by Indiana University in "Slavic and East European
   Series" (1957-1966); since 1967 under the sponsorship of The American
   Association for the Advancement of Slavic Studies. Columbus, Ohio.
   This bibliography seeks to present (on an annual basis) as complete a record as
   possible of North American publications in Slavic and East European studies,
   according to the present editor, David H. Kraus. It includes works, primarily in
   English but also in other languages, which are of research or information value
   and which were published in North America or, if published elsewhere, were
   written, edited or compiled by North Americans. The average number of entries
   per issue is five thousand. The following categories are represented: books, book
   reviews, portions of books, journal articles, review articles, and dissertations.
   An author index and a bibliographical index are provided. A basic tool for anyone
   involved in East European studies.   S. M. H.

2. Birkos, Alexander, and Lewis A. Tambs, eds. **Academic Writer's Guide
   to Periodicals.** Kent, Ohio, Kent State University Press 1973. 572p.
   (East European and Slavic Studies). $10.00cl.; $7.50pa.
   This is the second volume of a projected seven-volume series which, according
   to the publisher, is designed "to provide the academic writer with a guide . . . to
   the subject interests and editorial policies of the hundreds of journals extant in
   the humanities and social sciences." For each journal the following information
   is provided: editors' names, address of the editorial office, sponsors of the
   journal, frequency of publication, when founded, subscription rates, editorial
   interest, preferred manuscript length, author remuneration, languages of sub-
   mission, book review information, and where the journal is abstracted. This is
   a must reference for all academic libraries and scholars in the field.
   CSP, 15:4:617   R: J. W. S.

3. Birkos, Alexander S., and Lewis A. Tambs, eds. **East European and
   Soviet Economic Affairs: A Bibliography** (1965-1973). Littleton, Colo.,
   Libraries Unlimited, 1975. 170p. $10.00.
   A collection of English-language books and articles dealing with the economic
   affairs of Eastern Europe and the USSR. The compilers present a broad, compre-
   hensive bibliography of material available in most medium-sized and large libraries.
   The entries (1168 in all) are arranged geographically and subdivided by subjects.
   A list of publishing outlets for scholarly papers, and author, title, publisher, and
   periodical indexes are appended.   S. M. H.

4. Harvard University, Widener Library. **Slavic History and Literature.**
   4 vols. Catalogue of Slavic materials collection. Cambridge, Harvard
   University Press, 1970. 850p., 780p., 535p. 500p. (Widener Library
   Shelflist Series, no. 28-31). $190.00/set.

The Widener Library collection of Slavica is one of the largest in the world.
This bibliography of shelflist cards is particularly valuable to scholars in search
of material available in the United States.

5.   Horecky, Paul L., ed. **East Central Europe: A Guide to Basic Publications.**
        Chicago, University of Chicago Press, 1970. 956p. $27.50.

6.   Horecky, Paul L., ed. **Southeastern Europe: A Guide to Basic Publications.**
        Chicago, University of Chicago Press, 1970. 755p. $25.00.

The two weighty tomes will long be considered the most authoritative guides
to "basic" publications in all European languages. The first, *East Central Europe*,
covers Czechoslovakia, East Germany, Hungary, Poland and the Sorbians
(Lusatians) and Polabians. About sixty specialists contributed approximately
thirty-five hundred entries in European languages. The second, *Southeastern
Europe*, covers Albania, Bulgaria, Greece, Rumania, and Yugoslavia. More than
fifty experts submitted sections containing about 3,000 entries. A considerable
number of the contributors are natives of the regions about which they write.
        SR, 30:3:457-60   R: Sherman D. Spector

7.   Kanet, Roger E., comp. **Soviet and East European Foreign Policy:**
        A Bibliography of English- and Russian-Language Publication, 1967-1971.
        Santa Barbara, ABC-Clio Press, 1974. 208p. $15.75.

Approximately 3,200 items are listed, including journal articles as well as books.
This increases the value of the bibliography enormously. The entries are arranged
not by subject but in alphabetical order according to author, or by title if
author's name is not given. This means that the publications on any given subject
are scattered throughout the volume instead of being conveniently grouped in
one place. To make up for this, there is a long, detailed index, with many headings
and sub-headings.
        RR, 34:3:338-40   R: Thomas T. Hammond

8.   Kerner, Robert Joseph. **Slavic Europe: A Selected Bibliography in the**
        Western European Languages Comprising History, Languages and
        Literature. New York, Russell & Russell, 1969. (Repr. of 1918 ed.).
        402p. $11.50.

Originally published as volume 1 of the "Harvard Bibliographies, Library Series,"
this bibliography still retains its value, with 4,500 entries covering Russia and
all other Slav peoples. Chapters on each nationality are divided by subjects,
emphasizing historical and cultural topics. This bibliography complements the
three bibliographies by Paul Horecky and should therefore be available in
academic libraries.   S. M. H.

9.   Kolarz, Walter, ed. **Books on Communism: A Bibliography.** 2nd ed.
        New York, Oxford University Press, 1964. 568p. $4.80.

This book is the second edition, updated and enlarged, of a bibliography which
was published in 1959 under the same title and edited by the late R. N. Carew
Hunt. The first edition covered the years 1945-57, the present volume the years
1945-62. The new edition lists about 2,500 items. The contents of this useful
bibliography are divided into 52 "subject and country sections," of which the

first five deal with Communism and the world Communist movement, the next twenty with the Soviet Union, the next twenty-five with Communism and related questions in other countries, and the last two with official publications on Communism and relations with the Soviet Union and the Communist bloc which have appeared in the United Kingdom, the British Commonwealth, and the United States. It is a valuable addition to the scarce research tools available to scholars, students, and the broad public interested in the Soviet Union, the Communist bloc, and Communism in general.

SR, 24:2:363-4   R: Witold S. Sworakowski

10. Lazitch, Branko, and M. M. Drachkovitch. **Biographical Dictionary of the Comintern.** Stanford, Hoover Institution Press, 1973. 458p. $15.00.
This dictionary includes 718 biographical sketches in addition to the identification of 359 pseudonyms used by Communists. Each biographical sketch offers, as far as possible, basic data and a political biography of the person's career both within his party and in the broader arena of the Comintern. Forty-seven Communist parties are presented.

SR, 33:3:551-52   R: Kermit E. McKenzie

11. Lewanski, Richard C., comp. **A Bibliography of Slavic Dictionaries.** 4 vols. 2d rev. and enl. ed. Bologna, Johns Hopkins University, Editrice Compositori, Instituto Informatico Italiano, 1972-73. Vol. 1: *Polish.* 197p. Vol. 2: *Belorussian, Bulgarian, Czech, Kashubian, Lusatian, Old Church Slavic, Macedonian, Polabian, Serbocroatian, Slovak, Slovenian, Ukrainian.* 352p. Vol. 3: *Russian.* 396p. Vol. 4: *Supplement.* 409p. (Bologna Center Library Publications).
These four volumes, though awkward to use, are a valuable reference and research tool. Lewanski has made a solid contribution in making accessible to us bibliographical information on the rather impressive lexical resources of the Slavic field.

SR, 34:2:427-8   R: Thomas F. Magner

12. Lewanski, Richard C., ed. **The Literatures of the World in English Translation: A Bibliography. Vol. II: The Slavic Literatures.** New York, The New York Public Library and Frederic Ungar, 1967. 630p. $18.50.
This is the first comprehensive bibliography of English translations from Slavic literatures (in the sense of belles-lettres). It lists translations published up to 1960 from Belorussian, Bulgarian, Croatian, Czech, Kashubian, Lusatian, Macedonian, Polish, Russian, Serbian, Slovak, Slovenian, and Ukrainian. Anthologies, works by individual authors, and anonymous works are enumerated separately. Authors and titles are indexed.

SR, 27:4:690-1   R: Vasa D. Mihailovich

13. Meyer, Klaus. **Bibliographie der Arbeiten zur osteuropäischen Geschichte aus den deutschprachigen Fachzeitschriften 1858-1964.** Berlin, Otto Harrassowitz, 1966. 314p. DM8pa. (Bibliographische Mitteilungen des Osteuropa-Instituts an der Freien Universität Berlin. Vol. IX).

This bibliography attempts to make available the contents of German-language periodicals for the past century in the fields of East European history. It is a selective bibliography, which uses a chronological subject arrangement of more than four thousand articles from 55 periodicals and yearbooks.

SR, 26:4:701-2   R: Evelyn G. Lauer

14.   Meyer, Klaus, et al., comps. **Bibliographie zur osteuropäischen Geschichte: Verzeichnis der zwischen 1939 und 1964 veröffentlichten Literatur in westeuropäischen Sprachen zur osteuropäischen Geschichte bis 1945.** Edited by Werner Philipp. Berlin, Otto Harrassowitz, 1972. 649p. (Bibliographische Mitteilungen des Osteuropa-Instituts an der Freien Universität Berlin, Vol. X). DM65pa.

Essentially, this publication represents a very full and probably close-to-exhaustive inventory of 12,000 entries of books, *Festschriften*, and articles, which appeared in the principal languages of Western Europe between 1939 and 1964, on the history of Eastern Europe up to the end of the Second World War. The bibliography concentrates on the Soviet Union/Tsarist Russia and Poland, both from the beginning of independent statehood and within their changing and fluctuating borders and ethnic compositions. There are six main chapters: Eastern Europe (as a whole), Russia and the Soviet Union, Finland and the Baltic countries, the Ukraine and Belorussia, Asiatic Russia, and Poland.

SR, 33:2:408-9   R: Paul L. Horecky

15.   Peschl, Otto, comp. **Katalog der Bestände auf dem Gebiet der slawischen Philologie einschliesslich der Belletristik: Universitätsbibliothek Wien.** (Catalog of Holdings in Slavonic Philology Including Belles-Lettres: University Library of Vienna). Boston, G. K. Hall, 1973. 456p. $65.00.

The 30,000 entries comprise the collection of the Vienna University Library holdings on the literature of the Slavic peoples of Austro-Hungary. This rich mine of sources from the nineteenth century is particularly valuable because much of it is not available elsewhere in Western libraries. The bibliography, organized by nationalities, is based on public catalog arrangements of author and title entries.   S. M. H.

16.   Schöpflin, George, ed. **The Soviet Union and Eastern Europe: A Handbook.** New York, Praeger, 1970. 614p. $25.00.

In this reference, a sort of a minor encyclopedia, a team of contributors examine the political and economic systems of the Eastern European countries within the Soviet enclosure, the structure of their societies, and their cultural life. A brief introduction provides the historical background essential to an accurate understanding of the Soviet Union and Eastern Europe; it is followed by basic country-by-country information on the governments, economies, communications, and social structure of the Communist-ruled states in Central-Eastern-Balkan Europe. The rest of the book is devoted to an analysis of politics, military and strategic affairs, planning and economic policy, trade, social affairs, education, law, religion, and culture.

EEQ, 5:4:566-7   R: Joseph S. Roucek

17.　Seeman, Klaus-Dieter, and Frank Siegman. **Bibliographie der slavistischen Arbeiten aus den deutschsprachigen Fachzeitschriften 1786-1963**. Berlin, Otto Harrassowitz, 1965. 422p. (Bibliographische Mitteilungen des Osteuropa-Instituts an der Freien Universität Berlin, Vol. VIII). DM8.80pa.

The volume is a subject index to the complete contents, except for reviews, of only five Slavic journals: *Archiv für slavische Philologie, Zeitschrift für slavische Philologie, Wiener slavistisches Jahrbuch, Die Welt der Slaven*, and *Zeitschrift für Slavistik*. In addition, selected articles from twenty-six other periodicals are cited. Both items have author indexes.

　　　　SR, 26:4:701-2　　　　　R: Evelyn G. Lauer

18.　Shaffer, Harry G. **English-Language Periodical Publications on Communism: An Annotated Index**. New York, Research Institute on Communist Affairs, Columbia University, 1971. 53p. Mimeographed edition. $1.50.

The index covers periodicals which focus on Communism, on Communist countries, and on research in the social sciences and the humanities carried out in the Communist countries. There are 392 titles with brief information on the scope, address, and price of the periodicals.　　S. M. H.

19.　Stankiewicz, Edward, and Dean S. Worth. **A Selected Bibliography of Slavic Linguistics. Vol. II**. The Hague, Mouton, 1970. 530p. 108Dglds.

This work is the second volume of a two-volume bibliography of Slavic linguistics. In their format and scope, the two volumes are designed as the most ambitious and comprehensive work of its kind in the field of bibliographical research in Slavic linguistics, and the authors' goal is to serve teachers and graduate students alike. Volume I of the *Bibliography* appeared in 1966 [see review by G. Y. Shevelov in *SEEJ*, 11 (1967):399-45], and consists of sections on Slavic cultural pre-history, Balto-Salvic, Slavic accentology, common Slavic, comparative Slavic, Old Church Slavic, and South Slavic. Volume II treats West Slavic and East Slavic; it also contains a special section, "Bibliography of Bibliographies and History of Research." Within each of the two language groups, there is a breakdown into general studies and specific languages. Both volumes contain separate sections on abbreviations of sources and separate author indexes.

　　　　CSP, 14:3:564-7　　　　　R: G. Schaarschmidt

Chapter 2

Economics

20. Adams, Arthur E., and Jan S. Adams. **Men Versus Systems: Agriculture in the USSR, Poland, and Czechoslovakia.** New York, The Free Press; London, Collier-Macmillan, 1971. 327p. $12.50.
This book is a result of the authors' visit to the USSR, Poland, and Czechoslovakia during the summer of 1967. Most of it is made up of descriptions of all types of farms in those countries. The authors are perceptive observers, and the great variety of farms described give a real insight into collectivized agriculture. The chapters on Poland and Czechoslovakia are illuminating. The two countries present a paradox—Poland overwhelmingly devoted to private agriculture, Czechoslovakia the exact opposite.
        SR, 31:2:463-4   R: Martin McCauley

21. Brown, Alan A., and Egon Neuberger, eds. and intro. **International Trade and Central Planning: An Analysis of Economic Interactions.** Berkeley, University of California Press, 1968. 455p. $13.50.
This volume has undertaken to investigate its subject matter within a broad framework of analysis that encompasses all the major centrally planned economies—the Soviet Union, Eastern Europe, and China. It also examines the foreign trade activities of these countries from the standpoint of their interaction with the imperative of domestic economic planning. The three major papers dealing with the foreign trade of the Soviet Union are particularly rich in content. Also included are useful appendixes, a selected bibliography, and a subject index.
        SR, 28:4:662-3   R: Leon M. Herman

22. Dean, Robert W. **West German Trade with the East: The Political Dimension.** New York, Praeger, 1974. 269p. $17.50.
This is an essentially descriptive, straightforward account of Bonn's Eastern trade policy from 1954 to 1973. The first chapter discusses the general political and economic setting and presents a brief history of the evolution of Bonn's Eastern policy. The main part of the work constitutes a systematic coverage of the politics of trade with the GDR, the Soviet Union, and the other East European states, primarily Poland, Czechoslovakia, and Rumania. The fifth and concluding chapter deals with the political role of trade in an era of detente. It must be considered a valuable addition to the studies of East-West trade: there is nothing comparable available in English at this time. An appendix with six tables of pertinent trade statistics and an index further enhance the study's utility.
        EEQ, 9:1:119-20   R: Manfred Grote

23. Grzybowski, Kazimierz, ed. **East-West Trade**. Dobbs Ferry, N.Y., Oceana Publications; Leiden, A. W. Sijthoff, 1974. 307p. (Orig. publ. in *Law and Contemporary Problems*, vol. 37, 1972, by Duke University School of Law). $16.50.

Includes papers delivered at a symposium held at the Duke University School of Law. Papers examine specific topics (e.g., the 1972 US–USSR Trade Agreement), provide an overall look at trading relations between individual countries, and examine various legal and trading practices of individual countries.

S. M. H.

24. Ingram, David. **The Communist Economic Challenge**. New York, Praeger, 1965. 168p.

As a calm and well-written study, touching selectively on the main weaknesses and strengths of Communist economies, this book should prove useful for a wide audience of nonspecialists. Communist economic trends since 1963 have certainly not made the book obsolete: they have in fact strengthened the author's judgments.

SR, 25:4:708-9   R: Holland Hunter

25. Karcz, Jerzy F., ed. **Soviet and East European Agriculture**. Berkeley, University of California Press, 1967. 445p. (Russian and East European Studies). $10.00.

This volume consists of fourteen papers presented at the Conference on Soviet Agricultural and Peasant Affairs held in Santa Barbara in August 1965. Eleven of them deal with Soviet agriculture, mostly during the Khrushchev era, and one each with Yugoslavian, Czechoslovakian, and Polish agriculture. The papers are well written and readily accessible to any student of the subject.

SR, 27:4:674-5   R: Evsey D. Domar

26. Marczewski, Jan. **Crisis in Socialist Planning: Eastern Europe and the USSR**. Trans. from the French by Noël Lindsay. New York, Praeger, 1974. 247p. $18.50.

The main contribution of this book, which does not shirk from bold questions or conclusions, is its up-to-date discussion of *de jure* institutional change in East European socialism. A further contribution is the discussion of material not readily available in Western languages. The book is well-written and admirably compact.

CSP, 17:2-3:538-9   R: John P. Farrell

27. Mellor, Roy E. H. **Comecon: Challenge to the West**. New York, Van Nostrand Reinhold Company, 1971. 152p. (Searchlight Book, No. 48). $3.50pa.

The purpose of this book is to provide "the layreader and those . . . commercially involved in dealing with Comecon countries" with "a fund of basic information" about this Soviet bloc institution. Nearly half of this slender volume is devoted to a detailed, country-by-country account of the economic development patterns and the present industrial potential of the individual Comecon members. The book contains quite a lot of information, which could be of interest not only to a general reader or businessman but also to more serious students of economic relations in Eastern Europe.

SR, 32:1:179-80　　　　　　　R: Michael Gamarnikow

28.　Meznerics, Ivan. **Law of Banking in East-West Trade**. trans. by Emil Böszörményi Nagy. Budapest, Akadémiai Kiadó; Leiden, A. W. Sijthoff; Dobbs Ferry, N.Y., Oceana Publications, 1973. 427p. $22.50.

A Hungarian economist discusses various aspects of trade and commercial transactions between East European countries and the West; emphasis is placed on laws governing the operation of banks. The author provides not only relevant legal texts but offers extensive commentaries on the various laws. In the face of growing East-West trade, the book will serve individuals and businesses involved in these transactions.　　　　　　　S. M. H.

29.　Pisar, Samuel. **Coexistence and Commerce: Guidelines for Transactions between East and West**. New York, Toronto, London, and Sydney, McGraw-Hill, 1970. 558p. $17.50.

Pisar's book is addressed primarily to lawyers, businessmen, public officials, and others who have an interest in trade with socialist countries. They will find it a unique source of information and advice on the special commercial and legal problems encountered in that trade. A major contribution is the "code of fair practices" proposed by the author as a basis for improving the institutional framework within which East-West trade is conducted.

SR, 30:2:436-7　　　　　　　R: Joseph S. Berliner

30.　Stokke, Baard Richard. **Soviet and Eastern European Trade and Aid in Africa**. New York, Praeger, 1967. 327p. $15.00.

Stokke has produced an admirable survey of Soviet and Eastern European economic activity in Africa. He brings together in one place most of the data now available on the trade and aid relations between the European Communist countries and Africa, including data on some countries about which information is usually very difficult to find. The numerous tables of aid and trade figures are probably the most significant contribution of this monograph. The most interesting part of the study comprises Stokke's evaluations concerning the economic activity of the Soviet Union and Eastern Europe in Africa. He shows that commodity prices on goods purchased from Africa have been "by and large on a par with 'world market levels'." The author has produced a very interesting survey of the information available to date.

SR, 27:3:496-7　　　　　　　R: Roger E. Kanet

31.　Strausz, David A. **The Hop Industry of Eastern Europe and the Soviet Union**. Pullman, Washington State University Press, 1969. 242p. $8.00.

Strausz's book offers a lucid, highly readable description of the hop crop, including its climatic and ecological requirements and growing techniques. He provides a penetrating and well-documented appraisal of the successes, failures, and prospects of this highly specialized facet of agriculture in Eastern Europe. Moreover, he gives firsthand observations with nearly all the local authorities on hops. The book is thoroughly researched, well documented, and highly accurate.

SR, 29:3:550-1 R: Earl R. Leng

32. Wilcox, Henry. **Comecon and the Politics of Integration**. New York, Praeger, 1972. 200p. (Praeger Special Studies in International Politics and Public Affairs). $15.00.

This book is the "story" of Comecon as reflected in official pronouncements and press commentaries of member countries, chronologically covering the 1968-71 period. The purpose of the study is to compile a partial record of intrabloc relations. The study confirms that integration has not yet been defined, much less achieved, in Comecon. It also shows that the USSR, Bulgaria, and Poland tend to be the most enthusiastic supporters of closer economic cooperation within the bloc, as long as it does not lock them into positions as suppliers of raw materials. The author is to be commended for leaving no relevant documents and articles unturned (well over 500 are cited).

SR, 32:2:399-400 R: Paul Marer

33. Wilczynski, Jozef. **The Economics and Politics of East-West Trade**. New York, Praeger, 1969. 416p. $12.50.

This book is a very competent introduction to East-West trade. It is divided into three parts: 1) historical survey, 2) background on ideology, organization, exchange rates, and integration with central planning, and 3) analysis of trade issues—discrimination, dumping, bilateralism and settlements, gains from trade, and others. The author analyzes the political and economic forces in trade since 1945 and finds trade increasingly conditioned by economic self-interest. The East is defined as Comecon (including the four Asian observer nations but excluding Yugoslavia) and the West as the advanced capitalist world, including Japan, Australia, and New Zealand.

SR, 30:3:693 R: Alan Abouchar

34. Wilczynski, Jozef. **The Economics of Socialism: Principles Governing the Operation of the Centrally Planned Economies in the USSR and Eastern Europe under the New System**. Chicago, Aldine Publishing Co., 1970. 233p. $8.95.

This survey brings together, clearly and concisely, the elementary principles which govern the operation of the centrally planned economies of Eastern Europe and of the USSR. The author reviews the background of modern socialist economics and devotes a chapter to each of the following topics: planning and the market, profit, production and growth, accumulation, consumption, labor, land, pricing, money and banking, fiscal policy and control, domestic trade, foreign trade, international economic cooperation, and socialism versus capitalism. Each chapter is followed by a list of suggested references available in English. As a pedagogical tool, the book is useful on an undergraduate level.

SR, 31:3:691 R: Jan S. Prybyla

Chapter 3

Government and Law

35. Collier, David S., and Kurt Glaser, eds. **Elements of Change in Eastern Europe: Prospects for Freedom**. Chicago, Henry Regnery, 1968. 251p. (Foundation for Foreign Affairs Series, 12). $7.50.
This is the fourth in a series of volumes emerging from conferences that the Foundation for Foreign Affairs has held jointly with the Studiengesellschaft für Fragen mittel- und osteuropäischer Partnerschaft since 1962. Most of the essays in the present volume, prepared for a conference held in September 1966, are directed against a too easy and gullible acceptance of the spirit of détente on the part of the governments and the scholars of Western Europe and the United States. If the commitment of revisionists to human values has any substance, Kurt Glaser writes in his final chapter summarizing the conference, they must be on their way to conversion from Marxism altogether.
SR, 28:3:502-3   R: John C. Campbell

36. Farrell, R. Barry, ed. **Political Leadership in Eastern Europe and the Soviet Union**. Chicago, Aldine Publishing Co., 1970. 359p. $12.50cl.; $4.95pa.
This symposium comprises the following: A. G. Meyer, "Historical Development of the Communist Theory of Leadership." Carl J. Friedrich, "The Theory of Political Leadership and the Issue of Totalitarianism." Frederick C. Barghoorn, "Trends in Top Political Leadership"; plus five essays dealing with the theme "Leadership and Society."

37. Gripp, Richard C. **The Political System of Communism**. New York, Dodd, Mead, 1973. 209p. $3.95pa.
The author compares political structures and processes of fourteen Communist states, employing five hypotheses as organizing principles: intent to institute a Communist society, domination of the Communist Party, introduction of public-socialist ownership, provision for popular participation, and establishment of foreign policies supporting Communist states and revolutionary movements in non-Communist countries.
SR, 33:2:374   R: Howard R. Swearer

38. Grzybowski, Kazimierz. **The Socialist Commonwealth of Nations: Organizations and Institutions**. New Haven, Yale University Press, 1964. 272p. $7.50.
This is a vastly learned treatise on the legal intricacies of relations among Communist-ruled states, treated under the generic term "socialist commonwealth of nations." The author believes that the institutional and ideological aspects of the commonwealth are of secondary importance. For him the legal realities of inter-Communist relations are more significant than the ideological foundations upon which such relations are built. The driving force of the commonwealth, according to the author, is the USSR. This was true ten years

ago but is no longer the case. The Sino-Soviet conflict exacerbated those centrifugal tendencies. This study should become an indispensable addition to background material in the fields of Communist international relations and Communist views of international law.

SR, 24:3:549-51   R: Kurt L. London

39.   Hazard, John N. **Communists and Their Law: A Search for the Common Core of the Legal Systems of the Marxian Socialist States.** Chicago, University of Chicago Press, 1969. 560p. $8.75.

The author looks beyond exclusively Soviet features of law, and endeavours to find the common core of all Marxian socialist legal systems. He mentions fourteen states: nine East European, four Asian, and one American—Cuba. Subsequently, he proceeds with an analysis of several chosen institutes or sectors of law—e.g., land utilization, property in the production enterprise, inheritance, family, contract law, state planning, torts, and correction of criminals. The authoritarian system of government is common to all Marxian socialist states. Differences in the limitation of freedom of the individual in Marxian and other authoritarian states vary, but it is probable that some of the limitations in Marxian systems can also be found in other authoritarian systems. The result of the author's study is a readable and most interesting book.

CSP, 14:2:376-8   R: L. Kos-Rabcewicz-Zubkowski

40.   Ionescu, Ghita. **The Politics of the European Communist States.** New York, Praeger, 1967. 303p. $6.75.

This is a study of politics and not an experiment in political science. The author, knowing the East European countries, is quite aware of the limits on generalization, on broad comparisons, and—sacrilegious as it may seem to some—on factor analysis, institutional patterns, and model-building. The material in the first part of the book, on the "framework and network of power," is likely to be as familiar to the reader as to the author himself. Describing the totalitarian state in its classic Leninist-Stalinist form, the author makes a point of calling it the apparat-state. He takes up the interrelationship of party, army, political police, and other instruments for the coercion and mobilization of society. The weight of Ionescu's argument is that changes in the political system (he predicts them for East European countries) grow out of the requirements of modern society.

SR, 28:2:343-5   R: John C. Campbell

41.   McKenzie, Kermit E. **Comintern and World Revolution, 1928-1943: The Shaping of Doctrine.** New York, Columbia University Press, 1964. 368p. (Studies of the Russian Institute). $6.50.

The author has rendered a useful service by producing a careful survey of Comintern doctrine during the classic Stalinist period. The fact that the world Communist movement has shifted into a new era with changing problems and challenges in no way makes this study obsolete. Not only must an understanding of the present era be grounded in the past, but the common thread of ideological commitment cannot be underestimated. McKenzie's justification for studying doctrine is entirely sound when he reminds us that "whatever the phase of historical development of Communism, its leaders have always emphatically concurred on one point—the overweening importance of a correct world view. To ignore the actuality and content of this world view is to fail in an understanding of Communism."

SR, 24:1:138-9   R: Elliot R. Goodman

Chapter 4

History

42.   Adams, Arthur E., Ian M. Matley, and William O. McCagg. **An Atlas of Russian and East European History**. New York, Praeger, 1967. 204p. $6.00.
Against a skillfully constructed mosaic of physical and human geography, the authors survey the political, cultural, and economic development of the region focusing especially on four themes: the impact of the acceptance of Christianity, the thirteenth-century calamities and their consequences, the continuous absorption of influences from both the East and the West, and the development of a distinct type of sociopolitical culture in recent decades. Spatial patterns and the dynamics of specific historical events and processes are depicted on simple and in most cases quite legible maps. The book is an informative introduction to the history and historical geography of Eastern Europe.
      SR, 29:2:346-7   R: Joseph J. Tvaruzka

43.   Dvornik, Francis. **Byzantine Missions among the Slavs: Ss. Constantine Cyril and Methodius**. New Brunswick, N.J., Rutgers University Press, 1970. 485p. (Rutgers Byzantine Series). $17.50.
Dvornik's latest contribution to the literature on Byzantium and Slavdom, published simultaneously in Czech translation (Prague, 1970), is basically a critical evaluation of the current status of Cyril and Methodian studies. Father Dvornik takes advantage not only of his own ground-breaking research but also of the spate of Cyrillo-Methodiana published in connection with the eleven hundredth anniversary of the Moravian mission of the "Apostles of the Slavs" as well as the recent archaeological work in East Central Europe and the Balkans. In the present volume Dvornik is much more speculative than in his previous specialized works in this field, for he attempts to pull together the numerous loose threads of scholarship on the results of Byzantine missionary work among these newcomers to Eastern Europe. His well-argued hypotheses provide a necessary continuity in the work.
      SR, 30:4:876-7   R: George P. Majeska

44.   Gimbutas, Marija. **The Slavs**. London, Thames and Hudson; New York, Praeger, 1971. 240p. (Ancient Peoples and Places, vol. 74). $10.00.
Making abundant use of archaeological, literary, and linguistic evidence, the author traces the history of the Slavs from their putative beginnings in the early second millenium B.C. to the rise of the Slavic states in the ninth and tenth centuries A.D. A true Slavic culture emerged about 500, and the migrations (from the area north of the Carpathian mountains and the middle Dnieper river area) took place in the sixth and seventh centuries. The author deals admirably with the many controversies and problems of early Slavic culture.
      SR, 31:4:877-8   R: Ann Farkas

45.   Stone, Gerald. **The Smallest Slavonic Nation: The Sorbs of Lusatia.**
      London, Athlone Press; New York, Oxford University Press, 1972.
      201p. $12.00.
The Sorbs of Lusatia (they call themselves Serbs) have been the least known of
all the Slav nations. This volume contains chapters on their history, language
and literature, folkways and folklore, music, and a brief introduction deals with
the location of the Sorbs. Their history is almost exclusively social and cultural
history, centering on literature and folk culture.
      SR, 31:4:922-3   R: Peter Brook

46.   Vlasto, A. P. **The Entry of the Slavs into Christendom: An Introduction
      to the Medieval History of the Slavs.** Cambridge, Cambridge University
      Press, 1970. 435p. $19.50.
The book focuses on each of the Slavic groups at the moment of its integration
one way or another into what we call "Western civilization." Its best sections
are those that deal with Slavic peoples, such as the Wends and the future Slovenes,
who remained beyond even the secondary influence of Byzantine missionary
activities. Other sections of the book are of decidedly uneven quality. Many of
the hypotheses put forth by the author are intriguing, but they are rarely
cogently argued or well documented.
      SR, 30:4:876-7   R: George P. Majeska

Chapter 5

International Relations

47. Anderson, M. S. **The Eastern Question, 1774-1923: A Study in Inter-national Relations.** New York, St. Martin's Press, 1966. 435p. $9.00.
This is a judicious and useful survey of the Eastern question from Kutchuk-Kainardji to the end of the Ottoman Empire. It is a well-informed, integrative study based on obvious mastery of the vast amount of monographic literature, both Western and Russian, that has appeared on this subject in recent decades. Among the twelve chapters, which are arranged chronologically, are: The Ottoman Empire and the Great Powers, 1774-1798; The Napoleonic Wars and the Growth of Balkan Nationalism, 1798-1821; Anglo-Russian Relations and the Crimean War, 1841-1856; From the Treaty of Paris to the Bosnian Revolt, 1856-1876; The Near East Before the First World War, 1909-1914; The War of 1914-1918; The Peace Settlement, 1918-1923. The brief Conclusion of ten pages is note-worthy for its thoughtful reflections.
AHR, 72:4:1345   R: L. S. Stavrianos

48. Bromke, Adam, and Philip E. Uren, eds. **The Communist States and the West.** New York, Praeger, 1967. 242p. $6.50.
In this symposia several experts discuss the various aspects of the relations between the Communist countries and the West. R. Lowenthal, H. Mayo, H. Von Riekhoff, M. Kaplan, F. Michael, and others are contributors. The various arguments and citations presented here clearly reflect the depth of study as well as the breadth of scope of this book. It successfully complements such recent works on related aspects of European Communism as Gordon Skilling's *The Governments of Communist Europe* and *Eastern European Government and Politics* by Vaclav Beneš and associates.
EEQ, 1:4:419-22   R: Andrew Gyorgy

49. Epstein, Fritz T. **Germany and the East: Selected Essays.** Ed. by Robert F. Byrnes. Bloomington, Indiana University Press, 1973. 234p. $6.95pa.
For nearly half a century, Fritz Epstein has been active on both sides of the Atlantic as a scholar, teacher, editor, and bibliographer in the field of Central and East European history. This book brings together in one volume a translated edition of some of his own writings which had previously appeared in various German periodicals. The following essays are included: Political Education and Higher Educational Policy in the Soviet Union; East Central Europe as a Power Vacuum between East and West During the German Empire; The Question of Polish Reparation Claims, 1919-1922; Otto Hoetzsch as Commentator on Foreign Policy during the First World War; and Russia and the League of Nations. All essays are meticulously-documented research papers which are as fresh and useful today as at the time of their original appearance. Byrnes contributed an informative and affectionate introduction to Epstein, the man and the scholar.
CSP, 16:3:488-9   R: Ulrich Trumpener

50. U.S. Department of State. **Foreign Relations of the United States, 1946. Vol. 6, Eastern Europe; The Soviet Union.** Washington, GPO, 1969. 993p. $5.50.

51. U.S. Department of State. **Foreign Relations of the United States, 1947. Vol. 4, Eastern Europe; The Soviet Union.** Washington, GPO, 1972. 887p. $5.25.

52. U.S. Department of State. **Foreign Relations of the United States, 1948. Vol. 4, Eastern Europe; The Soviet Union.** Washington, GPO, 1974. 1161p. $10.80.

Each volume contains material and documents classified as "Multilateral Relations," and is followed by selected declassified documents pertaining to individual East European countries. The last volume (Vol. 4, 1974) contains the State Department documents of the year 1948. Ample footnotes are provided. For the text of treaties and agreements concluded between the United States and East European countries including the USSR, one will have to consult the *United Nations Treaty Series.*   S. M. H.

Chapter 6

Language and Literature

53. Čiževskij, Dmitrij. **Comparative History of Slavic Literatures**. Ed. by Serge A. Zenkovsky. Trans. by Richard Noel Porter, and Martin P. Rice. Nashville, Vanderbilt University Press, 1971. 225p. $10.00.

The richness of the author's scholarly experience and his authority in the field of Slavic literatures and Slavic-Western cultural relations, make this work a valuable contribution toward the clearing of the subject. Many students of Slavistics will be thankful to Čiževskij for pointing to the need of establishing connections between the Slavic East and the European and American West and providing an impressive repertoire of problems to be worked out on, as well as several samples of effective methods for their scholarly treatment.

      CSP, 15:3:419-20   R: V. Grebenschikov

54. Čiževsky, Dmitrij. **Survey of Slavic Civilization, Vol. l: Outline of Comparative Slavic Literature**. Boston, American Academy of Arts and Sciences, 1952. 143p.

The *Survey* "is to be regarded only as a preliminary essay," according to the author. The reader will find here a substantial survey of the main features and trends in Slavic literatures, and, most important of all, an insight into the numerous problems in a field which still awaits serious investigation.

      SCP, 15:3:419-20   R: V. Grebenschikov

55. Erlich, Victor. **The Double Image: Concepts of the Poet in Slavic Literatures**. Baltimore, Johns Hopkins Press, 1964. 160p. $5.00.

Erlich's book is a study of the poet's shifting image of himself and his work as illustrated in the careers of six major practitioners of poetry. There are: Pushkin, Krasiński, Briusov, Blok, Mayakovsky, and Pasternak. What emerges clearly from this excellent study is the persistence in many literatures during the nineteenth and early twentieth century of the notion that the poet's activity is of necessity estranged from normal human life—often to the detriment of the poet as a man.

      SR, 24:2:343-4   R: Edward J. Brown

56. Gribble, Charles E. **Medieval Slavic Texts. Vol. 1: Old and Middle Russian Texts**. Cambridge, Mass., Slavica Publishers, 1973. 320p. $12.95cl.; $6.95pa.

A concise and valuable survey of Old Rus' literature is provided in the introduction of this volume, which also contains lengthy excerpts and some complete texts useful in learning to read Old Slavic (Kiev Rus') chronicles, sermons, and epics.   S. M. H.

57. Jakobson, Roman, C. H. van Schooneveld, and D. S. Worth, eds.
    Slavic Poetics: Essays in Honor of Kiril Taranovsky. The Hague,
    Mouton, 1973. 575p. (Slavistic Printings and Reprintings, 267). 180Dglds.
The 51 essays in *Slavic Poetics* for the most part closely reflect Taranovsky's
interests. Indeed, many of them express a specific debt to remarks made by
him either in publications or in seminars he has taught at Harvard University.
Perhaps the book's chief significance is that it marks the first appearance in
a single volume of nearly all the leading metrics both within Russia and without.
It is a valuable sourcebook not just for its specific articles but also for indicating
the current state of research in the field it covers, pointing the way for others
interested in Russian versification and in poetics in general.
    SR, 34:1:202-3   R: Barry P. Scherr

58. Shevelov, George Y. **A Prehistory of Slavic: The Historical Phonology
    of Common Slavic.** New York, Columbia University Press, 1965.
    662p. (Columbia Slavic Studies). $18.50.
The publication of this book on the historical phonology of Common Slavic
(CS) adds a new volume to the enormous number of works which deal with
this subject. The bibliography gives more than 300 bibliographical references.
The book is not suited for classroom use because of its confusing presentation,
because of its haphazard choice of examples, and because of its failure to distinguish between commonly agreed upon analyses and highly controversial issues.
For specialists in Slavic linguistics the book has two merits: it contains an
enormous wealth of examples from different Slavic languages, glossed in
English and grouped together to exemplify specific phonological processes; and
it contains an enormous wealth of bibliographical material.
    SR, 25:4:679-86   R: Theodore M. Lightner

59. Shevelov, George Y. **Teasers and Appeasers: Essays and Studies on
    Themes of Slavic Philology.** Munich, Wilhelm Fink Verlag, 1971.
    336p. (Forum Slavicum, no. 32). DM 98.
This volume is a worthy sequel to the great scholar's unsurpassed *A Prehistory
of Slavic.* The twenty essays and studies were selected from those written by
Shevelov between 1949 and 1969; they are all "united by a certain approach,
which aims at understanding language as a dynamic, complex system of systems
in their interconnections and interactions, and seeks internal and external motivations behind changes." The author testifies to his fame as the leading scholar
in Ukrainian philology in "The Name *Ukrajina* 'Ukraine'," "Ukrainisches
vantaž," and other articles.
    SEER, 51:122:127-8   R: M. Samilov

60. Unbegaun, Boris O. **Selected Papers on Russian and Slavonic Philology.**
    Oxford, Clarendon Press, 1969. 341p. $9.95.
This representative collection of articles was assembled by Robert Auty and
Anne E. Pennington on the occasion of Professor Unbegaun's seventieth birthday.
The volume contains 26 articles which were written over a period of more than
35 years and are in part not easily accessible. Unbegaun is the most outspoken

Western partisan of the hypothesis that literary Russian is of Church Slavic and not East Slavic origin and the entire history of literary Russian a gradual and uninterrupted process of russification of Church Slavic. The editors are to be commended for having made this selection of his works accessible.

SEEJ, 15:3:355-6   R: Gerta H. Worth

Chapter 7

Political Theory and Communism

61. Black, Cyril E., and Thomas P. Thornton, eds. **Communism and Revolution: The Strategic Uses of Political Violence**. Princeton, Princeton University Press, 1964. 467p. $10.00.

There is not a single statement by a prominent Communist to indicate that the objective of the world revolution has been changed or abandoned, that the commitment to attaining this goal has been weakened, or that, despite changes in emphasis and perspective, faith in the ultimate outcome of the struggle has been lost. The present volume is a symposium to which twelve experts contributed. The text has the merit of combining history with analysis of current Communist activities. This book is a fountain of information, it is an extremely useful reference text, and it stimulates thinking. It is recommended to all students of Soviet strategy.

      SR, 24:2:335-6   R: Stefan T. Possony

62. Bromke, Adam, and Teresa Rakowska-Harmstone, eds. **The Communist States in Disarray, 1965-1971**. Minneapolis, University of Minnesota Press, 1972. 363p. (The Carleton Series in Soviet and East European Studies). $13.50cl.; $4.95pa.

This work is devoted to the impact of the Sino-Soviet conflict on the world community of socialist states, together with the spread of nationalism and polycentrism. But the major concentration is on Eastern Europe; of the sixteen chapters, eight of the eleven on countries are devoted to particular East European countries and three of the other five concern the overall problems of this area. Within this framework a general accounting of developments since the fall of Khrushchev is undertaken.

      SR, 32:1:180-1   R: R. V. Burks

63. Buzek, Antony. **How the Communist Press Works**. New York, Praeger, 1964. 287p. $7.50.

The book is unique in providing a fairly thorough survey of the workings of the Communist press. The author had the advantage of having observed its operation from the inside. He worked for Ceteka, the Czechoslovak news service, in Prague from 1950 to 1955 and as its London correspondent from 1955 to 1961, when he severed the connection. He has written a useful study of the ideology, structure, control, and functioning of the Soviet and East European press. It is focused upon the censorship and administrative manipulation and draws much of its material from the 1950s.

      SR, 27:3:498   R: Leo Gruliow

64. DeGeorge, Richard T. **The New Marxism: Soviet and East European Marxism since 1956**. New York, Pegasus, 1968. 170p. $6.00cl.; $1.95pa.

DeGeorge has written an admirable work of scholarship, a survey of developments in Marxist philosophy from Khrushchev's devaluation of Stalin to the end of 1967. It is conceived as an effort at synthesis, with chapters on such topics as the Marxist vision of man, Marxist ethics and Communist morality, and ideological conflicts and power politics. Greater attention is given to developments in the Soviet Union, which are usually contrasted with trends in the other countries. In general the contrast shows that the Soviet thinkers put more stress on the collective and the others more on the individual. In the field of ethics, DeGeorge finds, it follows that for the Soviet Marxist "the basic moral choice is not personal but social, the ultimate court of appeal is not one's conscience but society's decision." The implications of such thinking for established regimes are clear.

65. Degras, Jane, ed. **The Communist International, 1919-1943. Documents. Vol. III, 1929-1943**. London, Oxford University Press for the Royal Institute of International Affairs, 1965. 494p. $14.00.

The third volume of documents of the Communist International completes a valuable series. Beginning with a rather heavy concentration in the period of the early 1930s, the documents trail off after the Seventh World Congress, as the Comintern itself did, to the point where there is nothing at all in 1941, only a May Day manifesto in 1942, and the formal document of dissolution (1943) to open the archives.

RR, 25:3:317-8   R: John C. Campbell

66. Drachkovitch, Milorad M., and Branko Lazitch, eds. **The Comintern: Historical Highlights: Essays, Recollections, Documents**. New York, Praeger; London, Pall Mall Press, 1966. 430p. (Hoover Institution Publication). $10.00.

This is a collection of essays written by such experts as S. T. Possony, B. D. Wolfe, R. C. Thornton, B. Lazitch, and M. M. Drachkovitch on various aspects, structure, and function of the Third International, including certain documents pertinent to the International during the period of 1921-1923. Possony in his essay denies the Comintern's conception of the Communist International was different from Marx's conception of a workingman's international, no difficult task, and thus the greatest Marxist of them all proves to be no Marxist.

AHR, 73:2:441-2   R: George Barr Carson, Jr.

67. Drachkovitch, Milorad, et al., eds. **Yearbook on International Communist Affairs, 1966**. Stanford, Hoover Institution Press, 1967. 766p. (Hoover Institution Publications Series, 60). $25.00.

Publication of this yearbook is the beginning of a new publishing venture of the Hoover Institution. Except for the brief introduction by the editor, the entire volume is devoid of any attempt at analyzing the multifarious activities of Communists. The book is strictly descriptive and provides a vast assortment of data. The main portion of the work is taken up with résumés of individual Communist parties arranged by geographic regions. A chronology of major events in the Communist world (nearly fifty pages) follows. Then come summaries of major Communist conferences and succinct descriptions of the activities of Communist-front organizations. These are succeeded by a documentary section containing complete texts and excerpts from twenty-five major documents. This mammoth volume concludes with a bibliography of major English, Russian, French, and German publications on international Communism in 1966 and an extensive index.

SR, 28:2:342-3   R: Paul E. Zinner

68.   Dunayevskaia, Raya. **Philosophy and Revolution: From Hegel to Sartre, and from Marx to Mao.** New York, Delacorte Press, 1973. 372p. $8.95cl., $2.95pa.

If one seeks the central idea of Ms. Dunayevskaya's work, it may be found to be that of praxis—but the idea used as backdrop rather than analyzed in depth. It is around this issue that the author organizes her analysis of the relations between philosophy and revolution. In her view, of particular importance are the different resistance movements which from 1956 to 1970—in Warsaw and Budapest and Prague, Gdansk and Szczecin—have united workers and youth from various countries of Eastern and Danubian Europe in revolt against the inhuman oppression of local Marxist-Leninist regimes. They have embarked upon a movement for the liberation of all men. She asks, "is it not time for intellectuals to begin with where the workers are and what they think, to fill the theoretic void in the Marxist movement?"

SR, 33:4:784-5   R: Henri Chambre

69.   Fleron, Frederic J., ed. **Communist Studies and the Social Sciences: Essays on Methodology and Empirical Theory.** Chicago, Rand McNally, 1969. 481p. $5.95pa.

This collection of studies is a very useful and unique contribution to scholarly literature. It will make more "visible" hitherto obscure studies, some either unpublished or inaccessible. It should be useful reading for all scholars in our field who have not taken the trouble to "retool" and bring their knowledge of the philosophical, methodological, and technical context of their research up to a reasonable level. Also, in an era when rigor and logic in scholarship are once again threatened, perhaps by an anti-rational and anti-scientific "counterrevolution," it is good to be reminded that so many scholars are in their daily work in an extraordinarily difficult field to contribute to what David Easton referred to as "reliable understanding."

SR, 29:3:539-42   R: Frederick C. Barghoorn

70.   Johnson, Chalmers, ed. **Change in Communist Systems.** Stanford, Stanford University Press, 1970. 368p. $8.95.

This volume consists of eleven essays which were written on the basis of the workshop discussions held in the summer of 1968 at the Centre for Advanced Study in the Behavioral Sciences at Stanford, California. The aim of their joint endeavour was to explore the possibility of developing models to help explain many of the transformations that have occurred and are occurring in post-Stalin Communist systems, and to suggest research strategies for dealing with problems of change and diversity in the Communist world. The work must be rated as an important early step in the direction of systematic comparison of

Communist systems through the development of conceptual tools for explanatory and predictive analysis of developments in these systems.

      CSP, 13:2-3:293-6   R: Donald V. Schwartz

71.   Kolarz, Walter. **Communism and Colonialism: Essays.** Ed. by George Gretton. Intro. by Edward Crankshaw. New York, St. Martin's Press, 1964. 147p. $4.95.

Kolarz's twelve penetrating essays discuss the impact of the Communist tyranny on oppressed and captive nations and peoples and explain the Communist threat to mankind in its entirety. The work is permeated by deep humanitarian sentiments and strong religious conviction. Kolarz devotes particular attention to the status of the nations and nationalities within the Soviet Union itself. He criticizes the "elder brother" theory and points out that the non-Russian ethnic groups are being russified. These essays have been published posthumously—the author died prematurely in 1962.

      SR, 24:1:137-8   R: Stefan T. Possony

72.   Miller, Richard I. **Teaching about Communism.** New York, McGraw-Hill, 1966. 355p. $6.50.

This volume is intended as a handbook for teachers, school administrators, and other educators who are responsible for introducing courses on Communism. Its scope is broad, including a rationale for instruction, a survey of relevant curriculum practices, discussion of the major issues Miller believes should be included in instruction about Communism, and suggestions for pedagogy, for pre- and in-service education of teachers, and for strategy and tactics in establishing courses relating to Communism. Despite its weaknesses, it is the only available book of its kind and should be useful to curriculum planners and administrators in the schools.

      SR, 26:3:523-4   R: Howard Mehlinger

73.   Rothschild, Joseph. **Communist Eastern Europe.** New York, Walker, 1964. 168p. $4.50.

Rothschild's book concentrates on post-war events and is designed as an informative brief. The author concludes with some telling propositions. He believes that the events in Hungary in 1956 taught us a triple lesson: (a) Eastern Europe is too weak to be able to break away from Moscow; (b) the United States is not inclined to help the nations of the area if the risk is war; and (c) the Soviet Union is ready to face a showdown. However, he suggests that the West should support the trend toward greater independence of these nations by a policy of "rewards" while warning against attempts to punish them because they continue to remain Communist.

      SR, 25:3:547-8   R: Josef Korbel

74.   Staar, Richard F., ed. **Aspects of Modern Communism.** Columbia, University of South Carolina Press, 1968. 416p. $7.95.

This collection of writings attempts to summarize the stage of Communist bloc relations as of 1967; it does not deal with the impact of the Soviet invasion of Czechoslovakia. Most of the authors strive to present both a historical framework and a more than superficial assessment of present trends. On the whole,

they succeed better in the former aim than in the latter. While China and other
Asian Communist regimes are dealt with in separate essays, all of Eastern Europe
is treated as a whole in three essays on the topics of polycentrism, economic
integration, and the Warsaw Pact.

       SR, 29:1:124-5   R: Robert J. Osborn

75.   Staar, Richard F., ed. **Yearbook on International Communist Affairs,
1973.** Stanford, Hoover Institution Press, 1973. 651p. $25.00cl.;
$9.50pa.

Like the preceding volumes, the seventh *Yearbook* provides a reference work
of the highest order, and henceforth will be indispensable to all those who are
interested in the evolution of different components of the world Communist
movement. In this volume the editor has prefaced the accounts of individual
Communist parties and subsidiary international organizations with an introduction
in which he concisely summarizes the chief trends exhibited within the movement in 1972.

       SR, 33:2:373-4   R: François Fejtö

76.   Sworakowski, Witold S., ed. **The Communist International and Its
Front Organizations. A Research Guide and Checklist of Holdings
in American and European Libraries.** Stanford, Hoover Institution
Press, 1965. 493p. $10.00.

This large volume with over 2,300 entries will be valuable to anyone doing
research on the Comintern and its history, for it lists the books and pamphlets
available in American and European libraries.

       SEER, 45:104:266-7   R: F. L. Carsten

77.   Sworakowski, Witold S., ed. **World Communism: A Handbook, 1918-
1965.** Stanford, Hoover Institution Press, 1973. 576p. $25.00.

Since 1967 the Hoover Institution has issued an annual *Yearbook on International Communist Affairs,* beginning with coverage of the year 1966. This
volume is intended to fill the gap for the period from just before the founding
of the Comintern through 1965. In all, there are 106 separate pieces by 53
different authors. Not only do they trace the foundation and development of
the various national Communist parties, but they also deal briefly with international Communist organizations such as the Comintern, Cominform, the
Council for Mutual Economic Assistance, and the Warsaw Pact. It is a valuable
reference work, along with the other volumes in this series.

       SR, 33:3:550-1   R: Elliot R. Goodman

78.   Taborsky, Edward. **Communist Penetration of the Third World.**
New York, Robert Speller & Sons, 1973. 500p. $12.50.

The author has made an heroic effort to cover in a single volume the current
doctrines and policies of some nine Communist states vis-à-vis all the regions
of the Third World, embracing a veritable plethora of activities—overt and
covert. The attempt was worthwhile, and the results are useful to many who
labor in this field. It will be among the basic handbooks on the topic.

       SR, 33:2:370-1   R: Uri Ra'anan

79. Toma, Peter A., ed. **The Changing Face of Communism in Eastern Europe**. Tucson, University of Arizona Press, 1970. 413p. $4.95pa.
The aim of the book, according to its editor, is to analyze significant changes which have occurred in East European countries and the impact of these changes on their relations with the USSR and the West. The main theme for both purposes is pluralism: that it is not only deceptive but unscholarly to lump together the eight socialist countries of Europe into one geographic region governed by uniform political rules. For those to whom that proposition still needs proving, this book performs the task. Among the contributors are Stephen Fischer-Galati (Rumania), Joseph Fiszman (Poland), Marin Pundeff (Bulgaria), Jan Triska (Czechoslovakia), Bennett Kovrig (Hungary), George Klein (Yugoslavia), and Nicholas Pano (Albania). All specialists in the field of Soviet and East European affairs will profit by reading the book.
  SR, 30:3:679   R: John C. Campbell

80. Triska, Jan F., ed. **Communist Party-States: Comparative and International Studies**. Indianapolis, Bobbs-Merrill, 1969. 392p. $9.00.
The principal contribution of this work lies not so much in the substantive results of the authors' efforts—which are, by and large, neither novel nor breathtaking, and correspond in great measure to conclusions and observations made by other scholars using other methods—but rather in the attempt to open new avenues to the study of Communist systems. In the process they have produced a splendid book that eloquently demonstrates the possibilities and yet implicitly concedes the limitations of the quantitative and behavioral methods they employ. The principal theme of the work is integration and interaction among Communist states, which is also the central motif of at least six of the thirteen contributions. This study raises, however, numerous questions which are not answered or answerable.
  SR, 30:3:674-6   R: Vernon V. Aspaturian

81. Tucker, Robert C. **The Marxian Revolutionary Idea**. New York, W. W. Norton, 1969. 240p. (A Publication of the Center of International Studies, Princeton University). $5.95.
In this collection of carefully reasoned and documented essays, Tucker extends the highly original interpretation set forth in his *Philosophy and Myth in Karl Marx* (1961) to the phenomena of contemporary Marxism and Communist movements. Marx, he argues, located the source of revolutionary energy in the frustration of man in his capacity as a producer, not consumer. Marx, in the author's view, never outgrew his wish to abolish the occupational specialization founded in the division of labor; the liberation of human creativity was his main goal. These essays, always searching, and always written with urbanity, are among the most distinguished writings on Marxism which American scholarship has produced.
  SR, 29:2:330-1   R: Lewis S. Feuer

82. Wolfe, Bertram D. **Marxism: One Hundred Years in the Life of a Doctrine**. New York, Dial Press, 1965. 404p. $6.95.

The book is not a study of both "Marxism-in-theory" and "Marxism-in-action." It deals exclusively with some selected aspects of that part of Marx's heritage which reflects his determination to change the world by shaping the development of social and political events. The greatest single error of Marx was his belief that nationalism was not really an acting force in society. The author argues that this error left Marx's political heirs completely unprepared for the explosion of national feeling in the following century and made it impossible for them to explain how nationalism could become a successful rival to socialism, even in their own camp. Apart from this misconception about the course of history, "Marxism-in-action" involves many obscure assumptions and inconsistent claims, in particular in matters concerning war, peace, and the right to national defense. It is a useful study of Marx's pronouncements on contemporary international, political, and social events.

SR, 24:4:730-2   R: Z. A. Jordan

PART II

RUSSIAN EMPIRE PRIOR TO 1917 AND USSR; NON-RUSSIAN REPUBLICS; JEWS

Chapter 8

Russian Empire Prior to 1917 and USSR

GENERAL REFERENCE WORKS

Bibliographies and Serials

83. Berton, Peter, and Alvin Z. Rubinstein, with a contrib. by Anna Allott. **Soviet Works on Southeast Asia: A Bibliography of Non-Periodical Literature, 1946-1965.** Los Angeles, University of Southern California Press, 1967. 201p. $4.50pa.

This material includes an analysis of Soviet scholarship on Southeast Asia; a report entitled "Soviet Southeast Asian Studies, Language and Literature" by Anna Allott, and a section on the categories of works excluded from the bibliography and the various aspects of Soviet publishing on Southeast Easia. Also provided are lists and descriptions of Soviet periodical publications on Asia and Africa and general bibliographical tools. The bibliography itself lists 401 titles. Titles are in English followed by the Russian in transliteration, and any non-Russian languages are designated. This book is the third in the Far Eastern and Russian Research Series of the School of Politics and International Relations of the University of Southern California.

    SR, 31:2:451-2   R: Robert A. Karlowich

84. Gladney, Frank Y., ed. **Fifteen-Year Index to the Slavic and East European Journal, 1957-1971.** University of Illinois, Urbana-Champaign, American Association of Teachers of Slavic and East European Languages, 1972. 70p. $4.50pa.

85. **Guide to Russian Reprints and Microforms.** New York, Pilvax, 1973. 364p.

The *Guide* in its 8,214 entries restricts itself to Cyrillic alphabet imprints dealing with Slavic subjects as well as the few non-Cyrillic Slavic reprints. The publishers claim "to provide a near-complete, comprehensive register of existing reprints and microforms," but this statement should be qualified since some reprinters are omitted—or are covered selectively. Pilvax's intent to continue the service rendered through the *Guide* can only be applauded and cooperation among bibliographic centers and publishers encouraged.

    RR, 34:3:354-5   R: Wojciech Zalewski

86. Heitman, Sidney, comp. and ed. **Nikolai I. Bukharin: A Bibliography.** Stanford, Hoover Institution Press, 1969. 181p. $10.00.

An exhaustive guide to the works and life of Nikolai Bukharin.

87. Horecky, Paul L., ed. **Russia and the Soviet Union: A Bibliographic Guide to Western-Language Publications**. Chicago, University of Chicago Press, 1965. 473p. $8.95.

88. Horecky, Paul L., ed. **Basic Russian Publications: Annotated Bibliography on Russia and the Soviet Union**. Chicago, University of Chicago Press, 1962. 313p. $6.50.

The basic scheme of these two bibliographies edited by Paul Horecky is almost the same: General Reference Aids and Bibliographies; The Land; The People; History; The State; The Economic and Social Structure; The Intellectual (and Cultural) Life. In *Russia and the Soviet Union* the scheme has been expanded to cover also General and Descriptive Books; The Nations—the national question in general; Ukrainica; Baltica; and Other Nations. The methodology—including sequence of presentation—in both guides is well conceived and well elaborated.

SR, 25:2:370-2   R: Fritz T. Epstein

89. Klieber, Max, comp. **Institute Publications (1951-1968): Part I, Publication Index; Part 2, Subject Index; Part 3, Author Index**. Munich, Institute for the Study of the USSR, 1969. 160p.

For almost two decades, the Institute for the Study of the USSR offered émigré scholars an opportunity to share their knowledge of the USSR with Western specialists in journals and monographs published by the Institute. This endeavor led to one of the best collections by experts in all fields and subjects, which this bibliography has recorded for the scholar's use.

S. M. H.

90. Lesure, Michel. **Les Sources de l'histoire de Russie aux Archives Nationales**. The Hague, Mouton; and Paris, École Pratique des Hautes Études, 1970. 502p. (Études sur l'histoire, l'économie et la sociologie des pays Slaves, 15). 53Dglds.pa.

This valuable guide to materials in the Archives Nationales in Paris will be indispensable for many historians of Russia and useful for researchers in other fields as well. The bulk of the materials discussed or listed are for the period 1700-1917. The richest and best organized collections are from the Napoleonic era, but there are also significant pre-Petrine and post-revolutionary papers.

SR, 31:3:665   R: J. M. McErlean

91. Maichel, Karol. **Guide to Russian Reference Books**. Vol. 1: *General Bibliographies and Reference Books*. Ed. by J. S. G. Simmons. Stanford, Hoover Institution Press, 1962. 92p. (Hoover Institution Bibliographical Series, X). $5.00. Vol. II: *History, Auxiliary Historical Science, Ethnography, and Geography*. Ed. by J. S. G. Simmons. Stanford, Hoover Institution Press, 1964. 297p. $12.00.

If, as cannot be doubted, the high standard of the first two volumes of the six-volume reference work prepared by Maichel and Simmons is maintained, librarians and scholars will have a set at their disposal which will probably never be matched inside or outside Russia. The volumes go beyond the listing of bibliographical reference works; they include other reference tools such as bibliographies, indexes, encyclopedias, chronologies, biographies, terminological dictionaries, atlases, gazetteers, handbooks, and dissertation abstracts. The volumes still to be published will comprise social sciences, religion, philosophy, military science, and library science (Vol. III); humanities, literature, languages, music, and fine arts (Vol. IV); supplementary material and cumulative index (Vol. VI); publication of Volume V will precede the publications of Vols. III and IV. [Editor's note: As of 1977, however, no further volumes have been published.]

SR, 25:2:370-2   R: Fritz T. Epstein

92. Maichel, Karol, comp. **Soviet and Russian Newspapers at the Hoover Institution: A Catalog.** Stanford, Hoover Institution, Stanford University Press, 1966. 225p. $6.50cl.; $5.00pa.

Provides an inventory of the largest collection of Russian newspapers in the United States, which is available at the Hoover Institution. Also contains references to the holdings of Columbia University and the Library of Congress. Titles are arranged in alphabetical order with description of the holdings.

S. M. H.

93. Nerhood, Harry W., comp. **To Russia and Return: An Annotated Bibliography of Travelers' English-Language Accounts of Russia from the Ninth Century to the Present.** Columbus, Ohio State University Press, 1969. 367p. $10.00.

With admirable diligence, Nerhood has assembled an annotated bibliography of 1,422 English-language accounts of travelers to Russia and the Soviet Union. This bibliography is physically attractive, well indexed, and illuminated with brief comments on the contents of almost all of the individual works listed. However, a number of important seventeenth century accounts are missing (Brereton, Carlisle, and Fletcher, for example). Nerhood's work will probably be most valuable to students of British and American images of, and attitudes toward, Russia in the past century.

SR, 29:3:500-1   R: Robert O. Crummey

94. Schatoff, Michael, comp. **Half a Century of Russian Serials, 1917-1968: Cumulative Index of Serials Published Outside the USSR.** Ed. by N. A. Hale. Part 1: 1917-1956, A-M. Part 2: 1917-1956, N-R. Part 3: 1917-1956, S-Z, Supplement and Directories. Part 4: 1957-1968, A-Z, Directories. New York, Russian Book Chamber Abroad. Part 1: 1970, 173p. (2d ed., 1972, 173p.). Part 2: 1971, pp. 174-355. Part 3: 1972, pp. 356-558. Part 4: 1972, pp. 559-697. $13.85ea. pa.

The four volumes list over 3,700 serials published in the Russian language outside the USSR from 1917 to 1968. Unfortunately, the compiler fails to indicate the sources of his data and to give library locations for any of the serials covered.

SR, 33:2:410-11   R: Patricia K. Grimsted

95. Simmons, J. S. G., ed. **Russian Bibliography: Libraries and Archives; A Selective List of Bibliographical References for Students of Russian History, Literature, Political, Social and Philosophical Thought, Theology and Linguistics.** Middlesex, England, Anthony C. Hall, 1973. 76p. £1.00 or $3.00.

This is a listing of only the essential bibliographies which the beginning graduate student in Russian literature, linguistics, or a social studies field ought to become aware of quickly. This closely classified listing of approximately 700 items grew out of booklists used as handouts by the author in over 20 years of bibliography orientation lectures at Oxford.

SEEJ, 18:3:345   R: J. Thomas Shaw

96.   Smits, Rudolf, comp. **Half a Century of Soviet Serials, 1917-1968: A Bibliography and Union List of Serials Published in the USSR**. 2 vols. Washington, GPO, 1968. 861p.; 862-1661. $16.00/set.

This invaluable reference tool is a continuation of the Library of Congress's earlier *Serial Publications of the Soviet Union, 1939-1957*. Its 29,761 entries cover all known serial publications (except newspapers) published in the various Slavic languages of the Soviet Union since October 1917. The entries list Library of Congress call numbers and its precise holdings, as well as indicating libraries in the United States and Canada where partial or complete runs of a given serial will be found.   S. M. H.

Biographies

97.   Bulgakov, V. F. **The Last Year of Leo Tolstoy**. Trans. from the Russian by Ann Dunnigan. With an intro. by George Steiner. New York, Dial Press, 1971. 235p. $7.95.

Bulgakov's Tolstoy is, in the main, the Tolstoy of the standard biographies, since the diary has long been a principal source for them. We meet again the spartan champion of simplicity, love, and work, weeping easily and deeply concerned about everyone's troubles; the resolute enemy of property, conventional education, lawyers, doctors, human carnivores, high society pleasures, modern literature, and the claims of the flesh. The work also shows how busy Tolstoy was and how he was involved in countless activities.

AHR, 77:2:549   R: Arthur P. Mendel

98.   Byrnes, Robert F. **Pobedonostsev: His Life and Thought**. Bloomington, Indiana University Press, 1968. 495p. $15.00.

Byrnes's account of Pobedonostsev's life, career, and personal philosophy is straightforward, largely non-analytical, and generally unpsychological. The documentation is very full, the range of sources, both manuscript and published, is truly impressive, and the listing of Pobedonostsev's works alone will be invaluable to future scholars. The author's description of his part in the judicial reforms, his destruction of Loris-Melikov and the constitutional revision of 1881, his administration of the Holy Synod, and his work with primary education and the censorship provides a fascinating composite picture of the committed conservative in action. Pobedonostsev held an organic view of change, opposed introducing alien institutions where no natural base existed, and clung firmly to the unique need for autocracy in Russia.

SR, 28:3:486-7   R: Roderick E. McGrew

99.   Cohen, Stephen F. **Bukharin and the Bolshevik Revolution: A Political Biography, 1888-1938.** New York, Knopf, 1973. 495p. $15.00.
This is the most comprehensive biography of Bukharin in any language; the "Old Guard" Bolshevik represented the right wing within the CPSU sympathetic to the peasants' interests. This work will undoubtedly become the definitive study on Bukharin. Its thorough research ensures Bukharin his rightful place in the history of the USSR.   S. M. H.

100.   Crankshaw, Edward. **Khrushchev: A Career.** New York, Viking, 1966. 311p. $7.50.
Crankshaw's political biography of Khrushchev is broadly conceived, dramatically presented, and eminently readable. It should prove a boon to the general reader, and it should not be neglected by the specialist. The latter cannot fail to be stimulated, perhaps sometimes even provoked, by Crankshaw's wide-ranging, free-swinging, but often penetrating interpretations of Khrushchev's political life. The Khrushchev that emerges from the record is clearly recognizable. All the essential traits of the politician the world came to know later are there. Crankshaw's book abounds in insights into the phenomenon of Khrushchev. This alone makes it useful reading. Its freshness of style and literary quality, furthermore, make it enjoyable reading.
        SR, 26:3:492-3   R: Carl A. Linden

101.   Crowley, Edward L., et al., eds. **Party and Government Officials of the Soviet Union, 1917-1967.** Metuchen, N. J., Scarecrow Press, 1969. 214p. $7.50.
This book traces the composition of Soviet officialdom, including government and party organs. Chronologically arranged, it begins with the first congress of the RSDRP and the governments starting with November 7, 1917. An extensive general index helps to identify a certain person with either party or government position at a given time. A useful tool for students of Soviet affairs.
        S. M. H.

102.   Crowley, Edward L., et al., eds. **Prominent Personalities in the USSR: A Biographic Directory Containing 6,015 Biographies of Prominent Personalities in the Soviet Union.** Munich, The Institute for the Study of the USSR; Metuchen, N. J., Scarecrow Press, 1968. 792p. $35.00. The quarterly supplement is available for an annual subscription of $10.00.
The latest volume in the series of Soviet biographies, *Prominent Personalities in the USSR,* is the most comprehensive so far. From the biographical material on 130,000 Soviet citizens assembled in the files of the Institute, the editorial staff of this reference tool, headed by Andrew I. Lebed, culled data for 6,015 biographies, of which 4,300 represent updated entries and 1,715 are entirely new. The volume is organized under these main headings: education, career (positions), publications, awards. This is a welcome substitute for a non-existent Soviet who's who and as a time- and labor-saving device, it deserves to be given a very high rating. In addition to 730 pages of biographical data, it devotes 62

pages to listing the names of key personnel of major party, government, military, scientific, and other organizations. [*See also* item 126]
SR, 28:4:697-8   R: Sergius Yakobson

103.   Daniels, Rudolph L. **V. N. Tatishchev: Guardian of the Petrine Revolution**. Philadelphia, Franklin Publishing Co., 1973. 125p. $8.95.
Daniels has compiled a biography of the professional life of Tatishchev which through careful and painstaking work provides a full chronological record of Tatishchev's career in state service and his activity during removal or retirement from the bureaucracy. He includes also a discussion of Tatishchev's role in the affair of 1730 and informs us of the content of his subject's scholarly works.
SR, 33:4:772-3   R: Frederick I. Kaplan

104.   Deutscher, Isaac. **The Prophet Outcast: Trotsky, 1929-1940**. New York, Oxford University Press, 1964. 543p. $9.50.
In this final (third) volume of Trotsky's biography, Deutscher tries to overcome the sense of anticlimax that pervaded the last decade of his hero's life by restating a thesis, already familiar to readers of his earlier books, that Trotsky's personal tragedy was overshadowed by his prophetic genius. Add to this Deutscher's narrative power, his dialectical skill, and you have the formula which makes for compelling yet disturbing reading. Deutscher's trilogy sets a standard by which all future biographies of Trotsky will be judged.
JMH, 37:2:118-9   R: Alfred J. Rieber

105.   Fischer, Louis. **The Life of Lenin**. New York, Harper & Row, 1964. 703p. $10.00.
This Lenin biography is by far the most important and most useful study. Fischer brought many new advantages to his study of Lenin not the least of which was the simple fact that he knew Lenin and his retinue at first hand. Furthermore, he has not restricted his work to a personal memoir but has thoroughly researched his subject from logical sources. In no other work does Lenin emerge as the leader of the Soviet state with such clarity.
JMH, 37:3:410-11   R: Warren Lerner

106.   Getzler, Isreal. **Martov: A Political Biography of a Russian Social Democrat**. Cambridge, Cambridge University Press; Melbourne, Melbourne University Press, 1967. 246p. $12.50.
The first biography of the leader of the Russian Mensheviks, Iulii O. Tsederbaum, whose pseudonym was L. Martov. The book has the density of documentation, but unlike many others it provides sufficient analysis and interpretation so that it is clear and readable. The author has used unpublished materials from the Menshevik Project in New York, the Hoover Institution, Amsterdam, and elsewhere; periodicals and books; and interviews with the small and fast-vanishing band of Menshevik veterans of the Revolution. The book is a welcome and worthy addition to the large and growing shelf of scholarly English-language studies of the Russian revolutionary movement.
SR, 27:3:490-1   R: Donald W. Treadgold

107. Haney, Jack V. **From Italy to Muscovy: The Life and Works of Maxim the Greek**. Munich, Wilhelm Fink Verlag, 1973. 198p. DM48.

Michael Trivolis, better known as Maxim the Greek, was sent to Muscovy as a corrector of Slavonic biblical and liturgical translations, where he spent 26 years in prison, being released in 1551. He left behind some 360 works; only about 200 have been published. The book is in two parts: the first a biography, the second an account of his thought and culture as revealed in his works. The bibliography is excellent.

CSP, 17:2-3:525-6   R: F. J. Thomson

108. Haupt, Georges, and Jean-Jacques Marie. **Makers of the Russian Revolution: Biographies of Bolshevik Leaders**. Trans. from Russian by C. I. P. Ferdinand. Commentaries trans. from French by D. M. Bellos. Ithaca, Cornell University Press, 1974 (1969). 452p. $15.00.

The fifty-six brief autobiographies and biographies of the original guard of the Old Bolsheviks are translations from the *Entsiklopedicheskii slovar russkogo bibliograficheskogo Instituta Granat,* 7th ed. (Moscow, 1927-1929). The biographies are divided into two groups: 1) The Major Figures (Bukharin, Kamenev, Lenin, Stalin, Sverdlov, Trotsky, and Zinoviev), and 2) Men of October, subdivided into three categories: early Bolsheviks, former dissidents, and recruits from other parties and other lands. The appended list of periodicals, abbreviations, acronyms, organizations, and a general and name index are complete and useful.

History, RNB, 3:2:32   R: Stephan M. Horak

109. Hingley, Ronald. **Joseph Stalin: Man and Legend**. New York, McGraw-Hill, 1974. 482p. $15.00.

In the process of de-iconizing the tyrant Stalin, Hingley magnificently demolishes the legend built for so long and painstakingly by Stalin, his henchmen, and sympathetic Western writers. The work is also a compelling study of how myths and legends emerge and how they can distort the real person to the point of necessitating a complete rewriting of history. Such is the case with Stalin, who succeeded in creating his own illusory image of benevolent leader. The search for the origin of the myth begins with Stalin's childhood and continues through the circumstances of his death in 1953. To this end the author has examined some 400 books and sources, including the memoirs of former Stalin associates, using the method of confronting opposing views. Instructors and graduate students ought to submit this work to seminar scrutiny in order to test how legend is made and laid to rest.

AHR, 81:1:189   R: Stephan M. Horak

110. Hodnett, Grey, and Val Ogareff. **Leaders of the Soviet Republics, 1955-1972: A Guide to Posts and Occupants**. Canberra, Department of Political Science, Research School of Social Sciences, Australian National University, 1973. 454p. $4.00pa.

This extensive and updated guide to the Soviet leadership in government and party covers all 15 Soviet republics. The guide provides information on names and positions held on the regional and republic level and other pertinent data.

The generally broad coverage provides a valuable service for both the student and specialist. There is a name index.   S. M. H.

111.   Jenkins, Michael. **Arakcheev: Grand Vizier of the Russian Empire**.
       New York, Dial Press, 1969. 317p. $5.95.
Jenkins presents the first biography in any language of Count Aleksei A.
Arakcheev, the talented artillerist of Paul I's Gatchina regiments who became
under Alexander I, inspector of artillery in 1803, war minister in 1808, and in
the last decade of the reign a "grand vizier." Although Jenkins was not permitted
to consult the Arakcheev papers in the Soviet archives, he has used printed
materials to good advantage. The author's sympathy for Arakcheev's loyalty,
honesty, energy, Spartan simplicity, and lack of vanity makes him soft-pedal
his hero's ruthlessness and pedantic cruelty in enforcing discipline. Kiesewetter's
pre-World War I articles, using the same sources, give a better analysis of
Arakcheev's administration of the military colonies, but for students this is a
balanced and highly readable account of an important figure in Russian history.
       SR, 29:1:102-4   R: Allen McConnell

112.   Lerner, Warren. **Karl Radek: The Last Internationalist**. Stanford,
       Stanford University Press, 1970. 240p. $7.95.
To foreign observers of Soviet political life, K. Radek (1885-1939) appeared
to be one of the most talented spokesmen for Soviet foreign policy: in the
early 1920s as secretary of the Executive Committee of the Communist International, and again in the early 1930s as an editor of *Izvestiia* and diplomatic
trouble-shooter. Lerner presents Radek as an internationalist *par la force des
choses*: a Pole without a country, who never led a party organization whose
inescapable "national" identification was as a Jew.
       CSP, 13:1:109-11   R: D. LaBelle

113.   Lunacharsky, Anatoly Vasilievich. **Revolutionary Silhouettes**. Trans.
       from the Russian and ed. by Michael Glenny. With an intro. by
       Isaac Deutscher. New York, Hill and Wang, 1968. 155p. $5.00.
Writing between 1919 and 1923, Lunacharsky discoursed with wit and
perspicacity on the three Soviet greats of the moment—Lenin, Trotsky, and
Zinoviev—and on a series of his deceased associates of the Bolshevik or broader
Social-Democratic movement: Martov and Klekhanov; Sverdlov, the late Bolshevik Party secretary; Uritsky and Volodarsky, victims of assassination; and
two little-known but interesting figures of the "Proletarian Culture" movement,
F. I. Kalinin and Pavel Bessalko. If Lunacharsky could still call Lenin an "oppor-
tunist," Sverdlov "unoriginal," and Trotsky "more brilliant" than Lenin, there
is little wonder that nothing approaching the crisp maturity of these vignettes
has since appeared from the presses of the USSR. Deutscher's introduction
supplies a brief and useful sketch of Lunacharsky's own life and character.
       SR, 28:4:650-1   R: Robert V. Daniels

114.   MacKenzie, David. **The Lion of Tashkent: The Career of General
       M. G. Cherniaev**. Athens, Ga., University of Georgia Press, 1974. 268p.
       $11.00.

After meticulous research in the USSR and Europe, MacKenzie has written a political biography that not only delineates a bold and tragic figure but also provides new material on the Russian conquest of Central Asia and a new focus on Pan-Slavism and other major issues of nineteenth century Russia.

S. M. H.

115. Morgan, M. C. **Lenin**. Athens, Ohio, Ohio University Press, 1971. 236p. $8.75.

Although the title implies a biography, this is an unpretentious study, organized chronologically for the most part, which focuses on Lenin's ideology and politics. The narrative is leavened by occasional asides depicting the informal Lenin, and a sketchy biographical framework is provided. It is a skillful synthesis and useful reading for undergraduates.

SR, 32:2:386　　　　　　　　R: Robert D. Warth

116. Payne, Robert. **The Life and Death of Lenin**. New York, Simon and Shuster, 1964. 672p. $8.50.

For Payne, as for Possony, Lenin is a compulsively destructive revolutionary; however, whereas Possony attempts to provide a serious analytical foundation for his conclusion, Payne tends toward the superficial and the sensational. Motivation is reduced to a formula: Lenin's Asiatic ancestry (an atavistic urge to destroy) plus Nechaevism. Payne's biography of Lenin is an exciting introduction for the casual reader.

SR, 24:1:121-3　　　　　　　R: Saul N. Silverman

117. Payne, Robert. **The Rise and Fall of Stalin**. New York, Simon and Shuster, 1965. 767p. $10.00.

Payne uses a wide range of Russian and foreign materials on Stalin, including the documents and memoirs that have been published under Khrushchev. An attractive feature of the book is the several dozen of Stalin's letters and official documents that are reproduced and translated in the text. Payne is most interested in Stalin as a person, and in the blood he shed. Most space is allowed for such matters as Stalin's arrangement of the murder of Sergei Kirov and of the show trials in the Great Purges and Stalin's secret abduction of Hitler's burnt body, perhaps to perform the ritual of a Georgian vendetta. These are the delights of the book. The author is much less interested in institutional or social history. Foreign policy as well as the fighting and suffering of World War II are scanted. The forced collectivization of agriculture, with millions of victims, receives about three pages apiece. He knows that the dying Lenin was trying to have Stalin executed and that Stalin poisoned him first. He knows that Stalin was planning to murder practically everybody before his end, and strongly suggests that the Presidium, led by Beria, strangled him first. This penchant for dramatic assertions, standing by themselves or backed up by debatable arguments, weakens this enjoyable book.

SR, 25:2:343-4　　　　　　　R: Francis B. Randall

118. Pipes, Richard. **Struve: Liberal on the Left, 1870-1905**. Cambridge, Harvard University Press, 1970. 415p. (Russian Research Center Studies, 64). $10.00.

This is the first volume of a projected two-volume biography of Peter Struve, one of the most controversial intellectual and political leaders of late imperial Russia. A monarchist and Slavophil in his early youth, he became a rationalist and a liberal when influenced by Ivan Aksakov in 1885 and a leading spokesman for Social Democracy from about 1889 to 1900. Thereafter, he reverted to his earlier and more fundamental liberalism while editor of the émigré newspaper *Osvobzhdenie* and as a leader in the Union of Liberation. Pipes has performed a valuable service in publishing a complete bibliography of Struve's works (save newspaper articles) from 1892 to 1905. On the other hand, the author's sympathy for his subject sometimes leads him to overstate his case.

        CASP, 14:3:538-40   R: Dale LaBelle

119.   Possony, Stefan T. **Lenin: The Compulsive Revolutionary**. Chicago,
        Henry Regnery, 1964. 418p. (The Hoover Institution Series). $7.95.
Possony's Lenin is an intellectual fallen angel turned arsonist. Possony concludes Lenin was essentially a user, both of himself and of others. He destroyed in order to organize for destruction. The author establishes the case for Lenin's "compulsiveness," but in the end one wonders whether the term "compulsive" is really adequate. He sees Lenin's (indirect) contacts with the German authorities prior to 1917 as being of pivotal tactical significance during the 1917-18 revolutionary period. Possony's analysis does not conclusively demonstrate that the Germans actually were able to influence Lenin by these means, though they may have expected to do so; on this matter Possony is more accurate in his appended essay, in which he concludes that psychologically Lenin was essentially his own master.

        SR, 24:1:121-3   R: Saul N. Silverman

120.   Shub, David. **Lenin: A Biography**. Baltimore, Pelican Books, 1970.
        496p. $2.95pa.
This new printing of Shub's well-known biography of Lenin is an unabridged, revised edition of the work first published in 1948.

        S. M. H.

121.   Simmonds, George W., ed. **Soviet Leaders**. New York, Thomas Y.
        Crowell, 1967. 405p. $10.00.
The present collection of biographical sketches edited by Simmonds represents the first substantial effort at the individual assessment of the lesser Soviet leadership since Walter Duranty's *The Politburo* back in the Stalin era. G. Hodnett has contributed the lion's share of the political sketches—Brezhnev, Iosygin, Podgorny, Shelest, and Suslov, along with the economic administrators V. Novikov and D. Ustinov. R. Slusser handles the police leaders Shelepin and Semichastny, along with the chief military commissar Yepishev. The military ministers of defense, Zhukov, Malinovsky, and Grechko, plus the chief of staff Zakharov, the rocket chief Krylov, and the air force chief Vershinin and the diplomats (Gromyko, Kuznetsov, and Zorin) are summarized by S. Bialer. The list of persons includes also Khrushchev, Strogovich, Kantorovich and Liberman, together with Solzhenitsyn, Yevtushenko, and a half-dozen other leading literary figures.

        AHR, 74:5:1673-4   R: Robert V. Daniels

122.   Trotsky, Leon. **The Young Lenin**. Trans. by Max Eastman. Ed. and
        annotated by Maurice Friedberg. Garden City, N.Y., Doubleday, 1972.
        224p. $7.95.
In its pages Trotsky has examined all the evidence available in memoirs and
documents concerning Lenin's youth, and with patient and ironical persistence
reduces all the official legends and apocryphal made-to-order "memories" to
foolishness. Bolshevik political prudery is reticent and mendacious concerning
the political views of Lenin's father, Ilia N. Ulianov. Though this work of
sanitation is probably the chief merit of Trotsky's book, it contains much else
of value.
        SR, 32:4:816-7   R: Bertram D. Wolfe

123.   Tucker, Robert C. **Stalin as Revolutionary, 1879-1929: A Study in
        History and Personality**. New York, W. W. Norton, 1973. 519p. $12.95.
The study represents not only a scholarly contribution in itself, but is also
proof that "psychohistory" is being accepted as a legitimate tool to unlock
new vistas. Tucker's novel technique in Stalin's case reveals quite correctly
that three elements contributed equally to the horror of modern history known
as Stalinism: 1) the psychological structure of the man himself, 2) Marxian
philosophy as adopted and practiced by the Russian Bolsheviks, and 3) the
Russian historical framework, with all previous experiences in autocracy and
extremism practiced simultaneously by the regime on the top and the radical
intelligentsia on the lower level. Against such a multi-faceted background, the
author sketches the portrait of a tyrant who developed his dictatorial personality
from his original servile obedience toward his master and prophet—Lenin.
This is a most complete biography utilizing all essential material and presently
available sources. An announced companion volume will cover the period
1930-1953. This fine biography, written in superb and clear English, should
be read not only by scholars and students but also by the broadest public
inclined to believe that the Hitlers and Stalins are singular experiences of
the past.
        History, RNB, 2:1:2   R: Stephan M. Horak

124.   Ulam, Adam B. **Stalin: The Man and His Era**. New York, Viking Press,
        1973. 760p. $12.95cl.; $4.95pa.
Ulam has approached his formidable task within a rather conventional "life
and times" framework, but the finished product is a masterful synthesis that
equals or surpasses his highly regarded life of Lenin. The verve and pace of his
account seldom falter, even though he makes few concessions to the hypothet-
ical "general" reader, who would presumably choose a colorful and dramatic
chronicle to an intellectual feast overly rich in analysis and interpretation.
This is a thoroughly hostile biography of the great tyrant, and in view of the
Pandora's box opened by Khrushchev's speech in 1956, no other sort is tenable.
This is a fascinating biography written with grace, authority, and rare discernment.
        SR, 33:4:778-9   R: Robert D. Warth

125.   Valentinov, Nikolai (N. V. Volski). **The Early Years of Lenin**. Trans.
        and ed. by Rolf H. W. Theen. Intro. by Bertram D. Wolfe. Ann Arbor,
        University of Michigan Press, 1969. 302p. $12.50.

Valentinov is the Russian revolutionary who knew Lenin briefly but closely in 1904 in exile. The major portion of the biography is devoted to speculative analyses of how Lenin's family, homes, and literary favorites must have affected Lenin. Only two brief personal reminiscences are identified: Lenin's conversation about the merit of Chernyshevsky's style and Plekhanov's statement regarding his rejection of Lenin's argument that Russia had already entered its bourgeois phase of development.

SR, 29:1:700   R: Ellen Mickiewicz

126. **Who's Who in the USSR, 1965-66 (A Biographical Directory).** Eds.: Andrew I. Lebed, Heinrich E. Schulz, and Stephen S. Taylor. 2d ed. New York, Scarecrow Press, 1966. 1189p. $25.00.

This updated second edition of *Who's Who in the USSR* includes 5,000 key figures from every field of Soviet life today. The book serves as an indispensable tool for libraries, journalists, politicians, historians, and students of Soviet affairs. Over 100 researchers were involved in this monumental project, which is the only publication on the Soviet Union of its kind. It is not only used in the West but is also kept in the archives of the CPSU for internal use. [*See also* item 102]

Autobiographies, Memoirs

127. Alliluyeva, Svetlana. **Twenty Letters to a Friend.** Trans. by Priscilla Johnson McMillan. New York, Harper and Row, 1967. 246p. $5.95.

Alliluyeva disclaims all intention of writing a political book. Her express purpose is to tell the story of her family as she witnessed it in the course of growing up. The family chronicle is a well-established literary genre, and in this instance the intrinsic interest is obviously enhanced by the fact that the family concerned was Stalin's. The book, moreover, is basically about him. He appears and reappears, stalking in and out of the story, expressing views, making decisions, settling fates, being a "bad and neglectful" husband and father, while devoting "his whole being to politics and struggle." *Twenty Letters* shows that Stalin's love for Russia contained no small admixture of that "100-percent Russianism" which Lenin suspected in him. The time has come when we must revise the general view that Beria was no more than one of the many tools of Stalin's dictatorship, although he was a tool.

SR, 27:2:296-312   R: Robert C. Tucker

128. Barratt, G. R. **Voices in Exile: The Decembrist Memoirs.** Montreal, McGill-Queen's University Press, 1974. 381p. $18.50.

Barratt has made available in English a representative sample of the memoirs of the major participants in the Decembrist movement. These memoirs shaped Russia's historical memory and image of the episode of December 14, 1825, and of its aftermath, and they endowed its participants with the aura of martyrdom. The main "witnesses" relied upon are, quite rightly, M. A. Bestuzhev, V. I. Shteingel, I. D. Iakushkin, N. V. Basargin, N. I. Lorer, and A. E. Rozen.

CSP, 17:2-3:528-9   R: Marc Raeff

129.   Eastman, Max. **Love and Revolution: My Journey through an Epoch.**
       New York, Random House, 1964. 667p. $8.95.
Eastman went to Russia in 1922. His reputation as an advocate of the Revolution and various friendships brought him close to the inner circles of Bolshevism.
Later, as Trotsky's biographer and translator, and as friend and eventually husband
of Krylenko's sister, he occupied a sometimes unique vantage ground from which
he observed the struggle against Trotsky's opposition and the rise of Stalinism.
This book does not notably contribute to our knowledge of Soviet history
of the 1920s and 1930s, but it does illuminate it with an assortment of
historical footnotes. It is an eminently readable and informed testimony.
       SR, 24:3:528-9   R: Stephen F. Cohen

130.   Kerensky, Alexander. **Russia and History's Turning Point.** New York,
       Duell, Sloan and Pearce, 1965. 558p. $8.95.
This is by no means Kerensky's first attempt at autobiography; much of the
book will in fact seem familiar to those who have read *The Catastrophe* (1927)
and *The Crucifixion of Liberty* (1934). Through a half century of Soviet rule
Kerensky has remained remarkably faithful to the principles that guided his
policies during the revolution; consequently this book will be of genuine importance to Kerensky's biographers. In 1917 he operated on the assumption that
a majority of the Russian people share or could be made to share his views
and that Russia was fundamentally ripe for democratic government on the
Western model.
       SR, 29:1:93-5   R: Alexander Rabinowitch

131.   Miliukov, Paul. **Political Memoirs, 1905-1927.** Ed. by Arthur P. Mendel.
       Trans. by Carl Goldberg. Ann Arbor, University of Michigan Press,
       1967. 508p. $9.75.
As leader of the Kadet Party, Miliukov was at the center of Russian politics
from 1905 until he left the Provisional Government in May 1917. As historian,
expert in Balkan politics, he gained international recognition. Miliukov began
his memoirs in Vichy, France, during World War II. When he died in March
1943, they extended in complete form up to July 1917. Michael Karpovich and
Boris Elkin edited and published them in 1955. Mendel's English edition is a
good translation of that part of the 1955 Russian edition dealing with Miliukov's
political career from 1905 on.
       SR, 27:2:326-7   R: David B. Miller

132.   Trotsky, Leon. **My Life: An Attempt at an Autobiography.** Intro.
       by Joseph Hansen. New York, Pathfinder Press, 1970. 602p. $12.50cl.;
       $3.95pa.
Joseph Hansen, who wrote the introduction to this book, was Trotsky's secretary from 1937 to 1940. The story concentrates on Trotsky's life and writings
and describes chronologically the events from 1929 to 1940. Though useful
for the student of Soviet history, this nostalgic account offers little that is new
to the expert.   S. M. H.

Handbooks and Encyclopedias

133. Bezer, Constance A., ed. **Russian and Soviet Studies: A Handbook for Graduate Students.** Compiled by Thomas P. Raynor and Carolyn J. Rogers. Vol. 1: *Research Manual.* 106p. Vol. 2: *Financial Aid, Exchanges, Language and Travel Programs for the Soviet Union and Eastern Europe.* 99p. New York, Russian Institute, Columbia University, 1970. Mimeographed. $0.50/vol.

This handbook brings together information designed to serve three purposes: "to help with the student's initial orientation within the field," to "save time in locating services and sources," and to codify "practices sometimes found confusing."   S. M. H.

134. Crowe, Barry. **Concise Dictionary of Soviet Terminology, Institutions and Abbreviations.** New York, Pergamon Press, 1969. 182p. $5.50.

The entries in the dictionary are printed in Cyrillic and are followed by English translations and, in most cases, explanations. There are altogether some 1,700 entries in the dictionary, including cross references.

SR, 30:1:223   R: Dina B. Crockett

135. **Great Soviet Encyclopedia: A Translation of the Third Edition.** Vols. 1-8 and cont. Group Editorial Director of the Editorial and Translation Staff: Jean Paradise. New York, Macmillan, 1973– (Moscow, 1970–). $60.00/vol.

The *Great Soviet Encyclopedia* is a volume-by-volume translation of the third edition of *Bol'shaia Sovetskaia Entsiklopediia,* the first volume of which was published in 1970. The publisher's Foreword states that the "purpose of this translation is to convey the scope and point of view of the *Great Soviet Encyclopedia . . .* " To this end, the work of the English translators is subsequently verified by Soviet editors, and no further editorial comment or modification by the publisher is permitted. Because this official Soviet encyclopedia is being translated and verified exactly as it appears in the Russian edition, a point of view is conveyed by means of omissions (Trotskii, Bukharin, and Beriia, for example) or presentation (the American purchase of Alaska: "American capitalists embarked on rapacious exploitation of its natural wealth. The native population . . . was subjected to cruel oppression and doomed to gradual extinction" [*Vol. I*, p. 195]). Each volume is being translated separately, resulting in a separate English alphabetical sequence per volume. The index is indispensable.

136. Mickiewicz, Ellen P., ed. **Handbook of Soviet Social Science Data.** Foreword by Karl W. Deutsch. New York, Free Press. London, Collier-Macmillan, 1973. 225p. $14.95.

This is the first attempt in English to compile a comprehensive set of empirical data on the USSR, and it will be welcomed by all interested in placing the quantitative study of the Soviet system on a more stable basis. The handbook's nine chapters and their compilers include demography, agriculture, production, health, housing, education, "elite recruitment and mobilization, communications, and "international interactions." Each chapter begins with a brief headnote followed by numbered tables displayed in a readable manner, with source notes for each table at the end of the chapter. The more than two hundred tables are

conveniently listed with page references at the front of the handbook.
SR, 34:1:162-3   R: Robert Sharlet

Libraries, Archives, and Museums

137. Grimsted, Patricia Kennedy. **Archives and Manuscript Repositories in the USSR: Moscow and Leningrad.** Princeton, Princeton University Press, 1972. 436p. (Studies of the Russian Institute, Columbia University). $22.50.

The book represents the fruit of scholarly research in some of the institutions, personal examination of the facilities in many others, interviews with the archivists and librarians, and collation of the experiences of a great many scholars who have engaged in research in the Soviet Union. Although intended primarily for the foreign scholar working at home on Russian materials, the guide will undoubtedly prove of use to the Soviet scholar as well, since no other modern and comprehensive survey of its type is available.
SR, 33:1:148-9   R: Daniel Clarke Waugh

138. Walker, Gregory, et al., eds. **Directory of Libraries and Special Collections on Eastern Europe and the U.S.S.R.** Hamden, Conn., Archon Books, Shoe String Press, 1971. 159p. $9.00.

This directory of British libraries "is intended for librarians' clients as well as for librarians themselves." It discusses resources in the British Isles for the study of Eastern Europe and the USSR. Each entry (148 in all) includes place, name of the institution, address, name of librarian, and description of special features of each collection. American students and also scholars traveling to England will find this a useful guide to major British collections.
S. M. H.

Description and Travel

139. Adams, Charles Francis, ed. **John Quincy Adams in Russia: Comprising Portions of the Diary of John Quincy Adams from 1809 to 1814.** Intro. by Harry Schwartz, gen. ed. New York, Praeger, 1970 (1974). 622p. (Praeger Scholarly Reprints, Source Books and Studies in Russian and Soviet History). $25.00.

John Quincy Adams served as the first United States emissary to the court in St. Petersburg after recognition in 1809, and remained there until 1814. He enjoyed a close relationship with Alexander I, thus his description of the Tsarist court and of the life in the capital are particularly valuable to students of nineteenth century Russian history.   S. M. H.

140. Berry, Lloyd E., and Robert O. Crummey, eds. **Rude and Barbarous Kingdom: Russia in the Accounts of Sixteenth-Century English Voyagers.** Milwaukee, University of Wisconsin Press, 1968. 391p. $7.50.

This is a good edition of valuable sources: a selection of the most important writings on Muscovy by Englishmen who came as traders and diplomats following the discovery of the White Sea route by Richard Chancellor in 1553 and the establishment of the Russian Company a year later. It includes the account of Chancellor's voyage, in the Clement Adams version; the *First Voyage* (1557-58) of Anthony Jenkinson; Sir Thomas Randolph's brief description of his mission of 1568-69; the verse letter of George Turbeville, who was Randolph's secretary; Giles Fletcher's *Of the Russe Commonwealth*, first published in 1591; and Sir Jerome Horsey's *Travels*, a record of his almost continuous residence in Russia from 1573 to 1591. Texts are modernized but based on original manuscripts or first editions, with substantive variants recorded when they are not available elsewhere.

SR, 29:2:303-4   R: Benjamin Uroff

141. Buchanan, Sir George W. **My Mission to Russia**. New York, Arno
Press, 1970. (Repr. of 1923 ed.). 252p. $19.50.
The original edition of 1923 appeared in two volumes under the title *My Mission to Russia and Other Diplomatic Memories*. Buchanan served as British ambassador to Russia from 1910 to 1918. His personal account of the events in Russia during the war and revolution of 1917 represents a significant contribution to the history of Russia. He describes the events in Petersburg on an almost day-to-day basis.   S. M. H.

142. Golder, F. A. **Bering's Voyages: An Account of the Efforts of the
Russians to Determine the Relation of Asia and America**. 2 vols.
New York, Octagon Books, 1968. 371p. 290p. (American Geographical
Society, Research Series, no. 1). $17.50.
The volumes are facsimile reproductions of the original two volumes (published by the American Geographical Society in the 1920s), identical in nearly every respect. Most of the material presented concerns the voyages themselves, made in 1728 and 1741, respectively. Rather little is said about their purpose and the preparation for them. The first volume includes Bering's account of the voyage, the so-called "Short Account" presented to Empress Anne, and Nartov's report of Peter's statement of the purpose of the voyage. The second volume is given over almost entirely to Steller's journal of the sea voyage from Kamchatka to America and return, translated and in part annotated by Leonard Stejneger.

SR, 29:1:101-2   R: Raymond H. Fisher

143. Haxthausen, August von. **Studies on the Interior of Russia**. Trans.
by Eleanore L. M. Schmidt. Intro. by S. Frederick Starr. Chicago,
University of Chicago Press, 1973. 328p. $10.50.
Teachers and students of Russian history will welcome this abbreviated one-volume English translation of Haxthausen's celebrated three-volume German account of his travels in Russia in 1843. One will find there the descriptions of village life in central Russia and especially the extensive accounts of Iaroslavl and Nizhnii Novgorod provinces; discussion of the sectarian communities, analysis of colonization and national integration, and the lengthy essays on Moscow, the nobility, the religiosity of Russians, and the peasant commune. The translation reads well. The editor's notes are useful.

SR, 32:3:605-6   R: Nicholas V. Riazanovsky

144.   Herberstein, Sigmund von. **Description of Moscow and Muscovy**. Ed.
        by Berthold Picard. Trans. by J. B. C. Grundy. London, J. M. Dent,
        1969. 105p. $8.50.
Sigmund von Herberstein (1488-1566), a diplomatic envoy of the Habsburgs,
the Emperor Maximilian I, journeyed twice to Muscovy: in 1516, and again in
1526. He published first his memoirs in Latin in 1549. In his work Herberstein
speaks of the Russian fear that the visitors to their country are really spies, of
foul-ups in one's traveling plans in Russia, of forced drinking at receptions.
All of this makes one think of the old adage that the more things change, the
more they remain the same. As for Grundy's translation, it is on the whole
adequate.
        SEEJ, 15:1:141-2   R: Alex E. Alexander

145.   Hill, S. S. **Travels in Siberia**. New York, Arno Press, 1970. (Repr. of
        1854 ed). 2 vols. in 1. $30.00.
Hill, one of the first Westerners to cross Siberia from Moscow to Irkutsk, down
the Lena River to Iakutsk and then to the Sea of Okhotsk, described in detail
the land, the people inhabiting it, and the possibilities for trading. Of special
interest are his comments on the exile colony in Irkutsk.
                        S. M. H.

146.   Kennan, George. **Siberia and the Exile System**. Intro. by Harry Schwartz,
        gen. ed. New York, Praeger, 1970. (Repr. of 1891 ed.). 575p. (Praeger
        Scholarly Reprints, Source Books and Studies in Russian and Soviet
        History). $30.00/set of 2 vols.
George Kennan, widely recognized as the first American specialist on Russia,
together with George Frost, traveled eight thousand miles across Siberia from
June 1885 to March 1886. His account of this experience shocked the world
and aroused animosity in Russia for his revelation of the prevailing brutality
and harshness of the exile system. This book should be compulsory reading
material in any course on Russian history; for that reason, the new edition is
well justified.   S. M. H.

147.   Kennan, George F. **The Marquis de Custine and His Russia in 1839**.
        London, Hutchinson, 1972; Princeton, Princeton University Press,
        1971. 145. $6.60.
The American ambassador to the Soviet Union in the period immediately after
the Second World War, General Walter Bedell Smith, wrote in his introduction
to translated excerpts from Custine: "I could have taken many pages verbatim
from his journal and, after substituting present-day names and dates for those of
a century ago, have sent them to the State Department as my own official
reports"; George Kennan, a later successor, who took up his post in 1952, has
now published a study of the marquis and his book in which he declares that
"even if we admit that *La Russie en 1839* was not a very good book about
Russia in 1839, we are confronted with the disturbing fact that it was an excellent book, probably in fact the best of books, about the Russia of Joseph
Stalin, and not a bad book about the Russia of Breshnev and Kosygin."
        SEER, 51:123:313-5   ·   R: A. G. Cross

148.   Kohl, Johann G. **Russia: St. Petersburg, Moscow, Kharkoff, Riga, Odessa, the German Provinces on the Baltic, the Steppes, the Crimea, and the Interior of the Empire.** London, Chapman and Hall, 1844; repr. New York, Praeger, 1970. 530p. New intro. by H. Schwartz. New York, Arno, 1970. 530p. $17.75.

Kohl's extensive travelogue on Russia of the 1830s, reproduced here from a condensed 1844 English translation of the multivolumed German original, is well worth reprinting. In a valuable way much of Kohl's information is super-ficial—that is, devoted to externals and the physical environment. Some of it is the ageless trivia of the tourist. Often this trivia illustrates general points of significance. For example, Kohl noted the multinational complexion of the St. Petersburg drivers, their economic freedom, their hard life, and their careful supervision by an omnipresent police force.

JBS, 4:4:388-9   R: Earl W. Jennison

149.   Lansdell, Henry. **Through Siberia.** New York, Arno, 1970. (Repr. of 1882 ed.). 391p. $28.50.

The original publication comprised two volumes: I, 376p.; II, 373p. Lansdell, a minister who was interested in the Russian prison and exile system, undertook a journey through Siberia from May through September of 1879. He describes the system of punishment as effective and justifiable. Upon the publication of his travel account he was accused of being the paid agent of the Russian govern-ment who portrayed a completely distorted picture of the situation. Neverthe-less, some of his observations cannot be discounted altogether.

S. M. H.

150.   Ledyard, John. **John Ledyard's Journey through Russia and Siberia 1787-1788: The Journal and Selected Letters.** Ed. with an intro. by Stephen D. Watrous. Madison, University of Wisconsin Press, 1966. 293p. $6.50.

The focus of the study is Ledyard's journal which contains his notes made between St. Petersburg and Yakutsk and, after his arrest in Irkutsk, during his escorted expulsion westward to the Polish border. The journal and related letters provide the reader with a fascinating view of eighteenth century Russia as well as an insight into the explorer. A vivid image of a robust adventurer whose curiosity knew no bounds emerges from these pages.

SR, 27:2:340   R: George J. Demko

151.   Olearius, Adam. **The Travels of Olearius in Seventeenth Century Russia.** Trans. and ed. by Samuel H. Baron. Stanford, Stanford University Press, 1967. 349p. $8.95.

Of the many Western accounts of Muscovy written in the seventeenth century, the best is undoubtedly contained in the travel journal of Olearius. Between 1634 and 1643 he visited Russia four times and Persia once, on diplomatic missions from the Duke of Holstein. His description of the two countries first appeared in German in 1647. Baron's edition is the first in English since 1669. This is more of a popular than a scholarly edition, very useful but by no means definitive.

SEEJ, 15:2:255   R: Benjamin Uroff

152. Parkinson, John. **A Tour of Russia, Siberia and the Crimea, 1792-1794.** Ed. with an intro. by William Collier. London, Frank Cass, 1971. 280p. (Russia through European Eyes, no. 11). £4.00.

This book is a condensed version of the diary of John Parkinson, a clergyman and "Oxford don" who, as a companion to a young British nobleman, made a "grand tour" of Europe which led him via Stockholm to Russia. Since very few English travelers penetrated so deeply into the Russian empire and left accounts, his diary, though he lacks sensibility, is a useful supplement to other travel reports. Parkinson shows little sympathy for the Russians. He speaks of them "from first to last as a set of rascals." He states that they are "totally destitute of principle. . . destruction being an enjoyment and pleasure to them."

SR, 32:3:606-7   R: Walther Kirchener

153. Staden, Heinrich von. **The Land and Government of Muscovy: A Sixteenth Century Account.** Trans. and ed. by Thomas Esper. Stanford, Stanford University Press, 1967. 142p. $5.50.

154. Fletcher, Giles. **Of the Russe Commonwealth (1591).** Facsimile edition with variants. Ed. by John V. A. Fine, Jr., and Richard Pipes, with an intro. by Richard Pipes. Cambridge, Harvard University Press, 1966. 98, 8, 116p. $7.50.

155. Fletcher, Giles. **Of the Rus Commonwealth.** Ed. by Albert J. Schmidt. Ithaca, Cornell University Press, 1966. 176p. $6.00.

The publication of new editions of eye-witness accounts of Muscovy is a welcome announcement for readers of early Russian history and indicates the deepening interest of historians in pre-Petrine Russia. Two of the books deal with Fletcher, the Elizabethan diplomat and writer. The other concerns the experiences in Russia of Henrich von Staden, a German adventurer who served Ivan Grozny. All works represent solid contributions to the understanding of early Russian history, and the editors are to be commended for their labors.

SR, 28:1:127-8   R: C. Bickford O'Brien

156. Wilson, Francesca. **Muscovy: Russia through Foreign Eyes, 1553-1900.** New York, Praeger, 1971. 382p. $10.00.

In this book 28 travelers are individually discussed. Within the chronological limits indicated in the title, most of the great names are there: Fletcher, Olearius, Collins, Custine, Haxthausen, Wallace. The documents chosen describe the Russian scene and the Russian people.

SR, 31:1:150-1   R: Benjamin Uroff

ANTHROPOLOGY AND FOLKLORE

157. Alexander, Alex E. **Bylina and Fairy Tale: The Origins of Russian Heroic Poetry.** The Hague, Mouton, 1973. 162p. 38Dglds.

For his analysis the author has chosen six byliny which he considers representative ("Volkh Veslavich," "Alesha Popovich and Tugarin the Dragon," and others) and selected fairy tales from Afanasev's collection. He examines these on a variety of levels and concludes that the fairy tale not only bears an aesthetic relationship to the bylina, but that both genres also share the pattern of hero, donor, and marginal agent, difficult tasks, single combatant, and abduction by an amorous dragon. The author must be commended for the convincing way in which he demonstrates the numerous points of similarity between certain of the byliny and fairy tales. He maintains that they are no more and no less than a fairy-tale history of Kievan Rus'.

SEEJ, 18:1:87-8   R: Russell Zguta

158.   Duddington, Natalie, trans. **Russian Folk Tales**. Illus. by Dick Hart.
New York, Funk & Wagnalls, 1969. 144p. $4.95.
This book, a selection of 22 tales taken from A. N. Afanasiev's classical collection (1855-63), represents a small segment of Russian folk tales—some animal tales and tales of magic ("fairy tales"). Both of these types are international. The only tales that are typically Russian are the realistic tales and anecdotes that constitute over half the Russian folk-tale repertoire. However, none of these have been included in this collection.

SR, 29:3:563-4   R: Felix J. Oinas

159.   Dunn, Stephen P., and Ethel Dunn. **The Peasants of Central Russia**.
New York, Holt, Rinehart and Winston, 1967. 139p. (Stanford University Case Studies in Cultural Anthropology). $1.95pa.
The Dunns have composed an ethnographic account of the peasants of Central Russia based on recent Soviet sources. The authors' object is to describe broadly the life of the many millions of peasants who inhabit the region between the middle Volga and the Baltic and the changes being undergone. The peasants here do not form a whole society or culture, but rather what A. C. Koreber called a part-culture. The idea of a part-culture implies a whole to be completed elsewhere, and in the present case it was completed in the minor but functionally important cities and city life of traditional Russia.

SR, 27:2:337-8   R: Lawrence Krader

160.   Jones, Roy G. **Language and Prosody of the Russian Folk Epic**. The Hague, Mouton, 1972. 105p. (Slavistic Printings and Reprintings, 275). 32Dglds.
The study is based on the byliny of Trofim Riabinin as recorded by Gilferding in 1871. Jones discusses meter and rhythm, rhythmic units, repetition of prepositions, morphological variants within the line, epic formulas, and the development of the epic line in Russian. He defines the meter in terms of the obligatory stresses and demonstrates that the thirteen- and eleven-syllable lines dominate.

SR, 33:2:398   R: Felix J. Oinas

THE ARTS

Architecture

161.   Kopp, Anatole. **Town and Revolution: Soviet Architecture and City Planning, 1917-1935**. Trans. from the French by Thomas E. Burton. New York, George Braziller, 1970. 274p. $15.00.

Kopp, a practicing architect and urbanist, fruitfully exploited the brilliant and heretofore largely untapped journals of the era. From these and other sources he culled over 200 photographs, plans, elevations, and sketches, whose publication alone would have justified his effort. These are presented in chapters divided fairly equally between chronological and topical themes. The principal sections focus on those areas in which the architects of the twenties particularly distinguished themselves: public housing, workers' clubs, urban planning, and anti-urban schemes, including the pioneering linear cities. The monograph's consistent point of view is informed by thoughtful research and the visual acuity of a practiced architect.
SR, 29:1:744-5   R: S. Frederick Starr

162.   Senkevitch, Anatole, Jr. **Soviet Architecture, 1917-1962: A Bibliographical Guide to Source Material**. Charlottesville, University Press of Virginia, 1974. 284p. $13.50.
Senkevitch's bibliographic guide which he has assembled indicates just how vast is the range of published sources, and opens the prospect of more thoroughly grounded research on a variety of new and old topics. The volume does not purport to be a comprehensive index. Rather, the 1,000 separate entries— including monographs and journal articles, both Russian and Western—have been selected "primarily to satisfy initial bibliographic enquiries into the history and theory of Soviet architecture." They achieve this admirably well. The brief summaries of entries are generally useful and the indexing unusually thorough.
SR, 34:2:444-5   R: S. Frederick Starr

163.   Voyce, Arthur. **The Art and Architecture of Medieval Russia**. Norman, University of Oklahoma Press, 1967. 432p. $9.95.
Voyce presents not only the development of Russian art and architecture to about 1700 but also its Scythian, Iranian, and other antecedents. He has included political, economic, and social background with particular attention to Russia's dependence upon Byzantium's with Romanesque and even more with Oriental features, especially from Georgia and Armenia. Occasional late influences from China, India, and other Asian lands are indicated. The author treats also the decorative arts and crafts, including such aspects as metalwork, jewelry, embroidery, arms of armor, woodwork, carving, and ceramics. Numerous fine plates with descriptions, a glossary, a bibliography, and a detailed index make this work a handy reference tool.
AHR, 73:4:1120-1   R: Oswald P. Backus III

Fine Arts

164.   Frankel, Tobia. **The Russian Artist: The Creative Person in Russian Culture**. New York, Macmillan, 1972. 198p. (Russia Old and New Series). $5.95.
This is a well-written, well-organized history of the arts in Russia from the earliest period to the present day. Although designed for students and others new to Russian culture, the book will encourage readers to plunge in more deeply. The arts surveyed include woodworking, icon-making, architecture,

poetry, literary criticism, theatrical design and direction, music, ballet, and cinema.

SR, 33:3:612-3   R: Priscilla Johnson McMillan

165.   Johnson, Priscilla, and Leopold Labedz, eds. **Khrushchev and the Arts: The Politics of Soviet Culture, 1962-1964.** Cambridge, Mass., MIT Press, 1965. 300p. $7.50.

Thorough and well documented, it is the best factual blow-by-blow account of the *smutnoe vremia* of Soviet literature in the 1960s—a period of hope and despair, imposters and heretics, defenders of the true faith and alleged agents of schismatic churches, reticent writers of chronicles of days past and irritable temporal rulers. Among the documents included in the volume perhaps the most valuable are Khrushchev's angry remarks provoked by the "decadent" Soviet paintings exhibited at the Manezh on December 1, 1962, and Mikhail Romm's 1962 speech to motion picture and theater artists and technicians, in which the veteran film director denounced Stalinist obscurantism and anti-Semitism. It is also most useful to have, in chronological order, the attacks on Ehrenburg's memoirs by the Stalinist critic Ermilov and the denunciation of Evtushenko, the accused writers' replies, as well as the full text of Alexandr Tvardovsky's poem "Terkin in the Other World."

SR, 24:2:351-3   R: Maurice Friedberg

166.   Sjeklocha, Paul, and Igor Mead. **Unofficial Art in the Soviet Union.** Berkeley, University of California Press, 1967. 213p. $15.00.

Following an impressively thorough introduction to the role of political influence on Russian and Soviet art in the past, the authors of this text have described and documented one of the most interesting phenomena in contemporary art: the appearance in the Soviet Union of a bona fide unofficial and underground art. The authors have given us a scholarly, intriguing account. It is the most instructive work on Soviet art to appear since Camilla Gray's *The Great Experiment* (London, 1962) and is essential for any assessment of the place of the visual arts in Soviet life.

SR, 27:4:677-8   R: Arthur Sprague

Music

167.   Hanson, Lawrence and Elisabeth Hanson. **Tchaikovsky: The Man behind the Music.** New York, Dodd, Mead, 1966. 385p. $7.50.

The Hansons have written a very readable book intended for the general reader. It is a biography in the popular style. Anyone having a casual interest in music, anyone believing the "romance" of music and life, will read the book with pleasure and even some profit. There is no scholarly pretense, there are no annotations to identify the frequent quotes, no musical examples or learned analyses. The photographs in the American edition are better reproduced than those in the English edition (*Tschaikovsky: A New Study of the Man and His Music.*)

SR, 27:1:167-9   R: Boris Schwarz

168. Krebs, Stanley D. **Soviet Composers and the Development of Soviet Music.** New York, W. W. Norton, 1970. 364p. $11.50.

Part I of this book reviews Soviet cultural ideology in music, identifying its sources and tracing its development through the changing tensions generated whenever politics impinged on creative autonomy. Kreb's insight into cause and consequence clearly defines the methodology devised by the party to control creativity in music. A critical examination of the lives and works of some two dozen major Soviet composers occupies the bulk of the book. No other study in English compares with it for completeness.

SR, 30:3:699-700   R: Malcolm H. Brown

169. Schwarz, Boris. **Music and Musical Life in Soviet Russia, 1917-1970.** New York, W. W. Norton, 1972. 550p. $13.50.

This is a longish chronicle of Soviet musical life and the ways of the Soviet musical establishment; there is only cursory discussion of the music itself. The five main parts are called "Experimentation" (1917-21), "Consolidation" (1921-32), "Regimentation" (1932-53), "Liberalization" (1953-64), and "Collective Leadership" (1964-70). The author apparently finds the twenties the most interesting of times in Soviet music. His book should prove a useful complement to the still very small collection of credible books on Soviet music.

SR, 32:1:204-5   R: Stanley Krebs

170. Seaman, Gerald R. **History of Russian Music. Vol. 1: From Its Origins to Dargomyzhsky.** New York, Praeger, 1968. 351p. $9.00.

Despite the disappointing criticism in professional circles of this projected two-volume history of Russian music, it must be said that Seaman's book will be useful to those who, because of language barriers, are unable to read the Russian publications. The materials are arranged in a readable manner; each chapter is subdivided into many shorter sections, neatly subtitled in textbook fashion. The musical examples are provided with transliterated texts wherever words appear. The book is based entirely on secondary Russian sources.

SR, 29:1:745-7   R: Boris Schwarz

171. Swan, Alfred J. **Russian Music and Its Sources in Chant and Folk-Song.** New York, W. W. Norton, 1973. 234p. $12.50.

In this book, not quite ready for publication at the time of his death in 1970, Swan coordinates the several areas of his special expertise, placing them in a wider historical context planned to substantiate his personal view of Russian music. The importance of the book lies precisely in this expression of a personal view, even if it is not always borne out in an absolutely convincing fashion by the evidence adduced. Swan sees Russian music as growing out of folk song and liturgical chant. This book together with Stanley Kreb's *Soviet Composers and the Development of Soviet Music* (1970) and Boris Schwarz's *Music and Musical Life in Soviet Russia 1917-1970* (1972) supersede all earlier books on Russian music in English.   S. M. H.

172. Vodarsky-Shiraeff, Alexandria. **Russian Composers and Musicians: A Biographical Dictionary.** New York, Greenwood Press, 1969 (1940). 158p. $12.50.

Similar to Igor F. Belza's *Handbook of Soviet Composers* (London, Pilot Press, 1944. 101p.), this useful reference aid offers brief sketches of 82 composers and musicians arranged in alphabetical order. Many of the names included in this biography have become the victims of Stalin's purges and despite limited de-Stalinization their complete biographical data has not yet been made available in Soviet publications. Therefore, this reprint represents the only guide to Russian musicians.   S. M. H.

Theater

173.   Donskov, Andrew. **The Changing Image of the Peasant in Nineteenth Century Russian Drama**. Helsinki, Academia Scientarum Fennica, 1972. 204p.

The appearance of this book deserves great attention. Very little has been written about Russian peasant drama. The book's achievement is twofold: it provides a profound analysis of the basic peasant types in Russian drama of the nineteenth century and a morphological analysis of the language of different dramatists. The author focuses his attention on the leading dramatist of Russian sentimentalism, Nicolai Il'in. Then he turns to three plays of everyday life, written by A. Potekhin. Using the example of D. Kishenskii's play *Pit' do dna ne vidat' dobra*, he shows how peasant characters have changed. This work should be required reading for many self-styled "Slavic" linguists who occupy themselves with every problem except the study of the Russian language in detail and its peasant dialects in particular.

        CSP, 16:1:128-9   R: V. Revutsky

174.   Evreinov, Nikolai. **Life as Theater: Five Modern Plays**. Trans. and ed. by Christopher Collins. Ann Arbor, Ardis, 1973. 272p. $10.95cl.; $3.95pa.

A welcome addition to the body of Russian drama in translation in this collection of five plays by Evreinov (1879-1953). Theoretician, playwright, regisseur, and composer, Evreinov strongly influenced the development of both Russian and international avant-garde and absurdist drama through his views that life is basically theatrical, that the audience senses this and desires theatricality on the stage for self-escape and catharsis, and that drama itself should be realistic and more stylized as in the earlier forms of the puppet show. Along with the plays, Collins provides a lengthy and valuable general introduction to Evreinov's theater.

        SEEJ, 18:4:445-6   R: Kathryn Anne Brailer

175.   Sukhovo-Kobylin, Alexander. **The Trilogy of Alexander Sukhovo-Kobylin**. Trans. and with an intro. by Harold B. Segel. New York, E. P. Dutton, 1969. 264p. $6.95.

Segel's translation of the *Trilogy* of Sukhovo-Kobylin makes available in English for the first time a fascinating work of Russian drama from the mid-nineteenth century. In his introductory essay Segel covers the relevant scholarship, Russian and English, and analyzes the dramatic and philosophical structure of the trilogy. The translation itself reads well.

SR, 29:3:553-4   R: Joan Delaney

176.   Swift, Mary Grace. **The Art of the Dance in the U.S.S.R.** Notre Dame, University of Notre Dame Press, 1968. 405p. $15.00.

In nine chapters, of which the first is devoted to a concise survey of Russian ballet up to the Revolution, the author endeavors to provide a broad outline of the evolution of ballet in Soviet Russia and some of the Soviet republics up to 1964. An attempt is made to describe the ideological principles underlying Soviet ballet, and there are numerous quotations from political literature and official pronouncements. Concise synopses of ballets are given where appropriate, and there are some excellent illustrations. The book is a mine of information, but care must be taken in employment the bibliography, notes, and index.

SR, 29:2:356-7   R: Gerald Seaman

THE ECONOMY

General Studies

177.   Bornstein, Morris, and Daniel R. Fusfeld, eds. **The Soviet Economy: A Book of Readings**. 3rd ed. Homewood, Ill., Richard Irwin, 1970 (1962). 467p. $7.95. 4th ed., 1974. 543p. Paper.

This enlarged edition updates available material, including two essays by E. Liberman. It examines the three basic aspects of the Soviet economy: the fundamental strategy of planning, the role of Marxist ideology, and a summary view of the principles by which resources are allocated. Another part of the reader provides details about the operation of the Soviet planned economy, followed by aspects of macroeconomics of national product and growth, and essays on the changing nature of the system and possible future developments. The contributions of over twenty specialists and a well-selected bibliography make this reader useful to anyone interested in the Soviet economic system.

S. M. H.

178.   Campbell, Robert W. **Soviet Type Economies**. London, Macmillan, 1974. 259p. £4.50cl.; £2.25pa.

This work provides a general introduction to the working of the Soviet economic system. The book is basically an extension of an earlier work, *Soviet Economic Power*, re-appraising the economic development of the USSR in the light of recent research, and extending the work to include an assessment of the managerial reforms in the Soviet Union and to discuss developments in Eastern Europe and (marginally) China and Cuba. The author has provided an entertaining and instructive introduction to the performance of Soviet economic systems.

SEER, 53:132:470   R: A. H. Smith

179.   Gregory, Paul R., and Robert C. Stuart. **Soviet Economic Structure and Performance**. New York, Harper & Row, 1974. 478p. $7.95pa.

"This book is developed around four central themes and is, accordingly, subdivided into four parts: (1) the evolution of the Soviet economic system, (2) the process of resource allocation in the Soviet economy, (3) reform of the Soviet command economy, and (4) the economic performance and economic development of the Soviet economy." The book provides an introduction to the history and performance of the Soviet economy. An extensive bibliography is of great help in search for a specific subject. Its clear style and objective presentation make this study a most valuable source for the student of Soviet economic affairs. The book can also be recommended as a textbook for classroom use.   S. M. H.

180.   Hooson, David J. M. **A New Soviet Heartland?** New York, D. Van
        Nostrand, 1964. 165p. $1.45pa.
Hooson's thesis is simple and provocative: that in the deep interior of the Soviet Union east of the Volga Rive and west of Lake Baikal a powerful, secure Soviet bastion of industry and energy is developing at a tempestuous rate. The author succeeds in presenting a stimulating thesis and an important area in clear, readable, non-technical prose with well-marshaled evidence, judicial balance, and brevity.
        SR, 24:2:341-2   R: Chauncy D. Harris

181.   Hutchings, Raymond. **Soviet Economic Development**. Oxford, Basil
        Blackwell, 1971. 314p. £3.25cl.; £1.50pa.
This book covers much of the same material as previous text surveys of the Soviet economic system and its development, but it is different in being more chronological and less analytical than most, relying more on the telling detail than the judicious generalization to develop its message. Indeed, it is a distinctly idiosyncratic book. It is well written and raises a number of interesting points, but it gives somewhat the impression of a collection of asides to the main flow of discourse in our research efforts on the Soviet system.
        SR, 31:1:186   R: Robert W. Campbell

182.   Kaser, Michael. **Soviet Economics**. New York, McGraw-Hill, 1970.
        256p. $4.95cl.; $2.45pa.
The book is an original and imaginative treatment of the Soviet economy intended for the general reader as well as the college student. A large amount of material on Soviet economic history and practice is creatively integrated under three broad headings: ideology, mechanics, and objectives. Instructors and specialists on the Soviet economy will benefit from any stimulating insights. Although the book includes some technical discussion of various points, non-economists will find it accessible and rewarding, particularly for its integration of ideological, historical, political, and social aspects with the economic analysis.
        SR, 30:4:900-1   R: Morris Bornstein

183.   Katz, Abraham. **The Politics of Economic Reform in the Soviet Union**.
        New York, Praeger, 1972. 242p. $15.00.
The author has provided a very useful book for all students of Soviet society. His approach is to focus on the Kosygin economic reforms announced in September 1965, for the period of the Eighth Five-Year Plan. His combination of

political and economic considerations makes his approach interesting as a venture in programme assessment. His careful documentation from primary Soviet sources provides a helpful reference source as well as analysis of important programmes. A useful review of the Stalinist model for planning and management is provided as a frame of reference for assessing the nature of change implied by the proposed reform.

CSP, 16:2:301-2   R: John P. Hardt

184.   Kish, George. **Economic Atlas of the Soviet Union**. Ann Arbor,
        University of Michigan Press. 2d rev. ed., 1971. 90p. $12.50.
This is the second edition of a work first published in 1960. Most of the changes deal with shifts in the structure of urban centers, the addition of new towns of importance and the further diversification of industry in towns already in existence a decade ago. This work will be useful for students and others seeking a quick guide to Soviet economic development.

SEER, 52:126:156   R: Martin McCauley

185.   Schwartz, Harry. **The Soviet Economy since Stalin**. Philadelphia,
        Lippincott, 1965. 236p. $5.00.
This is a detailed, dramatic review of all the major economic campaigns conducted by the ebullient Khrushchev, together with a shrewd analysis of the factors that eventually led to his downfall. After a very brief review of the period 1924-52, the book presents a vivid account of the economic developments from 1953 to 1964. Many teachers will find the work useful for class assignments, and many scholars in other aspects of Slavic affairs will find it a highly readable guide to recent Soviet economic history.

SR, 25:4:708-9   R: Holland Hunter

186.   Sutton, Antony C. **Western Technology and Soviet Economic Develop-
        ment, 1917 to 1930**. Stanford, Hoover Institution Press, 1968. 318p.
        $10.00.
This book is the first detailed study of the large-scale infusion of Western technology and technical personnel into the Soviet economy during the 1920s. Part 1 contains a systematic review for each economic sector of the important commercial contracts involving "identifiable technical associations" concluded with Western firms or experts during the 1920s. In part 2 the author attempts to assess the overall effect of foreign concessions and technical assistance on Soviet economic development. The study shows that Soviet concessions involving foreign equity capital usually ended in expropriation or other failure for reasons often not spelled out by Sutton. The study is of value to students of the Soviet economy and of technological innovation in economic development, for it contains a great deal of interesting data and provides several insights into Soviet growth and the process of technological transfer.

SR, 29:2:337-8   R: Michael R. Dohan

187.   Sutton, Antony C. **Western Technology and Soviet Economic Develop-
        ment, 1930 to 1945**. Second volume of a three-volume series. Stanford,
        Hoover Institution Press, 1971. 401p. $12.50.

Sutton's study of the role of Western technology and technicians in the Soviet economy is a major contribution to a neglected but important aspect of Soviet growth. This volume carefully documents the wide use and critical importance of Western technology and technical skills in the high-priority sectors during the early five-year plans and summarizes the major technological transfers occuring through the Lend Lease agreement. The well-organized industry-by-industry review of Soviet use of Western technology and technicians shows the many methods and problems of transferring technology and the great impact that just blueprints and a dozen engineers can have on an industry.

      SR, 31:4:904-5   R: Michael R. Dohan

188.   Sutton, Antony C. **Western Technology and Soviet Economic Development, 1945 to 1965**. Third volume of a three-volume series. Stanford, Hoover Institution Press, 1973. 482p. $15.00.

This is the third volume, completing a comprehensive survey of the origins of applied technology since 1917. The survey is, of course, invaluable, whatever the conclusions one draws from it, in that it is a comprehensive look at major technologies in use in all sectors, rather than just a few scattered instances such as the turbodrill, which Granick has so thoroughly described. The overall picture that emerges is familiar from other contexts. In the high-priority sectors where Western technology has not been available—i.e., for military purposes—the USSR has managed to concentrate its innovative resources and to produce a good showing. Elsewhere, the major processes have been imported in one form or another, often with the active help of Western firms and their governments.

      CSP, 17:2-3:536-7   R: Norman E. Cameron

189.   Treml, Vladimir G., and John P. Hardt, eds. **Soviet Economic Statistics**. Durham, N.C., Duke University Press, 1972. 457p. $14.75.

This volume makes available the papers presented at a conference held at Duke University in November 1969 to examine Soviet statistical practices and to provide guidance for their more effective use by Western analysts. It is the first general assessment of Soviet statistics since the late forties. Several initial essays introduce Soviet statistical concepts and publication practice. The book should serve as a valuable reference work for specialists in the field.

      CSP, 15:4:621   R: C. H. McMillan

190.   Yanowitch, Murray, comp. **Contemporary Soviet Economics: A Collection of Readings from Soviet Sources**. 2 vols. White Plains, N.Y., International Arts and Sciences Press, 1969. vol. 1: 196p. $12.50. vol. 2: 179p. $12.50.

The two volumes contain forty articles that were translated and published previously in the journal *Problems of Economics*. The original Soviet source is given in each case. The first volume concentrates on the problems of macro-economic planning, and the second concerns itself generally with the functioning of various individual sectors of economic activity. Almost all articles were first published between 1967 and 1968. The book is valuable for the advanced student of Soviet economy.   S. M. H.

Economic History

191. Baykov, Alexander. **The Development of the Soviet Economic System.**
     Cambridge, Cambridge University Press, 1970 (1947). 514p. $15.00.
Baykov left Russia after the Bolshevik revolution. In this book he offers his
personal assessment of the first three years of the new regime, followed by the
history of economic changes and the development up to the Second World War.
These periods are examined: 1) Transitional Period and Periof of "War Communism,"
2) Period of Restoration and Preparation for the Reconstruction of the National
Economy, 3) Period of Extensive Industrialization, Collectivization of Agriculture
and Rationing, and 4) Period of Intensive Endeavour to Improve the Country's
Economy and Economic System. Not only the extensive bibliography, mainly
of Russian titles, but also the author's qualifications justify the new edition of
this valuable contribution.   S. M. H.

192. Cohn, Stanley H. **Economic Development in the Soviet Union.** Lexington,
     Mass., D. C. Heath, 1970. 135p. $10.00cl.; $2.95pa.
The book is concerned with measuring the explaining certain quantitative aspects
of Soviet economic growth since 1928. The author presents and analyzes many
statistical series on the growth of the national product, its sectors of origin,
and end uses; growth and regional distribution of the output of individual
commodities; employment and education; and factor productivity. Cohn's
focus is on statistical measures of growth, with limited attention to the explanation of growth policies. Specialists will find the book a handy reference source.
     SR, 30:4:900-1   R: Morris Bornstein

193. Feiwel, George R. **The Soviet Quest for Economic Efficiency: Issues,
     Controversies, and Reforms.** New York, Praeger, 1967. 421p. $15.00.
The author attempts to trace the major controversies on static and dynamic
efficiency and the major institutional reforms to achieve these goals from the
beginning of the Soviet period to the present. In the early chapters he covers
a considerable amount of the Western debates about static efficiency under
socialism; the industrialization and planning debates in the USSR in the 1920s;
and the subsequent debates about prices, investment criteria, and "planning
versus market." He has, nevertheless, tied these various discussions together
for the first time so that the continuity between these various battles can be
seen more clearly. The stage for the debates and actions in the 1960s is set by
a detailed discussion of plan implementation, incentives, and policy instruments.
The author suggests that the Soviet Union has not yet arrived at the proper
combination of elements.
     SR, 28:1:160-1   R: Frederic L. Pryor

194. Gershenkron, Alexander. **Europe in the Russian Mirror: Four Lectures
     in Economic History.** Cambridge, Cambridge University Press, 1970.
     158p. $4.95.
The author's central purpose is to see what certain aspects of Russian economic
history can tell us about some leading themes that have been advanced in the
study of European economic history. He examines Max Weber's hypothesis
regarding Protestant ethics as related to the Old Believers, Iurii Krizhanich's

views, and mercantilism as interpreted by Eli Heckscher—as it may pertain to the headlong reforms of Peter the Great. The book is marvelously stimulating, both for the insights provided and for a dozen fascinating questions it opened for exploration.

SR, 30:3:659-60   R: Henry L. Roberts

195.   Jasny, Naum. **Soviet Economists of the Twenties: Names to be Remembered**. Cambridge, Cambridge University Press, 1972. 218p. (Soviet and East European Studies). $12.50.

This is the last text written by the late Naum Jasny, who died in 1967. It was probably not yet ready in a definitive version, but the missing editorial stage was supplied by Michael Kaser and the final product is a timely book, rather a set of essays on the non-Bolshevik economists in the twenties. This brilliant lot of experts staffed the top levels of different Soviet economic agencies, and their influence may still be felt today in the renascent economic science in the USSR. But for all too long these "bourgeois specialists" were not studied and their role remained in the shadow, since they were tried in the early thirties and, in most cases, physically annihilated. This is a stimulating book for the scholar and for advanced seminars on Soviet industrialization and planning.

SR, 32:397-8   R: M. Lewin

196.   Liashchenko, P. I. **History of the National Economy of Russia to the 1917 Revolution**. Trans. by L. M. Herman. Intro. by Calvin B. Hoover. New York, Octagon, 1970. (Repr. of 1949 ed.). 880p. $17.00.

(Listed in P. Horecky's *Russia and the Soviet Union*.) A representative Marxist-Leninist interpretation, first published in Moscow, 1939.

197.   McKay, John P. **Pioneers for Profit: Foreign Entrepreneurship and Russian Industrialization, 1885-1913**. Chicago, University of Chicago Press, 1970. 442p. $11.50.

According to McKay, profit could be made by the foreigner coming into partnership with Russian capital and a modus vivendi with the tsarist government—an arrangement mutually profitable for all concerned. The foreigner profited by selling his superior technology, which Russia could not duplicate. Advanced technology was worth money and it saved money in lower production costs. His materials enabled the author to study the operations of some 200 foreign firms in Russia. He has made an original contribution and argued tellingly against some conventionally held interpretations. He has provided a mine of new facts and has described clearly for the first time how the foreign entrepreneur operated in Russia during the last years of tsarism. The book is clearly written and well organized. It must take its place as an essential monograph for the study of the economic history of Russia.

SR, 30:2:396-7   R: William L. Blackwell

198.   Nove, Alec. **An Economic History of the U.S.S.R**. Baltimore, Penguin Books, 1969. 416p. $10.00.

This valuable book is an extremely political economic history, for in the Soviet Union politics dominates economics. Thus the author feels justified in choosing to "concentrate on economic policies, decisions, events, organizations, and conditions" chiefly as they relate to the men, or man, at the top. This leads him to organize his study mainly around the specific pattern of events in time, as opposed to analytical or topical subdivisions. Nove uses qualitative data—debates, literature, stories, even jokes—with rare skill and sensitivity. This allows him to cut through the fog of propaganda and some academic discussions and give his reader a balanced view of Soviet economic experience.

        SR, 29:1:713-4   R: John P. McKay

199.   Pintner, Walter McKenzie. **Russian Economic Policy under Nicholas I.** Ithaca, Cornell University Press, 1967. 291p. $8.75.

This monograph is another of the much-needed studies filling in the background of Russian history of the nineteenth century; it adds significant detail about the period of the gendarme of Europe. What seems to be emerging is a new concept of Nicholas I. He is revealed by Pintner as a monarch faced with such a host of economic problems that he lapsed into what might be termed the timidity of poverty. As a result of Kankrin's as well as Nicholas I's inability to reform and to understand economic needs of the country, Russia steadily fell further and further behind the advancing nations of the West. The author has helped to show why this happened.

        AHR, 73:5:1580-1   R: John S. Curtiss

Economic Theory and Planning

200.   Bergson, Abram. **The Economics of Soviet Planning.** New Haven, Yale University Press, 1964. 394p. (Studies in Comparative Economics, No. 5). $7.50.

Every English-speaking student of the Soviet economy has been partly molded by Bergson, the father of Soviet national product and income statistics. In approaching Soviet economic institutions he considers, one after the other, the principal components of the Soviet national income and product accounts. Each such component consists, basically, of a ruble value at any date; this value is the product of a physical quantity and a price. Hence, by systematically considering the administrative processes by which plans are drafted, physical quantities are produced or used, and prices are determined in the individual Soviet accounts, Bergson claims to have catalogued the entire set of economic institutions. His book is a useful, even important source of institutional detail, but it is neither a satisfactory nor an unsatisfactory account of how the economic performance of Soviet institutions is to be appraised.

        SR, 24:4:738-42   R: Edward Ames

201.   Carr, Edward Hallett, and R. W. Davies. **Foundations of a Planned Economy, 1926-1929.** Volume 1, in two parts. London, 1969; New York, Macmillan, 1971. Part 1: pp. 1-542. Part 2: 453-1023. (A History of Soviet Russia). $12.50ea.

These two volumes represent the first half of the final series in Carr's mammoth history of Soviet Russia from the Revolution to 1929. Here Carr with the aid of a co-author, the economist Davies, covers in exhaustive detail the economic institutions and development of the USSR during the three years just before the

initiation of the First Five-Year Plan. The Carr-Davies work is most useful in
its descriptions of specific institutions: in agriculture, the details of land tenure,
the development of the cooperatives, and the early Kolkhoz arrangements;
in industry, the shifting relationships among ministries, syndicates, and trusts;
the status of private enterprise and the treatment of managerial specialists;
and the myriad of competing proposals and conflicting agency involvements
that lay behind the ultimate formulation of the First Five-Year-Plan.

SR, 31:2:428-9   R: Robert V. Daniels

202. Degras, Jane, and Alec Nove, eds. **Soviet Planning: Essays in Honor
of Naum Jasny**. Oxford, Basil Blackwell, 1964. 225p. 35s.

Eight of the ten chapters are independent essays more or less related to the
central theme of Soviet planning. Five of them were written primarily for students
of economics. As Nove points out, Western analysts have not uncovered so far
any theory of planning in the sense of a body of doctrine that underlies decision-
making by planners.

SR, 24:1:144-6   R: M. Gardner Clark

203. DiMaio, Alfred John, Jr. **Soviet Urban Housing: Problems and Policies**.
New York, Praeger, 1974. 234p. (Praeger Special Studies in International
Economics). $16.50.

The study provides a critical analysis of the Soviet housing policy and cites
experiences and problems stemming from a centralized and planned economy.
It should prove of considerable interest to Western Urbanologists facing and
comparing modern urban problems.

204. Ellman, Michael. **Planning Problems in the USSR: The Contribution of
Mathematical Economics to Their Solution, 1960-71**. Cambridge,
Cambridge University Press, 1973. 22p. (University of Cambridge Dept.
of Applied Economics, 24). $14.95.

This novel study attempts a critical exposition of the efforts made to overcome
the problems of the Soviet planning system. The book opens a new avenue for
further research. An extensive bibliography of literature in the Russian language
is useful for the specialist.   S. M. H.

205. Ellman, Michael. **Soviet Planning Today: Proposals for an Optimally
Functioning Economic System**. Cambridge, Cambridge University
Press, 1971. 219p. (University of Cambridge. Dept. of Applied Economics,
Occasional Papers, 25). $10.00cl.; $4.45pa.

The revival of Soviet economics after 1954 is the topic of this book. The Soviet
economist has today recognized that there may be a discrepancy between actual
Soviet prices and the "separating hyperplan" which mathematically represents
the alternatives from which planners choose when they select a "best" plan among
those available to them. This discrepancy—which does not exist in a competitive
market economy—makes it impossible for Soviet economists to interpret money
values of Soviet aggregates like "consumption" and "investment" as Western
economists can interpret corresponding Western aggregates. These topics, which

are an important part of Western economics, are still neglected in the Soviet Union.

SR, 32:2:398-9 　　　　　　　R: Edward Ames

206.　Hardt, John P., et al., eds. **Mathematics and Computers in Soviet Economic Planning.** New Haven, Yale University Press, 1967. 298p. (Yale Russian and East European Studies, no. 5). $7.50.

The well-designed symposium held at the University of Rochester in 1965 on "Mathematics and Computers in Soviet Economic Planning" suggests that, as of the mid-sixties, Soviet mathematical economists had hardly begun to cope with that challenge. The authors examine the state of the art in such areas as input-output analysis, linear programming, and the construction of multiperiod optimizing models.

SR, 30:4:903-4 　　　　　　　R: Leon Smolinski

207.　Moorsteen, Richard, and Raymond P. Powell. **The Soviet Capital Stock, 1928-1962.** Homewood, Ill., Richard D. Irwin, 1966. 671p. $9.75.

The work contains two independent but related essays. In part 1 the authors set out to measure 1) changes in the stock of Soviet capital and 2) the annual flow of productive services to the Soviet economy of the capital stock. In part 2 the authors estimate two important relationships between capital and output in the growth process. First, they estimate the Soviet investment rate, or the percentage of output in each year allocated to new capital. Second, with familiar techniques they estimate the proportions of growth that can be attributed to growth of capital, to growth of aggregate inputs, and the growth of input productivity resulting from economies of scale, increase in allocation efficiency, and improvement in technology. This study has been extended by the essay published in 1968 by Becker, Abraham S., et al. *The Soviet Capital Stock: Revisions and Extensions, 1961-1967.*

SR, 28:3:508-10 　　　　　　　R: Marvin R. Jackson

208.　Richman, Barry M. **Management Development and Education in the Soviet Union.** East Lansing, Bureau of Economic Research, Michigan State University, 1967. 308p. $7.50.

According to the author, the present and future needs of the Soviet economy require industrial managers of a new type who can apply general managerial skills, who understand the use of quantitative techniques for planning and control, and who are also knowledgeable in areas such as marketing, cost accounting, and industrial psychology. This idea is no doubt correct, but Soviet engineering education (which trains most future managers) does not yet include these kinds of instruction. Despite certain deficiencies the book's publication is to be welcomed. It is the only monograph in English dealing with the education of Soviet managers.

SR, 28:1:165-6 　　　　　　　R: Karl W. Ryavec

209.　Sharpe, Myron E., ed. **Planning, Profit and Incentives in the USSR.**
　　　White Plains, N.Y., International Arts and Sciences Press. Vol. 1:
　　　The Liberman Discussion: A New Phase in Soviet Economic Thought.
　　　1966. 314p. $10.00. Vol. II: *Reform of Soviet Economic Management.*
　　　1967. 337p. $10.00.
These two volumes contain a large sampling of Soviet views on the reform of
economic planning and administration. There are 31 articles and shorter statements by various Soviet economists analyzing the problems and suggesting
changes, and four documents describing the reform measures actually undertaken in 1965 and after. Nine of the articles are by Liberman himself. The volumes
will be a useful source for introducing those who do not read Russian to some
aspects of the economic revolution that has taken place in the USSR. It is convenient to have this much material gathered in the form of a book.
　　　　SR, 27:4:669-71　　　　　R: Robert Campbell

210.　Spulber, Nicolas. **Socialist Management and Planning: Topics in
　　　Comparative Socialist Economics.** Bloomington, Indiana University
　　　Press, 1971. 235p. (International Development Research Center,
　　　Studies in Development, No. 2). $10.00.
This is a collection of thoughtful and informative essays by a knowledgeable
economist. However, only three of the essays contain a large proportion of new
material. The balance of the book contains essays on industrial management
and on agricultural patterns, foreign trade, aid, and growth. Of these, the essays
on management of trade and on the history of CEMA deserve to be singled out
as comprehensive, informative surveys. A number of these essays could be used
in an advanced undergraduate course.
　　　　SR, 31:2:465-6　　　　　R: Judith Thornton

211.　Zaleski, Eugène. **Planning for Economic Growth in the Soviet Union,
　　　1918-1932.** Chapel Hill, University of North Carolina Press, 1917.
　　　425p. $15.75.
This is the American edition of a well-known French book which, since its
publication in Paris in 1962, has become one of the classics in Soviet economics.
It includes references to the industrial production and price indices, estimated
by the American economists. It also refers to some Soviet sources which have
recently appeared. Some additional bibliographical materials, particularly those
important for English-speaking readers, have been added. The book deals with
the period from 1918 to 1932. It examines the formation of the Soviet planning
system, the evolution of planning methods and the performance of the economy.
It is the best available source on the early planning efforts, on the introduction
and consolidation of one-year plans, on the drafting of the First Five-Year Plan,
on several subsequent increases in its targets, and on the dislocations which the
over-ambitious planning created. It should be included in the reading list for
any courses on Soviet-type economies, comparative economic systems, and the
economic history of the USSR.
　　　　CSP, 14:2:381-3　　　　　R: Zbigniew M. Fallenbuchl

212.   Zaleski, Eugène. **Planning Reforms in the Soviet Union, 1962-1966:**
       An Analysis of Recent Trends in Economic Organization and Management.
       Trans. from the French by Marie-Christine MacAndrew and G. Warren
       Nutter. Chapel Hill, University of North Carolina Press, 1967. 203p.
       $6.00.
Zaleski introduces his analysis with a study of the organizational shifts in the
Soviet economy in which he tries, with limited success, to determine the shifting
power and autonomy of Gosplan in the planning process. He follows this with
an extremely valuable chapter on the integration of short- and long-term planning
and the system of long-term "roling plans," subjects that have regrettably
received scant attention from Western analysts in the past. Subsequent chapters
trace the interaction between the debates on reforms and the actual measures
that have been carried out. The strength of his chronological approach is that
one can clearly see how the ideas of various protagonists were modified over
time in order to meet the objections of the various opponents.
       SR, 28:1:160-1   R: Frederic L. Pryor

Agriculture

213.   Hahn, Werner G. **The Politics of Soviet Agriculture, 1960-1970.**
       Baltimore, Johns Hopkins University Press, 1972. 311p. $12.50.
This study is one that should prove of considerable interest to students of
both Soviet politics and Soviet agriculture. It examines the agricultural issues
over which the Soviet leaders have been divided during the decade 1960-1970.
It provides one of the most informative and readable accounts available in
Western literature of the unfolding of some of the more important agricultural
problems of the decade and the role played therein by certain Soviet officials
either in complicating the problems or in attempting to resolve them.
       SR, 33:3:547-8   R: W. A. Douglas Jackson

214.   Jasny, Naum. **Khrushchev's Crop Policy.** Foreword by Alex Nove.
       Glasgow, George Outram, 1965. 243p. 35s.
The book consists of an introduction and eight essays of varying length treating
summer fallow, hay, oats, potatoes, maize, pulses, sugar beets for fodder, and
the evaluation of feeds. Each essay compares recent Soviet activity in respect
to the crop or practice at hand with that of Western nations. One cannot quarrel
with the book's central theme: that Khrushchev's attempts to get something
for nothing by mounting massive campaigns to alter the structure of land use
without regard to careful matching of crops and practices to regional peculiarities
were indeed foolish and wasteful. Jasny's persistent and heroic attempts to grapple
with these questions during the past half century are a great contribution, and
we are deeply in his debt for this.
       SR, 27:1:160-2   R: Jeremy Anderson

215.   Laird, Roy D., and Edward L. Crowley, eds. **Soviet Agriculture: The**
       Permanent Crisis. New York, Praeger, 1965. 209p. $7.00.

This is a collection of papers presented to the International Symposium on Soviet Agriculture held at the Institute for the Study of the USSR in Munich, in February 1964. Students of Soviet agricultural policy will find in this collection a rich store of statistical analysis concerning the "Ten Great Years" of the Khrushchev era, but they will also find more. There are first-hand accounts by people (*e.g.,* Boris Wjunov) who for many years actually tried to manage large sectors of the Soviet agricultural slum, and who eventually gave it up as a bad job. In short, the volume is indispensable for those who want to know more about the Soviet Union as it really is, rather than about the view one gets from *Intourist* Volkswagen.

RR: 25:1:99-100 R: Jan S. Prybyla

216. Lewin, Moshe. **Russian Peasants and Soviet Power: A Study of Collectivization.** Trans. from the French by Irene Nove with John Biggart. Preface by Alec Nove. Evanston, Ill., Northwestern University Press, 1968. 539p. $15.00.

No major event of Soviet history has been more thoroughly obscured by the official historiography than the collectivization of agriculture. One is therefore grateful for a knowledgeable, thorough, and fair-minded work of Lewin. The author finds the regime deficient not only in its understanding of peasant attitudes and aspirations but also in the development of its own programs and administrative structures. The primacy of considerations of power (being urban-oriented) and the tyranny of ideological abstractions over empirical economic data and analysis, which Lewin later describes as the essence of Stalin's agrarian policy, are an integral part of the same heritage. The most original and informative portions of the book are the chapters which detail the transition from NEP to general collectivization. Lewin's study adds a good deal to our specific understanding of the process of collectivization and its consequences.

SR, 31:2:429-31 R: Herbert J. Ellison

217. Millar, James R., ed. **The Soviet Rural Community: A Symposium.** Urbana, University of Illinois Press, 1971. 420p. $12.50.

This volume is a "must" for students of Soviet agriculture. The general standard is high, there is relatively little repetition, there are many valuable and clear statistical tables; altogether, this is a volume which no one interested in the Soviet rural sector should be without. Among contributors are George L. Yaney, Robert F. Miller, Jerzy Karcz, David W. Bronson, and Constance B. Krueger stressing the role of the agricultural specialists, agricultural administration, and income from private plots. The editor himself contributes a thoroughly documented survey of kolkhoz finance, with particular attention to the financing of investments.

SR, 31:3:693-4 R: Alec Nove

218. Ploss, Sidney I. **Conflict and Decision-Making in Soviet Russia: A Case Study of Agricultural Policy, 1953-1963.** Princeton, Princeton University Press, 1965. 312p. $6.50.

This is a valuable contribution to serious writing about contemporary Soviet domestic politics. It attempts to generalize about the nature of decision-making within the Soviet elite by examining phases in the formulation of agricultural policy from Stalin's death to 1963. An introductory chapter offers a controversial interpretation of agricultural politics from the end of the Second World War to 1953. The main thesis of the book is that decision-making with respect to agriculture was marked by recurrent conflict. "Liberals" (led by Khrushchev), who urged the adoption of more reasonable agricultural policies, were opposed—frequently with success—by "conservative," "orthodox," "neo-Stalinist" elements, who favored the traditional resource-allocation priorities and "managerial devices of authoritarian centralism."

SR, 25:2:355-7   R: Grey Hodnett

219.   Stuart, Robert C. **The Collective Farm in Soviet Agriculture.** Lexington, Mass., Lexington Books, D. C. Heath, 1972. 255p. $12.50.
The study concentrates on the structural and operational characteristics of the kolkhoz in the period after 1950. It contributes to the understanding of many institutional aspects of collective farming. Data from diverse sources are pieced together to give a fairly complete picture of kolkhoz structure. Of particular interest are data on the educational attainment of kolkhoz managerial personnel, the source and type of family income on kolkhozes, the structure of labor inputs to agriculture, and production costs and sales receipts of kolkhozes.

SR, 33:2:357-8   R: Lawrence J. Brainard

220.   Volin, Lazar. **A Century of Russian Agriculture: From Alexander II to Khrushchev.** Cambridge, Harvard University Press, 1970. 644p. (Russian Research Center Studies, 63). $18.50.
This volume of a detailed interpretive survey of Russian agriculture from the mid-nineteenth century through 1966 will be indispensable for both specialists and general readers interested in the Soviet area. Although the treatment is generally non-technical, even the more specialized student of Soviet agriculture will find Volin's interpretations of specific policies and practices interesting and thought-provoking. The book is divided chronologically into three main sections: the reign of Alexander II through the October Revolution, "war Communism" through the Stalin era, and the Khrushchev era and beyond. The author has relied primarily on information from published Soviet and pre-Soviet sources. Fortunately for the reader, the writing style is lively, and complex technical questions are handled in a clear, comprehensible manner.

SR, 31:1:184-5   R: Robert F. Miller

221.   Wädekin, Karl-Eugen. **The Private Sector in Soviet Agriculture.** Ed. by George Karcz. Trans. by Keith Bush. 2d rev. and enl. ed. Berkeley, University of California Press, 1973. 407p. $17.50.
This volume is a considerably revised and enlarged English translation of the author's *Privatproduzenten in der sowjetischen Landwirtschaft* (Cologne, 1967). Three chapters have been added which bring the historical account of Soviet policy toward "private" agriculture down to 1971. The first three chapters set forth the "ground rules" under which the private sector operates in the Soviet agricultural economy. The next four chapters assess the performance of Soviet private agriculture and explain its connection with the rest of the

economy. These are followed by a historical survey of policy toward the private sector from the death of Stalin in 1971 and a chapter of summary entitled "Conflict and Uneasy Coexistence."

SR, 33:2:356-7   R: Stephen P. Dunn

Industry and Production

222.   Abouchar, Alan. **Soviet Planning and Spatial Efficiency: The Prewar Cement Industry**. Bloomington, Indiana University Press, for the International Affairs Center, 1971. 134p. (Russian and East European Series, no. 39). $5.50.

This modest monograph is concerned with two problems in the regional planning of the cement industry of the Soviet Union during the 1930s. The first is the economic rationality of the location of cement factories, and the second is the degree to which cement was rationally distributed to consumers in order to avoid waste of transport.

SR, 33:1:157-8   R: David Granick

223.   Athay, Robert E. **The Economics of Soviet Merchant-Shipping Policy**. Chapel Hill, University of North Carolina Press, 1971. 150p. $7.50.

The book sheds light on the motives, ways, and means underlying the development of the Soviet merchant fleet and its implications for capitalist countries. It is the first book published in English which provides a systematic analysis of the economic foundations of Soviet shipping policy. The study is based on primary sources and it will have broad appeal to businessmen, economists, and political scientists interested in Soviet and East-West studies in general.

SR, 33:2:376-7   R: Josef Wilczynski

224.   Blackwell, William L. **The Beginnings of Russian Industrialization, 1800-1860**. Princeton, Princeton University Press, 1968. 484p. $12.50.

This is a work of intermediate synthesis that deals with a large topic and time span and provides full scholarly documentation. Blackwell's book may be considered as virtually a companion to the last sections of Jerome Blum's book on lord and peasant in Russia to 1860 and Alexander Vucinich's book on science in Russian culture to 1860. The study begins with a short sketch of industrial development before 1800, then proceeds to examine for the period 1800-1860 various aspects of the industrializing process: the role of the state and of private entrepreneurs, the growth of transportation and technology, the development of financial institutions and important branches of industry. It brings together a tremendous amount of data. The appendixes provide figures on, among other things, the changing population and social composition of Russian cities.

SR, 29:3:508-10   R: Ralph T. Fisher Jr.

225.   Blackwell, William L. **The Industrialization of Russia: An Historical Perspective**. New York, Thomas Y. Crowell, 1970. 198p. Paper.

This historical survey of Russian economic development from the middle of the nineteenth century to the present aims to provide students with "background usually lacking in more detailed and technical examinations of the contemporary economy of the U.S.S.R." The subject matter is therefore quite familiar as is the descriptive approach stressing political and social phenomena. Given his framework, the author has produced a good manual that should prove useful in classroom teaching situations.

> SR, 30:3:667   R: John P. McKay

226.   Conynghan, William J. **Industrial Management in the Soviet Union:**
        The Role of the CPSU in Industrial Decision-Making, 1917-1970.
        Stanford, Hoover Institution Press, 1973. 378p. $9.50.

This is a book with a broader horizon than its title suggests, and it should not be overlooked by students of Soviet politics or political scientists. It is a comprehensive evaluation of the record of the Soviet Communist Party's general political direction of the industrial and agricultural economy of the USSR. The study combines a well-drawn analytical perspective of party leadership of Soviet economic development from Lenin to Brezhnev with a perceptive case study of Khrushchev's ultimately abortive design for a major departure from past—principally Stalinist—direction of the economy.

> SR, 33:3:543-4   R: Carl A. Linden

227.   Falkus, M. E. **The Industrialization of Russia, 1700-1914.** London,
        Macmillan, 1972. 93p. (Studies in Economic History by the Economic
        History Society). 1.75s.

Although the author has illuminated the basic patterns of the industrialization process and discussed the relationship between industrial growth and various aspects of government policies, such as fiscal policies, tariff policies, the government's investments in creating the necessary capital overhead, he omited analysis of the government's monetary policies and the impact of the banking system. Nevertheless, he has provided an invaluable service to a broad audience of scholars and intelligent readers by presenting in a concise and penetrating manner many problems pertaining to the study of Russia's economic history.

> SEER, 52:127:292-4   R: Arcadius Kahan

228.   Fleming, H. M. Le, and J. H. Price. **Russian Steam Locomotives.**
        New York, Augustus M. Kelley, 1969. 112p. $11.00.

This book will appeal primarily but not exclusively to specialists in Russian transportation and to those who have a particular interest in the steam locomotive. Although the work is devoted mainly to steam locomotives of the post-1917 period, there is considerable information on other aspects of Soviet railway development. This is an updated version of a work originally published in 1960. The authors have relied on what secondary literature was available from the USSR.

> SR, 29:1:699   R: Richard M. Haywood

229.   Goldman, Marshall I. **The Spoils of Progress: Environmental Pollution**
        in the Soviet Union. Cambridge, MIT Press, 1972. 372p. $7.95.

The author finds that the Soviet Union has little to offer, either in theory or practice, that might lead to an improvement of environmental quality elsewhere.

Based on an extensive survey of Russian materials, the study concludes that environmental disruption has been as extensive in the Soviet Union as anywhere.
SR, 32:3:629-30   R: Robert G. Jensen

230.   Granick, David. **Soviet Metal-Fabricating and Economic Development**: **Practice Versus Policy.** Madison, University of Wisconsin Press, 1967. 367p. $8.50.
The great value of Granick's book lies in its demonstration that some of the more important and widely accepted generalizations in this area are of limited relevance for purposes of analyzing sectors during particular time periods. This study of Soviet metal-fabricating focuses largely on the first two Five-Year Plans and draws heavily on material appearing in industrial newspapers and magazines of that period, as well as on Soviet histories of machine building and a previously unutilized census of equipment. One gets the impression that the material for additional valuable industry studies lies buried in the Soviet industrial press of the prewar period. The study can be of considerable interest to all serious students of the Soviet economy.
SR, 26:4:692-3   R: Murray Yanowitch

231.   Gregory, Paul R. **Socialist and Nonsocialist Industrialization Patterns**: **A Comparative Appraisal.** New York, Praeger, 1970. 211p. $15.00.
This monograph is a technical econometric study. The author compares industrial development in the USSR and Eastern Europe with each other and with the experience of Western countries, taken to constitute the "normal" pattern, in order to test various hypotheses about the effect of the economic system on changes in industrial structure and foreign trade. Thus the analysis shows the differential growth of the heavy and light branches of Soviet industry after 1928, the emphasis on basic metals and nonmetallic minerals, the neglect of the food industry, and so forth. Eastern Europe followed much the same development strategy after World War II. The study will be of interest only to those trained in econometric techniques, and chiefly for its demonstration of the application of these techniques rather than for new substantive findings.
SR, 30:4:900-3   R: Morris Bornstein

232.   Hanson, Philip. **The Consumer in the Soviet Economy.** Evanston, Ill., Northwestern University Press, 1968. 249p. $7.50.
The author seeks to measure and compare Soviet consumption with consumption in other countries, especially the United Kingdom. Others, particularly Janet Chapman, have tried before him and have encountered similar difficulties.
This study appears to be the most sophisticated and thorough attempt to apply economic analysis to the economics of consumption and light industry in the USSR. That it is not entirely successful only illustrates how difficult such a project is.
SR, 29:3:547-8   R: Marshall I. Goldman

233.   Haywood, Richard Mowbray. **The Beginnings of Railway Development in Russia in the Reign of Nicholas I, 1835-1842.** Durham, N. C., Duke University Press, 1969. 270p. $9.00.

Although an excellent summary is provided of transportation development before 1835, most of the book is devoted to the debates that preceded each of the empire's hesitant steps into the railway era. In this book the most creditable character seems to be the builder of the Tsarskoe Selo Railway, Franz Anton von Gerstner. This is an informative and well-designed work, which incidentally offers useful insight into how decisions were reached in Nicholean Russia.

SR, 29:2:310-1   R: J. N. Westwood

234.   Hunter, Holland. **Soviet Transport Experience: Its Lessons for Other Countries.** Washington, D.C., The Brookings Institution, Transport Research Program, 1968. 194p. $6.00.

In this work the author continues his investigation of problems first explored in his previous monograph, *Soviet Transportation Policy* (1957). Besides presenting an excellent chapter and two appendixes on the commanding place of railroads in Soviet transportation, he gives fine summaries of both the place of trucks in freight transport and the growth of passenger traffic, as Soviet planners, reluctantly but decisively, enter the automobile age. The book presents an excellent, concise survey that should be of interest to scholars and students in various fields.

SR, 29:3:546-7   R: John P. McKay

235.   Hutchings, Raymond. **Seasonal Influences in Soviet Industry.** London, Oxford University Press, for the Royal Institute of International Affairs, 1971. 321p. $13.00.

This is the first full-length study of seasonality in Soviet industry, combined with some comments concerning seasonality in other sectors of the economy. The period covered is from 1924 through 1967, but useful data for subbranches of industry are only available from 1958 on. The author compares Soviet with Canadian seasonality on the ground that Canada is the most comparable country. The study has been carried out competently and quite painstakingly, but the only general result is the implied one that the nature of the Soviet Union's economic system has not had a great effect upon seasonality.

SR, 31:2:443-4   R: David Granick

236.   Liberman, E. G. **Economic Methods and the Effectiveness of Production.** Trans. by Arlo Schultz. Ed. by Leonard J. Kirsch. White Plains, N.Y., International Arts and Sciences Press, 1971. 183p. $15.00.

This volume presents Liberman's proposals for reforms in the planning and management of the Soviet economy. While enterprise managers would have greater freedom in certain areas of the production and in the use of inputs, they would still have to meet central fixed quotas, assortment and delivery assignments. Liberman hopes to achieve output while employing the initiative and knowledge available on the lower level of the Soviet economic structure.

SR, 33:3:555-6   R: Abraham S. Becker

236a.   Ofer, Gur. **The Service Sector in Soviet Economic Growth: A Comparative Study.** Cambridge, Harvard University Press, 1973. 202p. (Harvard Economic Studies, vol. 141. Russian Research Center, no. 71). $10.00.

The author has set himself the task of explaining why the Soviet Union has reached a relatively advanced stage of economic development but yet retains an industrial structure resembling those of considerably less developed economies. In particular, he asks, why is the share of the civilian labor force employed in services so low relatively to comparable industrialized countries. The study offers a large number of tables explaining the situation.

SR, 33:3:555-6   R: Abraham S. Becker

237.   Tugan-Baranovsky, Mikhail I. **The Russian Factory in the 19th Century**. Trans. from the 3d Russian edition by Arthur Levin and Clara S. Levin. Supervised by Gregory Grossman. Homewood, Ill., Richard D. Irwin; Georgetown, Ont., Irwin-Dorsey, 1970. 474p. $8.75.

The book still stands as the only major synthesis we have, and a first translation in English is fully justified, providing us with usable facts and interpretations above and beyond the historiographical status of the work as a landmark in the Marxist-Narodnik debates. The translation is clear and fluent and has been provided with a substantial glossary of Russian terms, but a rather thin index.

SR, 31:3:665-7   R: William L. Blackwell

238.   Westwood, J. N. **A History of Russian Railways**. London, George Allen and Unwin, 1964. 326p. 45s.

The study reviews the growth of Russian railways up to World War I. Maps and photographs supplement a compact account of tsarist efforts, drawing on primarily Russian sources, including early ministerial documents. The next four chapters review Soviet developments through 1959. The bibliography and footnotes will guide scholars to a rich variety of primary sources.

SR, 24:1:147-8   R: Holland Hunter

Labor and Trade Unions

239.   Brodersen, Arvid. **The Soviet Worker: Labor and Government in Soviet Society**. New York, Random House (c. 1966). 278p. $4.95cl.; $1.95pa.

The author offers a critical chronological survey of Soviet labor policies from 1917 to the present. Problems of ideology, economic policy, industrial development, education, and social stratification and mobility are raised and analyzed by the author, albeit briefly and somewhat superficially. The purpose—to offer Western readers, particularly college students, a "brief" introduction to the role of the working class in contemporary Soviet society"—has been achieved.

SR, 26:4:688-9   R: Peter J. Potichnyj

240.   Brown, Emily Clark. **Soviet Trade Unions and Labor Relations**. Cambridge, Harvard University Press, 1966. 394p. $6.95.

The author's major concern was to describe and appraise Soviet trade unions in "their own political and economic setting," primarily in the period since Stalin's death. A large part of the study is devoted to trade-union organization and activity at the national, regional, local, and plant levels, but the book also deals with some aspects of Soviet labor policy and industrial relations. The emphasis throughout is on government decrees—some of them not previously known—and trade-union statutes. This summation of the formal powers of trade unions is valuable indeed, but one wishes that the author had been perhaps a bit more critical in analyzing the material. She also overlooked the entire important area of agricultural trade unions.

> SR, 24:4:688-9   R: Peter J. Potichnyj

241.   Kaplan, Frederick I. **Bolshevik Ideology and the Ethics of Soviet Labor: 1917-1920. The Formative Years.** New York, Philosophical Library, 1969. 521p. $10.00.

The bulk of the book is devoted to a workmanlike and thoroughly documented description of what happened to Russian labor in the course of the "Bolshevization" of Russia in the critical years immediately after the October Revolution. The author's interests are mainly epistemological and/or psychological. Very important ontological considerations are not included.

> SR, 29:1:132   R: Thomas J. Blakeley

242.   McAuley, Mary. **Labour Disputes in Soviet Russia, 1957-1965.** Oxford, Clarendon Press, 1969. 269p. $6.75.

This book, which is restricted to the study of disputes at the industrial enterprise, is based primarily on the author's research in the USSR. The bulk of the book is concerned with a discussion of disputes over the legal rights of the employee; for example he may claim that he was illegally discharged, that his job should be classified in a higher wage category, that he was underpaid for overtime, or that his annual vacation should be given him in the summer. Wage rates, salaries, and hours of work are set by law and are not subject to dispute.

> SR, 29:1:715-6   R: Edmund Nash

243.   Potichnyj, Peter J. **Soviet Agricultural Trade Unions, 1917-70.** Toronto, University of Toronto Press, 1972. 258p. $12.50.

This book makes a useful and welcome contribution to the knowledge of the structure and functioning of Soviet agricultural institutions. It focuses on agricultural trade unions and the role they play in Soviet rural society and examines their organization and structure, membership, finances, conditions of labor, and aspects of social insurance. A 25-page bibliography complements this well-documented study.

> SR, 33:2:357-8   R: Lawrence J. Brainard

244.   Stanley, Emilo J. **Regional Distribution of Soviet Industrial Manpower: 1940-1960.** New York, Praeger, 1968. 209p. $15.00.

The book is basically designed to analyze the regional distribution of Soviet industry through the study of employment data. The focus is on graphic presentation in the form of maps and tables. On the basis of data for the years 1940 and 1960, industrial sectors of industry; maps are used to show the distribution of a particular sector by regions. Data were derived from national and regional statistical handbooks published in the Soviet Union in the late 1950s and early 1960s. The author points out that employment in machine manufacturing alone, which he uses as a case study, correlates well with the general pattern of industrialization.

> SR, 29:2:338-9   R: Theodore Shabad

245.   Swianiewicz, S. **Forced Labour and Economic Development: An Enquiry into the Experience of Soviet Industrialization.** London, Oxford University Press, 1965. 321p. $7.20. (Issued under the auspices of the Royal Institute of International Affairs.)

The continued practice in the post-Stalin period of forced labor camps in the Soviet Union is proven by the recurrent publicized sentencing of "guilty" persons to terms of forced labor. The author approaches the question of function in a rather a priori fashion, adopting as his stance a homemade economic determinism. The institution of forced labor acquires for him an aura of economic rationality from the point of view of the Stalinist development strategy.

SR, 26:3:505-6   R: Václav Holešovský

246.   Zelnik, Reginald E. **Labor and Society in Tsarist Russia: The Factory Workers of St. Petersburg, 1855-1870.** Stanford, Stanford University Press, 1971. 450p. (Sponsored by the Russian Institute, Columbia University). $15.00.

The work is one of the few on Russian history of European or American authorship that uses Soviet archives. The author also had at his disposal a rich fund of published sources. The book's aim is to "contribute to our ultimate understanding of the role of factory workers in the Russian Revolutionary movement, and of the social and political repercussions of industrialization as it was carried out in the context of the Russian autocratic system." Zelnik's people function within a Russian context of autocracy and nationalism rather than acting out predetermined roles as a European bourgeois ruling class and proletariat, creating a kind of industrial populism.

SR, 31:3:665-7   R: William L. Blackwell

Resources and Their Utilization

247.   Campbell, Robert W. **The Economics of Soviet Oil and Gas.** Baltimore, Johns Hopkins Press, 1968. 279p. (Published for Resources for the Future, Inc.). $8.50.

Campbell accomplishes admirably his dual purpose of assessing Russian capabilities and intentions for exporting petroleum and of simultaneously offering much relevant material on a matter of more general interest, namely, the effectiveness of the Soviet system's arrangements for factory use. The author asserts that underground gasification of solid fuels turned out to be a "wretchedly unproductive venture." This is the most perceptive account yet published on the issues arising in regard to Soviet international trade in petroleum and the economics of Soviet oil and gas.

SR, 28:3:510-1   R: Earl Brubaker

248.   Conolly, Violet. **Beyond the Urals: Economic Development in Soviet Asia.** New York, Oxford University Press, 1967. 420p. $13.50.

The author deals with a wide range of questions, such as the progress of industrialization in the eastern part of the Soviet Union, population and migration problems, the Central Asian cotton industry, labor problems on Asian construction sites, and development aspects of the Soviet-Chinese dispute. She correctly assesses the new Soviet policy toward development of the eastern regions realizing that the government "now clearly tends to favor investment in the western regions where the best returns can be expected on capital, rather than, for example, developing new projects in the labor and capital intensive industries of east and west Siberia where returns on both capital and labor are below the Soviet average." The book contains new insights for the specialist.

SR, 28:2:346-7   R: Theodore Shabad

249.   Dienes, Leslie. **Locational Factors and Locational Developments in the Soviet Chemical Industry.** Chicago, Dept. of Geography, University of Chicago, 1969. 262p. (Research Paper No. 119). $4.00pa.

The study examines the geography of the Soviet industry and in particular the development and location of the synthetic industries. The major objectives are to analyze the impact of technological change on the location and on the regional types of the chemical industry in general; to examine the planner's use of the chemical industry for regional developments, and to systematize and appraise the regional distribution at various time intervals, measure it against and correlate it with relevant developments. Little material and few published sources are available on the subject at hand. Numerous tables and an extensive bibliography of mainly Soviet literature offer further possibilities to explore several related yet not exhaustively discussed problems pertaining to Soviet industrial planning, location, and development.

S. M. H.

250.   Shabad, Theodore. **Basic Industrial Resources of the USSR.** New York, Columbia University Press, 1969. 393p. $20.00.

This useful book sketches the trends of production in four groups of raw materials—fuels, electric power, metals, and chemicals—from 1940 to 1965. This review is reliable and judicious. In general, it combines discussions of resources, usually in qualitative terms, with those of location, technology, and markets. The regional statistics and the clear maps are systematically cross-indexed. The bulk of the work consists of a regional industrial gazetteer. The regional groupings—political, economical, and geological—are rather artificial. They include the European parts of the Russian SFSR, the Trans-Caucasus, the Ukraine and Moldavia, Belorussia, the Baltic, the Urals, Siberia, the Kazakh SSR, and Central Asia. The work can profitably be used in conjunction with Chauncy Harris's *Cities of the Soviet Union* (Chicago, 1970).

SR, 30:4:904-5   R: Demitri B. Shimkin

Foreign Economic Policy

251.   Carter, James Richard. **The Net Cost of Soviet Foreign Aid.** Foreword by Raymond F. Mikesell. New York, Praeger, 1971. 134p. $12.50.

Using methods developed for the analysis of Western aid programs, Carter presents in this book an estimate of the net costs. He finds that between 1955 and 1968 the USSR delivered $3.1 billion in goods and services to non-Communist underdeveloped countries. After deducting what they got back in repayment of the loan-aid, and the benefit from price discrimination, the net cost is estimated to be only $680 million.

SR, 32:1:177   R: Joseph S. Berliner

252. Crosby, Alfred W., Jr. **America, Russia, Hemp and Napoleon; American Trade with Russia and the Baltic, 1783-1812.** Columbus, Ohio State University Press, 1965. 320p. $6.50.

Crosby's investigation of American trade relations with Russia from the treaty of Paris to Napoleon's defeat is an ideal one for a monograph: subject and period are delimited and the material generally accessible, except for some Russian sources.

        RR, 25:3:318-9   R: Isaac Stone

253. Foust, Clifford M. **Muscovite and Mandarin: Russia's Trade with China and its Setting, 1727-1805.** Chapel Hill, University of North Carolina Press, 1969. 424p. $10.00.

This detailed scholarly work concerns itself with the Russo-Chinese trade during the eighteenth century. It helps to understand the background of future Russian-Chinese relations. Its topical limits make the study useful for the graduate student specializing in Russia's expansion to the East.   S. M. H.

254. Freedman, Robert Owen. **Economic Warfare in the Communist Bloc: A Study of Soviet Economic Pressure against Yugoslavia, Albania, and Communist China.** New York, Praeger, 1970. 192p. $14.00.

The signal contribution of this book is its detailed documentation of the chronology and extent of Soviet economic pressure against the three "target" countries. We learn that the Soviet arsenal includes delay in trade negotiations, refusal to buy or sell key commodities, delay or refusal to ratify trade agreements or to deliver goods for which contracts had been signed, reduction or suspension of economic assistance and training of students from the "target" nation, and a complete embargo of trade.

        SR, 31:2:464-5   R: Paul Marer

255. Kirchner, Walther. **Commercial Relations between Russia and Europe 1400-1800: Collected Essays.** Bloomington, Indiana University Press, 1967. 332p. (Indiana University Publications: Russia and East European Series, Vol. 33). $5.00pa.

This brings together in one volume twelve articles originally published in English, German, and French during the past twenty years. However, the general reader, seeking a comprehensive survey of Russia's commercial relations with Western Europe, will be disappointed, because the articles presented here are uneven in scope. The introduction, written especially for this book, contains a general discussion of the problem, but is too short. Russian-Western relations during the sixteenth century are covered rather well, but the seventeenth and eighteenth centuries are neglected.

        SR, 27:1:132   R: Thomas Esper

256. Marer, Paul. **Soviet and East European Foreign Trade, 1946-1969: Statistical Compendium and Guide.** Computer programs by Gary J. Eubanks. Bloomington, Indiana University Press, 1972. 408p. (International Development Research Center Studies in Development, no. 4). $15.00.

The book embodies a description and some rigorous analysis of the methods and practices underlying the organization and presentation of foreign trade statistics in the socialist countries. The book is divided into four parts. Part 1, "Introduction and Summary," provides a guide to the data presented in part 2, "Statistical Series." The methodology used in constructing the tables is considered in part 3, "Notes and Documentation." Part 4 consists of seven appendixes, dealing with the United Nations and Comecon trade classifications, the problems of reconciliation, valuation, definitions, and unspecified Soviet exports; the last two appendixes contain standardized statistics on trade with the United States, Canada, Japan, and Australia, and a description of the Soviet and East European Foreign Trade Data Bank developed at the International Research Center.

SR, 33:1:156-7   R: Jozef Wilczynski

257.   Quigley, John. **The Soviet Foreign Trade Monopoly: Institutions and Laws.** Columbus, Ohio State University Press, 1974. 256p. $15.00.
The author analyzes the history, nature, and operation of the foreign trade monopoly in the Soviet Union. Much of the research for his book was done in the USSR. It copes with the subject in a competent, illuminating, and penetrating manner. It includes a number of documents. Most revealing are the "Conditions of Delivery of Goods for Export" of 1960. The reader is aided by a bibliography and an index. Quigley concludes that the "dismantling of the monopoly system seems unlikely in the foreseeable future."

RR, 34:2:220-1   R: Dietrich A. Loeber

258.   Rosefielde, Steven. **Soviet International Trade in Heckscher-Ohlin Perspective: An Input-Output Study.** Lexington, Mass., Lexington Books, D. C. Heath, 1973. 175p. $13.50.
The Heckscher-Ohlin theorem states that if a competitive market economy has plentiful labor and scarce capital, it will export labor-intensive goods and import capital-intensive goods. The Leontief paradox notes that the United States exports labor-intensive goods and imports capital-intensive goods, contrary to the theorem. Rosefielde has presented the standard two-factor approach so well that its weaknesses, as well as its strengths, are at once apparent. His book is a welcome addition to the list of works seeking to analyze the Soviet economy at the technical level that is applied to other economies.

SR, 34:1:168   R: Edward Ames

259.   Sawyer, Carole A. **Communist Trade with Developing Countries: 1955-65.** New York, Praeger, 1966. 127p. $10.00.
The author has attempted in her study to evaluate the importance of Communist—especially Soviet—trade for the economies both of the developing countries and of the Communist states themselves. She shows that, despite the enormous growth of this trade, it still represents a relatively small percentage of the trade of most of the developing countries. In speaking of the market which the Communist countries offer for the goods of the Third World, Miss Sawyer argues that there has been little shift in the products which are purchased. Food products—cocoa, coffee, and tropical fruits—and raw material still make up more than 90 percent of all Communist imports. Contrary to Communist claims

that they are willing to purchase the manufactured goods of developing areas, Western purchases of these goods in 1964 totaled more than $3 billion, compared with $180 million in Communist purchases.

SR, 26:4:693-4   R: Roger E. Kanet

260.   Smith, Glen Alden. **Soviet Foreign Trade: Organization, Operations, and Policy, 1918-1971.** New York, Praeger, 1973. 370p. (Praeger Special Studies in International Economics and Development). $21.50.

This book was written primarily for the use of businessmen interested in trade with the Soviet Union. Half of the text deals with the organizations involved in the conduct of foreign trade and the other half deals with Soviet trade policies and practices, both in general and specifically with the other socialist countries, the developing countries, and the West. A large part of the text is devoted to descriptions of the structure and functions of the various organizations that have been responsible for the conduct of trade at various periods.

SR, 33:1:155-6   R: Joseph S. Berliner

261.   Tansky, Leo. **U.S. and U.S.S.R. Aid to Developing Countries: A Comparative Study of India, Turkey, and the U.A.R.** New York, Praeger, 1967. 192p. $15.00.

The author attempts to examine the objectives, the character, and the effectiveness of Soviet and United States aid programs in three developing countries. He has placed more emphasis on the impact of the assistance on the economies of the recipient countries. He points out, for example, that by September 1965 the Soviet Union had accounted for almost twenty percent of public investment in the industrial sector in India during the second five-year plan and almost one-fourth during the third plan. In the UAR, 38 percent of the planned industrial development will be financed by the Soviet Union and Eastern European countries. In his conclusion, the author assesses the value of U. S. and Soviet assistance to the recipients.

SR, 26:4:693-5   R: Roger E. Kanet

262.   Wiles, P. J. D. **Communist International Economics.** New York, Praeger, 1969. 566p. $12.50.

This is probably the most important book to date in the burgeoning literature on the political economy of foreign trade of Soviet-type economies. In eighteen chapters and numerous quantitative examples, both empirical and theoretical, and stressing the USSR, Wiles covers all phases of the experience, including Marxist theory and Soviet institutions, balance of payments and exchange rates, efficiency criteria, trade structure and its terms, finance, international integration, and economic war. The book will be standard in the field for years to come.

SR, 32:1:177-8   R: W. Donal Bowles

EDUCATION

General

263. Ablin, Fred, ed. **Contemporary Soviet Education: A Collection of Readings from Soviet Journals.** Intro. by George S. Counts. White Plains, N.Y., International Arts and Sciences Press, 1969. 295p.

264. **Education in the USSR: A Collection of Readings from Soviet Journals.** White Plains, N.Y., International Arts and Sciences Press, 1963. 2 vols. 210p.; 212p. $12.00ea. Paper.

These volumes deserve a place on the personal shelves of scholars and teachers rather than only on those of well-endowed libraries.

        CSP, 11:1:130-2   R: D. Dorotich

265. Mickiewicz, Ellen Propper. **Soviet Political Schools: The Communist Party Adult Instruction System.** New Haven, Yale University Press, 1967. 190p. (Yale Russian and East European Studies, 3). $6.50.

This study is essentially a description and analysis of adult education under Khrushchev. The author discusses the Evening University of Marxism-Leninism, the *politshkola*, and the circle and independent study as ways and means in which adult education is carried on. Of these, independent study is, paradoxically, highly organized and the most advanced form of adult instruction. It may serve purposes other than education. Party schools and education are dealt with only in passing.

        SR, 29:1:135-6   R: Jaan Pennar

266. Noah, Harold J., ed. and trans. **The Economics of Education in the U.S.S.R.** New York, Praeger, 1969. 227p. $16.50.

A translation of most of the papers read at a 1964 conference on the economics of education. The papers deal with operational aspects of education policy, though some references are made to earlier studies on the economic benefits of education. The agenda of the conference was divided into three topics: 1) general problems of the economics of education, 2) the impact of education labor productivity, and 3) specific examples of educational planning. Some interesting light is shed (by Komarov and Samoilova) on the economic consequences of the post-1958 policy of increasing the proportion of university students enrolled on a part-time basis. The volume should prove most useful to the reader intent on understanding how education fits into general Soviet economic planning.

        SR, 29:1:141   R: Stanley H. Cohn

267. Redl, Helen, ed. and trans. **Soviet Educators on Soviet Education.** Foreword by Fritz Redl. New York, Free Press; London, Collier-Macmillan, 1964. 252p. $6.95.

A compendium of Soviet primary sources, mainly psychological and pedagogical. It is a welcome addition to the translations appearing in the *Current Digest of the Soviet Press* and in the magazine *Soviet Education*, to similar compendiums by George Kline (*Soviet Education*, 1957) and Dorothea Meek (*Soviet Youth*, 1957), and to translations emanating from the Foreign Languages Publishing House. These translations reveal once more the interesting attitudes of Soviet educators to heredity, discipline, family and morality, the parents' role in the schools, experiences in the boarding schools, children's literature, and youth organizations. The introduction is superb and should be read by all who study the Soviet system through direct observation.

SR, 24:3:574-6   R: George Z. F. Bereday

268.   Shneidman, N. N. **Literature and Ideology in Soviet Education.** Lexington, Mass., D. C. Heath, for Centre for Russian and East European Studies, University of Toronto, 1973. 207p.

The volume provides 1) a compact analytical treatment of such aspects as ideology in education; literature in primary, secondary and tertiary education; basic concepts—*ideinost', partiinost', narodnost', klassovost',* and their confused interrelation; the handling of Russian classics, with the aid of Lenin's seven articles on Tolstoi; scholarship versus political needs; and 2) curricula, detailed programmes, book lists, examination instructions, and other information on education pertaining to all levels. The bibliography and index are good. A scholarly and interesting work.   S. M. H.

History of Education

269.   Alston, Patrick L. **Education and the State in Tsarist Russia.** Stanford, Stanford University Press, 1969. 322p. $8.50.

This volume is a welcome addition to an all-too-brief list of modern works dealing primarily with education in the Russian Empire. Among the positive aspects of the study are the translation and interpretation of hundreds of documentary sources unavailable to most students of the subject. A second value is the attractive literary style in which these elements are presented, and the excellent selection, organization, and arrangement of a stupendous quantity of material.

SR, 29:1:108-9   R: William H. E. Johnson

270.   Shimoniak, Wasyl. **Communist Education: Its History, Philosophy and Politics.** Chicago, Rand McNally, 1970. 506p. $4.50.

The author's aims are not to analyze the process of narrow indoctrination in Communist ideology but rather "to present important Communist educational policies and practices and to analyze their role in social change." The author is able to use most of the languages of the countries he writes about, and he covers fourteen Communist nations, including Albania. However, the stress falls on the school in relation to society in the USSR. Shimoniak sketches the historical background of education in tsarist Russia, and then goes on to survey in historical context the aims, reforms, structure, administration, curriculum, and methodology of Soviet education. He pays particular attention to the influence of Communist policies on minority languages, chiefly in the Ukraine and Central Asia, the struggle of atheism versus religion in school and life, and the role of women in society. In sum, the author presents a creditable analysis of the Communist impact on the school, society, and the individual in the Soviet Union.

SR, 30:3:676-7 R: William W. Brickman

271. Sinel, Allen. **The Classroom and the Chancellery: State Educational Reform in Russia under Count Dmitry Tolstoi.** Cambridge, Harvard University Press, 1973. 335p. (Russian Research Center Studies, 72). $14.00.

The publication of a monograph on a phase of the history of education in pre-revolutionary Russia is a welcome event, since such works are rather rare, especially in English. The author concentrated his research on the work of D. A. Tolstoy as minister of education (1866-80). As a faithful servant of his tsarist master, he fought the influences of Catholicism, liberalism, and revolutionism. A dedicated Slavophile, he glorified the Russian tradition in education. The author analyzes in a dispassionate manner the successes and failures of Tolstoy's reforms in elementary, secondary, higher, and teacher education. Despite Tolstoy's positive contributions to Russian education, he "actually stimulated the phenomenon he wished to combat, the growth of antistate sentiment among the students." The book is interesting to read and adds considerably to the knowledge of the educational history of tsarist Russia.

SR, 33:4:774-5 R: William W. Brickman

272. Wiener, Leo, trans. **Tolstoy on Education.** With an intro. by Reginald D. Archambault. Chicago, University of Chicago Press, 1967. 360p. $6.00.

This useful anthology presents a selection of Tolstoy's more important pedagogical articles from the early 1860s. Tolstoy advocated an educational process which would, he felt, develop in the future adult an ability to live creatively within the social structure and even, if necessary, to reshape that structure. In these core ideas Tolstoy was, in a very real sense, a precursor of Dewey and A. S. Neill of Summerhill fame.

SEEJ, 14:1:92 R: Peter Rudy

Institutions and Organizations

273. Fitzpatrick, Sheila. **The Commissariat of Enlightenment: Soviet Organization of Education and the Arts under Lunacharsky, October 1917-1921.** Cambridge, Cambridge University Press, 1970. 380p. $13.50.

The study represents a meticulously documented and thorough account of the institutional aspects of Narkompros: its formulation of policies, internal workings, and relations with the party, the state, and the people from 1917 to 1921. Educational theory and the practice of education are considered here only secondarily. There are, however, two fine chapters on Proletkult and the arts. This book will remain a "must" for those interested in the subjects it discusses and the period it deals with.

SR, 30:4:887-8 R: Howard R. Holter

274.   Grant, Nigel. **Soviet Education**. Baltimore, Penguin Books, 1964. 190p.
$0.95pa. 3rd ed. Harmondsworth, Eng., Penguin Books, 1972. $1.65pa.
Grant's paperback is a useful account of the general features of the Soviet school
system, updated to about 1963, and generally reliable in its content and observations.
It is also a good, brief account of the system for anyone not interested in pursuing the
matter further. Specialists in comparative and Soviet education will find little new in
it, and beginning students are advised to use DeWitt or other detailed studies as their
introduction to the field. Recommended only for high school teachers.
        SR, 24:3:574-5   R: George Z. F. Bereday

275.   Jacoby, Susan. **Inside Soviet Schools**. New York, Hill and Wang, 1974.
        248p. $8.95.
The author visited several nursery schools, kindergartens, and elementary and secondary schools. She brings a fresh approach and accurate appraisal to the study of Soviet
education. In contrast to American education, Soviet schools are oriented toward
strict discipline and collectivized instruction. The administration of education is centralized in Moscow, and the objectives are unified in a comprehensive plan. The Soviet
government has a strong commitment to education, and parents strive to obtain the
best possible for their children.
        RR, 34:2:219   R: David A. Law

276.   Melinskaya, S., comp. **Soviet Science, 1917-1970. Part I: Academy of
        Sciences of the USSR**. Comp. at the Institute for the Study of the USSR.
        Ed. by Paul K. Urban and Andrew I. Lebed. Metuchen, N.J., Scarecrow
        Press, 1971. 322p. $7.50.
This guide contains three sections and several supplements. The first section outlines
the history of the USSR Academy of Sciences. The second examines its structure and
organization and lists the directors of its various branches and divisions. The third part
contains various lists, including registers of full, corresponding, and foreign members of
the Academy. A useful guide for the expert involved in research work within the USSR.
        S. M. H.

276a. Noah, Harold J. **Financing Soviet Schools**. New York, Teachers College Press,
        1967. 291p. (Studies of the Russian Institute, Columbia University. Compara-
        tive Education Studies, Teachers College, Columbia University). $8.50cl.;
        $3.95pa.
This study, the first of its kind in English, makes a beginning in closing a serious gap in
our knowledge of the economics of Soviet education. Schools of general education,
mainly elementary and secondary, rather than schools for specialized training, have
been chosen for detailed examination because they enroll the vast majority of students.
Perhaps the most significant result of this analysis is that since 1950 it has been these
schools of general education which have consistently been allocated a rising share of
total educational expenditures.
        SR, 27:3:504-5   R: Frederic Lilge

GEOGRAPHY AND DEMOGRAPHY
General and Regional

277.   Demko, George J., and Roland Fuchs, eds. **Geographical Perspectives in the
        Soviet Union: A Selection of Readings**. Columbus, Ohio State University
        Press, 1974. 742p. $30.00.

The 38 translated articles are grouped in nine categories, encompassing the various branches and the major themes of Soviet economic geography—history, philosophy and methodology, economic regionalization, resource management, agricultural, industrial, transportation, population, urban, and historical geography respectively. This collection provides a most illuminating and comprehensive view for the English readers of the content and theory of the various fields which together make up the core of the lively and vital field of endeavor which comprises Soviet economic geography in the last two decades and seems to be going from strength to strength.

> RR, 34:3:341-2   R: David Hooson

278.   Krasheninnikov, Stepan Petrovich. **Explorations of Kamchatka: North Pacific Scimitar.** Trans. with intro. and notes by E. A. P. Crownhart-Vaughan. Portland, Oregon Historical Society, 1972. 375p. $13.75.

The first definitive translation of Krasheninnikov's almost forgotten classic, *Opinsanie zemli Kamchatki* (1755), comes as a welcome contribution to the limited literature in English on this area. His three-year-long labor has yielded an encyclopedic compilation of notes on Kamchatka's mountains and rivers, fauna and flora, climate, aboriginal inhabitants, and a history of the Russian conquest, depredations, and subsequent revolts.

> SR, 32:1:161-2   R: John J. Stephan

279.   Mellor, R. E. H. **Geography of the U.S.S.R.** London, Macmillan; New York, St. Martin's Press, 1964. 403p. $12.00.

The book treats physical features, historical development, population, population distribution, settlement forms and administrative structure, agriculture, fuels and minerals, industry and transport for the Soviet Union as a whole. The study is a highly condensed survey of certain significant features of the Soviet Union. It is likely to become popular as a rapid introduction to that complex land for the general public.

> SR, 25:2:365-6   R: George Kish

280.   Shinkarev, Leonid. **The Land beyond the Mountains: Siberia and Its People Today.** New York, Macmillan, 1973. 250p. (Prepared by the Novosti Press Agency Publishing House, Moscow). $10.95.

The Soviet author, who wandered across Siberia for twelve years, describes in popular fashion the land and the people of this vast region stretching from the Ural Mountains to the Far East. He includes a brief historical essay and one on the growing industrialization with numerous illustrations and photographs. A short bibliography of works in the Russian language may be useful for the expert. Obviously, the thousands of concentration camps that are scattered across Siberia and the forced re-settlement of the land are nowhere mentioned in the book; however, the population figures tell the story plainly; from 9.8 million in 1927 to 19.5 million in 1967.

> S. M. H.

Population and Ethnology

281.   Armstrong, Terence. **Russian Settlement in the North.** Cambridge, Cambridge University Press, 1965. 224p. $9.50.

The volume undertakes to sketch the Russian advance into the north and to inquire into its causes and effects. In fact, it is just a kind of progress report based on competent and substantial studies by Russian and Soviet scholars. The author's concern is with settlement rather than exploration and conquest, or politics, economics, diplomacy, and such *per se*. He discusses the physical environment and the advent of the Russians into the north, settlement in this area (north of the Arctic circle in European Russia) under the tsars, and also the settlement since 1917 (up to 1959). Maps, appendices, and a working bibliography add to the usefulness of the book.

RR, 25:4:418-9   R: Raymond H. Fisher

282.   Dunn, Stephen P. and Ethel Dunn, eds. **Introduction to Soviet Ethnography**. 2 vols. Berkeley, Cal., Highgate Road Social Science Research Station, 1974. Vol. 1: 362p. Vol. 2: 345p. $10.00pa.

The purpose of this two-volume study is to introduce the reader to an unfamiliar intellectual tradition and to a little known body of factual data. The editors set forth the manner in which the intellectual tradition of Soviet ethnography differs from its Western counterpart. Their analysis assists the reader in understanding and interpreting the reprinted articles which follow. The pre-revolutionary Russian ethnographic tradition differed from the corresponding tradition in the West by the social affiliation of its practitioners, many of whom were political exiles. The editors also review Marxist theory and note that Soviet scholars work with a set of agreed-upon concepts, thus having a greater degree of methodological self-consciousness than their Western counterparts. The volumes conclude with a glossary of Russian terms, a list of abbreviations and an extensive bibliography of recommended readings in English. There are excellent maps, but the photographs are reproduced badly.

CASS, 9:1:127-8   R: James W. Van Stone

283.   Gibson, James R. **Feeding the Russian Fur Trade: Provisionment of the Okhotsk Seaboard and the Kamchatka Peninsula, 1639-1856.** Madison, University of Wisconsin Press, 1969. 337p. $15.00.

Gibson gives the account of the original Russian settlement, spurred on by the search for furs and sea otter skins, and of the two centuries of agonized effort to maintain the settlement. Attempts to establish agriculture in Kamchatka and along the Okhotsk coast failed almost completely because of the harsh climate and the inefficiency of peasants and administrators. This book is one of the best examples of scholarship in the field of Russian historical geography. A great quantity of archival and other material has been used, including reports of administrators and travelers. The 25-page bibliography is a model for the researcher in Russian geography.

SR, 29:4:695-6   R: R. A. French

284.   Gregory, James S. **Russian Land, Soviet People: A Geographical Approach to the U.S.S.R.** New York, Pegasus, 1968. 947p. $15.00.

The text is divided into two major parts: a general survey covering land forms, climate, vegetation, soils, agriculture, and industry, and a regional survey (approximately 500 pages) following a broad division into some thirteen regions. Although the author has visited the Soviet Union several times, he does not seem to have grasped the reality of Soviet life and experience and the nature of dissent that, in literary form or otherwise, has raised its head despite official efforts to suppress it. Does he really believe that the role British traditions and ideas play within the member nations of the Commonwealth is similar to that of "Russian ideology and technology," say in the Georgian SSR or in any of the Baltic republics?

       SR, 29:2:345-6   R: W. A. Douglas Jackson

285.   Harris, Chauncy D. **Cities of the Soviet Union: Studies in Their Functions, Size, Density, and Growth.** Chicago, Rand McNally, 1970. 484p. $9.95.

Over the last decade or so the typical Russian—previously a peasant—has become an urbanite, and the metamorphosis continues. Among other things, this process has created a significant geographical pattern, and this book is the most comprehensive and accurate analysis of that pattern yet to appear in English, probably in any language. The bibliography of this work, running to over a thousand items, is a major achievement in itself, and there is a very useful chapter which assesses, with considerable courtesy, post-war Soviet research on their own cities. The book will be an invaluable reference for anyone concerned with developments in general in the Soviet Union or the course of the world phenomenon of urbanization.

       SR, 30:431-2   R: David Hooson

286.   Leasure, J. William, and Robert A. Lewis. **Population Changes in Russia and the USSR: A Set of Comparable Territorial Units.** San Diego, San Diego State College Press, 1966. 43p. (Social Science Monograph Series, Vol. I, No. 2). $2.50pa.

This small volume is primarily a set of table providing data for 1851, 1897, 1926, 1939, and 1959 for regions in the Soviet Union with constant boundaries. The data include total population, urban population in settlements of 15,000 and over, average annual increase in the intercensal periods for both total population and urban population, labor force, literatre population, and percentage of the population made up of Eastern Slavs. The real contribution of the study is the elaborate adjustments to the 1961 regions of data for 1851, 1897, and 1926 reported for former political units with different boundaries. The resulting tabulations make possible for the first time comparisons for comparable regions of certain demographic data extending over more than a century.

       SR, 26:1:501   R: Chauncy D. Harris

Climatology and Ecology

287.   Borisov, A. A. **Climates of the U.S.S.R.** Ed. by Cyril A. Halstead; trans. by R. A. Ledward; foreword by Chauncy D. Harris. Chicago, Aldine Publishing Co., 1966. 255p. $10.00.

The volume, translated from a second, revised addition that appeared in Moscow in 1959, has been widely used in the Soviet Union as a reference aid and as a university textbook. A brief introductory history of the study of climate in the USSR is followed by a discussion of climate-forming factors and climatic elements. Two-thirds of the book is devoted to a regional survey of the country's climates, including climates of the bordering seas and largest inland bodies of water, the great latitudinal natural zones (tundra, forest steppe, desert) and the mountainous areas. The generally good translation has been marred by a

strangely undisciplined treatment of personal and place names, which because
of transliteration problems requires a particularly systematic approach.

> SR, 25:2:366-7   R: Theodore Shabad

288.   Gerasimov, I. P., D. L. Armand, and K. M. Yefron, eds. **Natural
Resources of the Soviet Union: Their Use and Renewal**. Trans. by
Jacek I. Romanowski. English edition ed. by W. A. Douglas Jackson.
San Francisco, W. H. Freeman, 1971. 349p. $12.50.

A translation of a Soviet collection of articles, primarily by geographers, pertaining
to the use of water resources, climate, vegetation, agriclutural land, and fish
and game supplies. It provides an illuminating overview of Soviet resource problems
and potentials with particularly informative sections on agricultural land,
forestry, and fishing.

> SR, 31:3:695-6   R: Robert N. Taafe

289.   Pryde, Philip R. **Conservation in the Soviet Union**. New York, Cambridge
University Press, 1972. 301p. $12.50.

This study has two stated objectives: 1) to review the major features of natural-
resource management and conservation in the USSR and identify major problems
resulting from Soviet approaches to resource management, and 2) to examine
these approaches "with the goal of acquiring insight into the contemporary
Soviet perception of what constitutes proper natural resource conservation."
These are ambitious goals. Pryde has succeeded reasonably well in meeting the
first but has faltered on the second. The book has 68 pages of appendixes,
including substantial excerpts from pertinent Soviet legislation, a good index,
and bibliographies for each chapter.

> SR, 34:1:168-9   R: Jeremy Anderson

GOVERNMENT AND STATE

Law

To 1917

290.   Dewey, Horace W., and Ann M. Kleimola, trans. and eds. **Russian
Private Law in the XIV-XVII Centuries: An Anthology of Documents**.
Ann Arbor, Dept. of Slavic Languages and Literatures, University of
Michigan, 1973. 260p. (Michigan Slavic Materials, no. 9). $5.50pa.

This selection of Russian civil law documents covering four centuries provides
an insight into the formation of Muscovy-Russia's political autocratic form of
government. The restrictions and subordination of private law to state law is
well demonstrated in this anthology. The book is recommended not only for
students of law but also for students of Russian history.

> S. M. H.

291.   Vernadsky, George, trans. **Medieval Russian Laws**. New York, Norton,
1969, (1947). 106p. $1.95.

(Listed in P. Horecky's *Russia and the Soviet Union*, #483). The volume
provides translations of *Rus' Justice* and similar legal documents. It also stresses
the ties between Kiev Rus' and Byzantine law. Appended is a valuable bibliography.

S. M. H.

1917 to the Present

292.   Berman, Harold J., ed. **Soviet Criminal Law and Procedure: The RSFSR
       Codes.** Intro. by Harold J. Berman. Trans. by Harold J. Berman and
       James W. Spindler. Cambridge, Harvard University Press, 1966. 501p.
       $11.95.

Berman's appraisal of the new Code of Criminal Procedure celebrates the passing
of secret "administrative" trials by the infamous "Special Boards" of the MVD,
NKVD, etc., but on the other hand apologizes for the continued absence of
judicial control over preliminary criminal investigation. He seems to defend the
Soviet judicial system. The translation of the criminal codes is satisfactory.
There are some novelties, and not everyone will agree with "correctional tasks"—
for corrective labor—without deprivation of freedom.

   RR, 25:3:309-10   R: Pauline B. Taylor

293.   Berman, Harold J., and John B. Quigley, Jr., trans. and eds. **Basic Laws
       on the Structure of the Soviet State.** Cambridge, Harvard University
       Press, 1969. 325p. $4.00pa.

This collection comprises translations of the most important Soviet laws as of
October 1968. The volume opens with helpful notes on the translation of Soviet
legal terminology, sources of the documents translated, and territorial subdivisions
of the Soviet Union. Part I includes the constitutions of the USSR and the RSFSR,
statutes on elections to the Supreme Soviet and on its permanent commissions,
legislation on local soviets, and the statutes of the Committee on Party-State
control. Part II contains laws on the procuracy and the judiciary, military tribunals, comrades' and conciliation courts, statutes on state arbitration, and
administrative commissions. This volume should be of considerable use to students
of Soviet government and politics.

   CSP, 14:2:375-6   R: Bohdan Bociurkiw

294.   Erickson, Richard J. **International Law and the Revolutionary State:
       A Case Study of the Soviet Union and Customary International Law.**
       Dobbs Ferry, N. Y., Oceana Publications, 1972. Leiden, A. W. Sijthoff.
       254p. $15.00.

In a closely reasoned, crisp study Erickson catalogues international law practice,
focusing on its reliance on custom as a source. He concludes that, in the main,
Soviet foreign policy relies heavily on established custom to implement its policy,
and to some extent seeks to create new custom to foster what remains of its
original revolutionary aims. Foreign Officers and specialists will want this study
on their shelves.

   SR, 32:4:831   R: John N. Hazard

295.   Feldbrugge, F. J. M., ed. **Encyclopedia of Soviet Law**. 2 vols. Dobbs
        Ferry, N. Y., Oceana Publications. Leiden, A. W. Sijthoff, 1974. Vol. 1
        (A-L), 429p. Vol. 2 (M-Z), 431-774pp. $95.00/set.
The work consists of alphabetically arranged descriptions of the laws and customs
of the Soviet legal system. The list of subject headings has been compiled on
the basis of a corresponding list in the *Index to Foreign Legal Periodicals* and
of the list contained in Soviet legal encyclopedias, so as to provide access of
approach, as far as possible, through both Western and Soviet concepts/terms.
                                      S. M. H.

296.   Feldbrugge, F. J. M. and J. Szirmal, eds. **Soviet Criminal Law, General
        Part**. Leiden University, The Netherlands, 1964. 291p. 32.50Dglds.
Presents a systematic description of the general part of Soviet criminal law from
a lawyer's point of view. It brings clarity to such confusing quirks of Soviet
legal writing as the roles of intent, aim, and motive, the distinction between
indirect intent and reckless negligence, and the nature of the "object" of a
Soviet crime. Readers interested in questions of criminal preparation and attempt,
concepts of imputability and mental illness, and effects of mistake, drunkenness
or *concursus*, will find the answers here, all thoroughly analyzed and documented.
        RR, 25:3:309-10   R: Pauline B. Taylor

297.   Fox, Irving K., ed. **Water Resources Law and Policy in the Soviet
        Union**. Madison, University of Wisconsin Press, 1971. 256p. $8.50.
The stated objective of this book is to provide "a useful introduction to the
situation in the Soviet Union and a contribution to our understanding of water
management in that country." The central feature of the volume is the translation
into English of a seminal monograph on Soviet water law. In 1965, O. S. Kolbasov,
a Soviet legal scholar, published his study of how water is allocated for competing
uses within the Soviet planning process. In December 1970, a set of "Principles
of Water Law of the USSR and Union Republics" was enacted by the Supreme
Soviet, and more detailed regulations were subsequently promulgated in the
various republics. The book contributes to this little explored area of Soviet
law and policy.
        CSP, 16:3:477-9   R: R. Brian Woodrow

298.   Grzybowski, Kazimierz. **Soviet Public International Law: Doctrines
        and Diplomatic Practice**. Leiden, A. W. Sijthoff; Durham, N. C., Rule
        of Law Press, 1970. 544p. 66Dfl. $18.50.
In a magisterial chronicle of a half century of development of Soviet doctrine
and practice in public international law, the author has brought together an
incredible amount of information in a small space. The "plus" of the book is
in the lead provided to documentation, organized under a series of headings
covering every aspect of the subject and even delving into broad fields of Soviet
constitutional law. There is ample footnoting, bibliography, and quotation,
not only from Soviet and Western sources but also from hard-to-use United
Nation records. Other notable features are the discussions of the Soviet concept
of *jus cogens*, the limits to application of the principles of self-determination,
the legality of aid rendered to anticolonial movements, the recognition of
government in exile and of incipient governments not yet in power in colonies,

the attention to be given to the protection of individual foreigners in relation to the attention to be focused upon breaches of the "new" rules, the attitude toward application of Soviet law in annexed and even leased territories, and the law of the sea and space. As such it will find a place in foreign offices, embassies, and libraries, and on the desks of those concerned with international affairs.

      SR, 30:2:428-9   R: John N. Hazard

299.   Hazard, John N., Isaac Shapiro, and Peter B. Maggs, eds. **The Soviet Legal System: Contemporary Documentation and Historical Commentary**. Rev. ed. Dobbs Ferry, N. Y., Oceana Publications, 1969. 687p. (Published for the Parker School of Foreign and Comparative Law, Columbia University). $17.50.

A collection of cases decided by Soviet courts and of excerpts from Soviet laws and from the writings of Soviet legal scholars. The book is divided into three parts: 1) "The Soviet State and Its Citizens," devoted chiefly to constitutional law, the agencies of public order, civil rights, criminal and civil procedure, and general principles of criminal law; 2) "Administering Soviet Socialism," devoted chiefly to land use, the system of industrial planning, contracts between state enterprises, collective farm law, labor law, and patent and copyright; and 3) "Private Legal Rights and Obligations of Soviet Citizens," devoted to personal property rights, inheritance, private contracts, torts and social insurance, marriage and divorce, and the rights and responsibilities of minors. There is a very useful bibliography of English-language writings on Soviet law.

      SR, 29:3:544   R: Harold J. Berman

300.   Johnson, E. L. **An Introduction to the Soviet Legal System**. London, Methuen, 1969; New York, Barnes & Noble, 1970. 248p. £3.25. $10.50.

In this brief work the late E. L. Johnson attempts to introduce Soviet law and legal institutions to the educated layman. Its title notwithstanding, the book treats the law in much greater detail than it does the legal system. Brief attention is also given to contract and tort, labor law, and the Soviet equivalent of corporation law; however, the area of civil rights is largely ignored. The book is notably without ideological bias, and it deserves a wide readership.

      SR, 30:4:896   R: Richard J. Johnson

301.   Kucherov, Samuel. **The Organs of Soviet Administration of Justice: Their History and Operation**. Foreword by John N. Hazard. Leiden, E. J. Brill, 1970. 754p. 96Dglds.

Part One of this history of Soviet justice, "Institutions of Justice," is a detailed, documented history of the development of the entire Soviet court system, civil, criminal, appellate and arbitral, as well as of "extraordinary courts," such as Revolutionary Tribunals and the Special Board of the NKVD. Part Two is devoted to "Men of Law," the judges, investigators, prosecutors and advocates who operate the system.

      RR, 31:2:182-4   R: Pauline B. Taylor

302.   LaFave, Wayne R., ed. **Law in the Soviet Society**. Urbana, University of Illinois Press, 1965. 297p. $4.75cl.; $1.95pa.

This is a symposium composed of seven essays. The selection of topics, dealing largely with the everyday life of Soviet citizens; the full utilization of original Russian sources; and the skillful presentation leave little to be desired. There is a critical review of the development of Soviet legal studies outside the Soviet Union; an essay on new trends in settling disputes in Soviet society by the use of informal sanctions with court decisions and by local group participation in decision-making; and an article on the new law of torts using actual cases. "Law and the Distribution of Consumer Goods in the Soviet Union" is perhaps the most interesting in the symposium, since it deals with the most vital issues in the life of Soviet citizens.

SR, 27:2:334-5   R: Jurij Fedynskyj

303.   Lapenna, Ivo. **Soviet Penal Policy. A Background Book**. Chester Springs, Pa., Dufour Editions, 1968. 148p. $3.50.

The author intends this book to be "a basic guide to Soviet penal policy." About half of it is devoted to a summary and evaluation of the main features of present-day Soviet criminal law and procedure, and about half to their historical and theoretical background in the period from 1917 to the death of Stalin. The author concludes that there is lacking in the Soviet Union a genuine system of law, a system of guarantees for the correct implementation of law, and the minimum legal standards recognized by civilized nations.

SR, 29:2:333   R: Harold J. Berman

304.   Ramundo, Bernard A. **Peaceful Coexistence: International Law in the Building of Communism**. Baltimore, Johns Hopkins Press, 1967. 262p. (Published in cooperation with the Institute for Sino-Soviet Studies, George Washington University). $6.95.

The author, a U. S. Army officer, has served with the Directorate of Foreign Military Rights Affairs in the U. S. Dept. of Defense. His work is not distorting, and he never in any way approaches the fiery polemics that have occasionally marred some of the lesser Soviet bloc juridical writings in the same field. The book does not break too much new ground in surveying Soviet legal literature, but it is thorough and comprehensive in the range of Soviet institutional practice, and it thus provides a valuable compendium of Soviet law-in-action in a still important field of applied international law.

SR, 29:4:705-6   R: Edward McWhinney

305.   **Soviet Criminal Law and Procedure: The RSFSR Codes**. Intro. and analysis by Harold J. Berman. Trans. by Harold J. Berman and James W. Spindler. Cambridge, Harvard University Press, 1966. 501p. (Russian Research Center Studies, 50). $11.95.

The bulk of the volume consists of a translation of the text of the latest RSFSR Criminal Code, Code of Criminal Procedure, and Law on Court Organization, as amended to July 1965. It is preceded by a 139-page introduction in which Berman analyzes and comments on the significance of the new legislation, its place in the history of Soviet legal development to date, and the technical impact on the average Soviet citizen of these major reforms in the administration of justice in the USSR. The result is a handy, highly condensed survey of the progression of Soviet official behavior up till now in this crucial area of social regulation and control.

SR, 25:3:542-3   R: George Ginsburg

306.   Tunkin, G. I. **Theory of International Law**. Trans. by William E. Butler. Cambridge, Harvard University Press, 1974. 497p. $20.00.

The most profound and comprehensive study of international legal theory yet produced by a Soviet jurist. The author is widely credited in Soviet circles with developing the legal basis for peaceful co-existence in the 1950s. This book is the fullest statement of his views.   S. M. H.

Politics and Government

To 1917

307.   Hosking, Geoffrey A. **The Russian Constitutional Experiment: Government and Duma**. New York, Cambridge University Press, 1973. 281p. $18.50.

This compact work offers an impressive quantity of new material on the State Duma from the Soviet State Archives. Particularly notable are the accounts of the progress of the land reform and small zemstvo bills, the naval staff and western zemstvo crises, and crises other than the Rasputin affair in the fading years of the Old Regime. The author also raises some basic questions on the movement of Russian society in the last decade before the Revolution. The study centers on the Octobrist Party as the key element for cooperation with the government.

SR, 33:2:352   R: Alfred Levin

308.   Levin, Alfred. **The Third Duma: Election and Profile**. Hamden, Conn., Archon Books, 1973. 210p. $8.50.

This monograph, like Levin's previous work, *The Second Duma* (1966), represents a welcome contribution to the history of the short-lived Russian attempt to set up a constitutional monarchy. The adoption of that new governmental form was neither easy nor successful as this study shows to the satisfaction of the inquiring scholar. It stresses the various aspects related to the election and function of the Third Duma. Although the law of June 3, 1907, retained the principle of representation for broad categories of the population, in essence it aimed to create a submissive and harmless body serving the regime rather than the people. To this end the law established an elaborate system of indirect elections, multiplication of voter categories (curia), and similar restrictions. Students of Russian history will appreciate this contribution that stimulates discussion and further inquiries.

AHR, 80:2:442-3   R: Stephan M. Horak

309.   Maklakov, V. A. **The First State Duma: Contemporary Reminiscences**. Trans. by Mary Belkin. Bloomington, Indiana University Press, 1964. 251p. (Russian and East European Series, Vol. 30). $6.50.

Maklakov's work is neither a memoir in the conventional sense nor a historical study but, rather, a critique of his former associates' political errors and thus, indirectly, an exercise in self-vindication. It is essentially an indictment of the Kadets, drawn up by a jurist of considerable forensic ability. Nevertheless, his writings are of undoubted importance for all students of Russian liberalism.

SR, 25:2:33-8   R: John Keep

310.   Paléologue, Maurice. **An Ambassador's Memoirs**. 3 vols. trans. by
        F. A. Holt. New York, Octagon Books, 1972. (1924, 1924, 1925).
        Vol. 1: July, 1914-June 2, 1915. 350p. Vol. 2: June 3, 1915-August 18,
        1916. 320p. Vol. 3: August 19, 1916-May 17, 1917. 346p. $45.00/set.
The author's account of his three years as French ambassador in Petrograd was first published in the *Revue des Deux Mondes* between January 1921 and July 1922. Although his interpretations of wartime and revolutionary Russia are not always to be taken seriously, his three volumes are still of interest and value to the historian.

SR, 32:2:388-9   R: Edward C. Thaden

311.   Pinchuk, Ben-Cion. **The Octobrists in the Third Duma, 1907-1912**.
        Seattle, University of Washington Press, 1974. 232p. (Publications
        on Russia and Eastern Europe of the Institute for Comparative and
        Foreign Area Studies, no. 4). $10.50.
The study proposes to examine one aspect of the Russian constitutional experiment—the Octobrist Party and its efforts to make the Duma Monrachy work. In essence the study restates the dilemma of Russian constitutionalism faced by the moderates when encountering the forces of reaction on the one side and of the revolution on the other. The Octobrists emerge as a largely artificial force. Despite its highly specialized nature, the book is quite readable and informative. The best parts of the book are on agrarian reform, national security, religious freedom, and Russian nationalism and its impact on the Octobrists and the Duma in general.

CSP, 17:2-3:531-2   R: Oleh W. Gerus

312.   Pospielovsky, Dimitry. **Russian Police Trade Unionism: Experiment
        or Provocation?** Foreword by Leonard Shapiro. London, Weidenfeld
        and Nicolson, for the London School of Economics and Political
        Science, 1971. 189p. £2.50.
This is the first monograph in English devoted to the *Zubatovshchina*, the most significant attempt within the Russian government before the revolution of 1905 to elaborate and implement a labor policy to come to grips with the burgeoning working-class movement and the challenge of revolutionary social democracy. No full scale Soviet study has appeared since the works of Ainzaft and Bukhbinder in the 1920s. The book, although of limited value, adds to our knowledge and re-evaluation of tsarist labor policy.

SR, 31:3:670-1   R: Jeremiah Schneiderman

313.   Riha, Thomas. **A Russian European: Paul Miliukov in Russian Politics**.
        Notre Dame, University of Notre Dame Press, 1969. 373p. $8.95.
The book is indeed a valuable—though limited—serious addition to the sparse literature on Miliukov, leader of the Kadet party. Basically, it is a carefully researched, objective, and well-written account of Miliukov's political fortunes.

A concluding chapter carries the story in brief to December 1918, when Miliukov left Russia, and also offers a variety of final considerations by the author.

SR, 29:1:109-10   R: Nathan Smith

314.   Romanov, A. I. **Nights Are Longest There: A Memoir of the Soviet Security Services**. Trans. by Gerald Brooke. Boston, Little, Brown, 1972. 256p. $7.95.

This volume represents a firsthand account of service in Smersh by a former officer of this agency, who writes under the pseudonym "A. I. Romanov." The author provides a useful account of the training, assignment, and operations of a junior-level Smersh officer. One's confidence in his veracity is enhanced not only by the general matter-of-factness of his tone but also by the internal consistency of his account.

SR, 32:4:827-8   R: Robert M. Slusser

315.   Smith, Edward Ellis, and Rudolf Lednicky. **"The Okhrana": The Russian Department of Policy**. Stanford, Hoover Institution, 1967. 280p. $10.00.

This volume is essentially a bibliography (containing 843 entries) of published materials and manuscripts in the Hoover Institution library relating to the activities of the Okhrana, the secret political police of the Russian Empire. On reading the annotations that describe the contents and indicate the conclusions of each listed item, one will find that many of the subjects discussed are startingly pertinent to the recent concern of the press and other media. No historian or student of organizations of political surveillance should overlook this volume. A glossary of Russian terms in the field, a list of periodicals and serials consulted, and an index are also included. A short introduction provides a summary of the history of the Okhrana.

SR, 30:3:663-4   R: Robert V. Allen

316.   Squire, P. S. **The Third Department: The Establishment and Practices of the Political Police in the Russia of Nicholas I**. Cambridge, Cambridge University Press, 1968. 272p. $11.50.

The volume is largely an administrative history that begins with a discussion of the political police regimes of earlier reigns and then discusses the establishment, organization, and functioning of the Third Department. The author has made use of an impressive collection of sources, chiefly annual reports of the department published in *Krasnyi arkhiv*; legislation creating and expanding its organization; and numerous memoirs, some written by its former members, and others by citizens who had had dealings with it. This study is a serious and judicious one, rather than a blanket indictment of the Russia of Nicholas I. As a result, it is a welcome contribution to the history of the period.

SR, 28:4:646-7   R: John Shelton Curtiss

317.   Starr, S. Frederick. **Decentralization and Self-Government in Russia, 1830-1870**. Princeton, Princeton University Press, 1972. 386p. $15.00cl.; $8.95pa.

This is a study of the "attempt to reconstitute the decrepit system of provincial government" which was part and parcel of the reform process begun after

Russia's defeat in the Crimean War. It provides an unprecedented depth of view into the variety of opinions and maneuverings within the government bureaucracy, which is too often treated in the literature as a monolith. The book reinforces the established view of a government dominated in the long run, by "suspicion of all public groups and institutions not directly under the guidance of the state."

SR, 33:3:538-9   R: Terence Emmons

318.   Vucinich, Wayne S., ed. **Russia and Asia: Essays on the Influence of Russia on the Asian Peoples.** Stanford, Hoover Institution Press, 1972. 521p. $15.00.

This volume presents a revised version of papers originally read in late 1967 at a conference on "The Russian Impact on Asia." The following peoples or countries are treated: Georgians, Armenians, Muslims in European Russia and the Caucasus, Siberian peoples, China, and Japan. These essays presented by experts are preceded by historical surveys of Russian attitudes toward Asia, Oriental studies in Russia, and the organizational vicissitudes of Soviet orientology.

SR, 33:1:139-40   R: Don C. Price

319.   Yaney, George L. **The Systematization of Russian Government: Social Evolution in the Domestic Administration of Imperial Russia, 1711-1905.** Urbana, University of Illinois Press, 1973. 464p. $13.50.

This fundamental reinterpretation of two centuries of Russian history traces the evolution of the bureaucratic state from the time of Peter the Great to the Revolution of 1905. The author rejects the stereotype of an impotent Russian peasantry and explains the vital role this historically neglected class played in government organization and evolution.

History, 2:2:26   R: Arthur E. Adams

1917 to the Present

320.   Adams, Arthur E. **Stalin and His Times.** New York, Holt, Rinehart and Winston, 1972. 243p. (Berkshire Studies in History). $3.25pa.

This study, based on a wide reading of the scholarship in the field, skillfully summarizes that reading in businesslike prose. Its aim is to summarize established ideas about Stalin and his times, rather than to introduce new points of view. The author tends to accept Stalinism as a necessary evil in the process of modernization, and he considers Western responses to the USSR in the early postwar years "probably panicky and premature."

SR, 33:1:145   R: Robert H. McNeal

321.   Armstrong, John A. **Ideology, Politics, and Government in the Soviet Union: An Introduction.** 3rd rev. ed. New York, Praeger, 1974 (1962). 236p. $8.00cl.; $3.50pa.

Armstrong has brought up to date his introductory text on Soviet government. Many of the revisions amount to carrying the story from the Khrushchev era to the present. Some interpolations add clarity or rebut conflicting views. Others (*e.g.*, on nationalities and on Party membership) provide data which have

only recently become available. Finally, a new chapter deals with "Interpretation of Domestic and Foreign Policy."
RR, 34:2:217-8   R: Alexander Dallin

322.   Barghoorn, Frederick C. **Politics in the USSR**. Boston, Little, Brown,
        1966. 418p. $2.95pa. (2d ed., 1972).
A pioneering attmpt to apply Gabriel Almond's structural-functional schema of
comparative politics to the Soviet polity. Barghoorn's attempt merits applause
and is, all in all, successful. His chapter on "Implementing Public Policy,"
a process blatantly ignored by most texts, goes far in explaining what happens
to policy when it is filtered through the labyrinthine channels of a highly
bureaucratic system. In "Soviet Justice," Barghoorn's personal encounter with
the KGB highlights an excellent treatment of a very complex subject. By shaping
his approach to the demands of Almond's model, Barghoorn has provided a
launching pad for others in the field to explore new directions.
        SR, 27:1:159-60   R: Henry W. Morton

323.   Cattell, David T. **Leningrad: A Case Study of Soviet Urban Government**.
        New York, Praeger, in cooperation with the Institute of Public Admini-
        stration, New York, 1968. 171p. $12.50.
This monograph provides a wealth of detail on the Leningrad administration
(in six chapters, seven charts, and twenty-four tables); it is based largely on sources
available only in the Soviet Union, including interviews from 1962 and 1966.
Chapter 2, "The Political Structure," will be of interest to all; chapters 3 and 4
deal with planning and with selected departments of local government; and chapter
5 describes at length the complexities of administering housing and also the
failures, such as the construction of "new slums." The work is a needed contribution to a neglected and difficult topic.
        SR, 28:4:669-70   R: Max Mote

324.   Conquest, Robert. **Russia after Khrushchev**. New York, Praeger, 1965.
        267p. $5.95.
In Conquest's model of the USSR, "the political world is limited to a few
thousand members of a self-perpetuating elite . . . trained for decades with the
purpose of enforcing its will against the tendencies of society as a whole,"
and in which there is "no mechanism for the social forces to express themselves."
Within the tiny elite, he finds four major factions—conservatives, modernizers,
Khrushchev's protéges, and moderates—and a few basic issues concerned with
the proper speed of economic modernization, methods of destalinization, the
propriety of liberalization, and the means of improving Party operations.
Conquest's conclusions about the current stability of the Stalin-molded system
need to be viewed within the wider context. His book is a desirable contribution
to our understanding of the Soviet Union, but it should be used in conjunction
with broader analyses of Soviet institutions.
        RR, 25:2:186-7   R: Louis Nemzer

325.   Cornell, Richard, ed. **The Soviet Political System: A Book of Readings**.
        Englewood Cliffs, N. J., Prentice-Hall, 1970. 392p. $7.95cl.; $4.95pa.

"To provide something more contemporary, more analytical to the study of the Soviet political system," the editor invited 28 well-known specialists to contribute essays which explain and analyze the Soviet political system within six main themes: 1) Understanding the Soviet Political System; 2) The Environmental Influences; 3) The Party and Political Leadership; 4) The Party and the Implementation of Decisions; 5) The Party and Supervision of Society, and 6) The Course of Change. Each essay is richly documented by the respective contributors (Aspaturian, Barghoorn, Brzezinski, Inkeles, Meyer, Roberts, and others). However, the study as a whole does not provide a bibliography or an index.   S. M. H.

326.   Daniels, Robert V., ed. **The Stalin Revolution: Foundations of Soviet Totalitarianism.** 2nd ed. Lexington, Mass., D. C. Heath, 1972 (1965). 233p. $2.50.

This collection of essays, written by Western and Soviet authors, illuminates the nature of the Soviet totalitarian system as seen by Westerners and such Soviet leaders as N. Bukharin, N. S. Khrushchev, L. Trotsky, and B. N. Ponomaryev. Western authors discuss such topics as "The Leader and the Party" (I. Deutscher); "The Problem of Industrial Development" (R. V. Daniels); "The Return of Inequality" (D. J. Dallin), and "Soviet Bonapartism" (C. J. Friedrich and R. A. Brazezinski). A highly recommended reader for students of Soviet government and politics as well as for the general public.   S. M. H.

327.   Day, Richard B. **Leon Trotsky and the Politics of Economic Isolation.** New York, Cambridge University Press, 1973. 221p. $10.95.

The author's basic goal in this work is to confront and destroy the historical myths that have surrounded Trotsky's program for economic development after the October Revolution. He demonstrates that after the Revolution and until 1925, having cast aside as irrelevant for the present situation his theory of permanent revolution, Trotsky preferred Russia's economic isolation, fearing dependence on concessions and credits from the capitalist West. He shows that even when Trotsky exchanged economic isolationism for integrationism, he still did not—as is commonly argued—reject the possibility of building socialism in one country. Instead, Trotsky argued after 1925 that Russia's political isolation did not require its economic isolation and that building socialism in the USSR was quite compatible with—in fact, necessitated—the use of the technical skills of the capitlist West.

SR, 34:2:399-400   R: Myron W. Hedlin

328.   Dornberg, John. **The New Tsars: Russia under Stalin's Heirs.** Garden City, N. Y., Doubleday, 1972. 470p. $10.00.

The book is based on the author's observations as a correspondent in Moscow (1968-1970). as well as on considerable historical research. He draws on the writings of such authors as Sigismund zu Herberstein, Adolphe Marquis de Custine, André Gide, von Staden, and many more. The result is an up-to-date account of the USSR enriched by perspectives in the past. Most of the book is devoted to the current Soviet repressions in the USSR, with emphasis on particular republics. The author writes about the overbearing Russian "superiority complex" with regard to the non-Russian nations. Lively, persuasive,

and informed, this is an important work for the general reader and the
student.
UQ, 28:3:297-8 R: Walter Dushnyck

329. Drachkovitch, Milorad M., ed. **Fifty Years of Communism in Russia.**
University Park, Pennsylvania State University Press, 1968. 316p.
(Hoover Institution Publication, no. 77). $7.50.
Over ninety percent of the material deals with Russia, the Russians, and Moscow,
though the writer, of course, believes he is really treating the entire Soviet Union.
Here and there, mention is made of the Ukrainians, Lithuanians, Armenians
and several other non-Russian nations in the USSR but, generally, half of the
population in that empire-state is virtually ignored. Not a single essay is devoted
to the non-Russian nations. Among contributors, in addition to the introduction
written by Drachkovitch, one will find such experts as Bertram Wolfe, Leonard
Schapiro, G. Warren Nutter, John N. Hazard, and Sidney Hook.
UQ, 24:4:371-3 R: Lev E. Dobriansky

330. Eissenstat, Bernard W., ed. **Lenin and Leninism: State, Law, and
Society.** Lexington, Mass., D. C. Heath, 1971. 322p. (Lexington
Books).
This volume is composed of papers delivered at the University of Oklahoma on
20-22 April 1970, and attempts to examine Lenin and his legacy from various
angles. There are some splendid essays and much light is shed on various aspects
of Lenin's policies and behavior. The volume is in five parts. The first considers
philosophy an ideology. The other parts deal with law and legality, economic
matters, Soviet mythology, and with Lenin's letters as an historical source.
SEER, 51:124:480-1 R: Martin McCauley

331. Fischer, George. **The Soviet System and Modern Society.** New York,
Atherton Press, 1968. 199p. (A Joint Project of the Bureau of Applied
Social Research and the Russian Institute of Columbia University).
$7.50.
Fischer's latest book is innovative in method, provocative in thesis and assertion, and somewhat inconclusive and speculative in logic and theory. It
constitutes a significant and valuable addition to the growing body of scholarly
literature on Communist systems that seeks to apply advanced methods of
analysis to the very poor data available and to substitute reasoned discussion
for moralistic polemic. The heart of the study is a quantitative analysis of the
composition, in terms of past work experience, of a sample of 306 incumbents,
1958, 1958-62, and 1962, of six categories of leadership posts at the all-union,
republic, and oblast levels of the CPSU. Using more than sixty statistical tables,
Fischer argues that there is a trend toward more top posts being held by men
of Dual Executive career experience. His study is a step in the right direction.
SR, 29:2:328-30 R: Frederick C. Barghoorn

332. Gruber, Helmut. **Soviet Russia Masters the Comintern: International
Communism in the Era of Stalin's Ascendancy.** Garden City, N. Y.,
Anchor Press/Doubleday, 1974. 544p. $3.95pa.

Gruber's anthology constitutes a welcome contribution to the otherwise exiguous field of documentary surveys on the Comintern stage in the history of the international Communist movement. This is the second of a projected three-volume sequence. It is a continuation of Gruber's earlier *International Communism in the Era of Lenin: A Documentary History* (Garden City, Anchor Books, 1967. 426p. 1972 ed. $2.50pa.). In the present volume Gruber treats the Comintern's "middle years," the 1924-31 period of Bolshevization, which coincided with Stalin's growing authority in the Party, and, as the result of the international movement's increasing dependence on Moscow, in the Comintern itself.

    RR, 34:1:98-9   R: Ivo Banae

333. Hammer, Darrell P. **USSR: The Politics of Oligarchy**. Hinsdale, Ill.,
    Dryden Press, 1974. 452p. $6.50pa.
Hammer, a political scientist, has produced an unusual work of multiple value. It is a stimulating and original essay on the functioning of the Soviet political system and a useful update, even for the specialist, on a variety of points ranging from the role of Supreme Soviet committees to the experiment in "popular justice." He begins with the workings of the system from the standpoint of local and regional administrators, and then moves through a discussion of the various bureaucratic structures to a concluding set of chapters on the process of top-level policy making in domestic and foreign affairs. Hammer speaks of the Soviet top leadership as being an oligarchy.

    SR, 34:3:607   R: Robert V. Daniels

334. Jaworskyj, Michael, ed. **Soviet Political Thought: An Anthology**.
    Sel., trans., and ed. by M. Jaworskyj. Baltimore, Johns Hopkins Press,
    1968. 621p. $15.00.
Jaworskyj emphasizes the theory of state and law as being of primary importance to Soviet political thought as a whole. He has done American readers of this generation a favor in recalling that the men of 1917 and even up to 1924 really believed in the immediate withering ot the critical instruments of politics, for this was so. Failure to understand this fact has caused some legal historians to misread the Soviet record. Jaworskyj's method of including large numbers of authors to prove wide variation of thought and that the production of political thought was not the monopoly of the political leaders makes for a rich volume. He has proved his thesis that the seeds of philosophy are not in the famous passages of Lenin, Stalin, and Khrushchev, but in the unknowns who first explored the way. The section treating the post-Stalin period is wholly new to readers of English alone. The volume is much enhanced by a 43-page introduction in the form of a summary of the assumptions of Marxist thought.

    SR, 28:1:153-4   R: John N. Hazard

335. Khrushchev, Nikita. **Khrushchev Remembers: The Last Testament**.
    With intro. and notes by Edward Crankshaw. Trans. and ed. by Strobe
    Talbott. Boston, Little, Brown, 1970, 639p. $12.95.
Khrushchev Remembers is undoubtedly a unique book; its publication as well as its authenticity created worldwide interest and confusion. American specialists on Soviet affairs invited by the State Department are reported as having taken

a positive stance. Among them are Harrison Salisbury, Foy Kohler, Henry
Shapiro, and others. The book's essential importance centers around Khrushchev's
activities in the Ukraine in the capacity of Stalin's emissary responsible for
bloody purges during the 1930s, and especially since 1937, when Khrushchev
liquidated the entire organization of the Communist Party of Ukraine. He
pledged to annihilate all "bourgeois nationalists on Ukrainian soil." Khrushchev
also accuses Stalin of anti-Semitism, but he himself never misses an opportunity
to make a disparaging remark about the Jews, insisting "that they be kept in
their places."

       UQ, 27:2:177-80   R: Walter Dushnyck

336.   Laird, Roy D. **The Soviet Paradigm: An Experiment in Creating a
      Monohierarchical Polity.** New York, Free Press. London, Collier-
      Macmillan, 1970. 272p. $7.95.

Laird's main purpose in setting forth a "monohierarchical paradigm" of the
Soviet polity is to introduce upper-level college students to the Soviet political
system as it had evolved by 1970. The paradigm underscores continuing tendencies in the Soviet polity toward greater centralization and unity, such as the
merger of the bureaucratic hierarchies of state and party and the "complete
carrying through" of this bureaucracy into Soviet society by means of numerous
"supportive adjuncts." The author describes the various ideologies that have
culminated in a new Soviet nationalism.

       SR, 33:1:152-3   R: Jan S. Adams

337.   Laqueur, Walter Z., and Leopold Labedz, eds. **The State of Soviet
      Studies.** Cambridge, Mass., MIT Press, 1965. 177p. $7.50.

Here is a collection of essays which on their original appearance in the London
Survey of January and April 1964 attracted so much interest that their
eventual appearance in book form was inevitable. The result is good. Among
those who discuss various aspects we find: Gleb Struve, Arthur E. Adams,
Robert Conquest, Alec Nove, and T. H. Rigby. Among the non-Americans
are Victor S. Frank (Britain), Basile Kerbley (France) and Jens Hacker (Germany).
In his concluding chapter Labedz recalls the sad decline of Western expertise on
things Soviet in the 1930s, when certain so-called experts lauded Stalin at his
worst, excusing even his purges. Western writers on Russia are far more objective
now, we are assured.

       RR, 25:2:206-7   R: Albert Parry

338.   Lazitch, Branko, and Milorad M. Drachkovitch. **Lenin and the Comintern.**
      Vol. 1. Stanford, Hoover Institution Press, 1972. 683p. (Hoover
      Institution Publications, 106). $17.50.

The authors deal with a dimension of the subject that never has been explored
seriously in depth: the unofficial and clandestine activities of the Comintern.
The description of the Comintern's official emissaries to the parties in Germany,
France, and Italy particularly, throws much new light on the opinions formed
and decisions taken in Moscow regarding these parties. Even more revealing
is the role played by a host of unofficial emissaries dispatched by Lenin, Zinoviev,

and the Comintern's Little Bureau to monitor the national sections and their leaders, often without their knowledge.

SR, 32:3:611-2   R: Helmut Gruber

339.   Linden, Carl A. **Khrushchev and the Soviet Leadership 1957-1964.** Baltimore, Johns Hopkins Press, 1966. 271p. $7.50cl.; $2.45pa.
This scholarly study presents a forceful though partial interpretation of Khrushchev's political character and of Soviet politics in the period 1957-64. In Linden's account Khrushchev never succeeded in consolidating his power after defeating "the anti-Party group" in 1957, so that Soviet politics remained basically unstable after that event just as before it. As a result, Khrushchev's grand strategy of improving living standards at home while pursuing détente abroad foundered. The interested layman will learn much about Soviet politics from this book, and anyone desirous of grappling with the still unresolved problems of Soviet politics will find here important materials to study.

SR, 27:3:492-4   R: Myron Rush

340.   Lyons, Eugene. **Workers Paradise Lost; Fifty Years of Soviet Communism: A Balance.** New York, Funk & Wagnalls, 1967. 387p. $6.95.
Appearing on the eve of Moscow's celebration of the 50th anniversary of the Bolshevik Revolution, this fact-filled work serves a good, constructive purpose. In recounting the history of the Soviet Union, the author provides a useful summary of the past fifty years. The strong aspects of the book are the author's easy narrative style and his exposure of numerous myths of Soviet origin promoted among the Western public unfamiliar with the realities existing in the USSR. Despite the author's pro-Russian bias in making "Russians a victim of Communism," this book deserves attention and careful reading.

UQ, 24:1:83-6   R: Lev E. Dobriansky

341.   Matthews, Mervyn, comp. **Soviet Government: A Selection of Official Documents on Internal Policies.** New York, Taplinger, 1974. 472p. $30.00.
A collection of official Soviet documents dating from 1917 to the present, which the author considers to be fundamental to the understanding of the Soviet political practice. The documents are divided into four main groups: state administration, law and the police, the peasantry, and the workers' labor legislation. This volume is useful in college libraries to support courses in Soviet history, politics, and law. The selection reflects the compiler's own view of the importance of the various documents included. His comments are helpful, yet not always shared by other specialists.   S. M. H.

342.   Meyer, Alfred G. **The Soviet Political System: An Interpretation.** New York, Random House, 1964. 494p. $5.95.
The author does not purport to have presented important new information, but he does attempt, with an unusual degree of success, to interpret the Soviet system outside of a vacuum and within the framework of comparative politics. Meyer sees in the Soviet Union many parallels with a giant Western business corporation. Both are bureaucracies, bureaucracy having been defined as "rational management on a comparatively large scale." The major difference

between the "USSR, Incorporated" and a large Western corporation is that
the former is bureaucracy-writ-large, the latter bureaucracy-simple. Meyer has
written a provocative and informative volume which should receive praise
from both layman and expert.

RR, 25:4:429   R: John H. Hodgson

343.   Narkiewicz, Olga A. **The Making of the Soviet State Apparatus.**
Manchester, Manchester University Press, 1970. 238p. $9.00.
The thesis of this study is that during the Civil War and New Economic Policy,
events at the local level had a decisive influence on shaping Bolshevik policy.
The author, drawing on the Smolensk archives as well as printed sources, contends
that the inefficiency of local administration, combined with rising unemployment and the mass migration to the town of peasants in search of non-existent
jobs, drove the authorities to act and, in the last analysis, made the decision to
collectivize agriculture inevitable. This is a useful if modest contribution to
our knowledge of early Soviet history.

SR, 31:1:168-9   R: Paul Avrich

344.   Nicolaevsky, Boris. **Power and the Soviet Elite: "The Letter of an
Old Bolshevik" and Other Essays.** Ed. by Janet D. Zagoria. New
York, Praeger, 1965. 275p. (Published for the Hoover Institution on
War, Revolution, and Peace). $6.95.
All those concerned with Soviet affairs are profoundly in debt to the late
B. Nicolaevsky, for without his tenacity and passionate devotion to digging
out the hidden truth, we would remain in ignorance of some of the facts most
essential for an understanding of Soviet politics. Yet his memory can best be
served by applying to his own work the same intrepid analysis which he brought
to the study of Soviet affairs. He told a considerable part of the truth as it was
known to him, but he did not always tell the whole truth, and on occasion his
interpretation of the evidence was colored or distorted by his own strongly
held theories or political views. The introduction to the volume by George F.
Kennan provides a profound and penetrating analysis of the moral dilemma of
Bolshevism which reached its climax in the purges and which underlay the struggle
for power with which Nicolaevsky's articles are primarily concerned.

SR, 25:3:529-31   R: Robert M. Slusser

345.   Odom, William E. **The Soviet Volunteers: Modernization and Bureaucracy in a Public Mass Organization.** Princeton, Princeton University
Press, 1973. 360p. $14.50.
This work is a four-part treatment of the largest mass voluntary organization
of the 1920s and 1930s, *Osoviakhim* (Society of Friends of Defense and Aviation-
Chemical Construction), which was finally replaced in 1952 by the more familiar
DOSAAF. The framework is an analysis of the organization as a modernizing
agency; in addition, it is a study of Soviet administrative organization. The
charts, tables, short chapters and frequent summaries, as well as the bibliography
and index, contribute to the book's value as a reference work. The study is
highly recommended for the reader who is interested in enhancing his appreciation of the entire history of Soviet organizations and style in administration.

CSP, 17:1:157-8   R: Max Mote

346.   Osborn, Robert J. **The Evolution of Soviet Politics**. Homewood, Ill.,
        Dorsey Press, 1974. 574p. $10.95.
Osborn combines a lucid writing style with a careful survey of Soviet political
history, a summary of recent findings of social scientists specializing in the
study of the USSR, and an eclectic methodological approach, to produce a
volume of value not only for the undergraduate student of Soviet politics, but
also for the scholar who specializes in the area. According to Osborn, there
was nothing inevitable about the development of the Soviet Union. However,
as important decisions were made in the years immediately following the Bolshevik
Revolution, limits were placed on the options open to political leaders in future
crisis situations. The author deals somewhat more fully with questions relating
to social stratification, social welfare programmes, and related matters than
do most authors of introductory Soviet politics texts.
        CSP, 17:158-60   R: Roger E. Kanet

347.   Pethybridge, Roger. **The Social Prelude to Stalinism**. New York, St.
        Martin's Press, 1974. 343p. $18.95.
So far scholars have tended to concentrate on the political and economic origins
of Stalinism. The author tries to supplement their work by emphasizing certain
aspects of Bolshevik thought, in contact with Russian society, which tended
to reinforce the movement toward an authoritarian political structure after the
Revolution. The topics selected in this book, such as illiteracy and small-scale
social structure, acted as severe brakes on the implementation of the Bolsheviks'
maximalist social theories, which are outlined in chapter 2. The final chapter
deals with Soviet bureaucracy and shows how the social influences mentioned
in previous chapters acted as strong consolidators of the centralized system.
In the conclusion an assessment is made of the balance among the personality
of Stalin, major political and economic developments, and the trends analyzed
in this book, as ingredients of "Stalinism."
        JMH, 47:3:598   (Abstract by the author)

348.   Reshetar, John S., Jr. **The Soviet Polity: Government and Politics
        in the U.S.S.R.** New York, Dodd, Mead, 1971. 412p. $4.50pa.
The Soviet Polity is an exploration of Soviet politics from the approach that
emphasizes "institutional structures, functional analysis, the nature of the
Soviet leadership, the principal components of Soviet political life, and the
definition of the major problems confronting the Soviet polity." The author is
able to follow the tortuous route of administrative developments and illuminates
both the fundamental continuity and the innovating change. His treatment of
the secret police, for example, is a model of balance and clarity, showing how
this structure maintains its cohesiveness through reorganization after reorganization. He also provided an excellent annotated bibliography. In sum, the book
is a welcome and lucid combination of the historical context and the Soviet
present.
        SR, 31:1:180-1   R: Ellen Mickiewicz

349. Rush, Myron. **Political Succession in the USSR.** New York, Columbia
University Press, 1965. 223p. (A Publication of the RAND Corporation
and the Research Institute on Communist Affairs of Columbia
University). $5.95.

The author's hypothesis is that Soviet politics always moves in a cyclical direction.
There is a stable phase of one-man rule, exemplified by the personal dictatorships
of Lenin (1917-12), Stalin (1929-53), and Khrushchev (1957-64). The authority
of such rulers is invariably enormous. On the other hand, each period of the
transfer of power is an unstable phase of succession crisis. But the succession
crisis is ultimately resolved in a final phase, which is marked by the emergence
of a new sovereign.

SR, 28:3:499   R: Sidney I. Ploss

350. Schapiro, Leonard. **The Government and Politics of the Soviet Union.**
New York, Random House, 1965. 192p. $3.95.

This slim volume epitomizes the traditional approach. The emphasis here is on
the historical, the institutional, the legal, and not on the behavioral. The chapter
on the "Origins of Bolshevism" is perhaps the best mini-treatment available
on the subject. The author presents a view of Russia over a fifty-year period
rather than of post-Stalin developments. Because of its focus on institutions,
it might serve as a complement to Barghoorn's study in advanced undergraduate
courses.

SR, 27:1:159-60   R: Henry W. Morton

351. Shub, Anatole. **An Empire Loses Hope: The Return of Stalin's Ghost.**
New York, Norton, 1970. 474p. $12.50.

This is a combination of eyewitness observations with expert research. The
author spent seven years in Eastern Europe and the Soviet Union, mostly as
a correspondent for the *Washington Post.* He knows more about psychology of
the people in that area than do many specialists. The main theme could be
expressed as follows: the process of de-Stalinization, initiated by Khrushchev,
was interpreted as the beginning of a thorough reform of the Soviet system,
at least by people in those East European countries which have traditionally
been oriented toward democratic and European social, political, and cultural
values. The Sino-Soviet split in the early 1960s raised another hope: that the
USSR would look for a détente in Europe and would grant greater freedom to
the satellite states within its empire. The return of neo-Stalinism after 1964,
and especially after the invasion of Czechoslovakia, proved that the reaction
of the Soviet leadership was quite the opposite to these general expectations.
This thesis is extremely well illustrated by Shub's description and analysis of
the important events of the turbulent decade.

CSP, 15:1-2:222-3   R: R. Selucky

352. Stewart, Philip D. **Political Power in the Soviet Union: A Study of
Decision-Making in Stalingrad.** Indianapolis, Bobbs-Merrill, 1968.
227p. $3.95pa.

This is an in-depth study of the decision-making machinery of the Stalingrad
(Volgograd) Oblast from 1954 to 1960. The author analyzes successively the
oblast party conference, the oblast party committee, the *obkom* plenum, the

obkom bureau, and the *obkom* first secretaries. Not very surprisingly, he concludes that it is the *obkom* first secretary who is the real center of authority and influence in the oblast. Stewart furnishes a wealth of materials on the structure and functions of the *obkom* and presents numerous tables correlating personal background variables with party leadership characteristics. The book is a worthwhile contribution to the literature on Soviet local politics.

> SR, 29:1:123-4 R: Robert F. Miller

353. Swearer, Howard R., with Myron Rush. **The Politics of Succession in the U.S.S.R.: Materials on Khrushchev's Rise to Leadership**. Boston, Little, Brown, 1964. 324p. $2.95pa.

This is a documentary case history intended primarily as an aid in college courses on Soviet politics. As such it should prove highly useful, but it will also be appreciated by both more mature specialists in Soviet studies and general readers interested in contemporary foreign politics. After a brief introduction justifying the study of Soviet "elite politics," there is a useful chapter discussing how they work when leaders are competing to assert their personal dominance ("the succession problem"), and setting the scene at the time of Stalin's death. The core of the book consists of five chronologically arranged chapters covering the period from Stalin's death to Khrushchev's assumption of the premiership in March 1958. Most of the documents are taken from *Pravda* and a few from other central publications, no use being made of the regional press. The translation and reproduction of names and titles is generally accurate and intelligent.

> SR, 24:4:734-5 R: T. H. Rigby

354. Tatu, Michel. **Power in the Kremlin: From Khrushchev to Kosygin**. Trans. by Helen Katel. New York, Viking Press, 1969. 570p. $10.00.

The author, a correspondent for *Le Monde* in Eastern Europe and, from 1957 to 1964, in Moscow, brings all his documented research to bear on casting some meaningful light on the hidden and dark political maneuverings within the Kremlin. The work is divided into five parts, but the first four form a highly minute examination of the four crises that led to Khrushchev's downfall: the U-2 affair in May 1960, the 21st Congress in 1961-62, the Cuban crisis in October 1962, and the crisis in 1964 that resulted in his ouster. The uninitiated reader will discover a wealth of reconstructed information shedding considerable light on the political maneuverings in the Kremlin.

> UQ, 26:2:200-2 R: Lev E. Dobriansky

355. Tucker, Robert C. **The Soviet Political Mind: Stalinism and Post-Stalin Change**. London, George Allen and Unwin, 1972 (rev. ed.). 306p. £3.50.

This new edition of Tucker's by now well-established work on Stalinism has as its purpose the reopening of old questions and the reconsideration of old answers in the light of additional information which has come to light. The author rightly stresses the continuities with the past, the Soviet political mind being a superimposition upon what is in many respects merely the more traditional Russian political mind. The first of the supplementary chapters constitutes an attempt to focus on approaches which have frequently downgraded the importance of the individual *persona* and emphasized merely the *function* of leadership. The second addition to the book, entitled "Stalin, Bukharin and History as a Conspiracy," reiterates the point that it was Stalin himself who masterminded the purges.

SEER, 53:130:133-5   R: Julian Birch

356. Wade, Rex A. **The Russian Search for Peace: February-October 1917**. Stanford, Stanford University Press, 1969. 196p. $6.50.

The tragic story Wade recounts has been told before, but never with such lucidity. He narrates dispassionately the sad tale of hope and frustration, idealism and naiveté that transpired. Rejecting the solution of a separate peace, the Petrograd Soviet elaborated a program for a general negotiated peace. But Russia's allies and Imperial Germany were by 1917 resolved to continue the war to a decisive military victory. The commitment of the Provisional Government to the Soviet formula after the formation of the First Coalition in May was vacillating. Wade's documentation is impressive, and his summation is judicious.

SR, 30:1:150   R: Robert Paul Browder

357. Wesson, Robert G. **The Russian Dilemma: A Political and Geopolitical View**. New Brunswick, N. J., Rutgers University Press, 1974. 228p. $12.50.

This book is informed by the view that Soviet Russia may be regarded as basically a continuation of the tsarist state. Russians today face the same major political problems as they did before 1917—namely, to hold together and rule the huge multi-national realm in the face of solvent forces of modernity, and to modernize economically (and militarily) without modernizing politically. The author's solution to the dilemma is for the Russians to shed their empire. They would then be free to develop their full potential. The Soviet political system is conservative and repressive. However, economic and/or military crises will force it to change radically.

SEER, 53:132:469   R: Martin McCauley

358. Wesson, Robert G. **The Soviet Russian State**. New York, John Wiley, 1972. 404p. $8.95.

This is a solid textbook written for the undergraduate course on Soviet politics. The first third of the book is devoted to the historical background of the contemporary system. There follow chapters on ideology, the party, state, economy, the "psychocultural front," law, the army, nationalities, and extensions abroad of the Soviet empire. A final chapter makes a judiciously cautious attempt to weigh the future prospects of this "aging revolution." A short list of suggested readings is appended to each chapter. The unifying theme is that a strain toward autocratic structures of rule has existed in both the tsarist and Soviet periods, created by the functional need to prevent disintegration in a vast Russian-dominated multinational empire.

SR, 32:2:396-7   R: Grey Hodnett

359. Wesson, Robert G. **The Soviet State: An Aging Revolution**. New York, John Wiley, 1972. 222p. $3.95pa.

This book is an abridged version of Wesson's other study, *The Soviet Russian State*, suitable for an introductory comparative government course. Wesson is not impressed by recent attempts to reformulate the questions one should ask about Soviet politics. His approach is broadly historical-descriptive, stressing similarities between the Soviet and tsarist regimes, and between these and earlier "imperial orders." On this level of analysis his work ranks well above most other introductory texts.

SR, 32:2:396-7   R: Grey Hodnett

Communist Party

360.   Avtorkhanov, Abdurakhman. **The Communist Party Apparatus.** Chicago, Henry Regnery, 1966. 422p. $10.00.

Anyone who is interested in the elitist nature of the CPSU should peruse Avtorkhanov's massive work on the party's organization and function very carefully. This is a specialist's handbook overflowing with tables and lengthy quotes and the intermittent insights of one who once served in the apparatus. The work is highlighted by an illuminating section on Soviet nationality policy.

SR, 27:1:159-60   R: Henry W. Morton

361.   **Current Soviet Policies. V: The Documentary Record of the 23rd Congress of the C.P.S.U.** Columbus, Ohio, *Current Digest of the Soviet Press*, 1973. $10.00ea. (*Current Soviet Policies*, vols. I through IV are published and available.)

This set of volumes belongs in every academic library regardless of size.

S. M. H.

362.   Hough, Jerry F. **The Soviet Prefects: The Local Party Organs in Industrial Decision-Making.** Cambridge, Harvard University Press, 1969. 416p. $12.50.

Hough has made an exhaustive empirical analysis of the actual day-to-day role of the party at the middle and lower levels in the economic and political structure over the last two decades. He concludes that it is much too premature to predict the death or the paralysis of the CPSU. The first secretary of the oblast is still not only the local "boss," but he and his staff are also the primary coordinators, arbitrators, and expediters in his region. City and *raion* party organs have less authority but still have a comparably powerful role. The author concludes that Soviet administration is a classic model of the prefectural system as opposed to the "pluralistic system of local-based coordination" exemplified by the United States. This volume represents one of the better studies on current politics in the Soviet Union.

SR, 29:2:332-3   R: David T. Cattell

363.   Hudson, G. F. **Fifty Years of Communism: Theory and Practice.** New York, Basic Books, 1968. 234p. $5.95.

The survey by Hudson, addressed to the non-specialist reader, is a straight forward, concise, yet reasonably comprehensive chronological account of the evolution of Communism. On the whole it is clear, simply written, and generally accurate, despite its occasional reliance on dubious sources. Nevertheless, Hudson brings out the important point of Soviet dissolution of the Polish Communist party in 1937, a clear prelude to the Nazi-Soviet Pact of 1939. His book is an adequate introduction to the subject.

        AHR 75:2:547-50   R: John M. Thompson

364.   McNeal, Robert H. **Guide to the Decisions of the Communist Party of the Soviet Union, 1917-67.** Toronto, University of Toronto Press, 1974. 329p. $15.00.

This guide contains 3,265 entries, each representing a Party decision. The entries, which appear in chronological order, include the following descriptions: entry number, decision title, and bibliographical location—that is, the reference to a published source. A subject index based on Russian terms enables the reader to find a desired item.

        CSP, 15:4:620   R: R. C. E.

365.   McNeal, Robert H., gen. ed. **Resolutions and Decisions of the Communist Party of the Soviet Union.** Vol. 1: *The Russian Social Democratic Labour Party, 1898-October 1917.* Ed. by Ralph Carter Elwood. Vol. 2: *The Early Soviet Period, 1917-1929.* Ed. by Richard Gregor. Vol. 3: *The Stalin Years, 1929-1953.* Ed. by Robert H. McNeal. Vol. 4: *The Khrushchev Years, 1953-1964.* Ed. by Grey Hodnett. Toronto, University of Toronto Press, 1974. Vol. 1: 306p.; Vol. 2: 382p.; Vol. 3: 280p.; Vol. 4: 328p. $75.00/set.

This set of four volumes is the indispensable reference work for the study of modern Russia in general and Soviet Communism in particular. It also amplifies the standard Soviet anthology in important respects and provides editorial explanation that is independent of Kremlin politics. The rich store of materials in these four volumes ranges from the formation of the party to the fall of Khrushchev, and it deals with a wide range of issues. The clearly organized volumes each contain a major introductory essay as well as shorter background essays on each party congress, conference, or Central Committee plenum.

        S. M. H.

366.   Moses, Joel C. **Regional Party Leadership and Policy-Making in the USSR.** New York, Praeger, 1974. 284p. $18.50.

This study relates the impact of social change and political leadership to regional policy-making and party elites in the USSR. It examines the potential capacity of Soviet regional parties to respond to demands for political participation within their own regions.   S. M. H.

367.   Planty-Bonjour, Guy. **The Categories of Dialectical Materialism: Contemporary Soviet Ontology.** Trans. by T. J. Blakeley. New York, Praeger; Dordrecht, D. Reidel, 1967. 182p. $12.50.

This study is concerned almost exclusively with the details of Soviet discussions on the major terms, concepts, and laws of dialectical materialism from 1953 through about 1961. The author centers on the intellectual contortions of Soviet philosophers as they wrestle with the inconsistencies and internal conflicts they have inherited from the various Marxist "classical" attempts to unite realism, materialism, and science with Hegelian dialectics. As the author correctly notes, moreover, though the level of discussion is "no longer lamentable," it is still mediocre (nor has the situation changed in this respect since 1961).

SR, 28:1:166-7   R: Richard T. De George

368.   Reshetar, John S., Jr. **A Concise History of the Communist Party of the Soviet Union.** Rev. ed. New York, Praeger, 1964 (1960). 372p. $2.50pa.

This work is built on the theme that Lenin provided the presumptions that culminated in Stalin's great purge. Lenin was as ruthless, obsessed, headstrong, self-righteous, and confident as his successors, not the kindly humanitarian driven to severity by circumstances, as he is sometimes pictured. Stalin's difference lay in his creation of the apparatus of oppression, the organization. The volume is aimed at the advanced student of Soviet affairs. This revised edition includes an added ninth chapter dealing with Khrushchev's regime.

AHR, 66:1:162-4   R: John N. Hazard

369.   Rigby, T. H. **Communist Party Membership in the U.S.S.R., 1917-1967.** Princeton, Princeton University Press, 1968. 573p. (Studies of the Russian Institute, Columbia University). $15.00.

In this book Rigby performs two important tasks. In a fifty-page introduction he has attempted to adapt the Almond framework of analysis to make it less ethnocentric in nature, and he has examined the general role of the party in these terms. In the rest of the book he has summarized in a most comprehensive manner all available statistical information about party membership over a fifty-year period. In fact, it is more an encyclopedia than a book to be read.

SR, 33:1:150-2   R: Jerry F. Hough

370.   Schapiro, Leonard. **The Communist Party of the Soviet Union.** 2nd ed., rev. and enl. New York, Random House, 1971. 631p. $3.45pa.

Reviewed in *Junior Slavica*, p. 78.

371.   Schapiro, Leonard, and Peter Reddaway, eds. **Lenin: The Man, the Theorist, the Leader: A Reappraisal.** New York, Praeger, 1967. 317p. (Published in association with the Hoover Institution on War, Revolution, and Peace, Stanford University). $7.50.

This book assembles a highly literate troop of English, Scottish, and Canadian scholars in a generally successful effort to render the enigmatic Lenin more intelligible by analyzing as separate topics many of the segments of his thought and politics. Readers are warned to familiarize themselves with Lenin's career as a whole before reading this study.

AHR, 73:5:1584-5   R: Stanley W. Page

372.   Tucker, Robert C., ed. **The Lenin Anthology.** New York, W. W. Norton & Co., 1974. 764p. $18.95cl.; $4.95pa.

This comprehensive volume includes essential writings of Lenin, each of them introduced with a brief interpretive commentary by Tucker. "The State and Revolution" and "Left Wing Communism" are presented in their entirety. A general introduction to the volume traces Lenin's career as a revolutionary, both in writings and in actions. Also included is a chronology, a bibliographic note, and an index. The student and expert alike will profit greatly from this well-selected anthology.   S. M. H.

373.   Unger, Aryeh L. **The Totalitarian Party: Party and People in Nazi Germany and Soviet Russia**. London, Cambridge University Press, 1974. 286p. $13.95.

This comparative study of totalitarianism in Germany and Russia largely concentrates on the propaganda put out by the two regimes and on the aims and claims of the two ruling parties. Throughout, and especially so in the conclusions at the end, the similarities between the two regimes are emphasized.

SEER, 53:133:623-4   R: F. L. Carsten

Police Terror, Propaganda, Espionage

374.   Andres, Karl. **Murder to Order**. New York, Devin-Adair, 1967. 127p. $3.95.

The author describes two case histories of political assassination ordered by a top Kremlin officiel (A. Shelepin) in peacetime in a neutral country. On October 12, 1957, a Soviet agent discharged a poison gas pistol at Dr. Lev Rebet. In 1959 Shelepin ordered the agent Stashynsky to murder Stepan Bandera, leader of the Organization of Ukrainian Nationalists (OUN). The murder was carried out on October 15, 1959, in Munich. Stashynsky later defected to the West, giving himself up to American authorities in West Germany. There followed a sensational trial, which exposed the Soviet policy of political assassinations and brazen slanders. Whoever reads this book will realize as never before that Soviet Russia is a monstrous tyranny.

UQ, 24:1:88-9   R: Austin J. App

375.   Barghoorn, Frederick C. **Soviet Foreign Propaganda**. Princeton, Princeton University Press, 1964. 329p. $6.00.

Barghoorn devoted his major analyses to the attempts by the Communists to use cultural diplomacy as instruments of their foreign policy. He defined their cultural diplomacy as "the manipulation of cultural materials and personnel for propaganda purposes," and accurately described this special and significant branch of intergovernmental propaganda as one much more highly developed by Communist states than by non-Communist countries. The author's short chapter on "Cultural Diplomacy under Lenin and Stalin" is especially valuable in placing in perspective the elements as noticeable in Soviet foreign cultural policy today which are repetitions or extensions of patterns set in earlier years, or characterizing Soviet cultural diplomacy from its inception. He still finds it "an important or even crucial Soviet instrument of power."

SR, 23:4:764-5   R: Howland H. Sargent

376.   Barron, John. **KGB: The Secret Work of Soviet Secret Agents**. London, Hodder and Stoughton, 1974. 460p. $12.95; New York, Reader's Digest Press, 1974. 462p. $10.95.

Barron's book consists of a series of case studies of KGB actions, with summaries setting forth the historical background and nature of KGB operations in the Soviet Union itself. It contains vivid details and is written in a lively style, offering much that should be new to most readers. Barron has been careful to cross-check his facts, and his accounts of KGB skulduggery in the Middle East, the United States, France, and Mexico carry the air of conviction.

      RR, 33:4:437-8   R: Robert M. Slusser

377.   Clews, John C. **Communist Propaganda Techniques.** Foreword by
         G. F. Hudson. New York, Praeger, 1964. 326p. $8.50.
The author discusses the ideological and political context of Communist propaganda, with emphasis upon an historical presentation. He gives us a great deal of useful historical-descriptive material. He discusses the Leninist doctrine of propaganda, relating it to general discussions of the nature and development of modern uses of mass communication, and he then proceeds to describe the development of the organization and structure of Soviet propaganda during the Stalinist and post-Stalinist periods, furnishing a great deal of factual material along the way about propaganda as an instrument of Soviet foreign policy and about various Soviet organizations, "fronts," and so on. The work should be especially beneficial in exposing the cynicism of contemporary Communist propaganda and in puncturing illusions regarding the moral foundations of a still dangerous movement.

      SR, 25:1:167-8   R: Frederick C. Barghoorn

378.   Conquest, Robert. **The Great Terror: Stalin's Purge of the Thirties.**
         New York, Macmillan, 1968. 633p. $9.95.
To read this book is unbearably painful and profoundly illuminating. The author has read, included, and documented everything, from Lenin's first decrees establishing forced labor camps for "enemies," then for "slothful workingmen" and those who "violate labor discipline," to the complicity that the post-Stalin leadership shares in the denunciations and purges of the "great terror." Every chapter, almost every page, has its separate shock. We witness the tortures of the men who were brought to confess, and examine the self-refuting nature of their confessions. It is a shattering experience to have to read this book, where all these crimes are brought together, but it is an instructive and necessary one. As historians we must be grateful to Robert Conquest for having undertaken this surely painful task, and having executed it with such thoroughness and skill. A minimum of twenty million lives are attributable to Stalin's peacetime measures from 1930 to 1953.

      SR, 28:2:335-6   R: Bertram D. Wolfe

379.   Conquest, Robert, ed. **The Soviet Police System.** New York, Praeger,
         1968. 103p. $5.00.
Not formally a history of the police but rather a systematic survey of its development, organization, and functions, the volume edited by Conquest is an attempt to provide in concise form the basic data needed for an understanding of the police's role in Soviet history and the functioning of the Soviet political system. The book's principal value lies in its documentation.

      SR, 32:4:825-7   R: Robert M. Slusser

380.   Dallin, Alexander, and George W. Breslauer. **Political Terror in Communist Systems**. Stanford, Stanford University Press, 1970. 172p. $5.95.
The authors have tried in their book to view the secret police's operations in the context of comparative Communist studies, itself a new and still exploratory field.
           SR, 32:4:828   R: Robert M. Slusser

381.   Deacon, Richard. **A History of the Russian Secret Service**. London, Frederick Muller, 1972. 568p. £5.80. New York, Taplinger, 1972.
Deacon focuses on the secret police's operations, especially espionage. His sources range from standard Soviet publications to the usual "well-placed informant who must remain anonymous" and he makes liberal, and at times uncritical, use of the press. He begins his account in remote pre-Soviet times, finding the origin of the attitudes which underlie the centuries-long history of the Russian secret police in the period of the Mongol Yoke.
           SR, 32:4:825-7   R: Robert M. Slusser

382.   Deriabin, Peter. **Watchdogs of Terror: Russian Bodyguards from the Tsars to the Commissars**. New Rochelle, N.Y., Arlington House, 1972. 448p. $11.95.
A former Soviet counter-intelligence officer who escaped in 1954, Deriabin offers a history of Tsarist and Soviet "bodyguards" (security police and agents) from *oprichnina* to the KGB. The book is not a scholarly work based on sources, but rather a popular account aimed at the general reader, providing details unknown heretofore and an extensive bibliography for further study.
                          S. M. II.

383.   Dewhirst, Martin, and Robert Farrell, eds. **The Soviet Censorship**. Metuchen, N.J., Scarecrow Press, 1973. 170p. (Published in cooperation with Radio Liberty Committee, New York, and the Institute for the Study of the USSR, Munich). $7.50.
The Munich Institute for the Study of the USSR, in cooperation with Radio Liberty (New York), organized a symposium on Soviet censorship in which a group of Soviet intellectuals, who have settled in the West since 1966, participated together with outstanding Western scholars. Discussions were held on: what is Soviet censorship; self-censorship; the system of formal censorship; unofficial censorship; censorship of music; censorship in the Soviet cinema; censorship and science; and on evading the censor. The editors' footnotes to the texts are excellent.   S. M. H.

384.   Hingley, Ronald. **The Russian Secret Police: Muscovite, Imperial Russian and Soviet Political Security Operations**. New York, Simon and Shuster, 1970. 313p. $7.50.
The question of continuity between tsarist and Soviet Russia underlies the whole book. Hingley sensibly notes that one of the links between the old and new political police is the lessons that Lenin and Dzerzhinsky, as experienced quarries of the Okhrana, passed on to the Cheka. The author shows how much more limited, and often humane, tsarist political police action was, compared

to Soviet. This is a competent account and a welcome addition to the growing
list of surveys of selected themes in Russian history.

      SR, 31:1:152-3   R: Robert H. McNeal

385.   Levytsky, Boris, comp. **The Stalinist Terror in the Thirties: Docu-
         mentation from the Soviet Press.** Stanford, Hoover Institution Press,
         1974. 525p. $14.50.

The core of the book is 234 biographical entries concerning purge victims, each
entry consisting of one or more excerpts from Soviet publications during the
period of the anti-Stalin campaign and rehabilitation of its victims. In addition
more general surveys of the impact of the purge are provided concerning such
groups as the military cadres and national Communist party leadership. An
imposing variety of sources is utilized, almost all in Russian (a few are in
Ukrainian), but with considerable attention to the Russian language press in
the non-Russian republics.

      CSP, 17:1:155-7   R: Robert H. McNeal

386.   Levytsky, Boris. **The Uses of Terror: The Soviet Secret Police, 1917-
         1970.** Trans. by H. A. Piehler. New York, Coward, McCann &
         Geoghegan, 1972. 349p. $7.95.

This work is a translation and updating of the second German edition, *Die
rote Inquisition* (1967), which brings the story down to 1970. A notable feature
of Levytsky's book is the extensive use he makes of émigré publications, which
provide detailed information on such matters as the struggle by the secret
police against nationalist guerrillas in the Ukraine and elsewhere in the period
after 1945.

      SR, 32:4:825-7   R: Robert M. Slusser

387.   Lonsdale, Gordon. **Spy: Twenty Years in Soviet Secret Service.** New
         York, Hawthorn Books, 1965. 220p. $4.95.

Lonsdale, a Communist who worked for Soviet intelligence in Europe and
America, incarnates the genuine espionage agent. Soviet training causes him to
center his attention on the "putrid West" rather than on his own activity.
Much more information regarding Soviet work in the Western world has been
contributed by "intelligence" literature of Soviet origin and by former Soviet
intelligence officers.

      RR, 25:4:416-8   R: Richard Wraga

388.   Marchenko, Anatoly. **My Testimony.** Trans. by Michael Scammell.
         Intro. by Max Hayward. New York, E. P. Dutton, 1969. 415p. $8.95.

This is an eyewitness account of prison life in the USSR. The book is especially
valuable because it is the first detailed account of Soviet prison life in the post-
Stalin era. It demonstrates that although the number of prisoners in Soviet
labor camps has decreased, the brutal instances have become worse. There now
appear to be four categories of prisoners in the USSR: 1) intellectuals arrested
for "anti-Soviet activities and propaganda"; 2) "nationalists" from various
non-Russian nationalities in the Soviet Union; 3) members of the many persecuted
religious denominations; 4) common criminals. After publication of *My Testimony*

in England in 1968, Marchenko was again arrested and is now most probably back in those Siberian prison camps that he so vividly describes in this book.

UQ, 26:1:82-3   R: M. W. Odajnyk

389.   Penkovsky, Oleg. **The Penkovsky Papers.** Intro. and comment by
        Frank Gibney. Foreword by Edward Crankshaw. Trans. by Peter
        Deriabin. New York, Doubleday, 1965. 412p. $5.95.

If genuine, *The Penkovsky Papers* (dealing with the trials of G. Wynne and O. V. Penkovsky in Moscow in 1963) are unique in the history of espionage. In the absence of the original and other information needed for analysis, we must accept *The Penkovsky Papers* on faith, basing this on our opinion of Frank Gibney, the editor and commentator, and Peter Deriabin, the translator. The trial, one of the more sensational espionage trials of our day, was similar in many respects to other Soviet trials. It raised questions, suggested doubts, and clarified less than it obscured. The case remains dim. Nor does the official Soviet record of the trial, published in Russia, subsequently shed any further light on the affair.

RR, 25:4:416-8   R: Richard Wraga

390.   Seth, Ronald. **The Executioners: The Story of Smersh.** New York,
        Hawthorn Books (1968). 199p. $5.95.

Personal experience in the shadowy world of espionage and counterespionage provides the basis for Seth's study of the Soviet security services in World War II, centering on the counterespionage agency known as "Smersh" ("Smert' shpionam," or "Death to Spies"). Since the author tends to equate Smersh with the secret police itself, his book includes a much broader treatment of the subject than might be inferred from its title. The author is knowledgeable and apparently enjoyed good contacts in Western counterespionage circles.

SR, 32:4:825-7   R: Robert M. Slusser

391.   Shub, Anatole. **The New Russian Tragedy.** New York, W. W. Norton,
        1969. 128p. $4.50.

This is a collection of a series of newspaper articles written by Shub immediately after his expulsion as *Washington Post* correspondent from Moscow in the spring of 1969. Shub's Russia is a composite of three exceedingly hostile worlds; that of the embattled foreign correspondent, hounded by the KGB; that of the increasingly persecuted and martyred dissident intelligentsia; and that of the Kremlin.

SR, 30:1:159-60   R: James C. McClelland

392.   **Soviet Intelligence and Security Services, 1964-70: A Selected
        Bibliography of Soviet Publications, with Some Additional Titles from
        Other Sources.** U.S. Senate, Committee on the Judiciary, 92nd Congress,
        1st Session. Washington, D.C., GPO, 1972. 289p. $1.25.

This bibliography is far more than a mere listing of titles; it includes concise analytical comments on many works, and thereby facilitates research on a multitude of fascinating and important topics.

SR, 32:4:825-6   R: Robert M. Slusser

393.   Tucker, Robert C., and Stephen F. Cohen, eds. **The Great Purge Trial.**
        Intro. by Robert C. Tucker. New York, Grosset and Dunlap, 1965.
        725p. $5.95.
It was an excellent idea of the editors to examine afresh the published record
of the March 1938 trial in which N. I. Bukharin and A. I. Rykov, the principal
surviving figures in the so-called "Right Opposition," were tried and condemned,
along with the former Trotskyite diplomat N. N. Krestinskii, the ex-chief of
the secret police, G. G. Yagoda, and a number of lesser figures. In the light of
all the relevant information known to them, and to attempt a new analysis
of the trial and its purpose, Tucker's interpretation shows that the trial served
a number of purposes, corresponding to the motives of the principal figures
involved. The introduction is concerned chiefly with the motives of the two men
whom Tucker regards as the principal antagonists in the 1938 trial, Stalin and
Bukharin. He followed Avtorkhanov for the statement that a plenum of the
Central Committee took place in September 1936, that at it a clash occurred
between Stalin and his opponents, and that as a result Bukharin and Rykov
won a temporary reprieve.
        SR, 25:2:353-5   R: Robert M. Slusser

394.   Wittlin, Thaddeus. **Commissar: The Life and Death of Lavrenty
        Pavlovich Beria.** New York, Macmillan, 1972. 566p. $12.95.
The first full-length biography of Beria, Soviet secret police chief from 1938
to 1953, has been written by Wittlin, a Polish-born writer who earlier published
an absorbing account of his imprisonment in Soviet concentration camps during
World War II, (*Reluctant Traveler in Russia,* 1952). The value of his book is
enhanced by rare photographs and a generous selection of relevant Soviet
documents.
        SR, 32:4:828   R: Robert M. Slusser

Dissent Movement

395.   Amalrik, Andrei. **Involuntary Journey to Siberia.** Trans. by Manya
        Harari and Max Hayward. Intro. by Max Hayward. New York, Harcourt
        Brace Jovanovich, 1970. 297p. $6.95.
In this work Amalrik narrates his earlier encounters with the Soviet repression
system. Most revealing, perhaps, is Amalrik's account of the real extent of
punishment resulting from a Soviet conviction.
        RR, 30:2:188-9   R: John A. Armstrong

396.   Brumberg, Abraham, ed. **In Quest of Justice: Protest and Dissent in
        the Soviet Union Today.** New York, Praeger, 1970. 477p. $10.95.
This compilation preserves material the bulk of which appeared in *Problems
of Communism* in 1968. The heart of the book contains documents prepared
by Soviet citizens, signed with names and addresses, and usually sent to appropriate "instances" in the Soviet government or the United Nations. Most of
the documents are links in the chain of repression, protest, secondary repression,
secondary protest—in such areas as literature, nationalities, religion, self-
expression, and intervention in Czechoslovakia. There are some records,

unofficial of course, of trials and board meetings, interrogations conducted by the police or party officials, and a few Soviet news articles. The documentary section is preceded by brief commentaries from foreign specialists and followed by a few samples of the underground literature of protest.

SR, 30:4:897-8 R: Leon Lipson

397. Chalidze, Valery. **To Defend These Rights: Human Rights and the Soviet Union.** Trans. by Guy Daniels. New York, Random House, 1974. 340p. $10.00.

Chalidze offers, in the opening chapters, features of Soviet law and the Soviet Union's position with respect to international conventions on human rights. Then he analyzes and exposes all the restrictions on basic human rights and freedom as related to social, religious and national minority aspects. Also, the treatment of prisoners and their prospects for the future are subjects of his concern. The author was a member of the USSR Human Rights Movement but is now—since 1972—a U.S. citizen. His moving account deserves a special place in college and public libraries. S. M. H.

398. Gaucher, Roland. **Opposition in the U.S.S.R., 1917-1967.** Trans. by Charles Lam Markman. New York, Funk & Wagnalls, 1969. 547p. $10.00.

This volume consists of the writings of anti-Bolshevik opposition groups from 1917 to 1967. It includes Whites, anarchists, social-revolutionaries from the period of the Civil War, opposition during the 1920s and 1930s coming from anti-collectivist forces, national and religious. It is an anthology of the resistance to the Soviet system. S. M. H.

399. Gerstenmaier, Cornelia. **The Voices of the Silent.** Trans. by Susan Hecker. New York, Hart Publishing Co., 1972. 587p. $10.00.

Gerstenmaier, a West German student of Soviet affairs and former editor of *Ost-Probleme*, has produced a detailed and comprehensive survey of several aspects of the struggle for elemental human rights and freedoms ensuing within the Soviet Union since the death of Stalin. She has made the personal acquaintance of many of the better-known figures involved in the Democratic Movement, and this volume not only serves as a general introduction to problems of dissent over the past twenty years but also fills in much information on the fate of those persons whose names have flashed briefly in the Western consciousness and then disappeared. Unfortunately, the Hecker translation contains too many errors and discrepancies.

SR, 32:3:623-4 R: Ted Crump

400. Hayward, Max, ed. **On Trial: The Soviet State Versus "Abram Tertz" and "Nikolai Arzhak."** Trans., ed., and with an intro. by Max Hayward. New York, Harper and Row, 1966. 183p. $4.95.

This is a disturbing book. It is a reminder that the Soviet Union, despite its obvious industrial and technological accomplishments, has yet to guarantee to its intellectuals that measure of freedom of expression which affords them the right to publish social and political criticism in a nonconforming, unorthodox literary style. Siniavski and Daniel, Soviet citizens who published abroad under the pseudonyms Tertz and Arzak, were arrested in 1965, charged with the crime of anti-Soviet agitation and propaganda, a violation of Section 1 of Article 79 of the Criminal Code of the RSFSR, tried, convicted, and sentenced to seven and five years, respectively. In this slim volume Hayward has ably translated the transcript of the trial.

SR, 27:1:157-8   R: Joseph J. Darby

401.   Litvinov, Pavel. **The Demonstration in Pushkin Square: The Trial Records with Commentary and an Open Letter.** Trans. by Manya Harari. Boston, Gambit, 1969. 176p. $4.95.

The main and central part of this book is a faithful account of two trials that took place in the Moscow City Court in February and September 1967, and that are somewhere in the middle of a chain of dramatic events, all connected with the struggle for freedom of expression, freedom of peaceful assembly and association, and other fundamental rights and freedoms contained in the Universal Declaration of Human Rights of 1948. It began with the arrest and trial of Daniel and Siniavsky in 1965-66, and ended, if there is an end to such prosecution in the USSR, with the arrest and trial of Pavel Litvinov himself, who was sentenced to five years' exile in Siberia in 1968. This is not a book for lawyers only. It is a document that should be read by everybody.

SR, 30:1:161-2   R: Ivo Lapenna

402.   Litvinov, Pavel, comp.**The Trial of the Four: A Collection of Materials on the Case of Galanskov, Ginzburg, Dobrovolsky and Lashkova, 1967-68.** English text ed. and annotated by Peter Reddaway. Trans. by Janis Sapiets, Hilary Sternberg, and Daniel Weissbort. Foreword by Leonard Schapiro. New York, Viking Press, 1972. 434p. $10.00.

This trial of January 1968 elicited so powerful a response among Soviet intellectuals that it may be said to have sparked the Soviet human rights movement. The protests which it generated exceeded in scope those following the 1966 trial of writers Andrei Siniavsky and Iulii Daniel. This book should be required reading for any serious student of the contemporary Soviet scene.

SR, 32:3:622-3   R: John B. Dunlop

403.   Medvedev, Roy A. **Let History Judge: The Origins and Consequences of Stalinism.** Trans. by Colleen Taylor. Ed. by David Joravsky and Georges Haupt. New York, Knopf, 1971. 566p. $12.50.

In the environment of the Soviet critical intelligentsia in which this was written, it is a wonder. Not only does it represent the first foray of the unofficial writers into the mainstream of Soviet history, it is a triumph of judicious scholarship over persecution, isolation and taboo. It demolishes official Soviet historiography and courageously raises basic questions defying the KGB and the fundamental structure of the system. This book should be a must not only for all students of Soviet and East European affairs, but also for the Western intellectual who is still confused about the real nature of the Soviet system.

RR, 31:2:179-81   R: Robert H. McNeal

404.   Medvedev, Zhores A. **The Medvedev Papers: "Fruitful Meetings between Scientists of the World" [and] "Secrecy of Correspondence is Guaranteed by Law."** Trans. by Vera Rich. Foreword by John Ziman. London, Macmillan. New York, St. Martin's Press, 1971. 471p. $11.95.

In 1962 Medvedev's manuscript (later published in the United States as *The Rise and Fall of T. D. Lysenko*) began to circulate in *samizdat*, and indeed by 1965 Lysenko's power had dwindled. His punishment for publishing the *Papers* was two weeks of "psychiatric detention" in May 1970 (described by Medvedev and his brother Roy in *A Question of Madness*, 1971). Many important topics are examined by Medvedev in the *Papers*: the internal and external passport system in the Soviet Union, the trials of publishing, the process of election to the Academy of Sciences, and the post office system. Fascinating as these insights are, the author's main emphasis is on two other themes—the obstacles to international travel, and the censorship of mail.

      SR, 31:3:697-8   R: Barry Mendel Cohen

405.   Medvedev, Zhores A. **Ten Years after Ivan Denisovich.** Trans. by Hilary Sternberg. New York, Knopf, 1973. 202p. $6.95.

Medvedev traces the gradual emergence of criticism hostile to Solzhenitsyn, the refusal to award him a Lenin Prize or to publish his later works, the appearance of his books abroad, his expulsion from the Soviet Writers' Union, and the reaction to his Nobel award. The reader is also provided with fascinating glimpses of such prominent representatives of the Soviet intelligentsia as Tvardovsky, physicist Kapitsa, cellist Rostropovich, all of whose paths crossed Solzhenitsyn's. Yet the most arresting aspect of this work is not its explicit informational content, but what it reveals about perceptions by Soviet intellectuals of the proper boundaries between freedom and order.

      RR, 33:4:446-8   R: Dorothy Atkinson

406.   Medvedev, Zhores A., and Roy A. Medvedev. **A Question of Madness.** Trans. by Ellen de Kadt. New York, Knopf, 1971. 223p. $5.95.

The book, written by twin brothers, represents a firsthand account of Zhores' involuntary confinement in a mental hospital because of his critical writings. His release was a result of vigorous protests from prominent Soviet as well as Western scientists and literary figures. This is the story of sensitively chronicled events which ended with Zhores' conditional release.   S. M. H.

407.   Reddaway, Peter, and Edward Kline, eds. **A Chronicle of Human Rights in the USSR.** New York, Khronika Press, 1973. No. 1: November 1972-March 1973. 80p. No. 2: April-May 1973. 77p. No. 3: July-August 1973. 78p. $3.00ea. Paper.

The editors have translated material that was published in the Soviet Union by the Russian Democratic Movement and appeared in either the *Chronicle of Current Events* or in other underground *samizdat* publications. Thanks to the efforts of Reddaway and a few others, the West is slowly seeing the true picture of Soviet life and the fate of the intellectuals who have the courage to oppose an oppressive system.   S. M. H.

408. Reddaway, Peter, ed. and trans. **Uncensored Russia: Protest and Dissent in the Soviet Union: The Unofficial Moscow Journal. A Chronicle of Current Events.** Foreword by Julius Telesin. New York, American Heritage Press, 1972. 499p. $10.00.

Reddaway has translated the first eleven issues of the *Chronicle of Current Events*, dating from April 1968 to December 1969. Instead of presenting the issues *ad seriatim*, Reddaway has had the bright idea of arranging the materials topically into seven parts. He succeeds in recounting how the *Chronicle*'s concern grew from its self-definition to include portraits and hardships of leading dissidents and unsung heroes—from central events in the capital to the movement's remote tributaries. The introduction is informative, concise, and sober.

SR, 32:3:595-600   R: Vera S. Dunham

409. Reve, Karel van het, ed. **Dear Comrade: Pavel Litvinov and the Voices of Soviet Citizens in Dissent.** New York, Pitman Publishing Corp., 1969. 199p. $4.95.

Dear Comrade is a significant document of political dissent in the USSR, directed against the portents of neo-Stalinism. It contains two important protest letters written by Pavel Litvinov, the grandson of the late people's commissar of foreign affairs, and letters and telegrams sent to Litvinov between December 1967 and May 1968. A concise introduction and careful annotations supplied by the editor enhance the value of this volume.

SR, 29:2:343-4   R: Bohdan R. Bociurkiw

410. Rothberg, Abraham. **The Heirs of Stalin: Dissidence and the Soviet Regime, 1953-1970.** Ithaca, Cornell University Press, 1972. 450p. $14.50.

The author has provided a far-ranging chornicle of the conflict between Soviet intellectuals and their government from the time of Stalin's death until virtually the present day. For the non-specialist, the book contains a readable and comprehensive glimpse into one aspect of recent Soviet history. It contains a wealth of material and information that will be of great interest to everyone who follows Soviet affairs.

SR, 32:1:212-3   R: Barry Scherr

411. Sakharov, Andrei D. **Progress, Coexistence, and Intellectual Freedom.** Trans. from the Russian by the *New York Times*, with intro., afterword, and notes by H. E. Salisbury. New York, Norton, 1968. 158p. $2.50pa.

Sakharov expresses his views on the democratization of the Soviet system. He takes a critical stand on the policy of coexistence which, according to him, serves Soviet needs only.   S. M. H.

412. Sakharov, Andrei D. **Sakharov Speaks.** Ed. by Harrison E. Salisbury. New York, Knopf, 1974. 245p. $6.95.

Following the foreword and introduction there are sections on "Progress, Coexistence, and Intellectual Freedom, June 1968" and "Manifesto II, March 1970," which first appeared in the book *Progress, Coexistence, and Intellectual Freedom*. The rest of the work consists of memoranda, a statement on "Let Soviet Citizens Emigrate," interviews with Swedish, Lebanese, and Western correspondents, including one with Mikhail P. Malyarov, the first Deputy Soviet Prosecutor, a letter to the Congress of the United States, and a sundry of statements dealing essentially with the human rights issue. The author shows also a considerable awareness of what is going on in the various non-Russian republics. Without question this work represents a refreshing source of humanistic ideas and thoughts.

   UQ, 31:1:61-4   R: Lev E. Dobriansky

413. Saunders, George, ed. **Samizdat: Voices of the Soviet Opposition.** New York, Monad Press, 1974. 464p. $13.00cl.; $3.95pa. Distr. by Pathfinder Press.

The book is divided into three sections. The first part, "From the Old Opposition to the New," includes memoir accounts by former members of the Left Opposition who survived Stalinist camps. The second section is on P. Grigorenko and his close associates A. Kosterin and I. Yakhimovich. The final section is devoted to *samizdat* documents which appeared between 1969 and 1972. The editor has brought together some important documents illustrating the evolution of the democratic movement among Russian, Ukrainian, and Latvian dissenters.

   RR, 33:4:439-40   R: Victoria E. Bonnell

414. Scammell, Michael, ed. **Russia's Other Writers: Selections from Samizdat Literature.** Foreword by Max Hayward. New York, Praeger, 1971. 216p. $6.95.

This book represents *samizdat* literature. Untouched by censorship, the essays are the most reliable sources of information about Soviet life. Works of nine authors of varying age, talent, and prominence have been selected for this collection.

   RR, 31:3:304-6   R: Herman Ermolaev

415. Siniavskii, Andrei. **For Freedom of Imagination.** Trans. by Laszlo Tikos and Murray Peppard. New York, Rinehart and Winston, 1971. 212p. $6.95.

This is a collection of essays of well-chosen and well-translated literary pieces, most of which are available only in the West. The essays on R. Frost and Pasternak are perhaps the most brilliant. The book is a small tribute to the man who, despite imprisonment and endless persecution, has the courage to express ideas that challenge the whole Soviet totalitarian system. S. M. H.

416. Yakir, Pyotr. **A Childhood in Prison.** Ed. with an intro. by Robert Conquest. New York, Coward, McCann & Geoghegan, 1973. 155p. $5.95.

The book consists of Yakir's moving account of his coming-of-age in the jungle of Stalin-era concentration camps. Laconic, terse, and matter-of-fact, Yakir's story is a classic which should be read by everyone concerned with modern Russian and Soviet history and politics.

   SR, 32:4:828   R: Robert M. Slusser

Diplomacy and Foreign Policy

Bibliographies and Biographies

417.   Clemens, Walter C., Jr. **Soviet Disarmament Policy 1917-1963: An Annotated Bibliography.** Stanford, The Hoover Institution, 1965. 151p. $4.00pa.
Designed to facilitate research on disarmament policy of the Soviet Union since 1917, this bibliography lists the most important primary and secondary material which has appeared in Russia, Europe, and North America.   S. M. H.

418.   Crowley, Edward L., ed. **The Soviet Diplomatic Corps, 1917-1967.** Metuchen, N.J., Scarecrow Press, 1970. 426p. $7.50.
This volume will be useful both to the historian of Soviet foreign affairs and to the practitioner of diplomacy with an interest in the USSR. It contains lists of past and present Ministers of Foreign Affairs and their deputies of personnel in the Ministry's various functional and geographic divisions, and of heads of foreign missions. It also provides a list of Soviet vetoes in the United Nations, and various organizational charts.   S. M. H.

419.   Hammond, Thomas T., comp. and ed. **Soviet Foreign Relations and World Communism: A Selected, Annotated Bibliography of 7,000 Books in 30 Languages.** Princeton, Princeton University Press, 1965. 1240p. $25.00.
This bibliography is a handy reference tool; it deserves a place on the desks of scholars. Four broad areas of bibliographical concern are announced: 1) Soviet foreign relations, economic as well as political with all countries since 1917; 2) Communist movement outside Russia since 1917; 3) certain specific aspects of Soviet foreign policy, such as ideology, propaganda, strategy and tactics, and espionage; 4) internal developments in all Communist countries except Russia.
          RR, 25:2:199-201   R: Melvin Croan

420.   Saran, Vimla. **Sino-Soviet Schism: A Bibliography, 1956-1964.** New York, Asia Publishing House, 1971. 162p. (Issued under the auspices of the School of International Studies, Jawaharlal Nehru University.) $10.00.
This is a most welcome Sino-Soviet bibliography listing 2,030 entries, including documents covering the crucial years of Sino-Soviet relations. Among the documents are speeches, statements, resolutions, communiques, letters, editorials, and reports of the Communist parties of the world. Western literature is also represented. The book is divided into three parts: Theory; International Communist Movement; and International Relations. Author and subject indexes are most useful.   S. M. H.

General Works

421.   Aspaturian, Vernon A., ed. **Process and Power in Soviet Foreign Policy.** Boston, Little, Brown, 1971. 939p. $10.00.

Over two-thirds of the 939 pages are written by Aspaturian, while the other
articles included in the volume bear such distinguished names as Theodore von
Laue, Henry Roberts, Arthur Schlesinger, Alexander Dallin, Zbigniew Brzezinski,
Robert Tucker, and others. All of the articles, with the exception of the introductory essay by Aspaturian, have appeared before in printed form, either as
parts of books or in scholarly journals; yet, in spite of the fact that they are
brought together as a mélange of views, the book still appears to be more
cohesive than a mere reader. The inclusion of works spanning the period between
1957 and 1968 forces students to focus not just on the text but also to place
the views presented within the context of the time in which they were written.
This essay should be the core of any required reading in Soviet foreign policy
courses.

      CSP, 15:3:412-3   R: Ivan Volgyes

422.   Berzins, Alfred. **The Two Faces of Co-Existence**. New York, Robert
       Speller, 1967. 355p. $6.95.

The author of this interesting book discusses Lenin's attitude toward capitalism
and democracies, explains the use of peace, friendship, and nonaggression pacts
as the tools of Soviet expansionist policy, and pays particular attention to
the Soviet policy toward Poland, Finland, Hungary, and the Baltic and Balkan
States, as examples. In the succeeding chapters he discusses the Communist
strategy and tactics according to Stalin and the Soviet policy of co-existence
after Stalin. Much of the information is already known to scholars, but its
arrangement and Berzin's comments deserve attention. The author ridicules
the new breed of scientists, the so-called Kremlinologists, whom he compares
to the latter-day soothsayers. He is amazed at the full-scale attention they give
to the activities of the men in the Kremlin and their complete disregard for the
many non-Russian nationalities forced to live under the rule of the Kremlin
bosses. The author suggests mutual scientific and cultural cooperation and direct
people-to-people contacts. He condemns complete opening of the gates of hte
non-Communist world without reciprocal action on the part of the Communists.

      AHR, 73:2:550-1   R: Edgar Anderson

423.   Eudin, Xenia Joukoff, and Robert M. Slusser, eds. **Soviet Foreign
       Policy, 1928-1934: Documents and Materials. Vol. 1**. University Park,
       Pa., Pennsylvania University Press, 1966. 353p. (Publication of the
       Hoover Institution on War, Revolution and Peace). $9.50.

The aim of this volume covering the period 1928-1931 is to present in the words
of the Soviet leaders themselves the most important points of Soviet foreign
policy without duplicating material previously published in English. The narrative summary, which introduces seventy documents selected from Soviet newspapers, periodicals, and Comintern reports, traces the course of events, but
devotes little space to close analysis.

      AHR, 73:1:186-7   R: Alfred J. Rieber

424.   Eudin, Xenia Joukoff, and Robert M. Slusser, eds. **Soviet Foreign
       Policy, 1928-1934: Documents and Materials. Vol. 2**. University
       Park, Pa., Pennsylvania State University Press, 1967. 423p. (Publication
       of the Hoover Institution on War, Revolution and Peace). $9.50.

This second volume opens with a Soviet press statement on the Soviet-Finnish nonaggression pact, January 1932, and ends with a *Pravda* commentary on the failure of the London Naval Conference in December 1934. The translations are of a high standard throughout. As happened both before and after this period, Comintern policy swung into line, and although the popular front was not officially adopted until 1935, its origin can be discerned here, if only in a murky haze.

SR, 28:1:1949   R: Jane Degras

(Note: These two volumes should be used together with Jane Degras' *Soviet Documents on Foreign Policy*. Vols. 1-3. London, Oxford University Press, 1951-1953.)

425.   Fischer, Louis. **Russia's Road from Peace to War: Soviet Foreign Relations, 1917-1941.** New York, Harper & Row, 1969. 499p. $12.50.
In attempting to interpret the Soviet behavior as a mixture of internal and external exigencies, of ideological commitments and hard realities, and of the Soviet leaders' own strictures, he succeeds in producing an integrated picture. Fischer is at his best in the analysis of Soviet foreign policy in the period he witnessed in Russia in the 1920s when he had access to documents that probably no other Western author was permitted to see and also to such key statesmen as Chicherin. The book may be controversial in some aspects, but it is that quality, combined with a sense of objectivity, that makes it thought-provoking and exciting reading for persons who are already well advanced in their knowledge of the complex story of Soviet foreign policy.

SR, 29:3:535-6   R: Josef Korbel

426.   Gamson, William A., and André Modigliani. **Untangling the Cold War: A Strategy for Testing Rival Theories.** Boston, Little, Brown, 1971. 222p. $6.95.
The two authors investigated the cold war as a sustained 18-year interaction process between two coalitions, the East and the West. Then they extrapolated and tested competing theories of major authors on both sides, the traditionalists as well as the revisionists, against the data generated by their interactional study. What emerged is an inventive, persuasive analysis of the two protagonists' mutual behavior from 1946 to 1963. All in all, conclude the authors on the basis of their data, obtained mainly from the *New York Times*, the responsibility for the cold war must be assigned to both parties equally.

SR, 31:2:436-7   R: Jan F. Triska

427.   Gehlen, Michael P. **The Politics of Coexistence: Soviet Methods and Motives.** Bloomington, Indiana University Press, 1967. 334p. $6.75.
This is a highly readable survey of recent Soviet foreign policies. While it does not take us very far into the politics of coexistence, this survey is on the whole a discriminating piece of work and should prove useful as a general introduction to the study of Soviet foreign policy.

SR, 28:1:155-6   R: Franklyn Griffiths

428.   Harvey, Mose L., et al. **Science and Technology as an Instrument of Soviet Policy**. Foreword by Ambassador Foy D. Kohler. Coral Gables, Fla., Center for Advanced International Studies, University of Miami, 1972. 219p. $5.95cl.; $4.95pa.

In the first part, this book presents translated extracts from Soviet articles and official documents on science and technology. In the second part, several authors offer analyses of the relationship between science and technology and Soviet foreign policy. The expert can gain from this book some insight into the Soviet technological potential, an increasingly major factor in the international arena.   S. M. H.

429.   Hoffmann, Eric P., and Frederic J. Fleron, Jr., eds. **The Conduct of Soviet Foreign Policy**. Chicago, Aldine-Atherton, 1971. 478p. $12.00.

The editors rely on the efforts of other social scientists to illuminate the problems posed by Soviet external behavior, modestly staying in the background and being content with supplying needed introductory remarks. Their work brings together most of the great articles written during the past fifteen years. Most of these articles have survived the test of time. The book is divided into seven parts, each dealing with a different basic topic: The Study of Soviet Foreign Policy; Domestic Politics and the Formation of Soviet Foreign Policy; Communist Ideology, Belief Systems and Soviet Foreign Policy; The Origins of the Cold War; Western Diplomacy and Soviet Foreign Policy; Competitive Coexistence and the Cold War; The Third World and Soviet Foreign Policy; and Retrospect and Prospect. This volume will remain constantly in demand as one of the finest sourcebooks for professors of political science specializing in the analysis of "the conduct of Soviet foreign policy."

CSP, 15:3:412-4   R: Ivan Volgyes

430.   Jacobsen, C. G. **Soviet Strategy—Soviet Foreign Policy: Military Considerations Affecting Soviet Policy-Making**. Glasgow, Glasgow University Press, 1972. 236p.

The author, who has researched relevant Soviet and Western publications, presents an analysis of Soviet military debates, Soviet strategic capabilities, strategic hardware, and the practical and psychological implications of different weapons systems. The book deals maily with the post-Khrushchev period.
S. M. H.

431.   Jelavich, Barbara. **St. Petersburg and Moscow: Tsarist and Soviet Foreign Policy, 1814-1974**. Bloomington, Indiana University Press, 1974. 480p. $12.50cl.; $4.95pa.

This volume represents, in reality, not one book but two. Out of the total of 457 pages, the first 288 are a scarcely re-edited reprinting of Mrs. Jelavich's earlier work, *A Century of Russian Foreign Policy, 1814-1914* (1964). The remainder, dealing with the Soviet period down through the 1960s is new. Of these two companion pieces the earlier one, covering the last hundred years of the volume, dealing with the Soviet period, may have its uses for textbook purposes; but it cannot be said to add much to the existing record of the external relations of the Soviet regime. This portion of the book is marred not just by a number of omissions but by a certain laconic, almost weary, inadequacy of

language at many points, such as to describe Stalin as a "controversial figure," who "appears to have been a tough, realistic, and determined statesman."
>   SR, 34:2:388-90   R: George F. Kennan

432.   Kanet, Roger E., and Ivan Volgyes, eds. **On the Road to Communism: Essays on Soviet Domestic and Foreign Politics.** Lawrence, University of Kansas Press, 1972. 212p. $8.50.
This volume consists of a collection of ten essays, mostly by American political scientists, that were originally presented at the Sixth Annual Bi-State Slavic Conference in November 1967. All essays pertain to some aspect of Soviet domestic or foreign policy.   S. M. H.

433.   Kohler, Foy D., et al. **Soviet Strategy for the Seventies: From Cold War to Peaceful Coexistence.** Coral Gables, Fla., Center for Advanced Studies, University of Miami, 1973. 241p. $5.95cl.; $4.95pa.
The central theme of all essays revolves around "peaceful coexistence," as it has been promoted and utilized from Lenin to Brezhnev. The first part analyzes the objectives and strategy of Soviet foreign policy. The book is a mine of useful material, although some important documents have been abbreviated to the point of confusing the undergraduate student. However, the study makes good reading and raises some interesting questions.   S. M. H.

434.   Kohler, Foy D. **Understanding the Russians: A Citizen's Primer.** New York, Harper & Row, 1970. 441p. $10.00.
The author was a U.S. Foreign Service officer from 1931 until his retirement as U.S. Ambassador to the Soviet Union in 1967. Kohler certainly knows Russia and the USSR, and his analysis of the system is cool and impartial. In a total of 26 chapters, densely studded with facts and quotations, he treats all aspects of Soviet life, with stress on U.S.-Soviet relations and a thorough examination of all the major foreign entanglements of the USSR. U.S.-Soviet confrontations may arise in a number of places, and only a firm stand on the part of the U.S. government, he believes, will deter the Soviet leaders from making a foolish decision which might precipitate a U.S.-Soviet armed conflict.
>   UQ, 26:3-4:312-3   R: Walter Dushnyck

435.   Kulski, W. W. **The Soviet Union in World Affairs: A Documented Analysis, 1964-1972.** Syracuse, Syracuse University Press, 1973. 526p. $17.50cl.; $5.95pa.
The book is particularly strong in its discussion of the limited influence of ideological beliefs on definitions of Soviet national interest, on the necessity of subordinating the interests of the international Communist movement to the state interest of the Soviet Union, and on the political and economic advice given by the USSR to Third World countries to avoid excessive economic radicalism in dealing with the West. In essence, Kulski's analysis demonstrates that Soviet specialists have a much more sophisticated, hard-headed, and non-ideological attitude in their perspective on international affairs than is commonly felt to be the case.
>   SR, 33:2:367-8   R: Robert E. Blackwell, Jr.

436.   Librach, Jan. **The Rise of the Soviet Empire: A Study of Soviet Foreign Policy**. New York, Praeger, 1964. 382p. $7.50cl.; $2.50pa.
The author has attempted to relate the complex story of Soviet expansion over the last forty-odd years and has succeeded in making his book comprehensive, informative, and interesting. The volume has two outstanding merits: it provides the general reader with a good synthesis of Soviet foreign policy, and it brings home to the specialist—too often engrossed in fascinating detail—the basic assumption underlying this policy. The author is at his best when relating Communist theory to practice, and his analysis in the first and the last two chapters is characterized by happy definitions and evaluations, especially of such concepts as "peace," "peaceful coexistence," and "national self-determination."
        JMH, 37:2:284   R: Piotr S. Wandycz

437.   London, Kurt L., ed. **The Soviet Impact on World Politics**. New York, Hawthorn Books, 1974. 312p. $13.95.
This book sets out to assess the Soviet impact on world politics and to warn the reader of the unrelievedly bleak record. Among contributors are: L. Schapiro, A. Ulam, H. Seton-Watson, A. Grosser, H. Hinton, Th. Wolfe, and others. With a distinctive unifying theme kept clearly in mind, they impose a refreshing improvement over most edited collections. It is self-evident that while the rest of the world changes, Soviet nature and purpose remain constant.
        RR, 34:3:340-1   R: David D. Finley

438.   Rosser, Richard F. **An Introduction to Soviet Foreign Policy**. Englewood Cliffs, N.J., Prentice-Hall, 1969. 391p. $8.50cl.; $4.95pa.
The author, being aware of the problem of sources and of the intricacy of differentiating between propagandistic agitation, ideological theorems, and the realistic pursuit of Soviet goals, proceeds methodically to acquaint his reader (undergraduate students, one may assume) with the principal moves of the Soviet policy-makers in the international arena, explaining their motivations and effectiveness. His discussion incorporates relevant matters of interest, such as geopolitics, the balance of power, and the Russian heritage, as well as Communist ideology. His study covers the entire period of the Soviet government's existence and all areas of the world in which it has been involved. Written with a sense of detachment, well balanced an organized, and in full command of relevant literature, it accomplishes Rosser's intent of providing a solid textbook.
        SR, 29:3:535   R: Josef Korbel

439.   Rubinstein, Alvin Z., ed. **The Foreign Policy of the Soviet Union**. 3rd ed. New York, Random House, 1972 (1960). 474p. $6.50.
(Listed in P. Horecky's *Russia and the Soviet Union*, #891.) Rubinstein provides a series of excerpts from Soviet documents together with his notes. In addition, five Western authors contribute to this still useful though somewhat outdated work. Advanced students of Soviet foreign affairs should be familiar with this collection, which has by now more historical value rather than providing a study of contemporary Soviet diplomacy.   S. M. H.

440.   Rush, Myron, ed. **The International Situation and Soviet Foreign
         Policy: Key Reports by Soviet Leaders from the Revolution to the
         Present.** Columbus, Ohio, C. E. Merrill Publishers, 1969. 358p. $4.95.
Rush, author of several books on the Soviet Union, did an excellent job collecting relevant documents that are judged basic to the process of the formulation
of Soviet foreign policy. Many documents are translated into English for the
first time, thus increasing the number of essential Soviet sources to which the
non-Russian-speaking reader has access. Academic libraries should not be without
this book.   S. M. H.

441.   Triska, Jan F., and David D. Finley. **Soviet Foreign Policy.** New
         York, Macmillan, 1968. London, Collier-Macmillan, 518p. $9.95.
The authors concern themselves with the systematic study of recurring patterns
in Soviet policies and especially with the dissection of the decision-making
process in the Soviet system. Disaffected by contradictory interpretations, they
attempt to overcome the primary limitation of historical and intuitive knowledge,
that of "perceptive relativity" (*i.e.*, that different observers perceive the same
phenomenon differently). They seek causality based on statistical experimentation and inference, assuming that the facts, relationships, and conclusions
thus established will compel agreement by all observers. To accomplish their
objective they employ a wide variety of such empirical methods and approaches
as content analysis, decision theory, role theory, bargaining and game theories,
a "multiple symmetry" model, as well as elaborate statistical and mathematical
techniques. They produced a provocative and stimulating study helping to
understand Soviet foreign policy.
         SR, 29:4:682-7   R: Charles Gati

442.   Ulam, Adam B. **Expansion and Coexistence: The History of Soviet
         Foreign Policy, 1917-67.** New York, Praeger, 1968. 755p. $12.95cl.;
         $4.95pa. (The second, revised edition is up-dated to 1973.) New
         York, Praeger, 1974. 797p. $15.95cl.; $6.95pa.
Ulam has written an interpretive history, one in which the emphasis is on
specific events, trends, external and internal circumstances, and the leaders
who have made policy. Largely chronological in its basic organization, the book
exhibits the hallmarks of historical scholarship in its thoroughness and judicious
presentation of information. Devoid of abstractions but not of interpretation as
to the contemporary implications and relevance of history, Ulam's book is a
one-man tour de force—a comprehensive and often brilliant study that surpasses
any other previous effort in making the history of Soviet foreign policy intelligible.
         SR, 29:4:482-7   R: Charles Gati

443.   Wesson, Robert G. **Soviet Foreign Policy in Perspective.** Homewood,
         Ill., Dorsey Press, Georgetown, Ont., Irwin-Dorsey Ltd., 1969. 472p.
         $9.50.
The discrepancy between ideology and practical foreign policy "outputs" in
Soviet relations with the rest of the world is a major theme in this work. The
resulting difficulties for Soviet foreign policy in many areas have been well
documented by the author. The book is for the most part organized chronologically, and attempts to deal with Soviet approaches to the world in terms of

state interest, as well as CPSU efforts to deal with the world Communist movement through the periods of "Lenin and Revolution," "Stalin and Nationalist Reversion," "Stalinism," "Competitive Coexistence," and "Conservative Communism."
The book's chief virtue is that it gives the broad lines of development of Soviet foreign policy.

SR, 30:1:157-9   R: Trond Giberg

444.   Wolfe, Bertram D. **An Ideology in Power: Reflections on the Russian Revolution.** Intro. by Leonard Schapiro. New York, Stein and Day, 1969. 406p. $10.00cl.; $2.95pa.

This volume is a collection of 25 essays originally published during the last 28 years by the eminent scholar Bertram Wolfe. Unifying these essays are the subject—the Russian Revolution, its antecedents and consequences—and the highly individual and dynamic style of the author. Central to Wolfe's view of history is the conviction that there are no general laws in accordance with which history proceeds. Rather, history is the juxtaposition of specific and often unexpected, hence unpredictable, events. In "Marxism and the Russian Revolution" he asserts that "contrary to what Marxism in all its varieties holds, the idea of revolution arose unexpectedly, unplanned, unthought of, taking its leading actors by surprise, creating for itself an explanation and an ideology or a complex of conflicting ideological fragments only after the fact." Wolfe gives an excellent analysis of the Soviet attempt to rewrite history, but what kind of dissonance, demoralization, or cynicism results from the effort?

SR, 29:3:521-2   R: Ellen Mickiewicz

445.   Zimmerman, William. **Soviet Perspectives on International Relations, 1956-1967.** Princeton, Princeton University Press, 1969. 336p. (Sponsored by the Institute of War and Peace Studies and Russian Institute. Studies of the Russian Institute, Columbia University.) $9.50.

In this volume the author tries to marry a social scientific conceptualization of the topic to historical data and therefore to historical explanation. Each of these methodological aspects of the study limits the other. Zimmerman's study emerges as the best monograph available to explain how the USSR's international relations specialists, rather than official decision makers, looked at the outside world and particularly the United States between 1956 and 1967. The study focuses on three persisting themes: the relevance of Marxist-Leninist ideology, continuity versus change, and spontaneity versus consciousness in Soviet foreign policy. The volume ends with one of the best available summaries of the diminished but still significant roles of Marxism-Leninism among Khrushchev's cautious successors.

AHR, 76:5:1577-8   R: David D. Finley

To 1917

446.   Allen, W. E. D., ed. **Russian Embassies to the Georgian Kings (1589-
        1605).** 2 vols. Texts trans. by Anthony Mango. Cambridge, published
        for the Hakluyt Society at the Cambridge University Press, 1970.
        Vol. 1: 368p. Vol. 2: 369-640pp. (Works Issued by the Hakluyt Society,
        Second Series, Nos. 138 and 139.) $18.50/set.
This new two-volume monograph represents a translation of the documents of
Russo-Georgian relations published in his time by S. A. Belkokurov. The translation is accompanied by substantial commentaries, and in preparing them the
author used not only other Russian materials but also Georgian sources. The
book is provided with an extensive introduction which presents an historic-
geographical background of the events dealt with in the translated documents.
        SR, 31:4:880-1   R: A. P. Novoseltsev

447.   Becker, Seymour. **Russia's Protectorates in Central Asia: Bukhara and
        Khiva, 1865-1924.** Cambridge, Harvard University Press, 1968. 416p.
        (Russian Research Center Studies, 54). $12.50.
This book gives the first full-length treatment of Russia's relations with the
small Moslem states of Bukhara and Khiva and their domestic history from the
conquest of neighboring Turkestan until their absorption into the USSR in the
1920s. In his chronological summary of Russia's dealings with its protectorates,
Becker has used a wide variety of published Russian and Western sources; neither
native Central Asian works nor Russian archival materials have been exploited.
The book is accurate, clearly written, and thorough; it is distinguished also by
scrupulous objectivity. A wide variety of illustrations and a complete, well-
organized bibliography complement the text. This study will prove most valuable
for those concerned with the problems of Central Asia and Russian expansion.
        SR, 28:1:142-3   R: David MacKenzie

448.   Cowles, Virginia. **The Russian Dagger: Cold War in the Days of the
        Czars.** New York, Harper & Row, 1969. 351p. $7.95.
The story of Russian intrigue and violence in the Balkans, 1840-1914, is a familiar
one. The author has expanded this account with a novel thesis concerning the
close connection that existed between expansionary Balkan policies and domestic
revolution in Imperial Russia. She maintains that "the two movements, subversion at home and subversion abroad, not only stimulated but fed one another"
in the revolutionary sense. This work has limited value for the specialist. It
gives the general reader an adequate though occasionally distorted and unbalanced
view of Russian relations with Southeastern Europe during the sixty years prior
to World War I.
        SR, 30:3:663   R: Bernard F. Oppel

449.   De Basily, Nicolas. **Diplomat of Imperial Russia, 1903-1917: Memoirs.**
        Stanford, Hoover Institution Press, 1973. 201p. 6p. black and white
        photographs (Hoover Institution Publications, 125). $6.00.
This is a well-written volume dealing with major political and social events during
a critical period of Russian history. There is an admirable chapter in which the
author lucidly describes some of the principal personalities of the Russian upper

class and nobility of St. Petersburg. The author has devoted part of his memoirs to a brief description of the four Dumas and their major leaders. There is a penetrating description of the fateful days of July 1914 in which European civilization, as De Basily knew it, was moving perilously toward a tragic abyss. What emerges is a poignant description of the tragic yet noble and placid Nicholas Romanov, whose political demise closely resembled a Greek tragedy.

SR, 34:1:149 R: Henry S. Robinson

450. **The Diplomatic Correspondence of British Ministers to the Russian Court at St. Petersburg, 1704-1776.** Chronological index and an introductory note by M. S. Anderson. Microfiche. London, Chadwyck-Healey, 1973. 9000p. £78.50. $198.00. Distributed in the U.S. by Somerset House, Inc. 417 Maitland Ave., Teaneck, N.J. 07666.

451. Grimsted, Patricia Kennedy. **The Foreign Ministers of Alexander I: Political Attitudes and the Conduct of Russian Diplomacy, 1801-1825.** Berkeley, University of California Press, 1969. 367p. $9.50.
No less than eight men served Alexander I in the capacity of foreign minister during his 25-year reign. Mrs. Grimsted's volume deals with the activities and ideas of each of Alexander's foreign ministers—not only with the relatively lofty processes of diplomacy but also with the more mundane procedures of the foreign office itself. Based largely upon archival materials in the USSR, Austria, England, France, and Poland, the book clearly demonstrates the personal rather than institutional or ideological nature of Russian diplomacy in the first quarter of the nineteenth century. This is a distinguished contribution to our understanding of both the Alexnadrian age and the working of Imperial Russian diplomacy.

SR, 29:3:510-1 R: Judith Cohen Zacek

452. Hsu, Immanuel C. Y. **The Ili Crisis: A Study of Sino-Russian Diplomacy, 1871-1881.** Oxford, The Clarendon Press, 1965. 230p. $7.20.
Hsu, already well known for his study of China's diplomatic history, has produced a useful study of the Ili crisis. It tells of the mission of Ch'ung-hou to Russia and his acceptance of the treaty of 1879, and shows how China, dissatisfied with the Ili settlement, refused to ratify it and succeeded in replacing it with the treaty of St. Petersburg of 1881, the result of negotiations by Tseng Chi-tse. The author's conclusion is that "the Ili settlement, though generally considered a Chinese victory, nevertheless awarded Russia considerable advantages." This is a careful, soundly documented, and illuminating piece of work with a useful bibliography, a glossary, and well-chosen maps.

SEER, 45:104:253-4 R: Ian Nish

453. Jelavich, Barbara. **Russia and the Greek Revolution of 1843.** Munich, Verlag R. Oldenbourg, 1966. 124p. (Südosteuropäische Arbeiten, No. 65). DM20.00.
This is a nice collection of meaningful documents, most of them hitherto unpublished, from the Bavarian state archives and the Haus-, Hof-, and Staatsarchiv in Vienna, presented in their original language (French, English, German) in 74 pages of appendixes, with a 48-page introductory text bearing the book's

title. Its conclusions are that the Russian emperor, despite his strong condemnation of the military coup which forced King Otho in 1843 to grant a constitution, abstained from intervening, because of his pro-Orthodox policies in Greece.

SR, 27:2:330-1   R: Stephen G. Xydis

454.   Kalmykov, Andrew D. **Memoirs of a Russian Diplomat: Outposts of the Empire, 1893-1917.** Ed. by Alexandra Kalmykov. New Haven, Yale University Press, 1971. 290p. (Yale Russian and East European Studies, 10). $12.50.

Between 1893 and 1914 the Russian diplomat A. D. Kalmykov lived in such places as Tabriz, Teheran, Bangkok, Ashkhabad, Tashkent, Uskub, Crete, and Smyrna. Although he never rose above the rank of general consul, his memoirs provide valuable information about the men who served Russia in the Asian Department at St. Petersburg and in diplomatic posts in Persia, Siam, Central Asia, and Turkey. He played an important role in negotiating peace between Siam and the French in Indochina; and during the First Balkan War his personal initiative and courage helped to prevent a massacre of the Christian population in Uskub (Skopje). A. Kalmykov edited these memoirs of her father, who died in 1941. They should be of particular interest to students of Asian and Balkan diplomacy and of general Russian history during the reign of Nicholas II.

SR, 31:3:670   R: Edward C. Thaden

455.   Kazemzadeh, Firuz. **Russia and Britain in Persia, 1864-1914: A Study in Imperialism.** New Haven, Yale University Press, 1968. 711p. $15.00.

This detailed history of Anglo-Russian relations begins with Russia's seemingly irresistible advance in Central Asia from 1865 to 1885. One by one the Muslim Khanates were conquered and annexed. But when a Russian force routed the Afghans and the Panjdeh oasis opening the road to Harat, the British prepared to fight, and Russia's advance halted. Iran (Persia) now found itself in an Anglo-Russian vise. A three-way struggle began, with Russia and Britain competing for influence and wealth in Persia while the Persian leaders tried to play the rivals against each other and make personal profits for themselves. The excellent study is based almost entirely on primary sources.

SR, 28:1:139-40   R: John Clinton Adams

456.   Lensen, George Alexander, ed. **Revelations of a Russian Diplomat: The Memoirs of Dmitrii I. Abrikossow.** Seattle, University of Washington Press, 1964. 329p. $6.95.

Abrikossow was a Russian Foreign Ministry official who rose to the upper middle ranks of the Russian diplomatic service. His assignments were usually closely associated with the Far East. He was in London during the Russo-Japanese War, in Peking in 1911-1912, in the Asian Section of the Foreign Ministry to 1916, and, subsequently, first secretary and chargé d'affaires in Tokyo from 1916 to 1925. During his last years in Japan he represented the defunct tsarist government, not the Bolshevik regime. The memoirs were written in English in the 1930s and 1940s. The editor has shortened and rewritten some sections so that the entire book now reads smoothly. It is a welcom addition to the growing amount of literature available on Far Eastern diplomacy and Russia in Asia.

SR, 24:3:534-6   R: Barbara Jelavich

457. Lensen, George Alexander, comp. **Russian Diplomatic and Consular Officials in East Asia: A Handbook of the Representatives of Tsarist Russia and the Provisional Government in China, Japan and Korea from 1858 to 1924 and of Soviet Representatives in Japan from 1925 to 1968.** Compiled on the basis of Russian, Japanese and Chinese sources with an historical introduction. Tokyo, Sophia University, in cooperation with The Diplomatic Press, Tallahassee, Fla., (1968). 294p. $15.00.

The volume gives each name in its Latin and Cyrillic forms, followed by the diplomatic, consular, or attaché assignments in the Far East with the appropriate dates. This master list is followed by a diagrammatic career analysis by post and year, with some supplementary information in footnotes. The work is carefully edited and published and will provide a handsome and useful addition to the reference shelves of libraries and interested individuals.

   SR, 29:1:110-1   R: John A. White

458. Mancall, Mark. **Russia and China: Their Diplomatic Relations to 1728.** Cambridge, Harvard University Press, 1971. 396p. (Harvard East Asian Series, 61). $12.00.

This is a rich and thoughtful book, of particular relevance to our own historic juncture. The pertinence to our time is in the pride of those old Chinese and Manchu rulers who viewed their Middle Kingdom as the world's center, to which all other peoples and state were but periphery and tributary. The author shows well the inability of the Russians to understand—less so to accept—this stand, and the Chinese-Manchu indignation at this inability. He delineates clearly the slow, hurtful process wherein both Peking and Moscow had to fit their disparate philosophies and state-styles to each other if the twain were indeed to meet.

   SR, 31:3:662-3   R: Albert Parry

459. **Mubadele—An Ottoman-Russian Exchange of Ambassadors.** Annotated and trans. by Norman Itzkowitz and Max Mote. Chicago, University of Chicago Press, 1970. 261p. $11.50.

In the present volume two specialists have collaborated to publish in translation the dispatches of the Turkish ambassador 'Abd ül-Kerim (1775-76) to Catherin II of Russia and of the Russian ambassador to Sultan 'Abd ül-Hamid I in the same years. Both had been involved in the conclusion of the peace of Kücük Kaynarca and had had to deal with the sultan, the one about war prisoners, the other about the position of the Crimea vis-à-vis Russia, neither with very striking success.

   SR, 30:3:662   R: Bertold Supler

460. Schwartz, Harry. **Tsars, Mandarins, and Commissars: A History of Chinese-Russian Relations.** Rev. ed. Garden City, N.Y., Anchor Press, Doubleday, 1973 (1964). 300p. $2.50pa.

A member of the editorial board of the *New York Times* for more than a decade, the author was also a noted specialist on Soviet affairs. In this study he offered an analytical survey of the Russo-Chinese disputes through the centuries and by doing so, provided us with a solid historical background of the contemporary Sino-Soviet conflict which aids in the understanding of the nature and complexity of the centuries-old rivalry. Politicians and students of Soviet foreign policy should welcome this new edition.   S. M. H.

461.   Smith, C. Jay, Jr. **The Russian Struggle for Power, 1914-1917: A Study of Russian Foreign Policy during the First World War.** New York, Greenwood Press, 1969 (1956). 553p. $17.00.

Drawing extensively on a large number of documents from the Imperial Foreign Office, Smith has produced the first detailed account of Russia's diplomacy during 1914-1917. He concentrates mainly on political issues, which reveal Russian aggressive aspirations. This book with its unsurpassed documentation remains a basic study of Russian war-time diplomacy.   S. M. H.

462.   Sorel, Albert. **The Eastern Question in the Eighteenth Century: The Partition of Poland and the Treaty of Kainardji.** New York, Fertig, 1969 (1898). 270p. $10.00.

"To become a European Power, Russia had to reckon with Prussia; for the solution of the Eastern Question, with Austria," states the author, who proposes to show how the alliance between Prussia and Russia was formed in 1764, and how Austria was led to accede to it. This is still a classic study on the topic.
S. M. H.

463.   Thaden, Edward C. **Russia and the Balkan Alliance of 1912.** University Park, Pennsylvania State University Press, 1965. 192p. $7.50.

This volume presents a study of Russia's role in the forging of the Balkan Alliance of 1912, which led directly to the two Balkan Wars of 1912-1913. The book is divided into six main chapters: "The Montenegrin Crisis of 1911," "Charykov and the Straits," "Russia and the Bulgarian-Serbian Rapprochement," "Bulgarian-Serbian Agreement," "Greece, Montenegro, and the Outbreak of War," and "The Balkan Allies and Europe." Chronologically, the story ends with the outbreak of the First Balkan War in October 1912. This brief study is a useful contribution to the literature in the field. It challenges a number of customary views on some significant issues, although the author's implication that the "aggressive interpreatation" of Russia's Balkan policy has remained dominant does not appear to be supported by the recent work of most Soviet and non-Soviet writers.
SR, 25:2:338-9   R: Terence Emmons

464.   Trani, Eugene P. **The Treaty of Portsmouth: An Adventure in American Diplomacy.** Lexington, University of Kentucky Press, 1969. 194p. $6.95.

This study is mainly of interest for the Russian diplomatic historian because of the details it provides concerning Japanese and American diplomacy and internal politics during 1904 and 1905. The author has used not only the available secondary literature and printed sources concerning the Portsmouth Conference, but also American and Japanese manuscript and archival sources. He did not have access to Soviet archives.
SR, 33:4:775   R: Edward C. Thaden

465.   White, John Albert. **The Diplomacy of the Russo-Japanese War.**
        Princeton, Princeton University Press, 1964. 410p. $8.50.
The book is based on a wide study of published documents and monographs
in Japanese, Russian, German, and French, and material from the Japanese
Foreign Ministry. It is divided evenly into three sections: prewar diplomacy, the
diplomacy of the war period, and the making of the peace. The chief impression
to be gained from the book is that of the ineptness and confusion of Russian
policy in comparsion with the far more realistic and clever Japanese approach.
Although the Russian government at this time pursued ambitions and aggressive
policies in Manchuria and Korea, adequate military and diplomatic preparations
were not made to back such actions. Japanese preparations for a possible armed
clash were, in contrast, excellent. The study will remain the standard account
until the Russian Foreign Ministry archives are freely available.
        SR, 24:3:534-6   R: Barbara Jelavich

With U.S.

466.   Barghoorn, Frederick C. **The Soviet Image of the United States**: A
        Study in Distortion. Port Washington, N.Y., Kennikat, 1969 (1950).
        297p. $11.00.
An interesting account surveying the Soviet propaganda picture of American
wickedness from the early years to the Korean war. The book is not an analysis
of propaganda techniques but rather a description of content, with excerpts
and anecdotes.
        SR, 10:3:231-2   R: Frederick L. Schuman

467.   Bennett, Edward M. **Recognition of Russia: An American Foreign**
        Policy Dilemma. Waltham, Mass., Blaisdell Publishing Co., 1970. 232p.
        $2.95pa.
Making excellent use of the important source materials that have now become
available, Bennett has retold the story with new insights, broad strokes of
perceptive interpretation, and graceful prose. Recognition of the USSR was
necessary and beneficial. Its tragedy lay in the unfounded optimism that motivated
many of the American negotiators, compounded by an apparent inability to
profit in the decade following from the lesson of 1933-36—the folly of utopian
hopes in dealing with the USSR. Unfortunately the volume is marred by the
absence from the bibliography of a number of authors hwo have made major
contributions to the subject.
        SR, 30:2:400-1   R: Robert Paul Browder

468.   Bishop, Donald G. **The Roosevelt-Litvinov Agreements: The American**
        View. Syracuse, Syracuse University Press, 1965. 297p. $7.50.
The author took what seems to have been an unpromising topic and wisely
chose to approach it with a wider frame of reference, to concern himself with
broader implications. The result is a meaningful work. The purpose, as stated,
is to examine the extent to which the promises that Litvinov made to the
United States at the time of recognition in November 1933 were implemented.
Not surprisingly, he finds that "in the cases of the agreements on interference

in internal affairs, legal rights of [American] nationals in the Soviet Union, and payment of the Soviet debts," the Soviets conspicuously failed to live up to their promises.

SR, 27:1:151-3   R: Michael Rywkin

469.   Bohlen, Charles E. **Witness to History, 1929-1969.** New York, W. W. Norton, 1973. 562p. $12.50.

This autobiographical account represents about one-third of the original notes. It is a wealth of incidents, details, and observations which contribute to the understanding of American-Soviet relations. There is also another factor: discretion, a shining virtue in a diplomat. The author argues that a more realistic assessment of the Soviet Union by American policy makers, such as urged by himself and Kennan, could not have made a great deal of difference whether in 1944-1945, or in the late fifties.

SR, 33:3:546-7   R: Adam B. Ulam

470.   Brzezinski, Zbigniew, and Samuel P. Huntington. **Political Power: USA/USSR.** New York, Viking Press, 1964. 461p. $7.50.

The purpose of the authors' dissections has been "to answer three broad questions: (1) What are the principal similarities and differences between the Soviet and American political systems? (2) What are the strengths and weaknesses of each system? (3) Are the two systems becoming more alike or less so?" The authors conclude that both countries represent the antithesis of the rigid European aristocratic social tradition: "the Soviet and American systems are effective, authoritative, and stable, each in its own way." This is a pioneering work in comparative political analysis.

SR, 24:1:134-6   R: William B. Ballis

471.   Davis, Lynn Etheridge. **The Cold War Begins: Soviet-American Conflicts over Eastern Europe.** Princeton, Princeton University Press, 1974. 427p. $15.00.

The slow but gradual erosion of U.S. influence in Central-Eastern Europe since 1945 is brilliantly described in this academic eulogy of the tragic series of steps undertaken by the U.S. decision-makers, utterly ignorant of or unabashed before Mackinder's classic dictum: "Who rules East Europe commands the Heartland; Who rules the Heartland commands the World Island; Who rules the World Island commands the World." That Soviet Russia does not as yet command the world is due to the recent development of the atomic bomb and its possible utilization by long-range jet planes; yet Mackinder's prophecy can become reality should the policy of Washington, "peace at any price," persist. Davis, using recently released documents of the State Department, details in her competent study how the views of U.S. officials on postwar peace precluded approval of Soviet efforts to establish Kremlin's colonialism in Eastern Europe through the imposition of Communist regimes.

UQ, 31:1:68-9   R: Joseph S. Roucek

472.   Deane, John R. **The Strange Alliance: The Story of Our Efforts at Wartime Co-Operation with Russia.** Bloomington, Indiana University Press, 1973. 344p. $3.50pa.

General Deane's account of his two years in Moscow as head of the United States Military Mission to the USSR was originally published as long ago as 1946. This is one of those rare books which can claim to have influenced public opinion. The American public, awakening from the euphoria of an alliance with Communist Russia, was by 1946 reverting to the old habits of hostility and fear. Deane's book showed the difficulty of any negotiation or even of any diplomatic contact with the Soviet Union, if these were conducted on the lines of traditional Western diplomacy. He realized that concessions made to the Soviets did not earn gratefulness. On the contrary, they were to the Soviets a sign of weakness and resulted in demands for even more concessions. But a determined stand by Britain and the United States often resulted in a Soviet climb down.

SEER, 53:132:467-8   R: H. Hanak

473.   Dobriansky, Lev E. **U. S. A. and the Soviet Myth.** Intro. by William
        G. Bray. Old Greenwich, Conn., Devin-Adair, 1971. 274p. $6.50.
The first five chapters of this work deal with the Soviet captive nations, with emphasis on Ukraine. Chapters 6 and 7 discuss Captive Nations programs in the United States, chapter 8 and 9 analyze diplomatic traps dealing with Moscow, and the last chapter outlines the objectives and achievements of the Ukrainian Congress Committee of America. The author cites examples of the shocking lack of knowledge in high circles about the nationality problem of the USSR. The book contains an excellent selected bibliography and index.

UQ, 27:2:175-6   R: Anthony T. Bouscaren

474.   Epstein, Julius. **Operation Keelhaul: The Story of Forced Repatria-
        tion from 1944 to the Present.** Intro. by Bertram D. Wolfe. Old
        Greenwich, Conn., Devin-Adair, 1973. 255p. $8.95.
The book begins with the story of a Lithuanian seaman, Simas Kudirka, who in 1970 made a dramtic leap to freedom from a Soviet ship onto the deck of a U.S. Coast Guard cutter in American waters. The bulk of the volume treats the forcible repatriation by British, American and French armies of hundreds of thousands of refugees from the occupied zones of Germany and Austria, a shameful sequel to and by-product of the alliance between the Western democracies and the Soviet totalitarian regime. Victims of this inhuman crime were not only war prisoners in German uniforms, but hundreds of thousands of civilians who had been brought forcibly as "slave laborers" from the USSR and other East European countries to Nazi Germany during the war. Epstein's book is an important contribution to the history of World War II, throwing long-needed light on the lamentable official policy of the USA in regard to refugees and POW's.

UQ, 30:3:181-2   R: Volodymyr Sawchak

475.   Farnsworth, Beatrice. **William C. Bullitt and the Soviet Union.**
        Bloomington, Indiana University Press, 1967. 244p. (Indiana
        University International Studies). $7.50.
The late W. C. Bullitt was an oddity who twice in a generation managed to get close to the center of American policy toward the Soviet Union. At the age

of 28, he obtained a place on the American delegation to the Paris Peace
Conference, where he maneuvered a mission to interview the new leaders of
Soviet Russia. In the FDR administration he helped arrange the recognition of
Russia in 1933, and accepted as a reward the ambassadorship to the Soviet
Union. The author interviewed Bullitt, his first wife, and other persons who knew
him. This volume is an extraordinarily able book.

     SR, 27:4:657   R: Robert H. Ferrell

476.   Filene, Peter G. **Americans and the Soviet Experiment, 1917-1933.**
          Cambridge, Harvard University Press, 1967. 389p. $7.95.
The author discusses American attitudes toward the "Soviet experiment" (as
distinguished from opinions about it) during the period of revolutions, "war
Communism," civil war, intervention, and the New Economic Policy, and briefly
during the first Five-Year Plan. He supplements these analyses of attitudes in
a second volume, which contains sixty views of Soviet Russia (1917-1965) by
persons from different walks of life. In the period of the NEP, as Filene points
out, some Americans assumed that the abandonment of "war Communism"
meant that the abandonment of Communism itself had begun. Later, after
several governments had recognized the Soviet government, some business
groups argued that recognition by the United States would benefit the American
national economy. The author does not seem to grasp fully the appalling in-
humanity of such Stalinist measures as the forcible collectivization, with circa
five million victims of this man-made famine.

     SR, 31:1:169-72   R: Harold H. Fisher

477.   Filene, Peter G., ed. **American Views of Soviet Russia, 1917-1965.**
          Homewood, Ill., Dorsey Press, 1968. 404p. $3.50pa.
This book, in fact, is a second volume which supplements the author's study,
Americans and the Soviet Experiment, 1917-1933. It contains sixty views of
Soviet Russia (1917-65) by persons from different walks of life and usefully
supplements studies of American-Soviet relations that concentrate on political
and economic matters.

     SR, 31:1:169-71   R: Harold H. Fisher

478.   Fleming, Denna Frank. **The Cold War and Its Origins, 1917-1960.**
          2 vols. Garden City, N.Y., Doubleday, 1970 (1961). 1158p. $17.50.
Fleming has with zeal and industry attempted the massive and intrinsically
desirable task of plotting the course of American-Soviet relations culminating
in the present cold war. An enormous amount of reference material, mostly
compiled from newspapers and magazine clippings, is contained in these two
stout volumes. The author is one of the first revisionists of the so-called Cold
War theory. One only hopes that some better qualified and more impartial scholar
will succeed where Fleming has failed.

     SR, 21:3:549-51   R: William Henry Chamberlin

479.   Gaddis, John Lewis. **The United States and the Origins of the Cold
          War, 1941-1947.** New York, Columbia University Press, 1972. 396p.
          (Contemporary American History Series). $12.50cl.; $3.95pa.

The author has provided us with one of the most interesting scholarly works on the origins of the cold war. The strength of the book lies in the careful research, superb organization, and the uniformly good writing. The book offers both the student and layman a wealth of clearly presented information. Furthermore, Gaddis has refrained from the prevalent self-righteousness which we have so far witnessed in the heated debate over this period. The book attempts to go beyond "revisionist" historiography. In fact, the author criticizes revisionist contributions to this crucial historical period for over-emphasizing the economic motivations of American policy-makers. He purports to differ by asserting that economics played only a minimal role in American-Soviet relations, and he virtually ignores economic factors in his own analysis. He claims that American public opinion was the key determinant in American policy toward the Soviets.

   SR, 33:4:780-1   R: Diane Shaver Clemens

480.   Harriman, W. Averell. **America and Russia in a Changing World: Half a Century of Personal Observation**. Intro. by Arthur M. Schlesinger, Jr. Garden City, N.Y., Doubleday, 1971. 218p. $5.95.

This volume includes Harriman's three lectures delivered at Lehigh University in 1970 and focuses mainly on the past fifty years of Soviet-American relations as seen by a statesman who himself was actively involved in the formulation and execution of U.S. policy. Despite the poor organization of the material, the book represents an important contribution to the growing literature in this field.   S. M. H.

481.   Herring, George C., Jr. **Aid to Russia, 1941-1946: Strategy, Diplomacy, the Origins of the Cold War**. New York, Columbia University Press, 1973. 365p. (Contemporary American History Series). $15.00.

The author presents a realistic picture of the place of lend-lease aid to the USSR in the policy of the United States. His fundamental thesis is that lend-lease for the USSR and Britain was intended mainly to facilitate the victory over Germany and was to terminate with the end of hostilities and not continue into the postwar period for reconstruction or any other purpose. Herring maintains that no amount of American aid to the Soviet Union could have brought about major Soviet concessions, particularly in East Central Europe.

   SR, 33:2:364-65   R: Karl W. Ryavec

482.   Herz, Martin F. **Beginnings of the Cold War**. Bloomington and London, Indiana University Press, 1966. 214p. $4.95.

This is, as the author says, "a modest effort . . . to summarize and highlight" the events that brought on the cold war. Of the first two chapters, one is prefatory and the second consists of an extract from Ambassador Charles Bohlen's minutes of Stalin's talks with Harry Hopkins shortly after V-E Day. The book has little to contribute to the renewed debate on the respective responsibility of the two sides for the emergence of the cold war, though it may help to refresh memories of the relevant events. Its chief value is as a supplementary text in college courses dealing with the cold war.

   SR, 27:3:492-4   R: Myron Rush

483.	Horelik, Arnold L., and Myron Rush. **Strategic Power and Soviet Foreign Policy**. Chicago, University of Chicago Press, 1966. 255p. $5.95.

The authors hold it to be crucial for the United States to maintain a margin of superiority large enough to offer hope of deterring not only war, but also "the dangerous employment of Soviet strategic power for political ends." They recognized the risks inherent in this recommended course of action, including the risk of stimulating a more dangerous arms race. The result of their study is well worth equally careful consideration.

       RR, 26:1:93-4   R: Warren B. Walsh

484.	Hurewitz, J. C., ed. **Soviet-American Rivalry in the Middle East**. New York, Praeger, 1969. 250p. $7.00.

This volume is based on sixteen papers by prominent specialists in Soviet and Middle Eastern affairs which were presented at a conference held at Columbia University in December 1968. The book is divided into four parts dealing with the topics "Struggle for Military Supremacy," "Economic Competition in the 1970s," "Cultural Contest," and "Quest for Stability." Most of the contributors take a pessimistic view of the possibility of a superpower détente in the Middle East and, by implication, in the rest of the world as well. The volume is an important and valuable contribution to a better understanding of the Middle East in the coming decade.

       SR, 29:3:536-7   R: O. M. Smolansky

485.	Jones, Robert Huhn. **The Roads to Russia: United States Lend-Lease to the Soviet Union**. Foreword by Edgar L. Erickson. Norman, University of Oklahoma Press, 1969. 326p. $6.95.

This is a documented, objective account of United States lend-lease to Russia. The study uses U. S. presidential papers, government reports, memoirs, and press accounts, with occasional references to a few standard official Soviet sources, to compile an admiring and somewhat heavy-breathing narrative of United States efforts to aid a suspicious and ungrateful ally.

       SR, 29:2:327-8   R: Holland Hunter

486.	Kennan, George F. **Soviet-American Relations, 1917-1920**. Vol. I: *Russia Leaves the War.* Volume II: *The Decision to Intervene.* [Originally published by Princeton University Press, 1956-1958.] New York, Atheneum, 1967. Vol. I: 544p., $3.95pa. Vol. II: 513p., $3.95pa.

With these two volumes on Soviet-American relations, Kennan proves that he possesses all the qualities expected from an historian in terms of ability to find and to analyze available material. His familiarity with the sources, the interviews with surviving individuals, his deep insight, and his fine literary style are impressive. These two volumes, along with the author's numerous other contributions, belong to the finest works on the study of American policy toward Soviet Russia. All students of Soviet affairs and those on international diplomacy should be familiar with George Kennan's works. S. M. H.

487.   Lasch, Christopher. **The American Liberals and the Russian Revolution.**
New York, Columbia University Press, 1962. 290p. $6.50.
The author labels representatives of the two different kinds of liberal response
to the war "war liberals" and "anti-imperialists." The same may be said for
liberal reaction to the revolution, although again there is an obvious division
that parallels the earlier one. In large part, the "war liberal" viewed the Bolshevik's separate peace and subsequent relations with the Germans as evidence
that they were not revolutionaries at all but foreign agents, while the "anti-
imperialists" argued that the Soviet leaders were not pro-German. But—and
this is the author's principal thesis—neither group was willing to recognize the
real implications for them of the revolution. This volume is closely reasoned
and carefully documented, based on a variety of primary and secondary sources.
        SR, 25:1:160   R: Robert Paul Browder

488.   Lukas, Richard C. **Eagles East: The Army Air Forces and the Soviet
        Union, 1941-1945.** Tallahassee, Florida State University Press, 1970.
        256p. $10.00.
This is a useful study, sketching in fair detail the story of American supply of
military aircraft to the Soviet Union under Lend Lease, and the use of Soviet
bases by American bombers. The study illustrates in many specific ways how
American military assistance to the Soviet Union for political and military
reasons interacted with other military and a variety of bureaucratic and political
problems. The book reads easily, and is recommended to those who would like
to know more about this chapter in Soviet-American relations, as well as to
those having a particular interest in the politico-military history of World War II.
        SR, 30:4:895-6   R: Raymond L. Garthoff

489.   Margulies, Sylvia R. **The Pilgrimage to Russia: The Soviet Union and
        the Treatment of Foreigners, 1924-1937.** Madison, University of
        Wisconsin Press, 1968. 290p. $7.50.
Miss Margulies is concerned, in a sense, with attitudes that influenced Americans
to make a pilgraimage "over into the future." She is especially interested in how
their attitudes were affected by exposure to the stratagems and manipulations
used by the Soviet ruling circles to persuade visitors that the future that Lincoln
Steffens had envisioned was actually coming to pass. The author, in her last
chapter, "Continuity and Change, 1924-1965," notes a certain continuity of
objectives, as well as of form and method, in the Soviet Union's treatment of
foreigners. She believes that fundamental changes are unlikely as long as the
USSR remains a closed society.
        SR, 31:1:169-73   R: Harold H. Fisher

490.   Mayer, Arno J. **Wilson vs. Lenin: Political Origins of the New Diplomacy,
        1917-1918.** Cleveland, World Publishing Co., 1964. 435p. (Meridian
        Books). $2.95pa.
Besides providing, for the Soviet specialist, a broader perspective in which to
place Lenin's early diplomatic moves, Mayer's study suggests, on re-examination,
that a full length parallel biographical work on Wilson and Lenin as statesmen
might be welcome.
        SR, 24:1:121-3   R: Saul N. Silverman

491.   Parker, W. H. **The Superpowers: The United States and the Soviet Union Compared.** London, Macmillan, 1972. 347p. £7.

The author takes the line of an economic geographer. The characteristic differences, he states in an opening paragraph, derive "from the disposition of land and sea over the surface of the globe," and the analysis unfolds from this brief. The first section deals with history, geography, and resources, followed by the economy—its organization, output and trade—and finally he turns to the structure of government and the roots of power. The book will be a welcome addition to the literature.

SEER, 52:128:474-5   R: Frank Spooner

492.   Paterson, Thomas G. **Soviet-American Confrontation: Postwar Reconstruction and the Origins of the Cold War.** Baltimore, Johns Hopkins University Press, 1973. 287p. $12.00.

The book is based on an exhaustive research of sources and unpublished manuscripts, mostly limited to American literature, but without the benefit of Soviet material. The author's political credo is manifest in the study. The book deserves the attention of the student and lay reader alike for its excellent bibliographic essay on unpublished manuscripts and as an example of an ideologically confused interpretation of events.   S. M. H.

493.   Rapoport, Anatol. **The Big Two. Soviet-American Perceptions of Foreign Policy.** New York, Pegasus, 1971. 249p. $6.95cl.; $2.95pa.

This small volume contains one of the most provocative studies dealing with Soviet-American relations during the last three decades. While not hiding his own views and sometimes even ignoring certain documents, the author, nevertheless, applied effectively a lucid, systematic analysis in the discussion of Soviet-American interaction. Therefore, this book can stimulate a discourse on Soviet foreign policy in the classroom far better than other similar studies lacking the perception of Soviet pseudo-dialectic.   S. M. H.

494.   Reilly, Alayne P. **America in Contemporary Soviet Literature.** New York, New York University Press. London, University of London Press, 1971. 217p. $8.95.

Reilly examines the way in which four authors—Andrei Voznesensky, Viktor Nekrasov, Valentin Kataev, and Evgenii Evtushenko—have recently written about the United Statse. Her thesis is that their works indicate a new approach to America by certain Soviet writers who no longer let ideology or preconceived notions stand in the way of an open and at times sympathetic appraisal of the successes and failures of American society. The book's findings are generally well supported by detailed stylistic and thematic analyses of works by the various writers. The book explores an interesting topic and provides some fresh insights into the nature of Soviet literature during the past decade.

SR, 31:1:199-200   R: Barry Scherr

495.   Slusser, Robert M. **The Berlin Crisis of 1961: Soviet-American Relations and the Struggle for Power in the Kremlin, June-November 1961.** Baltimore, Johns Hopkins University Press, 1973. 509p. $17.50cl.; $8.50pa.

496. Stettinius, Edward R. **Roosevelt and the Russians: The Yalta Conference.**
Ed. by Walter Johnson. Westport, Conn., Greenwood Press, 1970
(1949). 367p. $14.75.
Stettinius wrote this book in defense of President Roosevelt's action in Yalta.
In this most detailed account the author demonstrates how Stalin failed to honor
many of the agreements that were reached and signed before and during the
Yalta Conference. Yet Stettinius characterizes the Yalta Conference as "on
the whole a diplomatic triumph for the United States and Great Britain," and
claims that the USSR made more concessions than the United States. If there
is any merit to this publication it lies in the tragic failure on the part of some
politicians to understand the tactics of the Soviet rulers and the consequences
for the Western world.   S. M. H.

497. Ulam, Adam B. **The Rivals: America and Russia since World War II.**
New York, Viking Press, 1971. 405p. $10.95.
In this volume the author elaborates an approach voiced earlier in his *Expansion
and Coexistence*, with greater stress on the American side. It is a personal narrative—always informed, often clever, sometimes elegant—somewhat conde-
scending, barely tolerant of human foibles. It is much like a series of lectures
to Harvard undergraduates. It will provoke both approval and annoyance, which
is a good test of a fine book. Ulam is best in laying bare the American misjudgment of Soviet intentions and capabilities. He is concerned primarily with power
and politics. He recognizes but slights the strategic and economic factors, and
he ignores ideology altogether. And he fails to explore alternative Soviet and
American conceptions of the outside world—their roots and their implications.
          SR, 31:2:434-5   R: Alexander Dallin

498. Walters, Robert S. **American and Soviet Aid; A Comparative Analysis.**
Pittsburgh, University of Pittsburgh Press, 1970. 299p. $9.95.
There is very little that is new in this book. The discussion of Soviet aid depends
heavily on the existing English language literature, particularly on studies by
Joseph Berliner, Leo Tansky, and Marshall Goldman. Similarly, the discussion
of American aid is based on a large number of books and articles which are
now available on this subject. Even as a comparative study this is not the first
attempt. And yet, it is a very useful and interesting work. It puts together
materials which are scattered throughout many different places and presents
them in a well-balanced and highly readable form.
          CSP, 14:1:121-4   R: Zbigniew M. Fallenbuchl

499. Weissman, Benjamin M. **Herbert Hoover and Famine Relief to Soviet
Russia: 1921-1923.** Stanford, Hoover Institution Press, 1974. 247p.
$7.95.
In 1921 the Soviet Union was struck by a devastating famine. Although the
nation was in desperate need, the Soviet regime was suspicious of the motivation behind the offer of assistance from Herbert Hoover, whose strong anti-
Communist views were as well established as was his international reputation
as a relief administrator. As Weissman notes in his excellent study of this
complex episode, "to the Bolshevik regime, famine posed one of the most
crucial challenges since the seizure of power in 1917." In this highly unstable

situation, the Soviet leaders decided that acceptance of aid from their greatest ideological foes was less undesirable than the ravages of the famine. Lenin, on his part, was confident of his own ability to control events and outwit his opponents. Weissman has adroitly organized a large amount of data and presents it in lucid prose.

RR, 34:3:331-2   R: E. Berkeley Tompkins

500.   Welch, William. **American Images of Soviet Foreign Policy: An Inquiry into Recent Appraisals from the Academic Community**. New Haven, Yale University Press, 1970. 316p. $10.00.

Of central importance to Welch's analysis of the study of Soviet foreign policy is a proposed scheme for classifying images of Soviet policy according to two variables: constancy (how much does policy change?) and hardness (how hard is it?). The author's proposal for improving the discipline amounts to a plea for the empirical method—the rigorous definition and application of general concepts to particular data. The study is suitable for use in courses on Soviet and comparative foreign policy; it is obligatory reading for scholars in the field.

SR, 30:4:892-3   R: Philip S. Gillette

501.   Wilson, Joan Hoff. **Ideology and Economics: U. S. Relations with the Soviet Union, 1918-1933**. Columbia, University of Missouri Press, 1974. 192p. $10.00.

This serious study provides a solid background for the understanding of F. D. R.'s decision to extend diplomatic recognition to the USSR. The author discusses the attitudes prevalent within the American government and business circles toward trade with the Soviet Union. She concludes that on this issue the business community was rather divided and there was no coordination between economic and foreign policy, a fact which remains an endemic weakness of the U.S. policy toward the USSR. The study deserves a place in academic and public libraries.

S. M. H.

With Communist Countries

502.   Ambroz, Oton. **Realignment of World Power: The Russo-Chinese Schism under the Impact of Mao Tse-Tung's Last Revolution**. 2 vols. New York, Robert Speller, 1972. Vol. 1: 388p., Vol. 2: 406p. $25.00/set.

This study discusses the effects of the Chinese cultural revolution on the two great Communist rivals, the Communist movement, and international relations. The author believes that the Sino-Soviet conflict presents the West with a major opportunity for new initiatives in foreign policy. He argues that the United States can and should take advantage of it to weaken Soviet control over Eastern Europe and to perpetuate the status quo on Taiwan. "One of the purposes of the cultural revolution is the fostering and training of the new generation in hostility against the Soviet Union, perpetuation of the present state of affairs, and exclusion of any accommodation in the future." Ambroz deserves much praise for his detailed use of Yugoslav, West German, and Chinese Nationalist accounts, in addition to the more familiar sources.

      SR, 33:4:781-2   R: G. Paul Holman, Jr.

503.   An, Tai Sung. **The Sino-Soviet Territorial Dispute**. Philadelphia, Westminster Press, 1973. 254p. $8.95.

This study examines the background of the border problem, its exacerbation since the fighting along the Ussuri River in 1969, and the possibility that it will lead to war. An appendix containing English translations of Russo-Chinese treaties and protocols from 1689 through 1915 contributes well to its importance. The author contends, "the Sino-Soviet conflict, which began as an ideological dispute in 1960, has degenerated into a nationalistic clash based on territorial issues." Since Moscow enjoys enormous nuclear superiority, An doubts that Peking will attempt any military adventures, and estimates the probability of a Sino-Soviet war in the next decade to be only one in ten. Although the significance of the border problem is still unclear, the author does much to fill a serious gap in our understanding of the Sino-Soviet conflict.

      SR, 33:4:781-2   R: G. Paul Holman, Jr.

504.   Clubb, O. Edmund. **China and Russia: The "Great Game."** New York, Columbia University Press, 1971. 578p. 34 plates, 10 maps. $12.95.

The author has succeeded in what has become a rare endeavour for modern historians—to produce an overall, Toynbean survey of relations and contacts between Chinese and Russians, from the Mongol conquests in the thirteenth century to the Sino-Soviet Cold War attitudes of 1970. The product is a useful textbook on the subject and will be appreciated by students of international affairs as well as of history. The author has a talent for explaining in clear, concise prose what are in fact very complicated historical events. The book will be read with enjoyment by all people interested in the great game of Russian-Chinese relations.

      CSP, 14:3:568-70   R: I. E. Krepashevskii

505.   Gittings, John. **Survey of the Sino-Soviet Dispute: A Commentary and Extracts from the Recent Polemics, 1963-1967**. London, Oxford University Press, 1968. 410p. (Issued under the auspices of the Royal Institute of International Affairs). $11.75.

Instead of compiling editorials and official statements chronologically, the author has carefully culled the extensive Russian and Chinese materials for 1963-1967, grouping explicit references under thirty categories, such as "The Korean War," "The Sino-Indian Border Dispute, 1959," "The Sino-Soviet Border, 1962-4," and "Nuclear Weapons and Defense, 1958-9." Because these documents as issued contained a hodgepodge of current and retrospective charges and countercharges, this reordering is particularly helpful for quick reference and will be of use to the undergraduate reader and paper writer. The author prefaces each grouping, integrating where possible most recent Russian and Chinese materials.

      SR, 29:4:703-4   R: Allen S. Whiting

506. Halperin, Morton H., ed. **Sino-Soviet Relations and Arms Control.**
Cambridge, Mass., MIT Press, 1967. 432p. $10.00.
This volume binds together under hard covers a collection of articles already
distributed in one form by the Center for International Affairs of Harvard
University. The essays directly concerned with arms control questions offer
useful surveys by specialists of the manner in which Soviet and Chinese policies
on disarmament and arms control have diverged as part of the more general
Sino-Soviet split. Most of the authors cover developments into 1965, and therefore the book does not reflect the fact that the arms control issues have declined
in importance as occasions for Chinese and Soviet polemics in the most recent
period.
    SR, 27:1:153-4   R: Thomas B. Larson

507. Klochko, Mikhail A. **Soviet Scientist in Red China.** Trans. by Andrew
MacAndrew. New York, Praeger, 1964. 213p. $4.95.
Klochko's book, replete with wrathful criticism of how the Party runs and ruins
both Russia and China, concludes with the unduly optimistic prediction that
Communist rule in China will not outlive Mao. But carefully read, it provides
a number of facts about Soviet Russia and mainland China not heretofore
reported publicly, and is thus useful both as a check on hypotheses derived
from official sources as well as a unique record of personal observations and
experience. This is a significant contribution both to the study of the Sino-
Soviet dispute and of our knowledge of contemporary China.
    SR, 24:4:735-7   R: Thomas W. Robinson

508. Salisbury, Harrison E. **War between Russia and China.** New York,
W. W. Norton, 1969. 224p. $4.95.
This account of the centuries-old national hatreds between Russians and Chinese
is useful if exaggerated, but the suggestion that this deep-seated rivalry is
inevitably escalating toward a military denouement underestimates the role
that political leadership plays in deciding questions of war and peace. However,
the book is to be welcomed for the main themes it justifiably stresses: that
nuclear war between the Communist giants could be disastrous not only for the
participants but for the rest of the world as well.
    SR, 30:1:159   R: James C. McClelland

509. **Sino-Soviet Relations, 1964-1965.** Analyzed and documented by William
E. Griffith. Cambridge, Mass., MIT Press, 1967. 504p. (Center for
International Studies, Massachusetts Institute of Technology. Studies
in International Communism, No. 8). $3.95pa.
The work combines painstaking analysis and 34 basic documents (mostly
complete texts) on all aspects of Sino-Soviet relations. Although he admits that
a series of crises will continue to affect their attitudes toward one another
and the external world, he foresees no permanent reconciliation between the
two rivals. This is a solid contribution to a complex subject.
    AHR, 73:1:186-7   R: Alfred J. Rieber

510. Thornton, Richard C. **The Comintern and the Chinese Communists, 1928-1931**. Seattle, University of Washington Press, 1969. 246p. (Far Eastern and Russian Institute Publications on Asia, no. 20). $9.50.

This is an important and useful work, which presents considerable new material and successfully challenges previous interpretations on a number of points. Thornton is the first Western scholar to have been granted access to the six-volume stenographic report of the Sixth Congress of the Chinese Communist Party, held in Moscow in the summer of 1928. He also makes use of some recent works by Soviet authors.

        SR, 32:4:821-3   R: Stuart R. SChram

511. Treadgold, Donald W., ed. **Soviet and Chinese Communism: Similarities and Differences**. Seattle, University of Washington Press, 1967. 452p. $3.95pa.

The collection is very well organized, and the papers on various aspects of Red China and the USSR are interrelated to form a coherent and readable text. The essays were originally delivered at a conference of Russian and Chinese specialists held at Lake Tahoe, California, in June 1965; a conference designed "to examine and analyze the available facts on the basis of which alone can come authoritative comparisons of the two governments and societies." The volume consists of an introduction by Treadgold with his thoughts on the comparative study of Russian and Chinese Communism. This is followed by six sections of two or three papers each. This book should encourage further study of Sino-Soviet relations.

        CSP, 11:1:128-9   R: John W. Strong

With Western and Third World Countries

512. Allard, Sven. **Russia and the Austrian State Treaty: A Case Study of Soviet Policy in Europe**. University Park, Pennsylvania State University Press, 1970. 248p. $7.95.

As Swedish ambassador to Hungary, Rumania, and Bulgaria between 1949 and 1951 and to Hungary and Czechoslovakia from 1951 until 1954, Allard, before coming to Vienna, had numerous opportunities to observe Soviet aims and tactics in actual practice. The main emphasis of the volume is always on the foreign policy of the USSR and the seemingly sudden Soviet *volte-face* early in 1955, when, to the suprise of *cognoscenti* throughout the Western world, the Soviet Union not only agreed to sign a state treaty with Austria but actually took the initiative in pushing the treaty to conclusion. The author explains well this sudden change in Soviet tactics.

        SR, 31:2:462   R: R. John Rath

513. Balawyder, Aloysius. **Canadian-Soviet Relations between the World Wars**. Toronto, University of Toronto Press, 1972. 248p. $12.50.

The purpose of this book is to provide scholars and general readers with a long-overdue reference work on Canadian-Soviet relations during the interwar years. The most interesting chapter in the book is chapter 10, "The Comintern and the Communist Party of Canada." While the book is not balanced and some themes are not adequately developed, it is, nevertheless, a valuable reference work.

SR, 32:1:171-2   R: George Roseme

514.   Carroll, E. Malcolm. **Soviet Communism and Western Opinion, 1919-1921.** Ed. by Frederic B. M. Hollyday. Chapel Hill, University of North Carolina Press, 1965. 302p. $7.50.

After the death of Carroll in 1959, the manuscript was found among his papers. It has been edited and prepared for publication by Hollyday. The first two chapters present a summary of events between Soviet Russia and the West, especially Great Britain. Six of the eight chapters are devoted to the author's main topic, Western reaction to the Russo-Polish War. An entire chapter is devoted to the German reactions to the war.

RR, 25:1:96-7   R: Ross Horning

515.   Clissold, Stephen, ed. **Soviet Relations with Latin America, 1918-1968: A Documentary Survey.** London, Oxford University Press, 1970. 313p. (Issued under the auspices of the Royal Institute of International Affairs.) $12.00.

As stated in the introduction, "the documents included in this volume have been drawn from a wide range of Soviet and Latin American sources, some of them readily accessible, others—from the Comintern and Latin American Communist sources—less so." Many were taken from the *Current Digest of the Soviet Press.* The purpose of this collection of documents is to assist experts investigating Soviet foreign policy towards Latin American countries. The 199 documents are arranged by country and accompanied by explanatory notes and comments. An index of names and subjects is most useful. This novel study on Soviet foreign policy pertaining to Latin American countries represents another step forward for Western scholarship.   S. M. H.

516.   Cohn, Helen Desfosses. **Soviet Policy toward Black Africa: The Focus on National Integration.** Foreword by John N. Hazard. New York, Praeger, 1972. 316p. (Praeger Special Studies in International Politics and Public Affairs). $17.50.

The study is one of a number of bibliographical essays analyzing Soviet works on Africa. The emphasis is on the Brezhnev period and usefully brings some of the earlier studies up to date. The volume is well organized and readable. The author has thoroughly documented her basic thesis that pragmatism has replaced ideological considerations and that Soviet writers are increasingly less optimistic about the immediate future of Africa.

SR, 32:4:824   R: David T. Cattell

517.   Confino, Michael, and Shimon Shamir, eds. **The U.S.S.R. and the Middle East.** A Halsted Press Book. New York, John Wiley, Jerusalem, Israel University Press, 1973. 441p. (The Russian and East European Research Center and the Shiloah Center for Middle Eastern and African Studies, Tel Aviv University).

This volume is a symposium of papers presented at an international conference held at Tel Aviv University in December 1971 and devoted to an examination of the Soviet presence in the Middle East. It contains twenty papers by Western and Israeli scholars. The book is significant not only for its contents but also as an illustration of the limits of our understanding of Soviet motives and objectives after almost twenty years of Moscow' active involvement in the region.

SR, 33:2:371-2   R: O. M. Smolansky

518. Dallin, David J. **Soviet Russia and the Far East.** Hamden, Conn., Archon Books, 1972 (1948). 398p. $12.25.

Dallin sees Soviet policy toward China, Japan and Korea during the years 1931-1947 as a pattern of Communist imperialism resulting from its long-range planning, fifth-column infiltration, and ruthless suppression of any opposition in its march toward world domination. In this regard, little has changed since 1948, and Dallin's perceptive view of the Soviet system, behavior, and thinking is valid in 1976 as well. The author regards United States diplomacy and foreign policy as lacking in ability to comprehend the complexities involved.

519. Dyck, Harvey L. **Weimar Germany and Soviet Russia, 1926-1933: A Study in Diplomatic Instability.** New York, Columbia University Press, 1966. 279p. $6.75.

The relations between these two states were both close and erratic, both complementary and contradictory. The two countries were tied together by their hostility toward the order established by the Versailles Treaty; their economic needs were satisfied to a considerable extent by mutual trade; their security interests were to be met by secret military cooperation; and, last but not least, their designs against Poland were only an outgrowth of the Romanov-Hohenzollern policy of Poland's partition. Dyck's work represents a major achievement for its meticulous scholarship, unparalleled study of the enormous quantity of the archives of the German Foreign Office, and for a sound analysis and judgment. Until and unless the Soviet government opens access to its files, his book is likely to remain a definitive work on the thought-provoking topic of prewar Soviet-German relations.

RR, 26:3:302-3   R: Josef Korbel

519a. Fischer, Louis. **The Road to Yalta: Soviet Foreign Relations, 1941-1945.** New York, Harper & Row, 1972. 238p. $8.95.

This study is well organized, clear, and highly readable, though it does not add any new or revealing documents to the subject. A skillful combination of scholarship with a journalistic narrative, enriched by personal observations, gives the reader a better understanding of Soviet foreign policy and the causes of the Cold War. The author exposes Soviet imperialistic ambitions and in doing so he brings together a large amount of historical evidence dating back to the early years of the Soviet regime. The book can be easily understood by the layman and makes good reading for the student interested in the formation and execution of Soviet foreign policy.

S. M. H.

520. Jukes, Geoffrey. **The Soviet Union in Asia.** Berkeley, University of California Press, 1973. 304p. $8.75.

The book consists of a general study of Soviet interests in the Asian area on a broad basis, both inside and outside the Soviet borders. It can be recommended as a useful text for all those interested in the subject.

SR, 33:2:368-9   R: Klaus Mehnert

521. Kanet, Roger E., ed. **The Soviet Union and the Developing Nations.** Baltimore, Johns Hopkins University Press, 1974. 302p. $12.50.

This collection of ten articles, written by various authors specializing in Soviet foreign relations, surveys the Soviet Union's current policies toward the Third World. The authors of these surveys have neither the space nor information to go into Soviet relations with these areas in any depth. And because they are so close to the events, they find it difficult to draw conclusions, and therefore confine themselves to a few speculations. The volumes does not pursue any particular problems or thesis. Each author has defined his subject and worked independently. The result is a loosely organized summary of Soviet attitudes and policies toward the Third World, useful primarily for the classroom.

SR, 34:1:163-4   R: David T. Cattell

522.   Kapur, Harish. **Soviet Russia and Asia 1917-1927: A Study of Soviet Policy toward Turkey, Iran and Afghanistan.** New York, Humanities Press, 1967. 266p. $8.50.

• The study covers the first decade of Soviet Russian relations with the three border states of the non-Arabic Middle East. The bulk of the work deals with Soviet-Turkish relations, an area where the author appears at his best. Another part is devoted to Soviet-Iranian relations, and a small chapter to Soviet-Afghani affairs. The study is more descriptive than interpretive and should, therefore, be viewed with an understanding of the inherent qualities and limitations derived from such an approach.

SR, 27:1:152-3   R: Michael Rywkin

523.   Kapur, Harish. **The Soviet Union and the Emerging Nations: A Case Study of Soviet Policy towards India.** London, Michael Joseph, for the Graduate Institute of International Studies, Geneva, 1972. 124p. £3.50. Distr. by Humanities Press, New York, $10.50.

This study does not provide a detailed analysis of Soviet policy toward India, but it is valuable because the author pinpoints certain aspects of Soviet and Indian policies often neglected by other scholars, and offers some interesting and provocative interpretations. Soviet policy toward India was an effort to prevent the Communist leadership in Asia from passing into Chinese hands.

SR, 33:2:369-70   R: Surendra K. Gupta

524.   Klinghoffer, Arthur Jay. **Soviet Perspectives on African Socialism.** Rutherford, N.J., Fairleigh Dickinson University Press, 1969. 276p. $8.00.

This is a study in detail of the Soviet attitude toward the various strains of African socialism and Soviet politicians and scholars' interpretation of developments in Africa from 1955 to 1964. The guidelines for the Soviet line on Africa were set by Khrushchev, supplemented with an occasional article in *Kommunist*. It was left primarily to Ivan Potekhin and his African Institute, which was founded in 1959 and affiliated with the Soviet Academy of Science, to justify and explain Khrushchev's pronouncements in the light of Marxism-Leninism and to adapt them to African developments.

SR, 29:1:142-3   R: David T. Cattell

525.   Kohler, Foy D., et al. **The Soviet Union and the October 1973 Middle East War: The Implications for Détente.** Coral Gables, Fla., Center for Advanced International Studies, University of Miami, 1974. 131p.

Kohler, Leon Goure, and Mose L. Harvey discuss the tough policy pursued by the USSR in the Middle East crisis, which, perhaps for the first time, revealed to the world how Moscow sees the meaning of détente. This case study should receive close attention from scholars and politicians for its relevance to contemporary Soviet strategy.   S. M. H.

526.   Korbel, Josef. **Détente in Europe: Real or Imaginary?** Princeton, Princeton University Press, 1972. 302p. $10.00.
The author addresses himself pointedly to the underlying question of East-West relations, the meaning of détente. He does so by examining West European perceptions and policies vis-á-vis the Soviet Union; he then considers the intensification of cultural and economic ties; finally, he devotes considerable space to developments in West German *Ostpolitik*. Thus, although the book is by intent an essay, it is substantially a review of the European scene in the sixties. Korbel concludes on a cautious note. Either détente will be successful in breaking down the secretiveness of the East or it will lull the West into a potentially catastrophic complacency.
         CSP, 26:4:660-1   R: André Liebich

527.   Krammer, Arnold. **The Forgotten Friendship: Israel and the Soviet Bloc, 1947-1953.** Urbana, University of Illinois Press, 1974. 224p. $10.00.
The author analyzes the Soviet foreign policy during the period in which the USSR favored Israel over the Arab states. Searching for motives of the Soviet policy, Krammer suggests tha the Soviets implemented such a policy hoping to further their interests regardless of ideological contradictions, a policy practiced before and under different circumstances—the Hitler-Stalin Pact of 1939 for one. The extensive bibliography provides the reader with the possibility of pursuing the question of Soviet-Israeli relations in other areas and interpretations.
                              S. M. H.

528.   Landis, Lincoln. **Politics and Oil: Moscow in the Middle East.** New York, Dunellen Publishing Co., 1973. 201p. $12.95.
Landis sees Russian barter arrangements for the importation of Iraqui petroleum and Iranian natural gas as ominous portents of a dark future for the West. Although he acknowledges that such deals free Soviet-produced oil and gas for sale to Western markets and thus serve as an important source of hard currency (badly needed for the purchase of wheat and technology), he asserts that these economic arrangements are but an interim stage in Moscow's long-range design for domination of the Middle East. If successful, "Moscow would expect eventually to achieve a position of strategic economic dominance over the Middle East" and a "level of political authority as predominant power" in the region. Ideologically speaking, "the U.S.S.R. would be working toward a world energy delivery system within a world socialist planned economy."
         SR, 33:4:783-4   R: O. M. Smolansky

529.   Laqueur, Walter. **Russia and Germany: A Century of Conflict.** Boston, Little, Brown, 1965. 367p. $6.75.
This volume consists of a series of papers dealing with key episodes and problems. Sensibly, the author conceives of Russo-German relations not in narrowly diplomatic

terms, but as also encompassing mutual cultural and political influences. The book's emphasis centers around "a study in mutual misunderstanding," and while this phrase may apply to the years before the First World War and to those following the Second, it is to the inter-war period that he devotes major attention. If there is a central theme to the essays, it is the Soviet failure to understand German Nazism, and the failure of the Nazis to comprehend Marxism, Russia, and the Bolsheviks.

RR, 25:4:413-4   R: Alexander Dallin

530.   Lederer, Ivo J., and Wayne S. Vucinich, eds. **The Soviet Union and the Middle East: The Post-World War II Era**. Stanford, Hoover Institution Press, 1974. 302p. $9.95.

The papers presented at a Columbia University conference (1968) and at Tel-Aviv (1971) dealing with the Soviet attitudes toward the Middle East were published earlier. The gap left by the delay in publishing the proceedings of the Stanford conference (1969) has now been filled, and the result is a welcome addition to the literature on the subject. Among the various contributors, essays by John C. Campbell, George Harris, and Nadav Safran are particularly impressive.

SR, 34:2:401   R: O. M. Smolansky

531.   Legvold, Robert. **Soviet Policy in West Africa**. Cambridge, Harvard University Press, 1970. 372p. $13.00.

This study thoroughly analyzes the evolution and shifts in the USSR's relations with six West African states—Ghana, Guinea, the Ivory Coast, Mali, Nigeria, and Senegal between 1957 and 1968. During the first contact with independent Africa, according to Legvold, it was "an African nation's foreign policy, not internal development" which determined the Soviet attitude toward the country. The author points out the initial unfounded Soviet optimism about their opportunities in such "radical" states as Guinea, Ghana, and Mali. However, he notes that it was Guinea's independence and not Ghana's that "marked a turning point in Soviet relations with Black Africa." The organization of the book is very good, and judicious use has been made of various Soviet, African, and Western source materials. The book deserves a wide circulation in public libraires, embassies, and among students and teachers.

SR, 30:3:674   R: Ben C. Odum

532.   Lensen, George Alexander. **Japanese Recognition of the U.S.S.R.: Soviet-Japanese Relations, 1921-1930**. Tokyo, Sophia University, in cooperation with The Diplomatic Press, Tallahassee, 1970. 419p. $15.00.

The author painstakingly traces a series of attempts by the Japanese and Soviet governments to resume diplomatic relations following the Japanese Intervention in Siberia. These efforts finally resulted in Japanese recognition of the Soviet Union in 1925. But even after recognition, problems remained. Suspicion and mistrust rather than friendship characterized Japanese-Soviet relations for the remainder of the decade. Strictly speaking, this book is a history of Japanese-Soviet negotiations. Rather than dealing with the problem in the broad context of international relations, the author chose to limit himself to describing the events in the conference rooms. Despite some obvious weaknesses, this book offers a significant contribution to the diplomatic history of East Asia.

SR, 30:2:399-400 R: Tsuyoshi Hasegawa

533. Lensen, George Alexander. **The Strange Neutrality: Soviet-Japanese Relations during the Second World War, 1941-1945**. Tallahassee, The Diplomatic Press, 1972. 332p. $15.00.

The author's use of both the principal languages of his subject and his fondness for finding new sources have not heretofore been shown to better advantage. His search has been so thorough that he has been able to include sources not yet available for generation circulation, which the Japanese Foreign Office has permitted him to use without specific citation and which, therefore, appear in the footnotes only as "classified." The narrative is, to a great extent, an analysis of these sources, reinforced by a variety of secondary accounts.

SR, 32:2:391-2 R: John A. White

534. McSherry, James E. **Stalin, Hitler, and Europe**. Vol. 1: *The Origins of World War II, 1933-1939*. Vol. 2: *The Imbalance of Power, 1939-1941*. Cleveland, World. Vol. 1, 1968. 308p. $10.00; Vol. 2, 1970. 357p. $12.50.

From the continued sequence of paraphrases of the documents, the reader can secure a useful summary of the negotiations. The general reader who turns to this book will find it a helpful introduction; the scholar who turns to it for new information or insights will be disappointed. Though it covers somewhat less familiar ground, the second volume is very similar, and little needs to be added to the earlier comments.

SR, 27:4:660,
SR, 30:3:668 R: Gerhard L. Weinberg

535. Pennar, Jaan. **The U.S.S.R. and the Arabs: The Ideological Dimension**. New York, Crane, Russak, 1973. 180p. $9.75.

Proceeding from the assumption that ideology is an "indivisible component of the power struggle" in the international system, Pennar sets out to illustrate its significance in a case study devoted to Soviet-Arab relations. The various chapters trace the evolution of Communist theories on "national liberation" and the "noncapitalist path" of development, supplemented by a discussion of the ideological interaction between Moscow and Nasser, the Ba'th, and the Algerian FLN. In emphasizing the basic long-range incompatibility of Soviet and Arab nationalist interests—incompatibility which emerges particularly clearly in their ideological controversies—the author has performed a valuable service.

SR, 33:4:783 R: O. M. Smolansky

536. Ra'anan, Uri. **The USSR Arms the Third World: Case Studies in Soviet Foreign Policy**. Cambridge, Mass., MIT Press, 1969. 256p. $10.00.

Two case studies from the middle 1950s make up this book. One is the famous arms deal involving the Soviet Union, Czechoslovakia, and Egypt, the catalyst of a sea change in the military balance and the political climate of the Middle East. The other is the Soviet decision to arm Indonesia, a move which had certain parallels with the Egyptian case but no such durable results. The author has deliberately set out to test the generally accepted interpretations of diplomats, journalists, and scholars against all the old and new evidence he can find, some of it previously overlooked. Both studies are most helpful in increasing our knowledge of what really happened at this time of a major shift in Soviet policy toward the Third World.

SR, 29:1:702-3   R: John C. Campbell

537.   Rosenbaum, Kurt. **Community of Fate: German-Soviet Diplomatic Relations 1922-1928**. Syracuse, Syracuse University Press, 1965. 325p. $6.75.

The author made extensive use of the captured files of the German Foreign Office on microfilm at the National Archives for this fairly well-written retelling of the German-Soviet relations during the Weimar period. He concentrated particularly on the papers of Count Ulrich von Brockdorff-Rantzau, German ambassador in Moscow for most of the period. The material consists chiefly of details about major trends, events, and incidents which have been more than adequately described in earlier published works. Rosenbaum's contributions range from incidentals concerning the arrest in 1924 of the naive and anarchistical German students Kindermann and Wolscht by the Soviet authorities to interesting sidelights on how the Soviet and German governments handled the embarrassing revelations about their military collaboration published in 1926 by the *Manchester Guardian* and *Vorwärts*. The author also found confirmation in the documents he consulted of Gustav Stresemann's willing participation in the Reichswehr's secret rearmament, which took place partly on Russian soil, before and after these revelations. But the main lines of German and Russian policies during the period following the Brest-Litovsk treaty up to Hitler's ascendancy have been well known, and the book tells us nothing new about them.

SR, 25:1:165-6   R: Gerald Freud

538.   Rubinstein, Alvin Z. **The Soviets in International Organizations: Changing Policy toward Developing Countries, 1953-1963**. Princeton, Princeton University Press, 1964. 380p. $7.50.

Soviet policy towards developing countries can be studied in the context of the United Nations. This policy was inaugurated in July 1953 when the Soviet delegate to the UN Economic and Social Council announced that the Soviet Union was prepared to participate in the UN Expanded Programme of Technical Assistance for underdeveloped countries. As Rubinstein makes abundantly clear, Soviet participation in the functional agencies of the United Nations has the purpose of political propaganda. He points out how successful such a policy has been in the International Atomic Energy Agency and other branches of the UN.

SEER, 44:102:255-6   R: Harry Hanak

539.   Sen Gupta, Bhabani. **The Fulcrum of Asia: Relations among China, India, Pakistan, and the USSR**. New York, Pegasus, 1970. 383p. (Prepared under the auspices of the Research Institute on Communist Affairs and the East Asian Institute, Columbia University.) $8.95.

This study involves several Asian states in their relationship with the USSR and their relations among each other. Since the foreign policy of each state is closely linked with its domestic affairs, the international relations between China, India, Pakistan, and the USSR must also be viewed in the context of the internal situations in all respective countries as well as within the context of the global strategy of those countries. Extensive notes provide the reader with essential information concerning persons, events and bibliographical material.

S. M. H.

540.   Senn, Alfred Erich. **Diplomacy and Revolution: The Soviet Mission to Switzerland, 1918.** Notre Dame, University of Notre Dame Press, 1974. 2210. $9.95.

This volume describes the tangled web of events that led to the establishment and expulsion of the first Soviet mission to Switzerland in 1918. The Bolshevik efforts in Zurich and Bern during the last year of World War I assumed unusual significance, because Switzerland was one of the few places on the Continent where plans for the international Communist revolution could be prepared more or less openly. The Soviet-sponsored mission functioned in Switzerland from May to November 1918 under the leadership of J. A. Berzin. One of the intriguing themes that emerges from the volume deals with the difficulties of the Swiss government before expelling the Soviet mission.

SR, 34:2:395   R: James W. Hulse

541.   Smolansky, Oles M. **The Soviet Union and the Arab East under Khrushchev.** Lewisburg, Pa., Bucknell University Press, 1974. 326p. $15.00.

The author, long a student of Soviet-Arab relations, focuses on nine years of the relationship—from the arms deal of 1955 to the present. The 1955-1964 era is a crucial one, especially in the troubled emergence of Arab unity, and is punctuated by heroic episodes: the nationalization of the Suez Canal in 1956 and subsequent Anglo-French-Israeli invasion of Egypt; the lesser international crisis in Lebanon two years later; the rise and fall of Qasim's revolutionary regime in Iraq; the abortive experiment in trans-Arab statehood in the merger of Egypt and Syria as the United Arab Republic; the completion of the first stage of the High Aswan dam. The Soviet Union's part in these events and reaction to them are dealt with in extensive detail and with a sure hand. The central conclusion is that Khrushchev failed.

CSP, 27:1:160-1   R: Charles B. McLane

542.   Thompson, John M. **Russia, Bolshevism, and the Versailles Peace.** Princeton, Princeton University Press, 1967. 429p. (Studies of the Russian Institute, Columbia University). $11.50.

For the most part, the Paris Conference was briefed on Russian affairs by the diplomatic representatives of the former tsarist regime and by supporters or emissaries of the anti-Bolshevik forces inside Russia. Had these been united in their purpose, less time might have been spent at Versailles on the Russian question; certainly the wrangles there would have been less troublesome. Whether the outcome would have been different is a question to which the author does not address himself. He makes it clear that any territorial settlement imposed at a time when both Russia and Germany were too weak to have their say in the matter could not be expected to endure; and, indeed, with the exception of Bessarabia, Russia's frontiers were settled bilaterally, with Poland, Finland, the Baltic states, and in the south. The work deals in the main with two political questions, and of these its treatment is exemplary: power within Russia itself, that is, the case for and against Allied intervention once Germany was no longer valid, and what was to be done to meet the challenge and dangers of Bolshevism in a world exhausted and embittered by war.

      SR, 27:1:149-51   R: Jane Degras

543.   Ullman, Richard H. **Anglo-Soviet Relations, 1917-1921.** Vol. 1: *Intervention and the War.* Princeton, Princeton University Press, 1961. 360p. $7.50. Vol. 2: *Britain and the Russian Civil War: November 1918-February 1920.* Princeton, Princeton University Press, 1968. 395p. $10.00. Vol. 3: *The Anglo-Soviet Accord.* Princeton, Princeton University Press, 1972. 509p. (Published for the Center of International Studies). $17.50cl.; $9.50pa.

This first exhaustive study in English on Anglo-Soviet relations covers the period from the Bolshevik Revolution to the Compiègne Armistice in November 1918. The author elaborates with marked success on British policy which in sum was too pragmatic to deal effectively with the chaotic situation in Soviet Russia. Since official British records are still not available to historians, the study cannot claim to be complete; nevertheless, it is clearly and effectively written and represents a very desirable contribution to the period under discussion.

      SR, 21:2:351-2   R: Victor S. Mamatey

As the British discovered in 1919, drifting into intervention in a foreign civil war is a good deal easier than pulling out gracefully when victory appears impossible. This volume (the second in a three-volume series), which focuses on how Great Britain "extricated itself from a civil war in which it was the leading foreign participant," is particularly timely. Britain's role in Russia is carefully and effectively set forth, and this study is based not only on extensive private papers (except for those of Lloyd George and Churchill, which were not available) but also on recently opened British government records. In some places Ullman's work complements, in other duplicates, parallel studies of this period of Mayer and Thompson, but unless the papers of Lloyd George and Churchill reveal some unexpected surprises, this volume is clearly the definitive study of British policy toward Russia in this period.

      SR, 28:1:141-2   R: John M. Thompson

The publication of the third and final volume of Ullman's study of Anglo-Soviet relations provides a welcome relief from the polemics which have married historiography on this subject. It contains information concerning British policy during the Soviet-Polish War of 1920. The author's use of extensive excerpts from the private papers of British officials and from Soviet diplomatic correspondence makes this book a gold mine of valuable "raw" source materials. His chief aim in this volume is to evaluate the policies and diplomatic tactics of David Lloyd George and he describes his policy of "appeasement."

      SR, 32:6:820-1   R: Thomas C. Fiddick

544. Wheeler-Bennett, John W. **Brest-Litovsk: The Forgotten Peace, March 1918.** London, Macmillan, 1938; New York, St. Martin's Press, 1966. 478p. $8.00cl.; $4.95pa. New York, W. W. Norton, 1971. 478p. $3.25pa.
This is the best known and still most valuable treatment of the first Soviet-Germany Treaty which helped Lenin sustain the Soviet seizure of power in Russia in 1917. This book stands as one of the classics for that particular period and should be in college library collections.
JMH, 29:4:429   R: Dwight E. Lee

545. Wolfe, Thomas W. **Soviet Power and Europe, 1945-1970.** Baltimore, The Johns Hopkins Press, 1970. 534p. (A RAND Corporation Research Study). $15.00cl.; $3.95pa.
The study of Soviet policy toward both halves of a divided postwar Europe is arranged chronologically in three parts: the postwar Stalin period, the Khrushchev era, and the Brezhnev-Kosygin period's first half-decade. A main thesis of the book is that Soviet political objectives toward Europe with respect to neutralization of Germany, blocking the further build-up of NATO defenses, and preventing potential defections from the Soviet bloc remain basically unchanged since Stalin's time. This "hard" image of Soviet policy is amply documented from primary sources through careful weighing of alternative interpretations and contrary evidence. It should prove useful as a text in courses on Soviet foreign policy.
SR, 30:4:89203   R: Philip S. Gillette

HISTORY

Bibliographies and Source Materials

546. **Catherine II. Documents of Catherine the Great: The Correspondence with Voltaire and the Instruction of 1767, in the English Text of 1768.** Ed. by W. F. Reddaway. New York, Russell & Russell, 1971 (1931). 349p. $16.00.

547. Crowther, Peter A., comp. **A Bibliography of Works in English on Early Russian History to 1800.** New York, Barnes & Noble, 1969. 236p. $9.50.
In this bibliography 2,164 entries are organized under twenty major divisions (plus addenda through 1968): bibliography, historiography, general works, early Slavs, general history, foreign relations, law and institutions, social and economic history, archeology, anthropology, folklore, civilization, religion, education, the arts, language and literature, military history, naval history, regional history, and contemporary accounts. Each section is rationally subdivided and cross-referenced. The index is thorough. It unquestionably belongs in every library frequented by patrons interested in Russia prior to 1800.
SR, 30:2:454-5   R: Richard Hellie

548.   Meijer, Jan M., ed. **The Trotsky Papers 1917-1922.** Vol. 1: *1917-1919.*
        The Hague, Mouton, 1964. 858p. 90Dglds. Vol. 2: *1920-1922.* The
        Hague, Mouton, 1971. 894p. 150Dglds.
This publication comes not from the Harvard's Trotsky Archives but from that
of the International Institute in Amsterdam, which in 1936 acquired from Trotsky
some 800 documents (largely telegraphic communications and letters) covering
the period from 1917-1922. A comparison of these 800 items in the two
collections has shown that, with only one or two exceptions, they are identical.
While the documents involved here constitute only a portion of the Harvard
collection, this is probably the most important part since it covers the period of
Trotsky's greatest contribution to the permanent establishment of Soviet power.
Each document is reproduced in its entirety in Russian on the even numbered
pages, and facing it is a translation in English. Meijer's annotations add considerably
to the usefulness of the volume as a research tool.
          SR, 24:3:537-8   R: George Brinkley

The second volume, as skillfully translated and superbly edited as its predecessor,
provides 360 documents covering 1920 through 1922. The Trotsky vividly
recorded in these telegrams and memoranda is the military leader and administrator at the center of power, confronted with the daily crises of the fledgling Soviet
regime. Fully three-quarters of the documents in Volume Two appear here in
print for the first time.   S. M. H.

549.   Rieber, Alfred J., ed. **The Politics of Autocracy: Letters of Alexander
        II to Prince A. I. Bariatinskii 1857-1864.** Ed., with an historical essay,
        by A. J. Rieber. The Hague, Mouton, 1966 154p. (Etudes sur l'histoire,
        l'économie et la sociologie des pays Slaves, XII).
This slim volume contains 42 letters from Alexander II to Prince Bariatinskii,
a trusted friend and collaborator, and an important historical essay about the
autocracy's relationship to two vital questions: the Emancipation and imperial
expansion. Recently deposited in Columbia University's archives, the letters
provide fresh insight into Alexander's complex character and comment upon
the major foreign and domestic issues of the time. The essay, examining Alexander's
motives and methods of rule, also rescues from obscurity the colorful figure of
field Marshal Bariatinskii, conqueror of Shamil and exponent of Russian expansion in Central Asia.
          SR, 26:3:481   R: David MacKenzie

550.   Shapiro, David, comp. **A Select Bibliography of Works in English on
        Russian History, 1801-1917.** Oxford, Basil Blackwell, 1962. 106p.
        10s 6d.
(Listed in P. Horecky's *Russia and the Soviet Union*, #14). The bibliography
lists 1,070 books and articles relevant to the study of Russian history. Only a
few books are identified with references to critical reviews.
                          S. M. H.

551.   Smith, R. E. F. **The Enserfment of the Russian Peasantry.** Cambridge,
        Cambridge University Press, 1968. 180p. $7.25.

Smith's book essentially is a translation of 56 documents, from 1125-32 to 1649, each of them preceded by an introductory paragraph characterizing the document and sometimes explaining the more important Russian terms. The documents themselves carry no critical apparatus and it was not the intention of the book. There is a glossary that lists the English translations of 138 Russian terms followed by their Russian equivalents and explanations of the meanings. There is also an index of the Russian terms in the glossary, listing each with a numerical reference to its English equivalent. The book ends with a list of sources, with a closer characterization of some of them, and a general index.

     SR, 29:2:302   R: Marc Szeftel

552. **The Testaments of the Grand Princes of Moscow.** Trans. and ed. with commentary, by Robert Craig Howes. Ithaca, Cornell University Press, 1967. 445p. $10.00.

Howes' translation should be welcomed as a valuable addition to the resources of both academic teacher and scholar. The thirteen testaments, ranging from the time of Ivan Kalita to Ivan IV, represent one of the most important sources for the study of the political, legal, and social history of Muscovite Russia. The translation of the documents is satisfactory but the application of a method of simplification and modernization is evident.

     SR, 31:4:878-80   R: Jaroslaw Pelenski

553. Vernadsky, George, and Ralph T. Fisher, Jr., et al., eds. and comps. **A Source Book for Russian History from Early Times to 1917.** Vol. 1: *Early Times to the Late Seventeenth Century.* Vol. 2: *Peter the Great to Nicholas I.* Vol. 3: *Alexander II to the February Revolution.* New Haven, Yale University Press, 1972. Vol. 1: 306p. Vol. 2: 307-584pp. Vol. 3: 585-884pp. $35.00/set; $12.50ea.

This three-volume work represents the most comprehensive source book in English encompasssing various areas and fields of Russia's history. Documents and sources are accompanied by introductions and editorial explanations. The work is an indispensable tool to scholars and teachers alike.

     SR, 33:2:336-8   R: Daniel C. Waugh
                                     John T. Alexander
                                     John M. Thompson

General Surveys, Readers

554. Cherniavsky, Michael, ed. **The Structure of Russian History: Interpretive Essays.** New York, Random House, 1970. 448p. $6.95pa.

This symposium is divided into three parts: 1) Aspects of Medieval Russia, 2) Problems of the Russian Eighteenth Century: Gentry Monarchy and "Westernization"; 3) Aspects of Imperial Nineteenth-Century Russia. Seventeen authors discuss various aspects, problems, and interpretations related to the structure, formation and function of the Russian Empire. The topics stretched from the Byzantine influences to the socio-political structure of the Empire during the nineteenth century. The book represents a wealth of material for additional readings in courses of Russian history, civilization, culture, and socio-economic studies.   S. M. H.

555.   Dmytryshyn, Basil, ed. **Imperial Russia: A Source Book, 1700-1917.** 2nd ed. Hinsdale, Ill., The Dryden Press, 1974. 497p. $5.95pa. (First ed.: New York, Holt, Rinehart & Winston, 1967).
"The main purpose of this new edition is to include documentary material dealing with Russia's foreign relations. In pursuit of that goal texts of twenty-five major treaties have been included" (from "Preface to the Second Edition").

556.   Dmytryshyn, Basil, comp. **Modernization of Russia under Peter I and Catherine II.** New York, John Wiley, 1974. 157p. (Major Issues in History). $4.50.
Due to the profound influence on the course of Russian history exerted by Peter I and Catherine II, the author attempts to explain these developments through the selection of relevant decrees, observations made by foreigners, and assessments by historians reflected in contemporary Soviet historiography. Many documents have here been made available in English for the first time, an accomplishment which justifies its publication and recommendation for libraries to make this book available to students of Russia's history.
S. M. H.

557.   Ellison, Herbert J. **A History of Russia.** New York, Holt, Rinehart, & Winston, 1964. 644p. $8.95.
Writing on Russian history before 1917, many Western historians have endeavored to show how bad things in Russia had always been before Lenin ascended the Russian throne. Ellison is free of this tendency. Condemning "arrogant Great Russian chauvinism," he has no enthusiasm for the tsarist government, but he does endeavor to present an objective picture of the Russian historical past, to balance the failures and the achievements of prerevolutionary Russia. Especially sound is his analysis of the period 1906-1914, for which the prevailing cliché is "Stolypin reaction" but which in fact exhibited "immense achievements in many areas of national life." The author also devotes much attention to the situation of the national minorities in the Russian Empire and in the Soviet Union. The bibliography is reasonably complete.
SR, 24:2:323-4   R: Sergei Pushkarev

558.   Florinsky, Michael T. **Russia: A Short History.** 2nd ed. London, Collier-Macmillan, 1969 (1964). 699p. $9.95.
Florinsky's well-known two-volume survey, *Russia: A History and an Interpretation* (1953), has subsequently been condensed into one volume, *Russia: A Short History* (1964), as a textbook for students of Russian history. Florinsky follows the Russian historical scheme on the question of Russia's origin, terminology, and periodization. Otherwise, his survey properly scrutinizes Russia's past. This second updated edition makes one of the better textbooks for undergraduate instruction.   S. M. H.

559.   Hellie, Richard, comp. and trans. **Readings for Introduction to Russian Civilization: Muscovite Society.** Chicago, Syllabus Division, The College, The University of Chicago, 1967. 320p. $5.95.

The scope of this book covers Muscovite society as a whole, which Hellie follows group by group in nine chapters, involving many texts, some of them quite extensive. He has drawn heavily on the Law Code (Ulozhenie) of 1649, having translated *in extenso* chapters 7, 8, 11, 19, 20, and 22, next to a partial translation of chapters 10, 15, and 21. He also has translated the Toropets Administrative Charter of 1590/91, and the petition on forbidding foreign merchants to trade, 1648-49. Chapter 7 is devoted to "The Enserfment of the Peasantry," while chapter 8 deals with "Bondage in Muscovy."

　　　　SR, 29:2:302-3　　　　　　　　R: Marc Szeftel

560.　　Hunczak, Taras, ed. **Russian Imperialism. From Ivan the Great to the Revolution**. New Brunswick, N.J., Rutgers University Press, 1974. 396p. $17.50.

Ten specialists have joined in an attempt to explain the historical and geopolitical aspects of Russian expansionism. The centripetal tendencies of Tsarist Russia from Ivan II to the Romanov downfall and the Revolution are presented in ten chapters, in addition to the foreword by the editor and introduction by the late Hans Kohn. The most interesting details presented here are the treatment of the geopolitical aspects of Russian expansionism. The original Russian state which, according to V. O. Kliuchevski, controlled an area of some 15,000 sq. miles in 1462, expanded at the rate of 50 sq. miles a day for four hundred years. The ethnic Russians established domination over a large number of nations which actually outnumbered the dominant Russians. The details offered in this symposium have been evidently carefully researched. This is one of the first dependable studies on the expansion of the Russian empire.

561.　　Kerner, Robert J. **The Urge to the Sea; The Course of Russian History. The Role of Rivers, Portages, Ostrogs, Monasteries and Furs**. New York, Russell & Russell, 1971 (Repr. of 1942 ed. by University of California Press). 212p. $14.00.

This is the first American study attempting to explain Russia's territorial expansion from a geographical and geopolitical point of view. It is the first systematic treatment of the subject which has also drawn the attention of Russian historians, though they never elaborated on this aspect in a historical continuity. The study remains among the standard works explaining factors of Russian imperialism.

　　　　　　　　　　　　S. M. H.

562.　　Pipes, Richard. **Russia under the Old Regime**. New York, Charles Scribner's Sons; London, Weidenfeld and Nicolson, 1974. 361p. $17.50cl.; $6.95pa.

"The theme of this book is the political system of Russia. It traces the growth of the Russian state from its beginnings in the ninth century to the end of the nineteenth. . . . Unlike most historians who seek the roots of twentieth-century totalitarianism in Western ideas, I look for them in Russian institutions," states the author. The work's outline as expressed in the foreword makes it unique in American Russian historical literature only; the same views, analyses, and interpretations had been offered by Western European, especially Ukrainian national, historians. A novel aspect is the employment of analogies and comparisons in discussing the development of Muscovy-Russia. The author sees the roots of Bolshevism in the patrimonial system which led to "agro-despotism," in the subordination of the Russian Orthodox Church to the state's interest, in the absence of a bourgeoisie, and in the alienation of the intelligentsia from the system, which finally resulted in a bureaucratic police state. This is not exactly a textbook or a survey of Russia's history but rather a case study aimed at the advanced student.   S. M. H.

563.   Riasanovsky, Nicholas V. **A History of Russia.** 2nd ed. New York,
        Oxford University Press, 1969 (1963). 748p. $13.50.
(Review of first edition in SR, 22:4:753-4, R: M. T. Florinsky). The second
edition is updated to the Brezhnev-Kosygin period. The bibliography includes
new titles published between 1962 and 1968. No other significant changes have
been made in this edition.   S. M. H.

564.   Stephan, John J. **Sakhalin: A History.** Oxford, Clarendon Press, 1971.
        240p. $12.00.
This study is an impressive accomplishment of historical scholarship. The author
has conscientiously examined the available evidence in the libraries and archival
collections of Japan, the USSR, and Western Europe. He has successfully digested
these voluminous materials, and presents a concise, coherent, lucid, and impartial
account of Russian and Japanese policies and activities in an important part of
the Far East. Excerpts from key diplomatic documents, a convenient glossary
of Russian and Japanese place names, and a rich bibliography round out this
valuable study.
        SR, 31:2:433-4   R: Paul F. Langer

565.   Vernadsky, George. **A History of Russia.** 6th rev. ed. New Haven, Yale
        University Press, 1971 (1929). 531p. $3.95pa.
According to the author, "in the present edition the course of events and the
main trends of life in contemporary Russia have been related and analyzed.
The bibliography has been expanded in order to list a number of important
books published after 1960. The Appendix contains brief statistical data on
the Soviet Union for 1966." Vernadsky represents the so-called "Euro-Asiatic
school of thought" among Russian national historians.   S. M. H.

Archaeology and Historiography

566.   Chew, Allen F. **An Atlas of Russian History: Eleven Centuries of
        Changing Borders.** New Haven, Yale University Press, 1970. 127p.
        $5.45.
This revised edition will undoubtedly prove as helpful to students of Russian
history as the first edition. Although the addition of three new maps showing
vegetation, temperature and precipitation, and relief zones goes beyond the pro-
fessed scope of the *Atlas*, nonetheless it has enhanced the *Atlas*'s use as a complement to more comprehensive Russian history texts. The new appendix, "Name
Changes of Selected Russian Towns and Cities," will also be appreciated by
scholars.
        CSP, 13:4:440-1   R: E. R. Zimmermann

567. Gryaznov, Mikhail P. **The Ancient Civilization of Southern Siberia**.
Trans. from the Russian by James Hogarth. New York, Cowles Book
Co., 1969. 251p. 78 illus. in color; 92 illus. in black and white. $10.00.
The usefulness of this work warrants its translation into English. The author
offers a mass of original material from "The Neolithic Period," "The Bronze
Age" and "The Age of the Early Nomads." A chronological table, a list of
illustrations and an index add to the book's value. The translation itself is
satisfactory.   S. M. H.

568. Keep, John, and Liliana Brisby, eds. **Contemporary History in the**
Soviet Mirror. New York, Praeger, 1964. 331p. $7.50.
There is little evidence to date that the fall of Khrushchev will cause more than
a slight rewriting of the recent Soviet past; many of the main trends in post-
Stalin historiography will apparently continue. It is therefore particularly helpful to have this collection of essays, which is the fullest account in English of
developments between 1953 and 1961 in the Soviet treatment of recent history.
The writers generally agree that after Stalin, party controls over history were
modified but not fundamentally altered and that the output of recent Soviet
historiography deserves increased attention in the West.
SR, 24:3:540-1   R: John M. Thompson

569. Laqueur, Walter. **The Fate of the Revolution: Interpretations of Soviet**
History. New York, Macmillan, 1967. 216p. $5.95.
This is a critical and well-written commentary on changing interpretations of
the USSR by sundry Western and a few Soviet historians. Laqueur offers helpful
biographical sketches and summations of published works. Of particular interest
are Western evaluations of Lenin. This work deserves the careful attention of
historians and nonhistorians alike.
AHR, 73:5:1586   R: Frederick L. Schuman

570. Mazour, Anatole G. **The Writing of History in the Soviet Union**.
Stanford, Hoover Institution Press, 1971. 383p. (Hoover Institution
Publications, 87). $17.50.
As a supplement to his well-known *Modern Russian Historiography* (New
York, 1958) Mazour now offers a survey of Soviet historical writing on some major
themes and topics in Russian history. Almost everyone with an interest in the
field will be able to learn something from this volume. It may also stimulate
further experiments in this genre of scholarship. The author provides a gripping
description of the catastrophic impact of the Stalin cult on Soviet historiography
and assesses the progress made in overcoming it since 1956. Otherwise, his work
draws attention to the range of subjects treated by Soviet historians, and for
this reason will find its place on many library shelves.
SR, 31:3:684-6   R: John Keep

571. Okladnikov, A. P. **Yakutia before Its Incorporation into the Russian**
State. Ed. by Henry N. Michael. Montreal, McGill-Queen's University
Press, 1970. 499p. (Arctic Institute of North America, Anthropology
of the North: Translations from Russian Sources, no. 8). $20.00.

Okladnikov, the dean of Siberian archaeologists, first published this work in 1950; the English translation is taken from the 1955 edition. The book is based on his archaeological investigations in Yakutia, and covers the archaeology and ethnography of this Autonomous Soviet Socialist Republic into the seventeenth century. This work is a major source of information for scholars interested in eastern Siberia. Archaeologists will find the first half of the book extremely useful, since most non-Russian references emphasize the steppe cultures of southern Siberia at the expense of contemporary cultures to the east. The chapters on the Neolithic, Bronze, and Iron ages contain rich descriptions of the cultures of Yakutia during these periods, as well as discussions of foreign connections. The second part is devoted to studies of the origins of the Yakut people, the early history of the Yakuts, and the history of the Yakuts from their arrival on the Lena River until into the seventeenth century.

SR, 30:2:381-2   R: Ann Farkas

572.   Patrov, Vladimir. **"June 22, 1941": Soviet Historians and the German Invasion.** Columbia, University of South Carolina Press, 1968. 322p. $5.95.

The Soviet historian A. M. Nekrich in his book *June 22, 1941*, published in 1965, undertook to examine the origins of the German attack on the Soviet Union and to inquire into the causes of the initial Soviet military disasters, questions that have been largely ignored by Soviet historians. His book was withdrawn from circulation, and he was dismissed from his position in the Academy of Sciences and from membership in the Communist party. The "Nekrich Affair" is the subject of Petrov's book. He provides a searching analysis of the case, a full translation of Nekrich's work, as well as the texts of the praise and criticism it received in the Soviet Union. Petrov provides a useful case study of the problems faced by Soviet historians in any attempt to write "objective" history.

SR, 28:3:498   R: Leon Gouré

573.   Pundeff, Marin, comp. and ed. **History in the U.S.S.R.: Selected Readings.** San Francisco, Chandler Publ. Co., 1967. 313p. (Published for the Hoover Institution). $6.50.

This collection of readings has several merits. Included are selections by Marx, Engels, Plekhanov, Lenin, Pokrovsky, Stalin, and Khrushchev, as well as official pronouncements and decrees, all of which have provided guidelines for the writing and teaching of history in the Soviet Union. Some of the documents have been translated into English for the first time, and all have been provided with generally useful prefatory explanations for the beginning student.

SR, 28:4:656-7   R: Alexander Rabinowtich

574.   Pushkarev, Sergei G., comp. **Dictionary of Russian Historical Terms from the Eleventh Century to 1917.** Ed. by George Vernadsky and Ralph T. Fisher, Jr. New Haven, Yale University Press, 1970. 199p. $12.50.

This dictionary has been conceived as a very broad undertaking. Not only terms pertaining to Russian history from Kievan Rus' to 1917 have been carefully studied in it, but also West Russian terms used in the Grand Principality of Lithuania from the beginning of the fourteenth to the end of the sixteenth

century. Most entries offer much more than simple translations, for they are
followed by historical sketches which contain a wealth of information, at times
giving this dictionary the character of information, at times giving this dictionary
the character of a small encyclopedia of Russian historical terminology prior
to 1917. The translations are precise, the explanations pertinent, and the historical data accompanying them of basic importance. An immense scholarly and
teaching service has been performed by Pushkarev, Vernadsky, and Fisher.

    SR, 30:1:134-5   R: Marc Szeftel

575.   Rudenko, Sergei I. **Frozen Tombs of Siberia: The Pazyryk Burials
            of Iron Age Horsemen.** Trans. with a preface, by M. W. Thompson.
            Berkeley, University of California Press, 1970. 340p. 33 color, 147
            black and white plates. $30.00.

This volume is an English translation of S. I. Rudenko's *Kul'tura naseleniia
Gornogo Altaia v skifskoe vremia* (Moscow and Leningrad, 1953). Here Rudenko
described the barrows at Pazyryk excavated by him in 1929, 1947-1948, and
1949. The English version has been made from a text corrected by Rudenko and
is revised to include a new introduction by the author, an appended inventory
of each Pazyryk barrow with plate numbers of illustrated finds, and selected
additional bibliography, prepared by the translator, of references in English,
French, and German. Among the Pazyryk barrows were the graves of rulers
of the nomadic tribes inhabiting the mountain steppes of the Altai about the
middle of the first millennium B. C. Wood objects, leather, fur, textiles, carpets,
even the embalmed bodies of the tomb occupants and the carcasses of slain
horses buried near the graves—all were preserved. Thus the material culture
of these people can be studied in great detail in its own right, or in relation to
other nomadic tribes of the Eurasian steppes and to the high civilizations of the
Near East and China.

    SR, 30:3:657-8   R: Ann Farkas

576.   Szporluk, Roman, ed. **Russia in World History: Selected Essays by
            M. N. Pokrovskii.** Trans. by Roman Szporluk and Mary Ann Szporluk.
            Ann Arbor, University of Michigan Press, 1970. 241p. $7.95.

M. N. Pokrovskii (1868-1932), often referred to as the only Marxist historian
of rank in the USSR, reflects the development of Soviet historiography for the
last fifty years in a most remarkable way. The main value of this work is that
it makes light of Pokrovskii's essays available in English. The essays were
selected to present Pokrovskii's interpretation of Russia's history against the
background of world history. It is no surprise that most of the essays should no
longer be "available" in the Soviet Union, especially those critical of the early
years of the Soviet regime. A few titles to illustrate this point: "Bureaucracy,"
"Tsarism and the Roots of the 1917 Revolution," "The Prison of Nations,"
"Russian Imperialism in the Past and Present," "Historic Mission," and "Lenin's
Role in the Russian Revolution." The editor's introduction is a weighty contribution in itself. Scholars and students should pay attention to this work.

    UQ, 27:3:305-7   R: Stephan M. Horak

577.   Thompson, M. W. **Novgorod the Great: Excavations at the Medieval
        City, Directed by A. V. Artsikhovsky and B. A. Kolchin.** New York,
        Praeger, 1967. 104p. $13.50.
Thompson provides the first comprehensive account of the results of excavations
in Novgorod between 1951 and 1962. According to him, the excavations in
Novgorod represent one of the major landmarks in European archaeology.
The preservation of the wood by the humid conditions in Novgorod is in a way
comparable to that of the neolithic Swiss lakeshore dwellings of the fourth
millennium B.C. Among the most exciting finds are birchbark documents found
through most of the deposit except the bottom five and the two top street
levels. Dating from the mid-eleventh to the early fifteenth centuries, the over
four hundred examples from the excavation site are engraved or scratched on
the soft surface of the bark. The excavations in Novgorod have proved the
origins of the city and the way in which the people lived.
        SR, 29:1:99-100   R: Marija Gimbutas

Pre-Petrine Muscovy/Russia

578.   Barbour, Philip L. **Dimitry, Called the Pretender: Tsar and Great
        Prince of All Russia, 1605-1606.** Boston, Houghton Mifflin, 1966.
        387p. $6.95.
Barbour has related in a dramatic and colorful style the brief career of Dimitri
the Pretender. The narrative form employed by the author seems well suited
for dealing with the history of medieval Russia. His work should provide the
general reading public with a stimulating introduction to an unfamiliar area of
historical study. A relative sparsity of references and a condensed bibliography·
will limit this book's usefulness as a guide to further research. Nevertheless,
it is a valuable and welcome contribution to the literature of Russian history.
        SR, 27:1:135   R: Jack Culpepper

579.   Dallin, David J. **The Rise of Russia in Asia; [and] Soviet Russia in
        the Far East.** Hamden, Conn., Shoestring Press, 1971. 293p. $9.50.
These two books, first published in 1948 and 1949, are now reissued in unaltered
and unabridged versions. They deal with Russian policy in the Far East, with the
emphasis on the period since 1917. They are still valuable works contributing
to our knowledge of that aspect of the USSR history.
        SEER, 51:125:629   R: D. S. M. Williams

580.   Fennell, J. L. I., trans. and ed. **Prince A. M. Kurbsky's History of
        Ivan IV.** Cambridge, Cambridge University Press, 1965. 314p. $12.50.
In 1564, many years after he left Muscovy, Prince Kurbsky composed his
History of Ivan IV. In it he describes briefly the origin and youth of Ivan the
Terrible, deals at length with the Tsar's campaigns against Kazan and Livonia
in which Kurbsky himself participated, and then enumerates and describes
the many atrocities which the Tsar committed against the members of the priestly
caste and the boyars. The book thus contains remembrances of events which
occurred a dozen years or more earlier and also accounts of others of a later
date of which Kurbsky gained his knowledge indirectly. It has therefore all

the shortcomings of a secondary source. The Russian historian will be grateful for having Kurbsky's *History* easily available and expertly annotated.

SR, 25:4:691-2   R: Walther Kirchner

581.   Grey, Ian. **Boris Godunov: The Tragic Tsar.** New York, Charles Scribner's Sons, 1973. $8.95.

In this volume Grey chronicles the narrative history of the life of Godunov, drawing heavily from the classic accounts by Karamzin, Soloviev, and Platonov and the more recent scholarship of Zimin and Vernadsky. For those who know little of this period of history, his work can serve as a useful introduction. The serious reader will be better served by S. F. Platonov's study of Godunov's reign, reissued in 1973 in English translation by Academic International Press.

SR, 33:2:344-5   R: Joseph L. Wieczynski

582.   Grobovsky, Antony N. **The "Chosen Council" of Ivan IV: A Reinterpretation.** New York, Theo. Gaus' Sons, 1969. 171p.

Grobovsky attempts to prove that the Chosen Council as an institution, or as a private group or society, did not exist. He considers that they were merely well-intentioned individuals. The book will certainly remain in the bibliography on this subject, and it will remain because it is an interesting and bold attempt to solve one of the so-called mysteries of the reign of Ivan the Terrible.

SR, 30:1:136-7   R: Nikolay Andreyev

583.   Hellie, Richard. **Enserfment and Military Change in Muscovy.** Chicago, University of Chicago Press, 1971. 432p. $14.50.

The author is convinced that the enserfment of the Russian peasantry must be accounted for either on the basis of state decrees or of broad economic and social developments in which the state did not play the major role. With this in mind he surveys all suggested interpretations, from the amateur Tatishchev to historians such as Kliuchevsky and Platonov, who developed "non-decree" interpretations, continued by Soviet historians until the Stalin period. Yet his own position is: "A decree interpretation seems to be correct in the light of the evidence currently available." The value of the book lies not in Hellie's attempts at interpretation but in the industry with which he has assembled both factual and opinionated data provided by some 300 other authors.

SR, 31:3:658-9   R: Jesse D. Clarkson

584.   Kliuchevskii, V. O. **A Course in Russian History: The Seventeenth Century.** Trans. by Natalie Duddington. Intro. by Alfred J. Rieber. Chicago, Quadrangle Books, 1968. 400p. $8.95.

Based on the 1957 Soviet edition in Russian, this new version or translation flows smoothly and resounds the masterful style that made Kliuchevsky the most popular university teacher of history in Russia. In a solid, scholarly introduction, Rieber examines the work, life, and critics of Kliuchevsky the historian with a view to placing him in modern historiography. Both beginning and advanced students of Russian history will find the book valuable and highly readable, and because Kliuchevsky frequently differentiated between Russian and European experience, students of comparative historical methods will also be interested.

SR, 29:2:308-9   R: William K. Medlin

585.   Lantzeff, George V., and Richard A. Pierce. **Eastward to Empire:**
       Exploration and Conquest on the Russian Open Frontier, to 1750.
       Montreal, McGill-Queen's University Press, 1973. 276p. $15.50.
This posthumous book serves a useful function in pulling together the narrative
on that restless line of the eastern frontier from the rise of Muscovy to the
eighteenth century. In unadorned, spare language Lantzeff and Pierce have
summarized judiciously and fully the moderately well-known story of the
fighting, trading, bargaining, and initial settlement of the Russians, implying
a direct linkage and common purpose shared by Novgorodian and Suzdalian
princes, and eighteenth-century explorers of Kamchatka. All this is done
mainly from "published materials, both primary and secondary," used carefully
and thoroughly. No other book provides such a dependable and usable account,
although John Harrison's recent *Founding of the Russian Empire in Asia and*
America covers much the same ground less substantially but in more vigorous
prose.
       SR, 34:1:139   R: Clifford M. Foust

586.   Nørretranders, Bjarne. **The Shaping of Czardom under Ivan Groznyj.**
       London, Variorum Reprints, 1971. 188p. (Repr. of the 1964 Copenhagen
       ed., Variorum Reprint, 54). £6.00.
This book, by a Danish scholar, is important to all those interested in the reign
of Ivan IV, in the Tsar's ideas, and in the relation between theory and practice
in Ivan IV's statesmanship. The author's analysis of Ivan's letters to Kurbsky
(chapter 2) is masterly. He points out the close interrelations between the various
subjects mentioned in the Tsar's epistles. He rightly insists that Ivan is attempting
a scriptural, historical, political, and personal justification of his actions and adds,
"this personal justification is a long, connected argument in the form of a sort
of autobiography, and occupies a good fifth of the total text of the message."
This book is a lucid and most interesting attempt to discern a pattern of logical
continuity in the history of Russia in the sixteenth century.
       SR, 33:4:771-2   R: Nikolay Andreyev

587.   Pelenski, Jaroslaw. **Russia and Kazan: Conquest and Imperial Ideology**
       (1438-1560s). The Hague, Mouton, 1974. 368p. 90Dglds.
With the conquest of Kazan in 1552 the ethnic Russian state of Moscow became
a multinational empire. The book's context is the unstable balance of power
between the successor Khanates of the Golden Horde, Moscow, Lithuania-
Poland, and peripherial powers from Kazan's independence in 1438-45 to 1552.
The author shows that Kazan's submissiveness to Moscow was always episodic
and generally unwilling. Vasilii III established Moscow's predominance in
1523-24 by building the Russian fort, "Vasil'grad" on the Volga in Kazan
territory, and by transferring the center of Moscow's eastern trade from Kazan
to Nizhnii Novgorod. The book contains useful maps, pictures, bibliography,
and index. Tables of Turkic names in modern Turkish and Russian forms, chronological lists of rulers of Kiev, Vladimir-Suzdal, Moscow, and Kazan, and of
metropolitans of Moscow are appended.
       RR, 34:1:92-3   R: David B. Miller

588. Platonov, S. F. **Ivan the Terrible**. Ed. and trans. by Joseph L. Wieczynski. With "In Search of Ivan the Terrible" by Richard Hellie. Gulf Breeze, Fla., Academic International Press, 1974 (Leningrad, 1923). 166p. (The Russian Series, vol. 28). $11.50.

Wieczynski's translation gets high marks for accuracy and readibility, and Hellie's introduction is somewhat less successful. He devotes the greater part of his introduction to the protracted historiographical controversy over whether Ivan's policies were fundamentally rational or pathological. He presents the case for Ivan as a paranoid.

SR, 34:2:383-4   R: Samuel H. Baron

589. Platonov, S. F. **Moscow and the West**. Trans. and ed. by Joseph L. Wieczynski. Intro. by Serge A. Zenkovsky. Hattiesburg, Miss., Academic International Press, 1972. 171p. (Russian Series, vol. 9). $10.00.

Platonov's *Moskva i zapad* (Leningrad, 1925) is a minor classic, with equal emphasis on both words. It is limited in aim, being an essay rather than a monograph, a summary rather than an exploration. At the same time it is the definitive statement of the traditional "Westernizers" view of the relationship between Old Russia and Europe. Muscovy had to borrow from the West in order to compete with it. The editor's contributions include a map, notes to the text supplementing the author's own, a glossary, and an index.

SR, 32:1:161   R: Benjamin Uroff

590. Platonov, S. F. **The Time of Troubles: A Historical Study of the Internal Crisis and Social Struggle in Sixteenth- and Seventeenth-Century Muscovy**. Trans. by John T. Alexander. Lawrence, Kansas, University Press, 1970. 197p. $6.50cl.; $2.45pa.

Platonov's interpretation of the origins of the troubles is somewhat dated, and instructors who assign this work to their students will have to explain what is acceptable and what is not. The book has several useful appendixes: geneological tables, a chronological table, a glossary of terms, and annotated bibliography, and an index.

SR, 32:1:160   R: Thomas Esper

591. Presniakov, A. E. **The Formation of the Great Russian State: A Study of Russian History in the Thirteenth to Fifteenth Centuries**. Trans. by A. E. Moorhouse. Intro. by Alfred J. Rieber. Chicago, Quadrangle Books, 1970. 414p. $12.95.

The main value of the book lies in the new approach to explaining the rise of the Muscovite state and Russian autocracy. Presniakov describes the growth of the princely authority against the elaborated investigation of the social order of the period. Rejecting Solovev's theory of the development of an *udel* domain and the Slavophile "*obshchina* theory," Presniakov supports with a wealth of sources and documents the theory of hereditary domains, which later on disintegrated into a number of minor *votchina* principalities, independent of each other.   S. M. H.

592. Vernadsky, George. **The Tsardom of Moscow, 1547-1682**, in 2 v.
     A History of Russia, Vol. 5. New Haven, Yale University Press, 1969.
     873p. $20.00.

The appearance of this volume is the final step in Vernadsky's contribution to
the ten-volume *History of Russia* started in 1943 jointly by him and Michael
Karpovich. Since the epoch treated by Vernadsky was of crucial importance
for Russian historical development, it is not surprising that it required so much
space and attention, for the problems to be treated within those 135 years
are both numerous and intricate: Ivan the Terrible's tumultuous reign, the
Time of Troubles and the reconstruction of Muscovy, the evolution and the
consolidation of serfdom, the Ukrainian wars and the Union of the Ukraine with
Moscow, the drama around Nikon and the church schism, the great territorial
expansion into the "Eurasian space," and the gradual penetration of Western
culture. All this has been dealt with by a master's hand and very thoroughly.
The use of Russian prerevolutionary and Soviet materials, as well as Ukrainian
and Polish sources and monographs, has given the author's story a great degree
of objectivity.
        SR, 29:4:691-3   R: Marc Szeftel

593. Voyce, Arthur. **Moscow and the Roots of Russian Culture**. Norman,
     University of Oklahoma Press, 1964. 194p. $2.75.

The author has attempted to deal with Moscow from the mid-twelfth to the
early eighteenth century. In reality, he has concentrated on the period from
Ivan III to Peter the Great. The first chapter is a general survey of Russian history
during the Muscovite period. Subsequent chapters entitled The City, Daily Life,
Moscow Architecture, The Moscow School of Painting, and The Moscow School
of Decorative Arts explore in some depth the city, its people, and the culture—
primarily art—which emanated from it.
        SR, 27:1:171-2   R: Albert J. Schmidt

Imperial Russia

594. Alexander, John T. **Autocratic Politics in a National Crisis: The
     Imperial Russian Government and Pugachev's Revolt, 1773-1775**.
     Bloomington, Indiana University Press, for the International Affairs
     Center, 1969. 346p. (Russian and East European Series, vol. 38).
     $8.50pa.

As the title indicates, the focus of this study is on the government's reaction
to the revolt and on the measures taken to quell it and to deal with the institutional weaknesses laid bare by Pugachev's initial successes. Alexander's documentation is impressive in its completeness and breadth. He makes several interesting
observations, and he agrees with the conclusion reached by the investigating
commissions that there was no foreign intrigue or collusion behind Pugachev's
rising. The author shows that Catherine contemplated tactics of military and
diplomatic retreat in the last stages of the war with Turkey out of a desire to
free her hands to deal with Pugachev. In its limited purpose of accounting for

the concrete responses of the imperial government to the Pugachev revolt,
Alexander's book succeeds very well and will be of great value to students.

      SR, 29:3:507-8   R: Marc Raeff

595.   Alexander, John T. **Emperor of the Cossacks: Pugachev and the Frontier
          Jacquerie of 1773-1775.** Lawrence, Kans., Coronado Press, 1973.
          245p. $8.50.

Despite the book's title, Alexander has written what amounts to a chronological
narrative of the military events encompassing the *Pugachevshchina*, rather than
a biography of the instigator of the rebellion. The author concludes with an
attempt to introduce a comparative historical perspective, based on current
social science categories and terminology. The book is pleasantly written and
despite its narrow focus, readers will turn to it as a convenient English-language
account of the rebellion.

      SR, 34:1:142-3   R: David M. Griffiths

596.   Avrich, Paul. **Russian Rebels, 1600-1800.** New York, Schocken Books,
          1972. 309p. $10.00.

This study is an attempt to further explain and search for additional causes and
explanations of the Bolshevik revolution reaching as far back as two centuries.
Avrich discusses in detail the better-known rebels: Bolotnikov, Razin, Bulavin,
and Pugachev. Employing comparative and analytical insights, the author provides
a deeper understanding of the nature of all major Russian rebellions during the
17th and 18th centuries. The work is suitable for undergraduate students and
complements general textbooks.

      History, RNB, 1:4:84   R: Stephan M. Morak

597.   Barker, A. J. **The War against Russia, 1854-1856.** New York, Holt,
          Rinehart & Winston, 1971. 348p. $7.95.

Colonel Barker has written an interesting and lively book about the Crimean
War. He gives an excellent comparison of the British and French armies, in which
the former proved inferior in leadership, provisioning and housing the men,
and care of the wounded. The book is provided with a number of excellent
maps.

      SR, 31:1:155-6   R: John Shelton Curtiss

598.   Dukes, Paul. **Catherine the Great and the Russian Nobility: A Study
          Based on the Materials of the Legislative Commission of 1767.** New
          York, Cambridge University Press, 1967. 269p. $9.50.

The book begins with a useful sketch of the Russian government and nobility
prior to 1767. Next, the machinery of the commission is described in accurate
detail. Official policies toward economics, government, society, and culture
are reviewed, and opinions of the nobility about these same subjects are
presented. Finally, the influence of the commission on the rest of Catherine's
reign is assessed. In none of this can the author claim great originality; he picks
his way nicely among older historical authorities, using their arguments to settle
questions of interpretation. As for his source material, Dukes is interested only
in what the nobility said.

      SR, 27:4:645-6   R: Wilson R. Augustine

599.   Emmons, Terence. **The Russian Landed Gentry and the Peasant Emancipation of 1861**. Cambridge, Cambridge University Press, 1968. 484p. $13.50.

Aside from being informative and useful for students in Russian history courses, the study contains an insight into the Emancipation. Emmons gives almost all his attention to the liberal program, leaving corporate consciousness and heritage to the side, but he notes the close connection between all three phenomena and thereby makes his work a perceptive case study in the development of public opinion as well as a historical monograph. What is chiefly of interest in the book is the story of how the gentry's experience in 1856-1862 led many of them to find liberal principles meaningful.

SR, 29:3:512-3   R: George Yaney

600.   Fisher, Alan W. **The Russian Annexation of the Crimea, 1772-1783**. Cambridge, Cambridge University Press, 1970. 180p. $9.50.

This is a good narrative of the struggle of two powers to dominate the Crimea. Fisher has uncovered a wealth of information from Turkish archives and from published Turkish and Russian sources. He describes the problems of the Crimean peoples, who wished merely to follow their own interests, the Ottoman Empire which endeavored to maintain its hegemony, and the Russian Empire which sought to supplant it. Fisher is at his best when dealing with Ottoman and Crimean subjects.

SR, 30:2:392   R: Herbert H. Kaplan

601.   Golovin, Ivan G. **Russia under the Autocrat, Nicholas the First**. Intro. by Harry Schwartz, gen. ed. 2 vol. in 1. New York, Praeger, 1970 (Repr. of the 1846 ed.). 340p. (Praeger Scholarly Reprints, Source Books and Studies in Russian and Soviet History). $27.00.

This is more a personal account about Nicholas I's reign than a history in the traditional sense. Golovin is sharply critical of Nicholas's autocratic rule. He not only describes the general state of affairs in Russia during Nicholas' era, but also provides detailed insights into the function of the tsarist court. Golovin eventually emigrated to Lithuania, where he died. The author's personal experiences, which are expressed quite freely, are of great value to the historian of nineteenth century Russia.   S. M. H.

602.   Harcave, Sidney. **Years of the Golden Cockerel: The Last Romanov Tsars, 1814-1917**. New York, Macmillan, 1968. 515p. $12.50.

This study covers approximately a century of Romanov rule from Alexander I to the fall of Nicholas II and should have been entitled "The Decline and Fall of Russian Autocracy." To the average reader it is a fascinating and bewildering tale of political incapacity, overconfidence, and self-deception. The last century of Russian autocracy represented a trail that led logically, though not fatalistically, to catastrophe. The story of the last five reigns is presented succinctly, lucidly, and soundly. Great Russian nationalism, of course, while it soothed injured pride, often blinded political behavior; therein lies much of the tragedy of the last phase of Russian autocracy as rightly presented by this study.

AHR, 74:5:1663-5   R: Anatole G. Mazour

603. Harrison, John A. **The Founding of the Russian Empire in Asia and America**. Coral Gables, Fla., University of Miami Press, 1971. 156p. $7.95.

The author summarizes the history of the Russian drive across northern Asia and the northern Pacific from the ninth to the nineteenth century. He does so in three logical parts: 1) "The Land and the People"; 2) "The Gathering of Russia"; 3) "The Moving Frontier." Harrison succeeded in reducing a highly complex subject to a coherent narrative that can be understood and followed with interest by college students.

SR, 31:4:892   R: George Alexander Lensen

604. Jones, Robert E. **The Emancipation of the Russian Nobility, 1762-1785**. Princeton, Princeton University Press, 1973. 326p. $12.50.

This monograph is an expansion of Jones's doctoral dissertation. It explores various stages in the formulation of state policy toward the nobility during the period between the Manifesto of 1762, which offered noble servitors a conditional opportunity to leave state service, and the Charter of 1785, which redefined the group's legal and political status. Catherine's policies toward the nobility, Jones argues, owed less to the strength of noble opposition than to problems "she encountered in trying to provide Russia especially the vast and under-developed provinces, with a government capable of defending and promoting the national interest." The author's aim is "to relate Catherine's treatment of the nobility to the goals of her domestic policy and to her perception of the state's interests."

SR, 34:1:141-2   R: Joan Afferica

605. Kaplan, Herbert H. **Russia and the Outbreak of the Seven Years' War**. Berkeley, University of California Press, 1968. 165p. $5.75.

Employing a great deal of fresh source material, Kaplan skillfully pieces together the chain of events leading to the war. After noting how Empress Elizabeth had considered plans for partitioning Prussia as early as 1753, the narrative jumps ahead to 1755 and follows month by month the development of the empress's aggressive designs: the negotiation of the Anglo-Russian Subsidy Treaty, then its effective nullification by Russia, the rapprochement with France, the working of an offensive alliance with Austria, and finally, the initiation by Russia of the general European mobilization. The study represents a welcome and more than satisfactory response to the challenge issued by Professor Butterfield in 1955 to take an entirely new approach to the problem of the origin of the Seven Years' War.

SR, 28:1:129-30   R: David Lorimer Rankel

606. Kliuchevskii, Vasilii. **The Rise of the Romanovs**. Trans. and ed. by Liliana Archibald. London, Macmillan, 1970. 371p. $12.50.

According to A. G. Mazour (*Modern Russian Historiography*), Kliuchevskii, a student of S. M. Soloviev, is the most capable *Geschichtsmaler*, who embodies in his historical writing of supreme excellence a summary of all the efforts of Russian historians, beginning with Tatishchev in the eighteenth century." He did not show "any interest in problems of national minorities incorporated within the Empire, not even the Ukrainian people; he was truly a Great Russian historian." Kliuchevskii is representative of the methodological legal state school of thought, which considered the state to be the promoter of history. Discounting the role of the people, he is occasionally critical of some tsars and boyars, though not because of their indifference to the masses, but only when they failed to protect and promote the interests of the Russian Empire. The work, while concentrating mostly on the "Time of Troubles" and the reign of the first three Romanovs, reflects Kliuchevskii's almost exclusive preoccupation with Russia's expansion to the South, West, and into Asia. He glorifies conquests and finds no sympathy for victims.

UQ, 26:3-4:320-2   R: Stephan M. Horak

607. Kornilov, Aleksandr. **Modern Russian History from the Age of Catherine the Great to the End of the Nineteenth Century.** 2 vols. Trans. by Alexander S. Kaun. Bibliography by John S. Curtiss. New York, Russell & Russell, 1970 (1943). 310p. 284p. $20.00.

(Listed in P. Horecky's *Russia and the Soviet Union*, #506). Kornilov's work, *Modern Russian History, Being a Detailed History of Russia from the Age of Catherine the Great to the Revolution of 1917*, was translated by Alexander Kaun, with an introduction and a classified bibliography by Geroid T. Robinson, (New York, Knopf, 1924). Though somewhat neglectful of foreign affairs, the author offered a well-informed narrative of Russia's internal affairs during the nineteenth century, but he is sharply critical of the tsarist regime. This latest edition should be welcomed by all academic libraries that were unable to secure copies of the earlier editions.   S. M. H.

608. McConnell, Allen. **Tsar Alexander I: Paternalistic Reformer.** New York, Thomas Y. Crowell, 1970. 232p. $2.25pa.

In this brief biography, designed primarily for use in undergraduate history courses, McConnell has synthesized the vast bibliography of older wroks on Alexander I's reign as well as a number of recent works on some of the less well known aspects of the Alexandrine age. Although the book contains little that will startle scholars working on this period, it will certainly help destroy various stereotypes long cherished by nonspecialists, such as division of Alexander's reign into clear-cut "liberal" and "reactionary" phases. This volume will serve as an excellent supplementary text for courses in Russian history.

SR, 30:2:392-3   R: Judith Cohen Zacek

609. Mazour, Anatole G. **The First Russian Revolution, 1825. The Decembrist Movement, Its Origins, Development and Significance.** Stanford, Stanford University Press, 1965 (1937). 328p.

This work remains the only significant study of the Decembrists in English. The only change is the addition of a bibliographical supplement (compiled in 1961).

SEER, 45:105:558-9   R: Barry Hollingsworth

610. Mehlinger, Howard D., and John M. Thompson. **Count Witte and the Tsarist Government in the 1905 Revolution.** Bloomington, Indiana University Press, 1972. 434p. $17.50.

Deliberately eschewing any attempt at an all-inclusive analysis of Witte's historical role, Mehlinger and Thompson have limited their study to the crucial six
months in Witte's career which extended from the October Manifesto of 1905,
in the drafting of which he had a hand, to his forced retirement from the newly
created post of Chairman of the Council of Ministers in April 1906. Within this
restricted time span, however, their scrutiny of the historical record is intense
and rewarding. They have made effective use not only of the published materials
on Witte and the 1905 Revolution, but also of archival materials in the Soviet
Union and the West, incluidng the manuscript copy of Witte's *Memoirs* which
is one of the most valuable holdings in the Archive of Russian and East European
History and Culture at Columbia University.

        CSP, 15:4:584-5   R: Robert M. Slusser

611.   Oberländer, Erwin, et al., eds. **Russia Enters the Twentieth Century,**
           1894-1917. Trans. by Gerald Onn. New York, Schocken Books, 1971.
           352p. $12.00.

This collective work, by thirteen authors from Germany and Britain, appeared
first in German a year earlier than the English edition. It contains a lot of
information which would be useful to students, covering a wide range of political,
legal, economic, and cultural problems, taken essentially from the last two
decades of the imperial Russian regime. The part of the book which the student
is likely to find most useful is the last four chapters, which deal with intellectual,
religious, and cultural trends. Less satisfactory are chapters dealing with non-
Russian peoples.

        SR, 31:2:421-2   R: Hugh Seton-Watson

612.   Oliva, L. Jay. **Misalliance: A Study of French Policy in Russia during**
           the Seven Years' War. New York, New York University Press, 1964.
           218p. $6.00.

The author's purpose is "to analyze the origins, content, character, and results
of French policy in Russia from 1755 to 1762, in order to discover whether there
ever existed in the Franco-Russian relationship any elements of mutuality,
desirability, or durability." The author has fulfilled his promise in a lucid and
well-written exposition. Whereas France and Russia had both agreed to wage war
against Frederick II, they could not agree on the way it should be conducted
or on its purpose. After several years of military campaigns in which France
had suffered many defeats, she wanted peace—almost at any price. Russia, on
the other hand, was bent on further victories and wanted unrestricted freedom
in deciding the terms and time of peace negotiations. In the outcome France's
loss of influence and power in Europe was exacerbated by her defeats in the
colonies. France's disastrous policy allowed Russia to gain considerably in north
and eastern Europe.

        SR, 24:1:127-8   R: Herbert H. Kaplan

613.   Oliva, L. Jay. **Russia in the Era of Peter the Great.** Englewood Cliffs,
           N.J., Prentice-Hall, 1969. 184p. $5.95.

This volume may herald a new trend in classroom-oriented writing on Russian
history—away from the orthodox survey toward reinterpretations of more
restricted periods and topics. Addressed to students and general readers, the

author's concise study has something to offer the specialist, too. Its strengths include clarity of perspective, balance of generalization and specifics, and sprightly writing. He concentrates on the era rather than the man; he analyzes Petrine policies against the backdrop of early modern Europe. Also stimulating are his analysis of Petrine politics, especially the role of the nobility therein, and his examination of the social forces that supported and opposed Peter's reforms.

> SR, 29:3:505-6   R: John T. Alexander

614.   Papmehl, K. A. **Freedom of Expression in Eighteenth Century Russia.** The Hague, Martinus Nijhoff, 1971. 166p. 26Dglds. Paper.

This brief study is a welcome addition to the growing literature on Catherine's policies. Much of the story will be familiar to scholars—the increasing secularization of culture, the rapid increase in media of expression, the Legislative Commission's work, the law permitting private presses, and the repression of critics Radishchev and Novkov. But the author gives an unmatched account of the confusion of authorities vested with embryo censorship powers, of the trial and error that marked the moves of government and writers, and the unrecognized and changing assumptions on both sides.

> SR, 31:4:888-9   R: Allen McConnell

615.   Platonov, S. F. **Boris Godunov: Tsar of Russia.** Trans. from the Russian by L. Rex Pyles. Intro. by John T. Alexander. Gulf Breeze, Fla., Academic International Press, 1973 (Leningrad, 1921). 230p. (The Russian Series, vol. 10). $12.50.

By way of an introduction to *Boris Godunov*, Alexander contributes a well-researched, brisk, and informative account of Platonov's life and work—perhaps the most substantial to date in any language. Pyles' translation is passable, but marked by some awkwardness and occasional errors. Platonov's narratives sometimes have an old-fashioned ring, but they are basically clear and well told.

> SR, 34:2:383-4   R: Samuel H. Baron

616.   Presniakov, A. E. **Emperor Nicholas I of Russia: The Apogee of Autocracy, 1825-1855.** Ed. and trans. by Judith C. Zacek. With "Nicholas I and the Course of Russian History" by Nicholas V. Riasanovsky. Gulf Breeze, Fla., Academic International Press, 1974 (Leningrad, 1925). 102p. (The Russian Series, 23). $10.00.

Presniakov's essay on Nicholas I, written between 1923 and 1925, is "an interpretive essay which deals selectively with many features of the ruler's personality, purposes, programs, and policies," according to the translator. This is a valuable and stimulating piece of work and its translation should be a welcome addition to the literature for the English-speaking student. The translation is well done, and the book is enhanced by a brief essay by N. V. Riasanovsky.   S. M. H.

617.   Quested, R. K. I. **The Expansion of Russia in East Asia, 1857-1860.** Kuala Lumpur, University of Malaya Press, 1968. 339p. $9.75.

The seizure of the Far Eastern provinces, the subject of this volume, represents the biggest mouthful of the Chinese Empire that Russia was ever able to devour and digest. Quested has based her study upon many official documents—Russian, Chinese, British, French, and American. The period covered has not been comprehensively surveyed until now, even though the passing of this vast area to Russia was certainly one of the decisive events in the history of the Far East. Although the book encompasses a great deal of detail, the author has given a clear overall picture of the developments in policy-making at the diplomatic level without repeating slices of material found in published works in European languages.

SR, 29:2:311-2   R: Betty Miller Unterberger

618.   Raeff, Marc, ed. **Catherine the Great: A Profile.** New York, Hill and Wang, 1972. 331p. (World Profiles series). $6.50cl.; $2.45pa.

Raeff has made an effort to overcome the dearth of English-language scholarship on Catherine II by offering us a collection of twelve essays (ten in translation) designed to elucidate "most particularly Catherine's intellectual development and accomplishments and her influence on contemporary Russian cultural and social life." The essays read smoothly, and the translations are generally accurate. This volume stands as the most convenient and useful collection of scholarly essays on Catherine II available in any language.

SR, 31:4:886-7   R: David M. Griffiths

619.   Raeff, Marc. **The Decembrist Movement.** Englewood Cliffs, N.J., Prentice-Hall, 1966. 180p. (Russian Civilization series). $4.95cl.; $2.95pa.

The volume starts with an introduction by Raeff, followed by quotations from various sources, official accounts, testimonies, and constitutional projects drawn up by the Decembrists, and it ends with Pushkin's well-known poem, "Message to Siberia." The bibliography is rather perfunctory.

SR, 27:1:136   R: Anatole G. Mazour

620.   Raeff, Marc. **Imperial Russia, 1682-1825: The Coming of Age of Modern Russia.** New York, Knopf, 1971. 176p. (Borzoi History of Russia, vol. 4). $2.95pa.

This is the first of six volumes which together will comprise a new general history of Russia. The stated purpose of the series is to "overcome the main fault of general histories—the attempt on the part of one historian to cover the whole span of a complex and very long process within a very large society." In this volume Raeff is offering a compendium of his work and thought. He has taken essays scattered in numerous publications and brought them into a single brief volume. It should provide useful supplementary reading for courses on the middle period of Russian history to inform students of the views of our leading specialists on eighteenth-century Russia.

SR, 32:2:376-7   R: David L. Ransel

621.   Raeff, Marc, ed. **Peter the Great Changes Russia.** 2nd ed. Lexington, Mass., D. C. Heath, 1972 (1963). 199p. $2.50. (First published in 1963 under the title *Peter the Great, Reformer or Revolutionary?*) 109p.

Raeff's introduction, stressing the background of Russia prior to Peter's reign and the nature of Peter's reforms, is followed by a selection of excerpts from Russian and Western historians who examine various aspects and impacts of his reforms upon Russia's history and development. The conflicting views and interpretations of Peter's performance make excellent supplementary reading in survey courses on Russian history. The new edition includes an updated bibliographical survey. Numerous notes explain terms and nomenclatures and offer short characteristics of each contribution in terms of importance, views, and interpretation.   S. M. H.

622.   Raeff, Marc. **Plans for Political Reform in Imperial Russia, 1730-1905**. Englewood Cliffs, N.J., Prentice-Hall, 1966. 159p. (Russian Civilization series). $4.95cl.; $2.95pa.

This slender book begins with an introduction, comprising about a fourth of the contents, followed by documentary evidence of one sort or another. Among the sources gathered are the Russian "Magna Carta," or the "Conditions" which a group of members of the Supreme Privy Council fruitlessly attempted to impose on Empress Anna in 1730; there is the Panin Memorandum of 1762, representing the equally futile effort to curb arbitrary autocratic power in Russia; there are citations from Speranskii's constitutional projects and memoranda and similar documents relating to political reforms throughout the nineteenth century. The collection ends with the official pronouncement establishing the State Duma in 1905. There is a concise, admirably selected critical bibliography.

     SR, 27:1:135-6   R: Anatole G. Mazour

623.   Saul, Norman E. **Russia and the Mediterranean, 1797-1807**.   Chicago, University of Chicago Press, 1970. 268p. $8.75.

The book is a detailed study of diplomacy and war during the critical decade that opened with Napoleon's thrust into the Mediterranean and closed with the Peace of Tilsit. This decade witnessed an unprecedented alliance between Russia and the Ottoman Empire. Saul succeeds, through meticulous analysis of an impressive amount of archival material and other primary sources, in proving the existence of an intimate relationship between Russia's involvement in the Napoleonic wars and its interest in the Mediterranean and the Ottoman Empire. He presents a detailed, close study of intricate personal relations which influenced policy-making. His conclusions are concise and clearly drawn. The book is certainly a most valuable addition to the historical literature on the Russian thrust into the Mediterranean, and to the history of the diplomacy of the Napoleonic era.

     SR, 30:1:142-3   R: Ben-Cion Pinchuk

624.   Seton-Watson, Hugh. **The Russian Empire: 1801-1917**. Oxford, Clarendon Press, 1967. 813p. (Oxford History of Modern Europe). $10.00; text ed., $8.00.

This book may be considered to supersede the author's *The Decline of Imperial Russia, 1855-1914* (1952). It is based on a wealth of material, including sources and monographs, Russian and foreign. Its foremost virtue is objectivity; the author tries to give everyone the credit he deserves. He is especially careful about telling the story of the non-Russian borderlands, from Finland and the Baltic areas to the usually neglected Caucasus and Central Asia.

      AHR, 73:4:1201-2   R: Donald W. Treadgold

625.   Stavrou, Theofanis George, ed. **Russia under the Last Tsar**. Minneapolis, University of Minnesota Press, 1969. 265p. $7.50cl.; $2.45pa.

Most of the eight essays comprising this volume (originally lectures) will give the enterprising student enough material to enable him to sound as if he has read the authors at greater depth. Three essays bear on the question of Russia's constitutional development. Others deal with Pobedonostsev, Russian radical thought, development of science in Russia, and with the foreign policy in 1894-1914.

      SR, 29:1:107-8   R: George L. Yaney

626.   Tarlé, E. V. **Napoleon's Invasion of Russia, 1812**. New York, Octagon Books, 1971 (1942). 422p. $13.00.

The author, one of the most controversial Russian historians of modern times, who was also responsible for the purges of those historians who refused to become tools of Marxist dogma, is a well-known authority on Napoleon's invasion of Russia and the French Revolution. But in 1931 he too fell victim to the regime for his "errors"; he had identified Soviet foreign policy with that of tsarist Russia. Still later (1937), after Pokrovskii had been dethroned, Tarlé was summoned back to Moscow from his place of banishment. In *Napoleon's Invasion of Russia*, in contrast to his previous statements, the author concluded that the war against Napoleon was "solidly a national war." Tarlé initiated the glorification of Russia's past, subordinating history to official Stalinist policy.   S. M. H.

627.   Trotsky, Leon. **1905**. Trans. by Anya Bostock. New York, Random House, 1971. 488p. (Studies in the Third World Books). $15.00.

Bostock's smooth and accurate translation makes available in English this classic study of the Revolution of 1905, first published in German in 1908. The translation is from the 1922 Russian edition, which contains additional speeches and essays on the subject, composed by Trotsky between 1907 and 1922, as well as a vivid personal account of his exile in Siberia and subsequent escape. The book continues to be a significant historical source on the development of Trotsky's ideas and the polemics which grew up around them following that revolution.

      SR, 32:4:817-8   R: David A. Davies

628.   Warner, Philip. **The Crimean War: A Reappraisal**. New York, Taplinger, 1973. 232p. $9.95.

The author, in trying to correct some of the common errors about the Crimean War, has not been entirely successful, especially in his treatment of the diplomacy. The treatment of the campaign is better. He shows the British lack of planning and organization that proved so costly. The narrative is on the whole accurate. The British, who did poorly in 1855 and failed dismally in the final assault, lost much prestige. The Turks made a miserable showing. On the whole, an accurate judgment.

      SR, 33:1:135   R: John Shelton Curtiss

Revolution and Civil War

629.   Adams, Arthur E., ed. **The Russian Revolution and Bolshevik Victory**: **Causes and Processes**. 2nd ed. Lexington, Mass., D. C. Heath, 1972. (1960). 196p. $2.50pa.
While the first edition of this volume concentrates on the question of "why and how" the second revised and enlarged edition brings together essays, written by Western and Soviet authors, related to the "causes and processes." Such a confrontation of different and often conflicting views helps the student of Soviet history to realize the basic differences inherent in Western and Soviet thought, interpretation of history, and its meaning. This book should stimulate further discussions and questions among student and general readers alike.

S. M. H.

630.   Avrich, Paul, ed. **The Anarchists in the Russian Revolution**. Ithaca, Cornell University Press, 1973. 179p. $6.95cl.; $2.95pa.
These primary sources contain many documents appearing for the first time in English. They cover aspects of anarchist thought from workers' control to the future society. Most of the selections originated in 1917-1918 and come from the anarchist press; a few articles from the 1919-1921 period are also included. The documents reveal a political naiveté perhaps unsurpassed in the modern revolutionary movement.

CSP, 16:1:109-11   R: Charles Duval

631.   Bradley, John. **Allied Intervention in Russia, (1917-1920)**. New York, Basic Books, 1968. 251p. $6.50.
Bradley's book relates mainly the correspondence between the leaders of the Western governments and their diplomatic and military agents in Russia. Based chiefly on unpublished documents from British, French, and American archives, the book includes a bibliography and an index of personal names. The story starts with Allied efforts to get in touch with both the Bolsheviks and their Russian opposition, initially to restore the eastern front, possibly with Japanese help. To strengthen their weak Red Army, the Bolsheviks formed international Red units from war prisoners, which "ultimately consisted of some twelve nationalities and amounted to 182,000 men."

SR, 28:4:648-9   R: Sergei G. Pushkarev

632.   Brinkley, George A. **The Volunteer Army and Allied Intervention in South Russia, 1917-1921. A Study in the Politics and Diplomacy of the Russian Civil War**. Notre Dame, University of Notre Dame Press, 1966. 446p. $8.95.
The book is a political and diplomatic history of the civil war in southern Russia, focusing on "the interrelations between the intervening Powers and the Volunteer Army." It is a remarkable work of historical scholarship. The impressive bibliography also includes rich unpublished materials from the Columbia University Russian Archives and the Hoover Institution Library. Brinkley states that "Great Russian chauvinism" precluded a compromise between the Whites and the non-Russian nationalities striving for political independence.

SR, 28:4:648-9   R: Sergei G. Pushkarev

633. Daniels, Robert V. **Red October: The Bolshevik Revolution of 1917.**
New York, Charles Scribner's Sons, 1967. 271p. $6.95.
Daniels has set out to separate myth from reality in the October Revolution,
and all who value truth will be indebted to him. Instead of the inexorable march
of the masses toward inevitable victory, we see confusion on every hand, even
in the Bolshevik organization, and a welter of humanity as little willing to defend
the Provisional Government as to install the Bolsheviks in power. In the last
analysis, the Soviet regime is born as a result of chance developments and the
fact that the Bolsheviks are less disorganized than their enemies. There are
illustrations and charts; there is a bibliography with annotations, an index, and
a map of Petersburg; particularly useful is a chronology of events, clear and well
chosen. In every respect the book deserves a wider than college audience; it is
recommended also for the general reader and especially for secondary school
teachers.
SR, 29:3:518-9   R: Oliver H. Radkey

634. Daniels, Robert V., ed. **The Russian Revolution.** Englewood Cliffs,
N.J., Prentice-Hall, 1972. 184p. $5.95cl.; $2.95pa.
Historiographically speaking, Daniels has come closer than almost any other
scholar to making the Russian Revolution his own. His two best known publications, *The Conscience of the Revolution* and *Red October*, are authoritative
studies of the earliest years of the Soviet regime. This is a book of selected
extracts from older published accounts of the revolutionary year. There are
six sections: "The Fall of the Tsar," "The Provisional Government in Crisis,"
"The Social Revolution," "The Bolsheviks Prepare," "The October Uprising"
and "The Consolidation of Soviet Power." The selections bring out the flavor
of 1917, the folly, skill, desperation, and luck of its major participants, and the
all-engulfing compass of the revolution for the Russian people.
CSP, 15:3:398-9   R: Robert H. Johnston

635. Dziewanowski, M. K., ed. **The Russian Revolution: An Anthology.**
New York, Thomas Crowell, 1970. 222p. $3.25pa.
According to the editor, the purpose of this anthology on the Revolution is
"to present to American students seven selected passages from outstanding
writings about its crucial phases or aspects." It includes: "The Fall of the
Russian Monarch," by Sir Bernard Pares; "The Liberal Revolution Reappraised
by a Russian Conservative: The Conspirational Theory" (Katkov); "Lenin's
Return to Petrograd" (Sukharov); "The Kornilov Mutiny" (Chamberlin);
"The Capture of the Winter Palace" (Trotsky); "The Bolshevik Gamble"
(R. V. Daniels); and "The Bolsheviks in Power: The First Day" (J. Reed).
A chronological table and a selected bibliography enhance this well-balanced
anthology.   S. M. H.

636. Kenez, Peter. **Civil War in South Russia, 1918: The First Year of the
Volunteer Army.** Berkeley, University of California Press, 1971.
351p. $10.00.
This monograph represents the best study of the subject, and future writers on
the Civil War will have to turn to it. Like others, Kenez believes that the White
Russian forces were doomed to fail for two basic reasons: first, because their

leaders were unable to develop a program that might appeal to the masses; and second, because their Russian nationalism blinded them to the reality of imperial disintegration, thus making them unable to cooperate with the other major non-Bolshevik force, the national minorities.

   SR, 31:4:897-8   R: John M. Thompson

637. Melgunov, S. P. **The Bolshevik Seizure of Power.** Ed. and abridged by
   Boris S. Pushkarev. Trans. by James S. Beaver. Santa Barbara, American
   Bibliographical Center—Clio Press, 1972. 260p. $15.00cl.; $5.50pa.

Sergei Melgunov (1880-1956), well-known Russian historian and ardent foe of the Bolsheviks in 1917 and during the Civil War, continued his efforts to expose the Communists after his emigration from Soviet Russia in 1923 in such works as *Krasnyi terror v Rossii, 1918-1923*, and *Kak Bol'sheviki zakhvatili vlast'*, published in English as *The Bolshevik Seizure of Power*. This book is based on the study of contemporary newspapers, documents, and memoirs, as well as the author's own experiences. Central to Melgunov's view of the Revolution is the belief that the Bolsheviks, liberally subsidized by the Germans, were able to seize power in 1917 largely because of the failure of their rivals to take the threat of Bolshevism seriously and to provide adequate protection for the government.

   SR, 34:2:396   R: Alexander Rabinowitch

638. Miliukov, Paul. **Russia and Its Crisis.** Foreword by Donald W. Treadgold.
   London, Collier Books, Collier-Macmillan, 1969 (Repr. of 1962 ed.).
   416p. $2.95pa.

(Listed in P. Horecky's *Russia and the Soviet Union*, #134).

639. Mohrenschildt, Dimitri von, ed. **The Russian Revolution of 1917:**
   Contemporary Accounts. New York, Oxford University Press, 1971.
   320p. $8.95cl.; $3.50pa.

All but eight of the twenty-three articles in this collection have appeared in past issues of von Mohrenschildt's journal, *The Russian Review*. The eight remaining are extracts from published memoirs and histories of participants in or spectators of the tumultuous events of the revolutionary year or its immediate prelude. For better emphasis, they are divided into three sections: "On the Eve of the Revolution," "The Revolution and the Civil War," and "Epilogue."

   CSP, 14:2:372-3   R: Robert H. Johnston

640. Page, Stanley W., ed. **Russia in Revolution: Selected Readings in**
   Russian Domestic History since 1855. Princeton, N.J., Van Nostrand,
   1965. 299p. $3.75pa.

The editor includes several essays which illustrate the conditions which led to the Revolution of 1917. Five major sections present the views of contemporaries, latter-day historians, and other writers. Some of the readings are translated here for the first time. This volume can serve the beginning student of Russian history as useful supplementary literature.   S. M. H.

641. Pethybridge, Roger. **The Spread of the Russian Revolution: Essays on 1917.** London, Macmillan; New York, St. Martin's Press, 1972. 238p. $11.95.

The author has provided a brief and illuminating description of Russia in 1917 as a basically static society in which the means of mass communication, transportation, and distribution were inadequately developed. In general, the problems created by Russia's technological backwardness and widespread illiteracy are particularly well treated in essays on "Supplies," "The Press," and "Propaganda and Political Rumors." The book contains the traditional, incorrect assumption that the peasant "came as an afterthought" for Lenin.

      SR, 32:2:387   R: Esther Kingston-Mann

642. Pipes, Richard, ed. **Revolutionary Russia.** Cambridge, Harvard University Press, 1968. 365p. (Russian Research Center Studies, 55). $7.95.

The most novel contributions in this symposium (consisting of thirteen papers presented at Harvard University in 1967) are in the first of three categories into which the editor classifies the papers of his co-conferees—narrative studies, speculative essays, and analytical investigations of the motives of the revolutionaries. Among the contributors are: G. Katkov, J. Keep, J. Erickson, G. Kennan, E. H. Carr, A. Ulam, L. Shapiron and others.

      SR, 28:1:138-9   R: Robert V. Daniels

643. Rabinowitch, Alexander. **Prelude to Revolution: The Petrograd Bolsheviks and the July 1917 Uprising.** Bloomington, Indiana University Press, 1968. 229p. (Indiana University International Studies). $8.50.

The main problem—whether the Bolsheviks had provoked and organized the July demonstrations—is answered in this study clearly: Rabinowtich believes that a section of the Bolshevik party connected with the military organization and the Petersburg Bolshevik Committee was systematically preparing the disturbances which broke out on July 3, while at the same time the central committee of the party did all in its power to create the impression of urging on the soldiers and workers of Petrograd restraint and peaceful methods of political struggle in the extremely permissive conditions under the Provisional Government.

      SR, 31:4:896-7   R: George Katkov

644. Reed, John. **Ten Days That Shook the World.** Foreword by V. I. Lenin. Intro. by Granville Hicks. [New York, Modern Library, 1935.] New York, Random House, Vintage Books, 1965. 371p. $1.45pa.

The American journalist J. Reed, who later became a Communist, managed to get to Russia in time to witness the October Revolution. In this book he gives a detailed day-by-day account of events as they took place during that fateful time. This is an illuminating historical document that has become part of the essential literature for that period. It includes numerous original documents and propaganda leaflets not available anywhere else. Reed's enthusiasm for the Bolsheviks does not diminish the value of this rare first-hand account.

                            S. M. H.

645. Rosenberg, William G. **Liberals in the Russian Revolution: The Constitutional Democratic Party, 1917-1921.** Princeton, Princeton University Press, 1974. 534p. $25.00cl.; $9.75pa.

In this history of the Kadets, Rosenberg has combined great erudition and good sense to chronicle in considerable detail the failure of the most prominent party of political liberals in a twentieth-century revolution. The book is essentially comprised of two parts, one following in considerable detail the activities of the Kadets between February and October of 1917, the other the relations of the Kadets with the major anti-Bolshevik forces during the Civil War. The two main parts are supplemented by a background chapter on the party and two chapters on the dissolution of the party in emigration. This is as near a definitive history of the Kadets as might be hoped for.

RR, 34:2:212-3   R: Daniel Mulholland

646. Shukman, Harold. **Lenin and the Russian Revolution.** New York, G. P. Putnam's Sons, 1967. 224p. $5.95.

The author attempts "to set out the main course of the events which broadly constituted the revolutionary situation . . . in Russia during the last twenty years or so of Tsarist rule." The narrative of these events in concise and clear, and is notable for its critical balance. The author finds the tsarist government guilty of "an overweening propensity to govern solely through a centralized bureaucracy at a time when modernization was synonymous with democratisation," but he is equally critical of a political opposition which "clung to the idea of revolution, regardless of changes which may have rendered their point of view socially irrelevant."

SR, 31:2:427   R: Herbert J. Ellison

647. White, John Albert. **The Siberian Intervention.** New York, Greenwood Press, 1969 (1950). 471p. $15.25.

The author offers the most comprehensive treatment of the history of the Allied intervention in the Russian Revolution from 1918 to 1922. Although several other studies discussing the problem of intervention have been published since, this one still deserves its place on college libraries' shelves for its comprehensiveness, detailed treatment of various aspects, and its objectivity in the handling of such a sensitive topic. The main value, however, lies in the author's concentration on the Asiatic theatre of the civil war and intervention.

S. M. H.

648. Williams, Albert Rhys. **Journey into Revolution: Petrograd, 1917-1918.** Ed. by Lucita Williams. Foreword by Josephine Herbst. Chicago, Quadrangle Books, 1969. 346p. $8.95.

Williams was one of a small band of radical young journalists from the United States, veteranas of the American socialist and pacifist movements, who were drawn to Russia in the aftermath of the February Revolution. A onetime Congregational minister, Williams was a correspondent for the *New York Evening Post* when he arrived in Petrograd in early June 1917, knowing little about Russia and her past and speaking no Russian whatever. He was won almost immediately to the side of the Bolsheviks. Like his companion John Reed, Williams viewed the socialist struggle in Russia as his own. His first memoir

of events in 1917-1918, *Through the Russian Revolution*, a highly impressionistic glorification of the October Revolution, appeared in 1921. He was expanding and reworking this account at the time of his death. *Journey into Revolution*
is the product of this effort as brought to fruition by Williams' wife, Lucita.
While retaining the tendentious, propagandistic quality of its predecessor, this
book constitutes a significantly more ambitious and sophisticated attempt to
interpret the Russian Revolution to the Western public.

      SR, 29:1:93-4   R: Alexander Rabinowitch

RSFSR and USSR

649.   Amalrik, Andrei. **Will the Soviet Union Survive until 1984?** Preface
        by Henry Kamm. Commentary by Sidney Monas. New York, Harper
        & Row, 1970. 93p. $4.95.

Amalrik rejects as unrealistic wishful thinking the Western expectation of an
"inevitable liberalization" of the Soviet system or its "convergence with liberal
democracies." He seeks an analogy between the present Soviet regime and that
of Nicholas II on the eve of the revolution of 1905 and 1917. In the second
part of his essay, Amalrik develops his apocalyptic vision of the "inevitable"
Sino-Soviet war and the resulting collapse of the Soviet regime, accompanied
by internal anarchy and strife and the "break-up of the Russian Empire."

      RR, 29:2:328-35   R: Bohdan Bociurkiv

650.   Avrich, Paul. **Kronstadt 1921**. Princeton, Princeton University Press,
        1970. 271p. (Studies of the Russian Institute, Columbia University).
        $8.50.

In clear and energetic narrative, Avrich describes the most tragic attempt to
proclaim a republic of free soviets: the rebellion of the Kronstadt sailors.
He makes the point that it was not Kronstadt's position which had altered but
the nature of the soviets. Kronstadt was not a "white Guardist mutiny," as
some Soviet writers claim, nor was it "engineered by any single party or group."
The author concludes that the rebellion was spontaneous in its inception,
"anarcho-populist" in its program, and doomed, like the Paris Commune,
because of its lack of aggressiveness. His analysis of the rebellion adds greatly
to our understanding of this final challenge to the Bolshevik monopoly of
power.

      SR, 30:1:150-1   R: Ronald Grigor Suny

651.   Bethell, Nicholas. **The Last Secret: The Delivery to Stalin of over
        Two Million Russians by Britain and the United States**. Intro. by
        Hugh Trevor-Roper. New York, Basic Books, 1974. 224p. $8.95.

This remarkable book tells the story of a tragic and little-known episode: the
forcible repatriation of over two million Soviet men, women, and children who
found themselves in Allied hands in Europe in 1944-1947. In the chaotic atmosphere of post-war Europe, British and American authorities neglected both
their countries' tradition of asylum, coldly and uniformly treating two million
people as "traitors." The fate of these people was finally sealed in a secret
agreement at Yalta, where direct pressure from Stalin, combined with the

the presence in Red Army custody of British and United States prisoners-of-war, led to the decision that all Soviet citizens, irrespective of their wishes, should be dispatched to Russia. Many violent and tragic incidents followed this decision. In many instances mothers killed themselves and their children to avoid deportation.   S. M. H.

652.   Carr, Edward Hallett. **A History of Russia, Vol. VII: Socialism in One Country, 1924-1926.** Vols. 1 and 2. Baltimore, Penguin Books, 1970 (1958-1960). Vol. 1: 592p. $3.65pa. Vol. 2: 526p. $3.65pa. Vol. 3, Parts I and II. New York, Macmillan, 1964. 605p., 1050p. $17.50.

Volume Three, in two parts, completes Carr's monumental study of Soviet history up to 1926. His series "Socialism in One Country" has dealt exhaustively with the Soviet regime in the two-year period following Lenin's death—social and economic developments in Volume One; central and local politics in Volume Two; and now foreign policy and the Communist International in the two parts of Volume Three. This volume is in fact as much a history of the Communist movement and revolution around the world as it is a history of Soviet Russia. Carr's meticulous accumulation of details goes far beyond anything else yet written on any period of Soviet foreign policy. In his earlier volumes (*The Bolshevik Revolution, 1917-1923*—vols. 1-3; *The Interregnum, 1923-1924*—vol. 4) Carr developed his basic thesis of the duality of Soviet foreign policy, with its conflicting revolutionary and national-power strands. By implication, he shows us nonetheless how absorbed the Soviet leaders were in the immediate problems of the day, how much they overreacted to threats and setbacks, and how little sophisticated grasp of over-all strategy they had, apart from their stale and simplistic Marxist clichés.

SR, 25:2:341-3   R: Robert V. Daniels

653.   Dmytryshyn, Basil. **USSR: A Concise History.** 2nd ed. New York, Charles Scribner's Sons, 1971. 585p. $12.50.

This book's distinctive feature is that the last third consists of 41 appended documents, including in full such useful items as Lenin's "April Theses," the 1936 Constitution, and Khrushchev's 1956 "secret speech." Thus it serves particularly well the teacher who wants students to work through and savor some key primary sources of Soviet history. This volume serves the beginning student well.

SR, 32:1:169-70   R: John M. Thompson

654.   Fisher, Harold H. **The Famine in Soviet Russia, 1919-1923: The Operation of the American Relief Administration.** Freeport, N.Y., Books for Libraries, 1917 (1927). 609p. $20.00.

Facing various obstacles created by the Soviet regime, the poor system of transportation and the ideological histility of the Bolsheviks, ARA, in cooperation with several American organizations, saved the lives of millions of people by distributing food and clothing and by providing medical relief. This most generous act of the American people is not widely known in the United States and was never officially recognized in Soviet historical literature.

Therefore, the decision to reprint Fisher's account of the American action, which perhaps saved the Soviet system itself, is both justified and needed.

S. M. H.

655.   Heer, Nancy Whittier. **Politics and History in the Soviet Union.** Cambridge, MIT Press, 1971. 319p. $12.50.

That the Soviet historian has special political functions is well known, and the great value of Nancy Heer's study is that through painstaking research and perceptive writing she has filled in a picture which we knew only in outline. The author has chosen to concentrate on the single most sensitive theme in Soviet historiography—the rewriting of party history since 1956—as a means of clarifying the role of history in the Soviet system. In the area of history the party retrenched and has since tried to guide historians along a path of "contained revisionism." This study gives us the most detailed analysis to date of the complex role of the Soviet historian, who must balance scholarship with rationalizing official policies, perpetuating myths, and legitimizing political authority.

SR, 30:4:896-7   R: Lowell R. Tillett

656.   Krosby, Peter H. **Finland, Germany, and the Soviet Union, 1940-1941: The Petsamo Dispute.** Madison, University of Wisconsin Press, 1968. 276p. $6.75.

This is an exhaustive study of the question of Petsamo—an Arctic area rich in nickel deposits which for 24 years, from 1920 until 1944, was Finnish territory—as a "barometer" of Finnish-German relations, during a crucial year in the Second World War. The author has been careful in his research, which rests on German source materials, and he has been judicious, for the most part, in his appraisal of events. The book represents an important work which should be read by historians of the Second World War.

SR, 28:4:652-3   R: John H. Hodgson

657.   Mamatey, Victor S. **Soviet Russian Imperialism.** Princeton, N.J., Van Nostrand, 1964. 192p. (Anvil Originals, 68). $1.45pa.

This critical study explains in historical terms the evolution of Soviet imperialism. The author contends that Soviet imperialism is an empirically observable and pragmatically provable fact. The study can be most useful as introductory literature for the student and the general reader interested in understanding the Soviet system and its foreign policy in particular. The events which took place since 1964 make this slim work by no means obsolete; on the contrary, the author's observations remain valid even in 1975.   S. M. H.

658.   Pipes, Richard. **The Formation of the Soviet Union: Communism and Nationalism, 1917-1923.** Rev. ed. New York, Atheneum, 1968 (1954). 365p. $3.45pa.

Pipe's revised study is noteworthy in that he has been able to document in greater detail the serious clash of opinion among Communist leaders in Moscow precipitated by the conquest of Georgia. The bibliography has been brought up to date, as has the biographical information in the index. (For review of first edition see JMH, 29:1:153-4; R: George Barr Carson, Jr.).

S. M. H.

659.   Treadgold, Donald W. **Twentieth Century Russia**. 3rd ed. Chicago, Rand McNally, 1972 (1959, 1964). 563p. $9.95.
In this updated third edition, chapters 25 through 29 have either been rewritten or added, including the sections that cover Khrushchev's and Brezhnev's regimes. Although this is a history of the USSR, the title is erroneous: "Twentieth Century Russia" ceased to exist officially in 1917. The book offers a satis-factory background for the events of 1917 and gives a chronological account up to the early 1970s. However, the author neglects the issue of the non-Russian nationalities, underestimates the size and tragedy of the purges, and, though his academic honesty is never in doubt, the text appears to be written in the spirit of "co-existence." Recent revelations by Soviet dissident intellectuals make this version largely obsolete.   S. M. H.

MILITARY AFFAIRS

Bibliographies

660.   Parrish, Michael, comp. **The Soviet Armed Forces: Books in English, 1950-1967**. Stanford, Hoover Institution, 1970. 173p. (Hoover Insti-tution Bibliographical Series, 48). $7.50.
"This bibliography makes a systematic attempt to gather and organize publica-tions on Soviet armed forces into appropriate categories which would allow students to find the material in the subject area of their interests." Listed are books, articles, documents, and special studies. The bibliography includes 2,146 entries without annotations, yet it is adequately organized by subjects and topics. The author index refers to entries.   S. M. H.

661.   U. S. Department of the Army. **Soviet Military Power (Bibliography)**. New York, Greenwood Press, 1969 (1959). 186p. $13.00.
First published in 1963 by the Army Library, this is an extensive and updated bibliography on Soviet military affairs. The bibliography is arranged by specific subjects dealing with various aspects of the Soviet armed forces. An author index is included.   S. M. H.

To 1917

662.   Brussilov, A. A., General [Brusilov]. **A Soldier's Note-Book, 1914-1918**. West Point Military Library. Westport, Conn., Greenwood Press, 1971 (London, 1930). 340p. $13.00.
The author tells the story of the technical backwardness of the Russian army, which had too few cannons, too few shells, and almost no proper artillery training. Machine guns, airplanes, field communications, field transport, medical

equipment—all were gravely deficinet. There was no unity of command. The author holds that by May 1917 troops were refusing to obey orders on all fronts, so that the failure of the Kerensky offensive was already certain. The October Revolution was a logical consequence.

SR, 31:3:672-3   R: John Shelton Curtiss

663.   Curtiss, John Shelton. **The Russian Army under Nicholas I, 1825-1855.** Durham, N.C., Duke University Press, 1965. 386p. $10.00.
Perhaps the most valuable parts of Curtiss's book are those which deal with the organization of the military command, the training of the troops, and the life of officers and men during their service. On these matters there has hitherto been virtually no literature in English. Drawing copiously on Russian official sources and on military memoirs, the author has produced an admirable survey.

SEER, 44:103:512-3   R: Hugh Seton-Watson

664.   Delderfield, R. F. **The Retreat from Moscow.** New York, Atheneum, 1967. 257p. $5.95.
This book covers essentially common territory: the military defeat of Napoleon in 1812. The author reconstructs the campaign from the French point of view, continuing a successful series on Napoleon and his marshals. *The Retreat from Moscow* is a tribute to the courage and perseverance of the officers and men of the Grande Armée.

SR, 28:1:131   R: Major Albert S. Britt

665.   Duffy, Christopher. **Borodino and the War of 1812.** New York, Charles Scribner's Sons, 1973. 208p. $10.00.
This is first and foremost a book for the military history enthusiast. Duffy's work is primarily a detailed descriptive account based on a wide range of Russian and other sources, of the battle of Borodino, set within the framework of a rather brief sketch of the campaign as a whole. The work provides a competent account of the war as a whole, some valuable insights into the technical capabilities of the forces involved and how arms and troops were managed in combat, together with an enthralling reconstruction of the development of the fighting at Borodino.

SR, 33:4:773-4   R: Barry Hollingsworth

666.   Lensen, George Alexander. **The Russo-Chinese War.** Tallahassee, Fla., Diplomatic Press, 1967. 315p. $15.00.
Boxer attacks upon the Russians and their properties in Manchuria provoked a Russian retaliation sufficient to bring Manchuria under Russian dominance for several years. A very small part of this development is singled out in this book for a detailed description. Lensen devotes his account mainly to military action between the Chinese and Russian soldiers and railwaymen in Manchuria. For the reader who is fascinated by factual descriptions of military battles, this book will have some value.

SR, 30:1:148   R: Werner Levi

667. Longworth, Philip. **The Art of Victory: The Life and Achievement of Generalissimo Suvorov, 1729-1800.** London, Constable, 1965. New York, Holt, Rinehart & Winston, 1966. 350p. $7.50.
The book covers much the same ground as K. Osipov's biography of A. V. Suvorov, which was well translated into English in 1941, and which provides a comprehensive picture of Suvorov's achievements and personality. Perhaps the most interesting reflection of Suvorov's genius is to be found in his two treatises on military training: the "Suzdal' Regulations" (1762) and "The Science of Victory" (1796), in both of which he showed himself an innovator, determined to get the best out of his troops by caring for their health and well-being. His victories bore ample witness to the efficacy of his reforms. The reference notes to each chapter are scholarly and informative.
      SEER, 45:104:250-1   R: P. S. Squire

668. Miller, Forrestt A. **Dmitrii Miliutin and the Reform Era in Russia.** Nashville, Vanderbilt University Press, 1968. 246p. $7.50.
Miller's book is essentially a detailed description of the Russian military reforms planned and executed during the reign of Alexander II, together with an account of the exertions of D. Miliutin, minister of war during virtually all of Alexander's reign, to guide the emperor's reform measures through the labyrinth of bureaucratic and court intrigues. The book also contains admirably clear and thorough descriptions of the reform of the military district system (1862), the reorganization of the structure of military education (1863-70), and the introduction of universal military training (1874). The author's clear account of the military reforms is a useful and welcome addition to the field.
      SR, 29:3:513-4   R: Peter Czap, Jr.

669. Olivier, Daria. **The Burning of Moscow, 1812.** Trans. from the French by Michael Heron. New York, Thomas Y. Crowell, 1967. 221p. $6.95.
The book re-examines the well-worn question whether the fire was engineered by the French or the Russians or occurred accidentally as a by-product of war. The author argues that Count Rostopchin, the crafty governor of Moscow, gave instructions to the incendiaries directing the destruction of the city. Ms. Olivier had access to Russian documents recently made available to free-world scholars. At least it cannot be denied that in 1812, Russians were thinking of the psychological effect of a great event on the mind of their opponent.
      SR, 28:1:131   R: Major Albert S. Britt

670. Russell, William Howard. **Russell's Despatches from the Crimea; 1854-1856.** Ed. with an intro. by Nicolas Bentley. New York, Hill and Wang, 1967. 287p. $7.50.
Russell is called the first war correspondent for his coverage of the Crimean War from the sailing of the first British contingents in February 1854, one month before war was declared, to the signing of the armistice two years later. His despatches provide timely reading—this was a limited war, a bloody, costly war, a strange, frustrating war.
      SR, 27:1:149   R: Norman E. Saul

671.   Walder, David. **The Short Victorious War: The Russo-Japanese Conflict,**
        1904-5. New York, Harper & Row, 1974. 321p. $10.00.
This was not just "the last imperialist war," therefore I have placed it in its
context, diplomatic and economic as well as military. Britain supported her
new ally. The kaiser supported the tsar against the "Yellow Peril" but took
advantage of the weakening of Russia, France's military ally. When Britain
and Russia were on the brink of war, France, the ally of both, pulled them
back. The United States, opposed to Russian absolutism, was the first nation
to realize the dangers of a militarily successful Japan. Economically, Russia
was not ruined. Japan was nearly bankrupt, but despite military disasters and
the October Revolution, Russian stocks, high throughout the war, actually
rose when her Baltic Fleet was destroyed. Militarily, apart from aircraft, every
element of the Great War was present. European and U.S. observers, distracted
by Japanese gallantry and Russian ineptness, failed to appreciate the significance of this first glimpse of twentieth century warfare.
        JMH, 47:3:582

672.   Westwood, J. N. **Witnesses of Tsushima**. Tokyo, Sophia University,
        in cooperation with Diplomatic Press, Tallahassee, Fla., 1970. 321p.
        $15.00.
Unlike many other episodes in Russian military history, the great naval battle
of Tsushima, which undoubtedly marked the nadir of Russia's disastrous
embroilment in the Russo-Japanese War, has not lacked chroniclers. The author
has set out to correct the inaccuracies of earlier accounts of the battle and
especially to dispel the notion that the Russian navy in 1905 was hopelessly
inept and its opponent virtually flawless. Accordingly, Westwood demonstrates
that the Russian navy was by no means technically inferior to its rival, and
that in the naval action prior to Tsushima the Russians, although beset by some
unusually bad luck, performed quite creditably. To offset the absence of
Japanese sources in this study, the reader may consult the recent complementary study of Tsushima by N. F. Bush (New York, 1969) which is based substantially on Japanese sources.
        SR, 30:1:148-9   R: John W. Long

1917 to the Present

673.   Alexandrov, Victor. **The Tukhachevsky Affair**. Trans. from the French
        by John Hewish. Englewood Cliffs, N.J., Prentice-Hall, 1964. 201p.
        $4.95.
Alexandrov's account aims at popular appeal and dramatic impact rather than
scholarly precision. In general, the story as he recounts it is probably accurate,
and he has used all the major available sources. By now there can remain no
doubt that by indirect collusion the NKVD and the Gestapo planted false
documents with President Beneš, allegedly proving treasonous contact of
Tukhachevsky with the Nazis. Beneš, who accepted them as true, sent them
to Stalin, thus facilitating the dictator's purge of the Marshal and other generals.

In all, this book is recommended for insights into Soviet history, though not as the history of the Tukhachevsky affair.

SR, 24:1:126-7   R: Raymond L. Garthoff

674.   Armstrong, John A., ed. **Soviet Partisans in World War II**. Foreword by Philip E. Mosely. Madison, University of Wisconsin Press, 1964. 792p. $12.50.

The volume is divided into two parts with a total of eleven chapters. Part I, besides Armstrong's introduction, includes the following chapters: "Composition and Morale of the Partisan Movement" (Armstrong and K. DeWitt); "Partisan Psychological Warfare and Popular Attitudes" (E. Ziemke); "The Partisans in Soviet Intelligence" (A. Dallin, R. Mavrogordato, W. Moll); and "Air Power in Partisan Warfare" (G. L. Weinberg). Part II consists of five case studies. An appendix contains 74 Soviet partisan documents from German archives in translation, as well as a glossary of German and Russian military terms and abbreviations, a selected bibliography and an index. The work is an illuminating contribution to political science which the student of Soviet partisan warfare has long awaited.

UQ, 21:3:271-2   R: Lev Shankovsky

675.   Bialer, Seweryn, ed. **Stalin and His Generals: Soviet Military Memoirs of World War II**. New York, Pegasus, 1969. 644p. $10.00.

The vast majority of the works excerpted by Bialer were published after 1962, and only one as early as 1960. The book's value lies in the revelation to the general student of Soviet affairs of the treasure house of non-military information contained in the memoirs, which are simply too numerous and too lengthy for those not particularly concerned with World War II to follow. The most extensively used periodical source is *Voenno-istoricheskii zhurnal*. Bialer's coverage considerably exceeds the period of Soviet participation in World War II; about one-fourth of the translated material deals with the military during the Great Purge, the Nazi-Soviet Pact period, and the Finnish War. For both the prewar and the war period the selections are especially revealing on the nature of military leadership in the USSR and the interaction of civilian and military leaders. Zhukov's extraordinary power in 1941-1942, his later rivalry with Konev and other marshals, and Stalin's complicated personality are only a few of the key issues of Soviet affairs illuminated by the memoirs.

SR, 29:2:316-7   R: John A. Armstrong

676.   Carell, Paul. **Scorched Earth: The Russian-German War, 1943-1944**. Trans. from the German by Ewald Osers. Boston, Little, Brown, 1970. 556p. $12.50.

It is unusual to find a volume of military history so well written. This book, a sequel to the author's *Hitler Moves East*, continues its fascinating story of the Soviet-German campaigns of World War II. In addition to a wide range of published materials, including many Soviet military memoirs, the author has combed through the official archives and has collected diaries and accounts of many German participants. The author (in line with the main current of Soviet historiography) attributes decisive significance to the Battle of Kursk in the

summer of 1943. That battle, rather than Stalingrad, is held to have marked
the real turning point and the end of German prospects for victory.
> SR, 30:3:669   R: Raymond L. Garthoff

677.   Chaney, Otto Preston, Jr. **Zhukov**. Foreword by Malcolm Mackintosh.
        Norman, University of Oklahoma Press, 1971. 512p. $9.95.
Chaney's material leads him to provide a detailed and thorough treatment of
Zhukov's wartime role as a planner and commander of most of the key battles
on the Eastern Front. It is to this subject that the major part of the book is
devoted, the accounts being amplified by photographs and maps. But the
portrait of Zhukov as a person and the description of his political role, especially
in the hectic days of Khrushchev's climb to the pinnacle of power, unavoidably
remain sketchy and uncertain.
> SR, 31:3:679-80   R: Leon Gouré

678.   Chew, Allen F. **The White Death: The Epic of the Soviet-Finnish
        Winter War**. East Lansing, Michigan State University Press, 1971.
        313p. $12.50.
Chew's work is primarily a study of military tactics. His sources are impressive: published documents, memoirs, and secondary works in English, Finnish,
and Russian; archival materials in Washington and Helsinki; and personal interviews with a number of Finnish officers. The result is a far more detailed study
of the fighting than has hitherto been available in any major Western language.
> SR, 31:4:900   R: C. Leonard Lundin

679.   Chuikov, Vasili I. **The Fall of Berlin**. Foreword by Alistair Horne.
        Trans. by Ruth Kisch. New York, Holt, Rinehart and Winston, 1968.
        261p. $5.95.
The Soviet marshal Chuikov's promise to be sincere did not enable him to avoid
three biases. First, he sins by omission. He is completely silent about the Warsaw
uprising. His second bias is his ideological interpretation of what is not already
established doctrine. Finally, the marshal summarily dismisses everything
that the Germans have to say. On the other hand, he acknowledges some mistakes
made by Soviet commanders, what amounts to an unprecedented departure
from Soviet historiography. To be sure, the criticism consists largely of the
de-Stalinization of the historical events that he relates. Otherwise, the book is
a treasury of information unavailable elsewhere.
> SR, 27:4:662-3   R: Béla K. Király

680.   Clark, Alan. **Barbarossa: The Russian-German Conflict, 1941-45**.
        New York, Morrow, 1965. 522p. $10.00.
Essentially, *Barbarossa* is a military study of combat operations on a grand
scale. As a narrative it is tremendously exciting. The author is at his best when
he deals with the great battles on the eastern front, and the volume contains
much fine descriptive writing. He understands tactics and has a keen eye for
the relevant and important. He chooses four critical battles: Moscow, 1941;
Stalingrad, 1942; Kursk, 1943; and the Oder in 1945. The Germans, Clark

asserts, contrary to a widely held view, could not have taken Leningrad in September 1941 even if they had committed additional forces.
JMH, 37:4:505-7   R: Louis Morton

681.   Garder, Michel. **A History of the Soviet Army**. New York, Praeger, 1966. 226p. $7.50.
Colonel Garder is a first-class expert on Soviet military history, and his book is a first-class testimonial to the knowledge, historical insight, and conceptual vigor upon which his reputation rests. His account of Soviet military history begins with Peter the Great, for Garder believes that the Soviet Army is the product of two heritages, one based on the two hundred years of military experience accumulated before the revolution, the other on the experience of the Soviet regime itself. His analysis of the "classical heritage" serves as an introduction; the bulk of the book is devoted to a narrative account of the military and politico-military history of the Soviet regime up to the fall of Khrushchev; the concluding section contains much useful information on the personnel, structure, and doctrine of the Soviet armed forces today.
SR, 27:1:138-9   R: Matthew P. Gallagher

682.   Hart, B. H. Liddell, ed. **The Red Army, 1918-1945; The Soviet Army, 1946 to the Present**. Gloucester, Mass., Peter Smith, 1968. 480p. $6.75.
This collective volume, edited by a distinguished British military historian, is a reprint of a publication initially issued in 1956. It deals with the historical origins, evolution, and maturation of the Soviet army, and covers the period between 1918 and the early 1950s. The contributors include well-known international authorities on the subject, who treat the history of the Soviet army in a chronological and rather systematic fashion. The reader must be aware of the fact that this is not an updated source of information, especially on most recent developments concerning nuclear war capacity.
SR, 29:1:112-4   R: Roman Kolkowicz

683.   Higgins, Trumbull. **Hitler and Russia: The Third Reich in a Two-Front War, 1937-1943**. New York, Macmillan, 1966. 310p. $6.95.
In this book the noted military historian Higgins presents a view of the background and course of Hitler's war on the Soviet Union until the end of the Stalingrad campaign in the spring of 1943. Based on a thoughtful analysis of the memoir, documentary, and monographic literature, Higgins's book will serve both the scholarly community and the general public as an excellent introduction to this fascinating subject. He has taken advantage of some recently available information from the Soviet Union to give his picture of the eastern front a considerably more balanced approach than most previous Western writers.
AHR, 72:3:965   R: Gerhard L. Weinberg

684.   O'Ballance, Edgar. **The Red Army: A Short History**. New York, Praeger, 1964. 237p. $7.50.
This book is more a popularization than a scholarly analysis, but it is no less worthy of attention on that account. The author has a sound knowledge of

Soviet military history, a shrewd eye for relevancies, and a sprightly style of presentation. The book should be pleasing and useful not only to the general reader but also to the specialist, who will know enough about the complexities of the subject to appreciate the synthesizing skill with which the narrative has been put together.

SR, 27:1:138-9   R: Matthew P. Gallagher

685.   Orgill, Douglas. **T-34 Russian Armor**. New York, Ballantine Books, 1971. 160p. (Ballantine's Illustrated History of World War II, Weapons Book, no. 21). $1.00pa.

This is an account of the conception, birth, development, and wartime role of the tank. The T-34 was a fast, medium tank, with sloped and angled armor, an aspect to which the British and Germans had not then paid much attention, and almost forty thousand were produced, survivors being in action as late as 1967 in the Middle East. The book deserves to be consulted frequently.

SR, 31:3:680-1   R: Edgar O'Ballance

686.   Salisbury, Harrison E. **The 900 Days: The Siege of Leningrad**. New York, Harper & Row, 1969. 635p. $10.00.

Salisbury focuses not only on events in Leningrad and the actions, attitudes, and experiences of its leaders and citizens, but he portrays the siege against a detailed background description of the German invasion, Soviet policies, Stalin's mistakes and intrigues, as well as the military efforts to halt the German advance and later to relieve the city. The story ranges from the outbreak of the war and Soviet unpreparedness for it to Stalin's postwar purge of the Leningrad leadership. It is told on many levels as it shifts back and forth from Leningrad to the Kremlin, to the armies in the field; from high-level conferences to the personal experiences of lowly Soviet citizens and soldiers. Salisbury contributes his own comments and evaluation of events and personalities and some new material based on personal interviews with some of the leading participants of the siege.

SR, 28:4:651-2   R: Leon Gouré

687.   Seaton, Albert. **The Russo-German War, 1941-45**. New York, Praeger, 1971. 628p. $15.00.

This thorough study by a British colonel professionally familiar with both German and Soviet military establishments may well be the best one-volume account of the Soviet-German campaigns and the strategic thinking on both sides of the front. The lay reader will often be more interested in the author's suggestive opinions regarding the reasons for successes and failures than in the abundant technical detail; he will also do well to read the political sections with some caution. In essence, Seaton finds that Hitler lost the war when, by political misjudgment, he embarked on a two-front war. Hitler alone was responsible for the defeat at Stalingrad and for the rigid insistence on holding the ground, which cost Germany the initiative in the war. The author has done a valuable job in sifting the mountains of confusing evidence on the military aspects of German-Soviet war.

SR, 31:2:431-2   R: Alexander Dallin

688.   Skrjabina, Elena. **Siege and Survival: The Odyssey of a Leningrader.**
        Trans. and ed. by Norman Luxemburg. Foreword by Harrison E.
        Salisbury. Carbondale, Southern Illinois University Press, 1971.
        174p. $4.95.
In the annals of World War II, and indeed of modern wars, the 900-day siege
of Leningrad holds a special place in the long catalogue of disasters, horrors,
and fortitude in the face of seemingly impossible odds. Mrs. Skrjabina's contribution is mainly that of a young housewife and mother and a member of the
"intelligentsia" caught in the disaster. Essentially it is a diary of hunger and
death as they affected a Leningrad family, its friends and neighbors, and of
their personal struggle to survive.
        SR, 31:2:432-3   R: Leon Gouré

689.   Turney, Alfred W. **Disaster at Moscow: Von Bock's Campaigns, 1941-
        1942.** Albuquerque, University of New Mexico Press, 1970. 228p.
        $6.95.
Lt. Col. Turney traces Field Marshal von Bock's performance as commander
of Army Group Center in 1941, in the German advance from the Soviet
border to the outskirts of Moscow and, more briefly, in the South in the first
half of 1942. Using von Bock's detailed war diary as his major source and guide,
he is thus able to reconstruct how German planning, the decisions by Hitler
and by fellow commanders, the performance of German and Soviet troops,
and the balance of challenges and difficulties looked, both in victory and in
retreat, to one of the leading conservative Prussian professionals of the old
school. Some of the glimpses from the war diary are valuable, but there is
little else in the book that provides any novel insight or interpretation.
        SR, 30:1:155-6   R: Alexander Dallin

690.   Wagner, Ray, ed. **The Soviet Air Force in World War II: The Official
        History, Originally Published by the Ministry of Defense of the USSR.**
        Trans. by Leland Fetzer. Garden City, N.Y., Doubleday, 1973. 440p.
        $12.95.
"The original Russian text, as published in the Soviet Union, has been translated and edited by an American team. The history's scope is quite parochial;
it confines itself to major Soviet air campaigns only, and does not go into aspects of the war in which their air force was not the largest participant." The
Soviet author proceeds chronologically without mentioning sources or other
works. The American editor added several illustrations by courtesy of Sovfoto.
The main value of the work lies in making Soviet interpretations available to
the English-speaking reader.   S. M. H.

691.   Whaley, Barton. **Codeword Barbarossa.** Cambridge, MIT Press, 1973.
        376p. $10.00.
This book takes up the interesting question of what intelligence was actually
received by the Soviet Union about German intentions, when such information was transmitted, and how it was interpreted. As an effort at an analysis of
this difficult and fascinating subject, the book is indeed to be welcomed. In
a field that has often been the focus of idle speculation, dubious tales, and

outright fabrications, the author's attempt at a systematic and scholarly review makes a significant contribution.

SR, 33:2:361-2   R: Gerhard L. Weinberg

692.   Zhukov, Georgii K. **Marshal Zhukhov's Greatest Battles**. Ed. with an introduction and explanatory comments by Harrison E. Salisbury. Trans. from the Russian by Theodore Shabad. New York, Harper & Row, 1969. 304p. $6.95.

The book is not Marshal Zhukov's full memoirs. It is a somewhat limited selection of extensive excerpts from them concerning the battles of Moscow, Stalingrad, Kursk, and Berlin. Most of these selections are drawn from the Soviet *Voenno-istoricheskii zhurnal*, where they appeared during the years 1965 through 1967. The full edition of the Zhukov memoirs appeared in Moscow. On the whole, Zhukov's account is more free of intentional polemics than some of the other Soviet military memoirs. However, it is no substitute for the full Zhukov memoirs, but it is a good selection of interesting highlights of major campaigns.

SR, 29:1:111-2   R: Raymond L. Garthoff

693.   Zhukov, Georgii K. **The Memoirs of Marshal Zhukov**. New York, Delacorte Press, 1971. 703p. $15.00.

This is a translation of Zhukov's *Vospominaniia i razmyshleniia* (Moscow, 1971) in which he attempts to justify himself, blame others for failure, and answer a variety of critics and rivals. Although Zhukov praises Stalin's general leadership, force of personality, and steel nerves, he is far from the uncritical admirer that some Western writers portray. Stalin made some very serious mistakes: his all-out offensive on the entire front in the winter of 1941, the disastrous attempts to break the Leningrad blockade in the spring of 1942, and perhaps worst of all when the Soviet preemptive strike proved to be a great disaster, allowing the Germans to advance to Stalingrad and the Caucasus. There are some factual errors in Zhukov's narrative.

SR, 30:1:154-5   R: Michael Parrish

694.   Yeremenko, A. I. **The Arduous Beginning**. Trans. from the Russian *V Nachale Voiny* by Vic Schneierson. Moscow, Progress Publishers, 1966. 329p.

Marshal Yeremenko's memoirs of the beginning of the war, one of the first books by a senior Soviet commander about the Second World War, were first published in 1959. A revised edition appeared in 1964 and has now been translated into English. Both versions have given rise to controversy. Yeremenko, like most generals, likes to magnify his own imporatance, claim credit for what went right, rationalize his failures, and, in general, boast a good deal. Yeremenko is best known for his later command of the Stalingrad Front.

SR, 27:1:139-41   R: Michael Parrish

Navy

695.   Fairhall, David. **Russian Sea Power**. Boston, Gambit, 1971. (*Russia Looks to the Sea*. London, Andre Deutsch). 287p. $10.00.
Written by the *Manchester Guardian*'s defense analyst, who is quite familiar with both Western and Soviet sources, this book provides more than adequate information and perspective to a layman interested in the problems posed by the dramatic expansion of Soviet sea power. Fairhall's major thesis is that the Soviet Union, with its centralized planning, is better equipped than any other nation to coordinate its efforts in oceanographic research, merchant marine and fishing operations, and other activities supporting its naval power. The author fully recognizes the immense political effect of the Soviet presence in seas that had never seen the Red flag.
    SR, 31:1:183-4   R: Vladimir Petrov

696.   Herrick, Robert Waring. **Soviet Naval Strategy: Fifty Years of Theory and Practice**. Annapolis, U.S. Naval Institute, 1968. 198p. $9.00.
This is a solid study that represents a real contribution to our understanding of the development of Soviet military theory, with particular reference to naval strategy. The author's principal, and most controversial, conclusion is that "current Soviet naval strategy is an essentially deterrent and defensive one." Anyone interested either in current world military affairs or in the Soviet field, as well as the much smaller audience directly interested in Soviet military affairs, will find the book worth reading.
    SR, 28:4:649-50   R: Raymond L. Garthoff

697.   McGwire, Michael, ed. **Soviet Naval Developments: Capability and Contest**. New York, Praeger, 1973. 555p. $23.50.
The book is the result of a seminar held in 1972 at Dalhousie University and composed of both naval specialists and those in the adjacent but relevant fields of foreign relations, economic policy, and military theory. All participants were concerned with the significance of what seemed a break in the traditional pattern of Russian naval policy—a shift from the old task of coastal defense and support of the land forces to a posture of forward deployment that brought Soviet warships into the Mediterranean, Caribbean, and Indian Ocean. The first part of the book deals with the military and political theoretical contexts in which Soviet naval planners are working, while the second section contains a mass of technical and economic data. Part Three treats the development of Russian and Soviet naval doctrine in an historical context, while the following three sections consider the recent forward deployments of Soviet naval power. Thus, the reader is given the pertinent theoretical, historical, and professional background.
    CASS, 9:1:124   R: David R. Jones

698.   Woodward, David. **The Russians at Sea: A History of the Russian Navy**. New York, Praeger, 1966. 254p. $6.95.
This book offers an able and informative account of Russian sea power from the time of Peter the Great. It deals at much greater length with the history of the Imperial Russian Navy than with the Soviet period. Among the larger

points of interest to emerge from this study is that neither Imperial Russia nor
the Soviet Union followed the traditional path to sea power taken by the
Western maritime nations, which developed navies to protect their merchant
shipping. Rather, Russian and Soviet rulers alike looked to their navies to
serve the strategic interests and prestige of an essentially land-locked power.
With respect to the performance of the Russian Navy in past wars, Woodward
gives it average marks.

   RR, 25:4:414-6   R: Thomas W. Wolfe

Special Studies

699. Bloomfield, Lincoln P., Walter C. Clemens, Jr., and Franklyn Griffiths.
   **Khrushchev and the Arms Race: Soviet Interests in Arms Control
   and Disarmament, 1954-1964.** Cambridge, MIT Press, 1966. 338p.
   $10.00.

Under the sponsorship of the U.S. Arms Control and Disarmament Agency,
a team of experts at MIT's Center for International Studies spent eighteen months
investigating "Soviet Interests in Arms Control and Disarmament 1954-1964."
By using the available sources, shown in the extensive bibliography, the analysis
shows the chief factors in the period that appeared to influence Soviet arms
control policy—the military balance, the political pressures within the Communist
world, the economic cost of the arms race, and the power struggle within the
Kremlin. This is a valuable, original, and penetrating contribution to our understanding of international Communism.

   RR, 26:3:309   R: Joseph S. Roucek

700. Gallagher, Matthew P., and Karl F. Speilmann, Jr. **Soviet Decision-
   Making for Defense: A Critique of U.S. Perspectives on the Arms
   Race.** New York, Praeger, 1972. 102p. $12.50.

The authors conclude that defense policy is initiated at the top levels of the
party hierarchy, that the military has a preferential but subordinate position
in military policy formation, and that the scientists lack the institutional and
political advantages to play the kind of role their American counterparts have
enjoyed. To the analyst of Soviet foreign and military policies, these may be
commonplace assertions. But the supporting argumentation and evidence is
relatively fresh, and to the strategic analyst it cannot be repeated often enough
that Soviet military policies are the product of truly political processes.

   CSP, 16:1:116-8   R: Franklyn Griffiths

701. Garthoff, Raymond L., ed. **Sino-Soviet Military Relations.** New York,
   Praeger, 1966. 285p. $7.50.

In addition to editing this book, Garthoff wrote four of its eleven chapters
and imposed on the whole a unity and cohesiveness which bespeak the thoroughness with which he had worked out the plan that his collaborators have helped
him to implement. The problem of Sino-Soviet military relations is a many-
faceted one, with roots leading back to the early history of Stalin's relations
with the Chinese Communist party and the Kuomintang, and beyond this,

to the relations between Imperial Russia and Imperial China. The contributors
have succeeded admirably in assembling the evidence and analytical insights
upon which an appreciation of this momentous development of our times is
based.

SR, 27:1:138-9   R: Matthew P. Gallagher

702.   Garthoff, Raymond L. **Soviet Military Policy: A Historical Analysis.**
       New York, Praeger, 1966. 276p. $6.50.
The author tackles an elusive subject in his book on Soviet military policy,
one that concerns an aspect of Soviet activity which intertwines and interacts
with all the other activities by which the Soviet Union functions as a society,
a state, a member of the Communist camp, and a power in world affairs.
It is the distinctive achievement of his book that Garthoff succeeds in bringing
all these relationships clearly within the field of vision of the reader while
always maintaining a sharp focus on the main subject of study, namely, the
role of military power in Soviet policy. The book is broad in compass, deep in
historical perspective, and richly packed with information.

SR, 27:1:138   R: Matthew P. Gallagher

703.   Gouré, Leon, et al. **The Role of Nuclear Forces in Current Soviet
       Strategy.** Coral Gables, Fla., Center for Advanced International
       Studies, University of Miami, 1974. 148p. $8.95cl.; $4.95pa.
The contributors to this small though significant volume analyze Moscow's
planning regarding nuclear forces. They argue that the West makes a dangerous
mistake when accepting Soviet declarations at face value; that American behavior
is based on wishful thinking; that illusions prevail over realities. Soviet declarations and actions are two different things, and to take public statements seriously
is dangerously naive. The book deserves the attention of the American public
because it conveys a realistic picture of the Soviet regime and its global policies.

S. M. H.

704.   Kemp, Geoffrey, Robert L. Pfaltzgraff, Jr., and Uri Ra'anan, eds.
       The Superpowers in a Multinuclear World. Lexington, Mass., D. C.
       Heath, 1974. 300p. (International Studies Program Series, No. 1).
       $15.00.
The ten chapters of the book consist of revised and updated versions of papers
prepared for or delivered to a conference on "The U.S.—Soviet Strategic Balance
and Nuclear Multipolarity" held in May 1973 at the Fletcher School of Law
and Diplomacy, Tufts University. The first two chapters, by John Erickson and
Ra'anan, and the concluding chapter, by Pfaltzgraff, examine the Soviet-American
military-strategic relationship in the context of the May 1972 agreement on the
limitation of strategic arms (SALT I). Other chapters explore attitudes and
policies of third powers to the problem of nuclear weapons in international
affairs. Appendix A summarizes the conference discussion; and Appendix B
contains technical papers on Indian nuclear targeting options, aggregate offensive weapon ceilings at SALT II, notes on the Chinese nuclear program, and a
survey of Soviet and American nuclear delivery vehicles, 1946-1973. An index
of persons and subjects is included.   S. M. H.

705. Kolkowicz, Roman. **The Soviet Military and the Communist Party.**
Princeton, Princeton University Press, 1967. 429p. $9.00.

In probing the relations between the military and the Communist party of
the Soviet Union, Kolkowicz is not breaking new ground, but his book represents the most thorough, up-to-date, and sophisticated treatment of this subject.
Approximately one-third of the book deals with the nature of institutional
conflicts, including an examination of the structure, instruments, and methods
employed by the CPSU to control the military establishment. Another third
deals with specific issues of conflict that developed in the period 1953-1963.
Finally, the rise of the new technology and its present and possible future
effects are discussed. The author finds that a mild form of pluralism has grown
up in Soviet society and that the role and influence of the military are likely
to rise in the future.

       AHR, 73:3:864-5   R: Harry L. Coles

706. Lomov, N. A., ed. **Scientific-Technical Progress and the Revolution
in Military Affairs (A Soviet View).** Trans. and published under the
auspices of the U.S. Air Force. [Moscow, Voennoe Izdatel'stvo
Ministerstva Oborony SSSR.] Washington, U.S. GPO, 1973. 279p.
$2.25pa.

This book was written by a group of Soviet officers who were selected to
contribute to the *Communist of the Armed Forces* and other journals. It
describes the present stage in the development of Soviet military theory and
practice as related to general scientific progress. How nuclear weapons have
brought about a revolution in military thinking and the formulation of a new
strategy is the underlying theme. The book concludes: "The Soviet Armed
Forces are sparing no effort to carry out the missions posed by the 24th
Congress, under the leadership of the Communist Party . . . "

                       S. M. H.

707. **Marxism-Leninism on War and Army (A Soviet View).** Trans. and
published under the auspices of the U.S. Air Force. [Moscow, 1972.]
Washington, D.C., 1974. 335p. (Soviet Military Thought, Translation
Series, no. 2). $2.45pa.

This is a translation of the fifty (since 1957) revised edition of the standard
Soviet work on Marxist-Leninist concepts concerning the nature and origins
of war and the role of the armed forces in capitalist and socialist societies.
The American editor states that the text "was translated into English in the
Soviet Union" and that the American publication is "an exact reproduction"
of that translation. In the Soviet Union, as part of the series *Biblioteka ofitsera*,
the original is intended to serve as a reference and teaching guide for officers.
The content differs only marginally from that of previous editions. It is still
asserted that war is a product of class society; that the aggressive nature of
imperialism has not changed; and that a distinction has to be made between
just and unjust wars.   S. M. H.

708.   Milovidov, A. S., ed. **The Philosophical Heritage of V. I. Lenin and Problems of Contemporary War (A Soviet View)**. Trans. and published under the auspices of the U.S. Air Force. [Moscow, Voennoe Izdatel'stvo Ministerstva Oborony SSSR.] Washington, U.S. GPO, 1972. 292p. $2.35pa.

This compilation of Lenin's writings on war, its nature and its evaluation from the Marxist viewpoint, attempts to justify "wars of national liberation," which Lenin considered as promoting the cause of Marxist aims by weakening "capitalistic and imperialistic states." Lenin did not advocate permanent peace; he supported conflicts which in his view were "just wars." Wars which do not serve Communist interests are considered unjust."   S. M. H.

709.   Milsom, John. **Russian Tanks, 1900-1970: The Complete Illustrated History of Soviet Armoured Theory and Design**. Harrisburg, Stackpole Books, 1971. 192p. $11.95.

Milsom has compiled a complete and concise illustrated history of Soviet armored theory and design. He traces the evolution and development of Soviet armor from its early confused and amateurish fumblings to present-day practical and professional efficiency. This work should be on the reference bookshelves, within easy reach of all military students, commentators, writers, compilers, and planners.

SR, 31:3:680-1   R: Edgar O'Ballance

710.   Savkin, V. E. **The Basic Principles of Operational Art and Tactics (A Soviet View)**. Trans. and published under the auspices of the U.S. Air Force. Moscow, Voennoe Izdatel'stvo Ministerstva Oborony SSSR. Washington, U.S. GPO, 1972. 284p. $2.30pa.

The author reveals only partly the nature of the discussion and changes within the thinking of the Soviet military establishment. He examines more peripheral issues related to modern warfare and technology without providing details on Soviet armament and weaponry. However, he insists on the importance of maintaining strong ground forces supported by tanks and other conventional war equipment. Savkin concludes that achieving a nuclear balance with the U.S. makes Soviet conventional forces indispensable considering geopolitical factors affecting the Soviet Union.   S. M. H.

711.   Wolfe, Thomas W. **Soviet Strategy at the Crossroads**. Cambridge, Harvard University Press, 1964. 262p. $5.95.

This volume provides significant new insights into Soviet military thinking and Soviet elite politics. In examining the trends—primarily in the two years from the Cuban crisis to the fall of Khrushchev—Wolfe insists that some of the findings and some of the alignments of individuals must be considered tentative. Disagreements which exist between political and military leaders and among the military themselves can be shown to have existed in a wide variety of fields. There are many ambiguities and uncertainties in the Soviet leaders' own minds—some stemming from the novelty and complexity of the problems before them, others due to the specific nature of Soviet goals and perceptions.

It is precisely some sense of the way they see these problems that we gain from this highly competent and balanced analysis.

SR, 24:3:552-3 R: Alexander Dallin

RUSSIAN LANGUAGE

Dictionaries and Glossaries

712. Benson, Morton. **Dictionary of Russian Personal Names with a Guide to Stress and Morphology**. Philadelphia, University of Pennsylvania Press, 1964. 175p. (University of Pennsylvania Studies in East European Languages and Literatures). $4.75.

The dictionary contains approximately 23,000 surnames and a full list of Russian given names with their numerous diminutives. The introduction gives examples of the declension of surnames and of the stress movements in their declensions. It also sketches the relationships first between the stress of a surname and the stress of the word from which it is derived, and second between the stress of a surname and its final suffix. This work, the most comprehensive of its kind, has been compiled with scrupulous care.

SEER, 45:104:220-1 R: C. L. Drage

713. Galler, Meyer, and Harlan E. Marquess, comps. **Soviet Prison Camp Speech: A Survivor's Glossary. [Supplemented by Terms from the Works of A. I. Solzhenitsyn]**. Madison, University of Wisconsin Press, 1972. 216p. $10.00.

The publication of this dictionary fills an important gap and is a very welcome, as well as a long overdue, addition to the reference works now available to the researcher and student of Russian language, literature and history. As a reference work, it is almost unique and, as such, is highly recommended.

CSP, 14:4:734-5 (Editorial Board annotation)

714. Macura, Paul. **Russian-English Dictionary of Electrotechnology and Allied Sciences**. New York, Wiley Interscience Press, 1971. 707p. $32.50.

The dictionary contains about sixty thousand entries and is the largest of its kind. It will be most useful to anyone concerned with Russian electrotechnology.

SR, 31:4:949 R: Mark Alford

715. Paternost, Joseph. **Russian-English Glossary of Linguistic Terms**. University Park, Dept. of Slavic Languages, Pennsylvania State University, 1965. 230p. $4.00pa.

The photo-offset copy *Glossary* consists of 230 pages, each containing roughly 52 Russian items in the left column, and opposite each, in the right column, the English equivalent(s). This makes a total of around 11,960 Russian items, for which Paternost provides not only a gloss, but also an indication of verb aspect, of the separability of *-sja*, and the stress pattern. The *Glossary* is mainly intended to be of use to undergraduates either at the level of advanced grammar review or linguistic analysis of modern Russian. In addition the *Glossary* will have a very substantial interest for Russian teachers and researchers, and in general for anyone interested in the lexicon of Russian language study and analysis.

SEEJ, 10:1:93-5   R: Steven P. Hill

716.   Vitek, Alexander J. **Russian-English Idiom Dictionary**. Ed. by Harry H. Josselson. Detroit, Wayne State University Press, 1973. 328p. $19.95.

In this particular case, educated native speakers of Russian and English have worked together in an admirable combination of man and machine processing. The random sampling indicates that well over five thousand head-word items are included in the dictionary. Words are marked not only for stress but also for dieresis. The stylistic code, derived from the source material, encompasses 85 identifying levels of usage. Head words and English references are given in capital letters for easy identification. The dictionary should readily find its way into every Slavist's library.

SR, 33:4:838-9   R: Adele K. Donchenko

717.   Wheeler, Marcus. **The Oxford Russian-English Dictionary**. Ed. by B. O. Unbegaun with D. P. Costello and W. F. Ryan. Oxford, Clarendon Press, 1972. 918p. $18.00.

The Wheeler dictionary is superior to Smirnitsky's *Russko-angliiskii slovar'* in giving related forms, usually providing us with non-obvious oblique forms. Both dictionaries, however, attempt to present the basic Russian vocabulary along with colloquial expressions, idioms, and those technical words which might be encountered in the reading experience of an educated person. The Wheeler dictionary has some 70,000 entries, and Smirnitsky's about 50,000, though Smirnitsky is more generous with examples.

SR, 32:2:431-2   R: Thomas F. Magner

718.   Worth, Dean S., Andrew S. Kozak, and Donald B. Johnson. **Russian Derivational Dictionary**. New York, American Elsevier, 1970. 747p. $22.95.

This dictionary should prove an invaluable aid to the Russian linguist. It is likely to become as indispensable a work as the orthographic or the backwards dictionary, and as such its appearance is welcome. It is based on the 110,000-word corpus of the Ozhegov-Shapiro *Orfograficheskii slovar' russkogo iazyka* (4th ed., Moscow, 1959), but it is not as exhaustive as the Russian, and in fact it is rather a dictionary of Russian roots on vaguely etymological principles. Despite its flaws this dictionary is a useful and important work.

SEEJ, 18:4:455-6   R: Howard I. Aronson

History and Linguistics

719.   Baar, A. H. van der. **A Russian Church Slavonic Kannonik (1331-1332): A Comparative Textual and Structural Study, Including an Analysis of the Russian Computus**. (Scaliger 38B, Leyden University Library). The Hague, Mouton, 1968. 303p. 74Dglds.

Among the manuscripts belonging to the Joseph I. Scaliger collection, now housed in the University of Leiden library, there are nine in Russian Church Slavonic. Van der Baar has prepared a study of one of these, a *Kannonik*. His description of the manuscripts includes a paleographic study and remarks on the phonology, morphology, and syntax. His method of reproducing the text is excellent. He discovered no unusual or unexpected features, but has noted a great many instances where the language of the text deviates from that which is generally considered the norm for Russian Church Slavonic of the thirteenth and fourteenth centuries. This study will be of considerable interest to linguistics, paleographers, and students of ecclesiastical literature. There is a good bibliography attached.

SR, 30:1:213-4   R: J. V. Haney

720.   Borras, F. M., and R. F. Christian. **Russian Syntax: Aspects of Modern Russian Syntax and Vocabulary**. 2nd ed. New York, Oxford University Press, 1971 (1959). 444p. $13.00.
Russian Syntax is still a major resource for the student and teacher of Russian. Despite possible criticism of methodology and of details, it remains the single volume with the greatest range of useful information about contemporary Russian. The subtitle is more descriptive of the book's contents than is the main title, since most aspects of modern Russian other than strictly phonological or morphological questions are dealt with. It is probably best used as a reference work, but the inquisitive student may find himself browsing.

SEEJ, 16:2:251-5   R: Robert A. Rothstein

721.   Bratus, B. V. **Russian Intonation**. Oxford, Pergamon Press, 1972. 143p. (Pergamon Oxford Russian Series). $11.00.
This book is a manual for practical study, and as such it has many features to recommend it, as well as a few faults. The volume is divided into two unequal parts—the first offers a discussion of Russian intonational units, patterns, and variations, and the second part includes practice texts with arrows and other marks to indicate stress intensity and pitch modulation, and a double phonetic transcription of each line to help with pronunciation problems.

SR, 33:3:614-15   R: Roger Hagglund

722.   Forsyth, J. **A Grammar of Aspect: Usage and Meaning in the Russian Verb**. Cambridge, Cambridge University Press, 1970. 386p. $16.00.
Aspect enables a language like Russian, which seemingly has a primitive two-tense system, to create verbal structures of great complexity and delicacy. Forsyth addresses himself to the problem of defining, describing, and classifying Russian aspectual usage. After treating the theoretical problems of defining imperfective and perfective aspect, he considers the functions of procedurals and the validity of aspectual pairs, and then examines in detail the functioning of the aspects in various grammatical categories: the past tense, present and future tense, negative constructions, infinitive expression, and so forth. He provides a plenitude of illustrative examples with sufficient context to allow the reader to draw his own conclusions and match them with Forsyth's.

SR, 31:1:202-3   R: Thomas F. Magner

723.   Gardiner, S. C. **German Loanwords in Russian 1550-1690**. Oxford,
        Basil Blackwell, 1965. 330p. (Publications of the Philological Society,
        XXI).
This work is a most valuable contribution to the lexicology of Russian before
the time of Peter the Great. It comprises a discursive introduction which deals
with previous work in this field, with the primary sources consulted and with
previous work in this field, with the primary sources consulted and with the
historical background; a vocabulary in alphabetical order; and a chapter in
which the linguistic conclusions are given under the headings "Phonetics,"
"Morphology," "The semantic aspect," and "The function of German loanwords." The bibliography of primary Russian sources lists thirty items comprising
one hundred volumes. The author's archival researches make this an exhaustive
treatment of the subject.
            SEER, 45:105:537-9   R: H. Leeming

724.   Jakobson, Roman. **Selected Writings, Vol. II: Word and Language**.
        The Hague, Mouton, 1971. 752p. $31.00.
This volume of Jakobson's selected writings contains 61 studies covering the
forty-year period from 1929 to 1969 and ranging in length from two pages to
thirty or more pages. The range of subjects is vast: Russian verbal morphology,
declension and gender in Russian, aspects of phonology and grammar, notes
on the Gilyak language, Rumanian, Ukrainian, the concept of the zero sign,
translation, the fundamental concepts and methods of linguistics, the nature
of language, etymology, etc.
            SEER, 51:124:452-9   R: Dennis Ward

725.   Jones, Daniel, and Dennis Ward. **The Phonetics of Russian**. Cambridge,
        Cambridge University Press, 1969. 308p. $9.50.
Detailed analyses in English of the phonetic system of Russian are few indeed.
The standard works available in this field have been S. C. Boyanus' *Russian
Pronunciation* and *Russian Phonetic Reader* (1955), which is a rewriting of
the earlier *Manual of Russian Pronunciation*, and M. V. Trofimov and Daniel
Jones, *The Pronunciation of Russian* (1923). This work is a substantial rewrit-
ing of the 1923 work by Trofimov and Jones. It is divided into two main parts:
the first deals with the principle of phonetic theory and the transcription of
phonemes, and the second treats in detail the phonetic system of Russian.
The book can be used successfully at the undergraduate or graduate level.
            SR, 31:1:214-5   R: William W. Derbyshire

726.   Lewis, E. Glyn. **Multilingualism in the Soviet Union: Aspects of
        Language Policy and Its Implementation**. The Hague, Mouton, 1972.
        332p. (Contributions to the Sociology of Language, no. 3). 62Dglds. pa.
One essential element in Soviet language policy has been the concept of *dva
potoka*, or two streams, which seeks "to maintain a delicate if unstable equilib-
rium between promoting the modernizing, technological, and centralizing
functions of Russian, as well as simultaneously taking account of the tractable
fact of the practical necessity of the native languages for the vast majority,
and their emotional adherence to them." In obvious conflict with this policy
is the Soviet ultimate merging, which presumably would lead to the submerging

of all Soviet languages other than Russian. Only three percent of Russians know a second Soviet language, and they are undoubtedly Russians living in other republics. Otherwise, in the Ukraine, where Polish, Hungarian, and Moldavian minorities maintain their native languages and Russian, they omit Ukrainian from their curriculum. The author presents a large amount of information on all aspects of Soviet multilingualism: language policy, demographic factors, language maintenance, bilingual education, even theories of second language pedagogy.

      SR, 33:4:839-41   R: Thomas F. Magner

727.   Molinsky, Steven J. **Patterns of Ellipsis in Russian Compound Noun Formations**. The Hague, Mouton, 1973. 232p. 68Dglds.

Molinsky's book is the first attempt at an exhaustive grammatical analysis of some of the new types of compound nouns, and also the first extensive generative transformational treatment of the subject. As such, it can in the present state of linguistics be no more than a classificatory work; as is admitted, it "constitutes an initial step." It consists of two different sections. Part A categorizes "thematic abbreviated compounds," and Part B is a "schematic outline" of "thematic compounds," and combines a derivational classification with a historical sketch: due attention is paid to borrowings from Greek (mostly through Old Church Slavonic) and from Western European languages, and the extension of the thematic type in Modern Russian is discussed.

      CSP, 16:4:672-3   R: T. M. S. Priestly

728.   Nicholson, John Greer. **Russian Normative Stress Notation**. Montreal, McGill University Press, 1968. 169p. $11.25.

Nicholson's book is a critical survey of how the last three groups (native speakers, teachers, linguists) have dealt with this problem in print. Separate chapters are devoted to dictionaries, encyclopedic works, monographs and articles, and grammars and other sources. Included are earlier authors, such as Dal' and Sobolevsky, and recent Soviet and non-Soviet studies, ranging from the descriptive to the strictly normative. There is a bibliography, an index of Russian words, and an index of authors and editors. This monograph is the product of extensive detailed study and can be expected to serve as a source book for future researchers into the subject for many years. It is also of considerable pedagogical interest because it evaluates such standard references as the dictionaries by Ushakov, Avanesov, and Ozhegov, the Academy dictionaries, and the Academy grammar.

      SR, 28:4:693-4   R: Antonina Filonov Gove

729.   Norbury, J. K. W. **Word Formation in the Noun and Adjective**. Cambridge, Cambridge University Press, 1967. 219p. $4.95pa.

The author's primary aim is to provide a detailed description of "the procedures used in the formation of nouns and adjectives in Russian," and a listing of "the most common prefixes, suffixes, deaffixed stems and contracted stems used in these procedures." To this end, the book is organized into three parts—one discussion and two lists. It is, in fact, a useful treatment of word formation in modern Russian.

      SEEJ, 14:1:105-7   R: David Korn

730. Shapiro, Michael. **Russian Phonetic Variants and Phonostylistics.**
Berkeley, University of California Press, 1968. 55p. (University of
California Publications in Linguistics, vol. 29). $2.00pa.

731. Shapiro, Michael. **Aspects of Russian Morphology: A Semiotic Investigation.** Cambridge, Mass., Slavica Publishers, 1969. 62p. Paper.
In the first monograph Shapiro describes the old Moscow norm (OM), contemporary standard Russian (CSR), and two basic codes of the latter, the explicit
code (EXC) and the elliptic code (ELC). The notion of "iconic relationship"
is crucial in Shapiro's second monograph. Related elements in language are
iconically related if there is a factual similarity between them.
SR, 30:2:444-5   R: Herbert S. Coats

732. Stankiewicz, Edward. **Declension and Gradation of Russian
Substantives.** The Hague, Mouton, 1968. 173p. (Description and
Analysis of Contemporary Standard Russian, 4). 50Dglds.
This study is a serious one, based on extensive original research and containing
many original and provocative observations. Part I deals with "Declension and
Substantives," and Part II with "Gradation of Substantives and Derivation of
Personal Names." This volume is a serious contribution to Slavic scholarship
and one which deserves the attention of all who are interested in the structure
of Contemporary Standard Russian.
SEEJ, 14:2:236-40   R: Dean S. Worth

733. Unbegaun, Boris O. **Russian Surnames.** Oxford, Clarendon Press,
1972. 529p. $27.25.
The aim of the book is to discuss the modern system of Russian surnames in
both its morphological and its semantic aspects and does not pretend to be a
history of Russian surnames. It is the best all-around treatment in any language
of Russian names. The author describes how the Russian surname system d
developed out of the relatively fluid use of patronymics in *-ov, -in*, and the
nominal extension of *-ov*, that is, *-ovich* (fem. *-ovna*).
SR, 33:3:613-4   R: Thomas F. Magner

734. Vinogradov, V. V. **The History of the Russian Literary Language
from the Seventeenth Century to the Nineteenth.** Adapted and
intro. by Lawrence L. Thomas. Madison, University of Wisconsin
Press, 1969. 275p. $12.50.
V. V. Vinogradov presents a challenge to the reader—the problem of extract-
ing extremely valuable minerals from the crude ore which conceals them.
Thomas performed the useful service in condensing the original, putting it
into eminently readable English, and providing it with an index. Vinogradov's
work, *Ocherki po istorii russkogo literaturnogo iazyka XVII-XIX v.* (2nd rev.
ed., 1938), begins with the seventeenth-century crisis in the development of
the language and takes us through to the second half of the nineteenth century.
Thomas has written an introduction which gives a capsule account of the Russian
literary language from its beginnings to the point where Vinogradov begins.
SR, 30:4:906   R: Walter Vickery

735. Vinokur, Grigorii O. **The Russian Language: A Brief History**. Trans. by Mary A. Forsyth. Ed. by James Forsyth. Cambridge, Cambridge University Press, 1971. 147p. $12.00.

This book, which was first published in Russian in 1943 and revised and reduced somewhat in 1959, is essentially a philological account of the history of the written Russian language from the earliest chronicles in the eleventh century to the present time. Included are brief phonological sketches of the various eras of Russian and of the Russian dialects; a brief description of the inter-relationships of the Slavic languages; a brief history of Old Church Slavonic; and a very brief sketch of some phonological developments in some of the Slavic languages. In the past, Lomonosov's trend to orient the Russian language to the Old Church Slavonic influences prevailed. This book is recommended for the student or person who is interested in Russian philology, but not to one who is seriously interested in linguistics, except as a passing reference work.

        CSP, 16:1:126-8   R: Richard C. DeArmond

736. Ward, Dennis. **The Russian Language Today**. London, Hutchinson University Library, 1965. 297p. 25s. Chicago, University of Chicago Press, 1965. 297p. $3.00pa.

The purpose of this book is to describe the contemporary Russian language, or rather, since it is difficult to describe the whole of a language exhaustively in a small book, certain aspects of it, in particular recent or present-day develop-ments. It falls into two parts, "Sound and Symbol" (pp. 26-87), and "Forms and Usage" (pp. 91-266). Neither a grammar nor a treatise, the book takes the form of a series of essays which are complete in themselves.

        SEER, 44:102:200-3   R: C. L. Drage

Grammars and Textbooks

737. Doherty, Joseph C., et al. **Russian: Book One**. Boston, D. C. Heath, (1968). 303p. $6.50. **Russian: Book Two**. Boston, D. C. Heath, (1970). 382p.

Both volumes are intended to serve as a two-year introduction to the Russian language. The authors assume a five-period week. If less time is available, they suggest a three-year course. The two volumes together consist of an introduction and thirty-five lessons. Much of the text is devoted to drills, especially pattern drills. Each volume also contains appendixes giving declension and conjugation paradigms, lists of verbs dealt with in that volume, indexes, and a Russian-English and an English-Russian glossary. Those who are using the Doherty-Markus textbook will find the new edition a considerable improvement; those who are using another text will find little reason to switch.

        SR, 29:2:355-6   R: Rasio Dunatov

738. Gentilhomme, Y. **Russian for Scientists: A New Approach**. 4v. Trans. by J. F. Henry. Preface by Jean Train. Paris, Dunod, 1970. Vol. 1, 163p.; Vol. 2, 165-345pp.; Vol. 3, 347-507pp.; Vol. 4, 659p. Paper.

The first volume begins with the alphabet and consists of ten chapters treating various parts of Russian grammar. In volume two we find articles to be read

and translated. The third volume continues with articles to be translated, this time demonstrating the verb system, also dative and instrumental cases. The fourth volume continues discussion of verbs, with more articles for translation, followed by a table of units, a bibliography of recommended grammars, readers, and many dictionaries pertaining to specific fields of science, such as mathematics, nuclear physics, chemistry, and electricity. Concluding this final volume are grammatical, lexical, and subject indexes. This work is one of the few serious treatments of Russian language study purely for a science student, and because of its completeness it should be welcomed and highly recommended.
SR, 31:4:948   R: Noah D. Gershevsky

739.   Gould, S. H. **Russian for the Mathematician**. New York, Springer-Verlag, 1972. 211p. $8.80pa.
This little book is intended to teach mathematicians and students of mathematics exactly enough Russian to be able to read mathematical Russian. For this limited objective the book is completely successful. The author himself is a methematician and philologist who for many years directed the translation program of the American Mathematical Society.
SR, 32:2:432-3   R: Edwin Hewitt

740.   Harrison, William, Yelena Clarkson, and Stephen Le Fleming. **Colloquial Russian**. London, Routledge and Kegan Paul, 1973. 428p. $8.00cl.; $2.50pa.
This book is the latest in a series of language manuals devised primarily for the mature student working alone. A brief introduction deals with rules of Russian pronunciation, the alphabet, rules of spelling and reading practice. The manual is divided into 28 lessons, each consisting of four parts: reading text, vocabulary, grammar, and exercises. Highly motivated students should find it most rewarding.
CSP, 15:4:623   R: G. M.

741.   Koubourlis, Demetrius J. **Soviet Academy Grammar, Phonology and Morphology: A Computer-Aided Index**. Moscow, Idaho; University of Idaho Research Foundation, 1972. 170p. $2.25pa.
Slavicists now have an index to Volume I of the Soviet Academy *Grammatika russkogo iazyka*. Although the volume has a table of contents in the back, its 40] page length does not permit rapid retrieval of the desired information, and therefore this *Index* is a research tool whose appearance is welcome. It was compiled on the basis of the 1960 reprint of Volume I.
SEEJ, 17:4:479-80   R: Gary L. Harris

742.   Muravyova, L. S. [Murav'eva] **Verbs of Motion in Russian**. Moscow, Progress, 1973. 278p. £.95.
This is an excellent text for the instructor as well as the student of Russian. Murav'eva is one of the foremost Soviet experts on verbs of motion, and her work incorporates the now standard discussions of this important grammatical point along with the latest research in this area by a host of Soviet colleagues. The text is directed specifically at English-speaking students of Russian "who have worked through an elementary course . . . and wish to continue their

study of the language with or without a teacher." Indeed, the highly motivated intermediate student, equipped with a standard Russian-English dictionary, could easily master the text's essential points within a reasonable length of time and with a minimum of difficulty. Instructor-directed (and independent) study should leave few stones unturned.

    SEEJ, 18:4:450-1   R: Ray Parrott, Jr.

743. Phillips, Roger W. **A Concise Russian Review Grammar with Exercises.**
    Madison, University of Wisconsin Press, 1974. 108p. $2.95pa.
This little handbook aims to provide "a trouble-shooting approach" to grammar review for students at the stage between the elementary and advanced levels. A positive feature of the book is that it gathers together much of the collective wisdom and commonsense judgments that Russian teachers have been disseminating in classrooms in one way or another. Phillips has combined a sound analysis of the major and minor trouble spots with some effective translation and other exercises, and has presented this to us in a short, handy, and inexpensive textbook.

    SEEJ, 18:2:199-203   R: Maurice I. Levin

744. Rudy, Peter, Xenia L. Youhn, and Henry M. Nebel, Jr. **Russian:**
    A Complete Elementary Course. New York, W. W. Norton, 1970.
    522p. $7.50.
This attractively printed volume is designed to integrate the functions of an elementary grammar, introductory conversation, and graded reader. The authors have aimed at combining both audio-lingual and traditional methods and thus provide the basis for training in the fundamentals of aural comprehension, speaking, and reading. The book contains approximately 1,400 vocabulary items. Tape recordings are available from the publisher. According to its authors, the course has been tried out at Northwestern University over the past six years by both experienced and inexperienced instructors. The book has much to recommend it. Grammar explanations, though traditional, are clear and concise. The inclusion of an extensive body of literary readings adapted from Pushkin, Tolstoy, Chekhov, and Zoshchenko must be regarded as a positive asset.

    SR, 30:4:912-3   R: Clayton L. Dawson

745. Townsend, Charles E. **Continuing with Russian.** New York, McGraw-
    Hill, 1970. 426p. $9.95.
The appearance of this book represents a landmark in Russina textbook publishing; it is the first grammar textbook with *exercises* written specifically for the American student at the intermediate-advanced level. It is also the first Russian textbook for this level of study to be firmly based on some of the more important linguistic research on Russian of the past half century.

    SEEJ, 16:1:113-8   R: Robert L. Baker

746. Walker, Gregory P. M. **Russian for Librarians.** London, Clive Bingley,
    1973. 126p. Distr. by Linnet Books, Hamden, Conn. $8.50.
This book fills a need in library literature as a concise, well-organized survey for English-speaking librarians and staff who work with Russian materials. Beginning with a review of Russian grammar, the author presents clear

definitions, tables, and helpful exercises, using typical library words and phrases. Following this is a logical, although uneven, exposition on transliteration, cataloguing, acquisitions, standard reference books, and identification of East European languages.
SR, 33:4:842-3   R: Darlene J. Rácz

RUSSIAN LITERATURE

Bibliographies

747.   Field, Andrew. **Nabokov: A Bibliography**. New York, McGraw-Hill, 1973. 249p. $15.00.
This is a fourth bibliography of Nabokov's works to be published. There is no doubt that this bibliography is an improvement on the previous ones, that it is the work of a truly dedicated Nabokov fan, and that an enormous amount of labor must have gone into its compilation.
SR, 34:2:440-2   R: Gleb Struve

748.   Foster, Ludmila A., comp. **Bibliografiia russkoi zarubeznoi literatury, 1918-1968. (Bibliography of Russian Émigré Literature, 1918-1968)**. 2 Vols. Boston, G. K. Hall, 1971. Vol. 1: A-K, pp. 1-681; Vol. 2: L-ÎA, pp. 682-1374. $60.00.
This work embraces an awe-inspiring amount of data not only on belles-lettres published or mimeographed outside the Soviet Union between 1918 and 1968 in the original Russian, but also on works of literary criticism, linguistic studies, books and essays on Russian literary history, folklore, and the theater, as well as book reviews and memoirs. The book is bound to become a *vade mecum* for everyone interested in the literary achievements of the Russian emigration.
SR, 30:2:456-7   R: Sergius Yakobson

749.   Harvard University, Widener Library. **Twentieth Century Russian Literature**. Cambridge, Harvard University Press, 1966. 140p. (Widener Library Shelflist Number 3). $20.00.
This bibliography consists of classified listing by call number, alphabetical listing by author or title, and chronological listing.

750.   Line, Maurice B., Amrei Ettlinger, and Joan M. Gladstone. **Bibliography of Russian Literature in English Translation to 1945**. Bringing together *A Bibliography of Russian Literature in English Translation to 1900* by Maurice Line (1963) and *Russian Literature, Theatre and Art: A Bibliography of Works in English, Published Between 1900-1945* by Amrei Ettlinger and Joan M. Gladstone (1947). Totowa, N.J., Rowman and Littlefield. London, Methuen, 1972. 96p. $7.50.
(Original editions listed in P. Horecky's *Russia and the Soviet Union*.)

751.   Troitsky, N. A. **Boris Leontovich Pasternak 1890-1960: A Bibliography of the Works of B. Pasternak and Literature about Him Printed
in Russian**. Ithaca, Committee on Soviet Studies, Cornell University,
1969. 148p. $3.00.
This is a selective bibliography, but it surely is as complete a list of works in
Russian by and about Pasternak as could be compiled at this time. The publishing history of Pasternak's works is given chronologically. The section on
works about Pasternak is arranged alphabetically by author.
        SEEJ, 14:3:370   R: Dale Plank

752.   Zenkovsky, Serge A., and David L. Armbruster, comps. **A Guide to
the Bibliographies of Russian Literature**. Nashville, Tenn., Vanderbilt
University Press, 1970. 62p. $4.50.
This is a concise compilation of all known existing bibliographies of Russian
literature, in all languages, to 1970. There are two sections: General Bibliography, subdivided by source, and Literary Bibliography, subdivided by field.
Entries are arranged according to the Library of Congress Catalogue.
                        S. M. H.

753.   Zernov, Nicolas, comp. **Russkie pisateli emigratsii. (Russian Émigré
Authors: A Biographical Index and Bibliography of Their Works on
Theology, Religious Philosophy, Church History and Orthodox
Culture, 1921-1972)**. Boston, G. K. Hall, 1973. 222p. $19.50.
Of the large group of Russian writers who left their homeland between 1919
and 1922, and in lesser numbers in later years, many continued to be creative
abroad. Thanks to Zernov's laborious effort, we now have the first biobibliog-
raphical list of émigré authors, arranged in alphabetical order with an impres-
sive index of names (pp. 173-182). At least a dozen languages in addition to
Russian are represented, including English.   S. M. H.

                    General Surveys and Histories

754.   Barroshian, Vahan D. **Russian Cubo-Futurism, 1910-1930: A Study
in Avant-Gardism**. Paris, Mouton, 1974. 176p. 32Dglds.
This is an interesting and thoroughly documented study of a fascinating and
in many ways still puzzling phenomenon in Russian cultural history. The
author focuses his attention on the poetic work of the principal representatives
of cubo-futurism and he provides enlightening statements on Khlebnikov,
Maiakovsky, Burliuk, Kruchenykh, and Kamensky. He has discovered and
explored a wealth of material on futurism in the period immediately after the
revolution, when representatives of the avant-garde made a serious but futile
attempt to retrain artists and reform the public taste in accordance with their
own ideas.
        RR, 34:2:234-5   R: Edward J. Brown

755.   Čiževskij, Dmitrij. **History of Nineteenth-Century Russian Literature.**
2 Vols. Trans. by Richard Noel Porter. Ed. by Serge A. Zenkovsky.
Vol. 1: *The Romantic Period.* 236p. Vol. 2: *The Age of Realism.*
218p. Nashville, Vanderbilt University Press, 1974 (1964, 1967).
$15.00ea. cl.; $5.95ea. pa.

These two books are the central portion of what will eventually be a four-
volume history of Russian literature from the eleventh century to approximately 1920, the end of the Silver Age. Disregarding some controversial judgments by the author and his controversial views, these volumes remain an
important contribution—an invaluable reference work by a distinguished scholar
who has devoted his life to Russian literature.

      RR, 34:2:226-7   R: Richard Sheldon

756.   Fennell, John, ed. **Nineteenth-Century Russian Literature: Studies
of Ten Russian Writers.** Berkeley, University of California Press,
1973. 356p. $15.00.

This volume consists of eight studies of Russian writers—seven prose writers
and three poets—by six British Slavists, four of whom are associated with
Oxford University. The three poets—Lermontov, Tiutchev, and Fet—are the
subject of one essay by T. J. Binyon. H. Gifford is responsible for an essay on
Turgenev, and E. Lampert on Dostoevsky and Tolstoy. The volume opens with
the editor's essay on Pushkin, followed by A. de Jonge on Gogol. The closing
essay is by M. H. Shotton on Chekhov. The purpose of this volume is "to
investigate certain aspects of certain writers." Along with each essay is a
"select bibliography." In some cases it includes both the principal Russian
editions and the biographical and critical literature.

      SR, 34:1:191-3   R: Gleb Struve

757.   Freeborn, Richard. **The Rise of the Russian Novel: Studies in the
Russian Novel from Eugene Onegin to War and Peace.** New York,
Cambridge University Press, 1973. 289p. $18.50cl.; $8.95pa.

This study offers a sense of the complexity and scope of the Russian novel
between 1830 and 1870. The treatment is multi-faceted, flexible, and one might
even say random and casual. There is no straining to cover the important works
and significant biographical and literary events. The author's manner is one of
informed reticence, a reluctance to overstate, a willingness to entertain other
points of view, and a distaste for definitive solutions.

      SR, 33:1:185-6   R: Edward Wasiolek

758.   Gifford, Henry. **The Novel in Russia: From Pushkin to Pasternak.**
London, Hutchinson University Library. New York, Hillary House,
1964. 208p. $3.00.

The book gives a neat, comprehensive, enlightened view of the subject. Gifford
also produces a good conceptual "translation" of the Russian facts into an
idiom the educated English reader will understand. Some excellent parallels
with English literature help considerably. For example, Turgenev is compared
with Thackeray, Saltykov-Shchedrin with George Eliot, and the beginning of

Sholokhov's *The Quiet Don* is likened to Thomas Hardy. The author's judgments are usually sound and well sustained.

SR, 29:3:555-7   R: Victor Terras

759.   Gronicka, André von. **The Russian Image of Goethe: Goethe in Russian Literature of the First Half of the Nineteenth Century.** Philadelphia, University of Philadelphia Press, 1968. 304p. (The Haney Foundation Series, no. 3). $6.50.

The author devotes six increasingly larger chapters to the image of Goethe as fostered in the work of outstanding individual writers and critics (such as Zhukovsky, Pushkin, Lermontov, Belinsky, and Herzen), and of other writers somewhat arbitrarily associated with literary groupings (the Pushkin Pleiade, the Decembrists, and the Russian Romanticists). The reader is warned of numerous factual and interpretive errors present in this book.

SR, 29:3:554-5   R: A. G. Gross

760.   Gudzii, N. K. **History of Early Russian Literature.** Trans. by Susan Wilber Jones. Intro. by Gleb Struve. New York, Octagon Books, 1970. (2nd Russian ed., 1949). 545p. $17.50.

(Listed in P. Horecky's *Russia and the Soviet Union*, #1363). The work covers the period from the 11th-17th centuries, and contains an 82-page appendix of sample Rus' and Old Russian texts.   S. M. H.

761.   Ingham, Norman W. **E. T. A. Hoffmann's Reception in Russia.** Ed. and intro. by George Gibian. Würzburg, Jal-Verlag, 1974. 303p. (Colloquium Slavicum, no. 6). $20.25.

The book is organized chronologically into thirteen chapters, four of them tracing the publishing and critical history and thus constituting the framework. Seven chapters on individual authors are inserted in the proper chronological slots. Thus chapter 1, "The First Translations, 1822-1829," is followed by a substantial chapter on Pogorel'sky, the first Russian author, albeit a minor one, to show unmistakably the influence of Hoffmann. In the next period, 1830-1835, in which Hoffmann's fantasy began to be grasped in Russia, we find writers of such varying quality as Pushkin, Polevoi, Mel'gunov, Gogol, and Odoevsky. After the third survey, "Hoffmann Reappraised, 1836-1840," there is only a nonentity, Olin, and for the final years of Hoffmann's early vogue in Russia, A. K. Tolstoi and Lermontov. Needless to say, the kind and degree of influence varies greatly, and Ingham makes this clear.

RR, 34:2:227-8   R: Joan D. Grossman

762.   Jakobson, Roman, and Ernest J. Simmons, eds. **Russian Epic Studies.** New York, Kraus Reprint, 1970 (1949). 223p. $10.00.

This still useful work includes the following essays: "The Vseslav Epos" (R. Jakobson and M. Szeftel); "Classical Influence on the *Slovo*" (C. Manning); "Scandinavian Influence on the *Slovo*" (M. Schlauch); "The *Slovo* in English" (A. Yarmolinsky), and others. The volume should prove useful as additional reading material for the student of history and literature.

S. M. H.

763.   Kostka, Edmund R. **Schiller in Russian Literature**. Philadelphia,
        University of Pennsylvania Press, 1965. 314p. $7.50.
This is a book of considerable general interest. Kostka shows conclusively that
Schiller was one of the main sources of this extravagant idealism, and that his
influence continued to be felt for a surprisingly long time, right down to the
days of the Symbolish movement. The author has read widely in the original
texts and secondary literature and gives a good bibliography.
        SEER, 45:105:547-8   R: W. H. Bruford

764.   Lavrin, Janko. **A Panorama of Russian Literature**. New York, Barnes &
        Noble Books, Harper & Row, 1973. 325p. $16.50.
The scope of the book in relation to its size ensures a rather simplistic analysis
of individual works and authors. This survey is for neither the scholar nor the
advanced student. For the general reader and, with reservations, for the beginning student, however, it fulfills a need which Mirsky is too erudite and out-
rageous to meet.
        SR, 33:4:820-1   R: Doris V. Johnson

765.   Legters, Lyman H., ed. **Russia: Essays in History and Literature**.
        Leiden, E. J. Brill, 1972. 1964p. $12.50.
The essays in this volume are by a group of distinguished scholars of Russian
history and literature. They are based on public lectures given at the University
of Washington in Seattle during 1967-68 and 1968-69. Each essay is an original
piece of scholarly work and, according to the editor, reflects the current research
interest of the author. The volume concludes with Eric H. Boehm's "Bibliography: Current State and Prospects."   S. M. H.

766.   Maguire, Robert A. **Red Virgin Soil: Soviet Literature in the 1920's**.
        Princeton, Princeton University Press, 1968. 482p. $10.00.
This book is actually something like a *tolsti zhurnal* in itself. True, it contains
no fiction or poetry. But it has all other ingredients: literary criticism, literary
history, cultural history, aesthetic philosophy, history *tout court*, reviews.
There is an excursus succinctly summarizing the whole history of the *tolstyi
zhurnal* in Russia, and very well too. There are articles offering excellent,
thoughtful, and independent analyses of major writers who published in
Krasnaia nov; in fact, Maguire's chapter on Pilniak and V. Ivanov contains the
most literary and penetrating criticism of these writers. This is a splendid work
and a major contribution to our field.
        SR, 28:2:356-8   R: Hugh McLean

767.   Markov, Vladimir. **Russian Futurism: A History**. Berkeley, University
        of California Press, 1968. 467p. $12.00.
Markov's *Russian Futurism* is an event in the world of Slavic scholarship, since
it is the first history of Russian Futurism either in Russian or any Western
language. A wealth of bibliographical material is supplied, most of it still unavailable to Western scholars and untranslated. Over thirty pages of reproductions
are included: photographs and portraits of prominent Futurists, pages, drawings,
and book covers from some of the most characteristic Futurist publications.

Thus, all major poets such as Majakovskij, Khlebnikov, D. Burliuk, Kruchenykh, Shershenevich, and many others are presented as men and artists in installments, as it were, throughout the book.

SEEJ, 14:1:67-9   R: Xenia Gasiorowska

768.   Mihailovich, Vasa D., comp. and ed. **Modern Slavic Literatures. Vol. 1: Russian Literature.** (A Library of Literary Criticism). New York, Frederick Ungar, 1972. 424p. $15.00.

Mihailovich has examined a wide range of materials concerning each author (69 in all of the twentieth century)—articles, book reviews, textbooks in various languages—and selected from these materials excerpts that are pithy and stimulating. Many of these selections are translated from Russian for the first time, and the translations read well. For those who do not know Russian, the book will be invaluable as a short reference tool.

SR, 32:3:665   R: Richard Sheldon

769.   Roberts, Spencer E. **Soviet Historical Drama; Its Role in the Development of a National Mythology.** The Hague, Nijhoff, 1965. 218p. 26.50Dglds.

Besides general chapters on the changes in party policy towards historiography, Roberts devotes three chapters to specific dramas about cult-heroes: Sten'ka Razin, Peter the Great and Lermontov, and their subsequent tortuous fates at the hands of Soviet critics. The selection is a good one, for it serves to bring out the pitfalls of this genre of Soviet literature in all their variety. The author's strength lies on the historical side, and the documentation of his chosen historical figures is impressive.

SEER, 44:103:496-7   R: R. D. Thomson

770.   Slonim, Marc. **Soviet Russian Literature: Writers and Problems, 1917-1967.** Rev. ed. New York, Oxford University Press, 1967. 373p. $2.25.

Slonim's book is not something entirely new; originally it formed part of the second volume (*Modern Russian Literature: From Chekhov to the Present,* 1953) of his two-volume history of Russian literature. Revised, corrected, and enlarged, it was then published under its present title in 1964. Since then it has been once more revised and brought up to date—that is, its account of Soviet literature was extended from 1963 to 1967. Slonim's book is meant for the general reader, and it certainly provides such a reader with a good over all, vividly written survey of Soviet literature during the fifty years of its existence.

SR, 27:2:352-3   R: Gleb Struve

771.   Stacy, R. H. **Russian Literary Criticism: A Short History.** Syracuse, Syracuse University Press, 1974. 268p. $15.00cl.; $8.00pa.

The book is well-informed and on the whole well-balanced—a pioneer study of Russian literary criticism from Lomonosov to our days. It fills a notable lacuna in Western studies of Russian literature and will be found useful by English-speaking students. There is no bibliography in the book, but all the important relevant literature available in English is listed at the end of each chapter.

RR, 34:3:345-6   R: Gleb Struve

772.　Struve, Gleb. **Russian Literature under Lenin and Stalin, 1917-1953.**
Norman, University of Oklahoma Press, 1971. 454p. $9.95.
The present volume—revised, enriched, and expanded—grew out of the classic
Soviet Russian Literature, 1917-1950 (1951). The bibliography is excellent
and streamlined. The footnotes, honed and updated throughout, make fascinating reading all by themselves. Several revisions turn poignantly eloquent.
The altered language of the dedication to Mandelshtam, Babel, Pilniak, and
other victims of Stalinism reflects a clearer knowledge than that of 1951 of
their martyrdom. The author masterfully structures and controls a mass of
unwieldy materials. Incisive periodization is supported by a lucid grasp of what
the regime has done to the literary life of the country.
　　　　SR, 31:1:197-8　　　　　　R: Vera S. Dunham

773.　Thomson, Boris. **The Premature Revolution: Russian Literature and
Society, 1917-1946.** London, Weidenfeld and Nicolson, 1972. 325p.
£3.95.
This volume is broader in scope than its title suggests; it attempts a survey of
Russian culture, with an emphasis on literature, during the first thirty years
of Soviet rule. Although the approach appears to be straightforward and basically
chronological, the actual structuring of the book results in somewhat erratic and
uneven emphases on the materials. This is more than a survey of literature and
literary developments, and at the same time much less than that; though necessarily abbreviated and condensed, and at the same time, something less than a
connected and coherent general view of the main cultural and literary trends.
This volume should prove useful as supplementary reading in basic courses on
Soviet literature or Soviet culture.
　　　　SR, 33:4:836-7　　　　　　R: Harold Swayze

774.　Waliszewski, Kazimierz. **A History of Russian Literature.** Port
Washington, N.Y., Kennikat, 1969 (1927). 451p. $15.00.
The first edition of this popular history of Russian literature was published in
1900. Though written in journalistic form, the book provides adequate information on the various subjects and offers pertinent criticism, explanations, and
analyses that are not always found in other histories of Russian literature. It
makes good reading for the general reader who is not interested in academic
complexities.　　　　　　　　　　　　　S. M. H.

Critical Studies

775.　Amosoff, N. **The Open Heart.** Trans. by George St. George. New York,
Simon & Shuster, 1967. 248p. $4.95.
The Open Heart reaffirms Russian literature's traditional concern with the
individual and his subjective feelings, as against the wooden collectivism of
socialist realism. Medical subjects lend themselves ideally to this reaffirmation.
The main value of this book, however, is neither literary nor documentary. It
"humanizes" the Soviet medical scene and gives a glimpse of a surgical clinic
in the USSR.
　　　　SR, 27:2:336-7　　　　　　R: Mark G. Field

776.   Anderson, Roger B. **The Teller in the Tale: N. M. Karamzin's Prose;
       A Study in Narrative Technique**. Houston, Cordovan Press, 1974.
       238p. $8.95.
Anderson has undertaken "to discuss Karamzin's nonhistorical prose chronologically and systematically on the level of an intrinsic (textual) analysis";
his main thesis is "simply that Karamzin's choice of narrative point of view in
any given piece of fiction relates significantly to the unified message of that
work." As it turns out, this approach works best of all precisely with the
Letters. The book is informative but also thought-provoking; the style is lucid
and simple; the analytical tools are sharp.
   SEEJ, 18:4:428-9   R: Rimvydas Šilbajoris

777.   Baer, Joachim T. **Vladimir Ivanovič Dal' As a Belletrist**. The Hague,
       Mouton, 1972. 204p. (Slavistic Printings and Reprintings, 276). 42Dglds.
This book attempts a comprehensive summary of Dal''s writings from his first
major work, *Russian Fairy Tales* (1832), to his essentially valedictory *New
Scenes from Russian Life* (1868). The author gives an account of the major
thematic and formal features of Dal''s favored types of narrative, with special
emphasis on his use of *skaz* and his efforts to forge a literary language from
the speech of the common man. Regrettably, the editing of the book is unsatisfactory.
   SR, 33:1:187-9   R: John Mersereau, Jr.

778.   Bakhtin, Mikhail. **Problems of Dostoevsky's Poetics**. Trans. by
       R. W. Rotsel. Ann Arbor, Ardis Publishers, 1973. 249p. $8.95cl.;
       $3.95pa.
This 1963 edition (*Problemy poetiki Dostoevskogo*) of the original 1929 study
(*Problemy tvorchestva Dostoevskogo*) is still a provocative and strikingly
original work. The new edition is about 25 percent longer than the first, and
the chief addition consists of a sixty-page excursion into the sources of polyphonic art, which takes Bakhtin back to classical models, folk art, and ritual,
and to what he calls the carnivalization of life. The carnival attitudes to life
in its literary form has the effect of mixing styles, tones, and of uniting opposed
ideas; it is the matrix from which the polyphonic novel developed. Bakhtin is
part of "classical" Dostoevsky criticism, and serious students of Dostoevsky
who do not know Russian will now have an opportunity to judge for themselves
whose voice they hear in his novels.
   SR, 34:2:436-8   R: Edward Wasiolek

779.   Bayley, John. **Pushkin: A Comparative Commentary**. Cambridge,
       Cambridge University Press, 1971. 369p. $13.50.
What the author does is comment on most of Pushkin's works, using mixed
chronological and genre divisions of the subject. Those who are seriously
interested in Pushkin—students taking a course about him, amateur readers,
and lovers of Pushkin, and especially those whose vocation is the study of
Pushkin—will all want to read Bayley's comments when they approach a particular work by the poet.
   SR, 31:1:188   R: George Gibian

780. Bayley, John. **Tolstoy and the Novel.** New York, Viking, 1967. 616p. $6.95.

The book deals most extensively and successfully with *War and Peace*. Shorter chapters are devoted to *Anna Karenina, What is Art, Resurrection,* Tolstoi's shorter tales, particularly those concerned with the Caucasus and sex, and the book ends with a brief consideration of *Doctor Zhivago* in the tradition of Tolstoi's work, counterpart to a lengthy, obscure, and questionable introduction devoted to the course of Russian literature before Tolstoi and the "Inevitable Comparisons" between Tolstoi and Dostoevski. The reader will question numerous interpretations, assertions, and arguments but will have added greatly to his understanding and appreciation of Tolstoi through this sophisticated study.

SR, 26:3:510-1   R: Ralph E. Matlaw

781. Benson, Ruth Crego. **Women in Tolstoy: The Ideal and the Erotic.** Urbana, University of Illinois Press, 1973. 141p. $6.95.

On the basis of a study of several heroines in L. N. Tolstoi's fiction, Ms. Benson seeks to define Tolstoi's attitudes toward women, sex, love, marriage, and the family. The author bases her study primarily on those works of Tolstoi in which relationships between men and women are a central theme, and she includes some relevant remarks made by Tolstoi elsewhere. Benson describes Tolstoi's attitude as "ambivalent," and by this one understands her to mean that Tolstoi was both attracted to and hostile toward women. This "ambivalence," she claims, is inherent in his attitude toward every woman.

CSP, 16:4:661-4   R: Edward S. Lee

782. Birkenmayer, Sigmund S. **Nikolai Nekrasov: His Life and Poetic Art.** The Hague, Mouton, 1968. 204p. $10.00.

In this first book-length literary study of Nekrasov's work in English, the author gives a definitive and responsible statement regarding the poet's place in Russian nineteenth-century literature: Nekrasov was a mature, conscientious, and aesthetically effective artist, and no more a social reformer than Pushkin and Gogol had been. In part one Birkenmayer moves chronologically through the poet's life and reconstructs the man and his age in a careful and precise manner. In part two the author concentrates his attention on a literary discussion of Nekrasov's works and provides convincing evidence that his "Muse" was at her best in purely lyrical poems where the figure of Nekrasov-the-artist overshadows the social prophet. A list of primary sources and of critical and biographical works in Russian, English, French, and Polish is appended.

SEEJ, 14:3:381-2   R: Rolf Ekmanis

783. Brown, Clarence. **Mandelstam.** New York, Cambridge University Press, 1973. 320p. $13.95.

One of the joys of Brown's book is the personal tone. He has been involved with Mandel'shtam and his poetry since the mid-1950s when he was a graduate student at Harvard. After a "Preliminary," chapters 2-7 offer an authoritative compilation of all known facts concerning Mandel'shtam's biography up to 1925. The stark heading of chapter 8, where the material is presented in the form of chronicle entries, is all too clear: "1925-1938: Silence, prose, arrest, exile, sickness, death." The well-chosen photographs tell the story on their own. Brown confines his study of the poetry to that written before 1925, with only a few excursions into the final periods.

RR, 33:2:296-302   R: Robert P. Hughes

784.   Brown, Edward J., ed. **Major Soviet Writers: Essays in Criticism.**
        New York, Oxford University Press, 1973. 439p. $3.95pa.

The essays, dealing with circa forty Soviet Russian authors written by fourteen critics, are grouped into those concerned with poetry and those concerned with prose. Within each group they tend to cluster around a certain major figure. No effort was made to establish connections among the individual essays, but placed side by side they seem to interact in various ways so as to impart to certain paragraphs a new vibration. This is a collection that can only be described as distinguished.

SEEJ, 18:2:188-9   R: Richard Sheldon

785.   Brown, Edward J. **Mayakovsky: A Poet in the Revolution.** Princeton,
        Princeton University Press, 1973. 386p. (Studies of the Russian
        Institute, Columbia University). $16.50.

This is the first full-length biography of Mayakovsky in English. Moreover, it is truly a critical biography, predictably free from the pieties and the taboos which hamstring V. O. Pertsov's three-volume account. Brown's adeptness at literary analysis, at identifying the work's commanding images and disentangling its thematic and ideational strands, is evidenced by his dissections of Mayakovsky's long poems such as "The Cloud in Trousers," "The Flute Spine," "Man," and, most notably, "About That." It is first and foremost a richly textured *story*— a story of a major poet and a remarkable human being, told with authority, grace, and acumen.

SR, 34:1:199-200   R: Victor Erlich

786.   Burg, David and George Feifer. **Solzhenitsyn.** New York, Stein & Day,
        1972. 371p. $10.00.

The American author of *Justice in Moscow* and *The Girl from Petrovka*, Feifer, and the Russian-born Burg, who writes for English newspapers, have made a really first-rate contribution. Their book is a serious, thorough study which was written in spite of considerable personal risk and difficulty, not to mention Solzhenitsyn's almost total aversion to publicity. The book is well organized, and the mass of material—much of it unearthed in the Soviet Union firsthand by the authors—is well presented. Their book is not only a worthy tribute to Solzhenitsyn's talent and literary achievement, but a moving description of a man of profound religious faith and patriotism, and finally a convincing explanation of how that man has come to be a significant ethical force today in Russia and in the world.

SR, 32:4:859-61   R: Roger Hagglund

787.   Carden, Patricia. **The Art of Isaac Babel.** Ithaca, Cornell University
        Press, 1972. 223p. $8.50.

Carden treats Babel's devices essentially as those of narrative prose, with emphasis on message and expression, and she does it very well. She makes here the ingenious observation that Babel maintains his reader's interest by keeping him guessing about the artistic and moral point of each story. This book contains a good synthesis of earlier criticism, advances a number of new ideas, and provides a reliable basis for future scholarship. The treatment of the philosophical and psychological aspects of Babel's work is quite exhaustive.

      SEEJ, 18:3:322-3   R: Victor Terras

788.   Christian, R. F. **Tolstoy: A Critical Introduction**. Cambridge, Cambridge University Press, 1969. 291p. $9.50cl.; $2.95pa.

This book is supported by extensive scholarship in Russian sources and an expert, sensitive knowledge of the language. The result is a fresh approach to a comprehensive definition of Tolstoy's creative art and one which is expressed with maturity of judgment and original insights. Written with grace and occasional quiet humor, the book is an important contribution, and the pleasure it affords the reader is enhanced by the author's conviction, which suffuses the whole study, that Tolstoy "is a great novelist because he was a great man."

      SR, 29:1:751   R: Ernest J. Simmons

789.   Cioran, Samuel D. **The Apocalyptic Symbolism of Andrej Belyj**. The Hague, Mouton, 1973. 270p. (Slavistic Printings and Reprintings, 274). 56Dglds.

In chapter 1 ("The Context") Cioran describes the apocalyptic mood of the turn of the century as the background against which Belyi wrote. Chapter 2 ("The Family Apocalypse") also provides background and it is more successful. In chapter 3 ("Towards a Theory of Symbolism") Cioran attempts to systematize what he rightly calls the "confusing array" of knowledge found in Belyi's theoretical writings. The next chapter ("The Call of Eternity") discusses the four *Symphonies*, early, often denigrated, and the most obviously apocalyptic of Belyi works. The last chapter ("The Eternal Return") discusses theosophical, anthroposophical, biblical, mythological, psychological, and Nietzschean elements in *Kotik Letaev*. This volume is a valuable addition to the literature on Belyi.

      SEEJ, 18:3:321-2   R: Gerald Janecek

790.   Clive, Geoffrey. **The Broken Icon: Intuitive Existentialism in Classical Russian Fiction**. New York, Macmillan, 1972. 233p. $7.95.

Clive approaches a series of important novelists in terms of modern philosophical concepts. Existentialism is a philosophy that attempts to analyze and systematize the same sort of spiritual experiences to which only Russian literature in modern times has succeeded in giving convincing artistic life. The author concentrates on works of the following novelists: Gogol, Goncharov, Tolstoy, Dostoevsky, and Solzhenitsyn. The result is a suggestive and continually interesting book, extremely well written and quite illuminating. The book was not, however, written for specialists but rather for students and general readers.

      SR, 33:1:183-4   R: Joseph Frank

791.   Collins, Christopher. **Evgenij Zamjatin: An Interpretive Study**. The Hague, Mouton, 1973. 117p. 30Dglds. pa.

Collin's overall argument is that Zamjatin evolved from a scientific-minded intellectual heretic and revolutionary into a seeker after a new unity, in which modern attitudes and developments might be integrated with the traditional values and patterns of a more primitive, more natural life. Some of the most interesting and original pages in this study are devoted to analyzing Zamiatin's symbolism in Jungian terms. The bibliography and index are both useful.

        SEER, 53:130:111-2   R: D. J. Richards

792.   Cross, A. G. **N. M. Karamzin: A Study of His Literary Career, 1783-1803.** Carbondale, Southern Illinois University Press. London and Amsterdam, Feffer & Simons, 1971. 306p. $12.50.

The author has chosen to focus on Karamzin's ideas—social and political ideas as well as aesthetic—telling us where Karamzin got them, how he adapted them to the tastes of his Russian readers, and how he continued to press them on his readers even as the ideas themselves underwent transformation. Doubtless such works as the *Memoir and History of the Russian State* are discussed because one could hardly do justice to the spectrum of Karamzin's thought otherwise. Students of comparative literature, Russian intellectual history, and Russian literature courses where the emphasis is on themes, motifs, and *Geistesgeschichte* will find many illuminating passages in Cross's book. The study belongs on any general reading list devoted to eighteenth-century Russia.

        SR, 31:2:420-1   R: Horace W. Dewey

793.   Dalton, Margaret. **A. K. Tolstoy.** New York, Twayne Publishers, 1972. 181p. (Twayne's World Authors Series, no. 168). $5.50.

Dalton's study is a comprehensive treatment of Tolstoy's life and all his major works; even a considerable amount of lyric poetry has been included. The author notes that the novel *Prince Serebriannyi* served Tolstoy as a "practice run" for the later dramatic trilogy.

        SR, 31:4:937-8   R: William E. Harkins

794.   Dalton, Margaret. **Andrei Siniavskii and Julii Daniel: Two Soviet "Heretical" Writers.** Würzburg, Jal-Verlag, 1973. 190p. (Colloquium Slavicum, Beiträge zur Slavistik, no. 1). DM26pa.

The author's express intention in this study is to provide a "literary interpretation" of works which, she believes, have been "heavily distorted" by overemphasis on their political aspects at the expense of their literary content. The volume contains, in addition to discussions of the two writers' fiction and of Siniavsky's essay on socialist realism and *Mysli vrasplokh*, a brief biographical sketch of each writer.

        SR, 33:3:612   R: Harold Swayze

795.   Debreczeny, Paul, and Jesse Zeldin, eds. and trans. **Literature and National Identity: Nineteenth-Century Russian Critical Essays.** Lincoln, University of Nebraska Press, 1970. 188p. $8.50.

This volume contains five essays and an introductory article by Paul Debreczeny. The essays, all translated into English for the first time, are by Ivan Kireevsky (on Pushkin's poetry), Stepan Shevyrev (on Gogol's *Dead Souls*), Apollon Grigoriev (on Turgenev's *A Nest of the Gentry*), Nikolai Strakhov (on *War and Peace*), and Vladimir Soloviev (on Dostoevsky). The translators are to be commended for producing generally readable and what appear to be accurate versions. The texts are annotated, and a helpful index is included.

SR, 30:3:702-3 R: Arthur Levin

796. Dees, Benjamin. **E. A. Baratynsky**. New York, Twayne Publishers, 1972. 160p. (Twayne's World Authors Series, no. 202).
Dees's book is a carefully done, extremely succinct piece of work that merits the close attention of the specialist in the period and in Russian poetry. Curiously for a book in this Twayne series, it is not written so as to be accessible to the general reader of poetry or even the general Russian specialist. It is a highly condensed scholarly monograph rather than a work of criticism or even of scholarly criticism. After a brief biographical account, Dees gives a running analysis and commentary on Baratynsky's poems, in chronological order except for a chapter on the narrative poems.

SR, 34:2:431-3 R: J. Thomas Shaw

797. Driver, Sam N. **Anna Akhmatova**. New York, Twayne Publishers, 1972. 162p. (Twayne's World Authors Series, no. 198). $5.95.
Akhmatova has always been one of the most accessible of all the great modern Russian poets. A recently published selection of her verse in the exceedingly good translations of Stanley Kumitz will make her audience abroad even larger. This brief study of Akhmatova's poetry starts with dealing mainly with her early poetry. Driver's treatment is straightforward-orthodox, therefore systematic and informative; the reader gets a brief account of Akhmatova's life, a quick survey of Acmeism by way of literary background, and then a careful sorting of suits and sequences.

SR, 33:1:190-1 R: H. W. Tjalsma

798. Dunlop, John B., et al., eds. **Aleksandr Solzhenitsyn: Critical Essays and Documentary Materials**. Belmont, Mass., Nordland Publishing Co., 1973. 569p. $16.95.
This is the first well-organized symposium in English on the many facets of Solzhenitsyn's writing. The contributors—American, British, Canadian, French, German, as well as Russian expatriates—are all distinguished scholars in their respective fields, one of them a Nobel Prize winner in literature. Original studies constitute one-third of the material. The essays (35 in all) complement each other rather interestingly. The editors have compiled a volume which is entitled to a prominent place on the shelves of every serious educational institution. The last 114 pages of "Documentary Materials," which include a bibliography, are sufficient to make this work important and of lasting value to all scholars engaged in studying the thought and the writings of Solzhenitsyn.

CSP, 17:1:186-7 R: Alexander P. Obolensky

799. Dyck, J. W. **Boris Pasternak**. New York, Twayne Publishers, 1972. 206p. (Twayne's World Authors Series, no. 225). $6.50.
The author provides a general introduction to Pasternak and in so doing manages to at least touch on all aspects of his writing. Dyck devotes a chapter to his poetics as presented in the autobiographies and then goes on to discuss the

poetry, *Doctor Zhivago*, the short prose, and the translations. The book can
serve as a basic guide for the reader largely unfamiliar with Pasternak.
    SR, 32:4:857-8   R: Barry P. Scherr

800.   Ehre, Milton. **Oblomov and His Creator: The Life and Art of Ivan
       Goncharov**. Princeton, Princeton University Press, 1973. 295p. (Studies
       of the Russian Institute, Columbia University). $14.50cl.; $3.45pa.
The purpose of the book "is twofold: to make a major Russian novelist of the
nineteenth century more familiar to those who know him only through *Oblomov*,
and to reach beyond the standard clichés of Goncharov criticism to a contemporary
reading of his art," the basic assumption being that "the meanings of art are
intimately related to their forms." The author fulfills these aims not only competently but in a masterful fashion that is a model of criticism—fresh and original,
although drawing on Soviet scholarship, and well-organized—to give an accurate
and living picture of Goncharov and the interrelationship of his life and art. This
book belongs on the shelf (and in the hand) of anyone interested in the Russian
novel.
    CSP, 16:4:668-9   R: G. M. H. Shoolbraid

801.   Eng-Liedmeier, Jeanne van der, and Kees Verheul. **Tale without
       a Hero and Twenty-Two Poems by Anna Axmatova**. With unpublished
       poems by Anna Axmatova. The Hague, Mouton, 1973. 141p. 30Dglds. pa.
Both authors place their considerable expertise at the disposal of their audience
and succeed brilliantly in pointing out those beauties and merits of Akhmatova's
poetry that less acute readers might have missed. The collection contains the
following essays by the two authors: "Public Theme in the Poetry of Anna
Akhmatova," "Twenty-Two Poems of Anna Akhmatova"; "*Poema bez geroia*,"
and the concluding essay by Verheul entitled: "Some Marginal Observations of
the First Version of *Poema bez geroia*." All the contributions combine into one
set and, as a result, Akhmatova emerges as the powerful spokesman of a whole
generation, a vivid recorder of the predicament of intellectuals after the Revolution, and the study in general represents sensitive and sympathetic probing of a
type that still cannot be done in the poet's homeland.
    CASS, 9:1:180-9   R: Ludmila Koehler

802.   Falen, James E. **Isaac Babel: Russian Master of the Short Story**.
       Knoxville, University of Tennessee Press, 1974. 269p. $9.75.
With keen insight, Falen examines the tales within the context of Babel's personal
experience. Babel (1894-1941?) was a highly autobiographical writer for whom
questions of personal identity played a central role. The author also examines the
influences, particularly those derived from a Jewish cultural tradition, which
helped shape those traits.   S. M. H.

803.   Fanger, Donald. **Dostoevsky and Romantic Realism: A Study of
       Dostoevsky in Relation to Balzac, Dickens, and Gogol**. Cambridge,
       Harvard University Press, 1965. 307p. $7.50.
Fanger's book is a highly intelligent presentation of Dostoevsky as a romantic
realist, romantic in his concern with the alienated, the grotesque, the exceptional,
and the half-comprehended which expands to mythic significance; and realistic

in his concern with the prosaic materials in the life of the urban oppressed. He devotes about half his space to Balzac, Dickens, and Gogol, not as sources for Dostoevsky, although he is familiar with the studies of such relationships, but as parallel examples of what he considers to be a separate literary movement which has received less attention than it deserves. Fanger has written a book which was badly needed, and has written it very well.

SR, 24:3:561-2   R: Robert L. Belknap

804.   Fiene, Donald M., comp. **Alexander Solzhenitsyn: An International Bibliography of Writings by and about Him, 1962-1972.** Ann Arbor, Ardis, 1973. 148p. $8.95cl.; $3.50pa.

This bibliography is the most complete and up-to-date presently available and covers the period from 1962 to November-December 1972. It lists publications in Russian and English, by type and relative importance, mostly in chronological order. Book reviews are listed alphabetically according to the title of the periodical. The introduction lists all standard reference works consulted as well as the various transliterations and abbreviations used. In spite of its possible shortcomings, this bibliography should be welcomed by scholars, critics, and students alike.

CSP, 16:4:684-5   R: G. M.

805.   Gasiorowska, Xenia. **Women in Soviet Fiction, 1917-1964.** Madison, University of Wisconsin Press, 1968. 288p. $10.00.

Gasiorowska's study of women in Soviet fiction, written with grace, humor, and an impressive familiarity with her material, is a thorough and comprehensive treatment of Soviet literary heroines, but within narrowly circumscribed limits the author has set for herself. Having chosen to study women as they appear in Soviet fiction, the author realizes that she is dealing with the historical development of a literary stereotype and not with the true nature of existence for Soviet women since the Revolution. Gasiorowska has culled fifty years of Soviet literature, seeking the essence of the fictional women it has created. Unlike many Western scholars, her bent is to discover the generalizations in the literature, rather than the exceptions. Despite the post-Stalin relaxation in literature, Soviet writers have remained moralistic and prudish in their treatment of sex.

SR, 29:1:754-5   R: Jeri Laber

806.   Gibson, A. Boyce. **The Religion of Dostoevsky.** Philadelphia, Westminster Press, 1974. 216p. $6.95.

The author was a professor of philosophy at the University of Melbourne; he died in 1972. His book is the result of his lifelong interest in Dostoevsky. It compares favorably with the best known of the many essays on the subject by Berdiaev. Gibson is more sober, less eulogistic, and more useful as he presents Dostoevsky's development instead of a final credo. Strong in theology, the author is less secure in literature. He seems to suggest that Dostoevsky made use of polyphony precisely because, as a Christian moralist, he was primarily concerned with one central issue, the "wholly personal issue of pride." It is pride which makes an individual resent being seen by others as an object, and polyphony emerges as a struggle between subjectivities refusing to be objectivized. Gibson, although fascinated by Dostoevsky's genius, does not call him a great theologian.

SR, 34:1:193-4   R: Cesław Miłosz

807.   Gregg, Richard A. **Fedor Tiutchev: The Evolution of a Poet**. New York, Columbia University Press, 1965. 257p. $6.50.

This volume undertakes a biographical and psychological study of its subject by presenting a detailed analysis of his major and representative lyrics taken in chronological order. It is a reworked dissertation (at Columbia University) retaining the main body of its research, which has been incorporated into a critical study contributing well to Russian literary studies.

SR, 28:2:352-3   R: Richard Burgi

808.   Grossman, Joan Delaney. **Edgar Allan Poe in Russia: A Study in Legend and Literary Influence**. Würzburg, Jal-Verlag, 1973. 245p. (Colloquium Slavicum, Beiträge zur Slavistik, no. 3). DM30. pa.

This treatment of the influence of Poe in Russia offers Slavic studies and the study of comparative literature the answer to a question that has remained in doubt since the time of symbolism. The author has, in her thorough and carefully balanced study, indicated the submerged and forgotten paths by which the myth of the "*bezumnyi* Edgar" was disseminated in Russia, and she also sets herself the problem of the earlier discussed influence on individual Russian writers of Poe's work.

SR, 33:3:604-5   R: Johannes Holthusen

809.   Gustafson, Richard F. **The Imagination of Spring: The Poetry of Afanasy Fet**. New Haven, Yale University Press, 1966. 264p. (Yale Russian and East European Studies, vol. 2). $8.50.

Gustafson introduces relevant philosophical and biographical materials with great skill. His criticism is shrewd and full of insight. Even the interpretation of "On a Swing," which is rather startling, is ultimately convincing. It is the first full-length study in English of this major Russian poet.

SR, 28:2:352-3   R: Richard Burgi

810.   Hayward, Max, and Leopold Labedz, eds. **Literature and Revolution in Soviet Russia, 1917-1962; A Symposium**. London, Oxford University Press, 1963. 235p. 25s.

A better description of this book would be "studies in the changing literary situation of the Soviet writer," for the majority of these papers deal with the politics of Soviet literature, the crucial moments, the turning-points in the evolution of the literary situation of the Soviet writers; and it is these essays that are the most valuable in the book. As a result of the developments during the 1920s, the literature of modern Russia is now almost synonymous with the literary situation.

SEER, 44:102:213-5   R: R. D. B. Thomson

811.   Jackson, Robert Louis, ed. **Chekhov: A Collection of Critical Essays.**
         Englewood Cliffs, N.J., Prentice-Hall, 1967. 213p. (Twentieth Century
         Views). $4.95cl.; $1.95pa.
In his introduction Jackson sees as a fundamental philosophical orientation
and basic theme in Chekhov the clash of will and environment, freedom and
necessity, as revealed through his unheroic minor personalities. The introduction
also includes a brief history of Chekhov criticism. The first essay of the collection (B. Eikhenbaum, "Chekhov at Large") seeks to establish the thematic
relation of Chekhov's untraditional heroes to the ineffective protagonists in
the works of Pisemsky and Leskov. L. Grossman ("The Naturalism of Chekhov")
examines the influence of the French naturalists on Chekhov. A. Skaftymov
("Principle of Structure in Chekhov's Plays"), like D. Chizhevsky's essay, seeks
to associate Chekhov's style with his world view. Jackson ("The Seagull: The
Empty Well, the Dry Lake, and the Cold Cave") presents a Freudian analysis of
Konstantin, who is unable to cope with life, and interprets Nina's ability to take
her life into her own hands in an archetypal context. Several other essays offer
additional insights into Chekhov's world view.
         SR, 30:1:205-7   R: Thomas G. Winner

812.   Jackson, Robert Louis. **Dostoevsky's Quest for Form: A Study of
         His Philosophy of Art.** New Haven, Yale University Press, 1966.
         274p. $6.00.
The eleven chapters of this notable study contain an exhaustive, amply documented, and convincing presentation of the development of Dostoevsky's
aesthetic view in a general philosophic and religious context. The author leaves
no doubt about how deeply Dostoevsky was indebted for the formation as well
as the formulation of his basic aesthetic ideas to the thought of German idealism,
especially the moral-aesthetic speculations of Schiller, Schelling, and Hegel. Taken
all in all, this study is a truly outstanding achievement.
         RR, 26:3:301-2   R: Heinrich A. Stammler

813.   James, C. Vaughan. **Soviet Socialist Realism: Origins and Theory.**
         New York, St. Martin's Press, 1973. 146p. $9.95.
James's book is concerned with the gradual evolution of Lenin's views on the
functions of the press (and literature) to the final formulation of the well-
known theory of socialist realism at the First Congress of Soviet Writers in 1934,
and its subsequent application. The book is thus concerned with political theory
rather than literary development. The study is complemented by abundant
quotations from Soviet sources. Although the author's enthusiasm for his subject
is admirable, his final deductions seem hardly worth the energy expended on
reaching them.
         SR, 34:1:198-9   R: Margaret Dalton

814.   Karlinsky, Simon. **Marina Cvetaeva: Her Life and Art.** Berkeley,
         University of California Press, 1966. 317p. $7.25.
Of the many outstanding and talented twentieth-century Russian poets, perhaps
none has been so neglected and mistreated as M. Tsvetaeva. Karlinsky's book
attempts to correct this situation. After meticulously scanning all the material
available to him, the author has gathered for the first time a comprehensive

bibliography and in digested form related the significant events in the poet's life. Part One of this book discusses in detail the major period of Tsvetaeva's literary career, her relations with her contemporary fellow-writers, her loves and losses, her sad emigration, and even sadder return to her native land, where in 1941 she ended her life by her own hand. In Part Two the author writes of art. The long chapter on the technical aspects of Tsvetaeva's verse is informed and informative, even if its focus is limited to those technical features of special interest to the Formalists.

SR, 26:3:514-5   R: Richard F. Gustafson

815.   Kaun, Alexander Samuel. **Leonid Andreyev: A Critical Study**. New York, AMS Press, 1970 (1924). 361p. $9.50.
(Original edition listed in P. Horecky's *Russia and the Soviet Union*, #1477). This monograph is one of the best available in English as a critical evaluation of Andreyev's works.   S. M. H.

816.   Kemball, Robert. **Alexander Blok: A Study in Rhythm and Metre**. The Hague, Mouton, 1965. 539p. 80Dglds.
This long monograph in Blok's metrics is divided into four parts: Part I is "introductory," devoted to "Blok's Place in Russian Prosody." Part II presents a comparison between English and Russian versification. Part III is divided into six sections, treating rhythmic variations in the various meters, certain cases of "irregular" substitution in what are basically standard meters, tonic verse, and ending patterns in Blok's verse. Part IV covers again all of Blok's poetry, this time arranging the poems according to meters. The book is a fine beginning for this most difficult task.

RR, 25:4:421-3   R: Richard F. Gustafson

817.   Kramer, Karl D. **The Chameleon and the Dream: The Image of Reality in Čexov's Stories**. The Hague, Mouton, 1970. 182p. (Slavistic Printings and Reprintings, 78). 36Dglds.
The author has tackled his detailed exploration of the ambiguity which is central to Chekhov's world view and narrative technique with courage and panache, and his book ranks alongside Alexander Chudakov's *Poetika Chekhova* (1971) as one of the most important studies of this writer to appear for many years. Kramer writes in an intelligent, easy-flowing, readable style which permits detailed re-narration, where necessary, without laboriousness, and complex argumentation, without obscurity. Despite his deep understanding of and commitment to Chekhov, there is no uncritical idolization.

SR, 33:3:609-10   R: L. M. O'Toole

818.   Kryzytski, Serge. **The Works of Ivan Bunin**. The Hague, Mouton, 1971. 283p. (Slavistic Printings and Reprintings, 101). 56Dglds.
This volume is an attempt to answer the need for a complete and authoritative treatment in English of Ivan Bunin's life and work, and it has much to offer. The content of Bunin's prose and poetry is treated exhaustively, with frequent comments on matters of literary language and style. Bunin's biography is carefully worked out, and the reader receives a lively impression of the famous writer's personality. The author makes every effort to tie Bunin's literary

production to his life, and quite often to explain the former in terms of the latter. The student of Bunin will come away from this work with a comprehensive knowledge of what Bunin wrote and what he did in his life, and some notion of already existing criticism.

SR, 34:2:439-40   R: Edward J. Brown

819.   Labedz, Leopold, ed. **Solzhenitsyn: A Documentary Record**. Foreword by Harrison E. Salisbury. New York, Harper & Row, 1971. 229p. $7.95.

This is a meticulously annotated compilation of material on the career of Solzhenitsyn from his literary debut in 1962 to the furor over the Nobel Prize in the fall and winter of 1970. Included are attacks on Solzhenitsyn (and a few early defenses) from the Soviet press; various statements from Solzhenitsyn himself, including his correspondence with the Writers' Union; three "interviews" with the writer, numerous protests against his treatment gleaned from *samizdat*; and protests directed by foreign intellectuals to the Soviet authorities. Historians will turn frequently to these documents for vivid evidence of the sinister machinery that controlled Soviet literary life in the sixties and for an indication of what Soviet readers were like.

SR, 31:4:942-3   R: Deming Brown
(An enlarged edition of this work was published by Indiana University Press, 1973. 320p. $3.50pa. Reviewed in SEER, 52:129:613-5. R: D. Short).

820.   Ledkovsky, Marina. **The Other Turgenev: From Romanticism to Symbolism**. Würzburg, Jal-Verlag, 1973. 170p. (Colloquium Slavicum, Beiträge zur Slavistik, no. 2). DM24 pa.

The author begins with a study of the romantic elements in Turgenev's writing, linking these to the wide Russian interest in the "Gothic," proceeding to a discussion of nonrealist themes in his better-known works, and leading to a discussion of his relatively little-read "mysterious tales," which link him to Gogol on one side and the Symbolists on the other. It is a timely book, reinforcing one's impression that the realism ascribed to Turgenev was in fact a great curiosity about all dimensions of life, mitigated by an enduring skepticism regarding the powers of reason.

SR, 33:2:400-1   R: George Woodcock

821.   Lednicki, Wacław. **Tolstoy between War and Peace**. The Hague, Mouton, 1965. 169p. (Slavistic Printings and Reprintings, 52). 25Dglds.

The book deals specifically with Tolstoi's attitude toward the Russo-Polish "problem." Lednicki devoted many years of research to this vexing problem, as is evident by his other works. The purpose of this book is to show that Tolstoi's sympathetic attitude toward the Poles after *War and Peace* corresponds to his spiritual crisis. The first chapter is devoted to a careful examination of Tolstoi's Polonophobia in his earlier period. The author succeeds in proving that Tolstoi, like many of his compatriots, was infected with the xenophobia that was endemic to Russia. The other five chapters deal with Tolstoi's change, which was of a moral rather than a political nature. The book is well documented, and the thesis is fully proven.

SR, 25:3:359060   R: Louis J. Shein

822.   Linnér, Sven. **Dostoevskij on Realism**. Stockholm, Almqvist and
        Wiksell, 1967. 211p. (Acta Universitatis Stockholmiensis, Stockholm
        Slavic Studies, 1). Kr30.

This book is an attempt to investigate what Dostoevsky's views on "realism" actually were. To solve this problem, Linnér examines very carefully and conscientiously all of Dostoevsky's nonfictional writings (journalism, letters, and notebooks) from the time of his emergence from his Siberian *Katorga* (1854) to his death in 1881. Dostoevsky's novels are excluded from consideration of this question on methodological grounds. What Linnér's examination shows has long been well known, though it has not before been documented so carefully and so clearly. Dostoevsky's ideas on art were influenced by Belinsky's advocacy of "realism" in the 1840s. At the same time, his polemic with Dobroliubov in 1861, and some remarks in his letters, also bring him close to "a romantic and idealistic position." This contradiction between realism and idealism runs through all of Dostoevsky's thinking about art, and Linnér follows the course of his oscillations from one point of view to the other throughout the rest of his career.

SR, 29:1:748-9   R: Joseph Frank

823.   Lyngstad, Alexandra, and Sverre Lyngstad. **Ivan Goncharov**. New
        York, Twayne Publishers, 1971. 184p. (Twayne's World Authors
        Series, no. 200). $5.50.

This book offers many original insights and interpretations. The authors' scholarship is thorough; their literary judgments are often sound; the style is readable. They have touched upon the major issues of Goncharov's fiction, and their book deserves to be read.

SR, 31:4:937   R: Milton Ehre

824.   Magarshack, David. **Chekhov: A Life**. Westport, Conn., Greenwood
        Press, 1970 (1952). 433p. $10.50.

(Original edition listed in P. Horecky's *Russia and the Soviet Union*, #1484). This biography should be used with caution and the awareness that it is not always reliable. Ronald Hingley's *Chekhov: A Biographical and Critical Study* (1950) should be consulted together with this book.

S. M. H.

825.   Marshak, Samuel. **At Life's Beginning: Some Pages of Reminiscence**.
        Trans. by Katherine Hunter Blair. Foreword by Moura Budberg. Illus.
        by G. Philippovsky. New York, Dutton, 1964. 208p. $4.00.

This book takes the story of S. Ia. Marshak's life from his birth in 1887 to 1905 (he died in 1964). Marshak was one of the most beloved of Soviet writers. According to his Moscow obituaries, seventy million copies of his works had been published in the USSR during his lifetime. Marshak was equally famous as a translator and as a writer for children.

SR, 24:2:346-7   R: Edgar H. Lehrman

826. Matejka, Ladislav, and Krystyna Pomorska, eds. **Readings in Russian Poetics: Formalist and Structuralist Views**. Cambridge, MIT Press, 1971. 306p. $12.50.

The objective of this anthology is to "acquaint English readers with the methodological struggles in which the leading Russian theorists of literature engaged during the 1920's and early 1930's." Seventeen articles contributed by eleven experts transcend this somewhat narrow objective and acquaint the reader with the Formalist method *sui generis*. Apart from some shortcomings this book represents a valuable addition to the growing literature on Russian Formalism and a fine didactic tool for those whose language skills do not extend to Russian and Czech (original languages of contributions to this volume).

    SR, 31:3:735-6   R: John Fizer

827. Mochul'skii, Konstantin. **Dostoevsky: His Life and Work**. Trans. with an introduction by Michael A. Minihan. Princeton, Princeton University Press, 1967. 687p. $12.50.

Mochulsky's work has previously appeared in Russian and in French. A mixture of biography and criticism, it is one of the best books on the subject. The author's literary sensitivity and his sympathy with Dostoevsky's religious questionings combined to give him a rare insight into the novels. He expresses this perception not in amorphous rhapsodies but in judicious, analytical prose. The translation itself is accurate and reads well.

    SR, 28:4:675-7   R: R. M. Davison

828. Monter, Barbara Heldt. **Koz'ma Prutkov: The Art of Parody**. The Hague, Mouton, 1972. 143p. (Slavistic Printings and Reprintings, 211). 32Dglds.

This is a useful handbook and the author's translations are plentiful, well selected, and accurate. Her discussion of the genesis of the poet is knowledgeable. The thankless task of explaining the jokes and elucidating the allusions is tackled with resolution and efficiency.

    SR, 33:2:401-2   R: Richard Gregg

829. Moody, Christopher. **Solzhenitsyn**. New York, Barnes & Noble, 1973. 184p. $5.25.

Deceptively small in format, this book presents the most thorough general survey of Solzhenitsyn's fiction that has yet appeared. It concentrates on the works themselves, reducing biographical information to an essential minimum. Although it examines the writings as individual entities, the study is abundantly laced with cross-references comparing and contrasting their thematic and aesthetic characteristics. The book's most valuable contribution to our understanding of Solzhenitsyn is in demonstrating the multiple correlations of ideas, characters, and creative methods among his various works.

    SR, 33:3:611-2   R: Deming Brown

830. Moser, Charles A. **Pisemsky: A Provincial Realist**. Cambridge, Harvard University Press, 1969. 269p. $10.00.

This is a solid, scholarly volume, and certainly an important one for those interested in Pisemsky and his times. Among its virtues is an extensive and

extremely useful bibliography of works by and about Pisemsky, including an
exhaustive list of translations in a variety of European languages. Throughout
the book Moser follows the literary and personal relationships between Pisemsky
and a whole flock of the leading figures of the age—Turgenev, Ostrovsky, Nekrasov,
Grigoriev, and Dmitrii Pisarev, among others. The treatment of these relationships
is important not only for the light it throws on Pisemsky's literary fortunes, but
also for the total picture it provides of the shifting literary attitudes of the age.

     SR, 29:4:696-7   R: Karl D. Kramer

831.   Nabokov, Vladimir. **Speak, Memory. An Autobiography Revisited**.
        New York, Putnam's Sons, 1966. 316p. $6.75.
Everything about Nabokov narrated by Nabokov cannot be but fascinating.
It goes without saying that the legendary land and the charming people never
existed, but this becomes utterly unimportant. This is *Solus Rex*, written in
1939. Only the first part of it appeared in the émigré quarterly *Sovremennye
zapiski* (Spring 1940).

     RR, 26:4:405-6   R: Nina Berberova

832.   Nebel, Henry M., Jr. **N. M. Karamzin: A Russian Sentimentalist**.
        The Hague, Mouton, 1967. 190p. (Slavistic Printings and Reprintings,
        60). 32Dglds.
The book contains much useful and absorbing information about the intellectual
movements that contributed to Karamzin's development: the publishing and
cultural activities of the Moscow masons in the 1760s, and especially their
turning inward toward mysticism and the "wisdom of the heart" in the 1780s.

     SR, 28:4:672   R: Rimvydas Silbajoris

833.   Nilsson, Nils Ake. **The Russian Imaginists**. Stockholm, Almquist &
        Wisell, 1970. 117p. (Act Univ. Stockholmiensis; Stockholm Slavic
        Studies, 5). 30Sw.Kr.
The imaginists were altogether more sophisticated and ambitious than we have
allowed, as Nilsson shows in this admittedly introductory probe. Their aims and
practice are here placed by Nilsson in a new and balanced perspective. A small
anthology of illustrative poems is appended. The author discusses the following
Imaginists: V. Shershenevich, A. Mariengof, Essenin, R. Ivnev, and others.
Several poems have been included, four of them by Shershenevich. Much of the
Imaginist program sounds like a further extension of ideas originally introduced
by the Symbolists.

     SEEJ, 15:4:506-8   R: Evelyn Bristol

834.   Oulanoff, Hongor. **The Serapion Brothers: Theory and Practice**.
        The Hague, Mouton. New York, Humanities Press, 1966. 186p.
        (Slavistic Printings and Reprintings, 44). $8.25.
This is a full-length study of the twelve lively, gifted members of the Serapion
Brotherhood, most of whom are still active in Russian letters. Despite the
broader scope implied in its title, it is limited in reality to a study of selected
prose fiction written by six of the Serapions: Vsevolod Ivanov, Mikhail Zoshchenko,
Veniamin Kaverin, Nikolai Nikitin, Mikhail Slonimsky, and Konstantin Fedin. The
poetry and drama of the Serapions are entirely omitted. The book deserves credit

as the first sustained effort to deal with the contribution of the Serapion Brothers to prose fiction, and its excellent bibliography of more than thirty pages will undoubtedly serve as the principal starting point for all future work on the Brotherhood.

      SR, 28:1:174-5   R: William B. Edgerton

835.   Pachmuss, Temira. **Zinaida Hippius: An Intellectual Profile**.
         Carbondale, Southern Illinois University Press. Amsterdam,
         Feffer & Simons, 1971. 491p. $12.50.
A major figure of the twentieth-century Russian religious renaissance, Hippius is seen by Pachmuss as "one of the most stimulating minds of her time, a sophisticated poet, an original religious thinker and an inimitable literary critic," undeservedly neglected and misrepresented by literary critics and historians. The author's well-founded conclusion that Hippius' work embodies "the four chief aspects of the Russian cultural traditions—art, religion, metaphysical philosophy, and socio-political thought" is reflected in the arrangement and distribution of the chapters. The book has been extensively researched and is well documented. Especially valuable is the information taken from Hippius' numerous diaries, letters, and other archival materials.

      SR, 31:1:196-7   R: Olga Matich

836.   Peace, Richard. **Dostoevsky: An Examination of the Major Novels**.
         Cambridge, Cambridge University Press, 1971. 347p. $11.75.
Peace's discussion of *Notes from Underground* is mostly a restatement of the work; it is with the discussion of the four major novels that Peace really hits his stride. These eight chapters are a major achievement. In "The Ethical Reappraisal of Crime and Punishment" Peace analyzes the novel as a rejection by Dostoevsky both of the Underground Man, "the romantic dreamer . . . gone sour," and of the monism dominant in contemporary materialist ideas. "Motive and Symbol" are next examined in the novel and here there are many fresh observations. Peace discusses *The Idiot* under the headings "The Triumph of the Aesthetic" and "The Condemned Man." The analyses of *The Devil* and *The Brothers Karamazov* are also highly rewarding. Peace is especially good on uncovering hitherto unnoticed resonances and congruences, and also on Dostoevsky's use of names; in this latter realm he makes many remarkable and valuable discoveries.

      CSP, 16:4:664-6   R: Kathryn B. Feuer

837.   Piper, D. G. B. **V. A. Kaverin: A Soviet Writer's Response to the
         Problem of Commitment: The Relationship of** *Skandalist* **and**
         Khudozhnik Neizvesten **to the Development of Soviet Literature
         in the Late Nineteen-Twenties**. Pittsburgh, Duquesne University
         Press, 1970. 180p. $7.95.
This is a study of Kaverin's *Skandalist* (1928) and *Khudozhnik neizvesten* (1931). The author describes the different aesthetic schools and the state of Russian literary criticism in the decade preceding the twenties and against this background examines Kaverin's response to the pressures of Soviet literary doctrine. His thesis is that in these two works Kaverin depicted certain personalities

and issues that vitally affected the literary development of the decade. The study is a timely scholarly contribution to our understanding of Kaverin's works and of what happened to Russian literature in the twenties and the early thirties.

SEEJ, 16:2:236-8   R: Hongor Oulanoff

838.   Proctor, Thelwall. **Dostoevskij and the Belinskij School of Literary Criticism.** The Hague, Mouton, 1969. 198p. 32Dglds.

This volume attempts to study the literary criticism of Belinsky, Chernyshevsky, Dobroliubov, Pisarev, and Mikhailovsky, representatives of the socioliterary criticism "which, in a somewhat different form, continues to be predominant in Soviet criticism," with particular reference to the treatment accorded by these critics to the works of Dostoevsky. Proctor's study includes a good selected bibliography, conveniently divided into several sections, but there is no index. The book will in all probability be more useful for students of Belinsky and his school of literary criticism than for Dostoevsky scholars.

SR, 30:1:204-5   R: Temira Pachmuss

839.   Prutskov, Nikita I. **Gleb Uspensky.** New York, Twayne Publishers, 1972. 174p. (Twayne's World Authors Series, no. 190). $5.50.

Although Uspensky was clearly a most important figure in nineteenth-century Russian literature and social thought, no one could say that he is widely read today, especially in the West. Yet his agonized investigations of the life of the post-Emancipation peasantry tell us much not only about the Russian village in those years but also about the spiritual conflicts of the radical intelligentsia. At their best, his works are impressive literary monuments of a new type which has undergone a considerable revival recently in the Soviet Union.

SR, 33:1:189-90   R: Geoffrey A. Hoskins

840.   Randall, Francis B. **N. G. Chernyshevskii.** New York, Twayne Publishers, 1967. 178p. (Twayne's World Authors Series, no. 22). $4.50.

Randall has contributed a welcome study of Chernyshevsky to "Twayne's World Authors Series," which will include several works on Slavic writers. He gives the reader the essential facts of Chernyshevsky's biography and concentrates his attention on what he claims is a literary discussion on Chernyshevsky's practical criticism and especially the novel *Chto delat'?* Randall's analysis is chiefly of interest for Chernyshevsky's ideas, which had such great influence upon the Russian revolutionary movement both during his lifetime and later.

SR, 27:4:680-1   R: Charles A. Moser

841.   Reeve, F. D. **The Russian Novel.** New York, McGraw-Hill, 1966. 397p. $7.50.

Reeve's book is clearly addressed to the advanced scholar rather than to the student or the general public. The strength of the study lies in the twentieth century. The essays on Sologub's *Melkii bes* and Bely's *Petersburg* are excellent, and the one on Pasternak is certainly interesting. In particular, the book contains a good passage on the distinction between historical and novelistic vision.

SR, 29:3:555-8   R: Victor Terras

842.   Roberts, Spencer E., ed. and trans. **Essays in Russian Literature:
        The Conservative View: Leontiev, Rozanov, Shestov.** Intro. by
        Spencer E. Roberts. Athens, Ohio University Press, 1968. 392p.
        $7.50.
This volume consists of two essays by Lev Shestov, "Dostoyevsky and Nietzsche:
The Philosophy of Tragedy" and "Creation from Nothing"; one essay by
Konstantin Leontiev, "The Novels of Count L. N. Tolstoy"; and two essays
by V. V. Rozanov, "Pushkin and Gogol" and "How the Character Akaky
Akakievich Originated." The editor of these essays regards Leontiev, Rozanov,
and Shestov as representing the conservative view of the Russian intelligentsia.
The leitmotiv common to all three is their deep concern for the individual and
their distrust of European culture as epitomized by science and technology.
All three had a horror of scientism and technology, which dehumanized modern
man. The book is a useful addition to the literature on Russian thinkers and
writers who until recently were not too well known in the West.
        SR, 28:4:679-81   R: Louis J. Shein

843.   Rowland, Mary F., and Paul Rowland. **Pasternak's Doctor Zhivago**.
        Carbondale, Southern Illinois University Press. Amsterdam, Feffer &
        Simons, 1967. 216p. $4.95.
The Rowlands' book on *Doctor Zhivago* is an analysis of Pasternak's novel as
a work charged with profound symbolism and an example of "mythophoric
method." To the authors, "the range of Pasternak's symbols is literally limitless." The approach to *Doctor Zhivago* as a symbolic novel is perfectly legitimate,
and in the course of their study the Rowlands make some useful and original
observations.
        SR, 28:4:683-4   R: Gleb Struve

844.   Rozanov, Vasilii. **Dostoevsky and the Legend of the Grand
        Inquisitor**. Trans. and afterword by Spencer E. Roberts. Ithaca,
        Cornell University Press, 1972. 232p. $9.50.
Like Dostoevsky himself, Rozanov pushes questions and problems to their
extremes. The zest and vividness of his critique survives, despite the fact that,
writing in 1891, he was uncovering for the first time many aspects of Dostoevsky's
work which we, as post-Existentialist, post-Freudian readers, take for granted. The
commentary on the Legend itself is chiefly found in chapters 7 through 17. It
abounds in fascinating insights and emphases. Perhaps most interesting and enigmatic in the commentary is Rozanov's own attitude to the Inquisitor and his
creed. He finds it a "sad . . . truth that disharmony between outer reality and
the laws of moral judgment exists and is irreconcilable."
        CSP, 16:4:664-6   R: Kathryn B. Feuer

845.   Sandoz, Ellis. **Political Apocalypse: A Study of Dostoevsky's Grand
        Inquisitor**. Baton Rouge, Louisiana State University Press, 1971. 263p.
        $8.95.
Sandoz's thoughtful book deserves careful study. It is concerned with Dostoevsky's
"politics" only in the broadest sense of that word, being a study of his philosophical anthropology and religious metaphysics. As a result, the author brings in a
great deal of extrinsic theological, historical, and philosophical material to support

his interpretation of "The Legend of the Grand Inquisitor," where intrinsic evidence from the text itself would have served him even better. Sandoz adduces an impressive amount of literature relating to his theme. It is a distinct contribution to Dostoevsky scholarship.

SR, 31:2:507-9   R: Victor Terras

846.   Setchkarev, Vsevolod. **Ivan Goncharov: His Life and His Works.**
         Würzburg, Jal-Verlag, 1974. 339p. DM53 pa.

Setchkarev's book is the most detailed and complete scholarly study of Goncharov in English. He describes the concern of Goncharov's fiction as "existential" and "metaphysical" boredom. The absence of a firm aesthetic viewpoint permits Setchkarev to confuse the ideas or rhetoric of a work of literature with its poetics. Goncharov made his novels, like the great majority of nineteenth-century novels, "social." They became images of life as he knew it and, at their best, of life as we all know it.

RR, 34:2:228-9   R: Milton Ehre

847.   Shane, Alex M. **The Life and Works of Evgenij Zamjatin.** Berkeley,
         University of California Press, 1968. 302p. $7.95.

For more than forty years Zamiatin has enjoyed an international reputation as the author of *We*. Only within the past decade have English readers begun to discover some of the further reaches of his mind. D. J. Richards surveyed his life and works in a modest volume that came out in 1962 (*Zamyatin: A Soviet Heretic*). The major novellas and stories were translated by M. Ginsburg in 1966 (*The Dragon and Other Stories*). The essay "On Literature, Revolution, and Entropy" has been a *locus classicus* for students of "protest" writing ever since its publication in *Dissonant Voices in Soviet Literature* (1961). It has become evident that Zamiatin is a big, if not quite cosmic, talent. Now, with Shane's monograph, we have the first full-scale investigation, in any language, of the dimensions of that talent. Sixty pages of the book encompass a bibliography of works by and about Zamiatin—eight hundred items in all. This is an important book of generally good and often excellent quality.

SR, 28:4:681-2   R: Robert A. Maguire

848.   Simmons, Ernest J. **Introduction to Russian Realism: Pushkin, Gogol,**
         Dostoevsky, Tolstoy, Chekhov, Sholokhov. Bloomington, Indiana
         University Press, 1967. 275p. $6.50cl.; $2.65pa.

Simmons pursues a unified vision of some of the principal works of Russian literature through an emphasis on their realistic aspect, a legitimate and interesting point of departure. His emphasis is very much on the "real" rather than on the "ideal" side of the works under discussion. He succeeds well in presenting many characteristic examples of the concrete details of imagery, composition, and style, of which the realism of his authors is made. Simmons' book is not addressed to the scholar . . . presenting, rather, the view of an erudite and enlightened critic addressing the general public.

SR, 29:3:555-9   R: Victor Terras

849.   Simmons, Ernest J. **Introduction to Tolstoy's Writings**. Chicago,
       University of Chicago Press, 1968. 219p. $5.50.
Simmons, whose long biography of Tolstoy is well known, has now published
a short "biography of a literary career," a collection of introductions to various
editions of Tolstoy's writings composed over a number of years. Simmons
consciously recognizes the timeliness of Tolstoy's work but curiously short-
changes much of it. His chapters on the novels and stories are simplistic, but
satisfactory, perhaps, for the beginner, his intended reader. Tolstoy's ideas on
art, education, history, government, narcotics, and so forth, are recognized as
relevant but are not seen in their proper contexts or most interesting aspects.
       SR, 28:2:351-2   R: Richard F. Gustafson

850.   Stahlberger, Lawrence Leo. **The Symbolic System of Majakovskij**.
       The Hague, Mouton, 1964. 151p. (Slavistic Printings and Reprintings,
       14). 20Dglds.
This is a philosophical exegesis of Maiakovskii's work based largely on the
early longer works *Vladimir Maiakovskii: A Tragedy*, and "Man," but also on
the later "About This." According to the author, Maiakovskii's work can be
understood as an attempt to create a new myth (or tragedy) for modern man.
Its setting is the city. Nature, the old, or God's, creation is rejected. The poet
as hero suffers on behalf of the people and is thus identified with Christ, but his
martyrdom is masked by the images of the dandy and the clown. The poet feels
sympathetic toward animals because they lack a tradition and represent a primitive utopia toward which he strives.
       SR, 27:1:164-5   R: Evelyn Bristol.

851.   Styan, J. L. **Chekhov in Performance: A Commentary on the Major
       Plays**. Cambridge, Cambridge University Press, 1971. 341p. $14.50.
In the English-speaking world Chekhov's plays do not suffer from a shortage of
critical analysis. There are at least two full-length studies, those by David
Magarshack and Maurice Valency. However, this latest study completely justifies
its place in Chekhov criticism by being far and away the finest close analysis
of the four major plays—*The Seagull, Uncle Vanya, Three Sisters,* and *The Cherry
Orchard*. Styan offers compelling arguments for rejecting such standard Soviet
interpretations of Chekhov as the uplifting choral effect at the end of *Three
Sisters*, or Trofimov as the embodiment of the glorious wave of the future. Styan
succeeds in doing so by noting Chekhov's own way of balancing the pathetic
with the comic, the melodramatic with the practical, always creating a scene
which in its totality forces the audience to be objective and never fully acquiesce
in the view of any single member of the cast.
       SR, 31:2:511-2   R: Karl D. Kramer

852.   Terras, Victor. **Belinskij and Russian Literary Criticism: The Heritage
       of Organic Aesthetics**. Madison, University of Wisconsin Press, 1974.
       305p. $17.50.
The best virtue of this work is, in fact, its unswerving determination to zero
in on the central trait of Belinsky's criticism: its "organicism." What does
"organic" mean? Two related things: seeing literature "as a function of both
nationality and society, on the one hand, and as 'a living whole', on the other";

seeing Russian literature as an integral part of the national life and national consciousness, to which it gives both expression and direction. This is the essence of Belinsky's message as a critic. Everything else is commentary. This book derives its unquestionable validity from its concentration on this main critical argument of Belinsky's work. Both the friendly and the unfriendly student of Belinsky will find this study useful. Nowhere else is so full a treatment offered of most of what one needs to know about this famous spokesman of Russian literary thought.

      SR, 34:1:189-90   R: Herbert E. Bowman

853.   Terras, Victor. **The Young Dostoevsky (1846-1849): A Critical Study.** The Hague, Mouton, 1969. 326p. (Slavistic Printings and Reprintings, 69). 52Dglds.

This book is a major addition to the field, the best study to date of Dostoevskii's early work. The author moves comfortably through the Dostoevskii criticism, adducing materials where they are needed, but not compulsively; he also controls Dostoevskii's literary sources, and has an eye for connection and influences; but he relies chiefly on a conscientious and highly perceptive reading of the text.

      SEEJ, 15:2:217-8   R: Robert L. Belknap

854.   Troyat, Henri. **Tolstoy.** Trans. from the French by Nancy Amphoux. Garden City, N.Y., Doubleday, 1967. 762p. $7.95.

Troyat's popular biography of Leo Tolstoy, like his earlier lives of Russian writers, tends to resemble fiction. The story is told against a background of history and nature, the latter usually consisting of imagined scenery. This book gives a vivid picture of this aspect of Tolstoy, one that clearly endears the author of *War and Peace* to the modern reader.

      SR, 28:2:351   R: Richard F. Gustafson

855.   Verheul, Kees. **The Theme of Time in the Poetry of Anna Axmatova.** The Hague, Mouton, 1971. 233p. 42Dglds.

Not since the 1920s, with works like those of Eikhenbaum and Vinogradov, has there been such an original study in depth of some particular aspect of Akhmatova's poetry. Since Verheul's book also includes under the general theme of time such important related themes as memory, the past, and history, it is therefore quite comprehensive, ranging over the whole of Akhmatova's work. Further studies of Akhmatova's work will certainly depend in good measure on this book.

      SR, 32:3:662-3   R: Sam Driver

856.   West, James. **Russian Symbolism: A Study of Vyacheslav Ivanov and the Russian Symbolist Aesthetic.** London, Methuen, 1970. Distr. by Barnes & Noble, New York. 250p. $9.50cl.; $4.50pa.

Chapter I of this study offers a "brief and selective survey of the aesthetic theories which were the common heritage of the Russian symbolists and their detractors." Chapter II focuses on the aesthetic theories of V. Ivanov. The center of attention is meant to be Ivanov's famous "Two Elements in Contemporary Symbolism," but West often bogs down for long stretches in tedious summaries of peripheral essays by Ivanov. He concludes the chapter with a comparison of Ivanov's theories with those of Ernst Cassirer.

SR, 33:4:835-6   R: John E. Malmstad

857.   Winner, Thomas. **Chekhov and His Prose**. New York, Holt, Rinehart and Winston, 1966. 263p. $5.00.

There is no adequate full-length study of Chekhov's prose in English, and Winner's book will provide some important material for many who approach Chekhov for the first time. Yet the book falls quite short of a really incisive and provocative study of Chekhov's prose. Winner's stylistic analysis is always precise and informative. His steady concern for use of language reminds the reader that Chekhov's Russian is not the reverse side of the tapestry we see in translation. At the same time, there is more of an awareness of stylistic device and literary allusion in the author's workshop than a feeling for the totality of a literary work.

SR, 27:2:348-50   R: Robert Louis Jackson

858.   Woodward, James B. **Leonid Andreyev: A Study**. Oxford, Clarendon Press, 1969. 290p. $8.25.

Woodward's is the first significant Andreyev study to appear in English since A. Kaun's in 1924. The book has four parts: Introductory, Life and the "Apostate": 1898-1905, The Transcendence of Individuality: 1905-1911, and The Tragedy of the Idealist: 1912-1919. The author succeeds in placing Andreyev in the literary scene of the period, making him a lonely and essentially misunderstood man in his associations with other Russian writers. The book can be recommended to literary scholars and students of literature, for it deals with that period in the history of Russian culture which, with the exception of Gorkii, Briusov, Belyi, and Blok, has received scant attention in the West.

SEEJ, 15:1:116-7   R: Temira Pachmuss

859.   Yarmolinsky, Avrahm. **Dostoevsky: Works and Days**. New York, Funk & Wagnalls, 1971. 438p. $12.50.

Yarmolinsky's book is the third, substantially revised version of his original book on Dostoevsky which appeared in 1934. It is well written and makes for fascinating reading. In his treatment the biographic aspect prevails, and inevitably his attitude toward Dostoevsky the man spills over on Dostoevsky the artist.

SR, 31:2:508-9   R: Victor Terras

860.   Yarmolinsky, Avrahm. **The Russian Literary Imagination**. New York, Funk and Wagnalls, 1969. 2590.

This volume consists of a series of essays on various subjects. The individual articles are well written but the majority of them are not too deep to be devoted to expressing the humanity and the humane feelings of the authors whom he handles, such as Pushkin, Gogol, Turgenev, Chekhov, Babel, Evtushenko and Voznesensky. This is a well-balanced as well as informative book for the general reader.

UQ, 26:3-4:347-8   R: Clarence A. Manning

Anthologies

861. Carlisle, Olga Andreyev, and Rose Styron, eds. and trans. **Modern Russian Poetry**. New York, Viking Press, 1972. 210p. $6.95.
The collection reads quite easily, as is suitable for its intent. The survey is accompanied by an index with a chronological chart of Russian history, 1613-1968. The selections include pieces written by Mandelshtam, Tsvetaeva, Brodsky, Evtushenko, Mezhirov and others. Each poet is introduced by a short chatty essay, often incorporating family recollections and accounts of meetings between the editors and the poets.
> SR, 32:4:855-7   R: Sam Driver

862. Davie, Donald. **Russian Literature and Modern English Fiction: A Collection of Critical Essays**. Chicago, University of Chicago Press, 1965. 244p. $1.95pa.
It is first of all an anthology of Russo-English relations: discussions by Englishmen and Americans of Russian writers, and vice versa. But it is more than that too: Davie's modest introduction is really an excellent summary of the Anglo-American reception of Turgenev, Dostoevsky, and Tolstoy. This volume is a model of selection of both lively and useful materials.
> RR, 26:3:309-10   R: George Gibian

863. Drage, C. L., and W. N. Vickery, eds. **An XVIIIth Century Russian Reader**. Oxford, Clarendon Press, 1969. 346p. 55s.
The editors have clearly put this anthology together with the student in mind. The excellent vocabulary and notes covers words and expressions. And while assuming a rudimentary knowledge of Church Slavic, the editors are perfectly willing to point out aorists and unfamiliar declensions. Linguists will therefore find the book a treasure trove, and literature students, spared hours of deciphering, will be delighted with the extra time they have to analyze the texts as literature.
> SEEJ, 15:2:218-9   R: Michael Berman

864. Fennell, John, and D. Obolensky, eds. **A Historical Russian Reader: A Selection of Texts from the Eleventh to the Sixteenth Centuries**. Oxford, Clarendon Press, 1969. 228p. $5.00.
Not designed to serve as a comprehensive chrestomathy, the book serves to acquaint the student of Old Russian literature with the more important texts of that period. Thirteen selections represent a wide range of genres, including oratory, hagiography, didactic, military tale, biography, polemics, and correspondence. The book is well organized and neatly arranged. This collection will serve as an adequate introduction to Old Russian literature.
> SEEJ, 14:3:388-9   R: William W. Derbyshire

865. Field, Andrew, comp. **The Complection of Russian Literature: A Cento**. New York, Atheneum. Toronto, McClelland and Stewart, 1971. 324p. $8.95.
This is an interesting and well-chosen anthology of Russian literary criticism, slightly over half of it by Russian creative writers themselves, with a little literary gossip, psychological speculation, and paranoid slander thrown in

for spice. One might find this book interesting and rewarding, and one may
even in places overhear with excitement the impassioned discourse of Russian
writers speaking with each other on the moving subject of their literature.
      SEEJ, 16:3:356-7   R: Sidney Monas

866.   Field, Andrew, ed. **Pages from Tarusa: New Voices in Russian Writing.**
        Boston and Toronto, Little, Brown, 1964. 367p. $6.75.
Tarusskie stranitsy, a volume of prose fiction, poetry, criticism, and literary
miscellany, appeared in 1961 but was soon withdrawn from circulation. It was
received by the public (and the authorities, it seems) as a declaration of the
autonomy of art. Among the writers discussed, whose works are included, one
will find K. Paustovsky, Frida Vigdorova, V. Meyerhold, V. Kornilov, and
others. All translations are at least satisfactory. The author must be commended
for a job well done.
      SR, 23:4:782-3   R: Victor Terras

867.   Ginsburg, Mirra, ed. and trans. **The Ultimate Threshhold: A Collection**
        of the Finest in Soviet Science Fiction. New York, Holt, Rinehart
        and Winston, 1970. 244p. $5.95.
Mirra Ginsburg emerges in the 1970s as not only one of the most productive
but one of the finest translators of contemporary Soviet Russian literature.
Moreover, *Three Rolls, and One Doughnut; Fables from Russia Retold* (1952),
a collection of Russian, Ukrainian, Latvian, Armenian, and Jewish tales, has
already shown other facets of her craftsmanship. *The Ultimate Threshhold*
is the first English translation of Soviet science fiction which is increasingly
becoming popular with Soviet writers and young Soviet readers eager to escape
from the monotony of "Socialist realism."   S. M. H.

868.   Henry, Peter, comp. and ed. **Classics of Soviet Satire. Vol. 1: Anthology**
        of Soviet Satire. London, Collet's, 1972. 235p. £2.25.
Advanced Russian students, probably fourth-year, are apparently the audience
for this anthology of Soviet satire in Russian. There are notes appended to each
story. The editor's introductions to the volume and the stories give good basic
information about topics such as satirical journals of the '20s and details of
Soviet life which one has to know to understand the stories. The anthology
includes Maiakovskii (seven poems), Il'f and Petrov (five stories), Zoshchenko
(four stories), Kol'tsov (five stories), Kataev (four stories), and ten others.
      SEEJ, 18:4:444   R: Ellendea Proffer

869.   Olgin, Moissaye J. **A Guide to Russian Literature (1820-1917).** New
        York, Russell & Russell, 1971 (1920). 323p. $14.00.
The author has selected from the literary productions of the nineteenth and
twentieth century only those literary pieces which are of certain value because
of their artistic qualities, or represent some aspect of Russian life. Part I covers
the growth of a national literature; Part II, the "modernists"; and Part III,
"the recent tide" (1900-1917). The reprint of this anthology is well justified
for its selection and satisfactory translation.   S. M. H.

870.	Pomorska, Krystyna, ed. **Fifty Years of Russian Prose: From Pasternak to Solzhenitsyn.** 2 vols. Cambridge, MIT Press, 1971. Vol. 1: 278p.; Vol. 2: 354p. $10.00ea.

The first volume consists mainly of works by Boris Pasternak, Marina Tsvetaeva, Evgeny Zamyatin, Isaac Babel, and Boris Pilnyak. Volume two, emphasizing works written in the fifties and sixties, includes stories by Alexander Yashin, Yury Nagibin, Nikolay Zhdanov, Alexander Solzhenitsyn, Bulat Okudzhava, Vera Panova, and Yury Kazakov. The introduction to the anthology and the brief biographical sketches of the authors are useful. This well-designed and well-printed anthology will be of interest to the selective reader and a welcome addition to any collection of Russian literature.

    CSP, 15:3:425-6		R: N. N. Shneidman

871.	Proffer, Carl R., ed. and trans. **The Critical Prose of Alexander Pushkin, with Critical Essays by Four Russian Romantic Poets.** Bloomington and London, Indiana University Press, 1970. 308p. $8.95.

Proffer's book gives a selection of the critical works from Volume 7 of the 1956-58 "small" Academy of Sciences edition of Pushkin's works. His intent was to provide translations of all the substantial critical articles written by Pushkin, except things which largely duplicate each other in content or intent; in such cases he gives only one article, even when that means excluding one of the small number of substantial critical articles Pushkin published. In addition to 61 items from Pushkin's own writings, he includes one article each by Kiukhelbeker, Viazemskii, Ryleev, and Venevitinov, plus a number of brief selections from Viazemskii's notebooks. All these materials have value.

    SEEJ, 16:1:93-5		R: J. Thomas Shaw

872.	Proffer, Carl R., ed. **From Karamzin to Bunin: An Anthology of Russian Short Stories.** With a critical commentary and eleven translations by Carl R. Proffer. Bloomington, Indiana University Press, 1969. 468p. $12.50cl.; $4.95pa.

The selection of stories on the whole is fortunate. Not claiming to be a "history" of the Russian short story, the collection is representative and offers the reader the near "best." Among the authors one will find Karamzin, Pushkin, Gogol, Tolstoi, Gorky, Bunin, Garchin, Chekhov, Lermontov, and others. An important part of the book is the one entitled "Practical Criticism for Students," running to some fifty pages. Proffer's critical examination of the stories includes "information on style, structure, characterization, and theme." The analyses, especially of Karamzin's, Pushkin's, Tolstoi's and Bunin's works, could be singled out for praise. This book is intended "for the general reader."

    CSP, 12:4:487-8		R: Paul Varnai

873.	Setchkarev, Vsevolod. **Gogol: His Life and Works.** Trans. from German by Robert Kramer. New York, New York University Press, 1965. 264p. $6.00.

The first 91 pages provide a well-balanced and judicious treatment of the author's life, tracing it from birth (1809) and childhood in the Ukraine, through government service, teaching, and literary work in Petersburg, extended stays abroad,

spiritual crisis and creative failure, followed by slow suicide in Moscow in February of 1852. Concerning the stylized Ukrainian folk tales of *Evenings on a Farm near Dikanka*, which so delighted Pushkin and the rest of literary Petersburg during the early 1830s, it is pointed out that, although Gogol often borders on *Kitsch*, he manages to bring these stories off by interweaving lyric pathos with minutely "realistic" details, "The Overcoat," published in 1842 after several years of revision, is analyzed here as combining its author's highest literary skills. The present volume is now the best book on Gogol in English, clearly superior to the previous studies by Lavrin, Nabokov, and Magarshack.
> SR, 25:2:358-9   R: Robert L. Strong, Jr.

874.   Troyat, Henri. **Divided Soul: The Life of Gogol.** New York, Doubleday, 1973. 489p. $14.95.
The author's main object is to illuminate Gogol, the writer and the man. To this end he acquaints us not only with Gogol's upbringing, school years, foreign travels, and states of physical and mental ill health, but also his various human and literary relationships, amply documented by long quotations of a literary, philosophical, and personal nature. Particularly revealing are the references to Gogol's awe and admiration of Pushkin, his controversial friendship with the Aksakovs, Zukovskii, Pletnev, and Pogodin. Troyat's portrait of Gogol is so convincing that the reader's involuntary uneasiness is only redeemed by some pity, almost forgetting that this weird man was one of the greatest geniuses that ever lived. His biography of Gogol is an illuminating study and a remarkable literary achievement.
> CSP, 16:4:666-8   R: Paul Varnai

875.   Vickery, Walter N. **Alexander Pushkin.** New York, Twayne Publishers, 1970. 211p. (Twayne's World Authors Series, 82). $5.95.
Vickery's *Alexander Pushkin* gives an admirably concise introduction to the life and poetry; every word shows it is written by a scholar-specialist for a broad audience. It is written for the new reader who may need to be told the story before discussion can be meaningful. Vickery is at his best in his appreciation of the humorous long poems, in the chapter on *Evgenii Onegin*, and in the discussion of some of the experimental lyrics. At all times he speaks with responsibility, clarity, and easy command of the voluminous criticism and scholarship on both life and works.
> SEEJ, 18:1:72-3   R: J. Thomas Shaw

876.   Vickery, Walter N. **Pushkin: Death of a Poet.** Bloomington, Indiana University Press, 1968. 146p. $5.75.
Vickery has written a clear and eminently readable book on a complex and much-debated subject: the circumstances surrounding the duel and death of Pushkin. It is a subject that provokes an emotional response among Pushkinists and all those who have grown to love Pushkin's poetry. Vickery's carefully objective approach does not, in the final analysis, detract from Pushkin as a man, but pays tribute to the many—often contradictory—facets of his complex character. Pushkin's intolerable position both at home and in society and the inevitability of some final disaster becomes clearer as each piece of evidence is given. The last

chapters of the book are completely engrossing. Vickery's exposition is direct, fast-reading, and not weighed down with scholarly apparatus.
SR, 27:4:679-80   R: Sam Driver

877.   Yarmolinsky, Avrahm, ed. and intro. **Two Centuries of Russian Verse: An Anthology from Lomonosov to Voznesensky.** New York, Random House, 1966. 322p. $6.95.
A collection of over 350 of the finest Russian poems written between the early 1800s and the present day. Eighty-two poets are represented in this anthology—ranging from Pushkin and Lomonsov to the young Soviet poets who are now voicing protests against the Soviet totalitarian system.   S. M. H.

878.   Zenkovsky, Serge A., ed. **Medieval Russia's Epics, Chronicles, and Tales.** Rev. and enl. ed. New York, Dutton, 1974 (1963). 526p. $6.50pa.
A new edition of this well-selected anthology of translated Kievan Rus' and Russian texts covering the period from the eleventh to the seventeenth century is not only justified but welcomed by students and librarians, for the first edition has long been out of print. The introduction, short notes, the glossary, and a chronology of Russian history enhance the usefulness of this work that is essential to both the historian and the student of literature of pre-Petrine Russia.   S. M. H.

Individual Authors

879.   Amalrik, Andrei. **Nose! Nose? No-Se! And Other Plays.** Trans. and intro. by Daniel Weissbort. New York, Harcourt Brace Jovanovich, 1973. 228p. $2.95pa.
This collection of Amalrik's six plays represents the first absurdist literature to come from the Soviet Union. An autobiographical note of the author is also included. The translation reads well and reflects the author's style, sentiments and ability to convey linguistic nuances. S. M. H.

880.   Anatoli, A. [Kuznetsov]. **Babi Yar: A Document in the Form of a Novel.** Translated by David Floyd. London, Jonathan Cape. New York, Farrar, Straus and Giroux, 1970 (1966). 478p. $10.00.
The author used to live near Babi Yar, a ravine near Kiev, where the Nazis massacred almost 200,000 Jews, Ukrainians, and others during two years of occupation. The Soviet government, for reasons of its own, was never willing to publicize these events. Kuznetsov's episodic narratives first appeared in the magazine *Iunost'*, and were published in their entirety only in 1966 in the West. Floyd's translation is in many ways superior to Guralsky's translation of the 1966 edition.   S. M. H.

881.   Babel, Isaac. **You Must Know Everything: Stories 1915-1937.** Trans. from the Russian by Max Hayward. Ed. and with notes, by Nathalie Babel. New York, Farrar, Straus and Giroux, 1969. 253p. $5.95.
The present volume, along with a previous volume, *Isaac Babel, The Lonely Years, 1925-1939*, similarly edited and annotated [see SEEJ, 9 (1965): 459-62],

represents a body of helpful information about Babel the writer as well as about his personality. The editor's annotations pertinently introduce each of Babel's works. They will convey solid information to the general reader; the scholar may turn to it for handy reference.

SEEJ, 15:1:114-6   R: Hongor Oulanoff

882.   Baratynskii, Evgenii. **Selected Letters**. Trans. and ed. and preface by G. R. Barratt. The Hague, Mouton, 1973. 131p. (Slavistic Printings and Reprintings, 280). 44Dglds.

This collection of letters is a new welcome addition to the list of books and articles on Baratynskij which have appeared during recent years. It contains the 68 letters included in the 1951 Soviet edition of Baratynskij's works, plus six more which were first published in 1969 by Barratt. They cover the period from Baratynskij's early adolescence, 1813-14, to his death in Naples in 1844. The preface is informative if a bit repetitious. The notes are copious and contain much interesting and valuable material.

SEEJ, 18:1:70-2   R: Benjamin Dees
[Also reviewed by James West, SR, 33:4:832-3]

883.   Blok, Alexander. **Selected Poems**. Intro. and ed. by Avril Pyman. Illus. by Kirill Sokolov. New York, Pergamon Press, 1972. 366p. $11.50.

The book is a welcome addition to the all-too-small number of annotated Russian poetry texts published in the West and likely therefore to be available for several years at a stretch for use in the classroom. It contains a hundred lyrics, *Dvenadtsat'*, *Skify*, an extract from *Vozmezdie*, and a short prose passage, thus providing a selection twice as large as that in James Woodward's teaching text (Oxford, 1968), though smaller than the collection published in the same year by "Khudozhestvennaia Literatura," which is another stand-by for courses in Russian poetry. In addition to the poems there are 53 pages of introduction, 95 pages of notes, and an extensive bibliography covering, besides Russian works, publications on Blok and translations in English, French, German, and Italian.

SR, 33:2:402-3   R: James D. West

884.   Blok, Alexander. **Selected Poems of Aleksandr Blok**. Ed. by James B. Woodward. London, Oxford University Press, 1968. 186p. $6.00cl.; $3.00pa.

Woodward has admirably succeeded in his difficult and sensitive undertaking. He has achieved his purpose which, as he states in the preface "is to provide English speaking students of varying degrees of proficiency in Russian with an introduction to Blok's poetic works. It combines a wide range of poems illustrating the variety and development of his verse with an apparatus designed to facilitate understanding and appreciation." Using but a limited number of significant poems (there are fifty in all, only three of which are presented in full), he has managed to bridge Blok's, at times, elusive work and yet stresses organically the critical cycles of his poetry without overpowering the student with a mass of poems. The anthology will be welcomed by both students and teachers of Russian language and literature.

CSP, 12:2:212-4   R: C. V. Ponomareff

884a.   Blok, Alexander. **The Twelve and Other Poems**. Trans. from the Russian by Jon Stallworthy and Peter France. New York, Oxford University Press, 1970. 181p. $5.75.

The art and career of Alexander Blok seem more relevant today than at any time since his bitter death shortly after the revolution he welcomed. In his frantic travels through love, mysticism, depravity, and apocalyptic politics in a naive and vain search for the meaning of life, Blok is no stranger to today's Western intelligentsia. Besides *The Twelve*, the collection includes *The Stranger*, *On the Field of Kulikovo*, *The Scythians* and 46 other works. An introduction summarizes Blok's literary career and offers some insights into the theory and practice of translation. The book should serve as an excellent introduction to Blok's thought and imagery for the non-Russian reader.

> SR, 30:2:44-1   R: Christopher Collins

885.   Brodsky, Joseph. **Selected Poems**. Trans. by George L. Kline. Foreword by W. H. Auden. New York, Harper & Row, 1973. 172p. $5.95.

Brodsky is a metaphysical poet whose affinity with the English metaphysical school derives from kinship of intellectual attitudes and emotional susceptibilities as much as of taste. This allies him in the twentieth century with T. S. Eliot and W. H. Auden. Brodsky's imagination, like theirs, is capable of extraordinary leaps, as, for example, that of the remarkable conceit of "Refusing to Catalogue All of One's Woes." He is always restrained (compare his "New Stanzas to Augusta" with the Byronic poems to which he alludes), sometimes brilliantly epigrammatic, and often witty—with the serious, unfrivolous wit of his metaphysical forebears. G. Kline, collaborating with the poet, has translated most of his published work. He has done this with exemplary modesty and sensitiveness.

> SR, 33:4:837-8   R: Helen Muchnic

886.   Bulgakov, Mikhail. **Diaboliad and Other Stories**. Ed. by Ellendea Proffer and Carl R. Proffer. Trans. by Carl R. Proffer. Bloomington, Indiana University Press, 1972. 236p. $6.85.

This book contains the five stories of the *Diaboliad* cycle and six others published in the newspapers *Nakanune* and *Gudok*. Although these stories are largely satirical, some are extraordinarily moving, even lyrical in expression. Even if the quality of the writing varies—the plays seem far more mature. Regrettably, the translations are rather unsatisfactory.

> CSP, 15:3:433-5   R: A. C. Wright

887.   Bulgakov, Mikhail. **The Early Plays of Mikhail Bulgakov**. Ed. by Ellendea Proffer. Trans. by Carl R. Proffer and Ellendea Proffer. Bloomington, Indiana University Press, 1972. 418p. $11.50.

Bulgakov's main device is Aesopian language. A satirist brought up in a tradition still alive in the years before 1917, Bulgakov used Aesopian language as one did in the nineteenth century. But while daily life before the revolution changed so slowly that allusions remained pertinent to reality, the period treated by Bulgakov was marked by sudden and drastic changes in living conditions. This is one of the reasons why his barbs and allusions are not understandable for modern readers and hard to translate.

> SEEJ, 16:4:483-6   R: Elisabeth Stenbock-Fermor

888.   Bulgakov, Mikhail. **Flight: A Play in Eight Dreams and Four Acts**. Trans. with an intro. by Mirra Ginsburg. New York, Grove Press, 1969. 107p. $2.25.

The play originated in 1926-1928; although Gor'kii, Lunacharskii, and Stanislavskii fought hard to have this play produced at the Moscow Art Theater, censorship prohibited it in 1928 and so remained until 1957, when it was shown for the first time time in Volgograd. It gives a more or less balanced picture of "counterrevolutionaries."

The translator handles the Russian text expertly, emphasizing the literary impact of the translation.

SEEJ, 15:1:114-6   R: Hongor Oulanoff

889.   Bulgakov, Mikhail. **Heart of a Dog**. Trans. by Mirra Ginsburg. New York, Grove Press, 1968. 123p. $0.95pa.

Miss Ginsburg's translation on the whole is faithful, accurate, and not only literate but literary at the same time.

SEEJ, 15:1:73-5   R: Zoya Yurieff

890.   Bulgakov, Mikhail. **Selected Works**. Intro. by Avril Pyman. Oxford, Pergamon Press, 1972. 215p. $6.00.

The recent Bulgakov edition represents a synthesis of the series' interest in early Soviet literature and post-Stalinist works. Whereas the present edition presents, with one exception, Bulgakov's narrative prose of the 1920s, this prose was to become a "literary fact" in the 1960s when Bulgakov was officially rehabilitated. Pyman offers the reader two selections which have not been readily available in Russian: the grotesque science-fiction tale *Rokovye iaitsa*, and the short story *Psalom*, a moving lyrical tableau of solitude overcome by human communion. A third selection, the play *Beg*, while published by the Soviet Union, offers the advantage of certain accessibility at a reasonable price. In an extensive introduction, Pyman provides background for the selections.

CSP, 16:2:320-2   R: Robert L. Busch

891.   Chekhov, Anton. **Late Blooming Flowers and Other Stories**. Trans. by I. C. Chertok and Jean Gardner. New York, McGraw-Hill, 1964. 252p. $4.95cl.; $1.95pa.

This volume includes eight stories, ranging from Chekhov's earliest writings to his last story, "The Fiancée" (1903). The collection opens with "Late Blooming Flowers" (1882), which has never before been translated into English. Other stories are: "The Trick" "Verochka," "The Beauties," "Big Volodya and Little Volodya," "A Visit to Friends," and the unfinished "A Reward Denied." The English text is sometimes choppy and stilted and often fails to reflect either the smooth and easy flow or the subtleties of Chekhov's prose.

SR, 24:1:152-3   R: Thomas Winner

892.   Chekhov, Anton. **Letters of Anton Chekhov**. Ed. by Avrahm Yarmolinsky. New York, Viking Press, 1973. 290p. $12.50.

893.   Chekhov, Anton. **Letters of Anton Chekhov**. Ed. by Simon Karlinsky. Trans. from the Russian by Michael H. Heim in collaboration with Simon Karlinsky. New York, Harper & Row, 1973. 494p. $17.50.

Yarmolinsky's and Karlinsky's selections are of equal size, but the first selection comprises 413 letters, and the second only 185. The reason is that Karlinsky used only complete letters whereas Yarmolinsky abbreviated many. Both translations are careful, correct, and graceful.

SR, 33:3:607-9   R: Thomas Eekman

894.   Chekhov, Anton. **The Oxford Chekhov**. Trans. and ed. by Ronald Hingley. London, Oxford University Press. Vol. 1: *Short Plays*. 1968. 209p. Vol. 2: *Platonov; Ivanov; The Seagull*. 1967. 362p. $10.00. Vol. 5: *Stories, 1889-1891*. 1970. 257p. $5.95. Vol. 6: *Stories, 1892-1893*. 1971. 316p. $16.00. Vol. 8: *Stories, 1895-1897*. 1965. 325p. $5.60.

Hingley is uniquely qualified to translate Chekhov's writings. As a scholar of Russian history and literature, and an expert on Chekhov's works, he has a signal advantage over most of his predecessors. By and large his preparation has served him exceedingly well; and though no translation, by its very nature, can ever be completely satisfactory, the volumes present a most significant and welcome advance. The present five volumes are part of a "Complete Chekhov" in English, which is planned to encompass all dramatic works and all fiction, including those works not included by Chekhov in the first edition of his collected works. The text of this series, which is envisaged as a ten-volume edition, is based on the twenty-volume Russian edition (*Polnoe sobranie sochinenii i pisem*, Moscow, 1944-51), and is planned as a complete translation of this edition, with the exception of the notebooks and letters.

      SR, 32:3:659-61   R: Thomas G. Winner

895.   Chekhov, Anton. **Seven Stories**. Trans. by Ronald Hingley. London, Oxford University Press, 1974. 242p. $3.95pa.

Chekhov is considered the last of the great makers of Russian classics. He introduced a modern form and reflections upon modern times. The seven selected stories are perhaps most representative of Chekhov's restlessness, loneliness, and the emotions shared by men everywhere. *Peasants* (1897), *Cart* (1897), *The Privy Councillor* (1886), and *On the Road* (1886) are among the seven essays. The translations are masterpieces in themselves.

                         S. M. H.

896.   Chukovskaya, Lydia. **The Deserted House**. Trans. by Aline B. Werth. New York, Dutton, 1967. 144p. $3.95.

Olga Petrovna Lipatova, the heroine, is a warm, rather naive widow. Her entire being is centered in her work at a Leningrad publishing house and especially in her own son, Kolia. Time and again the narrative underscores her lack of political sophistication and her unquestioning faith in the Soviet state. She is a believer, but hers is a simple faith in people, not ideology. The style is simple and spare with a limited, plain vocabulary. The sentences are short and severe. Werth's fine translation is accurate and true to the spirit of the original.

      SR, 27:4:688   R: Thompson Bradley

897.   Dostoevskii, Fëdor. **The Adolescent**. Trans. with an intro. by Andrew R. MacAndrew. Garden City, N.Y., Doubleday, 1971. 585p. $10.00.

MacAndrew's *Adolescent* may be stylistically superior to Garnett's *Raw Youth*. Occasionally it is more accurate. But much more frequently MacAndrew unhappily sacrifices accuracy to verbal facility.

      SR, 31:3:733-4   R: Gordon Livermore

898.   Dostoevskii, Fëdor. **The Gambler, with Polina Suslova's Diary**. Trans. by Victor Terras. Ed. by Edward Wasiolek. Chicago, University of Chicago Press, 1972. 366p. $7.95.

The publication of *The Gambler* in Victor Terras's fine new translation is a welcome event. Of equal interest is the appearance in this book (also by Terras) of Polina Suslova's Diary, her story "The Stranger and Her Lover," and selected letters—all of this material relevant to the background and writing of *The Gambler*.

The whole book is prefaced by Wasiolek's lucid and discriminating introduction to the various sections. *The Gambler* draws heavily on the biographical materials of Dostoevsky's life. Yet as Wasiolek rightly observes, Dostoevsky uses his relationships between gambling and love that go far beyond the immediate and literary experience." Fundamental philosophical questions, too, involving basic moral and social issues, are found in *The Gambler*. All in all, the Wasiolek-Terras book is an important contribution to the study of Dostoevsky.

      SR, 34:1:194-5   R: Robert Louis Jackson

899.   Dostoevskii, Fëdor. **Memoirs from the House of the Dead.** Trans. with a preface by Jessie Coulson. London, Oxford University Press, 1965. 361p. (The World's Classics, 597). $2.75.

The preface is brief, accurate, and factual, introducing the reader to the sources of the novel. It is obviously meant for the general reader. *The Memoirs*, started already in prison, is a faithful story of the four years Dostoevsky spent in Siberia. It was not published until 1861, when Dostoevsky had already succeeded in obtaining permission to return to St. Petersburg. It immediately brought him worldwide fame. One of the main ideas of the novel is the assertion that the most terrible torment for the prisoners consisted in being deprived of their freedom and civil rights, and not in physical suffering. Dostoevsky's attention is concentrated not so much on his personal experiences as on the life and character of those surrounding him. The translation is a good one.

      SEEJ, 10:1:101-3   R: Joseph Suhadolc

900.   Dostoevskii, Fëdor. **Netochka Nezvanova.** Trans. by Ann Dunnigan. Englewood Cliffs, N.J., Prentice-Hall, 1970. 201p. $6.95cl.; $2.45pa.

Netochka Nezvanova, published in 1849 with the subtitle "The Story of a Woman," is one of Dostoevsky's first attempts at a novel. The work, however, remained unfinished. Dunnigan's translation is faithful to the ethos of the work; it is accurate, lucid, and readable.

      SR, 32:3:657-8   R: Robert Louise Jackson

901.   Dostoevskii, Fëdor. **The Notebooks for** *Crime and Punishment.* Ed. and trans. by Edward Wasiolek. Chicago, University of Chicago Press, 1967. 246p. $6.95.

The first volume, covering the three notebooks for *Crime and Punishment,* is well printed, indexed, and annotated by the editor and translator. The non-Slavic reader is given every possible help. The notebooks are divided into small sections, each prefaced by an essay which gives a useful summary of the comments of the section, compares the contents with the finished novel, and points out the insights afforded by the notebooks. A long introductory essay makes the best possible case for the notebooks as a means of understanding Dostoevski's art.

      SR, 26:3:511-3   R: Nathan Rosen

902.   Dostoevskii, Fëdor. **The Notebooks for** *The Idiot.* With an intro. by Edward Wasiolek. Trans. by Katharine Strelsky. Chicago, University of Chicago Press, 1967. 254p. $6.95.

Wasiolek has apparently worked from the printed Soviet texts of the notebooks, which were all published during the 1930s. Since then additional material for

Crime and Punishment and *The Possessed* has been found. The notebooks for *The Idiot* are especially baffling. Not only do they deal chiefly with the gestation of the novel rather than with the novel itself, but they reflect a most atypical confusion on Dostoevsky's part.

SR, 27:4:625-37   R: Nathan Rosen

903.   Dostoevskii, Fëdor. **The Notebooks for** *The Possessed*. Ed. and with an intro. by Edward Wasiolek. Trans. by Victor Terras. Chicago, University of Chicago Press (1968). 431p. $12.95.

The notebooks have, of course, been published in Russian, but scholarly interest in the author is not confined to those who can read the original. Language apart, this edition improves on the not very accessible Russian version by grouping the notes in a more orderly fashion than that in which Dostoevsky left them. For the most part Wasiolek has put the notes into chronological order, but some are grouped by subject. The most remarkable feature of these notebooks is the great distance between them and the final novel. The translation by Victor Terras suffers from only the occasional peculiarity, but the footnotes are rather more erratic. The book is invaluable to the student of Dostoevsky.

SR, 28:4:675-7   R: R. M. Davison

904.   Dostoevskii, Fëdor. **The Notebook for** *A Raw Youth*. Ed. and with an intro. by Edward Wasiolek. Trans. by Victor Terras. Chicago, University of Chicago Press, 1969. 570p. $15.00.

Ironically, Dostoevsky's creative process in writing *A Raw Youth*, his commonly acknowledge failure, is documented more fully than it is for any of his great successes. Notebooks are available in Russin in volume 77 of *Literaturnoe nasledstvo* (1965). This edition would seem of greatest profit to the general admirer of Dostoevsky—the reader with no specialized demands. The translator and editor have done much to make the text as readable and enjoyable as possible.

SR, 29:1:749-50   R: Robert T. Whittaker, Jr.

905.   Dostoevskii, Fëdor. **The Notebooks for** *The Brothers Karamazov*. Ed. and trans. by Edward Wasiolek. Chicago, University of Chicago Press, 1971. 279p. $9.50.

With the publication of this last volume, the working notebooks for all of Dostoevsky's major novels are now available in English. Unfortunately, the most detailed notebooks that have survived are those for Dostoevsky's weakest novel (*A Raw Youth*). For *The Brothers Karamazov* we have only a fragmentary account of the last stage of his work—which makes this the least interesting of the notebooks. Wasiolek's commentary is intelligent and informed, though his remarks are understandably brief.

SR, 31:1:192-3   R: Nathan Rosen

906.   Evtushenko, Evgenii. **The Poetry of Yevgeny Yevtushenko, 1953-1965**. Trans. and ed. by George Reavey. New York, October House, 1965. 215p. $6.50.

The volume consists of 54 poems selected and translated by Reavey and is a bilingual edition. The poems appeared between 1953 and 1965. The present volume will be welcomed by many students interested in current Soviet poetry.
RR, 25:2:210   R: Louis J. Sheim

907.   Evtushenko, Evgenii. **Stolen Apples**. Trans. by James Dickey, et al. Garden City, N.Y., Doubleday, 1971. 328p. $8.95.
The choice of poems is Evtushenko's own. Most of them are fairly recent, with only six early pieces ("Babii Iar," for one), the "social themes" of the poet and his age are seldom far from his mind. Not only events, but places fill the book, particularly its last two sections—Evtushenko's impressions of Italy and America. It is not entirely coincidental that the book should so seldom touch Russian themes.
SEEJ, 16:4:488-9   R: Jane Andelman

908.   Gogol, Nikolai. **The Government Inspector**. Adapted by Peter Raby. Based on a translation by Leonid Ignatieff. Minneapolis, University of Minnesota Press in association with Guthrie Theater Co., 1972. 120p. (Minnesota Drama Editions, no. 7). $5.75cl.; $1.95pa.
Raby's adaptation of the *Revisor* is in fact the script which the Guthrie Theater Company used for its 1973 season. It has been polished and refined in previous performances in Canada since 1967. The original five acts have been condensed into two, some scenes have been combined, and some dialogue has been shortened. The modifications are not major and in most cases make a faster pace. Evidently this publication is destined primarily for groups interested in giving readings or performances of a more modernized version of Gogol's play. As such, it is very good.
SEEJ, 17:1:71-2   R: Michael A. Curran

909.   Gogol, Nikolai. **Letters of Nikolai Gogol**. Selected, ed. and trans. by Carl R. Proffer with Vera Krivoshein. Ann Arbor, University of Michigan Press, 1967. 247p. $8.00.
More than thirteen hundred of Gogol's letters survive. Now for the first time we can sample them in English. Proffer has translated, with abridgments, some two hundred, and has provided annotations, a lively biographical sketch, and an extensive bibliography of writings on Gogol in the major European languages. The selection gives us a good idea of Gogol's various epistolary personalities. The book provides for the general reader a fascinating introduction to Gogol, and for teachers of survey courses in Russian literature it offers much illuminating material for parallel reading.
SR, 28:4:674-5   R: Robert A. Maguire

910.   Gogol, Nikolai. **Selected Passages from Correspondence with Friends**. Trans. by Jesse Zeldin. Nashville, Vanderbilt University Press, 1969. 271p. $5.95.
Selected Passages is one of those famous books that are read only by scholars and critics. For more than a century it has been ransacked for clues to Gogol's mind, character, and art. It is an important book, not merely because it came from a great artist, but because it falls within a tradition of Russian religious

writing that includes Dostoevsky, V. Soloviev, Berdiaev, and Merezhkovsky. In a well-crafted introduction, Zeldin gives the reader something of the context necessary for understanding the book: the story of its composition and of its critical reception. The reader must be warned of numerous mistakes that riddle the translation. Because this is the only translation of *Selected Passages*, it will probably be used in courses in Russian literature, history, and philosophy.

> SR, 29:1:150-1   R: Robert A. Maguire

911.   Gorkii, Maxim. **Fragments from My Diary**. Trans. by Moura Budberg. New York, Praeger, 1972. 265p. $8.95.

The collection is good: it is apparently a complete text containing several items excluded from Soviet editions, even from the standard *Polnoe sobranie sochinenii*. The translation is professional and the preface and introduction are brief and unpretentious.

> SEEJ, 17:3:337-8   R: Lauren G. Leighton

912.   Gorkii, Maxim. **The Petty Bourgeois**. Trans. by Igor Kosin. Pullman, Washington State University Press, 1972. 86p. $2.00pa.

As in his other plays (*The Enemies; The Barbarians;* and *The Children of the Sun*), Gorkii offers here a picture of human ruin and misfortune, but not without a plea for man's dignity. The play, of dubious literary value, succeeded because of its topical interest and the author's ability to combine misery with positive values.   S. M. H.

913.   Gorkii, Maxim. **Untimely Thoughts: Essays on Revolution, Culture and the Bolsheviks, 1917-1918**. Trans. with an intro. and notes by Herman Ermolaev. New York, Paul S. Eriksson, 1968. 302p. $6.95.

Gorkii's articles in *Novaia zhizn'* are generally considered as eloquent anti-Bolshevik propaganda. If they had been only that they might have achieved greater results, but Gorkii was concerned less with the realities of practical politics than with the will-o'-the-wisp of saving Russia and Russian culture. For him the real enemy was the Russian mob with its traditional disposition toward violence and vandalism, and his complaint was that all political parties, particularly the Bolsheviks, were guilty of irresponsible appeals to its baser instincts. The book is prefaced by a useful introduction covering Gorkii's relations with the Bolsheviks from the Revolution until his death. There are copious notes, mostly aimed at nonspecialist readers, and a competent index.

> SR, 29:2:353-4   R: R. D. B. Thomson

914.   Gumilev, Nikolai S. **Selected Works of Nikolai S. Gumilev**. Sel. and trans. by Burton Raffel and Alla Burago. Intro. by Sidney Monas. Albany, State University of New York Press, 1972. 248p. (Russian Literature in Translation, 1). $10.00.

The selection is good: representative poems from all Gumilev books of verse, one of his tragedies, critical articles, and occasional writings. Among the best poems included from his later period are "The Muzhik," "The Word," and "The Lost Tram." Monas has written a fine literary and historical introduction to this collection.

> SEEJ, 17:2:235-6   R: George Ivask
> [Also reviewed by Sam Driver, SR, 32:4:855-7]

915. Hippius, Zinaida. **Selected Works of Zinaida Hippius.** Trans. and ed. by Temira Pachmuss. Urbana, University of Illinois Press, 1972. 315p. $10.00.

This is the first full volume of prose works by Hippius to appear in English translation. It contains a preface, an introduction, and thirteen stories of varying length gleaned from prerevolutionary and émigré publications over a thirty-year period (1906-1936) and meant to represent the main trends and themes of Hippius' prose. The translation is careful and competent, though the English might at times have been less stilted and more spirited.

    SEEJ, 18:2:189-91   R: Roger M. Hagglund
    [Also reviewed by S. D. Cioran, CSP, 15:3:430-1]

916. Karamzin, N. M. **Selected Prose of N. M. Karamzin.** Trans. and with an intro. by Henry M. Nebel, Jr. Evanston, Northwestern University Press, 1969. 214p. $6.50.

Nebel has followed his monograph on Karamzin with a series of translations of Karamzin's tales and articles, for which he has provided an extensive introduction. He begins with a detailed and perceptive analysis of "Poor Liza" and traces Karamzin's deepening critical awareness and creative exploitation of sentimentalism's potentialities and extravagances through to the stories in *Vestnik Evropy*. All in all, six works and five articles have been translated.

    SR, 28:4:672-4   R: A. G. Cross

917. Kharms, Daniil, and Alexander Vvedensky. **Russia's Lost Literature of the Absurd.** Ed. and trans. by George Gibian. Ithaca, Cornell University Press, 1971. 208p. $6.50.

This valuable book is the first sizable English translation of the prose of Kharms, one of a fugitive group that flourished for about three years at the end of the '20s and called itself "Ob'eriu"; the first six letters derive, as the author explains, from *"Ob'edinenie real'nogo iskusstva,"* with the seventh thrown in for fun. Gibian provides a very helpful introduction of 38 pages, a translation of the Ob'eriu manifesto, and a bibliographical note which is extensive enough to explain *ob'eriuty*'s existence. The works include 28 pieces. Kharms was arrested in 1941 and died under the usual obscure circumstances the following year.

    SEEJ, 17:3:338-9   R: Clarence Brown
    [Also reviewed by Barry Scherr, SR, 31:2:513-4]

918. Korolenko, V. G. **The History of My Contemporary.** Trans. and abridged by Neil Parsons. London, Oxford University Press, 1972. 255p. $12.00.

Korolenko (1853-1921) was a Russian writer and publicist who gained the respect of his contemporaries for his *Istoriia moego sovremennika*, the crowning achievement of his literary career. This is an admirable translation—essentially an abridgment of volume 1 and the first four parts of volume 2 of Korolenko's *Istoriia*.

    SR, 32:2:389-90   R: Rolf H. W. Theen

919. Leontiev, Konstantin. **Against the Current: Selections from the Novels, Essays, Notes, and Letters of Konstantin Leontiev.** Ed. with an intro. and notes by George Ivask. Trans. from the Russian by George Reavey. New York, Weybright and Talley, 1969. 286p. $7.50.

Ivask's selections in this volume are generally well chosen and imaginatively arranged. Too much stress, however, is given to semi-autobiographical material of lesser interest today; there should have been more of Leontiev's ideas on culture and politics. Translation is adequate yet not without some errors.

SR, 28:4:678-9   R: Richard F. Gustafson

920. Mandelstam, Nadezhda. **Hope Abandoned.** Trans. by Max Hayward. New York, Atheneum, 1974. 687p. $13.95.

The author offers a biography of her husband, Osip E. Mandelstam, in this book, which is also a literary work in itself. She portrays the period, events, and personal experiences of the post-revolutionary generation of young Russian intellectuals, many of whom were subsequently either liquidated, imprisoned, or forced into exile. The author's powerful voice on behalf of justice cannot go unheeded in the USSR or the West. Hayward's translation is excellent.

S. M. H.

921. Mandelstam, Nadezhda. **Hope against Hope: A Memoir.** Trans. by Max Hayward. Intro. by Clarence Brown. New York, Atheneum, 1970. 432p. $10.00.

N. Mandelshtam is the most reliable witness of both the oppressive era and the life and work of her husband, Osip, with whom she courageously shared all torments, safely preserving his manuscripts and interpreting all he has written or said with the deep insight of a loving heart and a sharp mind. He wrote in 1933 a biting poem on Stalin. Instead of being shot immediately, Mandelshtam was condemned to live a tormented life for four years more until he died of exhaustion in a Vladivostok concentration camp, probably on December 27, 1938. Mandelshtam believed that art is joy, and life should be joy too, a free imitation of Christ. The recollections are translated well and the introduction is illuminating enough.

SR, 30:3:706-8   R: George Ivask

922. Mandelstam, Osip Emilevich. **Complete Poetry of Osip Emilevich Mandelstam.** Trans. by Burton Raffel and Alla Burago. Intro. and notes by Sidney Monas. Albany, State University of New York Press, 1973. 353p. $15.00.

923. Mandelstam, Osip. **Selected Poems.** Trans. by Clarence Brown and W. S. Merwin. London, Oxford University Press, 1973. 100p. £2.50.

924. Mandelshtam, Osip. **Selected Poems.** Trans. by David McDuff. Cambridge, Eng., Rivers Press, 1973. 182p. £2.25cl.; £1.00pa.

The reviewer of all three books concludes her extensive discussion with the statement: "However diverse in quality and usefulness the various translations considered may be, they do represent an upsurge of interest in Mandel'shtam

as a major European poet of the twentieth century, an interest which is as welcome as it is overdue."
<blockquote>SEER, 52:128:441-51   R: Jennifer Baines</blockquote>

925. Mandelstam, Osip. **The Prose of Osip Mandelstam: The Noise of Time, Theodosia, The Egyptian Stamp.** Trans. with a critical essay by Clarence Brown. Princeton, Princeton University Press, 1965. 209p. $5.00.

The book is notable both as a conscientious translation of some of the best and most difficult Russian prose of this century and as an example of solid scholarship. The first translation, *Shum vremeni* (1925), consists of a series of personal evocations of life in the period of the dissolution of Russian autocracy; and the second of life in the Crimea of "Denikin-Wrangel"; the third is a surrealistic story set in the "Kerensky summer" of 1917. The translations are provided with notes and an introductory "Critical Essay," in which Brown gives an outline of the poet's biography, briefly characterizes his poetry, and analyzes the style and structure of his prose. The translations, on the whole, are done carefully and sensitively.
<blockquote>SR, 26:3:513-4   R: Vadim Liapunov</blockquote>

926. Maiakovskii, Vladimir V. **The Bedbug and Selected Poetry.** Trans. by Max Hayward and George Reavey. New York, World, 1970 (1960). 317p. $6.95.

The first part of this book is a brief biography and critique of Maiakovskii's works. The second part offers more than a dozen of his best and most famous poems. The third is his playlet. *The Bedbug* is a satire of Stalinism, which can be seen as one of the reasons for Maiakovskii's suicide when conditions became intolerable. The translation is generally good and preserves much of the author's use of street jargon.   S. M. H.

927. Maiakovskii, Vladimir V. **Mayakovsky.** Trans. and ed. by Herbert Marshall. New York, Hill and Wang, 1965. 432p. $10.00.

To his own translations from the previous book (*Mayakovsky and His Poetry*, 1942), Marshall has added twenty-seven new titles. The book now has an introductory article, which is of a popular nature, but also a twenty-page chronology of Maiakovskii's life and works and a fourteen-page commentary on "About This." Marshall's translations are effective English pieces and retain Maiakovskii's tone and form as well, including his tendency to irregular and startling rhymes.
<blockquote>SR, 27:1:164-5   R: Evelyn Bristol</blockquote>

928. Nabokov, Vladimir. **Poems and Problems.** New York, McGraw-Hill, 1970. 218p. $7.95.

The first part of the book comprises 39 early poems written in Russian. They are provided with English translations made by Nabokov himself during his American period. The second part is made up of poems written in English and published at different times in the *New Yorker*. In the bibliography the author provides a note on the publication of each poem.
<blockquote>SEEJ, 16:2:244-6   R: Emmanuel Sztein</blockquote>

929.   Pasternak, Boris. **The Blind Beauty**. Trans. by Max Hayward and
       Manya Harari. With a foreword by Max Hayward. New York, Harcourt
       Brace & World, 1969. 128p. $3.95.
This is a play, half-finished by the author, and a posthumous edition. It portrays
the life of a noble Russian family of the nineteenth century and indirectly the
life of the common people of that period. *The Blind Beauty*, symbolically
representing Russia herself, is a maid blinded by an accident in a quarrel which
did not concern her directly. Hidden symbols offer students of Russian literature
rich material for discussion and for analyses of the author's *Dr. Zhivago*.
                              S. M. H.

930.   Pasternak, Boris. **Letters to Georgian Friends**. Trans. with an intro.
       and notes by David Magarshack. New York, Harcourt Brace & World,
       1968. 190p. $4.75.
This collection of letters will be of great interest to all students of Pasternak's
life and personality and to all admirers of his work. It covers the period from
1931 to 1959 and contains his letters to several Georgian poets, of whom the
two most outstanding, Paolo Yashvili and Titian Tabidze, perished during the
Stalin purges. There are also letters to their widows and some other Georgian
personalities. The book contains sixty letters of varying length, some of them
in excerpts only.
       SR, 28:4:683-6   R: Gleb Struve

931.   Pilniak, Boris. **Mother Earth and Other Stories**. Trans. and ed. by Vera
       T. Reck and Michael Green. New York, Praeger, 1968. 291p. $6.95.
This is the second translation of Pilniak's stories within two years. By happy
coincidence, only a few stories in the translation under discussion are found
also in the three collections published recently in Russian.
       SEEJ, 14:1:77-8   R: Michael Klimenko

932.   Pilniak, Boris. **The Tale of the Unextinguished Moon and Other Stories**.
       Trans. by Beatrice Scott. Intro. by Robert Payne. New York, Washington
       Square Press, 1967. 267p. $4.95.

933.   Pilniak, Boris. **Mother Earth and Other Stories**. Trans. and ed. by Vera T.
       Reck and Michael Green. New York, Praeger, 1968. 291p. $6.95.
The two books overlap in only one story, "The Tale of the Unextinguished
Moon"; they are geared each for a different purpose. The Scott-Payne displays
a medley of shorter stories which illustrate Pilniak's several manners: primitivism
("Above the Ravine"), ethnography ("The Birth of a Man"), ornamentalism
("St. Petersburg"), and others. By contrast, Reck and Green offer more leisurely
works which emphasize a lyrical Pilniak with roots in Turgenev and Bunin. The
first book gives us a better idea of Pilniak's range. But the second better serves
art. Each book, then, has different aims and fulfills them with differing degrees
of success.
       SR, 28:3:522-3   R: Robert A. Maguire

934.   Platonov, Andrei. **The Fierce and Beautiful World**. Intro. by Yevgeny
       Yevtushenko. Trans. by Joseph Barnes. New York, Dutton, 1970.
       252p. $6.95.

Five years ago Andrei Platonov was a nonentity. Now, after the Soviet publication of two collections of his stories from which the present translation is
derived, he is recognized at home and abroad as one of the great Russian writers
of the century. This resurrection is not really surprising, for the most vital
works of Soviet literature are precisely those that have been censored, restricted,
or somehow neglected. This first collection of his work in English is carefully
arranged to cover his entire career, from the twenties to the late forties. The
stories move from animal to man to machine. He writes with a sad love of life,
as an optimist convinced of the perfectibility of man but distressed by the
prevalence of misery. The striving for love and happiness is the central theme
of his stories. The translation is accurate and modest, but tends to simplify
elliptical passages.

     SR, 29:1:752-3   R: Gary Kern

935.   Pushkin, Alexander. **The Golden Cockerel and Other Stories**. English
        version by James Reeves. New York, Franklin Watts, 1969. 111p. $4.95.
Skazka o Tsare Saltane is the original title of this work. The poem, written for
children, tells the story of Tsar Saltan, his powerful son and a graceful swan.
With this collection of poems, English-language literature on Pushkin is greatly
enhanced.   S. M. H.

936.   Pushkin, Alexander. **Little Tragedies**. Trans. by Eugene M. Kayden.
        Yellow Springs, Ohio, Antioch Press, 1965. 96p. $3.50.
While somewhat monotonous, Kayden's verses are generally fluent enough and
rarely go against the natural rhythms of English speech. He uses a more modern
and a more colloquial idiom than A. F. B. Clark, which generally seems to be
quite proper and sometimes gives immediacy and action to the dialogue. Kayden's
effort is altogether a commendable contribution. The booklet will be enjoyed
by lovers of poetry, and to many Russian students who are trying to read the
original it will be a welcome aid.

     SEEJ, 10:1:100-1   R: Victor Terras

937.   Pushkin, Alexander. **Pushkin Threefold: Narrative, Lyric, Polemic
        and Ribald Verse**. Trans. by Walter Arndt. The originals with linear
        and metric translations. New York, Dutton, 1972. 455p. $12.50cl.;
        $4.95pa.
Pushkin Threefold offers a refutation—in performance as well as argument—of
the theory of translation argued for and exemplified in Vladimir Nabokov's
1964 translation of *Evgenii Onegin*. Arndt has accepted Nabokov's challenge:
his "threefold" includes 1) the Russian texts of the poems, together with 2) a
"linear" translation on facing pages, and in addition 3) a "metric" translation
which attempts to reproduce Pushkin's Russian poetry as English poetry in
the same poetic forms. The two sections of the book include a varied selection
of 74 lyrics and five longer works representing different genres: "Tsar Nikita,"
"Tsygany," "Zhenikh," "Tsar Saltan," and *Mednyi vsadnik*. These translations
of Pushkin's verse are on the whole so successful that one hopes Arndt will
continue to translate Pushkin's poetry into English.

     SEEJ, 18:3:313-4   R: J. Thomas Shaw

938.   Pushkin, Alexander. **Pushkin on Literature**. Ed. and trans. by Tatiana
         Wolff. London, Methuen, 1971. 554p. $24.00.
Wolff's work has obviously been a long labor of love; her preface says that work
on it began in 1947. She gives not only critical articles, but also literary criticism
from prefaces, including prefaces Pushkin chose not to republish, and also comments on literature in the letters and diaries. This book is divided into six sections
and includes 330 numbered items. This collection can be welcomed by all
interested in Pushkin, in Russian literature, in the history of literary criticism,
and in Romanticism.
         SEEJ, 16:1:92-5   R: J. Thomas Shaw

939.   **Russia's Other Writers: Selections from** *Samizdat* **Literature**. Sel.
         and intro. by Michael Scammell. Foreword by Max Hayward. New
         York, Praeger, 1971. 216p. $6.95.
This good collection of translated Soviet prose is a companion volume to
Russia's Underground Poets and *Russia's Underground Intellectuals*, by the
same publishers. All three volumes consist largely, although not exclusively,
of works available in the Soviet Union only through *samizdat*. Represented
here are: O. Mandelshtam, V. Rastopchin, V. Maksimov, and V. Vel'skii.
         SEEJ, 15:4:508-9   R: Deming Brown

940.   **Russia's Underground Poets**. Sel. and trans. by Keith Bosley, with
         Dimitry Pospielovsky and Janis Sapiets. Intro. by Janis Sapiets. New
         York, Praeger, 1969. 92p. $4.95.
A collection of 103 poems written by forty poets, practically all of whom are
unknown to popular audiences in the West, although Akhmadulina, Brodskii,
and Okudzhava are among them. The volume as such is perhaps a document
of the time.
         SEEJ, 14:2:230-1   R: Evelyn Bristol

941.   Shklovsky, Viktor. **Mayakovsky and His Circle**. Ed. and trans. by Lily
         Feiler. New York, Dodd, Mead, 1972. 259p. $8.95.
Shklovsky's reminiscences of the Futurist poet Mayakovsky impress us above
all by the personal warmth with which he writes of the poet's tragic life. They
are of great value in that they contain the theoretical reflections of a former
Formalist on Futurist art. And last, but not least, their poetically compressed
ciphered and allusive language speaks of Shklovsky's own turbulent passage
through revolutionary Russia.
         CSP, 16:2:322   R: C. V. Ponomareff

942.   Shklovsky, Viktor. **A Sentimental Journey: Memoirs, 1917-1922**.
         Trans. from the Russian by Richard Sheldon. With a historical intro.
         by Sidney Monas. Ithaca, Cornell University Press, 1970. 304p. $10.00.
This memoir, written fitfully over the period of 1919 to 1922 and first published
in Berlin in 1923, during Shklovsky's short-lived exile, is a fascinating performance.
A deliberately disjoined, fragmentary, digressive narrative, mixing scenes of
revolutionary turmoil and Civil War atrocities with lyrical meanderings, snatches
of literary theorizing, and vivid glimpses of the literary life in Petrograd, *A
Sentimental Journey* is a remarkable implementation of Shklovsky's Formalist

poetics, with its emphasis on discontinuity and displacement. Sheldon's introduction is informative and competent. Monas's historical introduction is
brilliantly perceptive; the notes are eminently helpful.

       SR, 30:1:209-10   R: Victor Erlich

943.   Soloukhin, Vladimir. **A Walk in Rural Russia**. Trans. by Stella Miskin.
       New York, Dutton, 1967. 254p. $6.50.

Although his literary career dates back to the late Stalinist years, Soloukhin
became well known in the Soviet Union only after the journal *Novyi mir*
published *Vladimirskie proselki* in 1957. *A Walk in Rural Russia* is a translation—or, more accurately, a partial translation—of that work. This account of
a forty-day walking tour the author made of his native Vladimir district in the
summer of 1956 gives fascinating glimpses of life in out-of-the-way places, most
of which are undoubtedly never visited by foreigners and rarely by residents of
the major cities of the USSR. The English translation is rather unsatisfactory.
It omits many portions of the original version which the author retained in later
editions; yet the translator fails to note that this is an abridged edition or to
provide information about the Russian edition from which the translation was
made.

       SR, 28:4:682-3   R: Harold Swayze

944.   Solzhenitsyn, Alexander. **August 1914**. Trans. by Michael Glenny.
       New York, Farrar, Straus and Giroux, 1972. 622p. $10.00.

The book's independent literary quality makes Solzhenitsyn's prose-film effort
one, if not the only one, of the major achievements of the 1972 literary season.
The novel is more mathematically than chronologically structured. The events
run in an intensified progression, and the characters of the novel have difficulties
in their attempts to alter this course. One feels, however, a deep pulse, soft and
powerful, that makes the 64 chapters an organic and lifelike unit; it is the pulse
of a human soul with its inherent and all-important goodness. *August 1914*
exhibits also traits which are familiar to the Baltic (and other non-Russian)
nationals, especially when Solzhenitsyn writes: "We oppress all the non-Russian
people in the empire but we don't seem to feel sorry for them."

       JBS, 3:2:143-4   R: Anatole C. Matulis

945.   Solzhenitsyn, Alexander. **The Cancer Ward**. Trans. by Rebecca Frank.
       New York, Dial Press, 1968. 616p. $8.50.

Miss Frank's translation of *The Cancer Ward* is on the whole quite accurate.
Often one admires the justness of the translator's choice among synonyms
and the deftness of her rendering of Solzhenitsyn's difficult syntax.

       SEEJ, 14:1:78-9   R: Patricia Carden

946.   Solzhenitsyn, Alexander. **Candle in the Wind**. Trans. by Keith Armes
       and Arthur Hudgins. Intro. by Keith Armes. Minneapolis, University
       of Minnesota Press, 1973. 141p. $6.95.

This is a translation of the play *Svecha na vetru*, which reflects Solzhenitsyn's
professional background as a mathematician and his interest in science and
technology. In the story he chooses an unspecified international setting in
order to express his fears and reservations about the consequences of a rapid

technocratization of humanity in general. The language is appropriate for the milieu of the technological intelligentsia who dominate the play. The translation is satisfactory, and the general reader should have no problem understanding the theme of the plot. [See "Solzhenitsyn's Play *The Candle in the Wind (The Light Which Is in Three)*," CSP, 13:2-3:179-192].　S. M. H.

947.　Solzhenitsyn, Alexander. **The First Circle**. Trans. from the Russian
　　　by Thomas P. Whitney. New York, Harper & Row, 1968. 580p. $10.00.
Solzhenitsyn's book is a fictionalized autobiography and recounts his experiences as a political prisoner in a scientific work camp during Christmas time in 1949. In the best tradition of the Russian novel, the book contains considerable historical information; it is, in fact, an intellectual history of the contemporary USSR. The author presents a masterly portrait of Stalin on the even of his death, when he was preparing still another purge. One of Solzhenitsyn's central themes is that freedom is not dead in Russia: it flourishes in the prison camps where people can say what they want. The book was completed in 1964.
　　　UQ, 25:1:80-1　　　　　　　R: Stefan T. Possony

948.　Solzhenitsyn, Alexander. **The Gulag Archipelago, 1918-1956: An Experiment in Literary Investigation, I-II**. Trans. by Thomas P. Whitney. New York, Harper & Row, 1974. 660p. $12.50cl.; $1.95pa. (Volume II: *The Destructive Labor Camps: The Soul and Barbed Wire*. New York, Harper & Row, 1975 691p. $15.00cl.; $2.50pa.).
Gulag, it may be recalled, is a symbolic Russian acronym for "Chief Administration of Corrective Labor Camps." Solzhenitsyn, himself a veteran of the Stalinist camps, has mockingly dubbed them Destructive Labor Camps. They housed ten to fifteen million prisoners at a time. From the beginning of the October Revolution to 1959, it is estimated, they cost no fewer than sixty-six million lives. *The Gulag Archipelago* is no mere anthology of horror stories. It is the real history of the Soviet Union during Stalin's regime and should be read by students, intellectuals, and all common people. Solzhenitsyn's ability to expose the real nature of the Soviet system has few rivals.　S. M. H.

949.　Solzhenitsyn, Alexander. **The Love-Girl and the Innocent**. A play trans. by Nicholas Bethell and David Burg. London, Bodley Head, 1969; New York, Farrar, Straus and Giroux, 1970. 131p. $4.95.
The play is about life in the Soviet labor camps. The play's hero, Rodion Niemov, an officer in the front line, refuses to submit to conditions of work and the treatment of prisoners. He is severely punished and at the end forced to operate by the "medieval" mechanism he has objected to, while the unfortunate girl whom he has come to love sees no way out but to knock at the door of the repulsive camp doctor who desires her. This play was accepted for performance in Moscow in 1962, but permission was withdrawn. The translators have managed to convey the feeling of the original Russian text with its vulgarism and "prisoner colloquialisms."　S. M. H.

950.   Solzhenitsyn, Alexander. **The Making of One Day in the Life of Ivan Denisovich**. Novel trans. by Gillon Aitken. Intro. and screenplay by Ronald Harwood. New York, Ballantine, 1971. 271p. $1.25pa.

One Day in the Life of Ivan Denisovich was published in the November 1962 issue of *Novyi Mir* with Khrushchev's express approval. With this short story, one of the greatest Russian writers of all times made his literary entry. In the novel Solzhenitsyn describes the developments, events, and his personal experiences that led to the infamous and tragic "day" of Ivan Denisovich.

S. M. H.

951.   Solzhenitsyn, Alexander. **Stories and Prose Poems**. Trans. by Michael Glenny. New York, Farrar, Straus and Giroux, 1971. 267p. $7.95cl.; Harmondsworth, England, Penguin, 1973. 205p. $1.25pa.

The book contains three of Solzhenitsyn's best-known short stories: "Matrona's House," "For the Good of the Cause," and "An Incident at Krechetovska Station"; plus three lesser-known stories: "The Easter Procession," "Zakhar-the-Pouch," and "The Right Hand." Sixteen moving and beautiful prose poems complete the volume.

CSP, 15:4:622   R: J. W. S.

952.   Sumarokov, A. P. **Selected Tragedies of A. P. Sumarokov**. Trans. by Richard Fortune and Raymond Fortune. Intro. by John Fizer. Evanston, Northwestern University Press, 1970. 229p. (Publications of Eighteenth-Century Russian Literature). $8.50.

Offers four of Sumarokov's nine tragedies: *Khorev, Hamlet, Semira,* and *Dmitrii the Impostor*. The volume lacks a bibliography and does not contain annotations to Sumarokov's tragedies. On the other hand, Fizer provides a brief but lucid guide to Sumarokov's life and person and to the principal tenets of his classicism. There are illuminating comparisons which help to define Sumarokov's artistic profile against the background of French classicism.

SEEJ, 16:1:91   R: Rimnydas Šilbaforis
[Also reviewed by Anthony Cross, SR, 30:4:906-7]

953.   Tolstoi, Leo. **Father Sergius, and Other Stories and Plays**. Ed. by Hagberg Wright. Intro. by Aylmer Maude. Freeport, N.Y., Books for Libraries, 1970. 426p. $11.75.

Father Sergius, together with *The Devil, Hajji Murad,* and *The Memoirs of a Madman*, was published only in 1911, in the collected edition of Tolstoy's posthumous works. It is the story of an aristocrat who became a monk and a hermit; however, being unable to find inner peace, he escaped from his cell to become a tramp in order to find what he could not find in his hermitage. This is one of Tolstoy's better studies dealing with man's spiritual pride and desires. *First Distiller* and *The Powers of Darkness*, the best-known and most highly esteemed of Tolstoy's plays (1887), are included among the plays. The book is intended for the educated public.

S. M. H.

954. Tolstoi, Leo. **The Law of Love and the Law of Violence**. Trans. by
Mary Koutouzow Tolstoy. Foreword by Baroness Budberg. New
York, Holt, Rinehart and Winston, 1970. 101p. $3.95.
"This work, among the last Tolstoy wrote and known to very few, illustrates
the imponderable quality of his genius." Tolstoy confesses in the preface, "The
only reason why I am writing this is because, knowing the one means of salva-
tion for Christian humanity, from its physical suffering as well as from the moral
corruption in which it is sunk, I, who am on the edge of the grave, cannot be
silent." The work reveals Tolstoy's dedication to pacifism, which is to him in
absolute accord with Christianity as he understood it.
S. M. H.

955. Tsvetaeva, Marina. **Selected Poems**. Trans. by Elaine Feinstein. Foreword
by Max Hayward. London, Oxford University Press, 1971. 103p. $7.50.
This volume is the first book-length publication of Tsvetaeva's poetry in English.
The selection was chosen entirely from the 1965 Soviet edition—much of it
verse from 1915-24, including pieces written to Mandelshtam, Akhmatova,
and Blok. The last forty pages contain an especially moving record in verse of
the painful termination of a love affair ("Poem of the Mountain" and "Poem
of the End").
SR, 32:2:427-8   R: Roger M. Hagglund

956. Turgenev, Ivan. **Home of the Gentry**. Trans. by Richard Freeborn.
Baltimore, Penguin Books, 1970. 208p. $1.65pa.
Home of the Gentry (*Dvorianskoe gnezdo*) is Turgenev's second novel, published
in 1859. The impossibility of happiness, and his "dream home" was supposed
to be one, is the novel's underlying theme. Turgenev believed that man is never
able to experience total happiness save as something ephemeral and inevitably
foredoomed. The novel's hero Lavretsky accepts Liza's view that "happiness
on earth does not depend on us." The translation is satisfactory, offering smooth
and enjoyable reading.
S. M. H.

957. Turgenev, Ivan. **Letters to an Actress: The Story of Ivan Turgenev
and Marya Gavrilovna Savina**. Trans. and ed. by Nora Gottlieb and
Raymond Chapman. Athens, Ohio University Press, 1973. 155p.
$7.50.
This book helps to clarify the relationship between Turgenev and Savins (1854-
1915), the famous self-taught actress of the Aleksandrinskii theater. The translation, based on the 28-volume *Polnoe sobranie sochinenii i pisem* (Moscow-
Leningrad, 1960-68), is both complete and accurate. Turgenev's letters tell a
story that "must stand with some of the great records of human loving"; we
are indebted to translators for making this story generally available.
SEEJ, 18:4:436   R: Jerome J. Rinkus

958. Turgenev, Ivan. **Turgenev's Spring Torrents**. Trans. by Leonard Schapiro,
with notes and critical essay. London, Eyre Methuen, 1972. 212p.
Schapiro's elegant, fluent translation of Turgenev's novella *Spring Torrents* is
what he calls "a small and humble tribute to a great master from one by whom
the craft of writing has never been pursued for its own sake so much as for the

utilitarian purposes of the record and analysis of facts." The background facts are neatly marshalled; points of craft are elucidated by reference to the manuscript variants; but his main preoccupation has been to demonstrate that *Spring Torrents* is "a synthesis, or perhaps symphony" of four dominant themes in Turgenev's life and work: the destructive force of sexual passion; the unattainability of happiness in mutual love; the deference of the weak to the strong; and the fear of enthusiasm.

> SEER, 51:123:300-1   R: Richard Freeborn

959.   Tiutchev, Fedor I. **Poems and Political Letters of F. I. Tyutchev.** Trans. with intro. and notes by Jesse Zeldin. Knoxville, University of Tennessee Press, 1974. 224p. $8.95.

Among Russian lyric poets, few have attained the excellence of Fedor I. Tiutchev, whose works have exerted a profound influence on modern Russian poetry, particularly on the symbolists and Boris Pasternak. Tiutchev's position in Russian intellectual history is of no less importance, for many of his concepts are typical of the nationalistic wing of nineteenth-century thought and of attitudes prevalent in the Soviet Union today. Students of Russian literature and thought will welcome Zeldin's translation of 220 Tiutchev poems and all four of his political letters.   S. M. H.

960.   Voznesenskii, Andrew. **Voznesensky: Selected Poems.** Trans. with intro. and notes by Herbert Marshall. New York, Hill and Wang, 1966. 129p. $4.50.

Marshall's translation contains 48 selections with fuller versions of some of those contained in the Blake-Hayward edition. His choice of vocabulary makes a strong appeal to the senses and he conveys *con brio* the shape of the poet's mind. This selection retains overall a greater fidelity in many specific turns of expression.

> RR, 26:2:195   R: Thomas E. Bird

961.   Zamiatin, Evgenii. **The Dragon: Fifteen Stories.** Trans. and ed. by Mirra Ginsburg. New York, Random House, 1967. 291p. $5.95.

What is most surprising about Zamiatin is that so large and varied a body of stories, plays, novels, and even essays could be sustained by means of a single technique. Reference here is, of course, to his life-long penchant for what has variously been called *ostranenie, Fremdsprachen*, "perspective by incongruity," and so on. The collection is a success in every way. Miss Ginsburg's introduction is concise but provides the information, and what is rarer, the mood needed to read the stories most sympathetically. She succeeded in showing Zamiatin in all his splendid diversity. It is hard to conceive of a better selection of the fiction with which Zamiatin might confront new readers.

> SR, 28:1:175-7   R: James M. Holquist

962.   Zamiatin, Evgenii. **A Soviet Heretic: Essays by Yevgeny Zamyatin.** Ed. and trans. by Mirra Ginsburg. Chicago, University of Chicago Press, 1970. 322p. $9.50.

Ginsburg offers a translation of Zamiatin's articles on cultural conflict by the Russian writer whose works were banned in Russia before and after the Bolshevik revolution. These essays are essential to a better understanding of one of the most original of Russia's literary minds of the 1920s. The translations are excellent and the selection of articles, essays, and reviews is well chosen, stressing Zamiatin's prophetic ability.   S. M. H.

963.   Zamiatin, Evgenii. **We**. Trans. by Mirra Ginsburg. New York, Viking
        Press, 1972. 204p. $6.95.
The translator's excellent fourteen-page introduction approaches the ideal in its factual accuracy, compositional balance, elegance of style, and infectious enthusiasm which cannot help but inspire even the most casual of readers. The translation of the novel itself testifies throughout to Ginsburg's awareness of Zamiatin's remarkable achievements in creating a "style of utmost taste" in excellent English. Therefore, this book is to be highly recommended to both the general reader and the student of Russian literature.
        SEEJ, 16:4:482-3   R: Alex M. Shane

PHILOSOPHY AND POLITICAL THEORY

Bibliographies

964.   Bourguina, Anna. **Russian Social Democracy, the Menshevik Movement:
        A Bibliography**. [In Russian]. Stanford, Hoover Institution Press, 1968.
        391p. (Hoover Institution Bibliographical Series, 36). $10.00.
This bibliography represents a most valuable research tool, bringing to the attention of interested scholars a wide range of scattered material that previously lacked bibliographic control. The guide, organized alphabetically within each chronological chapter, spans almost two-thirds of a century of writing from the beginning of the movement in 1903 until the end of 1965.
        SR, 29:3:524-5   R: Sergius Yakobson

965.   Sinclair, Louis. **Leon Trotsky: A Bibliography**. Stanford, Hoover
        Institution Press, 1972. 1089p. (Hoover Institution Bibliographical
        Series, 50). $35.00, photo offset of typescript.
In scope, Sinclair's volume is an ambitious undertaking. Part I, which amounts to more than half of the book (693pp.), lists all of Trotsky's writings chronologically; Part II includes a variety of information such as a concordance to books and periodicals, and lists of books and periodicals with locations; Part III includes a list of pseudonyms, translations by languages, a subject index, and so forth. This bibliography, however, is not without shortcomings. The whole system of listing is difficult to understand and on the whole too overloaded with insignificant details.
        SR, 32:4:818-9   R: Ladis K. D. Kristof

General Surveys

966. Edie, James M., et al., eds. **Russian Philosophy**. With the collaboration of George L. Kline. Chicago: Quadrangle Books, 1965. Volume I: *The Beginnings of Russian Philosophy: The Slavophiles; The Westernizers.* 434p. $7.50. Volume II: *The Nihilists; The Populists; Crisis of Religion and Culture.* 311p. $6.50. Volume III: *Pre-Revolutionary Philosophy and Theology; Philosophers in Exile; Marxists and Communists.* 521p. $8.50.

These three volumes are comprehensive (though of course not exhaustive) and break new ground by making available in careful, readable translations many works that were hitherto untranslated and often difficult to obtain even in Russian. They thus provide both an excellent text for anyone interested in teaching Russian philosophy and a good source book, useful for reference or general reading by those interested in Russian culture. The three volumes contain selections from 27 thinkers. They begin with some writings of H. Skovoroda, a little-known eighteenth-century Ukrainian religious philosopher, and end with a contemporary statement of dialectical materialism.

      SR, 25:2:361-3   R: Richard T. deGeorge

967. Haimson, Leopold H., ed. **The Mensheviks: From the Revolution of 1917 to the Second World War**. Chicago, University of Chicago Press, 1974. 476p. (Hoover Institution on War, Revolution and Peace, no. 117). $22.50.

According to the editor, "this volume is one of a series arising from the work of the Inter-University Project on the History of the Menshevik Movement." Among the contributors are David Dallin, George Denicke, Leo Lande, Boris Sapir, and Simon Wolin. The essays, written originally in Russian, were translated by Gertrude Vakar. Basically, this is a collection of memoirs, essays, reports, and statistics. Extensive notes and a complete name index add to the value of the material, which is useful for the student and scholar of Russian political history, Menshevism in particular.   S. M. H.

968. Larsson, Reidar. **Theories of Revolution: From Marx to the First Russian Revolution**. Stockholm, Almqvist and Wiksell, 1970. 381p. (Skrifter Utgivna av Statsvetenskapliga Föreningen i Uppsala, 53). Kr.35.

This book does not make for easy reading. Its heavy style may weary the reader. Still, this is a serious work, has some significant points to make, and should be of real interest to those concerned with the evolution of Marxism in prerevolutionary Russia. Essentially it is a systematic and analytical investigation of contending ideas within Russian Marxism from the 1880s to 1907. It limits itself to three critical issues: 1) the "objective" prerequisite conditions for the revolution, 2) the definition of an attitude toward the elite and the vanguard, and 3) the nature of the revolution itself and the revolutionary dictatorship. Within the frame provided by these issues the treatment is generally chronological.

      SR, 30:4:882-3   R: Henry L. Roberts

969.   Laszlo, Ervin, comp. and ed. **Philosophy in the Soviet Union: A Survey of the Mid-Sixties.** Dordrecht, D. Reidel; New York, Praeger, 1968. 208p. $10.00.

The purpose of Laszlo's book is to acquaint the philosopher and the student of Soviet affairs with the various aspects of Soviet philosophy and its recent accomplishments, and to provide evidence that this thought is of philosophical as well as social importance. The book contains thirteen articles, of which ten are systematic studies and three are concerned with the relation of Soviet and Western thought. The academic affiliations of the authors represent eleven institutions in four Western countries and West Berlin. The book is a useful secondary text for a course in Soviet thought.

    SR, 29:1:709-10   R: Mary-Barbara Zeldin

970.   Treadgold, Donald W. **The West in Russia and China: Religious and Secular Thought in Modern Times.** New York, Cambridge, University Press, 1973. Volume I: *Russia, 1472-1917.* 324p. $12.95cl.; $5.95pa. Volume II: *China, 1582-1949.* 251p. $11.95cl.; $4.95pa.

This is a book which seeks to understand one of the central phenomena of our time: the establishment of Communist ideologies in Russia and China. The author does not content himself with recent phases of the intellectual transformation that brought Communism to power, but surveys the centuries-long impact of Western ideas and ideals upon the two great peoples who, in the twentieth century, rejected their respective cultural traditions and went over in revolutionary fashion to Marxist doctrines. The most interesting feature of this book is the weight and attention Treadgold gives to religious encounters in the deeper past, and the common typology he finds in successive phases of the West's intellectual invasion of both Russia and China.

    SR, 33:2:342-3   R: William H. McNeill

971.   Utechin, S. V. **Russian Political Thought: A Concise History.** London, Dent, 1964. 320p. $6.00cl.; $1.95pa.

The author has attempted to write a concise history of Russian political thought in the form of a survey "intended for students of politics rather than of Russian history" and assuming "no more than a very elementary knowledge" of Russian history. Utechin has much that is cogent and stimulating to say about some of the thinkers he discusses, but at times he is erratic and he also includes a number of people who have little claim to figure in his volume.

    SEER, 44:102:220-2   R: Barry Hollingsworth

Non-Marxist Movements

972.   Avrich, Paul. **The Russian Anarchists.** Princeton, Princeton University Press, 1967. 303p. (Studies of the Russian Institute, Columbia University). $7.50.

This compact, lucid book is the first full-scale history in a Western language of the anarchist movement in Russia. Although the anarchists never managed to secure active widespread support, the literature by and on them is vast, and it is clear that very little has eluded the author. In addition to examining an impressive amount of published material in five languages, Avrich consulted the major anarchist archives in this country and abroad. The result is an admirable balanced, learned, and informative account of one of the more quixotic revolutionary movements in twentieth-century Russia. The author succeeded in describing their views and their pathetic fate with seriousness, detachment, and understanding.

        SR, 27:1:137   R: Abraham Ascher

973.   Brown, Edward J. **Stankevich and His Moscow Circle, 1830-1840.** Stanford, Stanford University Press, 1966. 149p. $5.00.
Brown is interested in discovering both the "true" N. V. Stankevich as a historical person and "the intellectual concerns and motives" of the man who created the idealized image of the saintly, mild, and contemplative Stankevich. The mystical Stankevich, Brown argues, is to be understood primarily in terms of the needs and aspirations of Stankevich's society and contemporaries. Stankevich's chief characteristics were a clear and perceptive mind, moral fervor combined with intellectual restraint, disinterestedness, and apparent abnegation of himself. Brown's contribution is to have separated fact from fiction in regard to Stankevich, having consulted the available literature during his two trips to the Soviet Union.

        RR, 26:76-8   R: Edward Thaden

974.   Callian, Carnegie Samuel. **The Significance of Eschatology in the Thoughts of Nicolas Berdyaev.** Leiden, Brill, 1965. 134p. 25Dglds.
This study is well organized. Part One deals with the historical background, and its four chapters elucidate the developmental connection between Berdyaev's eschatology and German philosophy and mysticism. Russian cultural renaissance, Christianity and Orthodoxy, and Marxist and Communist revolution. Part Two represents a systematic development of the theme, and its six chapters discuss the interdependence of eschatology and creativity, freedom, man, ethics, history, and metaphysics.

        RR, 25:3:316-7   R: Nikolai P. Poltoratzky

975.   Chaadaev, Peter Iakovlevich. **Philosophical Letters and Apology of a Madman.** Trans. with an intro. by Mary-Barbara Zeldin. Knoxville, University of Tennessee Press, 1970. 203p. $7.50.
With a taste for high style and a flair for color and imagery, Zeldin has produced one of the most successful and literate translations of the works of an important Russian thinker into English. The other translation of Chaadaev's works has been published by Raymond T. McNally, *The Major Works of Peter Chaadaev* (Notre Dame Press, 1969).

        SR, 30:3:664-5   R: Joseph L. Wieczynski

976.   Christoff, Peter K. **An Introduction to Nineteenth-Century Russian Slavophilism: A Study in Ideas.** Volume 2: I. V. Kireevskij. The Hague, Mouton, 1972. 406p. (Slavistic Printings and Reprintings, no. 23/2). 68Dglds.
This is the second volume in a series on Russian Slavophilism. The first volume, published in 1961, dealt with Alexei Khomiakov and his role in the Moscow Slavophile circle. The author presents the Slavophile doctrine as a major,

uniquely Russian contribution to the theory of knowledge. Kireevsky, who is the subject of the second volume of his Slavophile series, is viewed as the theoretician of the movement. He sees the Slavophiles as authentic philosophers of Orthodoxy, and this leads him to minimize their debt to German Idealism. His case is well served by his thorough knowledge of Eastern patristic philosophy and Russian monasticism.

SR, 33:1:134-5   R: Maria Banerjee

977.   Evans, John Lewis. **The Petraševskij Circle, 1845-1849.** The Hague, Mouton, 1974. 114p. 32Dglds.

In this book Evans gives a description of Petrashevsky's Fourierism, as well as Petrashevsky's views on his society and how to change it. He describes also the circle that met at Petrashevsky's residence and the social and political ideas of the circle members. He concludes with an account of the arrest, investigation, and punishment of the Petrashevtsy. The author does not, to any significant degree, look for elements of self-interest in the social and political beliefs of the Petrashevtsy.

SR, 34:2:387-8   R: Frederick I. Kaplan

978.   Galai, Shmuel. **The Liberation Movement in Russia, 1900-1905.** New York, Cambridge University Press, 1973. 325p. (Soviet and East European Studies Series). $22.50.

The monograph represents a comprehensive history of Russian liberalism from the late 1870s to 1905. It is distinguished by an impressive attention to detail, and it fully exhausts the published sources available to a Western historian. It thus now stands as the fullest and most reliable narrative on the subject.

SR, 33:1:137   R: Gregory L. Freeze

979.   Gerstein, Linda. **Nikolai Strakhov.** Cambridge, Harvard University Press, 1971. 233p. (Russian Research Center Studies, 65). $8.50.

In this study Gerstein takes a broader approach, leaning more toward Tolstoy's opinion that Strakhov (1828-1896) was destined for "pure philosophical activity." Actually, his intellectual range was so wide that the Russian term *myslitel'* might well be used. In this intellectual biography Strakhov emerges as a modest, apolitical scholar-critic surrounded by books. Like Tolstoy, he had a highly personal religious sense and angrily rejected the mediation of priests at the end of his life. A thorough list of primary and secondary sources is provided in the bibliography.

SR, 31:1:194   R: Robert L. Strong, Jr.

980.   Gleason, Abbott. **European and Muscovite: Ivan Kireevsky and the Origins of Slavophilism.** Cambridge, Harvard University Press, 1972. 376p. (Russian Research Center Studies, 68). $13.50.

Gleason adopts Karl Mannheim's thesis about German Romanticism as a conservative reaction to the French Enlightenment and Revolution, noting that in Russia, where the state was the product of a "revolution" at the summit, conservative ideologues were, in fact, oppositionists. The author limits his inquiry to those figures who entered Kireevsky's life. A biographical strategy suits the subject admirably: like many Romantic thinkers, Kireevsky was fascinated by the genesis of ideas and demanded that intelligence respond to the totality of experience. Kireevsky's final transformation from European into Muscovite is interpreted along psychological lines. Faced with the dilemma Kireevsky chose Russia, encasing her in a logical scheme by which her backwardness could be justified as fidelity to the past—a spiritual virginity superior to Western ripeness.

        SR, 32:1:167-8   R: Maria Banerjee

981.   Kropotkin, P. A. **Memoirs of a Revolutionist**. Ed. with intro. and notes
        by Nicolas Walter. New York, Dover Publications, 1971. 557p. $3.95pa.
Walter has provided an interesting and competent introduction, paying more attention to the period of Kropotkin's life (1886-1921) which is not covered by the *Memoirs*, which are left to speak more or less for themselves. The notes are extensive and informative, and there is an adequate index.

        SEER, 51:122:140-1   R: A. V. Knowles

982.   Lavrov, Peter. **Historical Letters**. Trans. with intro. and notes by James P.
        Scanlan. Berkeley, University of California Press, 1967. 371p. $9.50.
Scanlan's annotated translation is both faithful and scholarly. The most valuable and substantial of the five sections of Scanlan's introduction is the one that analyzes Lavrov's early philosophical essays and the character of his "Kantianized anthropologism." Scanlan's translation is a welcome addition to the expanding stock of nineteenth-century Russian social thought to the non-specialist.

        SR, 27:4:648-9   R: Philip Pomper

983.   Lukashevich, Stephen. **Konstantin Leontev (1831-1891): A Study in
        Russian "Heroic Vitalism."** New York, Pageant Press, 1967. 235p.
        $5.00.
Employing psychoanalytical insights as first formulated by Freud, the author attempts to show how Leontev's thinking was affected by the experiences of his childhood and adolescence. Therefore, this work is more a philosophical study than a historical study of one of the most remarkable Russian thinkers of the nineteenth century, whose intellectual heritage is still unclear. Lukashevich claims that only his approach is capable of explaining Leontev.

                                            S. M. H.

984.   Lukashevich, Stephen. **Ivan Aksakov, 1821-1886: A Study in Russian
        Thought and Politics**. Cambridge, Harvard University Press, 1965. 191p.
        (Harvard Historical Monographs, 57). $5.50.
This important monograph presents systematically a leading Slavophile's ideas on a wide range of topics, as those ideas developed from the 1860s to the 1880s. Making careful reference to the statements of the man himself, the author outlines Aksakov's thoughts on the relationship of peasant and landowner, on the limitations and the proper role of the zemstvos, on the legal reforms of the 1860s and other contemporary problems, as well as on his own theory of the community as a force composed of educated people without regard to class. Brief, pointed chapters analyze Aksakov's notions about Poles, Ukrainians, and Jews. The bibliography (pp. 173-187) is especially valuable for its brief critical

annotations of many items. The book is an important contribution to an understanding of Russian attitudes toward the West that continue to manifest themselves in a variety of ways.

SR, 26:4:698-9 R: Edward J. Brown

985. MacMaster, Robert E. **Danilevsky: A Russian Totalitarian Philosopher.**
Cambridge, Harvard University Press, 1967. 368p. (Russian Research Center, 53). $7.95.

MacMaster sees Danilevsky above all as a "totalitarian philosopher." By this he means that Danilevsky belonged to a group of nineteenth- and twentieth-century European and Russian thinkers who advocated the use of violence, war, or revolution to attain religious or metaphysical ends. The most interesting and suggestive discussions in this study concern Danilevsky's transformation from a Fourierist humanitarian radical in his youth to a "totalitarian fanatic" in mid-career. Danilevsky, like other radicals, sought a new form of modernity to take the place of the "dehumanized" and European one then being forced upon Russian society. This study is valuable for students of nineteenth-century Russian intellectual history.

SR, 28:3:487-9 R: Edward C. Thaden

986. McConnell, Allen. **A Russian Philosophe: Alexander Radishchev, 1749-1802.** The Hague, Nijhoff, 1964. 228p. 24.25Dglds.

This is a serious, useful, and interesting study. Giving a balanced account of Radishchev's life, thought, and enduring influence, it should be of interest to many others besides specialists in eighteenth- and early nineteenth-century Russian intellectual history. It does an excellent job of putting Radishchev into context. This, the second full-length life of its subject (in English), is quite different from the first, by David Marshall Lang. McConnell's work is more satisfactory to a scholar. His bibliography is remarkably complete, and he has made effective use of the many works listed. McConnell has done a very effective job of explaining the most important influences on his hero. His family background, his religious faith, and the several stages of his education are cogently set forth. So is the development of his ideology.

SR, 24:4:724-5 R: Roderick P. Thaler

987. McNally, Raymond T. **Chaadayev and His Friends: An Intellectual History of Peter Chaadayev and His Russian Contemporaries.**
Tallahassee, Fla., Diplomatic Press, 1971. 315p. $15.00.

The translator of the *Philosophical Letters* and the *Apologia of a Madman* offers in this volume a revised portrait of Chaadaev. McNally's aim is to "complement" rather than supplant the biography of Charles Quénet (1931) on the basis of unpublished manuscripts found in the archives of the Pushkin House and the Lenin Library. The main contention of this book is that Chaadaev's later thinking was significantly shaped by his efforts to substantiate the thesis about Russia's backwardness proclaimed in his first letter, and that this switch from attack to defense was a result of relentless probing by the Slavophiles.

SR, 32:4:809-10 R: Maria Banerjee

988. McNally, Raymond T. **The Major Works of Peter Chaadaev: A Translation and Commentary.** Intro. by Richard Pipes. Notre Dame, University
of Notre Dame Press, 1969. 261p. $7.95.
Chaadaev was not only an important figure in Russian intellectual history, but
he was also in a certain sense the starting point of that history. McNally's translation is excellent. He captures Chaadaev's eloquence and poignancy in an English
that yet manages to sound, like Chaadaev's French, slightly stilted and archaic.
     SR, 29:3:514-5   R: Sidney Monas

989. Pomper, Philip. **Peter Lavrov and the Russian Revolutionary Movement.**
Chicago, University of Chicago Press, 1972. 250p. $7.95.
Drawing skillfully on Amsterdam, Hoover, Columbia, and to a lesser extent,
Soviet archives, Pomper richly documents his novel interpretation of Lavrov's
personality. Although the book is somewhat fragmentary and disjointed in the
early chapters and skirts concentrated study of Lavrov's more scholarly works,
the author has given us a fine analysis of the interplay of personality, ideas, and
external circumstance.
     SR, 32:4:812-3   R: Arthur P. Mendel

990. Shestov, Lev. **Athens and Jerusalem.** Trans. with an intro. by Bernard
Martin. New York, Simon & Shuster, 1968. (Originally published by
Ohio University Press). 447p. $2.45pa.
Athens and Jerusalem, which was completed in 1937, brings together the various
strands of Shestov's earlier ideas, and is the culmination of his entire life and
spiritual odyssey. His point of departure is his critique of rationalism and
scientism, the twin evils of modern society. Distressed by the human tragedy
and looking for a balance between suffering and justice, he arrived at the conclusion
that such a balance can be maintained only by a God "with whom all things are
possible," a God who is "limitless possibility." Shestov struggles with the problem
of faith versus reason. The publishers and translator are to be congratulated for
making this work available in English.
     SR, 28:4:679-80   R: Louis J. Shein

991. Shestov, Lev. **A Shestov Anthology.** Ed. and intro. by Bernard Martin.
Athens, Ohio University Press, 1970. 328p. $10.00.
The famous Russian existentialist Lev Shestov is gradually becoming known in
the English-speaking world. The present anthology is an excellent introduction
to Shestov's central philosophical thought. Martin made an excellent choice in
the selections, and arranged them in such a way that the reader will gradually
be initiated into the aphoristic and often anti-rationalistic expressions of Shestov's
writings. Part I is arranged in a number of pensées, and Part II consists of ten
major essays. Most of these essays are now embodied in different works. Shestov's
main goal in life was to dethrone the Goddess of Reason and place on the throne
the God of the Bible.
     CSP, 17:2-3:557-8   R: Louis J. Shein

992. Thaden, Edward C. **Conservative Nationalism in Nineteenth-Century
Russia.** Seattle, University of Washington Press, 1964. 271p. $9.50.

In this study Thaden discusses, at least briefly, almost all important representatives of conservative Russian nationalism, and quite a few of these names appear for the first time on the pages of an English-language book. The first part of the book, "The Traditional and Romantic Background," deals with the thinkers of the 1830s and 1840s. In the second part, "The New Ideology," the author discusses the leading figures of the acme of national conservatism in the third quarter of the last century: A Grigoriev, N. Dostoevsky, and N. Strakhov. To the same era belongs N. Danilevsky. This is an objective and interesting survey of Russian conservative national thought.

   RR, 25:2:190-2   R: Serge A. Zenkovsky

993. Timberlake, Charles E., ed. **Essays on Russian Liberalism**. Columbia,
   University of Missouri Press, 1972. 291p. $9.00.
This collection of nine essays represents the fruits of the Bi-State (Kansas-Missouri) Slavic Conference held in Columbia, Missouri, in November 1969. Seven of them, of very unequal merit and interest, deal either with prominent persons or general topics such as I, Petrunkevich, F. Rodichev, V. A. Maklakov, and Kadet policy between 1905 and 1917.

   SR, 32:3:608-9   R: Leonard Schapiro

994. Venturi, Franco. **Roots of Revolution: A History of the Populist and
   Socialist Movements in Nineteenth Century Russia**. Intro. by Sir
   Isaiah Berlin. Trans. from the Italian by Francis Haskell. New York,
   Grosset and Dunlap, 1966. 850p. $3.45pa.
Venturi's study of the Russian Populist movement is still the most comprehensive and perhaps most authoritative account in any language. An impartial judgment, mature handling of this most complex aspect of Russian history, and consultation of primary sources combined with exhaustive research, make this work indispensable learning material for the student of Russian history. Recommended for both the student and the instructor, obligatory for the specialist, yet too advanced for the general reader. S. M. H.

995. Woehrlin, William F. **Chernyshevskii: The Man and the Journalist**.
   Cambridge, Harvard University Press, 1971. 404p. (Russian Research
   Center Studies, 67). $12.50.
Without government-sponsored martyrdom, Chernyshevsky, a *raznochinets*, could never have entered revolutionary heaven, haloed by liberals and radicals alike. Indeed, he probably never even would have written *What To Do?*—a novel which may be compared in its influence to *Pilgrim's Progress*. Already there is a vast literature on Chernyshevsky: there are his complete works, totaling sixteen volumes in Russian, and then there are, from Pypin and Plekhanov to Steklov and Nechkina, the multi-volumed studies, apologetic and tending toward hagiography. Woehrlin has written the fullest, most comprehensive, most judicious, and—as intellectual history—most "professional" account of Chernyshevsky's life and work available so far in English.

   SR, 31:3:667-8   R: Sidney Monas

996. Wortman, Richard. **The Crisis of Russian Populism**. New York,
   Cambridge University Press, 1967. 211p. $7.50.

Wortman depicts the breakdown of ideological unity in the populist movement after its failures of the late 1870s and early 1880s. After March 1, 1881, neither faith in revolutionary action nor faith in the peasantry gave promise of rapid realization of radical ideals. The author devotes more than half of the volume to the "psychological dimension of populism" during its crisis, as manifested in the works and lives of three writers for *Otechestvennye Zapiski*, A. N. Engelgardt, G. I. Uspensky, and N. V. Zlatovratsky. By the mid-1880s the "movement was broken" for the "single myth dissolved into many individual myths . . . " The volume is a useful one, for it introduces the student to a number of writers too often overlooked in studies of Russian populism.

        SR, 27:4:649-50   R: James A. Duran

Marxism in Russia and the USSR

997.   Ascher, Abraham. **Pavel Axelrod and the Development of Menshevism.** Cambridge, Harvard University Press, 1972. 420p. (Russian Research Center Studies, 70. Hoover Institution Publications, 115). $18.50.

In this book Ascher succeeds in presenting a very readable, solidly constructed, and reliable account of the activities and thoughts of the cofounder of the Russian Social Democratic Party, who was also the brain and soul of Menshevism. He dwells on the main stages of the life of his unusual personality, who was born into a very poor Jewish family and, thanks to his natural faculties, acquired knowledge and culture and, already as a young man, occupied a respected place on the Russian and international socialist Olympus. A born propagandist, Axelrod influenced people and exercised his leadership primarily by means of the spoken word.

        SR, 32:4:814-5   R: Boris Sapir

998.   Blakeley, Thomas J. **Soviet Theory of Knowledge.** Dordrecht, Reidel Publishing, 1964. 203p. (Sovietica, Monographs of the Institute of East-European Studies, University of Fribourg, Switzerland). 24Dglds.

Blakeley gives brief accounts of the history and role of epistemology in the evolution of Soviet philosophy, with particular stress on the cognitive functions and modes, methodologies, and historiography of the Soviet theory of knowledge. This work, although of great interest to the specialist, is written for the non-professional as well.

        SR, 25:1:172-3   R: Maxim W. Mikulak

999.   DeGeorge, Richard T. **Patterns of Soviet Thought: The Origins and Development of Dialectical and Historical Materialism.** Ann Arbor, University of Michigan Press, 1966. 293p. $6.95.

This book does a commendable job of summarizing and giving a detailed critique of the basic works of Marxist-Leninist philosophy from its German origins to its latest developments in the Soviet Union. DeGeorge points out that one must avoid the danger of systematizing the writings of Marx, Engels, and Lenin; nevertheless he manages to present the content of their works in a clear and organized way. Besides the intrinsic interest, DeGeorge presents a persuasive case for studying Soviet philosophy—not as the axioms from Soviet behavior may be deduced, but as a world view whose presuppositions and general conceptual mode cannot but influence the way in which Soviet citizens frame problems and solve them. The greatest merit of DeGeorge's book is the good common sense that comes forward at every point in it.

SR, 26:4:695-6   R: David Dinsmore Comey

1000.   DeGeorge, Richard T. **Soviet Ethics and Morality**. Ann Arbor, University of Michigan Press, 1969. 184p. $2.95pa.

In his introduction the author clearly delineates the predicament of the contemporary Soviet philosopher, who is faced with real moral problems but is able to deal with them only within the confines of a very dogmatic system and under the watchful eye of a none-too-sophisticated political establishment. Chapter 2 shows how the collectivist or generic notion of man underlies all Soviet ethical discussions. Chapter 3 deals with the notion of good and Chapter 4 with some of the basic values (freedom, duty, etc.) which the Soviets count among the norms of their system. Other chapters discuss "The New Moral Code," moral inculcation, and social control.

SR, 29:2:334   R: Thomas J. Blakeley

1001.   Frankel, Jonathan, ed., trans., and intro. **Vladimir Akimov on the Dilemmas of Russian Marxism, 1895-1903: The Second Congress of the Russian Social Democratic Labour Party; A Short History of the Social Democratic Movement in Russia**. Cambridge, Cambridge University Press, 1969. 390p. $10.00.

This volume contains two major tracts of Vladimir Akimov (Makhnovets), who was probably the most interesting and certainly the most attractive figure of the *Rabochee delo* group and of so-called Economism. While rescuing Akimov from undeserved oblivion and unraveling the hitherto intractable mystery of Economism, Frankel has also tried to put both into the historical context of Russian social democracy. In the process he has produced an excellent introductory essay called "The Polarization of Russian Marxism (1883-1903)." Akimov's tract *The Second Congress of Russian Social Democracy* contains much of what he was prevented from saying at the Second Congress of the RSDRP in 1903, in defense of his Economism. His *Short History of the Social Democratic Movement* is a scrupulous and richly documented comparative study of the Russian labor movement as it evolved in Vilno, St. Petersburg, and Kiev. This is the first major history of Russian social democracy. The volume is a fine work of scholarship and a major contribution to the study of Russian Marxism.

SR, 30:1:144-6   R: Israel Getzler

1002.   Jordan, Z. A. **The Evolution of Dialectical Materialism: A Philosophical and Sociological Analysis**. London, Macmillan; New York, St. Martin's Press, 1967. 490p. $12.00.

Jordan takes on the large task of setting the record straight on the origin of the doctrine that has become known as "dialectical materialism" and its development through the Stalinist period in the Soviet Union. In the first part of the book he clarifies the relations of Marx and Engels to Hegel, to the French positivists, and to each other. The doctrine of "dialectical materialism" was introduced and developed by Engels, who relied heavily on the philosophy of Hegel. The second part of the book examines Engels' doctrine in some detail and then traces its revision to Plekhanov and its transformation into an ideology at the hands of Lenin and Stalin. The text is solid, though Jordan underplays the importance of Lenin's *Philosophical Notebooks*, which is a source being mined more and more by contemporary Soviet philosophers. The third part analyzes the relation between dialectical and historical materialism, argues that they are in fact not logically related and concludes with analyses of the concept of scientific socialism and of historical materialism as a guide to action.

     SR, 28:1:166-7   R: Richard T. DeGeorge

1003.   Lane, David. **The Roots of Russian Communism: A Social and Historical Study of Russian Social-Democracy 1898-1907**. Assen, Van Gorcum, 1969. 240p. (Publications of Social History issued by the Internationaal Instituut voor Sociale Geschedenis, Amsterdam, Number 6). 37.50Dglds. (*Roots of Russian Communism*, in a new, revised edition, was published by Pennsylvania State University Press, 1975. 240p. $4.95pa.).

This study is strictly a sociological and statistical analysis of participants up to 1907. The author shows great resourcefulness in making use of the available data, employing impeccable methodology in constructing samples, defining concepts, computing margins of error, and cross checking his sources where possible. The result is probably the best picture we are likely to get of the distribution according to social class, education, occupation, age, and nationality. One is not surprised to find a heavy concentration of gentry, workers of peasant background, Great Russians, and persons of a younger mean age among the Bolsheviks, and of minority nationalities and city dwellers of all grades among the Mensheviks.

     RR, 29:2:215-7   R: Allan Wildman

1004.   Schwarz, Solomon M. **The Russian Revolution of 1905: The Workers' Movement and the Formation of Bolshevism and Menshevism**. Trans. by Gertrude Vakar. Chicago, University of Chicago Press, 1967. 361p. ("The History of Menshevism." A Publication of the Hoover Institution).

This is a useful book on a restricted theme. It is not an account of the 1905 revolution, nor even of the part played in it by industrial labor. It is concerned rather with the somewhat arid controversies that raged among Russian Marxists of the day as they sought to adjust their doctrines to rapidly changing circumstances. Schwarz was then a young Bolshevik militant who participated personally in some of these stirring events. He soon transferred his allegiance to the Mensheviks and has been closely associated with it ever since. The resultant study significantly enlarges our understanding of the Bolshevik-Menshevik debate of 1905. The author's detailed reconstruction of this complicated story, and of the first steps in Russian trade-union history, is of particular value since Soviet writers over the past years have endeavored to project a highly partisan picture of these events.

     SR, 27:2:319-20   R: John Keep

1005.   Senn, Alfred Erich. **The Russian Revolution in Switzerland, 1914-1917**. Madison, University of Wisconsin Press, 1971. 250p. $12.50.

The principal theme is the "defensist-defeatist" or "nationalist-internationalist" schism in the ranks of the S. D. and S. R. Russian exiles—a theme whose importance to events in Russia in 1917 and 1918 can scarcely be doubted. However, this theme sometimes almost disappears as he turns to examine the Polish political exiles and their relations with the Germans, Lenin's relations with various secondary non-Russian figures of the Second International and with the German government, Miliukov's brief visit to Switzerland in 1916, and so forth. Senn's approach to the great range of problems with which he deals is rigorously objective.

   SR, 31:1:164-5   R: C. Jay Smith

1006. Tompkins, Stuart Ramsay. **The Triumph of Bolshevism: Revolution or Reaction?** Norman, University of Oklahoma Press, 1967. 331p. $5.95.

Tompkins, the author of *The Russian Mind* (1953) and *The Russian Intelligentsia* (1957), is coming now with his concluding work, *The Triumph of Bolshevism*, which brings the story up to the revolution itself. This is an intellectual history of Russian Marxism: its origins, its application, its ascendancy. The author is primarily concerned with the motivations of the Russian Social Democrats and the ideological vagaries they pursued in emigration. He is relatively uninterested in the broader Russian panorama of the time, in the illegal underground, or in the actual events of 1905 and 1917. Tompkins allows himself to be more interpretive than many of his younger predecessors.

   SR, 27:4:653-4   R: Ralph Carter Elwood

1007. Ulam, Adam B. **The Bolsheviks: The Intellectual and Political History of the Triumph of Communism in Russia.** New York, Macmillan; London, Collier-Macmillan, 1965. 598p. $9.95cl.; $2.95pa.

Vigorously written, this study covers the ground with exemplary thoroughness from the nineteenth century to Lenin's death in 1924, roughly half the total space being allotted to the post-revolutionary epoch. Ulam bases his narrative on extensive research but carries his learning lightly; his judgments are fair and will command wide assent. If the interpretation is on the whole a familiar one, this is largely due to the state of the sources. All students of modern Russia will be grateful to Ulam for a highly stimulating account of the origins of Soviet Communism. Regrettably, there is no bibliography and no index.

   SR, 25:1:155-6   R: John Keep

1008. Wildman, Allan K. **The Making of a Workers' Revolution: Russian Social Democracy, 1891-1903.** Chicago, University of Chicago Press, 1967. 271p. (The Hoover Institution, Inter-University Project on the History of the Menshevik Movement). $7.95.

In his careful analysis of the emerging Social-Democratic movement, Wildman focuses upon the ambivalent relations between the rank and file factory workers and their intellectual mentors. According to Wildman, there was continuous contact between the two groups, and their destinies were inextricably intertwined. The Marxist intellectuals, through their untiring agitational work, stirred new hope among the factory hands and gave coherent expression to their dreams and aspirations. The book is sound and convincing, though the treatment of the intellectuals is much more thorough than that of the workers.

RR, 27:3:354-5   R: Paul Avrich

1009.   Wyndham, Francis, and David King. **Trotsky: A Documentary**. New York, Praeger, 1972. 204p. $12.50.
The purpose of this volume is to document in photographs, posters, and cartoons the life of Trotsky. Quite a few pictures have not been published before or are little known. The captions are brief but informative. The text is based on Trotsky's own and Isaac Deutscher's writings except for the period 1929-1940, for which it draws heavily on personal recollections of Trotsky's entourage.

SR, 32:4:818-20   R: Ladis K. D. Kristof

Intellectual and Cultural History

1010.   Andreyev, Nikolay. **Studies in Muscovy: Western Influence and Byzantine Inheritance**. Preface by Elizabeth Hill. London, Variorum Reprints, 1970.
This volume is a collection of fourteen articles, thirteen of which deal with the cultural history of Muscovy, predominantly in the sixteenth century. They offer only a selection from Andreyev's abundant scholarly production in different fields pertaining to Russian studies during a period of nearly forty years. All of the articles are of the same high competence and illuminating originality.

SR, 31:2:415-6   R: Marc Szeftel

1011.   Billington, James H. **The Icon and the Axe. An Interpretive History of Russian Culture**. New York, Knopf, 1966. 786p. $15.00.
This is an extremely interesting and well-written book. If in places it is difficult to read, it is largely because the author has introduced much material which is by no means new but which has been overlooked or ignored by most scholars heretofore. He has aimed at presenting an overall interpretation of Great Russian culture—the culture of the Russian North—and he has traced the two symbols of his title down into the period of the Communists in cogent fashion. It is only unfortunate that he, like most American and Western writers, should persist in applying the word "Russian" to the culture of Kiev, which is far more characteristic of Ukraine throughout its history than it is of Moscow and the Great Russians. The author does recognize, however, the independent character of Rus' in several places.

UQ, 23:1:82-3   R: Clarence A. Manning

1012.   Herzen, Alexander. **My Past and Thoughts: The Memoirs of Alexander Herzen**. 4 vols. Intro. by Isaiah Berlin. Trans. by Constance Garnett. New York, Knopf, 1968. 1908p. $30.00.
The memoirs cover the years 1817-1870 and contain, in addition to autobiographical material, Herzen's activities, thoughts, and writings in Russia and, after 1847, abroad. This publication is a potentially rich mine of information not only about the events in Russia but also about philosophical, social, and political movements in Western Europe. Herzen, the publisher of *Kolokol*, left

his imprint on Russian intellectual and social history so that *My Past and Thoughts* deserves the attention of students of Russian history and a place in every college library. This revised edition of the English translation, originally published in 1924, contains more than 200 pages of additional material selected from his *Collected Works* (Moscow, 1954-56).   S. M. H.

1013.   Lampert, E. **Sons against Fathers: Studies in Russian Radicalism and Revolution**. Oxford, Clarendon Press, 1965. 405p. 63s.
This is a lively, provocative book; both learned and entertaining, it shows a fine density of appropriately chosen dramatic detail worked into a sturdy but sufficiently playful and fluent style. It resembles Franco Venturi's *Roots of Revolution* in its point of view, as well as in its subject matter, though it is not so long, not so complete and exhaustive. It is about Chernyshevsky, Dobroliubov, and Pisarev, and in particular about the conflict between genera-tions. The chapters on Dobroliubov and Pisarev, especially the latter, are more interesting and more convincing than that on Chernyshevsky.
        SR, 24:4:725-6   R: Sidney Monas

1014.   Malia, Martin. **Alexander Herzen and the Birth of Russian Socialism, 1812-1855**. Cambridge, Harvard University Press, 1961; New York, Grosset & Dunlap, 1965. 486p. (Russian Research Center Studies, no. 39). $10.00cl.; $2.65pa.
Malia's study of Herzen, his philosophy and his role in the formation of Russian political and philosophical thought, is not only a singularly outstanding English-language work, but more so, the only extensive and scholarly study in any language. Herzen, the "father of Russian socialism," is also seen as a liberal, revolutionary democrat and promotor of national self-determination. This noble intellectual, publisher of *Kolokol*, was one of the first Russians who opposed Russia's oppression of Poles and Ukrainians. Malia's study should not be missed in any academic or public library.   S. M. H.

1015.   Miliukov, Paul. **The Origins of Ideology**. Trans. from *Ocherki po istorii russkoi kul'tury* (Paris, 1930-37), Volume 3, by Joseph L. Wieczynski. Gulf Breeze, Fla., Academic International Press, 1974. (The Russian Series, 19-1). $12.50.
This work has long figured as an essential element in the education of serious students of Russia. In 1948 M. Karpovich brought out the greater part of the second volume of this three-volume work in English translation. Fuhrmann's introduction ("The Two Worlds of Paul Miliukov") will convey to the student some useful information on Miliukov's life and work. Wieczynski deserves credit for a supple and lively translation. He has also furnished a set of notes which, though certainly helpful, tend to give more information than the student will want. By contrast, the editor has ommitted Miliukov's introduction and notes.
        JMH, 47:3:324   R: Samuel H. Baron

1016.   Pomper, Philip. **The Russian Revolutionary Intelligentsia**. New York, Thomas Y. Crowell, 1970. 216p. $3.25pa.

The subject of this study is in fact the *road to* or *roots of* the revolutionary fate of the intelligentsia. The early history dominates. Nearly half of the book, the most informative half, is devoted to the radical intelligentsia in the reign of Alexander II. The discussion of Marxism is therefore sketchy. Much of the interest and value of the book lies in its method. Men create, discover, and use ideologies "in a given historical context"; ideologies "reflect the diversity of human temperament and personality." The book is "designed for use in both survey and period courses." This monograph contains an excellent bibliographic essay and a good index.

   SR, 30:4:881-2   R: Alan Kimball

1017. Raeff, Marc. **Origins of the Russian Intelligentsia: The Eighteenth-Century Nobility**. New York, Harcourt, Brace and World, 1966. 248p. $2.45pa.

In this short, brilliant study Raeff analyzes the forces that shaped the behavior and attitudes of the eighteenth-century Russian nobility, especially of its educated component, who served as "fathers" to the first generation of the Russian intelligentsia. Drawing on a wealth of material, sources, memoirs, and diaries as well as the available secondary sources, the author examines in turn, in four chapters, the function of family and service in the lives of the pre-Petrine nobility; the changed occupational, social, and agricultural patterns of the nobility resulting from the revolutionary institutional and social reforms of Peter the Great and his successors; the impact of the educated nobleman's early life at home and at school on his later behavior and outlook; and finally, the way in which this societal context produced a special manner in which Western ideas and culture were assimilated by the Russian elite.

   SR, 27:2:317-8   R: George W. Simmons

1018. Raeff, Marc, ed. **Russian Intellectual History: An Anthology**. With an intro. by Isaiah Berlin. New York, Harcourt, Brace and World, 1966. 404p. $4.50pa.

The purpose of this anthology is to acquaint the English-speaking reader with the writings and ideas that have helped to shape the history of Russia. Most of the documents included are of the eighteenth- and nineteenth-century intelligentsia and never published in English. Among these are writings of F. Prokopovich, M. V. Lomonsov, M. M. Shcherbatov, N. I. Novkov, N. M. Karamzin, I. P. Pnin, P. Ia. Chaadaev, I. V. Kireevski, A. S. Khomiakov, K. S. Aksakov, K. D. Kavelin, L. N. Tolstoy, A. A. Blok, and M. O. Gershenzon. This volume will be most useful to students of Russian intellectual history and should serve as a handy reference for quotations as well.   S. M. H.

1019. Wolfe, Bertram D. **The Bridge and the Abyss: The Troubled Friendship of Maxim Gorky and V. I. Lenin**. [Published for the Hoover Institution on War, Revolution and Peace, Stanford University]. New York, Praeger, 1967. 180p. $5.95.

In Wolfe's story, the Gorky-Lenin relationship in its prerevolutionary phase was a debate between a God-seeking humanitarian and the angry atheist whom he so admired. After the Revolution their mutual affection turned into a *danse macabre* performed on a stage heaped high with the victims of civil war and famine, Cheka inquisitions, and random murder. Gorky, like most of the great literary figures, had resisted tsarist tyranny, and he resisted that of Lenin with equal tenacity. Wolfe's book, dealing with events of a half century ago, is as fresh as today's paper that tells of the current writers' trial in Moscow.

AHR, 73:5:1584-5   R: Stanley W. Page

PSYCHOLOGY AND PSYCHIATRY

1020.   Payne, T. R. **S. L. Rubinstejn and the Philosophical Foundations of Soviet Psychology**. Dordrecht, Reidel Publishing, 1969. 184p. Distr. by Humanities Press, New York. $14.25.

The reader who thinks it unfair to call Marxist-Leninist psychology a mystification should read Payne's book. "As the unifying principle in psychology Rubinstejn sees the so-called Marxist-Leninist theory of determinism. As a general theory, applicable to all parts of the material world, it is formulated as follows: the outer cause works through, and is refracted by, the inner conditions of the object on which it acts. In the light of this principle psychic events are the result of the interaction of the individual with the outer world."

SR, 33:4:786-7   R: David Joravsky

1021.   Rahmani, Levy. **Soviet Psychology: Philosophical, Theoretical, and Experimental Issues**. New York, International Universities Press, 1973. 440p. $17.50.

The author provides an elaborate survey of Soviet psychological research together with a critique of the theoretical foundation of the Soviet doctrinaire approach toward the methodology of research. He explains the Soviet concept of psychology and its function in various applications within the context of dialectical materialism. He does not, however, stress the degree to which psychology is used in the Soviet legal system and how frequently it is applied as an instrument of the KGB in dealing with dissident intellectuals. The study, with an excellent bibliography, is aimed at professionals and informed readers.

S. M. H.

1022.   Rollins, Nancy. **Child Psychiatry in the Soviet Union: Preliminary Observations**. Cambridge, Harvard University Press, 1972. 293p. $12.95.

This is the first book in English dealing with the theory, practice, and organization of child psychiatry in the Soviet Union. This study is not only of interest and value in the area of professional therapy, it also provides numerous insights into Russian cultural attitudes which have an effect on character and personality development. It should therefore attract the attention of an audience considerably beyond the scope of medicine.

SR, 33:4:787   R: Alec Skolnick, M.D.

1023.   Vygotsky, Lev Semenovich. **The Psychology of Art**. Intro. by A. N. Leontiev. Commentary by V. V. Ivanov. [Trans. from the Russian by Scripta Technica, Inc.] Cambridge, Mass., MIT Press, 1971. 305p. $12.50.

Vygotsky, one of the foremost Soviet psychologists, held that the psychology of art had in his day foundered on the rocks of subjectivism, from which he aimed to free it by placing it on a sound sociological and historical basis. His chosen method was to define the form of a work of art, to analyze the function of its elements and structure, and thence to arrive at general laws governing the aesthetic response.

SR, 32:1:202　　　　　　　　R: J. D. West

RELIGION

History

1024.　Cracraft, James. **The Church Reform of Peter the Great**. Stanford, Stanford University Press, 1971. 336p. $13.50.

This work traces Peter's ecclesiastical reforms from their inception at the close of the seventeenth century to the end of his reign in 1725. Biographical sketches of Peter and Feofan Prokopovich draw attention to their place within the broader perspective of contemporary European trends. The main strength of this work lies in its plan for painstaking adherence to the sources; however, the reader must be aware of numerous incorrect dates and mistranslations.

SR, 31:1:153-4　　　　　　R: Alexander V. Muller

1025.　Crummey, Robert O. **The Old Believers and the World of Antichrist: The Vyg Community and the Russian State, 1694-1855**. Milwaukee, University of Wisconsin Press, 1970. 258p. $10.00.

The Vyg community—which was organized in 1694 in the virgin forests between Lake Onega and the White Sea—became, thanks to the efforts of several dissenter leaders, not only a monastic settlement but also an important cultural institution in which the Old Believer writers produced some of their most important theological and historical works. Crummey performed a most rewarding task, finally initiating Western studies of this outstanding northern cultural center of non-Westernized Russia. He is primarily interested in the institutional history of Vyg. The book is attractive, has many useful plans, maps, and pictures which help the reader to understand the life of this semi-monastic settlement, and is supplied with an almost exhaustive bibliography.

SR, 30:2:390-1　　　　　　R: Serge A. Zenkovsky

1026.　Durasoff, Steve. **The Russian Protestants: Evangelicals in the Soviet Union: 1944-1964**. Teaneck, N.J., Fairleigh Dickinson University Press, 1969. 312p. $10.00.

The author presents in the first part of his book the historical background of Protestant denominations in Orthodox Russia beginning with 1575. The other five parts are concerned with the denominations of the Soviet period, their tribulations, problems, organizations, and statistics. The book combines the lucidity of popular presentation with a modest type of scholarship and documentation and is written with a sense of responsibility to the reader concerning

the sad truth of the curtailment of true freedom of worship in the Soviet
Union in general and as applied to the Evangelicals in particular.
SR, 31:3:698   R: B. B. Szczesniak

1027.   Kline, George L. **Religious and Anti-Religious Thought in Russia.**
Chicago, University of Chicago Press, 1969. 179p. $7.50.
The author's knowledge not only of Russian intellectual thought but also of
Western philosophy makes him a competent authority in this field, and it is
exactly this combination that makes the book of high value. The book is well
organized, and the author maintains a high standard of presentation throughout.
SR, 29:2:334-5   R: Michael Klimenko

1028.   Muller, Alexander V., trans. and ed. **The Spiritual Regulation of
Peter the Great.** Seattle, University of Washington Press, 1972.
150p. (Publications on Russia and Eastern Europe of the Institute
for Comparative and Foreign Area Studies, no. 3). $10.00.
The present new English translation is based on the official text from the
Polnoe sobranie zakonov. Muller has corrected it in accordance with the manuscript published by P. V. Verkhovsky in his work, *Uchrezhdenie Dukhovnoi
kollegii i Dukhovnyi reglament* (Rostov, 1916). Peter's manifesto of January 25,
1721, the oath taken by members of the Synod, the text of the law proper,
and the supplements are supplied. In general, the translation is accurate.
SR, 32:4:804-5   R: Robert Stupperich

Special Studies

1029.   Bennigsen, Alexandre, and Chantal Lamercier-Quelquejoy. **Islam in
the Soviet Union.** Intro. by Geoffrey E. Wheeler. New York, Praeger,
1967. 272p. (Published in association with the Central Asian Research
Centre, London). $7.00.
This book unfolds a broad survey of political change among the formerly Muslim
people of Russia for the purpose of determining what, if anything, survives from
the Islamic past and how much weight may be assigned such remnants today.
The authors evidently feel that a good deal may be found, but are cautious in
specifying its effect. Two chapters, 9 and 12, out of the sixteen, deal directly
with the practices of Islam. The others discuss problems of nationality and
civilization, with frequent reference to the "Islamic" character of selected
Soviet Asian groups. One of the most striking revelations of the book discloses
the vitality of regionalism in Soviet Asian political affairs.
SR, 28:1:143-5   R: Edward Allworth

1030.   Bourdeaux, Michael. **Patriarch and Prophets: Persecution of the
Russian Orthodox Church Today.** New York, Praeger, 1970. 359p.
$10.00.
This is a companion volume to the author's 1968 book *Religious Ferment in
Russia* (which deals with the opposition of the Evangelical Christian-Baptists
to Soviet religious policy since 1960). It separates commentary from documen-
tation; unfortunately, many documents are offered in an incomplete form,

though the editor frequently offers a brief summary of the parts left out. It is noteworthy that both Soviet and *samizdat* documents are included; dealing occasionally with the same problems, they offer contrasting versions of the same events and persons. Prefaced by an introduction on Church-State relations in the USSR, the documents are arranged in eight sections dealing with such aspects of the problem as features and consequences of Khrushchev's anti-religious campaign and the Church's reaction to it, the persecution of the clergy, the suppression of monasteries and seminaries, destruction of parish life, and reactions of the believers. The remaining sections contain protest documents written by various priests. This book will be read with intense interest by specialists and laymen alike.

SR, 30:1:164-5   R: Bohdan R. Bociurkiw

1031.   Bourdeaux, Michael. **Religious Ferment in Russia: Protestant Opposition to Soviet Religious Policy**. New York, St. Martin's Press, 1968. 255p. $8.95.

The book deals with the so-called Initiators' Movement, which began around 1962 among the Baptist communities in opposition to the government's attempts to gain control over the internal affairs of religious organizations. The book is a unique and profound study. It brings to the fore problems hardly touched by scholars previously, and poignantly stresses the problem of the Christian conscience in Russia. The book deals with the organized opposition of a small group of Baptists who dared to protest governmental pressure upon their personal lives and their organizations.

SR, 30:2:403-5   R: Michael Klimenko

1032.   Conquest, Robert, ed. **Religion in the U.S.S.R.** New York, Praeger, 1968. 135p. $5.00.

The purpose of the book edited by Conquest is to demonstrate the irreconcilable hostility of Communist ideology to any manifestation of religion. The author has listed many acts of the Soviet government regarding religion without any attempt to interpret or discuss their meaning. The first three parts, dealing mainly with the Orthodox Church, seem to be a theoretical treatment of religion and Communism. Part 4 deals with the non-Orthodox Churches and religion by discussing their religious life and activity.

SR, 30:2:403-4   R: Michael Klimenko

1033.   Dunlop, John B. **Staretz Amvrosy: Model for Dostoevsky's Staretz Zossima**. Belmont, Mass., Nordland Publishing, 1972. 176p. $4.75.

This book is one of the first monographs published in the West devoted to the specific image of one of the *startsy*: the justly renowned Amvrosy of Optina Monastery (1812-1891). The author introduces the reader to the inner world of Amvrosy, portraying his personal attitudes and his methods of spiritual guidance. The material used—derived from Amvrosy's letters and conversations—is skillfully arranged. All this makes the book very valuable for those who are interested in nineteenth-century Russian monasticism and even in questions of spiritual life and pastoral guidance.

SR, 33:2:399-400   R: Cyril Fotiev

1034.   Fireside, Harvey. **Icon and Swastika: The Russian Orthodox Church under Nazi and Soviet Control.** Cambridge, Harvard University Press, 1971. 242p. (Russian Research Center Studies, 62). $8.00.
Fireside has lifted the veil from what has been the least-known period in the recent history of the Russian Orthodox Church—its life under the Nazi occupation of the western areas of the Soviet Union during the Second World War. Using original German documents with superb competence, the author has clarified German policy—or rather the lack of it—toward the Russian Orthodox Church. Unlike the Soviet government, which quickly evolved a punitive antireligious policy, the new German regime never came to a unified solution of the religious question.
        SR, 31:1:175-6   R: Michael Bourdeaux

1035.   Fletcher, William C., and Anthony J. Strover, eds. **Religion and the Search for New Ideals in the USSR.** New York, Praeger, 1967. 135p. (Published for the Institute for the Study of the USSR). $5.00.
The book belongs to the tradition of the carefully documented monograph. Consisting of eleven essays by as many authors representing five countries, this volume was derived from papers presented at an international symposium, April 22-27, 1966, at the Institute for the Study of the USSR, in Munich. Significantly, religion seems to thrive in the face of governmental and party persecution, the desuetude of decades, the spread of rationalism, atheistic indoctrination in school and society, and open communal disapproval. This informative volume offers recent data, mainly from Soviet sources, documenting the persistence of all faiths in the hostile Soviet Communist atmosphere.
        SR, 27:1:172-3   R: William W. Brickman

1036.   Fletcher, William C. **Religion and Soviet Foreign Policy, 1945-1970.** London, Oxford University Press, 1973. 179p. (Published for the Royal Institute of International Affairs). $11.25.
The Church is seen in this monograph in the role of forming a favorable picture of the Soviet Union through the participation of its members in international peace conferences and ecumenical movements. The author explores the role of Soviet churchmen in the World Peace Council, the Christian Peace Conferences, the World Council of Churches, and relations with the Vatican.
        SR, 33:1:147   R: Cyril Bryner

1037.   Fletcher, William C. **The Russian Orthodox Church Underground, 1917-1970.** New York, Oxford University Press, 1971. 314p. $12.75.
Fletcher draws several conclusions from his study of underground Orthodoxy: it is a response to Soviet persecution; persecution of Orthodoxy does not succeed, for it does not eradicate religion but drives it underground; this underground opposition serves as insurance that organized religious institutions may continue to exist. This book rightly corrects and dismisses the view popularized by Harrison Salisbury and others that the "Church indulges in no undercover activities."
        SR, 34:1:151   R: Robert L. Nichols

1038.   Maloney, George A. **Russian Hesychasm: The Spirituality of Nil Sorskij**. The Hague, Mouton, 1973. 302p. (Slavistic Printings and Reprintings, 269). 68Dglds.

The book deserves recognition as a most systematic and factual study of Nil Sorsky, the spiritual leader of Russian Hesychasm in the fifteenth and sixteenth centuries. The author's elucidation of Nil's ascetic ideals shows the complex nature of his internal struggle for self-perfection, which was an important part of his teaching, and adumbrates the psychology of his thought processes. Section 2 also includes a brilliant analysis of the eight sources of passions.

SR, 34:2:382   R: Nikolay Andreev

1039.   Marshall, Richard H., et al., eds.**Aspects of Religion in the Soviet Union, 1917-1967**. Chicago, University of Chicago Press, 1971. 489p. $19.75.

The heart of the book consists of essays by seventeen scholars covering virtually every major aspect of the subject and every major group in the USSR (Orthodox, Moslems, Jews, Baptists, Catholics) as well as national churches (Georgian, Armenian) and even minor groups such as the Mennonites and the animistic Siberian tribes. There is an appendix containing the text of all the major laws pertaining to religion in the USSR, and a selected bibliography of English-language books on religion in the Soviet Union.

SR, 31:1:175   R: James P. Scanlan

1040.   Simon, Gerhard. **Church, State and Opposition in the U.S.S.R.** Trans. by Kathleen Matchett in collaboration with the Centre for the Study of Religion and Communism. Berkeley, University of California Press, 1974. 248p. $12.00.

This book is a translation of *Die Kirchen in Russland* by an outstanding expert on religion in Russia. It is of equal value to general readers and specialists in Soviet affairs. The first two chapters deal with the Russian church on the eve of the revolution. The next three chapters concern church-state relations and religious persecution at the present time. One chapter consists of an appraisal of Pastor Richard Wurmband's mission and its impact on the Western churches. The final part comprises documents translated from the Russian originals.

The best work now available in English by an individual author on contemporary Church-State relations in the Soviet Union.   S. M. H.

1041.   Zernov, Nicolas. **The Russian Religious Renaissance of the Twentieth Century**. New York, Harper & Row, 1964. 410p. $7.00.

Central to the author's arguments is the view that Russia achieved its national and cultural identity through the Orthodox Church, and for Zernov the tragedy of Russia's history arose out of events which undermined what he regards as the underlying religious unity of the Russian people: the schism of the seventeenth century, Peter's reforms, the emergence of the revolutionary intelligentsia, and the revolution of 1917. A large portion of this volume is devoted to discussion of the nature and role of the intelligentsia, described by the author as a group which tried to destroy religious unity by the "preaching of socialism based on materialism and atheism." In this connection Zernov stresses the importance of the *Vekhi* group, of the ex-Marxists Struve, Bulgakov, Berdiaev, and Frank. The book contains a useful appendix, which lists the leading figures of the religious movement and their major writings.

SR, 24:1:159-60   R: Harold Swayze

SCIENCE AND RESEARCH

Special Studies

1042. Boss, Valentin. **Newton and Russia: The Early Influence, 1698-1796.** Cambridge, Harvard University Press, 1972. 309p. (Russian Research Center Studies, 69). $19.00.

This is a welcome addition to the small literature in English on eighteenth-century Russian science. The author alludes to the sharp split between the Academy of Science, which was controlled by Germans and was anti-Newtonian, and the Russian amateurs outside the Academy, who were more receptive to Newton and played a key role in popularizing his ideas.

SR, 33:1:131-2   R: Herbert Leventer

1043. Fischer, George, ed. **Science and Ideology in Soviet Society.** New York, Atherton Press, 1967. 176p. $6.95.

Four contributors are reinforcing here a basic truth we should have perceived long ago: Soviet ideology is a very fuzzy and elusive thing; simply pointing to it does not explain why Soviet leaders have taken changing stands in various sciences, including no stand at all. The main effort of these authors is not to discover how and why Stalinists got involved in efforts to impose particular dogmas on particular sciences. Their attention is concentrated on the current process of disengagement, which began in 1950 with Stalin's emancipation of linguistics and is now observable, though halting and feeble, even in the social sciences. Sciences discussed are: sociology (George Fischer); philosophy (Richard DeGeorge); cybernetics (Loren Graham), and economics (Herbert Levine).

SR, 28:4:665-6   R: David Joravsky

1044. Graham, Loren R. **The Soviet Academy of Sciences and the Communist Party, 1927-1932.** Princeton, Princeton University Press, 1967. 225p. (Studies of the Russian Institute, Columbia University). $6.50.

The stated purpose of this well-written monograph is to tell the story of "the renovation of the Academy of Sciences" during the crucial period of the first Five-Year Plan with special attention to the details of the purging of the Academy with its concomitant terror. Much of the information has not previously been available in English or readily accessible in any language, which in itself makes the monograph a valuable contribution. Its value is increased because the author, who clearly recognized that neither the Academy nor what happened to it occurred in a vacuum, relates its story to a broader context—economic planning in the Soviet Union and the relations of governments to science and scientists outside the Soviet Union. Graham also emphasizes the relationship of the

Communist rulers to the Academy and treats in detail the steps by which they were successful in dominating the institution and its members.
RR, 27:4:476-7   R: Warren B. Walsh

1045.   Graham, Loren R. **Science and Philosophy in the Soviet Union.** New York, Knopf, 1972. 624p. $15.00.
Graham offers a discipline-by-discipline account of the interaction of science and Marxist philosophy in the work of the leading Soviet scientists, the controversies in which they have been involved, and the contributions they made to contemporary world science.   S. M. H.

1046.   Joravsky, David. **The Lysenko Affair.** Cambridge, Harvard University Press, 1970. 549p. $13.95.
Joravsky carefully examines in this study the role of theoretical ideology in the rise of Lysenkoism and the suppression of genetics in the Soviet Union. He demolishes the arguments that Lysenkoism was in some way inherently connected with Communist theory and that Lysenko's theories were grounded in valid scientific concepts. This is a profound and penetrating study that should stand unchallenged on the subject of Lysenkoism for some time to come.
SR, 30:4:898-9   R: Maxim W. Mikulak

1047.   Korol, Alexander. **Soviet Research and Development: Its Organization, Personnel and Funds.** Cambridge, Mass., MIT Press, 1965. 375p. $11.00.
This is a pioneering work in an area that is commanding increasing attention on both sides of the ideological frontier. Its central aim is to examine the magnitude and distribution of national resources allocated to scientific research and development in the Soviet Union. The author concludes that "Soviet state policies and practices have acted both as a powerful stimulant for the quantitative growth of scientific effort and as a depressant in many important qualitative potentialities of that," a conclusion with which economists would be the first to agree. This is an important book, not to be missed.
RR, 25:2:198-9   R: Jan S. Prybyla

1048.   Medvedev, Zhores A. **The Rise and Fall of T. D. Lysenko.** Trans. by I. Michael Lerner, with the editorial assistance of Lucy G. Lawrence. New York, Columbia University Press, 1969. 284p. $10.00.
This study of the Lysenko affair traces its history in considerable detail, naming names (and eloquently eulogizing the victims), quoting at some length from speeches, debates, articles, and reports, and explaining the scientific questions and issues in many of the events. This book is thus not only an extremely useful chronicle of what happened, but it also represents the courageous action of a scientist deeply involved, at his own risk, in the issues he describes. His chronicling of the injustices and stupidities committed in the course of the whole affair, together with his explanation of how it came about, constitutes a severe indictment of the Soviet system in its Stalinistic phase.
SR, 29:1:707   R: Beverly S. Almgren

1049.   Vucinich, Alexander. **Science in Russian Culture, 1861-1917**. Stanford,
        Stanford University Press, 1970. 575p. $18.50.
Vucinich's new book is a valuable contribution to the study of Russian history
and civilization and a worthy successor to his earlier volume, *Science in Russian
Culture: A History to 1860*. The author is concerned not only with science and
scholarship proper but also with relevant institutional structure and government
policies, Russian education as a whole, and indeed the entire intellectual and
cultural history of the period. This study will probably prove most useful as
a rich and rewarding account of numerous Russian scientists, scholars, and their
work. As such it is unmatched in the English language, and it has a distinct
contribution to make to the literature at large. Vucinich is in favor of science
and progress and against church and religion. The volume contains a rich
bibliography.
        SR, 31:1:159-60   R: Nicholas V. Riasanovsky

1050.   Zaleski, E., et al. **Science Policy in the USSR**. Paris, Organization for
        Economic Co-operations and Development, 1969. 615p. $15.00pa.
This is a collection of five research essays, each accompanied by several self-
contained appendixes. The topics range from organizational problems and the
financing of research within the general framework of Soviet economic planning
to the employment of scientists and engineers, from a brief history and description of the USSR Academy of Sciences to research in higher education and
industrial research and applied technology. This breadth of topics makes this
book a comprehensive and useful survey. The strength of the volume is in its
summary of information and discussion of the tools the Soviet regime employs
in planning research.
        SR, 29:1:139-40   R: Nicholas DeWitt

Space Exploration

1051.   James, Peter N. **Soviet Conquest from Space**. New Rochelle, N.Y.,
        Arlington House, 1974. 256p. $8.95.
The author, a former space systems analyst for Pratt & Whitney Aircraft, reveals
the little publicized implementation of militarism into the Soviet space program.
According to James, space research in the Soviet is determined, controlled, and
utilized exclusively by the Soviet armed forces. The program as such is part of
an overall Soviet strategic planning that is subordinated to Soviet global policy
and ideological aims as outlined by the CPSU programme.
        S. M. H.

1052.   Vladimirov, Leonid. **The Russian Space Bluff: The Inside Story of
        the Soviet Drive to the Moon**. Trans. by David Floyd. Foreword by
        Anatoli Fedoseyev. New York, Dial Press, 1973. 190p. $5.95.
The author makes it clear that the chief cause of the Soviet lag in the space-
exploration efforts was the gross interference of the Communist politicians
with that nation's scientists and engineers. Only the high talents and the incredible

ingenuity of experts allowed the late Sergei Korolev to achieve whatever was achieved before 1969—despite the rulers' ignorant caprices. And the reason the false impression in the West lingered so long was the colossal Western gullibility.

SR, 33:1:153-4   R: Albert Parry

SOCIOLOGY

General Studies

1053.   Dunn, Stephen P., ed. **Sociology in the USSR: A Collection of Readings from Soviet Sources.** White Plains, N.Y., International Arts and Sciences Press, 1969. 281p. $12.00.

All articles collected by Dunn have been previously published in *Soviet Sociology* and *Soviet Anthropology and Archeology*, and they thus reflect the official Soviet views on sociology. The articles are topically arranged: 1) Sociological Theory and Research; 2) Questions of Social and Nationality Policy; 3) Ethnic Processes and Relations; 4) Empirical Methodology and Social Statistics; 5) Empirical Studies of Worker Communities; 6) Rural Sociology and Agriculture; 7) Religion; and 8) Local Government and Administration. Soviet sociology has begun to emerge as an independent discipline only recently and is framed by Marxian doctrine and Soviet domestic policy. Therefore, its limits are obvious. Soviet sociology has little to offer its Western counterpart.

S. M. H.

1054.   Hindus, Maurice. **The Kremlin's Human Dilemma: Russia after Half a Century of Revolution.** Garden City, N.Y., Doubleday, 1967. 395p. $5.95.

Hindus brings to his task over forty years of reportage on Soviet life, and an intimate knowledge of the country and its peoples. The result is a remarkable panorama of Soviet life—the city, the village, the economy, and the social classes; and the plight of dissident intellectuals, the national minorities, and religious believers. The author is ever mindful of the material and cultural achievements of the Soviet government, but he is equally attentive to the manifold ways in which a dogmatic political ideology has combined with an enormously centralized power structure to create impossible dilemmas for those whose aspirations or cultural traditions are in conflict with the system. Because the book is informative and stimulating on so many themes, it can be strongly recommended both to specialists and general readers.

SR, 31:2:426-8   R: Herbert J. Ellison

1055.   Hollander, Paul, ed. **American and Soviet Society: A Reader in Comparative Sociology and Perception.** Englewood Cliffs, N.J., Prentice-Hall, 1969. 589p. $8.95.

The underlying idea of this book is basically sound and intellectuall productive: it is to provide assessments by American and Soviet sociologists or social scientists on their own society. This gives us a fourfold classification: American views on American society, American Views on Soviet society, Soviet views on American society, and Soviet views on Soviet society. These then are presented in eight major parts: social values, beliefs, and ideologies; the polity; social stratification; the family, marital and sexual relations; social problems; appraisals of sociology; and "Are the Two Societies Becoming Alike?" This reader might serve as collateral reading for a course on comparative modern society or a course on the Soviet Union.

SR, 29:1:710-11   R: Mark G. Field

1056. Inkeles, Alex, and Raymond A. Bauer. **The Soviet Citizen: Daily Life in a Totalitarian Society.** New York, Atheneum, 1968 (1959). 533p. $4.45pa.

This book resulted from examination of 3,000 questionnaires filled out by refugees from the Soviet Union in connection with the Harvard Project on the Soviet Social System (Russian Research Center Studies, no. 35). A wide spectrum of issues of daily life is investigated. The work constitutes a historical record of great importance pertaining to the nature of the totalitarian Soviet state.

S. M. H.

1057. Matthews, Mervyn. **Class and Society in Soviet Russia.** New York, Walter & Co., 1972. 366p. $12.50.

Matthews presents much of the available evidence on income inequality, differences in life styles, occupational prestige rankings, and social composition of students at different levels of schooling. Although the author mainly focuses on social and economic inequality, the volume also includes a useful discussion of recent Soviet demographic trends, a summary of rural-to-urban migration studies, and a heroic attempt to estimate the magnitude of Soviet youth unemployment.

SR, 33:2:377-78   R: Murray Yanowitch

1058. Nogee, Joseph L., ed. **Man, State, and Society in the Soviet Union.** New York, Praeger, 1972. 599p. $15.00cl.; $5.95pa.

This volume of essays by some thirty contributors, including Marx, Engels, Lenin, A. Amalrik, and V. Chornovil, attempts to assess the present-day Soviet system and society from various vantages such as ideology, politics, economy, judicial process, personal life, social groups, and national minorities. It is a combination of handbook and symposium and offers insights and analyses that are usually not available in ordinary textbooks. Despite the unevenness of the contributions, the book is highly recommended for classroom reading material. Nogee's introduction, a well-selected bibliography, and an extensive index add to the quality of the work.   S. M. H.

1059. An Observer. **Message from Moscow.** New York, Knopf, 1969. 288p. $5.95.

An anonymous Western student has written the most penetrating book of its genre. He concentrates on the delicate task of portraying the "mood" of the nation in the wake of the Czech invasion. The result is of necessity impressionistic, but it is based on an unusually long (three-year) sojourn and a wide range of acquaintances and friendships with Russians from all walks of life. What gives the book its special distinction is the author's ability to show the

Russian winter and traditional Russian backwardness as forces which affect attitudes, mores, and behavior much more powerfully than the incessant stream of propagandistic exhortations and official attempts at regimentation.

     SR, 30:1:159-60   James C. McClelland

1060.   Simirenko, Alex, ed. and intro. **Social Thought in the Soviet Union.** Chicago, Quadrangle Books, 1969. 439p. $14.95.

This collection of essays consists of an introduction and twelve chapters by as many contributors, covering social science ideology, philosophy, political science, law, historiography, economics, character education, psychology, psychiatry, structural linguistics, ethnography, and sociology. This is a valuable reference work and should be made available to every class in either comparative social science or Soviet area studies.

     SR, 29:1:137-8   R: Demitri B. Shimkin

1061.   Thaden, Edward C. **Russia since 1801: The Making of a New Society.** New York, John Wiley & Sons, 1971. 682p. $10.95.

Most of the book concentrates on domestic issues, such as agriculture, industry, education, science, music, literature, social classes, and bureaucracy. Only four chapters deal with the delicate and intricate problems of foreign policy. The book's basic strength is its clarity and impartiality. The author has given the most diligent attention to the nationality problem—before, during, and since the Revolution. This attention in a scholarly work to one of the most fundamental (and still largely neglected) problems in understanding modern Russian history is most welcome.

     SR, 31:1:154-5   R: Basil Dmytryshyn

1062.   Weinberg, Elizabeth Ann. **The Development of Sociology in the Soviet Union.** London, Routledge and Kegan Paul, 1974. 173p. $14.00.

The achievements of sociology in the Soviet Union since 1956 constitute the central theme of this book. Weinberg has gathered interesting and highly relevant information on the historical roots of Soviet sociology and on the present-day efforts of Soviet scholars to bring historical materialism and sociology into a symbiotic relationship and to effect a full separation of ideological and scientific approaches to social reality. This is a well-designed and precisely executed study, written in a dispassionate tone and with notable professional skill.

     RR, 34:2:218   R: Alexander Vucinich

Medical Care and Social Welfare

1063.   Field, Mark G. **Soviet Socialized Medicine: An Introduction.** New York, Free Press; London, Collier-Macmillan, 1967. 231p. $6.95.

Its wide scope and abundance of quoted sources make this publication valuable to anyone interested in the origins and development of the Soviet medical system. The book is notable for the well-rounded presentation of the many problems discussed. Its wide range of topics includes history, organization, health personnel, salaries, and clinical facilities. The author's primary sources are the published Soviet materials. In addition, he has used information collected from former Soviet physicians who emigrated to this country after the Second World War. The author presents both pre- and post-revolutionary conditions objectively and fairly, though critically. As to medical research, however, Field is quite critical of Soviet achievements. Through this medical portal one can see the whole of Soviet life, since the author very skillfully fits the medical system into the total Soviet structure.

SR, 26:4:691   R: Galina Zarechnak

1064.   Madison, Bernice Q. **Social Welfare in the Soviet Union**. Stanford, Stanford University Press, 1968. 298p. $8.50.

This book provides, in a highly readable and concise form, a picture of social welfare in the USSR, and is a distinctive contribution to our knowledge of Soviet society. The author reviews Soviet achievements and shortcomings, particularly in the areas of family and child welfare services. The study is divided into two parts: in the first section the author deals briefly with social welfare policy formation between 1917 and 1966; in the second part she turns to current practices, an analysis that is tempered and enhanced by her own expertise and two fairly extended stays in the Soviet Union. Her book is thus unique in this underexplored field.

SR, 28:3:519-20   R: Mark G. Field

1065.   Osborn, Robert J. **Soviet Social Policies: Welfare, Equality, and Community**. Homewood, Ill., Dorsey Press, 1970. 294p. $3.95pa.

Osborn examines three broad areas of post-Stalin Soviet social policies directed at this sector: 1) social security and the individual's claims to assistance and benefits in a system where the allocation of resources and the meaning of the concepts of welfare and social wage are determined centrally; 2) the motivations provided for the individual to select appropriate levels and type of education and employment and to remain committed to his work; 3) the organizing and shaping of the urban environment, where residential arrangements are made at promoting meaningful social interaction and at creating communities which would be conducive to social, occupational, and ethnic integration. The book clearly indicates that the political measures, which have resulted from values and ideas held by Soviet leadership, often resemble the policy solutions promoted by non-Communist governments.

CSP, 14:3:547-5   R: Barbara M. Kasinska

Social Problems and Social Change

1066.   Churchward, L. G. **The Soviet Intelligentsia: An Essay on the Social Structure and Roles of Soviet Intellectuals during the 1960s**. London, Routledge & Kegan Paul, 1973. 204p. $10.00.

This is a welcome contribution to an important and much misunderstood topic. Many of the disputes concerning the functions and attributes of Soviet intellectuals hinge on our definition of the intellectual. The author's definition is simple and unambiguous: "I regard the intelligentsia as consisting of persons with a tertiary education, tertiary students, and persons lacking formal tertiary qualification but who are professionally employed in jobs which normally require a tertiary qualification." To overcome the limitations of such a definition he also provides a typology of contemporary Soviet intellectuals based on their political attitudes, in an increasing order of alienation from the system. Thus he classifies them as careerist professionals, humanist intelligentsia, open oppositions, and the lost intelligentsia.

    SR, 34:1:160-1   R: Paul Hollander

1067. Connor, Walter D. **Deviance in Soviet Society: Crime, Delinquency, and Alcoholism**. New York, Columbia University Press, 1972. 327p. $12.50.

This work is built almost wholly on published sources. Consequently, it is strongest in analyzing the content of discussions in professional journals and the press, and in describing the formal mechanisms that have been set up to control deviance of different kinds. The most interesting and useful part of the book, therefore, is its exposition of public Soviet discussions of the causes of deviance and their remedies.

    SR, 32:3:625-6   R: Robert J. Osborn

1068. Inkeles, Alex. **Social Change in Soviet Russia**. Cambridge, Harvard University Press, 1968. 477p. (Russian Research Center Studies, 57). $12.50.

The richness and variety of Inkeles' ideas are presented in this collection of his major essays on the Soviet Union. The most lasting contributions to sociology are the articles on the nature of social structure. These are "Social Stratification and Mobility in the Soviet Union" (1950), "National Comparisons of Occupational Prestige" (with Peter H. Rossi, 1956), "Critical Letters to the Soviet Press" (with H. Kent Geiger, 1953), "Social Stratification in the Modernization of Russia" (1960), and "Developments in Soviet Mass Communications" (revised, 1967). Probably his greatest insight into the nature of modern social organization is represented in the essay, "The Totalitarian Mystique: Some Impressions of the Dynamics of Totalitarian Society," published in 1953.

    SR, 29:1:136-7   R: Alex Simirenko

1069. Meissner, Boris, ed. **Social Change in the Soviet Union: Russia's Path Toward Industrial Society**. Notre Dame, University of Notre Dame Press, 1972. 247p. $9.95.

The book, first published in German in 1966, consists of a major piece by the editor ("Social Change in Bolshevik Russia") and other chapters dealing with "Social Change in Russia prior to the October Revolution," "Educational Policy and Social Structure in the Soviet Union," "The Sociological Impact of Soviet Educational Policy," and a concluding essay by the editor on "Soviet Policy under Khrushchev's Successors." The main theme of the volume is the interaction between historical antecedents and industrialization and its impact on Soviet social and political structure. Among the highlights of the volume is an excellent and well-documented discussion of the re-stratification of Soviet society which culminated in a new, well-ordered hierarchical society.

    CSP, 17:2-3:537-8   R: Paul Hollander

1070.   Miller, Jack. **Life in Russia Today**. London, B. T. Batsford, 1969;
         New York, G. P. Putnam's Sons, 1969. 198p. $4.00.
This book makes an excellent supplement to the standard textbooks and books
of readings for introductory courses on the Soviet Union. The author seeks to
show how the Russians themselves view their own society. He portrays the
beliefs and ambitions, the satisfactions and frustrations of the ordinary Russian
and his family. For example, he remarks that "relations between people are not
a simple matter in any modern society. The additional complication in Soviet
society, caused by the informer system, especially in the sphere of friendship
and mutual trust, makes the whole country ill in a sense that may or may not
be definable by social psychologists or psychiatrists, but is real to the inhabitants."
The author, a senior editor of *Soviet Studies*, visited the Soviet Union before World
War II and a number of times since then.   S. M. H.

1071.   Shanin, Teodor. **The Awkward Class: Political Sociology of the
         Peasantry in a Developing Society: Russia, 1910-1925**. Oxford,
         Clarendon Press, 1972. 253p. $15.25.
This study contributes to the discussion, which has been renewed recently, of
the nature, causes, and consequences of differentiations and mobility of the
Russian peasantry through an examination of the many studies by Russian and
Soviet scholars in the quarter-century before collectivization. The book offers
a valuable introduction to a neglected but important body of theoretical and
empirical studies, and provides a framework for future comparative research on
stratification and change among peasants.
         SR, 32:3:621   R: Norman A. Moscowitz

1072.   Yanowitch, Murray, and Wesley A. Fisher, eds. **Social Stratification
         and Mobility in the USSR**. White Plains, N.Y., International Arts and
         Sciences Press, 1973. 402p. $20.00.
The selections which make up this book reflect the increasing horizontal and
vertical complexity of Soviet society, a consequence of ongoing occupational
differentiations which can no longer be contained within the descriptive formula
of "two classes, one stratum" (collective farmer, worker; intelligentsia). Within
this complex hierarchical system, processes of mobility are, as in other industrial
societies, conditioned by various elements of social origin. Represented here are
some of the best Soviet writings of the last decade on these issues, such as
Rutkevich, Filipov, Shkaratan, Liss, and Titma. Those who do read it will find
the effort worthwhile.
         RR, 34:3:337-8   R: Walter D. Connor

Women, Family, Youth

1073.   Brown, Donald R., ed. **The Role and Status of Women in the Soviet
         Union**. New York, Teachers College Press, 1968. 139p. $6.25.
This thin volume grew out of a "Symposium on Russian Women" held at Bryn
Mawr College and attended by a distinguished interdisciplinary group of scholars.
The editor has drawn together three useful long papers, the short commentaries,
a brief introduction and conclusion, excellent bibliographies, numerous tables,

and some interesting "discussion notes." The paper "Workers (and Mothers)" introduces the Soviet woman in her various roles; Vera Dunham describes her changing image in Soviet literature; and Bronfenbrenner's focus is "The Changing Soviet Family."

SR, 29:3:548-9   R: Robert Sharlet

1074.   Dodge, Norton T. **Women in the Soviet Economy: Their Role in Economic, Scientific, and Technical Development**. Baltimore, Johns Hopkins Press, 1966. 311p. $10.00.

The book is essentially a demographic study of the female population of the Soviet Union with respect to age, geographic distribution, education, social stratification, and employment. The data Dodge has assembled clearly indicate that the Soviet Union over the last five decades has made much headway toward guaranteeing equality of the sexes.

SR, 28:4:664-5   R: Nicholas DeWitt

1075.   Geiger, Kent H. **The Family in Soviet Russia**. Cambridge, Harvard University Press, 1968. 381p. $11.25.

The book is centered around three themes: 1) the views of Marx and Engels on the family; 2) the interpretation of these views by Soviet leaders, writers, and educators; and 3) the differences in "life styles" of families at various social levels in the Soviet Union. The book exhibits great insights; a study highly recommended to both the expert and layman.

CSP, 11:1:129-30   R: John Hofley

1076.   Kassof, Allen. **The Soviet Youth Program: Regimentation and Rebellion**. Cambridge, Harvard University Press, 1965. 208p. (Russian Research Center Studies, no. 49). $5.50.

This book answers well the need for a reliable, up-to-date survey of the Soviet youth program. It will serve those who want something broader in scope than what is so far available. The book is topically organized, deals mainly with the post-Stalin decade, and makes a more general appraisal of the whole range of youth activity, including the Pioneers. Along with adding fresh items from the Soviet press, it conveniently pulls together material that has been presented in various places by Kassof himself as well as by many other students of the Soviet social system. The author does not expect that in the next decade the essentially conservative program of the Komsomol will change much or become any less total in its effort.

SR, 25:1:169   R: Ralph T. Fisher, Jr.

1077.   Taubman, William. **The View from Lenin Hills: Soviet Youth in Ferment**. New York, Coward-McCann, 1967. 249p. $5.50.

This is an entertaining and illuminating book, instructive for the general public. Taubman's subject is student life at Moscow University in the year 1965-66. He conveys worthwhile information about many things, including the admission process, the system of courses and examinations, student recreation, the atmosphere and the daily routine in the dormitory, and discussions among students of various types and between students and party spokesmen. Throughout, the people he met are described with color and clarity.

SR, 28:4:667-8 R: Ralph T. Fisher, Jr.

Miscellaneous Special Studies

1078. Ambler, Effie. **Russian Journalism and Politics, 1861-1881: The Career of Aleksei S. Suvorin.** Detroit, Wayne State University Press, 1972. 239p. $12.50.

Suvorin (1834-1912) was the publisher of the important St. Petersburg newspaper *Novoe vremia.* The heart of the book is devoted to the journalist's career from 1861 to 1881, but it also contains substantial material on the relation between politics and journalism. The book describes Suvorin's evolution from a close associate of liberals and radicals to a rabid nationalist, anti-Semite, and political conservative after his purchase of *Novoe vremia* in 1876. The remainder of his life, to 1912, is treated in a brief epilogue.

SR, 32:2:380-1 R: Daniel Balmuth

1079. Hopkins, Mark W. **Mass Media in the Soviet Union.** New York, Pegasus, 1970. 384p. tables, charts, maps, photographs. $8.95.

This is a useful survey, covering the growth of the media, their structure, controls, functions, and practices. Students setting out to deal with baffling source materials from the Soviet media will find this book a helpful introduction to their work. The solid factual data incorporated in the book give it reference value, and the author's firsthand inquiries during his study and travels in the Soviet Union contribute much new and lively detail.

SR, 30:2:434 R: Leo Gruliow

1080. Male, D. J. **Russian Peasant Organization before Collectivisation: A Study of Commune and Gathering, 1925-1930.** Cambridge, Cambridge University Press, 1971. 253p. (Soviet and East European Studies). $12.50.

It is commonly ignored that the traditional Russian repartitional village commune organization, decadent and under attack before the revolution, not only survived it but became stronger and more equalitarian. With admirable industry, making the best of sketchy and unreliable data, Male has looked through the veil which the Bolsheviks pulled over this aspect of Soviet life and has drawn a picture of the village commune and its activities and relations to the Soviet state. There is little evidence of extensive economic differentiation in the village; it would seem that the great Soviet emphasis on class conflicts between rich, middle, and poor peasants was little more than an attempt to divide and weaken the peasant masses. The study should contribute to the understanding of the still somewhat mysterious Stalinist "transformation of the countryside."

SR, 30:3:668 R: Robert G. Wesson

1081. Shcherbatov, Prince M. M. **On the Corruption of Morals in Russia.** Ed. and trans. with an intro. and notes by A. Lentin. Cambridge, Cambridge University Press, 1969. 339p. $16.50.

Students can now read in English one of the most frequently quoted sources on eighteenth-century Russian social history. The text is accompanied by useful notes which introduce the reader to principal personages and events mentioned in the text and to a wide selection of secondary works on manners and politics in the eighteenth century. Appended to the translation are three letters relating to the period 1722-1727 and two tables by which Lentin seeks to demonstrate the eclipse of the "Old Nobility" in the eighteenth century. The bibliography contains many but not all primary and secondary materials relating to Shcherbatov's life and work.

      SR, 30:1:140-2   R: Joan Afferica

1082.   Taubman, William. **Governing Soviet Cities: Bureaucratic Politics and Urban Development in the USSR**. New York, Praeger, 1973. 167p. (Praeger Special Studies in International Economics and Development). $15.00.

The author draws upon the experience of a score of Soviet cities of varying size to develop the thesis, "the Soviet governmental system—in a sense a mammoth, complex organization—is riven up and down by bureaucratic politics." In developing his thesis Taubman provides new information on Soviet local politics and administration, especially on the changing role and importance of the city within the Soviet territorial-administrative hierarchy.

      SR, 33:4:788-9   R: B. M. Frolic

Chapter 9

Non-Russian Republics; Jews

GENERAL STUDIES

1083.   Allworth, Edward, ed. **Soviet Nationality Problems.** New York,
           Columbia University Press, 1971. 296p. $9.95.
This collective work is distinguished from previous studies of nationality in
tsarist Russia and the USSR by its focus on theoretical issues, its deliberate
avoidance of concrete treatment of "different nationalities as individual
groups," and its almost total dependence upon Soviet published materials. It
includes nine substantive chapters, covering theory (Allworth), imperial policies
(Raeff), Communist views (Kohn), implications for the Soviet state (Brezezinski),
legal reflections of national differences (Hazard), the Islamic legacy (Bennigsen),
and ethnicity and cultural differences (Rubel). An extensive bibliography
embracing Soviet and Western academic writings (but not the extensive émigré
literature), appendix data from the 1970 USSR census, and an index augment
the basic chapters.
           SR, 31:3:700-1   R: Demitri B. Shimkin

1084.   Bailey, Bernadine. **The Captive Nations: Our First Line of Defense.**
           Chicago, Chas. Hallberg, 1969. 191p. $0.75pa.
In 1969, 27 formerly independent nations, with a population of 1,161,373,000—
one-third of the world—were living under the Communist domination. Of the
fifteen so-called republics of the USSR only one is Russian. The others have
their own languages and cultures and yearn for independence, but are subjected
to a ruthless campaign of russification and have to endure Russian party members
in key political and educational positions. By every means, from enforced Russian
in the schools, to censorship, arrests, concentration camps and population transfers,
Soviet Russia under the pretext of Communist brotherhood tries to obliterate
the native cultures and incorporate them in "Mother Russia." This book ably
promotes the objective and deserves a wide distribution.
           UQ, 26:1:87-8   R: Austin J. App

1085.   Conquest, Robert. **The Nation Killers: The Soviet Deportation of
           Nationalities.** Rev. ed. New York, Macmillan, 1970 (1960, under the
           title: *The Soviet Deportation of Nationalities*). 222p. $6.95.
Conquest's book deals specifically with the relatively unknown Soviet deporta-
tions of entire peoples. Stalin transplanted to Siberia some 1.6 million people
simply because they were Chechens, Ingushi, Karachai, Balkars, Kalmyks, Volga
Germans, Crimean Tatars, and Meskhetians; and thus he depopulated 62,021
square miles of territory. This book describes how in the Soviet society the
Orwellian "unperson" was supplanted by the new category of "unnation."
Revealing as this book is, it tells the reader little about any amends that have

been made thus far to the former deportees. More particularly, it has virtually nothing to offer on the implications of such forced mass transplantations. The book tells much about important but heretofore obscure events and so it deserves attention.

JBS, 3:2:140-1   R: Nicholas Balabkins

1086.   Conquest, Robert, ed. **Soviet Nationalities Policy in Practice**. New York, Praeger, 1967. 160p. $5.25.
This is a well-documented survey of Soviet nationalities policy in theory and practice, from Lenin's 1903 Party program to the present. The volume embraces five chapters, heavily studded with references based almost entirely on Soviet sources. There is an editor's preface, an introduction, two appendices and a very extensive bibliography. The nationality problem in the USSR has indeed proved to be the Gordian knot of the Kremlin.

UQ, 25:4:399-401   R: Walter Dushnyck

1087.   Goldhagen, Erich, ed. **Ethnic Minorities in the Soviet Union**. New York, Praeger (for the Institute of East European Jewish Studies of the Philip W. Lown School of Near Eastern and Judaic Studies, Brandeis University), 1968. 351p. $8.75.
The eleven essays in this volume were originally presented at a symposium held at Brandeis University in the fall of 1965. Three of them, consisting of almost half of the book, deal broadly with the nationality problem in the Soviet Union in general. Each of the remaining eight essays deals with a specific ethnic group or national minority region. All of the essays are scholarly and informative, but they lack a common focus of attention. Also, the volume is highly unbalanced in its coverage; twice as many pages are devoted to the Jews as to the Ukrainians, and some important groups, for instance the Georgians, are simply left out.

CSP, 12:4:496-8   R: Ladis K. D. Kristof

1088.   Luckyj, George S. N., ed. **The Non-Russian Soviet Literatures, 1953-1973**. Oakville, Ont., Mosaic Press, 1974. 160p. $9.95cl.; $4.95pa.
This is the first scholarly account in English of the little-known but very important non-Russian side of Soviet literature. Behind its monolithic facade there lie hidden the forces of national cultural aspirations and universal artistic values unfettered by russification and socialist realism. Included are essays on Armenian, Belorussian, Latvian, Tartar, and Ukrainian literatures.

S. M. H.

1089.   Pennar, Jaan, Ivan I. Bakalo, and George Z. F. Bereday. **Modernization and Diversity in Soviet Education with Special Reference to Nationality Groups**. New York, Praeger, 1971. 395p. (Praeger Special Studies in International Economics and Development). $20.00.
This work includes masses of statistics from tsarist to post-Khrushchev times. Concerning the question of russification or linguistic diversity, it becomes clear that in tsarist times liberals advocated education in native languages, which the Soviets promoted actively in the 1920s, but only reluctantly thereafter. Without polemicizing, the authors present some evidence to suggest that under Stalin, and even after, Soviet personnel have been moved from non-Russian to Russian

areas, and vice versa, more to promote russification than for the sake of economic efficiency. In its present state the book is a source of raw or semi-processed materials for the specialist who already has the conceptual apparatus to handle them.

NP, 3:1:47-8   R: Earl W. Jennison, Jr.

1090.   Tillett, Lowell. **The Great Friendship: Soviet Historians on the Non-Russian Nationalities.** Chapel Hill, University of North Carolina Press, 1969. 468p. $12.50.

American East European historiography, while making progress in Russian and Soviet areas during the last two decades, almost completely neglected at the same time the non-Russian aspect of the USSR. Tillett's work represents, therefore, a remarkable breakthrough. Part I describes the making of the myth of friendship among Soviet nationalities, and Part 2, arranged topically, analyzes the substance of the myth. Laboring diligently through hundreds of Soviet works, articles and official documents, the author exposes the Soviet claims that Leninist nationality policy had created something entirely new in history—a multinational society without national conflicts—and that the party's nationality policy created the friendship among the peoples. A 34-page bibliography, an index, a glossary of historical terms, and a map of nationalities enhance the reference value of this pioneering contribution.

AHA, 76:5:1576-7   R: Stephan M. Horak

BALTIC REPUBLICS

Bibliographies and Encyclopedias

1091.   **Encyclopedia Lituanica.** Vol. 1, *A-C.* Vol. 2, *D-J*, Vol. 3, *K-M*. Boston, Juozas Kapočius, 1970-1973. 608p.; 576p.; 576p. $15.00/vol.

This projected six-volume encyclopedia, edited by S. Sužiedelis, is written in English. It aims to provide a "comprehensive and easily accessible source of information for those who wish to learn about Lithuania and its people." This work follows an alphabetical order, with its advantages and disadvantages. The quality of the translations is remarkably good. This encyclopedia is a must for university libraries and interested scholars.

SEEJ, 17:1:115   R: Valdis J. Zeps; (vols. 1-2)
Lit., 21:4:73-5   R: Antanas Klimas; (vol. 3)

1092.   Harvard University, Widener Library. **Finnish and Baltic History and Literatures.** Widener Library Shelflist Series. Cambridge, Harvard University Press, 1972. (Widener Library Shelflist Series, no. 40). 250p. $30.00.

Entries in this Widener Shelflist are limited to Finnish and Baltic history and literature and consist of classified listings by call number, alphabetical listings by author or title, and chronological listings. Particularly useful to researchers and students in search of dissertation material. S. M. H.

1093.   Jēgers, Benjamin̂s. **Bibliography of Latvian Publications Published Outside Latvia, 1940-1960**. Stockholm, Daugava, 1968-1972. Vol. 1, 337p. $12.50. Vol. 2, 406p. $16.80.
For the beginning date of his work the author has chosen 17 June 1940, the last day of Latvia's existence as an independent nation. Entries are alphabetical and consecutively numbered throughout the two volumes. The first volume (2,677 entries) describes books and pamphlets published in Latvian (2,344), followed by publications in other languages. Although this volume has no index, it can be used as a reference tool. The second volume covers serials, music, maps, programs and catalogs—each section arranged alphabetically. There is an appendix listing publications by non-Latvian publishers. The addenda increase the total number of entries in the two-volume set to 4,200. Scholars and librarians will find the work indispensable.
         JBS, 4:4:396-7   R: Emilija Ziplans

1094.   Kantautas, Adam, and Filomena Kantautas, comps. **A Lithuanian Bibliography: A Checklist of Books and Articles Held by the Major Libraries of Canada and the United States**. Edmonton, University of Alberta Press, 1974. 725p. $10.00.
The bibliography has been arranged by broad subject areas listing 10,168 numbered entries of books and articles written by 3,587 different authors in nearly every European language. Location symbols have been given showing which libraries possess the item, in addition to the author and title indexes.
                              S. M. H.

1095.   Parming, Marju Rink, and Tönu Parming. **A Bibliography of English-Language Sources on Estonia: Periodicals, Bibliographies, Pamphlets and Books**. New York, Estonian Learned Society, 1974. 72p. $5.50.
There are a total of 666 entries with short annotations. The bibliography has sufficient cross references. Author and short title indexes are provided. The use of the indexes is explained in the introduction. The stated objectives of the bibliography are to serve as a research tool; to guide librarians, scholars, and Estophiles in collection building; and to aid other bibliographers in their work.
         JBS, 6:1:81-2   R: Hilja Kukk

1096.   Rank, Aino. **A Bibliography of Works Published by Estonian Historians in Exile, 1945-1969**. Stockholm, Institutum Literarum Estonicum, 1969. 56p.
This bibliography covers books, periodical articles, and reviews written on history, archaeology, history of art, music, religion, and law. It represents the second volume of a series, following *Works by Estonian Ethnologists in Exile*, comp. by Helmut Hagar, Stockholm, 1965. 63p.
                              S. M. H.

1097.   Rank, Aino. **A Bibliography of Works Published by Estonian Philologists**. Stockholm, Institutum Literarum Estonicum, 1971. 117p.

This bibliography comprises a collection of items on Estonian literature and language and follows in content and makeup the author's previously published bibliography on the works of Estonian historians.   S. M. H.

1098.   Ziplans, Emilia E., et al., comps. **Baltic Material in the University of Toronto Library**. Toronto, University of Toronto Press (for the Association for the Advancement of Baltic Studies and the University of Toronto Library), 1972. 125p.
The bibliography lists 1,569 items as they appear in the library's catalog as of March 1972. The listing is under eleven subject areas, further subdivided under Estonia, Latvia, and Lithuania. Each entry in this bibliography has an entry number to which the well-made author and short title index refers.
    JBS, 4:3:279-80   R: Karl L. Ozolins

History

1099.   Berkis, Alexander V. **The History of the Duchy of Courland (1561-1795)**. Baltimore, Paul M. Harrod, 1969. 336p. $12.50.
Drawing upon the wealth of original documents in five languages, without ignoring the secondary commentaries, the author reconstructs the three phases of the history of Courland (Latvia): its early period (1561-1638), its golden age under Duke James (1638-1682), and its period of decline (1682-1795). The work traces the non-Indo-European origins of this people, through the settlement of the ancient Balts to the formation of Latvia as a nation and the formalization of her political institutions—the *Privilegium Gotthardium* and the *Formula Regiminis*. In this study Berkis includes a brief but excellent review of the intellectual and cultural life of Courland.
    EEQ, 5:2:262-5   R: Ash Gobar

1100.   Budreckis, Algirdas Martin. **The Lithuanian National Revolt of 1941**. Boston, Juozas Kapocius, 1968; distr. by Lithuanian Encyclopedia Press. 147p. $4.00.
The story of Lithuania's revolt of June 23, 1941 against the Soviet regime is not often told. The revolt, involving an estimated one hundred thousand armed Lithuanian rebels, took place at the outbreak of the German-Soviet war and war reported by the neutral press of Sweden. Budreckis expounds the clearly defined thesis that the Lithuanian revolt was a genuine patriotic uprising and that its sponsor, the Lithuanian Activist Front, cooperated with the Germans only for the purpose of re-establishing Lithuania's statehood, which the Soviets had destroyed in 1940. For this end the rebels were willing to make concessions to the Germans so far as Lithuanian national interests permitted them, but the Germans rejected the offered cooperation and suppressed the provisional government that the LAF had established.
    SR, 28:4:653-4   R: V. Stanley Vardys

1101.   Ezergailis, Andrew. **The 1917 Revolution in Latvia**. Boulder, Colo., *East European Quarterly*, 1974; distr. by Columbia University Press. 281p. (East European Monographs, no. 8). $12.50.

This work has as its central focus the revolutionary development of Latvia and the Latvian Social Democratic movement. While including an account of events in Latvia prior to the February Revolution, it concentrates on 1917, in particular describing and analysing the growth of Bolshevik influence both in Latvia and among Latvians in Petrograd and Moscow. The author explains why both before and during 1917 Latvia was more receptive to radical ideas than Russia proper and thus, in part, why the Bolsheviks were able early in the year to triumph in various worker, peasant, and military organizations. The book is basically for the specialist, and the author has made a contribution to both Latvian and Soviet history.

CSP, 17:4:677-8 R: Myron W. Hedlin

1102. Gerutis, Albertas, ed. **Lithuania; 700 Years**. Trans. by Algirdas Budreckis. 2nd rev. ed. New York, Manyland Books, 1969. 458p. $12.00.
This is a popular history of Lithuania and its people, covering the period from the beginning of statehood to the present. The translation is clear and precise, and the story can easily be comprehended by the general reader, which is the apparent aim of the author and translator—in particular to make Lithuanian-Americans aware of their national historical heritage.

S. M. H.

1103. Gimbutas, Marija. **The Balts**. New York, Praeger, 1968 (1963). 286p. (Ancient Peoples and Places, vol. 33). $8.00.
This volume provides non-specialized readers with all the information they are likely to need on the archeology of the Baltic tribes before the appearance of large-scale states in that area, before the beginning of the feudal period. The book is supplemented with brief chapters on ecology, folk religion, linguistic data, and the like. It can be confidently recommended, especially for its detailed and very interesting illustrations, some of which will provide a new esthetic experience to those unfamiliar with this area. Gimbutas' information, hitherto unavailable in English, will encourage students to dig further into a field which is strangely neglected in the West.

JBS, 5:1:51 R: Stephen P. Dunn

1104. Kirchner, Walther. **The Rise of the Baltic Question**. Westport, Conn., Greenwood Press, 1970 (1954). 283p. $11.00.
The author, in discussing the role which the eastern Baltic region played in world affairs, traces the history of sixteenth-century Livonia, where international conflicts were decided. This is a pioneering work in English.

JMH, 28:4:420-1 R: C. Leonard Lundin

1105. Nodel, Emanuel. **Estonia: Nation on the Anvil**. New York, Bookman Associates, 1964. 207p. $5.00.
Nodel's book is the first to be published in English on the struggle of the Estonian nation against Germanization and Russification from 1721 to 1940. The author has attempted chiefly to trace the attitude of the Baltic German nobility toward the emancipation of the Estonian people during the eighteenth and nineteenth centuries and to record its negative and positive impact upon the growth of

Estonian national consciousness. The book is of value to a student interested
in Baltic, particularly Estonian, problems.

　　　　SR, 24:3:542-3　　　　　　　　R: Edgar Anderson

1106.　　Ran, Leyzer, ed. **Jerusalem of Lithuania, Illustrated and Documented.**
　　　　3 vols. New York, 1974. (Available from Vilno in Pictures, Inc.,
　　　　34-40 93rd Street, Jackson Heights, N.Y., 11372.)
The editor of this amazing work, L. Ran, with his numerous helpers, devoted
25 years to this incredible and colossal undertaking. Through the ages Vilna
has always been the cosmopolitan capital of Lithuania. The first Jews may have
arrived in Lithuania as early as the twelfth or thirteenth century. Since the
fourteenth century, they have been granted privileges by Lithuanian rulers.
For centuries the most important Jewish community was in Vilna. Vol. I deals
with the 500 years of life and creativity in Jewish Vilna; Vol. II with Jewish
education, music, theater, Nazi occupation, and destruction of the Jewish
community and holocaust in which 80,000 people were murdered. Vol. III
offers four forewords, indexes, and an extensive bibliography. No historian of
Lithuania, no man interested in the history of Vilna&Vilnius can disregard this
book.

　　　　Lit., 21:3:74-9　　　　　　　　R: Antanas Klimas

1107.　　Rauch, Georg von. **The Baltic States; The Years of Independence**:
　　　　Estonia, Latvia, Lithuania, 1917-1940. Trans. by Gerald Onn.
　　　　Berkeley, University of California Press, 1974 (1970). 265p. $10.95.
Originally published in German (1970), its text in English is slightly enlarged.
Von Rauch is a fair-minded, objective historian. He has the great distinction
of being the first Baltic German historian who has had the courage to destroy
the age-old Baltic German historical tradition of the "deutsche Ostseeprovinzen"—
a tradition covering only Estonia and Latvia, which had remained directly or
indirectly under German rule for more than six hundred years. He has joined
the ranks of the modern historians who follow the Baltic conception of history
which covers the entire Baltic area, including Lithuania. The author should be
complimented for his great effort to overcome various difficulties in this complex
field of study, which will retain its value.

　　　　RR, 34:1:99-100　　　　　　　　R: Edgar Anderson

1108.　　Rutkis, Jānis, ed. **Latvia: Country and People**. Stockholm, Latvian
　　　　National Foundation, 1967. 683p. $17.00.
In this volume, 31 Latvian exiles from six countries have joined "to make facts
about Latvia and the Latvians readily available to interest foreign students."
This primary objective they have handsomely achieved. The contributors discuss
geology, climate, flora and fauna, geographical description of regions and towns,
followed by a lengthy analysis of the political system since 1918. The social
system and economy also receive detailed treatment, in addition to outlines of
the history of the Latvians and other Baltic peoples.

　　　　SEEJ, 14:2:257-9　　　　　　　　R: Rolf Ekmanis

1109.   Sabaliūnas, Leonas. **Lithuania in Crisis: Nationalism to Communism, 1939-1940.** Bloomington, Indiana University Press, 1972. 293p. $11.50. This work is distinguished by its concentration on the internal development in Lithuania and its rather critical evaluation of Lithuania's political and social developments in the period between the two world wars. The author argues that before the international crises that foredoomed Lithuania's independence there were internal ones—economic, social, political—that were reaching a peak at about the same time as the external one. The author to a large measure attributes the easy collapse of democratic Lithuania to emulation of West European political patterns and the disregard in which democracy was held in the world.

        SR, 31:3:711-2   R: Andrew Ezergailis

1110.   Sprudzs, Adolf, and Armins Rusis, eds. **Res Baltica: A Collection of Essays in Honor of the Memory of Dr. Alfred Bilmanis (1887-1948).** Preface by Professor Loy W. Henderson. Leiden, A. W. Sijthoff, 1968. 303p. 36Dglds. These essays, dedicated to Latvian scholar and patriot Bilmanis, and hence focusing on Latvia, take up various manifestations of an annexationist policy that tries not merely to subordinate its victims but also to include them with a willing acceptance of their Soviet russification. W. S. Hanchett contributes to the history of the collectivization of the Latvian peasantry. V. S. Vardys follows up with "Soviet Social Engineering in Lithuania." The remaining ten essays contribute to various aspects of the Baltic question.

        SR, 28:4:504-5   R: Stanley W. Page

1111.   Tomingas, William. **The Soviet Colonization of Estonia.** New York, Kultuur Publishing House, 1973. 312p. A detailed review of the events that led to the loss of independence of Estonia in June 1940. The introductory chapter provides a background of the emergence and history of Estonia until 1940. The last chapter, "Life in Estonia under the First Soviet Occupation 1940-1941," is followed by six appendixes containing texts of treaties concluded between Estonia and the Soviet Union. A selected bibliography and a list of periodicals are helpful to those who are interested in a further study of Estonian history.   S. M. H.

1112.   Vardys, V. Stanley, ed. **Lithuania under the Soviets: Portrait of a Nation, 1940-65.** New York, Praeger, 1965. 299p. $7.00. The seven Lithuanian authors, including one Italian, seem unanimous in the belief that the Lithuanian nation lived better in an independent state than it does now under Soviet rule. Vardys, who wrote four of the eleven articles, offers a frank account of years of Lithuanian independence, omitting none of the major problems, but he, above all, entertains no doubts that the happiest course for the Lithuanian nation would be political independence. This work must take a place on the bookshelf of anyone studying Soviet nationality policies.

        SR, 24:3:543-4   R: Alfred Erich Senn

1113.   Zins, Henryk. **England and the Baltic in the Elizabethan Era**. Trans.
         by H. C. Stevens. Totowa, N.J., Rowman and Littlefield, 1972. 347p.
         $16.00.

Zins's book, previously published in Polish, is of interest both to the general
European historian and to the student of Baltic history. We realize that in many
respects the Elizabethan era was a turning point in English history. Zins
distinguishes two fairly distinct periods in England's early relations with the
Baltic area. The first of these periods, from the end of the fourteenth century
to the end of the sixteenth century, covered England's prolonged struggle to
break down the monopoly of the Hanseatic League and to achieve a more independent position in her trading relation with the Baltic countries. During the
second period (from the beginning of the seventeenth century) the Baltic was
still of considerable, although diminishing, importance to England as a source
of essential naval stores. The book is quite useful and fills some serious gaps
in the existing historical literature.
         JBS, 4:2:160-1   R: Edgar Anderson

Government and Politics

1114.   **The Violations of Human Rights in Soviet Occupied Lithuania**: A
         Report for 1973. Glendale, Pa., Lithuanian American Community,
         Inc., 1974. 112p.

The report contains four chapters: 1) The suppression of Dissent; 2) The Suppression of Creative Freedom and the Cultivation of Cultural Heritage; 3) Violations of Freedom of Religion and Conscience; and 4) The Denial of National
Self-Determination. It presents available documentary evidence that in the
area of national and political rights an intensified police and ideological suppression prevails in Lithuanis.
         Lit., 21:1:75-6

1115.   Ziedonis, Arvidis, et al., eds. **Problems of Mininations: Baltic**
         Perspectives. San Jose, Cal., Association for the Advancement of
         Baltic Studies, 1973. 214p. $8.50cl.; $3.95pa.

The volume is made up of a heterogenous collection of social science papers
presented at the Third Conference on Baltic Studies, held at the University
of Toronto on 11-14 May 1972. Some of these are reproduced in full, others
abstracted. While all mini-nations face the same basic difficulties—inability to
defend themselves militarily and to achieve "industrial versatility"—the primary
concern of the subjected Baltic peoples has been the preservation of their
ethnic substance in view of the persistent pressure of russification. This pressure is especially strong in Latvia and Estonia where the post-war influx of
Russians dramatically undermined the numerical preponderence of the titular
nationality. Only in Lithuania does the situation seem to be, at present, less
aggravated.
         CSP, 16:4:648-9   R: Vincent C. Chrypinski

Foreign Policy

1116.   Kaslas, Bronis J., ed. **The USSR-German Aggression against Lithuania.**
New York, Robert Speller, 1973. 543p. $15.00.
The documentary materials contained in this work concern Lithuania's relations with Germany and the Soviet Union. As the book's title further suggests,
they focus on the destruction of Lithuania's independence engineered by those
two powers in 1939-1940, although many other documents peripheral to the
main events are also included. Many selections found in this volume have already
been published elsewhere, but others are brought to light for the first time. The
collection of documents consists of treaties, statutes, diplomatic correspondence,
excerpts from speeches and statements by former government members. Brief
comments by the editor attempt to clarify and interpret much of the documentary evidence.
JBS, 4:3:283   R: Leonas Sabaliunas

1117.   Senn, Alfred Erich. **The Great Powers, Lithuania, and the Vilna
Question, 1920-1928.** Leiden, E. J. Brill, 1966. 239p. (Studies in
East European History, vol. 11). 40Dglds.
The study is based on an impressive array of archival and printed sources and
it is objective, informative, and interesting. Senn divides his work into three
parts, preceded by a short but illuminating chapter on the background of
Lithuanian-Polish relations. The first part, called "Vilna and Versailles," centers
on the crucial years of the Zeligowski coup, the Hymans report, and the incorporation of "Central Lithuania" into Poland. The second, "Lithuania Intransigent,"
covers the years 1922-1925. The last section brings the story to 1928, when the
Vilna question receded into the background of European diplomacy. To a student
of East European history this is a very rewarding book.
SR, 28:2:334   R: Piotr S. Wandycz

1118.   Tarulis, Albert N. **American-Baltic Relations 1918-1922: The Struggle
over Recognition.** Washington, Catholic University of America Press,
1965. 386p. $8.95.
The three Baltic nations had been greatly inspired by President Wilson's high-
sounding promises of self-determination. It seems, however, that the doctrine
of national self-determination had been aimed mainly at the nations under
German, Austro-Hungarian, and Turkish rule, in order to disrupt the empires
of the Entente's adversaries. Wilson had hoped for the emergence of a new,
more democratic Russia, one which would make mutually satisfactory arrangements with all non-Russians trying to break away from the Russian Empire,
and was willing to apply his doctrine only to the Polish and Armenian nations,
with the possible inclusion of the Finns. Wilson, however, turned a deaf ear
to all the convincing and ingeniously conceived pleas of the Baltic national
governments for recognition and acted as a stumbling block to the recognition
of the Baltic republics by other powers.
SR, 25:4:700-1   R: Edgar Anderson

1119.   Watson, Herbert A. Grant. **The Latvian Republic: The Struggle For
Freedom.** New York, Hillary House, 1965. 102p. $4.00.

Watson, a retired British diplomat, has written a brief but valuable memoir of his experiences on a diplomatic mission to Latvia during Latvia's struggle to attain independence after the armistice of 1918. He is convinced that British aid, especially the presence of the Allied fleet in the Baltic waters "largely determined the fate of Estonia and Latvia." He does not belittle the native Latvian and Estonian efforts and finds that neither the Latvian nor the Estonian leaders were instruments or stooges of the British, as they are pictured in the Soviet Union, but represented strong popular opinion and had genuine support for independent statehood. Watson further considers that in 1940 the Baltic states lost their freedom, not because of their internal weaknesses, but rather because of their geographic position.

SR, 25:3:531   R: V. Stanley Vardys

Economics

1120.   King, Gundar Julian. **Economic Policies in Occupied Latvia: A Manpower Management Study**. Tacoma, Washington, Pacific Lutheran University Press, 1965. 304p. $5.00.

King's pioneering study provides a broad background for its principal theme. Its first part acquaints the reader with the resources of the Latvian economy and the influence on its development by different economic systems since the emergence of the Republic of Latvia in 1918. Half the book is devoted to a survey and analysis of the quantitative and qualitative dimensions of manpower and the accumulation of investments in skills and capital since World War II, after Latvia had been absorbed into the Soviet Union. The remaining portion of the book is devoted to the study of the roles of central, regional and plant management and their impact on production in the Latvian economy, and of the adequacy of living standards, minimum wages, and pensions.

SR, 25:4:700-1   R: Edgar Anderson

Religion

1121.   Paulson, Ivar. **The Old Estonian Folk Religion**. Trans. by Juta Kõvamees Kitching and H. Kõvamees. Bloomington, Indiana University; The Hague, Mouton, 1971. 237p. (Indiana University Publications, Uralic and Altaic Series, vol. 108). $9.50pa.

This book is the translation of a posthumous work by the Estonian scholar of the history of religion, Ivar Paulson (1922-1966). In this book Paulson views the religion in, and as dependent on, the people's natural surroundings. He first discusses the forest and water worlds, since the most ancient Estonian religious images and customs originated in the hunters' and fishermen's environment. This is followed by a discussion of the earth, sky or heaven, and the home circle (farm), which have been closely associated with the life of Estonians as agriculturists and cattle breeders during the last two millenia. The final essays are devoted to such universal questions as the soul, death, and the world beyond.

SR, 31:3:710-11   R: Felix J. Oinas

1122.   Rabinowitsh, Wolf Zeev. **Lithuanian Hasidism**. Foreword by Simon
         Dubnov. Trans. by M. B. Dagut. New York, Schocken Books, 1971.
         362p. $7.00.
This monograph, first published in Hebrew in 1961, is a scholarly, painstaking
account of the origins and spread of the Jewish Hasidic religious movement in
Lithuania and Belorussia, from its origins in the eighteenth century to its
destruction in the holocaust under the Nazi occupation. The translation of
this important study, which is based entirely on primary sources, is certainly
a major contribution to the existing English literature on Jewish life in Eastern
Europe.
         SR, 31:3:712-3   R: Ezra Mendolsohn

Language and Literature

1123.   Andriekus, Leonardas. **Amens in Amber**. New York, Manyland Books,
         1968. 85p. $4.00.
The modest shelf of Lithuanian verse in English translation has acquired a new
addition, a collection of poems culled from several volumes of Andriekus. The
dominant themes of his verse—the peregrinations of the Lithuanian diaspora,
the author's lament of homelessness, his *adoratio mystica*—are well represented
in the English-language collection. The translations by Demie Jonaitis, a poet
in her own right, are apt and are sometimes charged with greater intensity than
the originals.
         Lit., 14:3:78-9   R: J. Zemkalnis

1124.   Budina, Lazdina T. **Teach Yourself Latvian**. London, English Univer-
         sities Press, 1966. 335p.
This book is a Latvian course for the English-speaking student. It consists of
32 lessons, each of which has a reading passage, vocabulary, grammar, and
exercises. The grammatical rules are clearly expressed and skillfully graduated
and examples for practical application are given. This short Latvian course
will be of great help to the English learner.
         SEER, 45:104:264-5   R: Pauline Alksnis

1125.   Dambriūnas, Leonardas, et al. **Introduction to Modern Lithuanian**.
         Brooklyn, N.Y., Franciscan Fathers Press, 1966. 471p. $7.00.
This is a full introductory grammar of Lithuanian in English. It has a long
introductory chapter on pronunciation, spelling, accentuation, etc., followed by
forty lessons in which Lithuanian grammar is systematically presented. Every
fifty lesson is a review lesson with various exercises, drawings, reading selections,
but no new grammar. The keys and tapes are also available.
         Lit., 15:3:76-77   R: Antanas Klimas

1126.   Ford, Gordon B., Jr. **Old Lithuanian Texts of the Sixteenth and
         Seventeenth Centuries**. The Hague, Mouton, 1969. 43p. $5.00.

1127. Ford, Gordon B., Jr. **The Old Lithuanian Catechism of Martynas Mažvydas (1547).** Assen, The Netherlands, Van Gorcum, 1971. 104p. $13.10.

1128. Ford, Gordon B., Jr. **The Old Lithuanian Catechism of Baltramiejus Vilentas.** The Hague, Mouton, 1969. 421p. $30.25.

It is well known that Lithuanian is the most archaic of the living Indo-European languages—meaning that is has changed least from Proto Indo-European. On the other hand, Lithuanian was one of the last Indo-European languages to be written. The earliest texts go back only to the beginning of the sixteenth century. The first volume is a small selection of excerpts from several Old Lithuanian religious texts, which Ford uses in an introductory Baltic linguistics course. The latter presumably explains why the texts are not translated. It does, however, have an English glossary. The second book contains, after a brief biography of Mažvydas, the transcribed text and an English translation on the facing page. A list of Slavic loanwords found in the Catechism, with an indication of their Polish or White Russian source, completes the volume. The third volume is clearly the most important. It is patterned after Stang's study of Mažvydas, which it matches in richness of detail and clarity of presentation. This volume contains a facsimile of the original text (now located in the library of Vilnius State University) published in 1579, followed by a transcription and an English translation on the facing pages. In addition to a brief biography of Vilentas, the remainder of the monograph is a thorough linguistic analysis of the text, including sections on phonology, morphology, syntax, and a list of the Slavic loanwords found in the Catechism. The sections on phonology and morphology are the most interesting. We are all in Ford's debt for making available the two most important early Lithuanian texts.

     JBS, 5:2:152-3   R: Michael Kentowicz

1129. Magner, Thomas F., and William R. Schmalstieg, eds. **Baltic Linguistics.** University Park, Pennsylvania State University Press, 1970. 188p. $13.50.

This volume, dedicated to Alfred Senn, the Nestor of American Baltistics, on his seventieth birthday, consists almost entirely of papers read at a conference on Baltic linguistics, held at Pennsylvania State University in 1968. There are articles devoted to each of the individual Baltic languages and, in addition, a number on comparative Baltic and the relation of Baltic to Slavic and Indo-European in general. This is a book which should probably be read by all specialists in the field, since many of the papers propose new and interesting solutions to some classic problems in Baltic languages.

     CSP, 13:2-3:267-73   R: Michael J. Kentowicz

1130. Matulis, Anatole C. **Lithuanian Culture in Modern German Prose Literature.** Lafayette, Ind., Purdue University Press, 1966. 166p.

The author selects Hermann Sudermann, Ernst Wiechert, and Agnes Miegel "as representative authors of modern German prose ... all exhibiting the national Lithuanian character in their works," and describes and documents how these writers interpret the national-cultural profile of the Lithuanian people. He begins with an historical survey of Lithuanian elements in German culture and literature, emphasizes the popularity of the Lithuanian German prose works that portray the Lithuanian national character, and concludes that the preoccupation with, and fascination for, the Lithuanian culture by German men of letters "opened for the Lithuanian nation the portals to the modern world of literature." The main body of this study is devoted to an analysis of Sudermann's, Wiechert's, and Miegel's conception and portrayal of the Lithuanian people, language, customs, religion and mythology, as well as the village milieu and life.

JBS, 5:2:154-5   R: Albert A. Kipa

1131.   Oras, Ants. **Estonian Literature in Exile**. Bio-bibliographical appendix by
Bernard Kangro. Lund, Eesti Kirjanike Kooperativ, 1967. 88p. $2.50.
This is an extensive critical essay devoted to the Estonian letters produced outside Estonia from 1945 to 1967. It is informative to read in the introduction to this last book that quantitatively Estonian literature in exile exceeds the Estonian literature produced behind the Iron Curtain. The comparative bibliography of Estonian post-war publications compiled by Bernard Kangro shows deadening restrictions of the Communist regime have cramped literary production; less than 65,000 pages of belles-lettres published in Soviet-occupied Estonia since 1945 as against 95,000 pages of refugee literature. Oras writes with vision, coherence, and analytical depth.

SR, 28:4:691-2   R: Aleksis Rannit

1132.   Rubulis, Aleksis. **Baltic Literature: A Survey of Finnish, Estonian, Latvian,
and Lithuanian Literatures**. Notre Dame, University of Notre Dame Press,
1970. 215p. $8.50.
The book on Baltic literature briefly but adequately discusses the principal literary movements and their major representatives. Each Baltic nation and trend is represented by examples of prose and poetry of first-rate quality. Among the most outstanding Estonian writers are the romantic poetess Koidula (1843-86), the realist prose writers Vilde (1865-1933) and Tammsaare (1878-1940). In considering Latvian writers, the author begins with Neikens (1826-63) and includes every prominent author up to the present. The founder of Lithuanian *Kunstdichtung* was Donelaitis (1714-80). Rebulis also discusses Krėve, Mykolaitis-Putinas, Radauskas, and Landsbergis. The study is quite useful, especially since it is the first and only one of its kind in English.

SR, 30:2:451-2   R: Alida Cīrule

1133.   Schmalstieg, William R., and Antanas Klimas. **Lithuanian-English Glossary
of Linguistic Terminology**. University Park, Pa., Dept. of Slavic Languages,
Pennsylvania State University, 1971. 115p. $4.00.
This glossary was prepared for students and research scholars in the fields of Baltic and Lithuanian linguistics. The terms were taken from Lithuanian linguistic books and periodicals published within the last fifty years and also from textbooks, dictionaries, and wordlists. It contains 3,915 entries with English definition and appears to be extremely accurate and complete.

SEEJ, 16:3:385   R: Gordon B. Ford, Jr.

1134.   Šilbajoris, Rimvydas. **Perfection of Exile: Fourteen Contemporary Lithuanian Writers**. Norman, University of Oklahoma Press, 1970. 332p. $8.50.
The fourteen essays that constitute this introduction to contemporary Lithuanian literature seem to have been conceived as a separate studies rather than an organic whole. A brief survey of Lithuanian letters since the eighteenth century has been added. This volume will give the English-speaking reader a good idea of the present

status of Lithuanian literature on this side of the iron curtain. The essays that stand out are those on Škema, Mackus, and Landsbergis. In these essays both ideology and structure are examined with acute perception and great dedication. The short essay on Mekas is also a full-fledged contribution. *Perfection of Exile* opens the door to a rich world of a previously little-known literature, with its "small people and their great questions."

> SR, 31:1:217-8   R: Biruté Ciplijauskaité

1135.   Ziedonis, Arvids, Jr., et al., eds. **Baltic Literature and Linguistics.** Columbus, Association for the Advancement of Baltic Studies, Ohio State University, 1973. 251p. $8.50cl.; $3.95pa.

This fourth volume in a series published by the Association for the Advancement of Baltic Studies is a collection of essays which were presented as papers at the inter-disciplinary Third Conference on Baltic Studies held on 11-14 May 1972 at the University of Toronto. Divided into three sections dealing with Baltic literature, Baltic folklore, and Baltic linguistics, it should appeal to a fairly large circle of readers.

> CSP, 16:4:686   R: G. M.

1135a.   Ziedonis, Arvids, Jr. **The Religious Philosophy of Jānis Rainis, Latvian Poet.** Waverly, Ia., Latvju Grāmata, 1969. 344p. $6.80.

Jānis Rainis, whose real name was Jānis Pliekšans (1865-1929), is one of the outstanding—if not the most outstanding—of Latvian writers. Ziedonis's book is the only comprehensive study of Rainis in English and the only one which deals with the writer's religious philosophy. He did not belong to any organized religion, but he was very concerned with ethical issues, and his literary heroes are the torchbearers of his ethical ideas. Ziedonis supports his investigations by careful study of the complete works of Rainis, *Raksti* (Works) in 17 volumes, and by drawing on the research of other authors who have studied Rainis. The book also has an extensive index and bibliography.

> SR, 30:2:451   R: Alīda Cīrule

BELORUSSIA

History

1136.   Lubachko, Ivan S. **Belorussia under Soviet Rule, 1917-1957.** Lexington, University Press of Kentucky, 1972. 219p. $10.00.

The Belorussians were relatively late in developing a national consciousness in the modern sense. Their awakening coincided roughly with the advent of Bolshevism in Russia. During the early 1920s, Lenin succeeded in gaining the support of Belorussian nationalists, thanks to his relatively sympathetic nationality policies. This détente between Moscow and Belorussians came to a bloody end in the 1930s with the introduction of Stalin's purges, which literally decimated the Belorussian nation. No fewer than one million Belorussians perished in the hecatomb, while Belorussian nationalism suffered a fatal blow in three waves of purges (1929-1931, 1932-1933, and 1936-1938). Lubachko's book is well documented, his style is clear, and his conclusions are conservatively cautious. Eight maps, an impressive bibliography, and a thorough index make this study a lasting contribution that can be appreciated by scholars and students alike.

> CRSN, 1:2:196-7   R: Stephan M. Horak

[On Belorussian history see Nicholas P. Vakar, *Belorussia: The Making of a Nation. A Case Study.* Cambridge, Harvard University Press, 1956. 296p. $6.50. and his *Bibliographic Guide to Belorussia.* 1956. Reviewed in JMH, 29:2:172-3].

Language and Literature

1137.   Bykov, Vasily. **The Ordeal (A Novel).** Trans. by Gordon Clough.
         New York, Dutton, 1972. 170p. $5.95.
The Ordeal was first published in the Soviet Union in 1970. The main character
is the soldier Sotnikov, whose war-time experience of fighting Germans as a
member of a Soviet partisan unit and later as a prisoner of war in a German camp
is the theme of the novel. What makes this work unique is its realistic description
of war-time events, heretofore excluded from officially sanctioned Russian
literature. The translation is satisfactory.   S. M. H.

1138.   McMillin, Arnold Barratt. **The Vocabulary of the Byelorussian Literary
         Language in the Nineteenth Century.** London, The Anglo-Belyorussian
         Society, 1973. 336p. £2.00.
This is a study of a neglected aspect of the origins and development of a "new"
literary language based mainly on the literary works of Dunin-Marcinkievich,
which are taken to be typical of the general pattern. After a preface, a comprehensive bibliography and a short introduction, the author gives in Part II a detailed
study of the vocabulary, followed in Part III by a statistical analysis (3,378 words)
and conclusions. A list of Russicisms, Ukrainisms, Polonisms and unrecorded
forms in the works of Dunin-Marcinkievich is given in the appendix, as well as
an index of works from nineteenth century texts. It is a useful contribution to
Belorussian studies.
         CSP, 16:4:684   R: G. M.

1139.   Rich, Vera, trans. **Like Water, Like Fire: An Anthology of Byelorussian
         Poetry from 1828 to the Present Day.** London, George Allen & Unwin,
         1971. 347p. (UNESCO Collection of Representative Works, European
         Series). £4.50.
This is the first anthology of Belorussian poetry to appear in English. Vera Rich
is known for her three books of original poetry in English as well as translations
from Ukrainian, Polish, Old English, and Old Norse. She has been translating
Belorussian poetry for about twenty years. The book contains 221 poems by
41 authors. Contemporary Soviet Belorussian poetry is represented most extensively and is translated most adequately. The book can be useful and even
enjoyable for general readers.
         SR, 32:4:863-4   R: Anthony Adamovich

UKRAINE

Bibliographies and Encyclopedias

1140.   Pidhainy, Oleh S., and Alexandra I. Pidhainy, eds. **The Ukrainian
         Republic in the Great-European Revolution, Vol. V: A Bibliography.**
         Preface by M. Mladenovic. Toronto, New Review Books, 1971. 376p.
         Part II, 1975. 357p. $34.50/set.
The book constitutes the first major scholarly effort to provide a systematic
bibliography of the Ukrainian Revolution. Several earlier bibliographies on the

subject, which appeared in the Soviet Ukraine and the West, were handicapped by the narrowness of their scope and the partisanship in their selectivity. The approximately 11,000 items, in Ukrainian and other languages, relating to the period from 1907 to March 1917, alone, should demonstrate rather conclusively even to a sceptical reader the vitality and historical significance of the subject. Unfortunately, the editors did not see fit to annotate their material.

      CSP, 14:2:356-9   R: O. W. Gerus

1141.   Sokolyszyn, Alexander, comp. **Ukrainian Selected and Classified Bibliography in English.** New York, Munich, Ukrainian Information Bureau, 1972. 157p. (Mimeographed edition).

This bibliography deals with a wide range of topics: history, literature, politics, religion, economics, geography, law, education, language, etc. It is a mimeographed publication and marred by several oversights.

1142.   **Ukraine: A Concise Encyclopedia, Vol. 1.** Prepared by the Shevchenko Scientific Society. Ed. by Volodymyr Kubijovyč. Foreword by Ernest J. Simmons. Toronto, University of Toronto Press, published for the Ukrainian National Association, 1963. 1185p. $37.50.

We have here the most useful single volume of information on the Ukraine available in English, a volume which is both reliable and readable.

      SR, 24:1:164-7   R: Lowell R. Tillett

1143.   **Ukraine: A Concise Encyclopedia, Vol. 2.** Prepared by the Shevchenko Scientific Society. Ed. by Volodymyr Kubijovič. Foreword by Ernest J. Simmons. Toronto, University of Toronto Press, published for the Ukrainian National Association, 1971. 3,394p. $60.00.

Nearly a hundred Ukrainian scholars have supplemented and updated material available in *Entsyklopediia Ukrainoznavstva* (3 vols., 1949-52), producing a comprehensive library of information about the Ukraine in English. The value of the work is enhanced by the extensive bibliographies which include Soviet works, by the numerous illustrations and maps in color, and by the up-to-date charts and graphs. This encyclopedia is a monument to the scholarship of Ukrainians living outside the homeland, and is an essential compendium of information for all who are interested in Ukrainian studies.

      SR, 31:2:456-7   R: Lowell Tillett

1144.   Weres, Roman. **Ukraine: Selected References in the English Language.** 2nd ed. Chicago, Ukrainian Research and Information Institute, 1974. 312p. (Ukrainian Reference Series, no. 1). $10.00.

This volume contains 1,958 entries, listing works, both monographic and serial, relating to the history, economy, and culture of the Ukrainian people. Annotations indicate the nature and scope of books and articles listed. Author and subject indexes are provided.   S. M. H.

History

1145.   Adams, Arthur E. **Bolsheviks in the Ukraine: The Second Campaign, 1918-1919**. Port Washington, N.Y., Kennikat Press, 1973. 440p. $17.50.

This is a reprint of a comprehensive study first published in 1963 by the Yale University Press, which is based on a wealth of published materials and on the Trotsky Archives. Much of the book describes the Bolsheviks' unsuccessful attempt to administer and defend the Ukraine against the Whites (January to June 1919). Once in power, the Ukrainian Communist Party "remained insensitive to Ukrainian needs and stubbornly reluctant to adapt itself to Ukrainian realities."

   JMH, 37:1:112-3   R: David MacKenzie

1146.   Elwood, Ralph Carter. **Russian Social Democracy in the Underground: A Study of the RSDRP in the Ukraine, 1907-1914**. Assen, The Netherlands, Van Gorcum, 1974. 304p. 65Dglds.

This work is not a study of the Ukrainian political thought and parties of the last three decades preceding World War I; it centers on the activities of the RSDRP in Ukraine. The Ukraine was an interesting testing ground considering its history, its tradition, its rapid industrialization at the end of the nineteenth century, together with the emerging native Ukrainian nationalism, which had to be dealt with not only by the tsarist regime but also by Lenin and all other Russian-based socialist movements and parties. Elwood reveals his perception of these events: "Adding particular interest to a study of the RSDRP in the Ukraine is the fact that the Bolsheviks lost the Ukrainian revolution of 1917. Some of the reasons for this defeat can be found in the pre-war period—both in the organization and composition of the party and also in Lenin's nationality and agrarian policies formulated before he came to power."

   UQ, 31:3:299-300   Stephan M. Horak

1147.   Fedyshyn, Oleh S. **Germany's Drive to the East and the Ukrainian Revolution, 1917-1918**. New Brunswick, N.J., Rutgers University Press, 1971. 401p. $15.00.

The author tries to evaluate the interplay of the German *Ostpolitik* and the Ukrainian striving for national self-determination during the eventful years of the Ukrainian Revolution in 1917-18. Whereas most of the primary sources cited are not new, but have been used already in related writings, the broader aspects of the German war aims and of the German occupation policy with particular reference to the Ukraine, were never before integrated and presented in such a systematic fashion. This is the first comprehensive scholarly work on the topic in English, thus it provides a welcome base for a further exploration of this field.

   SR, 31:1:166-7   R: Ihor Kamenetsky

1148.   Gajecky, George, and Alexander Baran. **The Cossacks in the Thirty Years War. Vol. 1: 1619-1624**. Rome, Analecta OSBM, Series II, Section I, 1969. 140p.

This work is an investigation of the participation and military contribution of Ukrainians in the Thirty Years' War (1618-1648). Sources for this book were obtained mainly from The Vatican, Vienna, and Prague archives. The organization is chronological according to the yearly campaigns, as was the military practice of that century. Special attention is given to the campaigns in which Cossacks participated. On the basis of the material of this work, the reader comes to the conclusion that Cossack units played a significant role in the first phase of the Thirty Years' War. The authors have made a valuable contribution to historiography of this era.

   PR, 18:3:91-3   R: Jaroslav Rozumnyj

1149. Hrushevsky, Michael. **A History of Ukraine.** Ed. by O. J. Frederiksen. Preface by George Vernadsky. Hamden, Conn., Archon Books, 1970 (1941). 629p. $15.00.

This book represents the reprinting of the first and thus far the only translation of Hrushevsky's condensed *History of Ukraine.* The story is presented in a popular style for the general reader and student who is interested in a general survey of Ukrainian history. The English-speaking reader does not yet have access to Hrushevsky's prolific writings: his *Istoriia Ukrainy-Rusy*, in 10 volumes, his almost two thousand other works, articles and documents which he edited, almost all written in Ukrainian. This survey, dating from about 1900, presents the history of Ukraine from the so-called populist point of view, which is by now largely obsolete. An inadequate translation makes for heavy reading.

          S. M. H.

1150. Klein, Richard G. **Ice-Age Hunters of the Ukraine.** Chicago, University of Chicago Press, 1973. 140p. $6.50cl.; $2.95pa.

This deceptively small volume makes available a fine survey of a fairly extensive archaeological literature not readily accessible to those who do not read Russian and Ukrainian. It was only in later mid-Pleistocene times that human beings managed to adapt successfully to middle latitude regions of the Old World. By about 75,000 years ago, human biological and cultural evolution had advanced sufficiently to allow man to remain in Europe during the harsh climatic conditions of the last major glacial advance. The contemporary sites in the Ukraine, quite naturally according to its geography and geomorphology, are "open air sites" which provide an interesting and valuable comparison and contrast to those of Western Europe. The opening up of the Ukrainian literature may go some way to stimulate further research into this question.

   CSP, 16:3:466-7   R: Derek G. Smith

1151. Mackiw, Theodore. **Prince Mazepa, Hetman of Ukraine, in Contemporary English Publications, 1687-1709.** Chicago, Ukrainian Research and Information Institute, 1967. 126p. $3.00.

The book is far more than the title indicates. It discusses, with many digressions, those usually very brief items about Mazepa that appeared in English print, but this is very thin material and of little value either for understanding Mazepa or for a history of the English press and memoirs. Far more interesting are Mackiw's much more extensive presentations of non-English materials from scores of often obscure continental sources. Mazepa scholars will find much of value in the collection.

AHR, 73:5:1579-80   R: Heinz E. Ellersieck

1152.   Perfecky, George A., ed. **The Hypatian Codex, II: The Galician-Volynian Chronicle; An Annotated Translation.** With an editor's preface. Munich, Wilhelm Fink Verlag, 1973. 159p. Genealogical table. (Harvard Series in Ukrainian Studies, vol. 16). DM38 pa.

Perfecky offers a "free (but faithful) rather than a literal interpretation of the chronicle." He has been quite scrupulous, with the result that in many respects his translation is much more accurate than the Cross version of the *Povest' vremennykh let* and is free from the occasional blunders of Panov's 1936 modern Russian translation of portions of the Galician-Volynian Chronicle. The historical information in the notes (and often in brackets in the text) derives almost entirely from the secondary works of Hurshevsky and Pashuto, whose source in some cases was none other than this same chronicle.

SR, 33:4:769-71   R: Daniel Clarke Waugh

1153.   Peters, Victor. **Nestor Makhno: The Life of an Anarchist.** Winnipeg, Echo Books, 1970. 133p. $3.75.

The meteoric career of Nestor Makhno and the rapid rise and fall of his anarchist movement in the Ukrainian revolutionary ferment of 1917-1921 provide very colorful subject matter for the historian and biographer. The principal contribution of the work is to provide a readable, if brief, account based not only on the limited published sources and the anarchist press but also on eyewitness reports. It explains also why Makhno did not become a Ukrainian folk hero.

CSP, 13:4:425-6   R: John S. Reshetar

1154.   Pidhainy, Oleh S. **The Formation of the Ukrainian Republic: The Ukrainian Republic in the Great East-European Revolution.** Vol. 1. Toronto, New Review Books, 1966. 685p. $10.75.

This massive and well-documented study of the first year of the Ukrainian revolution, which began timidly and somewhat uncertainly in March 1917, is a welcome addition to what is still a rather limited body of literature on the tragic history of the Ukrainians—the second largest of the Slavic nations. In spite of some interpretative shortcomings, Pidhainy's work merits careful study by students of the Ukrainian problem.

CSP, 11:2:290-2   R: Oleh S. Fedyshyn

1155.   Polons'ka-Vasylenko, Natalia. **Ukraine-Rus' and Western Europe in 10th-13th Centuries.** London, Association of Ukrainians in Great Britain, 1964. 47p. + 16pp. of illus. $2.00.

This deceptively slim but lucid treatise on the little-known relations between ancient Rus'-Ukraine and Western Europe in the Middle Ages provides a fascinating insight into the close political, dynastic and cultural ties of Kievan Rus' with Western Europe.   S. M. H.

1156.   **Russian Oppression in Ukraine: Reports and Documents.** London,
        Ukrainian Publishers Ltd., 1972. 576p. $8.00.
This voluminous book contains seventeen essays on various aspects of Soviet
policy in Ukraine, in addition to several reports and eyewitness accounts. Each
essay includes an extensive bibliography. Photos documenting the Soviet terror
and famine of 1932-33 complement the text.   S. M. H.

1157.   Stachiw, Matthew, and Jaroslaw Sztendera. **Western Ukraine at the
        Turning Point of Europe's History, 1918-1923.** 2 vols. New York,
        Shevchenko Scientific Society, 1969-1971. (Shevchenko Scientific
        Society, Ukrainian Studies, English Section, vol. 6).
This work is the only study in English which uses original sources to show the
conflicting interests over Western Ukraine, namely, among the Poles, Russians,
Austrians, Jews and Ukrainians during the last crucial years of World War I
and at the Peace Conference in Paris. By briefly sketching the history of Western
Ukraine, the work lays a viable foundation for understanding the social, economic,
political and religious differences which brought these groups to the battlefield
where eventually was decided the fate of an independent Western Ukraine. The
inside story of the Paris Peace Conference is especially well presented in Volume II.
The political negligence of the Council of Four becomes transparent through
excerpts from the minutes of the closed door sessions they held.
        UQ, 27:3:77-8   R: N. N.

1158.   Tys-Krokhmaliuk, Yuriy. **UPA Warfare in Ukraine.** Preface by Ivan
        Wowchuk. Trans. from the Ukrainian by Walter Dushnyck. New York,
        Society of Veternas of Ukrainian Insurgent Army of the U.S. and
        Canada, 1972. 449p.
In the introduction the author offers general information about Ukraine prior
and during World War II. Then he proceeds with the history of the formation
and activities of the Ukrainian Partisan Army (UPA) fighting both invaders,
Nazi Germany and Soviet Russia. The UPA continued the fighting until 1950.
The story of this struggle of the Ukrainian underground is hardly known in the
West, and therefore this study is a welcome contribution to the history of the
Second World War.
        UQ, 29:2:185-7   R: Joseph S. Roucek

1159.   Yaremko, Michael. **Galicia-Halychyna: From Separation to Unity.**
        Intro. by Clarence A. Manning. Toronto, New York, Paris, Shevchenko
        Scientific Society, 1967. 292p. (Shevchenko Scientific Society,
        Ukrainian Studies, vol. 18; English Section, vol. 3). $7.50.
This is a scholarly and comprehensive work covering the history of Galicia from
earliest times to the present, being in fact the first English-language study of that
part of the Ukraine. The author discusses Galicia's history in four chapters:
The Princely Period (907-1340); Galicia under Polish Occupation (1349-1772);
Galicia under the Habsburgs (1772-1918); and Galicia from 1914 to 1945.
The author provides both analytical insights and panoramic views of Galicia in
a popular approach.
        UQ, 24:2:172-4   R: Roman V. Kuchar

Government and Politics

1160.   Bilinsky, Haroslav. **The Second Soviet Republic: The Ukraine after World War II**. New Brunswick, N.J., Rutgers University Press, 1964. 539p. $12.50.

The author of this study analyzes the political, socioeconomic, and cultural development of the Ukraine for the past twenty years and ponders its effect on the attitudes of Ukrainian toward the problem of separation. Some of the best chapters describe the rapid industrial strides of the Soviet Ukraine, the improved standard of living of its population, and the rise of Ukrainians to positions of power not only in their own and other republics but in the central part and state organs as well. But his carefully documented analysis also points to such discriminatory policies as a decline in the relative share of investment in Ukrainian industry and the various psychological and institutional pressures in behalf of Russification; the absence of courses in Ukrainian literature and and history in the republic's primary and secondary schools; the failure to provide Ukrainian-languages schools for Ukrainians living outside their republic; and the failure of Ukrainians to achieve a proportionate share of professional and academic personnel and of student in higher educational institutions.
    SR, 26:3:493-5   R: Michael M. Luther

1161.   Dzyuba, Ivan. **Internationalism or Russification? A Study in the Soviet Nationalities Problem**. Preface by Peter Archer. Ed. by M. Davies. London, Weidenfeld and Nicolson, 1968. 240p. 42s.

The author's main thesis is that Lenin's nationality policy called for a free and unrestricted Ukrainian culture as a part of the international proletarian culture. He accuses the present Soviet regime of violating Lenin's principles. He details his charges that the Leninist nationalities policy has been grossly violated, beginning with Stalin and through Khrushchev's regime to that of Brezhnev and Kosygin. He asserts that a policy of persecution and oppression is hardly an answer to widespread discontent. He is vehement in stating that the turmoil and upheaval in Ukraine is a direct result of the Russification of the non-Russian peoples and rejects the charges of "bourgeois nationalism" leveled against Ukraine. The present Moscow policies in Ukraine are the direct heritage of tsarist traditions.
    UQ, 24:3:270-2   R: Walter Dushnyck

1162.   Hodnett, Grey, and Peter J. Potichnyj. **The Ukraine and the Czechoslovak Crisis**. Canberra, Dept. of Political Science, Research School of Social Science, Australian National University, 1970. 154p. Paper.

This study is an attempt to evaluate the role of Ukraine in the Czechoslovak events of 1968. The authors, after an examination of the extended relations between Ukraine and Czechoslovakia, discuss in detail the crisis of 1968. They analyze the role of the leadership of the Communist Party of Ukraine, noting that especially Shelest and Podgorny were extremely hostile to, and even afraid of, the reform movement in Czechoslovakia. Their conclusions suggest that the ties between the Slovaks and Ukraine have since become closer and more friendly. This well-documented study illuminates not only the 1968 events but also the particular involvement with the Ukrainian question.   S.M.H.

1163.   Mazlakh, Serhii, and Vasyl' Shakhrai. **On the Current Situation in the Ukraine**. Ed. and trans. by Peter J. Potichnyj. Intro. by Michael M. Luther. Ann Arbor, University of Michigan Press, 1970. 220p. $8.95.
The work of Mazlakh and Shakhrai, published originally in Ukrainian in Saratov in 1919 under the title *Do Khvyli*, was a bibliographical rarity and unavailable until 1967, when it was reprinted by the Prolog Research Association in New York. It is still banned in the Soviet Union. The translation by Potichnyj now makes this unusual and significant work available to a broader public. The book is significant because it is undoubtedly the first theoretical formulation of national Communism. The authors desired an independent, separate, and equal Ukraine, and saw this goal as compatible with Marxism. Indeed, they offer a Marxist interpretation of Ukrainian developments. The work culminates in the final chapter, entitled "Questions for Comrade Lenin," in which Lenin is asked pointed why his policies did not correspond with what he had written earlier on the nationality question. Lenin did not respond.
         SR, 31:1:172-5   R: John S. Reshetar, Jr.

Foreign Policy

1164.   Stercho, Peter G. **Diplomacy of Double Morality: Europe's Crossroads in Carpatho-Ukraine, 1919-1939**. New York, Carpathian Research Center, 1971. 495p. $15.00.
This book will for some time serve as an authoritative source work on Carpatho-Ukraine for the critical period covered. Methodically arranged, the work is suitably divided into nine chapters dealing with various aspects of the history of that land. Virtually every page is heavily footnoted with source and documentary proof for the author's observations and historical narrative. Explanatory maps are conveniently provided, and supporting tables of statistical data enable the reader to appreciate with more precise accuracy the more pointed observations made by the author.
         UQ, 28:3:294-7   R: Lev E. Dobriansky

Economics

1165.   Bandera, V. N., and Z. L. Melnyk, eds. **The Soviet Economy in Regional Perspective**. New York, Praeger, 1973. 368p. $20.00.
This is a collection of essays concerned with regional aspects of Soviet economic development. The paucity of literature on the subject in the West makes this volume's contribution all the more notable. The essays vary in approach, scope and objectivity, but are invariably of a high level of scholarship. The subjects range from a general consideration of the policy and rules of regional allocation to studies, all from the angle of Soviet regional diversity, on income and productivity, industrial organization and management, agriculture and pricing, specialization and autarky, law. Significantly, no studies of specific regions have been included except for the Ukraine, and the two papers on the latter

area deal essentially with one topic: the export of capital from the Ukraine to other parts of the Soviet Union.

CASS, 9:1:120   R: S. Lamed

1166.   Koropeckyj, I. S. **Location Problems in Soviet Industry before World War II: The Case of the Ukraine.** Chapel Hill, University of North Carolina Press, 219p. $11.95.

This is an interesting and important analysis of a neglected aspect of Soviet development. The problem analyzed is whether the USSR was correct in stressing the development of heavy industry "behind the Urals" during the 1928-1940 period. The author has assembled and analyzed a good deal of primary regional economic evidence concerning these matters, especially as they related to the Ukraine. Under Stalin heavy industry expanded in the Ukraine but not as rapidly as elsewhere; in particular, the Ural-Kuznetsk Combine created a "second iron and steel base" for the USSR. This study makes a notable contribution to our understanding of the Soviet investment policies.

SR, 31:4:909-10   R: Holland Hunter

1167.   Melnyk, Zinowij Lew. **Soviet Capital Formation: Ukraine, 1928/29-1932.** Munich, Ukrainian Free University Press, 1965. 182p.

The book represents a notable contribution, although in a rather narrow field and covering a short period of time, to Western studies of Soviet internal finances. Well supplied with tables and well documented, it sets a useful standard for the future regional studies of the Soviet economy which we badly need. A case is made out for the view that Ukraine was being exploited by the rest of the USSR.

SEER, 45:105:568-71   R: Raymond Hutchings

Religion

1168.   Hordynsky, Sviatoslav. **The Ukrainian Icon of the XIIth to XVIIIth Centuries.** Trans. from Ukrainian by Walter Dushnyck. Philadelphia, Providence Association, 1973. 212p. (193 black and white, 24 color illus.).

This is the first monograph ever to appear on this subject. The book is significant also because it brings the little known Ukrainian icon to the attention of the world historiography of art. The author discusses the Ukrainian icon in its historical development and also concentrates on the distinguishing characteristics of icons from different parts of Ukraine, particularly Galicia, where many of them survived. His discussion of the technical aspects of the icon and its origin in Byzantium is useful for the general reader.

UQ, 30:3:289-90   R: Arcadia Olenska-Petryshyn

1169.   Medlin, William K., and Christos G. Patrinelis. **Renaissance Influences and Religious Reforms in Russia: Western and Post-Byzantine Impacts on Culture and Education (16th and 17th Centuries).** Geneva, Librairie Droz, 1971. 180p. (Études de philologie et d'histoire, 18). Paper.

The authors have attempted to explain the mechanics of the cultural change which came about in Muscovy and particularly in the Ukraine in the sixteenth and seventeenth centuries. The biographies of Maxim the Greek and Peter Mohyla receive more attention than the social and economic forces which the chosen methodology would suggest shifted Rus' from "traditional forms of belief" to "rationality." While the book presents many theses, its main point appears to be that Rus' was forced by historical conditions to choose from among three frameworks for its future development: the Western, the neo-Byzantine, and the traditional Muscovite. The authors seem to feel that Rus' (and Ukraine then) chose the middle way while Muscovy followed her example only much later.

      SR, 31:1:150   R: George P. Majeska

1170.   Solovey, Meletius Michael. **The Byzantine Divine Liturgy: History and Commentary**. Trans. by Demetrius Emil Wysochansky, O. S. B. M. Washington, D. C., Catholic University of America Press, 1970. 346p. $12.75.

Father Solovey's book was written in Ukrainian and first published in the Roman *Analecta* of the Basilian order (1964). The publication of an English translation certainly will be welcomed by the large number of Roman Catholics of the Eastern rite now living in America and using English as their language of study, and sometimes of prayer as well. After a first part devoted to the origins of Christian liturgy and the early development of the Byzantine rite, Father Solovey gives a systematic interpretation of the Eucharistic liturgy as it is used today in both the Orthodox Church and the Roman Catholic Ukrainian Eastern rite, giving occasional preference to certain usages adopted in the latter. In general, the author is well aware of the vast literature on this subject. All scholars committed to Byzantine and Slavic studies will find in this book the first scholarly and historical treatment of the subject available in English.

      SR, 31:1:149-50   R: John Meyendorff

Language and Literature; Fine Arts

1171.   Dovzhenko, Alexander. **The Poet as Filmmaker: Selected Writings**. Ed. and trans. by Marco Carynnyk. Cambridge, MIT Press, 1973. 323p. $8.95.

A. P. Dovzhenko (1894-1956) was a famous Ukrainian artist: cartoonist, painter, playwright, but above all a film director. His films—*Zvenyhora, Arsenal, Earth* and others—occupy a prominent place in the history of the cinema and are considered to be classics. The form of Dovzhenko's notebooks is fragmentary; sometimes only an isolated sentence appears in the text. Yet this does not downgrade the value of his writings. On the contrary, the author's comprehensive language creates a powerful mosaic, giving the reader a fascinating panorama of the time and its people. Carynnyk's edition is the first English publication of Devzhenko's notebooks, which have already been published in the Soviet Union (both in Russian and Ukrainian) and in other countries.

      CSP, 16:3:497-9   R: Jan Uhde

1172.   Kulish, Panteleimon. **The Black Council**. Trans. from Ukrainian and abridged by George S. N. Luckyj and Moira Luckyj. Intro. by Romana Bahrij. Littleton, Colo., Ukrainian Academic Press, 1973. 125p. $7.50.

The English edition of this best known of Kulish's historical novels presents a remarkable insight into the Ukrainian Cossack state. It exposes its bright as well as dark features. The translation is done with craftsmanship, letting the English-speaking reader gain a glimpse of the rich literary heritage of Kulish.

S. M. H.

1173.   Luckyj, George S. N. **Between Gogol and Ševčenko: Polarity in the Literary Ukraine: 1798-1847**. Munich, Wilhelm Fink Verlag, 1971. 210p. DM38.

This book concentrates on the crucial period in the first half of the nineteenth century when Ukrainian writers were struggling to decide whether to make their special contribution to Russian or whether to develop a complete Ukrainian literature in the Ukrainian language. As the title implies, Gogol made the first choice and Shevchenko the second. Luckyj's book should be required reading for all who refuse to face the facts about the Ukraine—or think they already have them.

SR, 34:1:189   R: William B. Edgerton

1174.   Luckyj, George S. N., ed. **Modern Ukrainian Short Stories**. Parallel text edition. Littleton, Colo., Ukrainian Academic Press, 1973. 228p. $8.50.

This volume reflects mainly the modernist trends in contemporary Ukrainian literature, but deserves special attention. Here it must be mentioned parenthetically that the writers who provided the English text for the Ukrainian stories (especially G. Luckyj, P. Kilina, and G. Tarnavsky) are outstanding craftsmen in the field of translation.

CSP, 17:2-3:559-61   R: O. Zujewskyj

1175.   Pidmohylny, Valerian. **A Little Touch of Drama**. Trans. by George S. N. Luckyj and Moira Luckyj. Intro. by George Shevelov. Littleton, Colo., Ukrainian Academic Press, 1972. 191p. (Ukrainian Classics in Translation, no. 1). $7.50.

This is a novel of universal human feelings, of eternal human problems. The Hero, Yuri Slavenko, a biochemistry professor, could have appeared in the Soviet Ukraine in the 1930s or anywhere else in the world. The novel has only two protagonists: Slavenko and Marta. The author uses numerous themes very successfully to describe the everyday life of the Soviet Ukraine in the 1930s, and proves that neither the people of the Soviet Union nor their style of life differs much from people elsewhere. The work is aptly supported by a short and informative foreword by G. Luckyj and a detailed analysis of the novel by G. Shevelov. The translation is successful.

CSP, 15:4:613-4   R: V. Revutsky

1176.   Struk, D. A. **A Study of Vasyl' Stefanyk: The Pain at the Heart of Existence**. Foreword by G. S. N. Luckyj. Littleton, Colo., Ukrainian Academic Press, 1973. 200p. $8.50.

Struk's monograph of Stefanyk, the foremost Ukrainian prose writer, is a critical confrontation of the oversimplified and tendentious views on Stefanyk which classify him as either a typical nineteenth-century populist writer or a writer about social injustice. The author's main purpose in this study is to provide supporting documentation for Stefanyk's universality as a writer whose prime concern was the portrayal of human pain and anguish, using as his subject the Ukrainian peasant. It is a welcome contribution as the first comprehensive work on Stefanyk, not only in English but also in critical bibliography in general.

SR, 33:2:403-4 R: Jaroslav Rozumnyj

1177. Ukrainka, Lesya. **Selected Works.** Trans. by Vera Rich. **Life and Work,** by Constantine Bida. Toronto, University of Toronto Press, 1968. 259p. $7.50.

It is only fitting that the task of translating the works of the greatest Ukrainian poetess and of the greatest of women writers should be entrusted to a woman. The book consists of two parts: *Life and Work* by Bida, and *Selected Works* translated by Rich. In sections on poetry and drama, Bida first gives a brief survey of these genres in Ukrainian literature prior to Lesya Ukrainka's appearance on the scene. Then the intricacies of Ukrainka's style, meter, and methods are discussed. Like Shakespeare, she turned to antiquity for most of her subjects. The translations are accurate and accomplished in a rich, flowing style.

SR, 29:1:146-7 R: Victor O. Buyniak

Education

1178. Kolasky, John. **Education in Soviet Ukraine: A Study in Discrimination and Russification.** Toronto, Peter Martin, 1968. 238p. $3.50pa.

Kolasky (a veteran Canadian Marxist formerly highly sympathetic to the USSR) accumulated very strong evidence of the existence of an opposition to Soviet policy among Ukrainian intellectuals during his two years' study in Kiev. The bulk of his work consists of statistics, some available in Soviet publications received abroad but many hitherto unknown, on the relative education of nationalities.

SR, 28:4:503-4 R: John A. Armstrong

Dissent Movement

1179. Browne, Michael, ed. **Ferment in the Ukraine: Documents by V. Chornovil, I. Dandyba, L. Lukyanenko, V. Moroz and Others.** Foreword by Max Hayward. New York, Praeger Publishers, 1971. 267p. $15.00.

The volume contains documents of protest and is a sequel to the well-known *Chornovil Papers.* Of special interest are the documents on the Jurists' Case of 1961, news of which Soviet authorities had hitherto succeeded in suppressing. The seven Ukrainian defendants sought to combat Russian great power chauvinism and bureaucratism and to demand the exercise of Ukrainian rights as provided for in the Soviet constitution—including the right of secession. They were tried in secret in May 1961 in a KGB prison and not in a courtroom. The volume also includes the complete text of the remarkable "Report from the Beria

Reservation" by the historian and writer Valentyn Moroz, who was sentenced to a nine-year prison term and to five years of exile in 1970 following a secret trial.

SR, 31:4:910-2   R: John S. Reshetar, Jr.

1180.   Chornovil, Vyacheslav, comp. **The Chornovil Papers**. Intro. by
         Frederick C. Barghoorn. New York, McGraw-Hill, 1969. 246p. $6.95.
The Chornovil Papers ia an annotated translation of Chornovil's lengthy petitions enumerating in detail the violations of the constitution and of criminal
law and procedure committed in the course of the arrests, investigation, and
trials by the very guardians of Soviet legality. Written from the standpoint of
internationalism and loyalty to the Soviet constitution, the papers represent
one of the strongest indictments of the continuing official violations of the
legally "guaranteed" rights of individuals and nationalities ever to emerge from
the USSR.

SR, 29:2:343-4   R: Bohdan R. Bociurkiw

1181.   Kolasky, John. **Two Years in Soviet Ukraine: A Canadian's Personal
         Account of Russian Oppression and the Growing Opposition**. Toronto,
         Peter Martin, 1970. 264p. $6.95cl.; $3.95pa.
This work is more than the memoir of a disillusioned Communist or a tourist's
report. It is a remarkable account based on close personal observation and on
lesser-known Soviet published sources. Kolasky knew his way about, had
personal contacts with many Soviet citizens, and proved to be a perceptive observer. He attended meetings and visited out-of-the-way places, and the book
abounds with experiences, encounters, and exchanges presented in a highly
vivid way. Kolasky discusses the unconscionable role of Russians in the Ukrainian
Ministry of Culture who are said to strangle that culture, the limited editions of
Ukrainian books, the paucity of Ukrainian films, the difficulty in obtaining
recordings of Ukrainian songs and subscriptions to publications, and the numerous
acts of bigotry and discimination by Russians that he witnessed. It is a grim and
disturbing account.

SR, 31:1:172-5   R: John S. Reshetar, Jr.

1182.   Moroz, Valentyn. **Boomerang: The Works of Valentyn Moroz**. Ed. by
         Yaroslav Bihun. With an intro. by Paul L. Gersper. Baltimore, Smoloskyp
         Publishers, 1974. 272p. $3.25.
Boomerang is a little book that tells of the life and works of Valentyn Moroz
and why he became an international *cause célèbre:* a fighter for universal
freedom and a martyr of the Soviet totalitarian system. Although Moroz's writings
are concerned almost exclusively with the oppression and persecution of the
Ukrainian people, his story and fight against tyranny typify the enslavement of
all other non-Russian nations. In 1965 he was arrested and sentenced to four
years at hard labor, which he spent in the Yavas concentration camp compound
in Mordovia. It was there that Moroz wrote his first significant essay, *A Report
from the Beria Reserve*. He also wrote *A Chronicle of Resistance, Amid the Snows*
and *Moses and Dathan*, all dealing with his prison experiences, the russification

of Ukraine, and man's eternal quest for freedom of justice. On June 1, 1970, he was arrested again and sentenced to nine years at hard labor and five years of exile from Ukraine.

UQ, 30:3:287-9   R: Walter Dushnyck

1183.   Moroz, Valentyn. **Report from the Beria Reserve: The Protest Writings of Valentyn Moroz**. Ed. and trans. by John Kolasky. Chicago, Cataract Press, 1974. 162p. $2.95.

The works of Valentyn Moroz appeared thus far in three collections; the first, *Boomerang* (1974), the second in Ukrainian in 1975. Included in both collections are such well-known essays as *Report from the Beria Reserve, Moses and Dathan, Chronicle of Resistance, In the Midst of the Snows, The First Day* and *Instead of Final Statement*. This collection also contains a foreword and a translator's note by Alexander S. Yesemin-Volpin and John Kolasky.

UQ, 31:1:60-1   R: Walter Dushnyck

1184.   Prychodko, Nicholas. **Stormy Road to Freedom**. With a foreword by Igor Gouzenko. New York, Vantage Press, 1968. 356p. $5.95.

N. Prychodko, Ukrainian political refugee, now a Canadian citizen, became known to English-speaking readers first with his own story described in his book, *One of the 15 Million*. The present book is in the form of a novel, a drama-packed account of the Ukrainian family of Hlobas, whose members are caught up, torn apart, and scattered in the turmoil of the brutal enslavement of Ukraine by Communist Russia. The story is a vivid and genuine illustration of life under Stalin's regime. The author unveils a vast panorama of life with moving clarity: how ordinary men and women in Ukraine lived, loved, and laughed throughout years of terror, Siberian slave labor camps, tortures by the Soviet secret police, the NKVD, the German-Soviet war, life in DP camps in West Germany, and—for some—finally exit to freedom, emigration to the United States.

UQ, 24:1:82-3   R: Walter Dushnyck

1185.   Stetsko, Slava, ed. **Revolutionary Voices: Ukrainian Political Prisoners Condemn Russian Colonialism**. Foreword by Ivan M. Lombardo. Munich, Press Bureau of ABN; 2nd ed., 1971 269p.

This is a well-compiled and comprehensive record of the writings, appeals and petitions of a number of Ukrainian political prisoners, most of whom are now in a Soviet prison, a concentration camp or—that new form of Soviet jail—a psychiatric ward. Many of these appeals appeared in *Ukrains'kyi visnyk*, a *samvydav* Ukrainian publication, and a surprising amount eventually were smuggled out of Ukraine to the West. The editor deserves much praise for her editing of this timely and important volume. The book also contains several pictures of the imprisoned Ukrainian intellectuals.

UQ, 29:3:297-9   R: Walter Dushnyck

CAUCASIAN REPUBLICS

Bibliographies

1186.   Avakian, Anne M., comp. **Armenia and the Armenians in Academic Dissertations: A Bibliography**. Berkeley, Calif., Professional Press, 1974. 38p.

The compiler has relied mainly upon records available at the University of California Library at Berkeley. Owing to the wide dispersion of the Armenian diaspora and of scholarly Armenological centers, there is a risk of duplication by research workers, so this new guide to academic dissertations on Armenian subjects is a valuable scientific tool.

SEER, 53:123:475   R: David M. Lang

History

1187.   Gidney, James B. **A Mandate for Armenia**. Kent, Ohio, Kent State University Press, 1969. 270p. $7.50.

The book tells the story of Armenia since the end of World War One, with particular reference to America's interest in the settlement of the Armenian question. It covers such issues as the treatment of Armenia at the Paris Peace Conference, Turkish policy toward Armenia, and the final collapse of Armenia's attempt to remain an independent state. This is an informative, cohesive, and objective presentation of events from 1917 to 1923. The author concludes that Armenia can exist only in union with the Soviet Union or with Turkey; prospects for an independent Armenia are almost nil. A well-selected bibliography consisting of unpublished material, official publications, and general works provides a sufficient foundation for this lucidly written, tragic story of a much-suffering nation. Recommended for the general reader and undergraduate student of East European history and diplomacy.   S. M. H.

1188.   Hovannisian, Richard G. **Armenia on the Road to Independence, 1918**. Berkeley, University of California Press, 1967. 364p. $8.50.

This study is a detailed account of the eighteen months from the Russian March revolution of 1917 to the conclusion of the Mudros Armistice between Turkey and the Allied powers in November 1918: the period of the creation and collapse of the emphemeral Transcaucasian Federative Republic and of the proclamation of the independence of its three component republics, Georgia, Azerbaijan, and Armenia in May 1918. As a prologue to his study, the author has supplied a brief and rather perfunctory survey of Armenian history, as well as three chapters on Russian and Turkish Armenia and on the war years 1914-17. An appendix contains excerpts from contemporary Allied statements on the Armenian situation during World War I. Voluminous notes, maps, and photographs accompany the text. The book is based on extensive research, including works in Armenian, Turkish, and Russian, as well as West European languages, and the bibliography is impressive.

SR, 27:2:320-1   R: Nina G. Garsoian

1189.   Hovannisian, Richard G. **The Republic of Armenia. Vol. 1: The First Year, 1918-1919.** Berkeley, University of California Press, 1971. 547p. $15.00.

The author confirms the conclusion of Firuz Kazemzadeh that the Armenian Republic was founded in late May 1918 simply to make the best of a bad situation. The first winter (1918-1919) in the Armenian Republic was a demographic disaster second only to the massacres of 1915-1916. The author states that about two hundred thousand people, almost 20 percent of the republic's population, died of hunger or disease by mid-1919. The disaster would have been greater had it not been for the help of American Near East Relief. During the remainder of the book the reader is lost in a sandpile of details; therefore, this book will probably be read only by specialists in the field.

   SR, 31:3:731-2   R: May K. Matossian

1190.   Lang, David Marshall. **The Georgians.** New York, Praeger, 1966. 244p. (Ancient People and Places, no. 51). $7.50.

Although Lang is not primarily an archaeologist, he has conformed to the general emphasis of the series to which this volume belongs by concentrating on the earlier period and giving an extensive and conscientious account of the prehistoric and pre-Christian eras. Three chapters are devoted to this epoch as against one apiece for the history, art, and literature of the nine centuries (ca. 330-1236) terminating in the Mongol conquest of Georgia. The author has given us a great deal of information on the recent state of Georgian studies and provided a pleasant introduction to the subject.

   SR, 27:1:133-5   R: Nina G. Garsoïan

1191.   Suny, Ronald Grigor. **The Baku Commune, 1917-1918: Class and Nationality in the Russian Revolution.** Princeton, Princeton University Press, 1972. 412p. (Studies of the Russian Institute, Columbia University). $15.00.

While materials relating to the Baku Commune (April-July 1918) abound, there has been no basic scholarly monograph on the subject in a Western language. The author has completed this undertaking with commendable patience amidst bewildering and often contradictory source materials and has striven to present the emotion-filled story with impartiality. The study should become a noteworthy contribution to the history of the Caucasus and of the first Soviet administration in that area.

   SR, 31:3:673-5   R: Richard G. Hovannisian

CENTRAL ASIAN REPUBLICS

Bibliographies

1192.   Allworth, Edward. **Nationalities of the Soviet East: Publications and Writing Systems. A Bibliographical Directory and Transliteration Tables for Iranian- and Turkic-Language Publications, 1917-1945, Located in U.S. Libraries.** New York, Columbia University Press, 1971. 440p. $17.50.

This volume is a bibliographical guide to 26 Iranian and Turkic national groups in the USSR. It contains a listing of some 3,300 books and periodicals in 26 languages, and the libraires in the United States in which they may be located. The volume also provides transliteration tables for the languages into the Roman alphabet. The work is an extremely valuable research and reference guide.

S. M. H.

History, Archaeology

1193.   Allworth, Edward, ed. **Central Asia: A Century of Russian Rule**.
New York, Columbia University Press, 1967. 552p. $12.95.
Here several highly competent specialists endeavor to tell "what has happened to the land and its people and why, during the last hundred years, Russian-style civilization has been superimposed upon the traditional Central Asian culture." Allworth's initial chapter, "Encounter," epitomizes certain difficulties displayed throughout the book. Describing the contacts and clashes between the Russians and natives, he covers a period from ancient Novgorod to 1865. In separate sections he takes up first encounters, military inroads, trade, slavery, cultural and intellectual exchanges, diplomatic exchanges, and government policy. The book is best on specific topics. The chapters on people, languages, and migra-tions; geography, industrialization, and agriculture; nationalism and social and political reform movements; intellectual and literary developments; musical tradition and innovation; and architecture, art, and town planning are all of high merit.
SR, 26:3:486-7   R: Richard A. Pierce

1194.   Bacon, Elizabeth E. **Central Asians under Russian Rule: A Study in Culture Change**. Ithaca, N.Y., Cornell University Press, 1966. 273p. $6.50.
Much of the book deals with the pastoral nomads (Kazaks, Kirghiz, Kara-Kalpaks, and Turkomans) and settled oasis peoples ("Sarts," or Tajiks and Uzbeks) in turn by periods: prior to the Russian conquest in the mid-nineteenth century, under tsarist rule, and after 1917. The closing chapters treat "Russian Influence on Central Asian Languages" and "Central Asian Cultures as of 1965." There are notes, bibliography, index, twelve illustrations, and two maps.
AHR, 72:4:1449   R: Donald W. Treadgold

1195.   Chadwick, Nora K., and Victor Zhirmunsky. **Oral Epics of Central Asia**. Cambridge, Cambridge University Press, 1969. 366p. $12.50.
This book is a conglomerate of two studies. The first is a reprint, with small adjustments, of Nora K. Chadwick's survey, "The Oral Literature of the Tatars." The second part, written by Zhirmunsky, complements Chadwick's survey with the results of more modern research. In the chapter on the epic tales he deals with those Turkic epics that were either omitted by Chadwick or treated inade-quately by her.
SR, 29:1:149-50   R: Felix J. Oinas

1196.   Demko, George J. **The Russian Colonization of Kazakhstan, 1896-1916**. Bloomington, Indiana University Publications; The Hague, Mouton, 1969. 271p. (Uralic and Altaic Series, vol. 99). $9.50.

In 208 pages of text, of which nearly half consists of maps and statistical tables, the author reviews the chief aspects of Russian settlement in Kazakhstan and attempts incidentally to derive from it—for the comparative history of migrations—theoretical lessons. A brief historical and geographical overview is the aim of the first part, which traces the chief stages of Russian penetration. There follows in the second part the depiction of the peasant immigration, for which the author strives to draw up in the third part—the fullest and most detailed—an agricultural, economic, and human balance sheet. A brief conclusion is followed by statistical tables, notes, and a rather uneven bibliography.

SR, 30:2:430-1   R: Fr.-X. Coquin

1197.   Donnelly, Alton S. **The Russian Conquest of Bashkiria: A Case Study in Imperialism**. New Haven, Yale University Press, 1968. 114p. (Yale Russian and East European Studies, 7). $6.50.

The author finds five major causes for Russian movement toward the southeast and into Bashkiria: the necessity for terminating harmful raids by the nomads, the desire to increase government income through tribute, Peter's interest in metallurgy, his intention to trade with the East, and official and unofficial migration of Russians into the area. Donnelly has made a valuable contribution to the history of the Russian empire.   S. M. H.

1198.   Frumkin, Grégoire. **Archeology in Soviet Central Asia**. Handbuch der Orientalistik. Part 7, vol. 3, sec. 1. Leiden, E. J. Brill, 1970. 217p. + 58p., 19 maps, 40 illus., 67 plates. 96Dglds.

This book sets out to review the principal developments of the past two to three decades in the archaeology of Kazakhstan, Kirgizia, the Fergana Valley, Tadzhikistan, Uzbekistan, and Turkmenistan. The author concentrates almost exclusively on synthesizing the work of Russian scholars, thus making available, often for the first time, archaeological materials excavated from sites previously dealt with only in the Russian literature. The author unfortunately provides the reader with a continual apologia for the Russian archaeologists' point of view. The book contains a most useful and comprehensive annotated bibliography of the Russian sources, from which the specialist must in the end derive his direct discussions.

SR, 30:3:656   R: C. C. Lamberg-Karlovsky

1199.   Masson, V. M., and V. I. Sarianidi. **Central Asia: Turkmenia before the Achaemenids**. Trans. and ed. by Ruth Tringham. New York, Praeger, 1972. 219p. $12.50.

Two Soviet archaeologists have provided an up-to-date account of man's efforts and successes in exploiting the deserts and moutain valleys from the first Pleistocene traces to the middle of the first millenium B. C. It is well illustrated and has selected chapter bibliographies through 1969, which include relevant Western publications and give Russian titles in translation.

SR, 32:1:156   R: Chester S. Chard

1200.   Wheeler, Geoffrey. **The Modern History of Soviet Central Asia**. New
York, Praeger, 1964. 272p. $7.00.
The author has furnished a necessary identification of the place and its people.
He has also defined briefly the impressive cultural traditions as well as the
distinctive international role which have characterized the region during its
long history. The Soviet government inherited this typically colonial problem
and has, like the Imperial government before it, pursued goals in Central Asia
that were essentially its own rather than those of the largely non-Russian local
population.

RR, 25:4:430-1   R: John Albert White

Social and Political Conditions

1201.   Allworth, Edward, ed. **The Nationality Question in Soviet Central
Asia**. New York, Praeger, 1973. 221p. $16.50.
This volume is based in good part upon the work of the graduate seminar in
Soviet nationality problems conducted at Columbia University during 1971-
1972, eight of whose members appear as authors. All in all, fifteen contributors
discuss various aspects of Soviet nationality policy in Central Asia, stressing such
subjects as literature, ethnic intermarriage, assimilation trends, national identity
and ethnic consciousness. A selected list of recent (1951-71) books in English
about Central Asia and the general Soviet nationality question and short biographical sketches of the contributors complete this study. Appended are a number
of valuable maps and tables, many appearing in English for the first time. The
editor deserves credit for the cohesiveness of the work, which ought to receive
serious attention from students and specialists.   S. M. H.

1202.   Massell, Gregory J. **The Surrogate Proletariat: Moslem Women and
Revolutionary Strategies in Soviet Central Asia, 1919-1929**. Princeton,
Princeton University Press, 1974. 448p. $18.50.
Relying heavily on a full range of documentary, contemporary, and recollective
literature in Russian, Massell has written a masterful historical and analytical
account of Soviet efforts during the 1920s to develop a productive strategy for
social change in Central Asia. Basically this is a study of the modernization of
a traditional society, with an added, complicating dimension: modernization in
Central Asia was not self-imposed by native leaders but was the result of outside
(Soviet Russian) vision and planning. The native reaction, extensively presented
here, was understandably indifferent at best and hostile and violent at worst.
The "Failure" of Central Asia to respond positively to Marxist-Leninist perceptions of social and political norms forced the Bolsheviks to search for different
"access-routes to Central Asia's societies" in order to bring about the desired
social and political transformation. That Muslim women came to be viewed as
a surrogate proletariat in Soviet eyes becomes abundantly clear as Massell delves
into the process by which the regime sought to modernize Central Asia.

SR, 34:2:398-9   R: Edward J. Lazzerini

1203.   Nove, Alec and J. A. Newth. **The Soviet Middle East: A Communist Model for Development**. New York, Praeger, 1967. 160p. $6.50.
The authors have explored a subject that has so far been very inadequately studied: the economic development of Transcaucasia and Soviet Central Asia. By assembling a large number of official figures in well-arranged and comparable tables, and still more by commenting on and analyzing the data, the authors have rendered a valuable service. The picture that emerges from their study is clear. Starting from abysmally low levels, the Soviet Middle East has made very rapid economic, especially industrial, and social progress. According to the authors, per capita incomes range from 50 to 70 percent of that of the RSFSR. There is a serious methodological error: almost all per capita figures include Russians, Ukrainians, and other immigrants as well as the native population, and are therefore hardly more meaningful than in such societies as French Algeria, where a high national average hid huge differences between the two constituent groups.

        SR, 26:3:503-5   R: Charles Issawi

1204.   Rakowska-Harmstone, Teresa. **Russia and Nationalism in Central Asia: The Case of Tadzhikistan**. Baltimore, The Johns Hopkins Press, 1970. 325p. $10.95.
This is a case study of the Soviet nationalities policy as applied to the Muslim peoples of Soviet Central Asia. After a brief chapter giving the historical background of the Tadzhik people from the earliest times up to the Revolution, the author embarks on a detailed examination of the various aspects of the Soviet experiment: the formation of the Tadzhik SSR; the ethnic structure of the republic; the nature and extent of Soviet control; and the reactions of the indigenous elite to Russian, socialist, political, economic, and cultural regimentation. The book ends with an essay defining the ultimate object of the Russian experiment and assessing its achievements. The book provides great insight into Soviet policy and methods and into native reaction to them up to 1956, and it is thus a valuable introduction to the study of subsequent developments.

        SR, 30:1:156   R: Geoffrey Wheeler

JEWS

Bibliographies

1205.   Fluk, Louise R., comp. **Jews in the Soviet Union: An Annotated Bibliography**. New York, The American Jewish Committee; Institute of Human Relations, 1975. 44p. $1.50pa.
This bibliography is a selection of the most significant and accessible writings, both scholarly and popular, on Soviet Jewry published in English between January 1, 1967 and September 1974. It includes 314 entries—books, pamphlets, and articles.   S. M. H.

1206.   Pinkus, B., and A. A. Greenbaum, comps. **Russian Publications on Jews and Judaism in the Soviet Union, 1917-1967: A Bibliography.** Ed. with an intro. by Mordechai Altshuler. Jerusalem, Society for Research on Jewish Communities, the Historical Society of Israel, 1970. 275p. (English) and 113p. (Hebrew).

In view of the forced assimilation policy pursued by the Soviet authorities in dealing with the Jewish nationality, it is scarcely surprising that the Soviet Union has published no comprehensive bibliography on Jewish theses. The vacuum was only partly filled in 1961 by the bibliography *Jewish Publications in the Soviet Union, 1917-60*, which, however, carried no listing of works on Jewish subjects written in the Russian language. The obvious need is now satisfied by this work—an invaluable, if not indispensable, research tool for scholars in the field. The bibliography is divided into three broad, carefully arranged and demarcated sections. The first lists 52 bibliographic compilations, mainly printed in the Soviet Union. The second is composed of books and pamphlets on Jewish subjects. The final section identifies 163 newspapers and periodicals which at one time or another in Soviet history have focused upon Jews or Judaica.
SR, 30:3:711-2   R: William Korey

1207.   Rothenberg, Joshua, comp. **An Annotated Bibliography of Writings on Judaism Published in the Soviet Union, 1960-1965.** Foreword by Erich Goldhagen. Waltham, Mass., Institute of East European Jewish Studies, Brandeis University, 1969. 66p. Paper.

This bibliography is not only an extensive compilation of Soviet writings, books, pamphlets, and articles on Judaism, but it also reflects the changing attitude of the Soviet regime toward the Jewish question. That anti-Semitism in the Soviet Union is on the rise becomes inescapably clear. This trend is in line with Soviet foreign policy, on the one hand, and with the promotion of the policy of russification at home, on the other.   S. M. H.

History

1208.   Baron, Salo W. **The Russian Jew under Tsars and Soviets.** New York, Macmillan, 1964. 427p. (Russian Civilization Series). $7.50.

Traditionally Muscovy-Russia was against Jewish settlement until, ironically, the partitions of Poland confronted Catherine II with nearly a million Jewish subjects in the western provinces of her empire. The manner in which the tsarina and her successors dealt with this growing Jewish hinterland oscillated between attempted vocational and cultural "amalgamation" under Nicholas I and Alexander II, and cynical and brutal quarantine, the constriction of space and opportunity in the Pale of Settlement, under Alexander III and Nicholas II. Yet for those Jews who envisaged the Bolshevist Revolution as the *annus mirabilis* of emancipation, the years following 1917 proved a total disillusionment. Baron makes clear that the Soviet regime soon revived tsarist anti-Semitism. Even today the Kremlin's suspicion of Jewish nationalism remains, and with it overt hostility to Jewish communal and religious self-expression.
JMH, 37:2:230-1   R: Howard M. Sachar

1209. Bobe, M., et al., eds. **The Jews in Latvia**. Tel Aviv, Association of
Latvian and Estonian Jews in Israel, 1971. 384p. $16.50.
This collection of articles deals with the life and annihilation of the prewar
Latvian Jewry. Its quality is uneven by scholarly standards, but it is important
that raw materials on Jews in independent Latvia be collected before the death
of the last survivors. The book fulfills that purpose. Laserson's description of
political life in interwar Latvia is well written and is of the greatest interest to
the outsider. He was a Zionist Socialist deputy in three of the four Latvian
Saeimas (Parliaments). The Latvian Jewish community in the years 1920-1940
was hopelessly divided ideologically, with all views represented, from Communists
to conservatives. The community was also divided linguistically (Hebrewists
vs. Yiddishists, not to mention the assimilationists). A short overview of Estonia's
tiny Jewry (5,000 as compared to Latvia's 100,000) is also given. The post-
1945 reestablishment of a Baltic Jewry is recognized, but is not discussed,
since 1943 clearly represents the end of a period.
　　　　　JBS, 4:2:170-1　　　　　　　　　R: Rein Taagepera

1210. Dawidowicz, Lucy S., ed. and intro. **The Golden Tradition: Jewish
Life and Thought in Eastern Europe**. New York, Holt, Rinehart and
Winston, 1967. 502p. $8.95.
In a concise, highly informative essay, Dawidowicz traces the origins of the various
Jewish reactions to the sudden encounter with a Gentile world that was hitherto
so distant except as an ever-looming threat. To some of Eastern Europe's Jews
the partial emancipation (after the French Revolution) appeared as a propitious
time for complete assimilation. In fact, the former goal may help explain the
attraction of so many East European Jews to a variety of reformist and revolutionary political causes. But there were also those who saw in political emancipation an opportunity to remain Jews by choice rather than coercion. The nineteenth century witnessed the birth of a specifically Jewish socialism (the Bund),
of a sophisticated neo-orthodoxy in religion, and of modern Jewish nationalism
(Zionism). World War II resulted in the all but complete disappearance of the
Bund. The religious orthodoxy, perhaps surprisingly, is holding its ground, while
Zionism emerged triumphant with the establishment of the state of Israel.
　　　　　SR, 26:3:518　　　　　　　　　R: Maurice Friedberg

1211. Kochan, Lionel, ed. **The Jews in Soviet Russia since 1917**. London,
Oxford University Press, Published for the Institute of Jewish Affairs,
London, 1970. 357p. $7.95.
The Jews in the Soviet Union have gone through six distinct and generally well-
known phases since the Revolution. They made an extremely important contribution, both quantitatively and qualitatively, to the various revolutionary parties
and subsequently participated in large numbers in the early Soviet government
and party apparat on all levels. However, during the sixth phase there has been
the introduction of a quota system of sorts for Jews in Soviet state, industrial,
and educational institutions. Aspects of these various phases, as well as the role
of Jews in Soviet society and their plight, have been treated in a scholarly and
convincing fashoin by seventeen leading Western authorities in this collection
of essays.
　　　　　CSP, 15:4:571-7　　　　　　　　R: D. Pospielovsky

1212. Mendelsohn, Ezra. **Class Struggle in the Pale: The Formative Years of the Jewish Workers' Movement in Tsarist Russia**. Cambridge, Cambridge University Press, 1970. 180p. $8.50.
Thus far the Jewish movement has been examined exclusively through the prism of Russian sources and perspectives. The rich literature in Yiddish remained unused. Now with Mendelsohn's informative book the internal history of the Jewish labor movement suddenly comes alive and takes on sharp new contours. The first chapter on the legal status, demography, and social-occupational stratification of Jews in tsarist Russia is in itself a valuable new contribution. Though the story of the shift from propaganda circles to economic agitation is well known, Mendelsohn provides a wealth of concrete details on techniques and associational forms which the Russian sources can scarcely convey.
   SR, 31:1:163-4   R: Allan K. Wildman

1213. Nedava, Joseph. **Trotsky and the Jews**. Philadelphia, Jewish Publication Society of America, 1972. 299p. $6.00.
The author examines Trotsky's attitude toward the Jewish problem in various periods: up to 1914, when Trotsky was concerned with the Jewish Bund; from 1914 to 1926, when he experienced "complete alienation" from the issue; from 1926 to 1932, when doubts about a Soviet Marxist and especially a Stalinist solution to the Jewish problem assailed him; and after 1932, as the rise of the Nazis placed the question in a new setting. Nedava treats Trotsky as a Jewish internationalist who, rejecting his own Judaism, was nevertheless impelled by it to transform into a sacred imperative the quest for the equality and dignity of man.
   SR, 33:3:548-9   R: Henry J. Tobias

1214. Shulvass, Moses A. **From East to West: The Westward Migration of Jews from Eastern Europe During the Seventeenth and Eighteenth Centuries**. Detroit, Wayne State University Press, 1971. 161p. $8.95.
Shulvass's monograph deals with the migration of East European (mostly Polish) Jews to Western Europe and the New World in the period before the great migration. There was a steady if undramatic movement of Jews from East to West, whose most important consequence was the introduction into Western Jewish communities of learned East European rabbis and scholars.
   SR, 31:3:712-3   R: Ezra Mendelsohn

1215. Smolar, Boris. **Soviet Jewry Today and Tomorrow**. New York, Macmillan, 1971. 228p. $5.95.
Born in Russia and well acquainted with the earlier phases of the Soviet period, Smolar is able to connect the current problems of Russian Jewry with both pre- and post-revolutionary experience. The author expresses fears that Jewish identity may disappear in the Soviet Union.
   SR, 32:1:176   R: Lyman H. Legters

1216. Tobias, Henry J. **The Jewish Bund in Russia: From its Origins to 1905**. Stanford, Stanford University Press, 1972. 409p. $16.50.
It was the Bund which, in 1898, organized the first conference of the Social-Democratic Workers Party of Russia, one faction of which, led by Lenin, dissolved

the Bund some twenty years later, and left it to Stalin to murder many of its members. Tobias has done a pioneering work by describing step by step the conscious policy of Lenin's Bolsheviks to force the Bund out of the RSDWP, which in 1905 represented thirty thousand members. An extensive bibliography increases the value of this study.

SEER, 53:130:128-9   R: Lucjan Blit

Education

1217. Schulman, Elias. **A History of Jewish Education in the Soviet Union.** New York, Ktav Publishing House, 1971. 184p. (Institute for East European Jewish Studies, Brandeis University, 3). $10.00.

In this study Schulman makes it clear that Jewish educational officials in the Soviet Union had to emphasize that their work on behalf of the Yiddish language had no connection with Yiddish-speaking activities outside the USSR. They feared the accusation of nationalism. One such official, M. Levitan, said, "The 160,000 pupils who study in the Soviet Yiddish schools must be enclosed within one frame with the 23,000,000 children who study in the schools of the Soviet Union in all languages." Schulman virtually ends his book with the early 1930s, when the Yiddish-language schools reached their zenith, only to yield within a few years to governmental suppression.

SR, 31:2:447-8   R: Lionel Kochan

Religion

1218. Rothenberg, Joshua. **The Jewish Religion in the Soviet Union.** New York, Ktav Publishing House and the Philip W. Lown Graduate Center for Contemporary Jewish Studies, Brandeis University, 1971. 242p. $10.00.

This is an immensely important book, a milestone in the study of Jews in the Soviet Union. It has the brilliant and possibly unique virtue of confining its purview strictly to the religious aspects of its subject, without succumbing to the temptation to confuse the issue with cultural and national repressions suffered by Jews in the USSR. Not that the author is unaware of these other matters. The tragedy of the situation is that Jews in the Soviet Union suffer not only religious disabilities but also severe restrictions owing to Soviet cultural and nationality policies. This book is absolutely essential for an accurate understanding of their situation.

SR, 31:3:700   R: William C. Fletcher

Dissent Movement and Anti-Semitism

1219. Eliav, Arie L. **Between Hammer and Sickle.** Updated ed. New York, New American Library, 1969. 237p. $1.25pa.

Eliav, who served for three years as first secretary of the Israeli Embassy in Moscow, is a keen observer who has traveled widely throughout the Soviet

Union and met with a great variety of Jews in all walks of public life. His two chapters on Jewish "types" and on the rarely visited Jewish communities of Lithuania, Georgia, Daghestan, Central Asia, and Birobidzhan are especially perceptive. The work highlights the extraordinary contradiction in Soviet policy: on the one hand, the authorities attempt to obliterate any sense of Jewish self-identity; on the other hand, the government insists on maintaining Jewish nationality identity in the required internal passport.

      SR, 29:1:706-7   R: William Korey

1220.   Gilboa, Yehoshua A. **The Black Years of Soviet Jewry, 1939-1953.** Trans. by Yosef Shachter and Dov Ben-Alba. Boston, Little, Brown, and the Graduate Center for Contemporary Jewish Studies, Brandeis University, 1971. 418p. $15.00.

Gilboa affirms that the Soviet governmental antagonism to Jewish culture beginning in the thirties—temporarily interrupted by the war—reached its climax in the 1950s. Only with the death of Stalin in 1953 was even greater tragedy averted. His book, scrupulously documented and temperate in tone, has the qualities that make it a work of abiding reference. It is also extremely readable. So far as present evidence allows, here is a remarkable contribution to our knowledge of the campaign against "worthless cosmopolitans," the Crimean affair of 1952, the Prague trial at the end of that year, and the "doctor plot" early in 1953. Gilboa brings Stalin's Jewish policy into perspective with Soviet developments in general—as indeed he does throughout this most valuable work.

      SR, 31:2:447-8   R: Lionel Kochan

1221.   Gitelman, Zvi Y. **Jewish Nationality and Soviet Politics: The Jewish Sections of the CPSU, 1917-1930.** Princeton, Princeton University Press, 1972. 573p. $20.00.

The author, in a heavily researched and lengthy work, seeks to examine Jewish national existence in the first generation of Soviet power. He concerns himself particularly with the Jewish experience "as a history of the modernization and secularization of an ethnic and religious minority resulting from attempts to integrate this minority into a modernizing state." The bulk of the volume deals with the *Evsektsiia's* major tasks to destroy the old order, the Bolshevization of the Jews, and the reconstruction of Jewish national life. He presents well the difficulties of the Jewish Bolsheviks with their dilemmas—to assimilate or to help build a pluralistic culture within the Communist framework.

      SR, 33:3:549-50   R: Henry J. Tobias

1222.   Glazer, Nathan, et al. **Soviet Jewry: 1969.** New York, Academic Committee on Soviet Jewry, (1970?). 95p. $0.75.

This is a collection of papers prepared for and given at the Second Conference of the Academic Committee for Soviet Jewry, held in Washington in 1969. In addition to the introduction by Glazer, there are five essays: 1) Jewish National Consciousness in the Soviet Union (M. Decter); 2) Myths, Fantasies and Show Trials: Echoes of the Past (W. Korey); 3) Soviet Foreign Policy and Anti-Semitism (J. Armstrong); 4) Anti-Semitism as an Instrument of Soviet Policy (A. Inkeles), and 5) The Jews and Soviet Foreign Policy (H. Morgenthau). Commentary and summaries are provided by M. Friedberg. One will also find a number of original texts pertaining to Russian anti-Semitism translated into English for the first time.   S. M. H.

1223.   Korey, William. **The Soviet Cage: Antisemitism in Russia**. New York, Viking Press, 1973. 369p. $12.50.
This work consists largely of a number of articles published or presented to various scholarly bodies over the last few years. The articles have been updated by the inclusion of additional material. At the heart of the book is the author's account of the 1970 Leningrad trial for the attempted hijacking of a Soviet plane, and the subsequent, related trials in Kishinev and Riga. These marked the zenith of the official Soviet attempt to crush the renaissance of Jewish national feeling in the USSR. But the trials had unwelcome repercussions and intensified the movement to such a degree that only a complete return to Stalinist repression could have stopped it.
             SR, 34:3:614-5   R: Lionel Kochan

1224.   Rubin, Ronald I., ed. **The Unredeemed: Anti-Semitism in the Soviet Union**. Foreword by Abraham J. Heschel. Chicago, Quadrangle Books, (1968). 317p. $10.00.
This is a valuable collection of essays, documents, and eyewitness accounts, all bearing on the precarious position of Jews in the Soviet Union. Among contributing essays one will find of special value M. Decter's "The Status of the Jews in the Soviet Union," "Passover and Matzoh—A Case History of Soviet Policy," and W. Korey's "Soviet Law and the Jews."
             SR, 28:4:666-7   R: Israel Getzler

1225.   Samuel, Maurice. **Blood Accusation: The Strange History of the Beiliss Case**. New York, Knopf, 1966. 286p. $5.95.
The author offers some significant historical insights. From a painstaking examination of the court record he delineates a satisfying, human account of the uncertainty, apprehension, and confusion of the defense and the almost natural involvement of the regime in a major conspirative effort. Beiliss himself is presented as a relatively insignificant figure in the entire proceeding as his contemporaries saw him. And the essential lack of clarity in the verdict on the blood-guilt charge becomes apparent.
             SR, 28:3:489-90   R: Alfred Levin

1226.   Schroeter, Leonard. **The Last Exodus**. New York, Universe Books, 1974. 432p. $10.95.
Schroeter's book in many respects is a pioneering work. Although the dissident movement, and particularly some of its outstanding figures, have known wide public attention, scholarly and systematic research on the subject is lacking, partly because of the inadequacy of sources. The author has used an impressive collection of Soviet underground *samizdat* publications, personal interviews, official and semi-official Soviet and Western publications, and Western news media, as well as his direct contacts with many of the people in the Jewish movement. The result is a book that for the first time provides an extensive account of the awakening and the activities of the Jewish national movement in the Soviet Union. In a sense *The Last Exodus* is a collection of case studies

of persons and small groups who triggered a mass movement. He provides illuminating examples of the transition from assimilation to the defining of national self-affirmation that many Soviet Jews have gone through in the last few years.

SR, 34:2:402   R: Ben-Cion Pinchuk

1227.   Shaffer, Harry G. **The Soviet Treatment of Jews.** New York, Praeger, 1974. 232p. (Praeger Special Studies in International Politics and Government). $13.50.

This book does offer a commendably objective analysis of the facts presented, concentrating on the Brezhnev-Kosygin era. Shaffer deals with such topics as the identity of anti-Semitism and anti-Zionism, the treatment of Judaism as a religion, discrimination in education and employment facilities, and their right to emigrate.

SR, 34:3:614-5   R: Lionel Kochan

PART III

EASTERN EUROPE
(INCLUDING THE GDR
AND THE BALKAN PENINSULA)

Chapter 10

East European Countries—General Studies

GENERAL REFERENCE WORKS

1228.   Blejwas, Stanislaus A., comp. and ed. **East Central European Studies: A Handbook for Graduate Students (A Preliminary Edition)**. Columbus, Ohio, American Association for the Advancement of Slavic Studies, 1973. 301p. $6.00pa.

The handbook includes a collection of essays by prominent scholars and a guide to research resources and reference aids, professional sources and services. Also provided is a list of major libraries, archives, and institutions in the United States and abroad; special research centers are identified according to country of specialization. Of particular interest is the inclusion of Jewish and Ukrainian studies.   S. M. H.

1229.   Carlton, Robert G., ed. **Newspapers of East Central and Southeastern Europe in the Library of Congress**. Slavic and Central European Division, Reference Department, Library of Congress. Washington, D. C., 1965. 204p. $1.00.

This mimeographed bibliography of nearly 800 titles represents the Library of Congress holdings of newspapers published after the First World War in Albania, the Baltic States (from 1918 to 1940), Bulgaria, Czechoslovakia, Hungary, Poland, Rumania, and Yugoslavia. Details of holdings are given, and there is a list of sources followed by a guide to places of publication, a language index, and an index of titles. Individual titles are numbered.

   SEER, 45:105:577   R: A. Helliwell

1230.   Horecky, Paul L., ed. **East Central Europe: A Guide to Basic Publications**. Chicago, University of Chicago Press, 1970. 956p. $27.50.

1231.   Horecky, Paul L., ed. **Southeastern Europe: A Guide to Basic Publications**. Chicago, University of Chicago Press, 1970. 755p. $25.00.

1232.   Jelavich, Charles, ed. **Language and Area Studies: East Central and Southeastern Europe, A Survey**. Chicago, University of Chicago Press, 1969. 483p. $11.50.

This volume surveys graduate training and needs in the United States, analyzes the present state of undergraduate programs, and reveals the current "state of the art" in at least fifteen disciplines. This task has been undertaken by the nineteen contributors.

   SR, 30:2:457-8   R: Sherman D. Spector

1233.   Krallert-Sattler, Gertrud, ed. **Südosteuropa-Bibliographie. Vol. III: 1956-1960. Part 1: Slowakei, Ungarn, Rumänien.** Munich, R. Oldenbourg, 1964. 519p. DM39.00.

First published in 1956 for the years 1945-50 under the direction of Fritz Valjevec, this bibliography is most useful, for it lists social science, humanities, and some purely scientific literature dealing with all of Socialist Europe except Poland and the Soviet Union. Titles (books and articles) are grouped topically under geographic headings, and the majority, which are in Eastern European languages, are translated into German. It is, however, a selective bibliography.

SR, 26:4:701-2   R: Evelyn G. Lauer

1234.   Krallert-Sattler, Gertrud, ed. **Südosteuropa-Bibliographie. Vol. III: 1956-1960. Part 2: Albanien, Bulgarien, Jugoslawien, Südosteuropa und Grössere Teilräume.** Munich, R. Oldenbourg, 1968. 634p. DM42.00pa.

This volume is an addition to the bibliography the Südost-Institut in Munich has been publishing since 1956 to cover in five-year segments the post-war publications on Southeast Europe. The scope of the bibliography has made it a fundamental tool for scholars concerned with the part of Europe that includes Slovakia, Hungary, Rumania, Yugoslavia, Bulgaria, and Albania. The hefty volumes cover books, articles, and dissertations in all relevant languages. Part 2 of the 1956-60 volume contains 559 entries for Albania, 2,477 for Bulgaria, 5,086 for Yugoslavia, and 901 for the area as a whole. The majority of entries represent, of course, publications from within the countries concerned and herein lies the special value of the bibliography.

SR, 29:2:363-4   R: Marin Pundeff

1235.   Kraus, David H., et al. **National Science Information Systems: A Guide to Science Information Systems in Bulgaria, Czechoslovakia, Hungary, Poland, Rumania, and Yugoslavia.** Cambridge, MIT Press, 1972. 325p. $12.50.

This study of the organizational aspect of national information systems in six East European countries is divided into two parts. The first three sections present an overview of the common characteristics of the six national systems. The remaining sections provide brief but detailed accounts of the national information systems of the individual countries. Each chapter describes the development, organization, and education programs of the national system, a directory of the country's information centers, a list of publications of these centers, and a brief bibliography. This detailed work is important for the researcher and student of East European affairs.   S. M. H.

1236.   **Selected Lists of Central and East European Periodicals Reviewing Western Publications: Albania, Austria, Bulgaria, Czechoslovakia, Finland, German Democratic Republic, Hungary, Poland, Romania, Switzerland, Yugoslavia.** Foreword by George Barany. Columbus, Ohio, Pub. by Association of American University Presses for the American Association for the Advancement of Slavic Studies, 1974. 72p. $5.00. Order from: Ellen Noble, Exec. Asst., Association of American University Presses, One Park Avenue, New York, N.Y. 10016.

GEOGRAPHY

1237.   Hoffman, G. W., ed. **Eastern Europe: Essays in Geographical Problems.**
London, Methuen, 1971. 502p. £5.00.
This volume is a collection of ten papers presented at a conference on East-
Central and Southeast European geography at Austin, Texas, in April 1969.
Hoffman has prepared his own regional synthesis as an introduction, and has
included the prepared comments and spontaneous remarks following each
presentation, and numerous statistical tables and maps. Further, each author
and commentator is briefly identified, and a list of the conference participants
is given. The varied subjects of the papers reflect the interest and work of
British and American scholars on Eastern Europe, an area long neglected by
Western geographers. The chapters are of considerable value in supplementing
the few textbooks of this part of Europe. This work reflects the role of ideology
in shaping or changing the cultural landscape and man's participation within it.
SEER, 51:122:153-5   R: F. W. Carter

1238.   Osborne, R. H. **East-Central Europe: An Introductory Geography.**
New York, Praeger, 1967. 384p. $7.50.
After two introductory chapters, which examine "The Peoples" and "The
Geographical Background," the author takes up the East European countries
in alphabetical order, from Albania to Rumania. After a short introduction he
sketches what he terms the "historical background," and he follows this with
descriptive accounts of the land, climate, soils, agriculture, industry, population,
transportation, and trade. The detail is immense, and the level of accuracy is
high. This compendium of geographical information on Eastern Europe is a
very useful one to have, and it will be widely used as a reference work. It is as
a factual and descriptive survey that this book is to be recommended.
SR, 27·3·497-8   R: Norman J. G. Pounds

HISTORY

1239.   Bannan, Alfred J., and Achilles Edelenyi. **Documentary History of
Eastern Europe.** New York, Twayne Publishers, 1970. 392p. $7.50.
The purpose of this book is to provide a collection of source materials on
Eastern Europe (excluding USSR) "from the first Slavic invasion before 1000A.D.
to the Czech Crisis of 1968," which could be used "for a comprehensive undergraduate course." The need for such a collection is obvious to anyone who
teaches in this area. There are 88 sources, including selections from chronicles,
law codes, constitutions, treaties, letters, travel accounts, and analyses by
scholars of events, episodes, or periods of history.
SR, 31:3:702   R: Charles Jelavich

1240.   Brown, J. F. **The New Eastern Europe: The Khrushchev Era and After.**
New York, Praeger, 1966. 306p. $2.25pa.
Brown examines in detail the decade that followed 1956 events in Eastern
Europe, by individual countries, describing political, economic, cultural, and
diplomatic events. Well written, this book is probably the best single effort of

this kind since the publication of Seton-Watson's *East European Revolution* (1951) and then being updated by Joseph Rothchild's *A History of East Central Europe* (1974).

SR, 26:2:326-8   R: R. V. Burks

1241.   Carsten, F. L. **Revolution in Central Europe, 1918-1919.** Berkeley, University of California Press, 1972. 360p. $11.95.

For the German-speaking lands the research in this study is based mainly on all the major archival collections; for Hungary and Czechoslovakia it is based mainly on secondary sources in Western languages. Conclusions are drawn sharply and frequently.

SR, 31:4:914-5   R: Istvan Deak

1242.   Deak, Sinian I., and P. C. Ludz, eds. **Eastern Europe in the 1970's.** New York, Praeger, 1972. 260p. $15.00.

The essays in this volume were prepared for a conference, "New Perspectives in Understanding East Central Europe," held at Columbia University in 1971. The papers are by scholars from many nations, and after each paper are a number of analyses by yet other international scholars. Essays cover politics, economy, international relations, nationalism, etc.

CSP, 15:4:622   R: Anne Woodbridge

1243.   Fejtö, François. **A History of the People's Democracies: Eastern Europe since Stalin.** Trans. by Daniel Weissbort. New York, Praeger, 1971. 374p. $13.50.

This book is a continuation of Fejtö's earlier *Histoire des democraties populaires* (1952). Taken together, the two volumes span the history of Eastern Europe from 1945 through 1970, covering every aspect of the life of the Communist regimes—the social and cultural, as well as the political and economic. The work reveals a voluminous mastery of detail. Fejtö also offers much that is suggestive and exciting in the way of interpretation. He views Chinese influence as a major, if behind-the-scene, factor in East European politics after 1956. Fejtö's new work is a most useful acquisition.

SR, 31:3:702-3   R: R. V. Burks

1244.   Heymann, Frederick G. **Poland and Czechoslovakia.** Englewood Cliffs, N.J., Prentice-Hall, 1966. 181p. (The Modern Nations in Historical Perspective. Spectrum Books). $4.95cl.; $1.95pa.

Heymann has gained reputation as an author of two comprehensive monographs on problems of late medieval Bohemia. But he is just as familiar with Polish history as with that of the Czechs and Slovaks. When referring to sources of tensions that marred the attempts to coordinate the foreign policies of Poland and Czechoslovakia between 1918 and 1938, he writes with discretion to balance conflicting points of views. His brief description of Poland under the Nazi heel and his sympathetic comment on Polish revival and reconstruction can be counted among the finest passages of this book.

AHR, 72:4:1444   R: Otakar Odlozilik

1245.   Hösch, Edgar. **The Balkans: A Short History from Greek Times to the Present Day**. Trans. from the German by Tania Alexander. London, Faber&Faber, 1972. 213p. $13.75.
The book presents the Balkan peninsula from historical and geographical points of view. In a territory where many people have different traditions, the formation of a political unit based on the idea of "nation" poisoned the atmosphere and had disastrous consequences. The author points out that this led to the artificial creation of new states in a milieu where geography does not provide a natural impulse for the political unification of the peninsula. The book explains the cultural influences on the area: Byzantine culture; Italo-Slav Adriatic culture; Central Europen influences in the northern area. This work is a fine example of a concise but comprehensive history of juxtaposed nationalities, cultures, religions and social customs. It certainly aids in a better understanding of this troubled area of the world and is an important contribution to the history of the Balkan peninsula.
　　　　　　CSP, 15:1-2:225-7　　　　　　R: Charles Wojatsek

1246.   Jelavich, Charles and Barbara Jelavich. **The Balkans**. Englewood Cliffs, N.J., Prentice-Hall, 1965. 148p. $4.95.
Two themes run through this work as the authors survey the complex history of the Balkans: a nationalism that imposed a history of conflicts upon the area, and the great powers' repeated intervention in its history. Whether during the centuries of the absolutist Ottoman rule, or during the struggle for national independence, or during the short interwar period of full statehood, or the contemporary era of profound political and social changes—throughout history these two forces, nationalism and big-power intervention, served at one time or another either as factors of constructive growth and encouragement or as elements of political fragmentation and economic retardation.
　　　　　　SR, 25:3:547-8　　　　　　R: Josef Korbel

1247.   Jelavich, Charles, and Barbara Jelavich, eds. **The Balkans in Transition: Essays on the Development of Balkan Life and Politics since the Eighteenth Century**. Hamden, Conn., Archon Books, Shoe String Press, 1974 (1963). 451p. $15.00.
This volume includes most of the papers presented in the summer of 1960 to a conference attended by 75 scholars specializing in Balkan studies. The aim of the volume is to find common features which characterize the development of the entire Balkan region from the middle of the eighteenth century to the present, moving away from the regional and nationalistic approaches that have so far dominated Balkan studies. Those who wish to read a good introduction to the problems of the Balkans will find this book to be an almost ideal choice, because it offers a fresh approach to familiar problems.
　　　　　　SR, 33:3:593-4　　　　　　R: Peter F. Sugar

1248.   Lendvai, Paul. **Eagles in Cobwebs: Nationalism and Communism in the Balkans**. Garden City, N.Y., Doubleday, 1969. 396p. $6.95.
Lendvai offers a sophisticated analysis of the Balkan's oldest and most endemic political problem: the irrepressible force of nationalism. The central theme of the book is clearly stated: "The Balkans have been a traditional storm center.

The twin assault of a Communist takeover and Soviet domination has not 'solved' the national problem. On the contrary, it has intensified national animosities." The author concentrates on the Yugoslav, Albanian, and Rumanian case studies of dissidence and defiance, showing almost conclusively that the rise of nationalism has led to a dramatic decline of Soviet influence not only in this region but also (by ideological osmosis) in neighboring countries.

> SR, 29:2:323-4   R: Andrew Gyorgy

1249.   Levine, Herbert S. **Hitler's Free City: A History of the Nazi Party in Danzig, 1925-39.** Chicago, University of Chicago Press, 1973. 223p. $7.50.

In a way, Danzig, as the author of this admirable history of the Free City's Nazi Party puts it, "is a miniature Third Reich." There was the systematic nazification of Danzig's institutions; there was the increasing pressure put on the Jewish community; there was steady radicalization of the leadership. Yet Danzig was different, too, for a modest degree of League of Nations supervision—or at any rate, a pretense of it—remained until the end. Thus Danzig also showed in microcosm what might have happened in Germany had Nazi control been less total. It is a concise book; even its length is exactly right. If we had more like it, history would be in better shape.

> EEQ, 9:2:245-7   R: Joachim Remak

1250.   McClellan, Woodford D. **Svetozar Marković and the Origins of Balkan Socialism.** Princeton, Princeton University Press, 1964. 308p. $7.50.

S. Marković (1856-1875) managed to compress a staggering amount and a stunning intensity of socialist work into his 28 years of life. A parliamentary and economic reformer, a literary critic and political journalist, a socialist theoretist and organizer of cooperatives, a national revolutionary and cosmopolitan intellectual, Marković more than any other individual propelled the education of Serbian youth of his day into the mainstream of European materialism and socialism. In a closely argued and lucidly written study based on wide and deep research in Yugoslav and Soviet archives and libraries, McClellan presents a judicious and intriguing portrait of this bold and magnetic pioneer of Serbian socialism. This is, in sum, a valuable book on an important subject.

> SR, 25:1:162-4   R: Joseph Rothschild

1251.   McNeill, William H. **Europe's Steppe Frontier, 1500-1800.** Chicago, University of Chicago Press, 1964. 252p. $5.50.

In this volume, remarkable both in conception and achievement, McNeill takes a fresh look at the crucial period in the history of Danubia and Pontic Europe. Forming the westernmost extension of the great Asian steppe, this region, roughly covering modern Hungary, Rumania, and the Ukraine, was the frontier where the agricultural settler met the mounted nomad. But this frontier was not static or merely defensive, and during centuries of constant movement it produced a bewildering array of major and minor powers, princes, nations, and tribes. The rivalry between Catholicism and Orthodoxy and the conflict with Islam further complicated the picture. As a result, the traditional historiography of the region has seldom escaped the confinement of nationalism and religious hatreds. The author's presentation is lucid and judicious, and his arguments most convincing. Without a doubt, it is "must" reading for all students of southeastern Europe.

SR, 24:2:323-3   R: Gunther E. Rothenberg

The author rightly dismisses the validity of simplistic arguments and interpretations and justly explains the popular roots and mass appeal of fascism in Hungary and particularly in Rumania. He recognizes the anti-modernism of the ideologies propounded by men like Szalasi and Codreanu but indicates that this anti-modernism appealed to, and also reflected, the inherent conservatism of the masses with its corollary anti-urban and anti-Semitic ramifications.

EEQ, 5:2:270-2   R: Stephen Fischer-Galati

1252.   Obolensky, Dimitri. **The Byzantine Commonwealth: Eastern Europe, 500-1453**. London, Weidenfeld and Nicolson; New York, Praeger, 1971. 445p. (History of Civilization Series). £4.00; $15.00.

This study is of a great significance for Byzantine and Slavic historians as well as for the general reader for whom the *History of Civilization* series is intended. It is the thesis of Obolensky's study that the political ideas, religion, literature, language, and art transmitted from Byzantine to Europe during the Middle Ages created a universal civilization which may best be described as a "Commonwealth." The "bonds" of the Commonwealth were a belief in the supremacy of the universal emperor, the Orthodox religion, and a Slavic literary culture based largely on translations of Greek religious works. This is a rich book of great importance to students of Slavic history.

SR, 31:3:657-8   R: Dorothy Abrahamse

1253.   Obolensky, Dimitri. **Byzantium and the Slavs: Collected Studies.** Preface by Ivan Dujcev. London, Variorum Reprints, 1971. 408p. $22.00.

This is a collection of works originally published in various periodicals and collections in the years 1945 to 1967. The studies are arranged in four thematic sections representing the main spheres of the author's scholarly activity: Byzantium and Eastern Europe, Byzantium and Russia, Cyril and Methodius, and the dualist movement in Eastern Europe. Altogether there are thirteen studies probing into the history and culture of the South Slavic lands and Kiev Rus'.

SEEJ, 18:2:178-9   R: F. Svejkovský

1254.   Orlow, Dietrich. **The Nazis in the Balkans: A Case Study of Totalitarian Politics**. Pittsburgh, University of Pittsburgh Press, 1968. 235p. $7.50.

This book represents a careful scholarly attempt to examine a single organizational expression of Nazi intrusion into the Balkans. In fact, the author deals only with the history of one organization, the *Südosteuropa-Gesellschaft*, as an example of the extension of Nazi foreign policy in the Balkans. The author provides us with many valuable theoretical insights into the functioning of bureaucratic systems. The work contributes to our knowledge of the functioning of Nazi bureaucratic machinery and of the strategy of "unofficial" German intrusion into the Balkans.

AHR, 75:4:1151-2   R: M. George Zaninovich

1255.   Ristelhueber, René. **A History of the Balkan Peoples.** Ed. and trans. by Sherman David Spector. New York, Twayne Publishers, 1971. 470p. $7.50.

With all its drawbacks this French study is still the best obtainable. Not only does it have the bulk of the central themes reasonably clear, but it manages to include an enormous number of special terms and to put over a whole series of subtleties in an amazingly restricted space. No serious student can put it down without having acquired a meaningful knowledge of the ethnic clashes, religious complications, and power politics of the area over the centuries. The interwar chapters reach an impressive level of achievement.

AHR, 80:5:1361   R: Michael Hurst

1256.   Rothschild, Joseph. **East Central Europe between the Two World Wars.** Seattle, University of Washington Press, 1974. 420p. (A History of East Central Europe, vol. 9). $14.95cl.; $7.95pa.

The editors of the series state that the task to be accomplished in eleven volumes is to provide "the scholar who does not specialize in East Central European history and the student who is considering such specialization with an introduction to the subject and a survey of knowledge deriving from previous publications." Rothschild had been assigned to write a history of the interwar period of all countries between the Baltic Sea and Greece, with only a brief discussion of the Baltic states. The author chose a mixture of handbook and interpretative monograph, which proved to be the right approach, though with some unavoidable difficulties (as in the selection of the subjects most characteristic in a given country). The book is destined to become trendsetting and controversial at the same time. Its intention, structure, methodology, and a general overview are summarized in a 25-page introduction, followed by condensed chapters on ten states.

S. M. H.

1257.   Seton-Watson, Robert W. **The Southern Slav Question and the Habsburg Monarchy.** New York, Fertig, 1969 (1911). 463p. $14.00.

(Listed in P. Horecky's *Southeastern Europe*, #2384). R. Seton-Watson, who is considered the foremost British authority on the Balkan Peninsula, provides valuable information on the Zagreb and Friedjung trials. This volume, together with the author's other works, belongs on the shelves of academic libraries of any size.   S. M. H.

1258.   Stoianovich, Traian. **A Study in Balkan Civilization.** New York, Knopf, 1967. 222p. $2.95pa.

The publication of this volume adds to the helpful collection of paperbacks that can be used for courses dealing with the Balkans. However, unlike the Jelaviches' *The Balkans* (1965), Stavrianos' *The Balkans, 1815-1914* (1963), or Hoffman's *The Balkans in Transition* (1963), it is neither conventional history nor, like Hoffman's work, a geographical and developmental survey, although it combines elements of both. This is a provocative book with too many ideas for its brief compass. But despite these faults Stoianovich is original, creative, and even daring—adjectives that fit relatively few contemporary academics.

SR, 28:2:330-1   R: Joel M. Halpern

1259.   Sugar, Peter F., and Ivo J. Lederer, eds. **Nationalism in Eastern Europe**. Seattle, University of Washington Press, 1969. 465p. (Far Eastern and Russian Institute Publications on Russia and Eastern Europe, no. 1). $15.00.

The volume concentrates on the history of nationalism in the nineteenth and twentieth centuries, and contains separate chapters on each one of the East European countries: Albania (T. Zavalani), Bulgaria (M. Pundeff), Czechoslovakia (J. Zacek), Greece (S. Zydis), Hungary (G. Barany), Rumania (S. Fischer-Galati), and Yugoslavia (I. Lederer). In addition, P. Sugar supplies a comprehensive overview of "External and Domestic Roots of Eastern Nationalism." There is no separate bibliography, but each chapter is provided with footnotes containing bibliographical information. The writing is clear and concise, the tone is moderate, the quality even.

SR, 29:1:719-21   R: Stanley Z. Pech

1260.   Van Creveld, Martin L. **Hitler's Strategy, 1940-1941: The Balkan Clue.** London, Cambridge University Press, 1973. 248p. $16.25.

The author has produced a detailed, informative analysis of "the Balkan clue" to Hitler's strategy in 1940-1941. The interpretation is supported by impressive documentation, including German and Italian military sources, although there are inevitable gaps in the masonry. While recognizing the deep roots of the plan to invade the Soviet Union, the author sees Hitler under the influence of a transitory "peripheral" strategy in the Mediterranean during most of the second half of 1940. This represented an attempted continuation of the German offensive against Britain after it became evident that a direct assault on the British Isles was no longer feasible in the summer of that year. In the final analysis, the Balkans became to Hitler what the "Spanish ulcer" had been to Napoleon.

CSP, 16:4:650-1   R: T. Murray Hunter

1261.   Wolff, Robert Lee. **The Balkans in Our Time.** Cambridge, Harvard University Press, 1974 (1956, 1967). 647p. $15.00.

During World War II the author served in the Balkan division of the Office of Strategic Services and undertook three trips to various parts of the Balkans. His narrative is based on his own observation and background knowledge and tells mainly about Yugoslavia, Rumania, and Bulgaria. In the 1974 edition almost two-third of the text is given to detailed discussion of developments from 1939 to the late 1960s. The book is recommended to the student and lay reader for general information relating to events in the Balkans since the beginning of World War II.   S. M. H.

GOVERNMENT AND POLITICS

1262.   Gati, Charles, ed. **The Politics of Modernization in Eastern Europe: Testing the Soviet Model.** New York, Praeger, 1974. 389p. $22.50.

This book is based on a conference held at Columbia University in March 1973. For the most part Gati's book is a success. There has been an attempt to offer both comparative and thematic articles such as those by C. E. Black, V. V. Aspaturian, R. Sharlet, Z. Y. Gitelman, R. Kanet, I. Volgyes, and W. E. Griffith and case studies such as those by Gati (Hungary), O. Ulc (Czechoslovakia), T. Gilberg (Romania) and L. Cohen (Yugoslavia). This book is a timely and thoughtful work which is likely to be basic for any future research.

      CSP, 17:2-3:530-41   R: Alan Whitehorn

1263.   Mastny, Vojtech, ed. **East European Dissent.** Vol. 1: *1953-1964.*
            Vol. 2: *1965-1970.* New York, Facts on File, 1972. 292p. $4.95ea.,
            $8.95/set pa.
The two volumes contain a collection of documents revealing the existence of dissent and covering the years 1953 through 1970. The editor has included not only typical expressions of dissent but also all forms of opposition, including armed uprising. The material, chronologically arranged, is taken from *Facts on File*. There is no attempt to analyze events. The collection will enable the student to examine first-hand information, which he can then put in proper perspective by reading monographs discussing these events.

                                      S. M. H.

1264.   Nagy-Talavera, Nicholas M. **The Green Shirts and the Others: A History**
            of Fascism in Hungary and Romania. Stanford, Hoover Institution
            Press, 1970. 427p. $9.95.
The author devotes about two-thirds of the study to fascism in Hungary, placing the movement and its ideologists and practitioners in the proper historic perspective. The most significant contribution made by the author is his attempt to find parallels between the two movements and to ascribe certain qualities to them in terms different from the conventional dismissal of fascism as an unrepresentative, freak political phenomenon in Eastern Europe.

1265.   Roberts, Henry L. **Eastern Europe: Politics, Revolution, and Diplomacy.**
            New York, Knopf, 1970. 352p. $6.95.
This book is a compilation of essays written by Roberts during various phases of his career; thus, it reflects the range of his substantive interests. The principal utility and relevance of the book is its contribution in documenting the intellectual history of a major scholar in the Slavic field.

      SR, 30:3:678   R: M. George Zaninovich

1266.   Staar, Richard F. **The Communist Regimes in Eastern Europe.** 2nd
            rev. ed. Stanford, Hoover Institution Press, 1971 (1967). 304p. $3.95pa.
Although this little reference book presents hardly anything new, it remains quite a useful volume, introducing the reader to the basic political, social, and economic factors influencing the development and course of eight East European satellites. Recapping post-1945 history, Staar deals, country by country, with the current situations in these countries; for each country he explains how the Communist Party came to control and how Party decisions are implemented. Numerous tables show trends from 1945 to 1967 and are updated

in the second edition to 1970, in politics, the economy, and other important features of national life. It is quite a handy reference work for a general reader and student interested in that part of Europe.

UQ, 24:4:377-8   R: Joseph S. Roucek

1267.   Sugar, Peter F., ed. **Native Fascism in the Successor States, 1918-1945.** Intro. by Lyman H. Legters. Santa Barbara, American Bibliographic Center—Clio Press, 1971. 166p. $9.50cl.; $4.50pa.
These papers were originally prepared for a conference sponsored by the Graduate School of the University of Washington in April 1966. Contributors were: Fritz Fellner and R. John Rath (Austria); Jan Havranek and Joseph F. Zacek (Czechoslovakia); György Ranki and George Barany (Hungary); Henryk Wereszycki and Piotr S. Wandycz (Poland); Emanuel Turczynski and Stephen Fischer-Galati (Rumania); and Dimitrije Djordjević and Ivan Avakumovic (Yugoslavia).

SR, 31:3:709-10   R: Nicholas M. Nagy-Talavera

FOREIGN POLICY

1268.   Byrnes, Robert F., ed. **The United States and Eastern Europe.** Englewood Cliffs, N.J., Prentice-Hall, 1967. 179p. $4.95cl.; $1.95pa.
The selection of Eastern Europe for discussion at the Thirty-first American Assembly, held in April 1967, reflects a current, somewhat fashionable preoccupation with a part of the world about which in the words of Byrnes, "the ignorance of the American people . . . is colossal." The contributors know their subject, and one will find among them S. Kertesz, A. Rubinstein, N. Spulber, R. Burks, K. London, J. Campbell, and finally Byrnes himself. They write on the land and peoples in history, politics and political change, economic modernization, social forces and cultural change, Eastern Europe in the Communist world, Europe, East and West, and American opportunities and dilemmas.

SR, 28:1:157-8   R: Paul Zinner

1269.   Campbell, John C. **American Policy toward Communist Eastern Europe: The Choices Ahead.** Minneapolis, University of Minnesota Press, 1965. 136p. $4.50.
Campbell brings into the picture the question of Germany and its paramount importance to developments in Eastern Europe. He also attaches greater importance to the revival of nationalism. Analyzing Poland and Yugoslavia as special cases in Communist development, Campbell then turns to a review of American foreign policy toward Eastern Europe, discussing its passage through the phase of containment, to declarations of liberation, and since Eisenhower's second administration, to a policy of gradualism. With sound judgment he presents various alternatives which may be pursued at the diplomatic, cultural, economic, and military levels.

SR, 25:3:547-9   R: Josef Korbel

1270.   Harris, David. **A Diplomatic History of the Balkan Crisis of 1875-1878: The First Year.** Hamden, Conn., Archon Books, 1969 (1936). 474p. $13.50.

This well-written book, fortified with numerous footnotes containing a wealth of additional material, has proven its value over a long period of time. It deals with a brief but critical period of the Balkan Peninsula's diplomatic history, which was followed by another Russo-Turkish war, the St. Stefano Treaty, and finally by the Congress of Berlin. Most recently published works have little to add to this exhaustive study.   S. M. H.

1271.   Helmreich, Ernst Christian. **The Diplomacy of the Balkan Wars, 1912-**
          1913. New York, Russell & Russell, 1969 (1938). 523p. $15.00.
The main value of this study lies in the fact that the author obtained valuable information from personal interviews with numerous statesmen whose policy affected either directly or indirectly the Blakan wars. As such the book remains a valuable contribution to the subject, and its reprint will be appreciated by the student of East European affairs.   S. M. H.

1272.   Iatrides, John O. **Balkan Triangle: Birth and Decline of an Alliance**
          across Ideological Boundaries. The Hague, Mouton, 1968. 211p.
          (Studies in European History, vol. 12). 35Dglds.
This study gives a general description of the relations between Yugoslavia, Greece and Turkey, which culminated in the treaties of Ankara (February 28, 1953) and Bled (August 9, 1954), the former being a treaty of friendship and collaboration and the latter a pact of alliance. The primary factor in the 1954 rapprochement was the fear of aggression from the Soviet Union or her East European satellites. Articles 2 and 5 of the treaty provide for mutual assistance in case of an attack against any one signatory, with mutual consultations to follow immediately. With whatever expectation the alliance had been formed, within one year the realities of political and national antagonism had rendered it ineffectual.
          SR, 28:4:655-6   R: William Peter Kaldis

1273.   Kovrig, Bennett. **The Myth of Liberation: East-Central Europe in**
          U.S. Diplomacy and Politics since 1941. Baltimore, Johns Hopkins
          University Press, 1973. 360p. $11.50.
The worth of this book is not in puncturing a myth but in analyzing its place in the continuing evolution of U.S. policy on East Central Europe over a quarter-century. Despite the existence of a large body of writing on the subject, there has long been a need for a cool and comprehensive account, and Kovrig has now written it. The book deals fully with the Hungarian revolt, less so with the Prague Spring.
          SR, 33:1:158-9   R: John C. Campbell

1274.   Remington, Robin Alison. **The Warsaw Pact: Case Studies in Communist**
          Conflict Resolution. Cambridge, Mass., MIT Press, 1971. 268p. (Studies
          in Communism, Revisionism, and Revolution; formerly Studies in
          International Communism), no. 17]. $10.00.
The book is a study in coalition politics and focuses mainly on three specific examples of conflict (Rumania, Czechoslovakia, and East Germany). Fifteen

documents round out the text. One is impressed with the analysis of the December 1970 crisis in Poland.

> SR, 31:3:703-4　　　　　　R: Richard F. Staar

1275. Whetten, Lawrence C. **Germany's Ostpolitik: Relations between the Federal Republic and the Warsaw Pact Countries.** New York, Oxford University Press, 1971. 244p. $6.50pa.

The purpose of this study is to trace the transition in West German relations with the Warsaw Pact countries by examining the positions of the principal states on the key divisive issues of the two decades–1950-1970. In line with this objective the author surveys the ups and downs of Bonn's *Ostpolitik*, culminating in the signing of the treaties with Moscow and Warsaw in the second half of 1970. The study is largely descriptive.

> SR, 33:3:572　　　　　　R: Andrzej Korbonski

ECONOMICS

1276. Berend, Ivan T., and Gyorgy Ranki. **Economic Development in East-Central Europe in the 19th and 20th Centuries.** New York, Columbia University Press, 1974 (Budapest, 1969). 402p. $18.00.

This translation of a Hungarian-language work has long been awaited by scholars in the field, not only because the original was a distillation of more than a decade of research by Hungary's most distinguished team of economic historians and a signal contribution to the literature, but also because of the paucity in English of publications, of whatever quality, on the economic history of East-Central Europe. Despite some transliterational as well as translational lapses, the book remains a very impressive piece of scholarship. Since it is destined to serve for a long time as the definitive work in its area, used often as a reference book, one wishes it had been treated with more care by its publisher.

> CSP, 17:2-3:542-4　　　　　　R: Scott M. Eddie

1277. Bornstein, Morris, ed. **Plan and Market: Economic Reform in Eastern Europe.** New Haven, Yale University Press, 1973. 416p. $15.00.

This is the second volume of essays based on a conference sponsored by the Comparative Economic Program at the University of Michigan (the first volume, edited by A. Eckstein, was *Comparison of Economic Systems*, 1972). The book stresses the methodology of measuring and evaluating system change. It is addressed primarily to the specialist and the graduate student.

> S. M. H.

1278. Gorove, Stephen. **Law and Politics of the Danube: An Interdisciplinary Study.** Foreword by Hans Kohn. The Hague, M. Nijhoff, 1964. 156p. 20.75Dglds. pa.

This is a legal and historical study of the status of navigation on the Danube River. Potentially, it constitutes a great avenue of commerce. However, because of political disagreements among the many countries through which it flows, its full potential for navigation has never been realized. The Danubian Conference was called at Belgrade in 1948 to draft a new Danube Statute. According to

Gorove, by 1960 the volume of traffic had risen to 23.1 million tons. Despite the inclusion of statistical data on traffic, however, the author fails to make clear how the new Danubian Statute functions. This is not an economic and technical study, but a political and legal one.

SR, 26:3:499-500   R: Victor S. Mamatey

1279.   Grossman, Gregory, ed. and intro. **Money and Plan: Financial Aspects of East European Economic Reforms**. Berkeley, University of California Press, 1968. 188p. $6.00.

This collection of seven essays grew out of a Workshop on Communist Money and Finance held at Berkeley in December 1966. Essays deal with the following countries: Poland (A. Brzeski); USSR (J. Montias); Hungary (J. Fekete); Czechoslovakia (P. Pesek and V. Halešovský). E. Babitchev analyzes the so-called Comecon bank, and G. Garvy together with G. Grossman offer an extensive introduction. This is a valuable book.

SR, 29:1:719   R: John Farrell

1280.   Kaser, Michael, and Janusz G. Zielinski. **Planning in East Europe: Industrial Management by the State; A Background Book**. London, The Bodley Head, 1970. 184p. $4.95.

This is a background book, according to its own subtitle, and it offers, in small type and unencumbered with footnotes, a succinct and precise description of the East European systems before and after the reforms of the mid-1960s, from central planning to worker consultation, via tiers of authority, finances, price-setting, and success criteria for management. Any student working in this general area should be acquainted with this valuable study, where he will find the most important facts he will need for further analysis.

SR, 31:1:238   R: J. M. Montias

1281.   Pryor, Frederic L. **Public Expenditures in Communist and Capitalist Nations**. Homewood, Ill., Richard Irwin Press, 1968. 543p. $8.50.

The stated purpose of the study is to ascertain the determinants of public expenditures in both intertemporal and interspatial dimensions. The main expenditure categories analyzed are military, welfare, health, and educational outlays. Briefer consideration is given to expenditures for research and development, administration, internal security, and foreign economic assistance. Seven market and seven centrally planned economies in Europe and North America are compared, with Yugoslavia classified within the market grouping. Trends and levels of expenditures are examined with respect to behavioral properties of substitution, centralization, stability, and incidence. The author uses both deductive and inductive analytical techniques. Pryor has clarified understanding of a vital sphere of economic life and cleared the road for future research endeavors in the field.

SR, 28:3:507-8   R: Stanley H. Cohn

1282.   Selucky, Radoslav. **Economic Reforms in Eastern Europe: Political Background and Economic Significance**. Trans. by Zdenek Elias. New York, Praeger, 1972. 179p. (Praeger Special Studies in International Economics and Development). $15.00.

This volume, written by one of the leading Czechoslovak reformers, gives the reader a comprehensive picture of all the complex problems involved in a switch-over from an arbitrary command economy to a more rational system geared to the market mechanism. The very fact that the author was an active participant in the seemingly unequal struggle between the would-be reformers and the entrenched party bureaucracy gives additional weight to his arguments.

  SR, 32:3:632-3   R: Michael Gamarnikov

1283.   Spulber, Nicolas. **The State and Economic Development in Eastern Europe**. New York, Random House (1966). 179p. $3.95.
This little book consists of three essays. Two, previously published elsewhere and still overlapping a bit despite revision, deal with the developmental process over a period of a century, 1860 to 1960. The third is a comparison of Rumania and Indonesia, showing some striking similarities, especially in the role played by "outsiders," the Jews in the former and the Chinese in the latter. The author covers the postwar period in Eastern Europe only briefly, summarizing his much more detailed study of *The Economics of Communist Eastern Europe* (1957). He does not discuss the recent reforms.

  SR, 26:3:497-8   R: John C. Campbell

NATIONAL MINORITIES

1284.   Chary, Frederick B. **The Bulgarian Jews and the Final Solution, 1940-1944**. Pittsburgh, University of Pittsburgh Press, 1972. 246p. $9.95.
This book is not only a welcome contribution to the literature on East European Jews but also the first in-depth study on the fate of the Bulgarian Jews. This heavily documented study revolves around the principal question, "Who saved the Bulgarian Jews?" Despite the author's ability to collect a mass of information, his conclusions are unclear; he refuses to give credit where credit is due—for example, to the Bulgarian Orthodox Church and to the countless sincere Bulgarians from top to bottom of the social structure.

  History, RNB, 1:5:106   R: Stephan M. Horak

1285.   King, Robert R. **Minorities under Communism: Nationalities as a Source of Tension among Balkan Communist States**. Cambridge, Harvard University Press, 1973. 326p. $14.00.
The subtitle of this book is more descriptive of its contents than is the main title. King is less interested in the political, cultural, and socioeconomic conditions *per se* of the ethnic minorities in the several Balkan Communist states (including Czechoslovakia and Hungary!) than he is in ascertaining how the relations between a *Staatsvolk* and the ethnic minorities in any particular Communist state become a source of international tension between and among several Communist states. King's thesis is that Communism has not solved the nationality problem in Eastern Europe. Cases of Communist interstate tension which are studied in this book in order to illustrate and confirm its main thesis are the Czechoslovak-Hungarian conflict, the Rumanian-Hungarian controversy, and the Yugoslav-Albanian disagreement.

  SR, 33:4:805-6   R: Joseph Rothschild

1286. Lendvai, Paul. **Anti-Semitism without Jews: Communist Eastern Europe.**
Garden City, N.Y., Doubleday, 1971. 393p. $7.95.
Lendvai's study examines the present conditions and status of Jews in Poland,
Czechoslovakia, Hungary, and Rumania. Despite the enormous numerical de-
crease of Jews since World War II (to about 0.2 percent of the total population),
many of the problems remained, including anti-Semitism in various forms. In
addition to a large number of documents appended, the author offers his own
analysis, which is not entirely supportable by history. Nevertheless, the book
provides a wealth of information for future historians.
S. M. H.

1287. Trunk, Isaiah. **Judenrat: The Jewish Councils in Eastern Europe under
Nazi Occupation.** Intro. by Jacob Robinson. New York, Macmillan,
1972. 664p. $14.95.
The study centers on the question: why and how the Councils (Judenrat) worked
and whether Jewish-Nazi cooperation was decisive in the destruction of European
Jewry. To arrive at an answer to this problem, the author spent five years of
study and research in various Jewish archives in the United States, Israel, and
Germany, in addition to making a personal collection of notes and summaries
of documents assembled in Poland during the years 1946-1950. The notes cover
62 pages. Moreover, Trunk utilized 927 questionnaires that were filled out by
survivors. The author set for himself the task of writing an objective history of
the Councils; his intention was not to pronounce judgment on those institutions,
but rather to probe deeply into the entire complex topic.
UQ, 29:3:306-9   R: Stephan M. Horak

LANGUAGE AND LITERATURE

1288. Gömöri, George, and Charles Newman, eds. **New Writing of East
Europe.** Chicago, Quadrangle Books, 1968. 270p. $6.95.
This book is a loosely structured anthology of poetry, fiction, and essays. The
central theme seems to be a literary vision, not unlike those encountered in
Western literatures but focusing on slightly different areas. It is a sharp vision,
"armed" with the thought of Marx, Freud, and more contemporary thinkers,
but at the same time it is a fragmentary vision, fractured, as it were, by the
realities of war, Nazism, and Communism which intruded upon it. The main
merit of the volume is that it brings writers of various nationalities together in
a brotherhood of common despair.
SR, 29:3:560-1   R: Paul Debreczeny

1289. Kimball, Stanley B. **The Austro-Slav Revival: A Study of Nineteenth-
Century Literary Foundations.** Philadelphia, American Philosophical
Society, 1973. 83p. $4.00pa.
The study focuses on the literary foundations of the Serbs, Croats, Slovenes,
Czechs, and Slovaks; three lesser foundations—those of the Poles, Ukrainians,
and Lusatian Serbs—are treated in an appendix. The main theme is the survey

of the vital role language and literature played in the various Austro-Slav national revivals, and especially how the early literary institutions promoted this process.

NP, 2:2:87-8 R: Joseph S. Roucek

FINE ARTS

1290. Blumenfeld, Yorick. **Seesaw: Cultural Life in Eastern Europe**. New York, Harcourt, Brace & World, 1968. 276p. $5.95.

The title of this book, in a metaphorical way, and the subtitle, in a descriptive way, suggestively convey its content. It shows how the cultural activity in the Communist-dominated part of the European continent is in constant motion: toward total subservience by the governing political power, toward freedom of artistic and intellectual self-examination, self-discovery, and self-expression on the part of the creators, the consumers, and the whole culturally aware intelligentsia. Blumenfeld's spectrum is wide—encompassing literature, all the visual arts, music, theater, film, mass media, as well as philosophy. The study embraces all countries belonging to the socialist bloc. It makes good supplementary reading for any student of Slavic literatures and civlizations.

SR, 29:4:722-3 R: Tymon Terlecki

1291. Weitzman, Kurt, et al. **A Treasury of Icons: Sixth to Seventeenth Centuries—From the Sinai Peninsula, Greece, Bulgaria, and Yugoslavia**. New York, Harry N. Abrams, 1968. 107p. 220 plates. $35.00.

In four separate essays by leading scholars and with 220 illustrations—58 in color—this book introduces a little known but extremely important mode of Byzantine artistic expression, the sacred image or icon. It presents an excellent selection of works and serious evaluations by leading authorities. Because icons and artists moved from area to area, the volume has been organized according to modern geographical boundaries. Selections from the unique cache of icons preserved at the Monastery of St. Catherine on Mt. Sinai illustrate Weitzmann's rich introduction to the theological and artistic bases of Byzantine icon painting. Many works, not published before or recently restored, are included. The plates are large and generally clear; there are numerous details. A catalog and bibliography of the icons completes this volume, which is useful to the scholar and the general audience alike.

SR, 29:3:499-500 R: Herbert L. Kessler

THE SOCIETY

1292. Fischer-Galati, Stephen, ed. **Man, State, and Society in East European History**. New York, Praeger, 1970. 343p. $11.00cl.; $4.95pa.

The book's scope is limited to the period from the fall of Constantinople to the outbreak of World War II. Topically, the distribution (of readings) is: political (including diplomatic and military); cultural (including religion); and socioeconomic. There is a useful bibliography of English-language books. Fischer-Galati mixes historical documentation with explanations by current scholars. These selections are often devoted to generalized analysis of semi-sociological types in keeping with the title *Man, State, and Society*. The selection of primary and secondary texts is generally very good. The book offers students some practical experience with primary materials and gives them a framework for generalization about Eastern Europe.

ECE, 1:2:208-9   R: Daniel Stone

1293.   Grant, Nigel. **Society, Schools and Progress in Eastern Europe**. Oxford, Pergamon Press, 1969. 363p. $7.00pa.

This book is divided into two equal parts, each containing eight chapters. In the first part three chapters are devoted to discussion of the social, political, and historical background of Eastern Europe, and another one to the Marxist theory of education and Soviet educational practice. The remaining chapters in the first part deal with the common characteristics, aims, structure, and control of Communist education in Eastern Europe. The second part discusses the curriculum, structure, and to some extent the overall development of the national systems of education in Poland, East Germany, Czechoslovakia, Hungary, Rumania, Yugoslavia, Bulgaria, and Albania from their prewar antecedents to the mid-1960s. The book provides a reasonably good introductory text, and to some extent even a reference source. It contains over forty tables of contemporary courses of study, diagrams of national school systems, and an extensive glossary.

SR, 31:1:210   R: Ginutis Procuta

1294.   Gutkind, E. A., ed. **Urban Development in East-Central Europe: Poland, Czechoslovakia, and Hungary**. Ed. by Gabriele Gutkind. New York, Free Press; London, Collier-Macmillan, 1972. 339p. (International History of City Development, vol. 7). $25.00.

1295.   Gutkind, E. A., ed. **Urban Development in Eastern Europe: Bulgaria, Romania, and the U. S. S. R.** Ed. by Gabriele Gutkind. New York, Free Press; London, Collier-Macmillan, 1972. 457p. (International History of City Development, vol. 8). $19.95.

The two volumes represent a collective work of leading Polish, Czechoslovak, Hungarian, Bulgarian, Romanian, and Soviet authorities on the subject. The books seek to describe and analyze the origins and development of towns. At the end of each volume is a long list of bibliographic sources, mainly writings of the twentieth century, which examine the field of town evolution from many angles. They are indispensable for current field work by the geographer in the region, for they bring together much material that is scattered in many sources and in many places.

SR, 33:3:562-3   R: F. E. Ian Hamilton

1296.   Jackson, George D., Jr. **Comintern and Peasant in East Europe 1919-1930**. New York, Columbia University Press, 1966. 339p. $8.50.

The strength of Jackson's monograph is in the presentation of hitherto uncovered information on the interrelationship between the Comintern and the Communist parties of the area, on the development of Moscow's peasant strategy and the serious differences in Moscow over some of the substantive aspects of that strategy, and on the activities of Krestintern, the "Red Peasant International." The major theme of the book is the development of Comintern policy toward the agrarian movements in Bulgaria, Polan, Yugoslavia, Rumania, and

Czechoslovakia (Hungary is left out). Through Krestintern, Moscow's policy was to challenge the agrarians' populist ideology, one which the author considers "new and original."

SR, 27:1:155-7   R: Charles Gati

1297.   Scott, Hilda. **Does Socialism Liberate Women?: Experiences from Eastern Europe.** Boston, Beacon Press, 1974. 240p. $7.95.
The book is a rather thorough documentation of the author's negative answer to the question in the title. Chapter 1, which describes the situation in present-day Czechoslovakia, serves as an introduction. Chapters 2 and 3 provide an interesting discussion of socialist ideas about women from Marx and Engels onward. Chapters 4 to 9 deal with the status of women as it has developed in Eastern Europe, and particularly in Czechoslovakia, since World War II. The last chapter states the author's conclusions about the relation between socialism and women's liberation.

SR, 34:3:619-20   R: Marianne A. Ferber

Chapter 11

Individual Countries

ALBANIA

1298. Pano, Nicholas C. **The People's Republic of Albania.** Baltimore,
Johns Hopkins Press, 1968. 185p. $6.50cl.; $2.95pa.
This volume is part of the "Integration and Community Building in Eastern
Europe" series, edited by Jan Triska. It serves well as an introduction to Albanian
modern history and politics, especially to the interested layman and the beginning
student in the field.
       SR, 29:1:127-8   R: Brian O'Connell

1299. Skendi, Stavro. **The Albanian National Awakening, 1878-1912.**
Princeton, Princeton University Press, 1967. 498p. $13.75.
Skendi has reconstructed in this study the complex process (of Albanian national
identity and cohesion) whereby Albanians overcame the factors of fragmentation
and achieved a sense of national needs and interests and, by 1912, independence.
He has handled the subject in three parts—"The Groundwork (1878-1881),"
"The Struggle for National Affirmation (1881-1908)," and "Toward Independence
(1908-1912)"—divided into eighteen chapters and provided with an introduction
("Albania's Legacy") and a "Conclusion." The study is based on far-reaching
research in Austrian, Italian, French, and English archives, the contemporary
press, and secondary sources in relevant languages. Skendi's study should be
greeted as a major event in Albanian historiography.
       SR, 26:4:680-2   R: Marin Pundeff

1300. Thomas, John I. **Education for Communism: School and State in the
People's Republic of Albania.** Stanford, Calif., Hoover Institution
Press, 1969. 131p. $6.50cl.; $2.60pa.
This is a concise technical report on education in Albania since 1944, based
on Albanian sources. In four sections it examines the relevant background
until World War II, the developments to 1961 under Yugoslav and then Soviet
influence, the present structure and operation of the educational system of the
country, and the role of the Communist Party in intramural and extramural
education. The study is supplied with twenty tables providing the necessary
statistics and six figures charting the organizational structure as of 1938, 1946,
1960, and 1969, as well as the lines of administrative authority. A bibliography
(pp. 121-131) lists the sources used. In content, Thomas has found the obvious:
the education in Albania under the Communists has been thoroughly politicized.
       EEQ, 4:2:110-1   R: Marin Pundeff

BULGARIA

General Reference Works

1301. Pundeff, Marin V., ed. **Bulgaria: A Bibliographic Guide**. Washington, D. C., Slavic and Central European Division, Reference Department, Library of Congress, 1965. 98p. $0.55pa. [Reprinted by Arno Press, 1968.] $5.50cl.

This bibliography is divided into two parts: the first is a discussion of sources, grouped into various categories, and the second is an alphabetical listing of all the sources discussed in the previous section. The individual entries contain all the pertinent bibliographical data, including the Library of Congress call numbers. Entries for holdings located in American libraries are followed by the library's symbol, as used in the National Union Catalog.

SR, 28:3:531-3   R: Miroslav Rechcigl, Jr.

Economics

1302. Dobrin, Bogoslav. **Bulgarian Economic Development since World War II**. New York, Praeger, 1973. 186p. $16.50.

Dobrin emphasizes the heavy price the Bulgarian economy has paid for its mindless aping of the Soviet developmental model. The result was a virtual caricature of that model, without the Soviets' compensating physical resources to attenuate the shocks of distorted development. Agriculture was left to stagnate while being forced to provide capital accumulation and labor for industrialization. Yet industrial growth was insufficient to provide employment for all the labor power driven from the farms. There were some genuine achievements in Bulgarian industrialization, but sustained growth became possible only when the country began to stress the production of primary products, for which she had traditionally been best suited.

CSP, 16:4:651-4   R: Robert F. Miller

Government and Politics

1303. Brown, J. F. **Bulgaria under Communist Rule**. New York, Praeger, 1970. 338p. $11.00.

Brown presents in this book a comprehensive account of Communism in Bulgaria in the last two decades. The once volatile Bulgarians have remained politically docile during the last generation. Bulgaria has neither deviated from the political standards set by the Soviet Union nor produced visible internal combustions of any consequence. Her immobilism has left her in the shadows of European politics. The impact of Stalin's death on the Bulgarian Communist hierarchy is well analyzed in Brown's work. It successfully resolved the eternal problem of reconciling the chronological survey with the functional problems of politics. Because of the high quality of scholarship, Brown's book will certainly take its due place alongside the more significant studies on East European politics.

SR, 31:4:933-4   R: Nissan Oren

1304.   Oren, Nissan. **Bulgarian Communism: The Road to Power, 1934-1944.**
         New York, Columbia University Press, 1971. 288p. (East Central
         European Studies of Columbia University and Research Institute on
         Communist Affairs, Columbia University). $12.50.
This volume treats the history of the BCP from the Zveno-Military League coup
in 1934 to the Communist seizure of the Bulgarian government on September 9,
1944. In presenting the party's history within the context of more general political developments in Bulgaria, it illuminates certain themes important to Bulgarian
history as a whole. Considerable attention is given to quarrels over personalities
and tactics. In particular, the complicated conflicts between Communist ideology
and national interests in Southern Dobrudja, Western Thrace, and Macedonia are
presented in a manner that is both succinct and clearly understandable, even
though the author adds little that is new.
         SR, 32:4:848-9   R: Wayne S. Vucinich

1305.   Oren, Nissan. **Revolution Administered: Agrarianism and Communism
         in Bulgaria.** Baltimore, Johns Hopkins University Press, 1973. 204p.
         (Integration and Community Building in Eastern Europe, no. 8).
         $8.50cl.; $4.00pa.
This book offers the most readable short political survey of contemporary
Bulgaria, from the end of World War I to the present. Although based mostly
on previously published research, the product is a powerful and convincing
summary of the rather tragic fate of modern Bulgaria. The main emphasis is
on the conflict between the peasant majority and the Communist minority.
         SR, 33:3:602-3   R: L. A. D. Dellin

1306.   Zhivkov, Todor. **Modern Bulgaria: Problems and Tasks in Building an
         Advanced Socialist Society.** New York, International Publishers, 1974.
         238p. $10.00cl.; $2.75pa.
Zhivkov is the First Secretary of the Central Committee of the Bulgarian
Communist Party and the Chairman of State of the People's Republic of Bulgaria.
The book contains a selection of his speeches of which the most interesting is
the report to the 10th Party Congress of April 20, 1971, entitled "The New Party
Program." The only value of this book lies in the fact that it bring into English
some speeches of the Bulgarian leader, although the dull repetiion of Marxist
phraseology may interest the specialist on contemporary Bulgarian affairs, too.
         S. M. H.

History

1307.   Georgiev, Emil, et al. **Bulgaria's Share in Human Culture.** Sofia,
         Sofia Press, 1968. 129p. 10 col. pl.
A common theme pervades the four articles of this book: the rationalizing,
democratizing, humanizing, and revitalizing effect of the contact between
Byzantine civilization and the South Slavic barbarians. The book thus emerges
as a study of the results of contact between peoples of different cultures or at
different levels of cultural development (Byzantine and Bulgarian). Though
marred by an excessive Bulgarian nationalism, it offers an interesting insight both

into Bulgarian medieval culture and into the image of the past that Bulgarian
elites are striving to communicate to their own people and to the world.
        SR, 29:2:322-3   R: Traian Stoianovich

1308.   Meininger, Thomas A. **Ignatiev and the Establishment of the Bulgarian
        Exarchate, 1864-1872: A Study in Personal Diplomacy.** Madison,
        State Historical Society of Wisconsin for the Department of History,
        University of Wisconsin, 1970. 251p. $3.50.
The establishment of the Bulgarian exarchate involved one of those prolonged
negotiations in which the relations of the two peoples directly concerned—the
Bulgarians and the Greeks, in this case—were greatly complicated by the conflicting interests of the powers—primarily Turkey and Russia, but also Austria-
Hungary, France, Britain, and Prussia. At the center of these negotiations was
Count N. P. Ignatiev, the Russian ambassador in Constantinople. The author
provides a careful and lively account of these negotiations on the basis primarily
of Russian and Bulgarian published sources.
        AHR, 76:4:1186   R: C. E. Black

Language and Literature

1309.   Aronson, Howard I. **Bulgarian Inflectual Morphophonology.** The
        Hague, Mouton, 1968. (Slavistic Printings and Reprintings, 70).
        32Dglds.
This book represents a major contribution to the existing literature on the inflection of contemporary standard Bulgarian. Aronson has given us a concise yet
detailed account of many areas of Bulgarian inflection which were inadequately
described in the previous literature. The combination of a systematic descriptive approach and extensive listings of relevant material makes his book the most
useful single treatment of his subject available in any language.
        SEEJ, 14:3:392-3   R: Joseph A. Van Campen

1310.   Kirilov, Nikolai, and Frank Kirk, eds. **Introduction to Modern
        Bulgarian Literature: An Anthology of Short Stories.** New York,
        Twayne Publishers, 1969. 480p. $6.95.
There are 36 selections from 28 authors, all but five of whom were living at the
time of compilation. The four oldest authors include Vazov, Strashimirov, Pelin,
and Yovkov. On the whole, the collection is quite readable and entertaining,
though the verbosity of Bulgarian writers, noted by Pinto, is in evidence.
        SEEJ, 15:2:231-2   R: James F. Clarke

1311.   Lord, Albert B., and David E. Bynum. **A Bulgarian Literary Reader.**
        The Hague, Mouton, 1968. 200p. 25Dglds.
The introductory essay provides a capsule background of Bulgarian literature
up to the time of Khristo Botev and Ivan Vazov, where the selections begin.
Each selection is preceded by a brief biographical sketch in English. The
introduction and sketches are quite good. The glossary, with its concise introduction, is excellent. It provides not only meanings but all the grammatical
information a student needs: accents, plurals for nouns, verbal conjugations,

phonological alternations, and so forth. The selections themselves are representative both in time and variety, a merit especially noteworthy since the compilers have intentionally not duplicated texts otherwise available, especially those in Vivian Pinto, *Bulgarian Prose and Verse* (London, 1957).
SR, 29:1:761-2   R: James E. Augerot

1312.   Moser, Charles A. **A History of Bulgarian Literature, 865-1944.** The Hague, Mouton, 1972. 286p. (Slavistic Printings and Reprintings, 112). 60Dglds.

A thorough history in English of Bulgarian literature has long been needed. C. A. Manning and Roman Smal-Stocki were the first to attempt to fill this lacuna with their *History of Modern Bulgarian Literature* (1960). Moser's *History* surpasses their work in both comprehensiveness and erudition. It was not until after 1878 that Bulgarian literature began to mature and branch out, as Moser notes. He stresses that Bulgarian literature from 1878 to 1896 was still geared to serve social ends. The last two chapters of the book, dealing with the period 1896-1944, are fascinating as well as unique contributions to the history of Bulgarian letters. The eighteen-page bibliography includes general histories of the periods discussed, as well as monographs on individual Bulgarian writers.
SR, 34:2:450-1   R: Sina Maria Dubowoj

The Society

1313.   Georgeoff, Peter John. **The Social Education of Bulgarian Youth.** Minneapolis, University of Minnesota Press, 1968. 329p. $10.00.

The book consists of two parts: a description and analysis of the social education of Bulgarian youth, and relevant background primary materials in English translation. The author gives a detailed representation of all existing Bulgarian educational institutions, which are modeled mainly on Soviet patterns. However, apart from striking similarities, some of the problems and needs of the Bulgarian educational system are shown to be quite different, thereby justifying this special study. Against this background, the author deals with the social education, defined as the introduction of youth into the traditions, values, mores, ethics, and ideology that characterize Communist society. Social education is examined in all aspects in schools, in the curricula and methods aimed at the preparation of young people as the trained manpower of a Communist society, loyal citizens of the state, and ardent devotees of the party.
SR, 28:4:668   R: Christo Ognjanoff

CZECHOSLOVAKIA

General Reference Works

1314.   Parrish, Michael, ed. **The 1968 Czechoslovak Crisis: A Bibliography, 1968-1970.** Santa Barbara, Cal., American Bibliographical Center— Clio Press, 1971. 41p. $6.00pa.

This is an extensive bibliography of books, pamphlets, monographs, special studies, documents, and journal articles from worldwide sources covering Soviet military intervention in Czechoslovakia in 1968.　S. M. H.

1315.　Rechcigl, Miloslav, Jr., ed. **Czechoslovakia: Past and Present.** Vol. I: *Political, International, Social, and Economic Aspects.* Vol. 2: *Essays on the Arts and Sciences.* Published under the auspices of the Czechoslovak Society of Arts and Sciences in America, Inc. The Hague, Mouton, 1968. 1,889p. 350Dglds.
[All essays contained are listed in: SR, 29:3:567-9.]

1316.　Shawcross, William. **Dubček.** New York, Simon & Shuster, 1970. 317p. $7.95.
The author did an unusual research job inside Czechoslovakia. He interviewed politicians, writers, students, workers, and the family and friends of Alexander Dubček, in addition to reading carefully and judiciously everything available on Dubček or by Dubček himself. The result is an excellent political biography by a first-class British journalist.
　　　　SR, 31:1:222-3　　　　　　R: Stephen Borsody

1317.　Spinka, Matthew. **John Hus: A Biography.** Princeton, Princeton University Press, 1968. 344p. $10.00.
Intended as a companion volume to the author's *John Hus' Concept of the Church* (Princeton, 1966), this book is nevertheless complete in itself, as a presentation of both the life and thought of the Czech reformer, superseding Spinka's *Jan Hus and the Czech Reform* (1941). The story of the Bohemian reform movement, its continuation by Hus, the latter's struggles with ignorant authorities and malicious rivals, and then the great epic of Hus at Constance, his rigged trial and perfect martyrdom—all are set forth with an ardor that will please many.
　　　　SR, 28:4:644-5　　　　　　R: Howard Kaminsky

1318.　Sturm, Rudolf. **Czechoslovakia: A Bibliographic Guide.** Washington, D. C., Library of Congress, 1967. 157p. $1.00pa. [Reprinted by Arno Press, 1968.] $6.00cl.
The bibliography is divided into two parts: the first is a discussion of sources, grouped into various categories, and the second is an alphabetical listing of all the sources discussed in the previous section. The individual entries contain all the pertinent bibliographical data, including the Library of Congress call numbers. Entries for holdings located in American libraries are followed by the library's symbol, as used in the National Union Catalogue.
　　　　SR, 28:3:531-3　　　　　　R: Miloslav Rechcigl, Jr.

Fine Arts

1319.   Kimball, Stanley Buchholz. **Czech Nationalism: A Study of the National Theatre Movement, 1845-83.** Urbana, University of Illinois Press, 1964. 186p. (Illinois Studies in the Social Sciences, vol. 56). $5.00cl.; $4.00pa.

This is essentially a statistical approach to the growth of national consciousness among the Czechs of the Habsburg Monarchy in the nineteenth century. It describes the attempts of successive committees of Czech leaders to organize the building of a Czech National Theater in Prague. The author's carefully prepared lists, tables, and appendixes provide a good index to the quantitative growth of Czech nationalism in the period. The work does provide a substantial body of detailed, well-digested data for students of the history of Bohemia in the nineteenth century.

SR, 24:3:546-7   R: Joseph F. Zacek

1320.   Large, Brian. **Smetana.** New York, Praeger, 1970. 473p. $16.50.

The English-reading public at last possesses a definitive study of the most important and historically significant Czech composer based on manuscript material in Prague, including unpublished diaries, letters, contemporary reviews, and photographs. This fortunate amalgamation makes the book useful on several levels. The casual reader will find whatever information meets his needs or curiosity, thanks to a well-organized presentation. The specialist will discover a wealth of previously unknown material with its exact documentary source. The subject matter is made doubly attractive by well-chosen illustrative plates that provide as much insight as the author's text. Another helpful feature is his summary of the opera plots, especially welcome to English readers.

SR, 30:4:917-8   R: Edith Vogl Garrett

1321.   Rechcigl, Miloslav, Jr., ed. **The Czechoslovak Contribution to World Culture.** The Hague, Mouton, 1964. 682p. 58Dglds.

This huge volume, which is really an encyclopedia as well as a collection of papers, is very valuable. Among many useful surveys of general topics, music in Czechoslovakia from earliest times to the present, painting, political science, engineering until 1940, and various other subjects are swiftly summarized. A second class of papers is the monographic article: for example, the mission of St. Amand in the seventh century, fifteenth century printers in Bohemia, and the Czechoslovak grain monopoly system. A third group comprises essays of opinion and interpretation. Libraries are urged to make certain they have this volume for reference purposes.

SR, 24:3:571-2   R: George Gibian

Economics

1322.   Šik, Ota. **Czechoslovakia: The Bureaucratic Economy.** White Plains, N.Y., International Arts and Sciences Press, 1972. 138p. $10.00.

The greater part of this book is an English translation of the 1968 Czech telecasts by the author, then a member of the Central Committee of the Communist

Party, the deputy premier, and the head of the Commission for Economic Reform in Czechoslovakia. The author, now a professor at the St. Gallen Institute for Economics in Switzerland, severely criticizes Czechoslovakia's economic performance under rigid central planning. He predicts a general return to highly centralized Stalinist planning in the Comecon countries.

        SR, 32:2:409-10   R: Jan M. Michal

1323.   Teichova, Alice. **An Economic Background to Munich: International Business and Czechoslovakia, 1918-1938.** New York, Cambridge University Press, 1974. 422p. $27.50.

This book presents a detailed study of the available foreign capital in the interwar economy of Czechoslovakia. The financial links are extended to foreign interests. Important cartels are studied and analyzed and their influence on output, prices, and foreign trade of the Central and Southeast European states is shown. The work is based on solid research in Czech and other European archives and provides numerous data, statistics and tables. The usefulness of the study is enhanced by an extensive bibliography; it will be most helpful to the student of East European economic affairs.   S. M. H.

1324.   Wright, William E. **Serf, Seigneur, and Sovereign: Agrarian Reform in Eighteenth-Century Bohemia.** Minneapolis, University of Minnesota Press, 1966. 216p. $6.00.

This is the first book in English on Maria Theresa and Joseph II's agrarian reforms in Bohemia. This is therefore a most welcome book, especially as it is written in a lucid and lively style and with admirable clarity and succinctness. In 1740 most Bohemian peasants enjoyed little personal freedom, and those who held land normally did so on very precarious tenures and in return for heavy labor dues. Although Joseph II's last and most ambitious reform, the tax law of 1789, proved abortive, his other (and his mother's) actions had been more successful: by 1790 all Bohemian peasants were personally free, and those on crown and ecclesiastical lands held hereditary leases to their property and owed practically no labor dues. Wright describes, step by step, how this came about.

        SR, 26:4:679-80   R: Emile Karafiol

Government and Politics

1325.   Bittman, Ladislav. **The Deception Game: Czechoslovak Intelligence in Soviet Political Warfare.** Syracuse, N.Y., Syracuse Universtiy Research Corporation, 1972. 246p. $9.95.

The author is fully qualified to impart his knowledge of Czechoslovak and Soviet intelligence work. He served in the Czechoslovak branch for fourteen years, part of them in a high position in D-Department (Department of Disinformation). All activities were closely supervised, and those of special importance were directed by the Soviet Intelligence. Their network, though mainly spread over West Germany, extended the world over—focused as it was on unmasking such American political designs as overthrow of a left-wing government in Indonesia and intrigues in the Congo. The book throws interesting light on the qualities and qualifications of Czechoslovak agents. Luckily, Bittman was in Vienna during the Soviet invasion of Czechoslovakia in 1968 and escaped to the United States. The American reader is now the beneficiary of his deception-game experiences.

        SR, 32:3:642   R: Josef Korbel

1326.   Ello, Paul, comp. **Czechoslovakia's Blueprint for "Freedom": "Unity, Socialism and Humanity," Dubček's Statements—The Original and Official Documents Leading to the Conflict of August, 1968.** Washington, D. C., Acropolis Books, 1969. 304p. $4.95cl.; $2.95pa.
The publication of some of Alexander Dubček's statements on the path of socialism in Czechoslovakia prior to the Warsaw invasion is a significant event. The author insists that the four texts he has chosen provide a "blueprint for the further development of a Socialist political order." The translations themselves are adequate, preserving something of the original style, which is difficult, often obtuse, and replete with the jargon of East European political figures. Ello provides each document with an introduction and an analysis based on the speech itself.

        SR, 29:3:538-9   R: Jack V. Haney

1327.   Golan, Galia. **The Czechoslovak Reform Movement: Communism in Crisis, 1962-1968.** Cambridge, Cambridge University Press, 1971. 349p. $16.50.
This is an amazing feat of scholarship. The author lists and interprets correctly even such obscure phenomena of the liberalization battle as the "Standpoint of the Party Organization on the District of Usti and Orlici Concerning the Situation on the Cultural and Artistic Front of 1965," or the less obscure but secrecy-shrouded frolicking of good old Allen Ginsberg as the King of May. Nothing seems to have escaped the gazelle eyes. Her book renders very well the tragedy of Czechoslovakia between 1962 and 1968.

        CSP, 16:2:308-9   R: Josef Škovorecky

1328.   Golan, Galia. **Reform Rule in Czechoslovakia: The Dubček Era, 1968-1969.** New York, Cambridge University Press, 1973. 327p. $18.50.
Reading the story of the proposed reforms, and their shattering collapse, one is impressed by their completeness, consistency, and imaginativeness, as well as puzzled by the relative ease with which brutal force relegated them to the archives of history. Democratization of economy, as the author characterizes a set of progressive proposals in the economic sector, cannot succeed without changes in the political life, and this in turn must materially affect the position and the role of the party. Political freedom cannot exist without a system of independent justice. This book is one of the best on this subject. The author presents the case in its entirety, giving the reader a concise picture and inviting him to ask questions on prospects and methods of change in a Communist society. Based exclusively on original sources, mainly newspapers and journals, her narrative has a ring of authenticity, strengthened by a sense of detachment, together with an understanding of a noble effort that failed.

        SR, 33:4:799-800   R: Josef Korbel

1329.   Jancar, Barbara Wolfe. **Czechoslovakia and the Absolute Monopoly of Power.** New York, Praeger, 1971. 330p. $17.50.

The focus of the book lies in formulating a new concept for an analysis of the power structure in a Communist system. The author suggests that the Soviet-type state should be called an "absolute monopoly" rather than a "totalitarian system," since its main characteristic is the absolute concentration of all powers in the hands of the ruling group of the ruling party. The core of that "absolute monopoly" is the unity of power and ownership. The case of Czechoslovakia has been taken as the evidence that this absolute monopoly of power might be destroyed by a consistent structural reform. Jancar says that what occurred in Czechoslovakia during the 1960s was the progressive erosion of the absolute monopoly; before this erosion reached its climax, Soviet intervention prevented the transformation of "monopoly" socialism into a pluralistic one. This is an excellent study based on both theoretical and empirical analysis.

> CSP, 15:1-2:239-40   R: R. Selucky

1330.   Journalist "M." **A Year Is Eight Months.** Intro. by Tad Szulc. Garden City, N.Y., Doubleday, 1970. 201p. $5.95.

A sober presentation of factual evidence and its stimulating interpretation of that evidence, this book by "M," a Communist journalist, represents a manifest effort at balance and fairness. Familiar topics are treated from a fresh point of view, and the complexities of the development between the fall of 1967 and August 1968 are analyzed and meaningfully evaluated. The book shows penetrating historical insight, especially in the explanation of the facillation and irresolution of the KSC leadership that was caused by the uneasy compromise reached among the liberals, the Dubček center, and the dogmatists. "M" stresses the spontaneity and gradual nature of the process of liberalization initially carried out, for the most part, by the intellectuals and youth through the mass media.

> SR, 30:1:177-8   R: Radomir Luza

1331.   Kennan, George F. **From Prague after Munich: Diplomatic Papers, 1938-1940.** Princeton, N.J., Princeton University Press, 1968. 266p. $6.50.

Kennan has included in this volume selected German, Czech, and Slovak documents, the text of the Nazi Germanization plan designed to solve the Czech question "once and for all," and materials containing explanations of the conflicts between the Czechs and the Slovaks. The greatest value of the book, however, is Kennan's perception of the climate of opinion at the time of writing his confidential letters from his post at Prague (and later Berlin) to the State Department. Kennan's firsthand account of the first great Czechoslovak tragedy that began in 1938 makes the work mandatory reading for those who want to go beyond superficial descriptions of events.

> SR, 29:1:119-20   R: Josef Kalvoda

1332.   Loebl, Eugen. **Stalinism in Prague: The Loebl Story.** Trans. by Maurice Michael. American edition. ed. and with an intro. by Herman Starobin. New York, Grove Press, 1970. 330p. $6.00cl.; $1.95pa.

Eugen Loebl, former deputy foreign trade minister, is one of three Communist defendants of the Slánský trial to survive. Here he unveils the decisive role of the Soviet advisers in the preparation of the trial and describes the techniques of interrogation, consisting of a "combination of continual hunger, repeated interruption of sleep, and of having to stand or walk in small, hard leather slippers throughout the day." His account of the pogromlike atmosphere and of the ideology behind the purges incorporates the essentials of his own experience.

SR, 30:1:177   R: Radomir Luza

1333.   Pelikán, Jiří, ed. **The Czechoslovak Political Trials, 1950-1954: The Suppressed Report of the Dubček Government's Commission of Inquiry, 1968.** Stanford, Calif., Stanford University Press, 1971. 360p. $10.95.

In April 1968, in its third attempt since 1955, the Communist party of Czechoslovakia set up a special commission to investigate the background of the show trials of the period 1949-1954 under strict rules of secrecy. For the first time in the history of a Communist party in power, access was given to the secret party archives, including the minutes of the meetings of the highest party organs. The final report, prepared by the Piller Commission, has never been published. This published text has the obvious merit of being an authentic report written by a large group of historians, lawyers, and economists. The most significant portion of the last section reveals the characteristics of the 1968 Czechoslovak experiment.

SR, 31:1:221-2   R: Radomir V. Luza

1334.   Piekalkiewicz, Jaroslaw A. **Public Opinion Polling in Czechoslovakia, 1968-69: Results and Analysis of Surveys Conducted during the Dubček Era.** Foreword by Barry Bede. New York, Praeger, 1972. 357p. $18.50.

The author is concerned with the degree to which the regime and its policies were supported by the population between March 1968 and March 1969. In examining this problem, he relies on the data collected in some twenty public opinion polls conducted by him in Czechoslovakia during that year. In all, about 35,000 people were interviewed, selected largely at random. Attitudes toward continued reform, support of party leaders, and willingness to respond to polls, for example, remained constant after the invasion and began to decline only gradually in the months thereafter.

SR, 32:4:837-8   R: Jane P. Shapiro

1335.   Remington, Robin Alison, ed. **Winter in Prague: Documents on Czechoslovak Communism in Crisis.** With an intro. by William E. Grifffith. Czech and Slovak trans. revised by Michael Berman. Cambridge, MIT Press, 1969. 473p. $12.50.

The Remington work, like most documentary collections, has a lasting value, and its importance is likely to increase if new evidence should come to light (for example, a report on the Dubček-Brezhnev conversations) that would enable us to re-evaluate the events of 1968. The stated purpose of the collection is to document the experiment of Prague's attempt "to sweep the ashes of Stalinism from the Czechoslovak road to Socialism."

SR, 29:1:729-30   R: Josef Kalvoda

1336. Slánská, Jozefa. **Report on My Husband**. Trans. from the Czech and with an introduction by Edith Pargeter. New York, Atheneum, 1969. 208p. $5.95.

Mrs. Slánská gives a personal account of the experiences of the widow of the former secretary-general of the Communist party of Czechoslovakia who was hanged as a spy and traitor in 1952 and was posthumously rehabilitated in 1963. During the "liberalization process" in Czechoslovakia in 1968, illegalities and terror of the Stalinist trials were denounced in broadcasts and publications. Slánská mentions in her report that her husband was arrested and liquidated on orders from Moscow, although she herself could not believe it at the time it happened. However, the innocent victims of Slánský, who also included some Communists, are not even mentioned in her book.

      SR, 29:1:729-31   R: Josef Kalvoda

1337. Sterling, Claire. **The Masaryk Case**. New York, Harper & Row, 1970. 366p. $7.95.

The argument of this book is that Czechoslovak Foreign Minister Jan Masaryk, whose body was found in a courtyard of Czernin Palace in the early morning of March 10, 1948, was probably murdered by agents of the Soviet security police in order to prevent him from escaping to the West. Mrs. Sterling is a journalist composing a "whodunit," albeit with far-reaching political overtones, for a popular audience. All facts collected in this book point to assassination rather than suicide. Scholars will perhaps find the book's greatest value in Mrs. Sterling's twenty interviews with persons involved in the incident who were still alive in 1968. The work is without footnotes but is provided with a brief bibliography.

      SR, 29:1:728-9   R: R. V. Burks

1338. Svitak, Ivan. **The Czechoslovak Experiment, 1968-1969**. New York, Columbia University Press, 1971. 241p. $10.95.

Svitak is a Czech intellectual who was known in Novotny's Czechoslovakia as something of a maverick, ready to display prominently his non-conformism—and suffer consequences. He was expelled from the Party. He is a philosopher by profession, but by inclination he is a political moralist. This book is a collection of essays written by a controversial figure. He is a Marxist, but in reading his book one discovers contradictions and confusion, typical of the subjective views of a single individual to be found anywhere in the "socialist camp."

      CSP, 14:1:133-4   R: B. Korda and I. Moravcik

History

1339. Betts, R. R. **Essays in Czech History**. London, Athlone Press, University of London, 1969. 315p. $8.75.

Most of the essays are about political, religious, and philosophical ideas, which are not so much studied as appreciated, in the light of Betts's own understanding of life—apparently a blend of quasi-Marxism with semi-Methodism—and his ideas about what happened in the late Middle Ages. The latter center about such notions as the rising middle class, the new economy of the marketplace, the domination of governments by bankers and merchants, and so forth. The other essays in the collection include "The Influence of Realist Philosophy on Jan Hus and his Predecessors in Bohemia," "National and Heretical Religious Movements," "Society in Central and Western Europe," and others.

SR, 30:1:172-3   R: Howard Kaminsky

1340.   Boba, Imre. **Moravia's History Reconsidered: A Reinterpretation of Medieval Sources**. The Hague, M. Nijhoff, 1971. 167p. $6.50pa.
This monograph focuses on one of the rapidly changing entities of Central Europe: Moravia, or, as it is also known, the Great Moravian Empire. Boba is convinced that most if not all previous students of this area have been wrong in their approach to the subject in so vital a matter as political geography of the ninth century. Moravia, he contends, was not situated north of the Danube and the Sava rivers but south in *Pannonia orientalis*.

SR, 31:2:453-5   R: S. Harrison Thomson

1341.   Brock, Peter, and H. Gordon Skilling, eds. **The Czech Renascence of the Nineteenth Century: Essays Presented to Otakar Odložilik in Honor of his Seventieth Birthday**. Toronto, University of Toronto Press, 1970. 345p. $10.00.
This *Festschrift* dedicated to the old master of Czech history united seventeen scholarly studies of American, Czechoslovak-émigré, and Czechoslovak authors in an interesting and highly competent volume. Appended is a selected bibliography of Professor Odložilik's works and an index. Contributions deal with such aspects as literature, sociology, journalism, politics, and history of the Czech people.

SR, 31:3:715-7   R: Friedrich Prinz

1342.   Bruegel, Johann Wolfgang. **Czechoslovakia before Munich: The German Minority Problem and British Appeasement Policy**. New York, Cambridge University Press, 1973 (1967). 334p. $14.95.
Bruegel's study of the Czech-German problem, *Tschechen und Deutsche 1918-1938*, published in Munich in 1967, has been justly hailed as a major addition to the literature on Central Europe between the wars. The shortened English edition examines two decades of Czech-German relations from 1918 until the Munich agreement. The author presents two closely related series of domestic and international developments. The material is skillfully arranged chronologically; the narrative is organized in two parts, the dividing line being the rise of Nazism in 1933. The examination becomes a general indictment of the ineptness in British policy. The analysis is cogent and displays sound scholarship based on primary evidence. On the whole, Bruegel's materials confirm our present knowledge about interwar developments in Central Europe.

ECE, 1, part 2.   R: Radomir V. Luza

1343.   Comenius, John Amos. **The Labyrinth of the World and the Paradise of the Heart**. Newly translated by Matthew Spinka. Ann Arbor, Czechoslovak Society of Arts and Sciences in American and Department of Slavic Languages and Literatures of the University of Michigan, 1972. 148p. and appendix (facsimile of Amsterdam ed., 1663). (Michigan Slavic Translations, no. 1). Paper.

Comenius (1592-1670) is, next to John Hus and Thomas Masaryk, probably the most prominent figure in Czech cultural history. The most striking fact about his intellectual outlook was its combination of rationalism with utopianism and mysticism. On the one hand, he was an intellectual sponsor of the seventeenth-century scientific revolution, and Trevor-Roper identifies him as one of the three foreign *philosophes* of the English Puritan Revolution. On the other hand, his mystical writings played a part in the religious ferment in Russia, and with Jacob Boehme he belongs among the Western progenitors of modern Russian mysticism.

      SR, 32:3:641   R: Zdenek V. David

1344.   Heymann, Frederick G. **George of Bohemia: King of Heretics.** Princeton, Princeton University Press, 1965. 671p. $15.00.

This is the first monographic treatment in a Western language of George Poděbrady, one of the most significant rulers in Czech history. [See also O. Odložilik's *The Hussite King* (1965).] Heir of the religious nationalism of the land of John Hus, prominent candidate for the imperial crown, George lived his life (d. 1471) under excommunication or threat of excommunication, intermittently under attack or threat of attack from all his neighbors. George must be reckoned among the great figures of central European history.

      SR, 25:2:347-8   R: S. Harrison Thomson

1345.   Kaminsky, Howard. **A History of the Hussite Revolution.** Berkeley, University of California Press, 1967. 580p. $15.00.

This is a fascinating ideological and sociological analysis of Hussite history seen as a movement of reformation and revolution. Kaminsky sees the two as intimately tied together. He sets the Hussite revolt in the larger context of "world-historical terms" both in its relationship to late medieval history and to the old order." The author, deeply versed in Czech *Hussitica*, offers to the West the harvest of the profuse scholarship and interpretations locked in Czech books and journals. His extensive and lengthy footnotes are especially helpful.

      SR, 29:3:502-3   R: Marianka Fousek

1346.   Kerner, Robert Joseph. **Bohemia in the Eighteenth Century: A Study in Political and Social History with Special Reference to the Reign of Leopold II, 1790-1792.** [Reimpression of the 1932 edition with a new introduction by Joseph F. Zacek.] Orono, Me., Academic International, 1969. 412p. (The Russian Series, vol. 7). $12.50.

Zacek's introduction to this classic study of Bohemia's history refreshes and updates the literature related to that period of Czech history. This is mainly a study in political and social history and economic conditions during the reign of Leopold II. Kerner used extensively the archives of Vienna and Prague, and the bibliography is in itself a worthwhile contribution.

                           S. M. H.

1347.   Kirschbaum, J. K., ed. **Slovakia in the 19th and 20th Centuries.** Toronto, Slovak World Congress, 1973. 368p.

The papers in this volume were delivered at the Conference on Slovakia held in Toronto during the Slovak World Congress in June 1971. The papers are written from the position that the Slovaks are "a distinct central European nation" and thus have the right to self-determination and equality of rights.
CSP, 16:4:682   R: Anne Woodridge

1348.   Kovaly, Heda, and Erazim Kohak. **The Victors and the Vanquished.** New York, Horizon Press, 1973. 274p. $8.95.
The authors' narrative is simple and moving. It is an intimate account of their own lives, full of horror, tragedy and hope. It is at the same time the story of a generation whose mentality and attitudes were formed under the pressure of war and Nazi terror. It is the story of a generation which, in spite of all the horrors, did find the strength to start an unprecedented movement of national reconciliation which was ultimately put down by the Soviet invasion. The second part of the book stresses not the events themselves, but rather their inner logic. It analyzes the rise to power of the Communist party and its transformation into a destructive, anti-human force, and the emergence of a strong thrust toward reconiliation in the framework of a specific model. The book is worthwhile reading and is recommended in the first place to all radical intellectuals.
CSP, 15:4:605-7   R: B. Korda

1349.   Levine, Isaac Don. **Intervention.** New York, David McKay, 1969. 152p. $4.95.
Levine analyzes the causes and consequences of the Soviet invasion of Czechoslovakia. To get answers to the question "Why did Moscow do it?," he went to all the Balkan countries and visited several West European centers where he interviewed important political personalities. Sometimes he identifies those persons; on other occasions, for obvious reasons, his informant preferred to remain anonymous. His general conclusion appears to be that the Soviets are preparing themselves for war, and in order to have their rear secured, they had to have their troops in Czechoslovakia. By the invasion they have achieved their objective, although they had to pay a price for it politically. The author is a seasoned student of Communist affairs, and his journalistic style makes the book easy and interesting reading.
SR, 29:1:729-30   R: Josef Kalvoda

1350.   Littell, Robert, ed. **The Czech Black Book.** New York, Praeger, 1969. 303p. $6.95.
What happened in Czechoslovakia from August 21 through August 27 of 1968 is dramatically described in this extraordinary document, prepared by members of the Institute of History of the Czechoslovak Academy of Sciences. It is a compilation of eyewitness testimony, official announcements and documents, broadcasts from the free Czechoslovak radio stations, newspaper articles, statements from participants in official government and party proceedings, and notes from high-level clandestine meetings. The work was originally printed in Czech as *Seven Days in Prague*. The editor and translator, R. Littell, has brought a copy of the original document out of Czechoslovakia.
UQ, 26:3-4:345-6   R: Joseph S. Roucek

1351.   Luža, Radomir. **The Transfer of the Sudeten Germans: A Study of Czech-German Relations, 1933-1962.** New York, New York University Press, 1964. 365p. $7.50.

The subtitle of this book gives a somewhat more accurate picture of its content than does the title. The bulk of the volume deals not with the actual transfer of the Germans from Czechoslovakia in 1945 but with the background of this momentous event in East European history. The author's thorough examination of the economic and social foundations of the Czech-German problem, the rise of Nazism in Czechoslovakia, the Czech crisis of 1938, Munich and the German occupation, and Czech resistance at home and diplomatic action abroad provides the necessary foundation for understanding and appraising the difficult decision made by the Czechoslovak government in exile, and ultimately endorsed by the major allied governments, to transfer more than three million Germans from Czechoslovakia. The study is based on exhaustive research in Czech and German literature and the book is a valuable contribution to post-1919 Czech history and to the study of international affairs.

   SR, 25:4:701-2   R: H. Gordon Skilling

1352.   Mamatey, Victor S., and Radomir Luža, eds. **A History of the Czechoslovak Republic, 1918-1948.** Princeton, Princeton University Press, 1973. 534p. $22.50cl.; $9.75pa.

This book is a product of many hands, with fourteen authors contributing seventeen chapters grouped in three themes: "The Czechoslovak Republic 1918-1938," "Occupation War and Liberation 1938-1945," and "Czechoslovakia between East and West 1945-1948." Among the authors, two German scholars, Jorg Hoensch and Gotthold Rhode, wrote carefully balanced accounts of, respectively, the Slovak Republic during 1939-1945 and the Protectorate Bohemia-Moravia. This volume devotes two full chapters to the Slovaks. It contains several maps, pictures, and photographs.

   EEQ, 8:3:389-91   R: Stanley Z. Pech

1353.   Masaryk, Tomas. **The Making of a State: Memories and Observations, 1914-1918.** Ed. and intro. by Henry Wickham Stee. New York, Fertig, 1969 (1927). 461p. $15.00.

Masaryk, who created a new state by the force of his own will, narrates events that brought about the freedom of Czechoslovakia. He describes how he organized abroad the fight and support of the Czech people and of Western statesmen, including Woodrow Wilson. This volume remains an indispensable work for the study of the history and formation of Czechoslovakia. Masaryk's comments and observations of these events are analytical, critical, and extraordinarily erudite, revealing the author's thoughtful mind and character.   S. M. H.

1354.   Masaryk, Tomas G. **The Meaning of Czech History.** Ed. by René Wellek. Trans. by Peter Kussi. Chapel Hill, University of North Carolina Press, 1974. 169p. $9.95.

This handsome volume contains a balanced collection of essays written from 1895 to 1910 by Masaryk. This is a valuable contribution to our understanding of Masaryk and modern Czech history. In his writings Masaryk attempted to formulate a national program anchored in the universal humanistic idea and in Czech history. He contended that the national revival was a natural extension of the Czech past, developing the religious and moral ideas of the Czech Reformation of the fifteenth century, when the Hussite movement established principles commonly known as Protestant a whole century before the Reformation. The seven essays do not aim at a comprehensive analysis of the various aspects of the Czech revival. Instead, they are carefully selected to illustrate and support Masaryk's theses.

CASS, 9:1:133   R: Radomir V. Luža

1355.   Mastny, Vojtech. **The Czechs under Nazi Rule: The Failure of National Resistance, 1939-1942**. New York, Columbia University Press, 1971. 274p. $10.00.

In part 1, Mastny describes the fall of Czechoslovakia. The major topics which run throughout parts 2 and 3 are the consolidation of the occupation regime and the rise of Czech resistance. Part 4 closes the narrative with the description of the persecution of the Czechs following the assassination of Acting Reich Protector Reinhard Heydrich in the early summer of 1942. Mastny's central thesis is simply stated: the Czechs failed to challenge the Nazi authorities with an effective resistance. By 1942 the resistance movement was destroyed, never to play a significant role until the end of the war.

SR, 34:3:628-30   R: Radomir V. Luža

1356.   Mňačko, Ladislav. **The Seventh Night**. Foreword by Harry Schwartz. New York, E. P. Dutton, 1969. 220p. $5.95.

This is an attempt by a Slovak journalist to place the August invasion in the context of Czechoslovak history since the war. The author was one of the country's leading columnists and a Communist since youth. He points to frequent errors in judgment on his part and offers a candid, if perhaps exaggerated, picture of his role in the implementation of Stalinist tyranny in his country. He hints darkly at a "new Yalta, a new division of spheres of interest by the two greatest powers" (USA and USSR). His is a voice of despair, despair that the socialist internationalism in which he and countless other Communists believed has become socialist imperialism.

SR, 29:3:538   R: Jack V. Haney

1357.   Odložilik, Otakar. **The Hussite King: Bohemia in European Affairs; 1440-1471**. New Brunswick, N.J., Rutgers University Press, 1965. 337p. $10.00.

This is the second major study in one year of George of Poděbrady, the Utraquist king of Bohemia (1458-71). Odložilik's book has much in common with Frederick G. Heymann's *George of Bohemia: King of Heretics* (Princeton University Press, 1965). Written by a recognized authority in the field, it is the product of mature scholarship. It is thoroughly grounded in the vast body of source material, primary and secondary, published and unpublished, especially the monumental studies of such distinguished forerunners as Palacký, Tomek, and others. The author concentrates on the skein of religious, political, and military involvements—on George's attempts to mediate between Catholics and

Utraquists within the kingdom and to maintain his throne against the Papacy and his secular rivals. Scholars will consult the version that suits their individual needs best; nonspecialists will find Odložilik's study manageable.

SR, 25:3:532-3   R: Joseph F. Zacek

1358.   Olivová, Věra. **The Doomed Democracy: Czechoslovakia in a Disrupted Europe, 1914-38.** Trans. by George Theiner. Intro. by Sir Cecil Parrott. London, Sidgwick and Jackson, 1972; Montreal, McGill-Queen's University Press, 1972. 276p. £4.50; $12.50.

Olivová's book is a remarkable piece of scholarship. It deserves to be studied carefully not for new information about interwar Czechoslovakia but for fresh, analytical insights which originate from a respectable scholar living in ideologically besieged Prague. Characteristic of the spirit of the "Czechoslovak Spring," the book was first published in Czech during that exhilarating though short-lived experience of freedom of expression. It is remarkably free of boring Marxist jargon and dogmatic schematism. Singularly well translated and introduced by an outstanding British scholar, it is a welcome contribution to the field of Slavic studies.

SR, 32:2:408-9   R: Josef Korbel

1359.   Pech, Stanley Z. **The Czech Revolution of 1849.** Chapel Hill, University of North Carolina Press, 1969. 386p. $10.00.

Pech's book is an important work. Not only is it the sole account in English, but it is also the only scholarly monograph with critical apparatus that covers the entire revolution in any language. It is based on documents the author collected in several archives in Prague, a large number of contemporary newspapers and other published contemporary sources, and studies of various aspects of the revolution by Czech and other historians. The author makes it clear that the revolution in Bohemia bore little resemblance to those in Moravia, Silesia, and Slovakia. Especially commendable are the sections in which the author discusses the national, liberal, and social aspects of the revolution. His book is "must reading" for all serious students of the revolutions of 1848-49 in general and for those of Central Europe in particular.

SR, 31:1:218-9   R: R. John Rath

1360.   Polisensky, J. V. **The Thirty Years War.** Trans. by Robert Evans. Berkeley, University of California Press, 1971. 305p. $10.00.

By publishing a Czech scholar's comprehensive study of the Thirty Years' War, the University of California Press contributed significantly to the progress of international exchanges which no barriers or "curtains" should hinder. The terse title covers a multitude of problems which vexed Western and Central Europe for several decades as dissatisfaction accumulated prior to the outburst in 1618, and then during the successive diplomatic and armed conflicts up to 1648. The author presents the highly complicated story on three levels. Some chapters are devoted to general problems; others deal with the intricacies of public life in Bohemia, or with developments in one area, the domain of Zlin in southeastern Moravia. The book is a significant contribution to the knowledge of the struggles for continental hegemony in which most Western and Central European countries became involved.

SR, 31:3:704-5   R: Otakar Odložilik

1361.   Ripka, Hubert. **Munich: Before and After, a Fully Documented Czechoslovak Account of the Crises of September 1938 and March 1939.** Trans. by Ida Sindelková and Comdr. Edgar P. Young. New York, Fertig, 1969 (1939). 523p. $14.00.

(Listed in P. Horecky's *East Central Europe: A Guide to Basic Publications*, #893). Ripka's account of events leading to, and related to, the Munich agreement is the first work produced by a prominent Czech journalist who joined Beneš's government-in-exile in London. The book contains important documents not available in any other study dealing with the Munich settlement. This account complements George F. Kennan's *From Prague after Munich. Diplomatic Papers, 1938-1940.* (Princeton, Princeton University Press; London, Oxford University Press, 1968. 266p. $6.50)   S. M. H.

1362.   Steiner, Eugen. **The Slovak Dilemma.** New York, Cambridge University Press, 1973. 229p. (International Studies. Published for the Centre for International Studies, London School of Economics and Political Science). $13.95.

This volume is one of the most levelheaded investigations of Slovakia's past and present in any major European language. The first part, terminating in 1948, presents a balanced picture of Slovakia. The second period, 1948-1970, depends more on firsthand observation made while the author was working as a journalist in Slovakia than on references to sources.

SR, 33:3:569-70   R: Yeshayahu Jelinek

1363.   Szulc, Tad. **Czechoslovakia since World War II.** New York, Viking Press, 1971. 503p. $14.00.

While serving as the *New York Times* foreign correspondent in Prague in 1968, Szulc was an eyewitness to Czechoslovakia's exciting experiment with "socialism with a human face" as well as its subsequent suppression by the Soviet invasion and occupation of the country. It is the first-hand information he gathered in this capacity that constitutes the main part of the present volume. To tell the absorbing story of the Czechoslovak crisis of 1968 was evidently the author's principal purpose in writing the book. However, in a commendable search for historical perspective and endeavor to explain what happened in 1967 and 1968 in terms of the Communist sins of the past, Szulc felt it necessary to preface his account of the 1968 events with a long historical survey covering the entire period of 1945-1967. This book ranks among the best volumes on Czechoslovakia written in recent years.

SR, 30:4:916-7   R: Edward Taborsky

1364.   Wechsberg, Joseph. **The Voices.** Garden City, N.Y., Doubleday, 1969. 113p. $3.95.

The Voices is essentially an account of what the distinguished journalist heard over the Czechoslovak underground radio after the invasion by Warsaw Pact forces. The author, born and raised in Czechoslovakia, treats his subject with deep feeling and emotion. The book is of interest as a personal account of the dramatic days of August.

      SR, 29:3:538   R: Jack V. Haney

1365.   Wiener, Jan G. **The Assassination of Heydrich.** New York, Grossman Publishers, 1969. 177p. $6.95.

This monograph deals with one of the most dramatic events in modern Czechoslovak history—the assassination of SS Obergruppen-führer Reinhard Heydrich, Acting Reich Protector of Bohemia and Moravia, and head of the German security police, by Czech parachutists in May 1942. The author approaches the complex subject from a subjective viewpoint. His aim is not to analyze the event but simply to tell a patently moving story. The volume reveals nothing new. It merely corroborates the known, and facts are presented at second hand. There is no bibliography and it has almost no references to sources, yet it remains of some interest to the general reader.

      SR, 29:1:727-8   R: Radomir Luža

1366.   Zacek, Joseph Frederick. **Palacký: The Historian as Scholar and Nationalist.** The Hague, Mouton, 1970. 137p. (Studies in European History, no. 5). 28Dglds.

The author has succeeded admirably in presenting a scholarly biography of František Palacký's accomplishments as a historian and as the chief leader of the Czech national movement. Zacek has done this by making a critical "synthesis of the published material" and combining it with the results of his own "researches into the pertinent primary sources." All in all, the study is an excellent one.

      SR, 33:2:379   R: R. John Rath

Language and Literature

1367.   Beneš, Oldřich, ed. **Seven Short Stories.** Prague, Orbis, 1965. 142p. Kčs.5,pa.

Seven Short Stories is completely devoted to recent Czech and Slovak stories, including superb examples by two maniacal figures, neo-Dadaists or neo-surrealists, Bohumil Hrabal and Ivan Vyskočil, who, along with Linhartova, are perhaps the most promising of the younger Czechoslovak story writers. This volume gives biographical notes on the authors.

      SR, 27:2:353-4   R: William E. Harkins

1368.   **Czech and Slovak Short Stories.** Selected, trans., and with an intro. by Jeanne W. Nemcova. London, Oxford University Press, 1967. 296p. $3.50.

This well-selected anthology is, by and large, well translated and has an intelligent introduction, and it presents us with more new stories than we would probably expect; nearly half the narratives chosen are recent ones. The collection

does help a great deal in bringing our understanding of the Czech (if not the Slovak) story up to date.
SR, 27:2:353-4   R: William E. Harkins

1369.   Doleẑel, Lubomir. **Narrative Modes in Czech Literature.** Toronto, University of Toronto Press, 1973. 152p. $10.00.
The author, a well-known member of the second generation of Czechoslovak structuralists and an expert in modern Czech prose, presents here a collection of essays with special attention to problems of composition in modern Czech narrative prose. The book offers both more and less than the title promises: it devotes the introduction to a typology of discourse, based on the dichotomy of narrator's and character's discourse which forms the "deep level" of the verbal structure of every narrated prose text, and then investigates certain devices of modern (except for Komenský) Czech literary prose.
SR, 34:2:445-6   R: Walter Schamschula

1370.   French, Alfred, comp. **Anthology of Czech Poetry.** Intro. by René Wellek. Ann Arbor, Department of Slavic Languages and Literatures of the University of Michigan, and Czechoslovak Society of Arts and Sciences in America, 1973. 372p. (Michigan Slavic Translations, no. 2). $4.50pa.
This first volume of a projected two-volume anthology of Czech poetry covers the six centuries between the emergence of poetry in the Czech language in the early fourteenth century and the foundation of the Czechoslovak Republic in 1918. It is an interesting and valuable anthology and represents, both in scope and conception, a considerable advance over most of its predecessors. This being a bilingual anthology, the Czech prototypes are printed along side the English translations, which are the work of a whole team of translators. On the whole, most translations fulfill one'x expectations.
SR, 34:1:204-5   R: Emil Kovtun

1371.   French, Alfred. **The Poets of Prague: Czech Poetry between the Wars.** London, Oxford University Press, 1969. 129p. $5.75.
There is no question that the Czech poets Seifert, Nezval, Halas, Hora, and the Catholic Zahradniček rank among the finest lyric poets of the twentieth century. French's study of the leading Czech poets between the two world wars not only presents an excellent account of the experimentation in Czechoslovakia during that period but also manages to convey the spirit, if not the word, of some dozen or so Czech poems in English translation. French's conclusions about the generation of poets between the wars could easily be applied to the recent generation of Czech poets before 1968: "They were full of frustrated energy and weighed down by frustrated hopes, for the times were against them."
SR, 30:4:915-6   R: E. J. Czerwinski

1372.   Jakobson, Roman. **Studies in Verbal Art: Texts in Czech and Slovak.** Published on the Occasion of the Author's Seventy-fifth Birthday by the Czechoslovak Society of Arts and Sciences in America and the Department of Slavic Languages and Literatures of the University of Michigan, Ann Arbor, 1971. 412p. (Michigan Slavic Contributions, no. 4). Paper.

This is a collection of essays on Czech, Russian, English, French, and German literature and poetics published by Jakobson in periodicals and books between 1921 and 1965. Many of them have been shortened. It is good to have Jakobson's articles on Czech literature together in one volume; these articles reflect the fashions of the 1930s.

SEER, 51:124:472-3   R: R. B. Pynsent

1373.   Miko, František. **The Generative Structure of the Slovak Sentence**: **Adverbials**. Translated by S. Kostomlatský. The Hague, Mouton; Bratislava, Publishing House of the Slovak Academy of Sciences, 1972. 150p. 38Dglds. pa.

The author deals in detail with the generative conception as related to the problem of adverbials, but he also approaches some central questions of syntax and suggests certain changes. According to the author, "with the best use of all the knowledge obtained by traditional studies, we intend to effect a confrontation of the generative model of language with traditional structural views on a larger scale as is customary in generative literature." This case study is of interest not only to the student of Slovak language but also to the specialist in linguistics.

S. M. H.

1374.   Mňačko, Ladislav. **The Taste of Power**. Trans. from the Slovak by Paul Stevenson. New York, Praeger, 1967. 235p. $5.95.

The present novel comes to us highly touted as an exposé of the corruption of Communist power. The narrative chronicles, in a series of flashbacks, the rise, decline, and death of a high Stalinist official. At first the honest and heroic leader of a partisan detachment fighting the Germans, he is transformed by power into an egomaniac, satyr, and, worst of all, an incompetent politician.

SR, 27:3:501-2   R: William E. Harkins

1375.   Selver, Paul, comp. and trans. **An Anthology of Czechoslovak Literature**. New York, Kraus Reprint, 1969 (1929). 301p. $12.00.

(Listed in P. Horecky's *East Central Europe*, #1140.) This representative anthology of Czechoslovak literature offers insight into the development of Czech and, to a lesser degree, Slovak literature.   S. M. H.

1376.   Součková, Milada. **A Literary Satellite: Czechoslovak-Russian Literary Relations**. Chicago, University of Chicago Press, 1970. 179p. $7.95.

More a series of loosely connected essays than a systematic presentation of literary give-and-take between Czechoslovakia and Russia, this small book nonetheless brings together many disparate facts. The author's views are often enlightening and almost always judicious. The book consists of fourteen informative essays dealing with the beginnings of Panslavism in Bohemia and Slovakia.

SEEJ, 15:3:390-1   R: Michael Berman

1377.   Součková, Milada. **The Parnassian: Jaroslav Vrchlický**. The Hague, Mouton, 1964. 151p. (Slavistic Printings and Reprintings, vol. 40). 20Dglds.

Součková's book on a poet who, from the mid-1870s to the mid-1890s, was the leading figure on the Czech literary scene has been conceived as an interpretative study with biographical data reduced to the minimum. In carrying out her proposed task, the author has avoided digression from the selected topics or piling up of technical details and has produced a succinct, penetrating monograph, really a masterpiece.

SR, 24:2:350-1   R: Otakar Odložilik

Religion

1378.   Hus, John. **The Letters of John Hus**. Trans. by Matthew Spinka. Manchester, Manchester University Press; Totowa, N.J., Rowman and Littlefield, 1972. 233p. $12.00.

This publication of Hus's letters in English translation complements Spinka's other books on John Hus. The letters are from Hus's last decade (1404 to 1415), the period of his public exposition and career. The letters provide an insight into the personality of the reformer who responded to criticism by attempting to show that he was in fact defending the true Christian ideal. Spinka's notes to each letter are helpful and illuminating. [Related titles by Spinka: *John Hus: A Biography* (Princeton University Press, 1968, 344p.). and *John Hus and the Czech Reform* (Hamden, Conn., Archon Books, 1966 (1941). 81p.).]

S. M. H.

1379.   Lochman, Jan Milič. **Church in a Marxist Society: A Czechoslovak View**. New York, Harper & Row, 1970. 198p. $5.95.

Lochman's book addresses itself to the Christian-Marxist dialogue as it developed in Czechoslovakia and indicates the chief cause of its decline—the Soviet-led occupation of August 1968. The book provides background information on the history of Czech Protestantism, but Lochman's chief interest is to examine the problems faced by the church at what he calls "the end of the Constantinian era"—that is, the end of the historical epoch in which the church received either official or tacit support from the state. Theoretically, Lochman, a liberal Marxist who has left Czechoslovakia in 1968, deftly states a core of views which Christians and Marxists share: that man is a social creature for whom history is significant and that he is on his way to a promised future of greater justice.

SR, 30:1:162-4   R: James P. Scanlan

1380.   Spinka, Matthew, ed. **John Hus at the Council of Constance**. New York, Columbia University Press, 1965. 327p. (No. LXXIII of Records of Civilization: Sources and Studies). $8.75.

1381.   Spinka, Matthew. **John Hus' Concept of the Church**. Princeton, N.J., Princeton University Press, 1966. 432p. $12.00.

In *John Hus* Spinka provides a translation of Peter of Mladoňovice's narrative of Hus's imprisonment, trial and death. He also translated a group of letters and other documents of Hus belonging to the same period. In *John Hus' Concept* Spinka explains that he wished to commemorate the five hundred and fiftieth anniversary of Hus's execution, also to pay a debt of gratitude for the inspiration he has derived from the example and teaching of Hus. This study, which contains a useful exposition of the thought of Hus and of teachings current in his day, should be considered, perhaps, as primarily a scholar's personal tribute to Hus's memory. As such it deserves and will be received with respect.

      SEER, 45:105:556-8   R: A. N. E. D. Schofield

1382.   Weltsch, Ruben Ernest. **Archbishop John of Jenstein (1348-1400): Papalism, Humanism and Reform in Pre-Hussite Prague.** The Hague, Mouton, 1968. 254p. (Studies in European History, vol. 8). 30Dglds.
This biography portrays a man frustrated by the powerlessness of his office and unable to realize his goal of a church independent from the state and a clergy obedient to his command. Weltsch revises the severe judgment which historians have passed on the archbishop. He does not deny that Jenstein enjoyed festivities and easily quarreled with his colleagues and the king, but he shows that Jenstein's difficulties sprang from the papal schism. The schism affected Jenstein's relations with both the king and the clergy. The inclusion of fifty pages of Jenstein's writings adds to the book's value in the study of fourteenth-century Bohemia and the archbishop of this period.

      SR, 28:3:490   R: Johannes Klassen

1383.   Zeman, Knox Jarold. **The Anabaptists and the Czech Brethren in Moravia, 1526-1628: A Study of Origins and Contacts.** The Hague, Mouton, 1969. 407p. 70Dglds.
The book deals with the meeting of two specific sects, or churches, of the Reformation period of the sixteenth century on the territory of the margraviate of Moravia. The groups dealt with show some particular similarities and differences which apparently led to peculiar attempts and expectations for (at least temporarily) very close relationship, at times even seeming to lead to a melting process, at others to sharp antagonism. The complicated and, in relation to earlier expectations, largely negative results of the two important religious developments have been presented in detailed and many-sided clarification by Zeman in this highly useful work.

      SR, 30:1:131-3   R: Frederick G. Heymann

The Society

1384.   Krejči, Jaroslav. **Social Change and Stratification in Postwar Czechoslovakia.** New York, Columbia University Press, 1972. 207p. (Political and Social Processes in Eastern Europe Series). $11.00.
The book's main section is an examination of the new social stratification pattern which was effected under Communist rule. The author clearly demonstrates that social differences do exist in socialist societies, and that the citizens of these societies are willing to recognize this fact. Communist rule facilitated the growth of a small, powerful concentration of political and economic power, which had been unknown in the Czechoslovakia of the interwar period.

      SR, 32:4:838   R: Jane P. Shapiro

1385.   Kusin, Vladimir V. **The Intellectual Origins of the Prague Spring:**
        The Development of Reformist Ideas in Czechoslovakia, 1956-1967.
        Cambridge, Cambridge University Press, 1971. 153p. $8.95.
Kusin's book is the first attempt to analyze the intellectual origins of the 1968
Czechoslovak reform. The author describes the development of reformist ideas
in Czechoslovakia since 1956 in many fields of human activity: in economics,
political science, legal theory, history, sociology, philosophy, and last but not
least in the whole cultural sphere. The Czech concept of "socialism with a human
face" did not fall from the sky. It had been elaborated upon for a decade by the
efforts of hundreds of scholars, writers, politicians, as well as economists, and
widely discussed since the early 1960s in many Czechoslovak journals, books
and newspapers. Kusin suggests that the reform stream was so strong that the
pre-January establishment was unable to suppress it. This reform movement
was interrupted by an outside force.
        CSP, 15:1-2:239-40   R: R. Selucky

1386.   Kusin, Vladimir V. **Political Grouping in the Czechoslovak Reform**
        Movement. New York, Columbia University Press, 1972. 224p.
        (Political and Social Processes in Eastern Europe Series). $11.00.
The author offers a survey of seven major nongovernmental political interest
groups, their internal development during 1968, and the influence each seems
to have had on the 1968 KSC-led reform movement. He argues that interest
groups do exist in Communist-ruled states. He focuses most fully on the intelligentsia and concludes that though it was not tightly organized, it seems to
have had the greatest impact on the reform movement.
        SR, 32:4:837   R: Jane P. Shapiro

1387.   Rodnick, David. **The Strangled Democracy: Czechoslovakia, 1948-**
        1969. Lubbock, Texas, Caprock Press, 1970. 214p. $7.95cl.; $4.95pa.
Though this is not a scholarly study, the general reader will find it highly
informative and educational. The book offers an analysis of the Czechoslovak
society since 1948 with emphasis on its ability to resist Communist indoctrination. Rodnick, a native of Czechoslovakia, collected material for his study
during prolonged visits to his homeland in 1948 and 1969.
        S. M. H.

GERMAN DEMOCRATIC REPUBLIC

General Reference Works

1388.   Childs, David. **East Germany.** New York, Praeger, 1969. 286p. $7.50.
The book was apparently conceived as something very like a handbook. Each
chapter is an information-packed treatment of a major segment of East German
life, and together they add up to a compendious array of data on the basis of
which the author draws sound but not very startling conclusions. The density
of information, including statistical data studding the text, makes for a rather

plodding treatment on the whole; but the attentive reader will emerge with a quite reliable picture of East Germany.

EEQ, 4:2:232-3   R: Lyman H. Legters

1389.   Hersch, Gisela, comp. **A Bibliography of German Studies, 1945-1971: Germany under Allied Occupation, Federal Republic of Germany, German Democratic Republic.** Bloomington, Indiana University Press, 1972. 603p. $12.50.

Part 4 of this bibliography includes books and articles related to the German Democratic Republic (pp. 374-498), under such headings as: History, Foreign Relations, Domestic Politics, Political Parties, Military and Police Force, the Legal System, Religious Life, Economic Conditions, Social Structures, Cultural Developments, Mass Media, and Education. No annotations are offered. The index includes authors, titles and subjects. The bibliography is limited exclusively to German-language publications.   S. M. H.

1390.   Price, Arnold H., comp. **East Germany: A Selected Bibliography.** Washington, Library of Congress, 1967. 133p. $1.00pa.

Price's bibliography lists books and journals, especially those published since 1959. To some degree, the book represents a sequel to Fritz T. Epstein's bibliography published in 1959 under the same title. This is a useful guide for the advanced student and the expert on the GDR.

S. M. H.

1391.   Stern, Carola. **Ulbricht: A Political Biography.** Trans. by Abe Farbstein. New York, Praeger (1965). 231p. $5.95.

This is the first full-scale Western biography of the man who has survived all the vicissitudes of the Stalinist and post-Stalinist periods to become the senior statesman of the Soviet bloc. The author describes Ulbricht in the preface to the American edition as "a politically dangerous and spiritually warped German petty-bourgeois who has been helped to undeserved power by the upheavals of this century." The author has based her study for the most part on reliable printed sources. The translation is on the whole sound.

SR, 26:4:684-5   R: H. A. Turner

Economics

1392.   Köhler, Heinz. **Economic Integration in the Soviet Bloc: With an East German Case Study.** New York, Praeger, 1965. 402p. $15.00.

The author demonstrates how the present trade status of East Germany was shaped by her extensive reparation commitments, by the subsequent acceptance of the Soviet economic model, and to some extent, by trade policies dictated by the ideological and political realities in the Russian sphere. Without a doubt, the inclusion of East Germany in the Russian Communist domain represents a fundamental factor in the political economy of Eastern Europe and beyond. The monograph offers a thoughtful view of the economic substratum at the base of that political maverick.

SR, 28:1:163-4   R: V. N. Bandera

Government and Politics

1393.   Hanhardt, Arthur M., Jr. **The German Democratic Republic**. Baltimore,
         Johns Hopkins Press, 1968. 126p. $6.00cl.; $2.45pa.
This volume is part of the Integration and Community Building in Eastern
Europe series, edited by Jan Triska. It will serve well as an introduction to the
modern history and politics of the G.D.R., especially to the interested layman
and the beginning student in the field.
         SR, 29:1:127-8   R: Brian O'Connell

1394.   Herspring, Dale Roy. **East German Civil-Military Relations: The
         Impact of Technology, 1949-72**. New York, Praeger, 1973. 217p.
         (Praeger Special Studies in International Politics and Government).
         $17.50.
Herspring has presented an important pioneering study of the military in the
German Democratic Republic. He seeks answers to such questions as: what types
of individuals occupy leadership positions in the *National Volksarmee* (NVA)
and what skills—"readiness" or "expertness"—prevail in the individual officer
of the NVA? Throughout his book the author refers to the combination of these
two skills—one political, the other military—as "dual executive." It is possible,
as Herspring maintains, that the party considers political control of the NVA
as more important than control of the economic system. Only further studies
of this aspect and others of the East German political system will prove the
validity of Herspring's conclusion and, perhaps, produce a further refinement
in methodology.
         CSP, 17:1:170-1   R: E. R. Zimmermann

1395.   Ludz, Peter C. **The Changing Party Elite in East Germany**. Foreword
         by Zbigniew Brzezinski. Cambridge, MIT Press, 1972. 509p. $15.00.
The author traces the changes in the structure of the East German society to
changes which have taken place within the Socialist Unity Party of Germany
(SED). These reflect, as well as explain, the social and political turns in the GDR
better than other attempts to analyze and interpret the course of development
in that part of Germany since the end of World War II. The author credits the
SED's elite with the ability to modernize and direct the society into the
projected future. The book is a translation of the 1968 German edition; it is
slightly revised in the present version but not updated. Included are a bibliography and name and subject indexes.   S. M. H.

History

1396.   Baring, Arnulf. **Uprising in East Germany: June 17, 1953**. Trans.
         by Gerald Onn. Intro. by David Schoenbaum. Foreword by Richard
         Lowenthal. Ithaca, Cornell University Press, 1972. 194p. $8.75.
Baring's book presents a case study in the political sociology of revolution.
Analyzing both the background and the actual course of the East German up-
rising, he pinpoints the particular circumstances that made for a revolutionary

situation and depicts the dynamics of an upheaval that required massive Soviet intervention to put down.

SR, 32:3:404 R: Melvin Croan

1397. Krisch, Henry. **German Politics under Soviet Occupation**. New York, Columbia University Press, 1974. 312p. $15.00.

This study is intended as "a detailed examination of Soviet policy in the immediate postwar period in Germany as that policy affected German political life." It covers only the period from April 1945 until May 1946 during which the Communist and Socialist parties were first separately established and then merged into the Socialist Unity Party (SED). As this was the only period in the history of the Soviet Zone in which the options were sufficiently open to justify the application of the word "politics," the title is apt.

CASS, 9:3:405-6 R: Robert Spencer

Literature

1398. Flores, John. **Poetry in East Germany: Adjustments, Visions, and Provocations, 1945-1970**. New Haven, Yale University Press, 1971. 345p. (Yale Germanic Studies, 5). $12.50.

Flores's book on East German poetry from 1945 to 1970 is the first comprehensive study of the subject in English. The author set out to summarize the development of poetry in the GDR under the somewhat arbitrary headings "adjustments," "visions," and "revisions." His work represents a piece of good solid research and will serve well as an introductory survey of East German poetry until such time as a more balanced and definitive study appears.

SR, 31:2:515 R: Helmut Winter

The Society

1399. Baylis, Thomas A. **The Technical Intelligentsia and the East German Elite: Legitimacy and Social Change in Mature Communism**. Berkeley, University of California Press, 1974. 314p. $12.50.

Baylis treats the East German technical intelligentsia as a whole. The first part of his study describes the technocrats' political characteristics, their experience as a "stratum" under Communist rule, and the efforts of the East German regime to socialize the various milieus in which they work. The second section of the book deals with technocratic recruitment into the political elite and touches upon the thorny issue of its "representation" in the highest party bodies. Baylis's judicious study offers much interesting material for further speculation.

SR, 34:3:620-1 R: Melvin Croan

HUNGARY

General Reference Works

1400. Bako, Elemer. **Guides to Hungarian Studies**. 2 Vols. Stanford, Hoover
Institution Press, 1973. Vol. 1: 636p. Vol. 2: 639-1218pp. $35.00/set.
This large publication has been prepared as a source of information and as a
research tool for students of Hungarian history, society, culture, and economics.
It includes books, journals, scholarly and popular articles, reviews, reports, maps,
and music—written in Hungarian and Western languages. No library can be with-
out this bibliography listing publications published before 1965.
NP, 2:2:88-90   R: Joseph S. Roucek

1401. **Bibliotheca Corviniana: The Library of Matthias Corvinus of Hungary**.
Introductory essays and commentaries by Csaba Csapodi and Klára
Csapodi-Gárdonyi. Trans. by Zsuzanna Horn. Trans. revised by Alick
West. Published with the assistance of UNESCO. New York, Praeger,
1969. 398p. 143pl. $55.00.
The systematic building of the Corvina collection began around 1467. An avid
reader himself, Matthias (1458-1490) began by collecting relatively plain,
undecorated books, purchased primarily for the sake of the text itself. After
his marriage to Beatrice of Aragon in 1476, the already strong Italian influence
on court life at Buda came to enjoy a virtual monopoly. Csapodi places the total
number of volumes at 2,00 to 2,500. The work constitutes an authoritative and
indispensable source for anyone dealing with the spread of fifteenth-century
Italian humanism into East Central Europe.
SR, 30:1:182-4   R: Thomas R. Mark

1402. Erdei, Ferenc, ed. **Information Hungary**. Oxford, Pergamon Press,
1968. 1,144p. (Countries of the World Information Series, vol. 2).
£12 10s.
The editor is vice-president of the Hungarian Academy of Sciences; the contributors are all prominent Hungarian scholars, literati, and public officials. This
reference book is divided into eleven major sections covering such topics as
the country's geography, history, governmental apparatus, economy, health,
education, science, literature, the fine arts, and international activities. It
contains maps and beautiful illustrations of Hungarian paintings and folk art.
Much of the information is presented here for the first time in English. Much
of the interpretation reflects official viewpoints.
SR, 29:2:362   R: Charles Gati

1403. Robinson, William F. **The Pattern of Reform in Hungary: A Political,
Economic and Cultural Analysis**. New York, Praeger, 1973. 467p.
$21.50.
Robinson has written a superb book, one which will be a basic handbook for
anyone interested in post-1956 Hungarian political, economic, and cultural
developments. The first part of this massive book is devoted to a discussion of
early impulses, the half-hearted and ultimately unsuccessful reforms between
1957 and 1961, and the extensive preparatory (1963-1968) which preceded

the introduction of New Economic Mechanism (NEM). The second part deals with the economic reform in operation, its achievement and its problems. The author analyzes what he considers to be the positive trends: a spectacular revival of Hungarian agriculture, foreign trade, and the discovery of the "third sector."

CSP, 16:2:307-8   R: Eva S. Balogh

1404.   Tezla, Albert. **Hungarian Authors: A Bibliographical Handbook.**
Cambridge, Harvard University Press, Balknap Press, 1970. 792p.
$25.00.
In 1964 Texla published his *Introductory Bibliography to the Study of Hungarian Literature.* Of the nearly 1,300 entries, about one-third were listings of primary works—that is, selected editions of authors' works and anthologies. Most of the entries dealt with broad background studies of Hungarian literature, language, and culture. Now, in his *Hungarian Authors*, Texla shifts the emphasis to individual authors and those secondary studies that deal specifically with them. The result is a massive work that contains 4,646 entries for 1962 authors, from the beginnings of Hungarian literature to today. This work must be welcomed by novice and master alike as an indispensable tool for any serious study of Hungarian literature outside Hungary.

SR, 31:1:236-7   R: Thomas R. Mark

1405.   Tezla, Albert. **An Introductory Bibliography to the Study of Hungarian Literature.** Cambridge, Harvard University Press, 1964; London, Oxford University Press, 1965 290p.
Although this bibliography of 1,295 primary and secondary sources of Hungarian literature is designed primarily for those students in the United States who are beginning their studies or undertaking research in this subject, it also serves as a most useful basic reference book for all those engaged in research on Hungarian literature outside Hungary, because each item is provided with information as to the whereabouts of copies of the work not only in the major libraries of the United States, but in those of Western Europe as well.

SEER, 44:103:501   R: Lóránt Czigány

Fine Arts

1406.   **Bartók, Béla: Letters.** Ed. by János Demény. Trans. by Péter Balabán and István Farkas. Translation revised by Elisabeth West and Colin Mason. New York, St. Martin's Press, 1971. 466p. $20.00.

1407.   Ujfalussy, József. **Béla Bartók.** Trans. by Ruth Pataki. Translation revised by Elisabeth West. Boston, Crescendo Publishing, 1972. 459p. $9.00.
The volume of *Letters* is the first collection of Bartók documents in English. The present volume contains sixty new documents in its total of 289. An appendix offers a helpful but unfortunately incomplete chronological list of Bartók compositions. The translation is excellent on the whole.

The Ujfalussy book is a quite important contribution to the Bartók literature. It gives an excellent sociopolitical commentary that is carefully related to

Bartók's career, clarifying the background for all those who are not very familiar with the Hungarian scene of his day. The author ably explains the changing circumstances of Bartók's life, including the pressures and attacks that often drove him to withdrawn from public appearances in Budapest.

      SR, 32:2:438-40   R: Hans Tischler

1408.   Berkovits, Ilona. **Illuminated Manuscripts in Hungary: XI-XVI Centuries**. Trans. by Zsuzsana Horn. Rev. by Alick West. New York, Praeger, 1969. 110p. 47 black and white pl., 45 col. $27.50.

The volume presents a factual and extremely readable account of the manuscripts examined. An extensive bibliography is also included. The list of illustrations is very useful and is presented in a scholarly fashion. The manuscripts are from three famous Hungarian libraries: the National Széchenyi Library and the University Library (both in Budapest), and the Cathedral Library (Esztergom).

      SR, 30:2:460-1   R: H. Richard Archer

1409.   Fehér, Zsuzsa D., and Gabor Ö. Pogány. **Twentieth Century Hungarian Painting**. 4th rev. ed. Budapest, Corvina Press, 1971. 19p. and 48 col. pl. 80s.

The paintings represent 33 artists, from the turn of the century through World War II. All but seven of the works reproduced are in the Hungarian National Gallery, so the illustrations supplement material about the gallery published in Budapest (A. S. Barnes & Co., 1970) and in the painting section of the catalogue for the exhibition "Art Hongrois, 1896-1945," which was held at that museum in 1969.

      SR, 33:1:170-1   R: Martha Kingsbury

1410.   Kampis, Antal. **The History of Art in Hungary**. Trans. by Lili Halápy. Budapest, Corvina Press, 1966. 399p. 80Ft.

This book is the first attempt to present the comprehensive art history of an East European nation, from its roots through its developing stages up to the present. Kampis makes good use of all newly available source material. He strives to examine the various internal influences on the development of Hungarian art, as well as the role played by neighboring cultures, and attempts to find the characteristically Hungarian traits. This is a useful and valuable study for experts as well as for foreigners interested in the subject. Lists of plates, artists, and places complete the book.

      SR, 28:2:349-50   R: Sandor Kiss

1411.   Kodály, Zoltan. **Folk Music of Hungary**. Enl. ed. rev. by Lajos Vargyas. Trans. by Ronald Tempest and Cynthia Jolly. Trans. rev. by Laurence Picken. New York, Praeger, 1971. 195p. $6.50.

Kodády was not only one of Hungary's great composers but along with Bela Bartók was responsible for collection of folk songs. Before his death in 1967, Kodály made extensive notes for a revised version of the first English edition of his classic work of folk-song studies. These changes have been incorporated into the present edition. Although many of the chapters in this new edition interest in, or general knowledge of, Hungarian folk music, the numerous

musical examples and especially the clear English translations make this edition
of definite value.
SR, 32:2:440 R: Elizabeth Suderburg

Economics

1412. Berend, Ivan T., and György Ránki. **Hungary: A Century of Economic
Development.** Trans. by Richard Allan. Newton Abbot, England,
David & Charles; New York, Barnes & Noble Books, 1974. 263p.
$18.50.
The process of Hungarian economic development has been a slow metamorphosis of the country from a predominantly agricultural society to one in which
industry has the foremost position. The authors conclude the industrialization
of the country has been the logical outcome of an inevitable process, periodically
marked by state intervention which culminated in the socialist transformation
of Hungary. The foundations for the industrialization of the country center
around the years of the *Ausgleich.* At this time foreign banks and financial
groups invested heavily in Hungary, providing the necessary capital accumulation for an economic "take-off." Although an abundance of tables and statistics
are used throughout the book, the only reference to their source is an almost
casual mention at the end of the book that they were derived from yearbooks
and government statistics. The bibliography is adequate.
EEQ, 9:2:247-9 R: James V. Fitzgerald, Jr.

1413. Fischer, Lewis A., and Philip E. Uren. **The New Hungarian Agriculture.**
Montreal, McGill-Queen's University Press, 1974. 138p. $10.00.
The authors of this stimulating book have attempted to "examine the evolution of the Hungarian countryside since the advent of socialism," to trace
"the main features of a socialist rural landscape and to draw some conclusions
about its structure and functions." They achieve all three objectives with
admirable clarity in a text of only 120 well-written pages. The first two chapters
provide a brief summary of the geographical and historical context within which
the land reformers operated when, after the Second World War, they began to
reshape the face of Hungarian agriculture, changing not only the social and
economic relations of the rural population, but also the landscape itself. In
addition to a brief historical sketch, there are useful chapters on the land reform
of 1945 and on the collectivization drive of the fifties. The second half of the
book deals with the impact of the New Economic Mechanism, which modified
the stark rigidity of the earlier collectivization. This work is mainly based on
field studies carried out between 1966 and 1971 in Somogy in the Dunantúl.
CSP, 16:4:657-60 R: F. B. Singleton

Education

1414. Földes, Éva, and István Mészáros, eds. **Comenius and Hungary:** Essays.
Budapest, Akadémiai Kiadó, 1973. illus. 240p. $11.00.

The volume is the first in a Western language to deal with Comenius's work at Sárospatak, where the Czech-Moravian educator lived between 1650 and 1654 and where he first had the opportunity to put some of his pansophic ideas into practice. It represents the work of German, Czechoslovak, and Hungarian scholars and it will help to evaluate practical application of Comenius's theoretical ideas.

SR, 33:2:380   R: Eva S. Balogh

Geography

1415.   Pecsi, Marton, and Bela Sarfalvi. **The Geography of Hungary**. London, Collet's, 1964. (Originally printed in Hungary. Budapest, Corvina Press, 1964). 299p. maps, photographs. $3.00.

This study contains 81 very useful black and white maps, two folded color maps, and 61 photographs. Its twelve chapters discuss such topics as the evolution and present aspect of the relief, mineral resources, climate, soils, population and settlement, industry, agriculture and ofrestry. Most valuable is the excellent regional discussion called "Landscape Units of Hungary." It also presents changes in the demographic and economic development of Hungary.

EEQ, 1:4:401-3   R: George W. Hoffman

Government and Politics

1416.   Kovrig, Bennett. **The Hungarian People's Republic**. Baltimore, Johns Hopkins Press, 1970. 206p. (Intergration and Community Building in Eastern Europe). $7.50cl.; $2.95pa.

Much of the book relies on evidence published in the United States, or at least in the West. While there are a number of references to articles which appeared in periodicals published in Hungary, these references are often used to support arguments regarding shortcomings of the Hungarian People's Republic. Kovrig fails to give Hungary full credit for its economic achievements. However, he is quite correct in pointing out that the "implantation of a 'socialist conscious- ness' seems to be as remote as ever."

EEQ, 5:3:424-5   R: Mario D. Fenyo

1417.   Shawcross, William. **Crime and Compromise: Janos Kadar and the Politics of Hungary since Revolution**. New York, Dutton, 1974. 311p. $10.00.

This is an account of the political career and the private life of Janos Kadar, who emerged after 1956 "as a pragmatic politician who tries to win the coopera- tion of his countrymen, not through fear and terror, but by granting concessions and by raising the standard of living." To this end Kadar introduced the so-called New Economic Mechanism (NEM) to increase productivity. Shawcross offers for the first time a coherent and well-documented Kadar biography. The study should be of interest to academic libraries as well as to the general public.

S. M. H.

Foreign Policy

1418.   Dreisziger, Nandor A. F. **Hungary's Way to World War II**. Astor Park,
        Fla., Danubian Press, 1968. 239p. (Problems Behind the Iron Curtain
        Series, no. 5). $5.00cl.; $4.00pa.
This is the first Western-language history of Hungarian foreign policy in the
interwar years. Moreover, the present study is based on documentary collections
recently published in Hungary, which C. A. Macartney (author of *History of
Hungary, 1929-1945*) was not able to see. Dreisziger writes well; he is moderate,
judicious, and a thorough researcher. He does away with many Western myths,
such as the quasi-dictatorial rule of Admiral Horthy and Hungary's enthusiasm
for armed collaboration with Hitler's Germany. He also points to the incon-
sistency of Communist historians who call the Hungarian leaders "fascists"
and then scold them for refusing to take up arms against fascist Germany. He
makes amply clear the dual aim of post-1933 Hungarian foreign policy: trying
to resist the expansion of German influence and, at the same time, seeking to
revise Hungary's frontiers.
　　　　AHA, 75:2:545　　　　　　　　R: István Deák

1419.   Fenyo, Mario D. **Hitler, Horthy, and Hungary: German-Hungarian
        Relations, 1941-44**. New Haven, Yale University Press, 1972. 279p.
        (Yale Russian and East European Studies, no. 11). $10.00.
Fenyo's work deals with German-Hungarian relations between 1941 and 1944—
that is, between Hungary's entry into the Second World War and the fall of
the Horthy regime in October 1944. The author had to deal all the time with
the Hungarian internal scene; the politics of the Hungarian Nazi-sympathizers
and those who opposed them. Its value lies in concentrating on a relatively
short period; therefore, the book is a useful tool for every student who wishes
to study the history of the Second World War in East-Central Europe in detail.
　　　　EEQ, 8:2:242-4　　　　　　　R: Nicholas Nagy-Talavera

1420.   Radványi, János. **Hungary and the Superpowers: The 1956 Revolution
        and Realpolitic**. Foreword by Zbigniew Brzezinski. Stanford, Hoover
        Institution Press, 1972. 197p. $5.95.
This well-written volume discusses mainly problems of Hungarian diplomacy
after 1956, Hungarian-American relations in the same period, and specifically
the Kádár government's endeavors for recognition of the Hungarian delegation
by the General Assembly's Credentials Committee. The author was a member
of the Hungarian foreign service for two decades and was Hungarian chargé
d'affaires in Washington from 1962 to 1967. He was an inside observer of, or
an active participant in, most events discussed in the volume. This special background he has supplemented by thorough research of documents and other
publications available in the United States. This book is "must" reading for
students interested in the working conditions of Communist diplomacy and
the linkage between Communist party organs and the implementation of
foreign policy.
　　　　SR, 32:3:647-8　　　　　　　R: Stephen D. Kertesz

History

1421.   Aczel, Tamas, ed. **Ten Years After: The Hungarian Revolution in the Perspective of History.** New York, Holt, Rinehart and Winston, 1967. 253p. $5.95.
The twelve thoughtful essays collected in this volume seek to define the historical meaning of the Hungarian uprising of 1956. The authors represent a great variety of viewpoints, but all agree that the uprising achieved enduring results notwithstanding the fact that it was defeated. As R. Aron put it: "The revolutionaries were defeated, but their action survives because it was *wirklich*, as Hegel would have said, that is, genuine and efficient." One theme, particularly relevant to the Hungarian revolution, receives special emphasis; this is nationalism, a complex motivating force of collective action which finds no place in the Marxist scheme but which all Marxist regimes felt impelled to come to terms with or turn to advantage.
        SR, 27:2:324-5   R: Paul Kecskemeti

1422.   Balázs, Éva H. **Berzeviczy Gergely, a Reformpolitikus (1763-1795).** Budapest, Akadémiai Kiadó, 1967. 388p. 70Ft.
G. Berzeviczy (1763-1822) was one of the precursors of the nineteenth-century Hungarian reform movements. His views differed, however, in many respects from the gentry liberalism that sustained the Hungarian reform movements of the pre-March era. The descendant of a noted gentry family of northeastern Hungary, he sympathized from his youth with the reforms of Joseph II. He was especially interested in the possibilities of modernizing the stagnant Hungarian economic system. In his principal treatise of 1806 he pointed out, however, that economic reforms were tied necessarily to the emancipation of the peasants and to the improvement of their economic and social conditions. This study is a most successful portrayal of the early life and personal development of Berzeviczy to 1795, done by a noted Hungarian historian. Western students of Hungarian history will welcome the rich documentation in the appendix, which occupies over 150 pages. A useful index of names has also been included.
        SR, 29:1:731-2   R: Paul Bödy

1423.   Barany, George. **Stephen Széchenyi and the Awakening of Hungarian Nationalism, 1791-1841.** Princeton, Princeton University Press, 1968. 487p. $15.00.
Széchenyi's life was replete with paradoxes. A rich aristocrat and cosmopolitan who remained unswervingly loyal to the Habsburg dynasty, a man who till the age of thirty hardly knew Hungarian and was scarcely familiar with his "fatherland," he was to become the national awakener of modern Hungary. Barany uses fully all the ingredients of modern analytic biography. The book is based on thorough research. The 1,500 footnotes embrace the entire literature on Széchenyi, including the 24 massive volumes of his collected works, letters, and papers. The book is more than the biography of an outstanding person, for Széczenyi is skillfully placed within his age. Barany finds that his subject's character and ability coincided with the needs of an age ripe for reform, and he expertly interweaves the other figures and problems of the first part of the Hungarian "Reform Age" with Széchenyi's activities and concerns. This book

is the best Széchenyi biography as well as the most competent work on Hungary's "Reform Age" ever to appear in the West.

SR, 33:3:683-4   R: Peter Hanak

1424. Bayerle, Gustav. **Ottoman Diplomacy in Hungary: Letters from the Pashas of Buda, 1590-1593.** Bloomington, Indiana University Publications, 1972. 204p. (Uralic and Altaic Series, vol. 101). $6.00pa.

The letters of the pashas of Buda, written mostly in Hungarian, are to be found in great numbers in the Austrian and Hungarian archives. Their publication started about half a century ago, when 451 letters written between 1553 and 1589 appeared in the volume compiled by Sándor Takáts *et al.* This present volume contains 107 letters in their original Hungarian text, but with English summaries.

SR, 33:1:167-8   R: F. Szakály

1425. Böddy, Paul. **Joseph Eötvös and the Modernization of Hungary, 1840-1870: A Study of Ideas of Individuality and Social Pluralism in Modern Politics.** Philadelphia, Transactions of the American Philosophical Society (New Series, Volume 62, Part 2). 1972. 134p. $5.00.

Böddy's book is more than a worthwhile addition to Hungarian historiography in English. Partly based on archival research carried out during a year's stay in Hungary, Böddy's monograph is an important contribution to Hungarian historiography in any language. Despite the position and prestige Eötvös had achieved as a politician and as a writer, he was bound to fail against the overwhelming forces of class prejudice, narrow-mindedness, and Hungarian nationalism. To speak of modernization of Hungary in the second half of the nineteenth century is to invite controversy.

EEQ, 8:1:110-2   R: Mario Fenyo

1426. Ignotus, Paul. **Hungary.** New York, Praeger, 1972. 333p. (Nations of the Modern World Series). $11.50.

Although not an historical survey in the traditional sense, this is a work that should be read by everyone interested in Hungarian history and culture. The author has produced in this book a work that is perhaps too selective and impressionistic, yet at the same time it is enlightening and refreshing. He is at his best when dealing with the impact of literature and the literati on Hungarian history.

SR, 33:3:575-6   R: Steven Bela Vardy

1427. Janos, Andrew C., and William B. Slottman, eds. **Revolution in Perspective: Essays on the Hungarian Soviet Republic.** Berkeley, University of California Press, 1971. 181p.

The six essays, by five authors, contained in this volume were presented to the Berkeley Conference commemorating the fiftieth anniversary of Belá Kun's short-lived Hungarian Soviet Republic of 1919. Taken as a whole, the essays represent a synthesis of the known facts in 1969. Kenesz's essay, "Coalition Politics in the Hungarian Soviet Republic," may be singled out for its lucidity and the freshness of its presentation.

SEER, 51:124:483-4   R: F. T. Zsuppan

1428.   Kiraly, Bela K. **Hungary in the Late Eighteenth Century: The Decline of Enlightened Despotism.** New York, Columbia University Press, 1969. 295p. (East Central European Studies). $9.75.
The principal merit of the book is that it provides for the American reader an analysis of Hungarian feudal society in the late eighteenth century. The author gives a balanced account of the Hungarian class structure, of Hungarian institutions, their relationship to the Habsburg central government, and of the religious controversies in eighteenth century Hungary. In the second section of his study, the author discusses diverse aspects of the noble revolt of 1790. The principal ingredient of that revolt was the partially successful political initiative of the Hungarian lesser nobility, designed to counteract the political and social innovations of Joseph II. By implication the author also demonstrates the reasons for the weakness of Western liberal influences in Hungarian political life and society.
                 EEQ, 4:1:112-3   R: Paul Böy

1429.   Lackó, M. **Arrow-Cross Men, National Socialists: 1935-1944.** Budapest, Akadémiai Kiadó, 1969. 112p. (Studia Historica, Academiae Scientiarum Hungaricae, 61). $6.00.
This volume is an abridged and inferior version of the original work in Hungarian (1966). Missing are, among other things, the fine analysis of the 1939 secret parliamentary elections and the biography of Ferenz Szálasi, the Arrow-Cross leader. The author, a Marxist, freely admits that the Arrow-Cross had a wide base, even among workers, and that at one point the Arrow-Cross miners almost brought the Hungarian economy to a standstill while vainly hoping for a German invasion of their country. On the other hand, the book swarms with unsupported statements of collective behavior of various social groups.
                 SR, 30:1:185   R: István Deák

1430.   McCagg, William O. **Jewish Nobles and Geniuses in Modern Hungary.** Boulder, Colo. *East European Quarterly*, 1972; distr. by Columbia University Press, New York. 254p. (East European Monographs, no. 3). $9.00.
The eye-catching title seems somewhat ambitious. The term "genius" escapes precise classification. The author's effort to explore "whether the overall experience of the Jewish nobility can afford us some explanations of the galaxy of Hungarian geniuses to which the group contributed" is a provocative experiment. Designed not to close questions but rather to stimulate further investigation, his independent-minded work, with a wealth of data on industrialization, assimilation, and education during Hungary's liberal era, is a welcome challenge to students of modernizing backward societies.
                 SR, 33:3:576-8   R: George Barany

1431.   Mindszenty, Jozsef Cardinal. **Memoirs.** New York, Macmillan, 1974. 341p. $10.00.
The bulk of the autobiography, translated from German by Richard and Clara Winston, gives matter-of-fact descriptions of the struggle between the church and the Communist government, the Cardinal's removal, torture, trial, imprisonment, brief freedom in 1956, followed by 15 years in asylum at the U.S. embassy

in Budapest, his travel to Vienna. More a manifesto in historical context than
an autobiography, Mindszenty describes his lifelong uncompromising fight
against the enemies of his church. Even at the age of 82 he did not desire
security in "complete and absolute exile," but rather sought leadership in
a crusade. At a time of an incipient détente between East and West, political
and ecclesiastical leaders, including the Holy See, advised against the publication of the memoirs. However, the Cardinal felt compelled by his conscience
to disregard the advice and publish the autobiography.

     HSN, 7(1975):3

1432.   Molnár, Miklós. **Budapest 1956: A History of the Hungarian Revolution.**
       Trans. by Jennetta Ford. London, George Allen & Unwin, 1968.
       303p. £4.25.

The French original of this work was published in 1968. Molnár's book establishes
the complete interdependence of events in the people's democracies and their
dependence on the will of the USSR. The logic of the Hungarian revolution
and the rhythm of its development are part of an indissolubly interlinked chain
of events: the ferment in the Soviet Union after Stalin's death, Imre Nagy's
"new course" of 1953-55, the fall of Malenkov, the fall of Imre Nagy, the
Twentieth Congress of the CPSU, Poznań, the new Hungarian movement of
defiance, inflexible neo-Stalinism, revolution in Hungary, ferment in Czechoslovakia, and Rumania's own peculiar foreign policy. The present book is an
excellent, systematic, and scholarly treatment written with the insight of a
participant and scholar.

     SR, 32:4:842   R: Belá K. Király

1433.   Pryce-Jones, David. **The Hungarian Revolution.** New York, Horizon
       Press, 1970. 127p. $4.95.

This book is essentially a pictorial chronicle. Numerous photographs showing
crowds milling in the streets, Soviet tanks in action, scenes of fighting, and
key personalities, convey the drama and agony of the unequal struggle; the text
provides a running commentary. The longest chapter (pp. 61-103) is devoted to
a day-by-day account of the two weeks of Hungary's revolutionary upheaval
(October 23 to November 4, 1956). The narrative is punctuated by well-chosen
brief quotations from prominent as well as anonymous participants in the revolutionary events. The book does give an evocative, searching record of one of
the most tragic episodes in recent history.

     SR, 30:3:687   R: Paul Kecskemeti

1434.   Szinai, Miklós, and Lászlo Szücs, eds. **The Confidential Papers of
       Admiral Horthy.** Budapest, Corvina, 1965. 439p.

Despite Horthy's assurance in his *Memoirs* (1957) that he had personally destroyed
most of his private papers, a considerable part of his papers fell first into the hands
of the Germans, then, at war's end, into those of the Russians, to be returned in
1959 to the Hungarian People's Republic. A Hungarian edition of a selection of
these documents published in 1963 has now been succeeded by a slightly
condensed English translation. It contains seventy-odd documents out of a total
of some 440 papers now kept in the Hungarian National Record Office. The
topics of the published papers vary widely: from foreign affairs to Horthy's

private musings on such things as racial health, the honor of an officer, or the many dangers threatening the well-being of his family, class, and nation. They also make excellent reading for those who appreciate Central European drama.
SR, 24:3:547-8   R: István Deák

1435.   Tókés, Rudolf L. **Béla Kun and the Hungarian Soviet Republic: The Origins and Role of the Communist Party of Hungary in the Revolutions of 1918-1919.** New York, Praeger; London, Pall Mall Press, 1967. 292p. (Hoover Institution Publications). $7.50.
Tókés's book, concerned with Béla Kun, discusses his role in the creation of the Hungarian Soviet Republic. The author utilized the documents and periodicals available to Western scholars, and his thorough research makes this work a real contribution. His treatment traces the development of Hungarian Communism from the extreme socialists of the Hungarian labor movement, and discusses the role of the Hungarian prisoners of war who became members of the Bolshevik faction of the RSDLP and who first established the Communist Party of Hungary in Russia during October-November 1918. The work has eleven appendices, making available for the first time several documents in English translation; an excellent bibliography; and a good, brief biographical section on the leaders of the Hungarian labor movement to August 1919.
SR, 27:2:323   R: Ivan Volgyes

1436.   Vardy, Steven Bela. **Hungarian Historiography and the Geistesgeschichte School.** Cleveland, Arpad Academy Publications, 1974. 96p. (Studies by Members of the Arpad Academy, no. 1). $4.00.
This study deals basically with the nature of interwar Hungarian historiography. Its basic thesis is that—contrary to the generally accepted belief by interwar and more recent historians—the so-called *Geistesgeschichte* School, while undoubtedly the most important one, was not the only worthwhile orientation or school in the historiography of interwar Hungary. In addition to the English and Hungarian version of the text, the work also includes an extensive bibliography on Hungarian historiography, as well as a detailed name and subject index.
S. M. H.

1437.   Volgyes, Ivan, ed. **Hungary in Revolution, 1918-19: Nine Essays.** Lincoln, University of Nebraska Press, 1971. 219p. $12.50.
This volume of essays gave nine recognized experts the opportunity to express themselves on certain aspects of the 1918-19 events in Hungary. The result is a welcome contribution to the growing literature on the subject. The first three essays set the stage for the establishment of the Hungarian Soviet Republic. Other contributors cover a great variety of topics dealing with the internal policies, nationality problem, and foreign relations. The book will be read for many years to come.
SR, 32:3:645-6   R: Peter F. Sugar

Literature

1438.   Aczel, Tamas. **The Ice Age.** New York, Simon & Schuster, 1965. 287p. $5.95.

The Ice Age, written by the onetime poet laureate of Communist Hungary, recaptures the mood of Budapest in the early fifties–above all, the fear gripping every aspect of life. The only escape from the all-pervading gloom was the acrid, black, Budapest humor, which turned every pompous dogma into absurdity– a sense of humor Aczel brings alive in his book. The plot of the novel concerns the arrest of an outstanding physician. The author treats this central event in a circular fashion, detailing more and more of its repercussions.

SR, 29:3:560   R: Paul Debreczeny

1439.   Ady, Endre. **Poems of Endre Ady.** Intro. and trans. by Anton N. Nyerges. Buffalo, Hungarian Cultural Foundation, 1969. 491p. (State University of New York, Buffalo, Program in Soviet and East Central European Studies, no. 1). $10.00.

Nyerges's volume of Ady translations is pioneering in this subject and impressive in its scope. The documentary portions of this volume–the long, learned intro-duction and the section of priceless photographs at the end–are excellent. The translating is uneven at best.

SR, 30:2:448   R: Emery E. George

1440.   Leader, Ninon A. M. **Hungarian Classical Ballads and Their Folklore.** Cambridge, Cambridge University Press, 1967. 367p. $12.50.

Leader's work aims 1) to provide an accurate description of the main Hungarian classical ballads in their several versions and 2) to examine the characteristics, recurrent themes, motifs, and underlying folk beliefs of Hungarian classical ballads and relate them to their international parallels, with particular reference to English and Scottish balladry. The excellent introduction provides an histor-ical survey of Hungarian ballad research, describes the chief collections, outlines regions of collection, discusses the Székelys' and Csángos' role in preserving old ballads, and classifies Hungarian ballads into old and new. A selected bibliog-raphy is appended, as well as indexes of motifs, ballad titles, and authors cited. Leader's work is an excellent introduction to the Hungarian subject matter of ballads and related folklore.

SR, 30:1:215-6   R: Barbara Krader

1441.   Nagy, László. **Love of the Scorching Wind: Selected Poems, 1953-1971.** Trans. by Tony Connor and Kenneth McRobbie. New York, Oxford University Press, 1973. 84p. $9.75.

This collection of selected poems by Nagy clearly dispels the notion that in the translation of literature, it is poetry that does not come through. Perhaps in this case this is because the two translators are distinguished poets themselves. Certainly the grace, verve, and scope of vision possessed by Nagy are apparent in each of these carefully shaped poems. A foreword by George Gömöri is invaluable to the reader who is encountering Nagy for the first time. A bibliography of Nagy's work and a few pages of notes on particular references round out this valuable and delightful book.

CSP, 17:1:166-7   R: Carol Shields

1442.   Quinn, David B., and Neil M. Cheshire. **The New Found Land of Stephen Parmenius: The Life and Writings of a Hungarian Poet.** Toronto, University of Toronto Press, 1972. 250p. $8.50.

This volume introduces Parmenius, his work, and the circle in which he moved in his adopted England. It reprints in edited form the poets two surviving poems and a long letter written from Newfoundland offering on facing pages new English translations of the Latin original. The works are thoroughly annotated and are preceded by a full critical and historical introduction. Parmenius was one of the few Renaissance Latinists to take the new lands and the voyages to them as the subject of epic poetry. This volume is based on his intimate association with Hakluyt and the English explorers.

HSN, 5(1974):2

1443.   Reményi, Joseph. **Hungarian Writers and Literature: Modern Novelists, Critics, and Poets.** Ed. with an intro. by August J. Molnar. New Brunswick, N.J., Rutgers University Press, 1964. 512p. $12.00.

The book is well structured and balanced. It starts with two historical surveys, which are followed by essays on fifteen writers and poets of the nineteenth century. In the third part, 27 novelists, poets, and critics of the twentieth century are presented, of whom seven are contemporary writers. Finally, three essays comment on Hungarian humor, on the tragic sense, and on English translations. Reményi's style is smooth, convincing, and often brilliant; technical but never cumbersome. He is a bold critic with the obvious detachment of the scientist even when discussing such controversial writers as Ady and Dezsó Szabó. His concern is with literary art—wherever it may be.

SR, 24:1:155-6   R: Károly Nagy

1444.   Riedl, Frederick. **A History of Hungarian Literature.** London, William Heinemann, 1906. [Gale Research, Detroit, 1968.] 293p. $14.50.

F. Riedl (1856-1921) was a well-known Hungarian literary historian. His approach is overwhelmingly nationalistic. "Hungarian literature," he writes, "is, in fact, the record of Hungarian patriotism. The ideas of nation, fatherland, and race are much more pronounced in it than in other literatures." The book has value only for someone who does not read Hungarian yet wishes to study, not Hungarian literature, but a chapter in the development of Hungarian literary scholarship. For those interested in Hungarian literature, a good basic textbook would be that of Joseph Reményi (1964).

SR, 30:1:216-7   R: Paul Debreczeny

1445.   Weöres, Sándor, and Ferenc Juhász. **Selected Poems.** Trans. with intro. by Edwin Morgan and David Wevill. Harmondsworth, Penguin Books, 1970. 136p. $0.95.

This anthology is divided into two parts: the first contains the poems of Weöres (born 1913) is the last typical representative of contemporary Hungarian poetry, and Juhász (born 1928) is the most outstanding poet of the post-war generation deeply rooted in the best traditions of Hungarian poetry. The translators have done an admirable job.

SEEJ, 15:4:515-6   R: Marianna D. Birnbaum

POLAND

General Reference Works

1446.   Beneš, Václav L., and Norman J. G. Pounds. **Poland**. New York, Praeger, 1970. 416p. $10.00.
The first two parts of this handbook-study, entitled "History" and "Land and the Resources," were written by Pounds, and Beneš wrote the remaining two parts on "The Polish Republic" (born after World War I) and "The People's Republic." This well-written book is supplemented by 11 maps and 26 illustrations. There are some helpful appendixes, including one on place-name variations, as well as a bibliography and an index.

SR, 31:3:714-5   R: W. J. Wagner

1447.   Bromke, Adam, and John W. Strong, eds. **Gierek's Poland**. New York, Praeger, 1973. 220p. $15.00.
This volume, which originally appeared as a part of a special issue of the *Canadian Slavonic Papers* in 1973, is a part of the "Carleton Series in Soviet and East European Studies." It is unique in that of the seventeen contributors, eight are active in Polish society and politics. Five others are living in Canada. With the exception of military affairs, almost all major topics—domestic, politics, economic reform, agriculture, theatre, religion, foreign policy—of interest in contemporary Poland are touched upon in this volume.

CSP, 16:4:682   R: R. C. E.

1448.   Hoskins, Janina W., comp. **Early and Rare Polonica of the 15th-17th Centuries in American Libraries: A Bibliographical Survey**. Boston, G. K. Hall, 1973. 193p. $19.50.
The survey lists *circa* 1,200 entries; since many of the books are represented by more than one copy and so kept by more than one library, the total number of volumes recorded is twice as large and amounts to *ca.* 2,400 items. The language of the books is mostly other than Polish. This is a very valuable addition to the number of standard books on Polish bibliography and a must for every reference library with an East European division.

PR, 18:3:90-1   R: Leszek Kukulski

1449.   Hoskins, Janina W., comp. **Polish Books in English, 1945-1971**. Washington, D. C., G. P. O., 1974. 163p. $1.55pa.
This bibliography contains more than 1,000 English-language books and pamphlets published in Poland or translated into English outside Poland from 1945 to 1971. The bibliography covers the social sciences and the humanities.

S. M. H.

1450.   Maciuszko, Jerzy J. **The Polish Short Story in English: A Guide and Critical Bibliography**. Detroit, Wayne State University Press, 1968. 473p. $15.00.
This book covers the period from 1884 (first recorded translation) through 1960, listing some 600 items painstakingly traced in obscure periodicals, out-of-print anthologies, and ephemeral publications. It is a book badly needed in everyday work by any scholar or student of Polish literature, providing him with a most useful tool in his research and, at the same time, pointing out new directions which many of our students will certainly follow.
            SEEJ, 14:3:397   R: Jerzy R. Krzyżanowski

1451.   Taborski, Boleslaw. **Polish Plays in English Translations: A Bibliography**. New York, Polish Institute of Arts and Sciences in America, 1968. 79p. $2.50pa.
Taborski's useful compilation lists by authors (79 in all) all known published and unpublished Polish plays in English translation up to September 1967. Each author rates a brief biographical sketch. Every play is annotated with publication and/or production dates, the translator's name and his address if the play is unpublished, the number of characters and a succinct but revealing plot summary. A selected bibliography in English on Polish drama and dramatists is included, along with an author index.
            SR, 28:2:360-1   R: Irene Nagurski

1452.   Teets, Bruce E., and Helmut E. Gerber, eds. **Joseph Conrad: An Annotated Bibliography of Writings about Him**. DeKalb, Northern Illinois University Press, 1971. 671p. $20.00.
The bibliography contains 1,977 entries which are arranged by year and cover the period between 1895 and early 1967. There is also a checklist of Conrad's works, an index to primary titles, and indices to secondary works, periodicals, and newspapers, and foreign languages.
            PR, 29:1:98-100   R: Robert Bense

Fine Arts

1453.   Knox, Brian. **The Architecture of Poland**. New York, Praeger, 1971. 161p. + 216 photographs. $18.50.
Knox has written an informative and perceptive guide to the architecture of Poland. It is organized topographically, by regions and their principal cities. Within these limitations a chronological development is rather freely maintained. This book is not only a most welcome traveling companion but also a useful tool in English for the nonspecialized art historian.
            SR, 31:3:715   R: J. L. S. Lozinski

1454.   Kott, Jan. **Theatre Notebook: 1947-1967**. Trans. from the Polish by Boleslaw Taborski. Garden City, N.Y., Doubleday, 1968. 268p. $5.95cl.; $2.95pa.
This is a collection of essays and reviews divided into two parts. The first, preceded by a lecture on "A Genealogy of Polish Drama," consists of 24 reviews

of plays staged in Poland; the second gives us impressions of a roving critic who had the good luck to see theatrical performances not only in Western Europe and the USSR but also in such countries as China and Tunisia. Kott is fascinated by the political implications of the theater and has an uncanny perception of them.

      SR, 28:4:687-8   R: Wiktor Weintraub

1455.   Zachwatowicz, Jan. **Polish Architecture.** Trans. from the Polish by
          Marek Latynski. Warsaw, Arkady, 1967. 155p. 376pl. 300zł.
This beautiful book afford a concise and coherent account of ten centuries of Polish architecture—that is, of the entire history of the modern Polish state. Its format is simple: eight textual sections, each dealing with a major stylistic phase, followed by a series of photographic studies of outstanding buildings of that epoch. The text isefl bears every evidence of first-rate translation, since even technical terms are accurately transposed into the modern American idiom. The plans and photographs are uniformly excellent.

      SR, 28:4:670-2   R: James Marston Fitch

Economics

1456.   Feiwel, George R. **Poland's Industrialization Policy: A Current
          Analysis: Sources of Economic Growth and Retrogression.
          Industrialization and Planning under Polish Socialism. Vol. 1.**
          New York, Praeger, 1971. 748p. $25.00.

1457.   Feiwel, George R. **Problems in Polish Economic Planning: Continuity,
          Change, and Prospects. Industrailization and Planning under Polish Socialism**
          Vol. 2. New York, Praeger, 1971. 454p. $20.00. (Vols. 1 and 2, $39.50).
The two volumes are part of Praeger's *Special Studies in International Economics and Development* series. Feiwel presents an extensive study of Polish economic development since World War II. He analyzes the following aspects: the nature of the planning economy, dynamics of a centrally planned economy, shifts in patterns of resource allocation, all three five-year plans with their implications and problems, economic reforms in perspective, financing of investments, blueprints for 1971-75, changing the system for the 1970s, and optimism in planning. A selected bibliography of 39 pages contains mainly Polish sources and monographs. This study is essential for students of East European economics.

                          S. M. H.

1458.   Korbonski, Andrzej. **Politics of Socialist Agriculture in Poland, 1945-
          1960.** New York, Columbia University Press, 1965. 330p. (East
          Central European Studies of Columbia University). $7.50.
Korbonski's unique contribution to scholarship is his explanation of the collapse of collectivization in Poland. The policy was introduced for ideological rather than economic reasons and under pressure from Moscow during W. Gomulka's imprisonment. Collectivization did not increase agricultural production and served merely to alienate the peasants, who hated the entire program. Upon his return to the leadership of the party, Gomulka acknowledge the failure

of Communist agricultural policy and permitted the immediate dissolution of the collectives; he was convinced that there could be no rise in the standard of living as long as collectivization continued.

JMH, 37:4:522-3   R: Charles Morley

1459.   Podolski, T. M. **Socialist Banking and Monetary Control: The Experience of Poland.** New York, Cambridge University Press, 1973. 392p. (Soviet and East European Studies Series). $28.50.

In addition to the description of bank control over enterprise behavior, Podolski also suggests that the bank has little power to control the overall level of spending and thereby the rate of inflation through the use of traditional monetary policy tools. He argues that Polish enterprises have resorted to the use of illicit trade credit, that the velocity of money in Poland is quite variable and accommodates itself to the needs of the enterprise.

SR, 33:1:161   R: Joyce Pickersgill

1460.   Zielinski, Janusz G. **Economic Reforms in Polish Industry.** New York, Oxford University Press, 1973. 333p. (Institute of Soviet and East European Studies, University of Glasgow. Economic Reforms in East European Industry Series). $21.00.

This is not an easy book to read—certainly not one for the general reader and rather heavy going even for the average undergraduate. But for all serious students of East European economics this study is a valuable addition to the existing literature on this subject. Zielinski's analysis quite often transcends the narrower boundaries of economic reforms in Polish industry to deal with more general aspects of Communist planned economies and their uphill struggle to evolve more rational methods of planning and management. This book is undoubtedly the best and the most comprehensive study of economic reforms in Poland published in the West. It is also a gold mine of statistical information on various aspects of the Polish economy.

SR, 33:4:795-6   R: Michael GAmarnikov

Education

1461.   Fiszman, Joseph R. **Revolution and Tradition in People's Poland: Education and Socialization.** Princeton, Princeton University Press, 1972. 382p. $15.00cl.; $7.50pa.

This is a study of Polish teachers made by the author during visits between 1965 and 1969. After describing some of the basic characteristics of Polish society under Communism, the author discusses ways of educating teachers, their life and status, their socialization, and their attitudes toward religion and the official Marxist-Leninist ideology. Even if Polish teachers experience considerable difficulties, their objective performance is quite impressive in comparison with many other parts of the world, including even North America. The major value of the book is in offering a good insight into the role-ambiguity of teachers under authoritarian rule of atheists in a traditionally Christian society.

CSP, 16:1:122-4   R: Alexander Matejko

1462.   Singer, Gusta. **Teacher Education in a Communist State: Poland,**
         1956-1961. New York, Bookman Associates, 1965. 282p. $6.00.
After briefly describing the Polish educational system, the author provides the
historical context of teacher education during 1918-1956. Then follows a
detailed treatment of the organization and curriculum of teacher education and
of the impact of the 1961 reform on the development of teacher training, with
special stress on the role of the Polish United Workers' Party. Also useful are
the numerous charts and statistical tables and the thirty-page bibliography.
         SR, 29:1:141-2   R: William W. Brickman

Government and Politics

1463.   Blit, Lucjan. **The Origins of Polish Socialism: The History and Ideas**
         of the First Polish Socialist Party, 1878-1886. Cambridge, Cambridge
         University Press, 1971. 160p. (International Studies, published for the
         Centre for International Studies, London School of Economics and
         Political Science). $10.00.
This brief book examines the origins, short-lived activities, and precipitous
demise of the Polish Social Revolutionary Party—Proletariat. Decidedly
internationalist in its program, the party represented the first appearance of
an antipatriotic faction in Polish Marxism and may be viewed as the spiritual
antecedent of the SDKP i L (Social Democratic Party of the Kingdom of
Poland and Lithuania) of the 1890s. The author treats the early history of the
Proletariat as a biographical reflection of its founder and principal spokesman,
Ludwik Waryński. Blit's work opens to students of Marxism who are not versed
in Polish the intriguing Polish chapter in the early history of European socialist
parties.
         SR, 31:4:920   R: Lawrence Orton

1464.   Groth, Alexander J. **People's Poland: Government and Politics.** San
         Francisco, Chandler Publishing Co., 1972. 155p. (Chandler Publications
         in Political Science). $3.95pa.
This is a useful little book, with no pretension to a novel theoretical approach.
Its main objective is to serve as an introduction to Poland's politics, and it contains
a comprehensive survey of political, economic, and social developments in that
country from the Communist takeover in 1944 until Gierek's ascendancy to
power in 1970. A good balance is maintained in describing political institutions
and processes—domestic as well as external.
         SR, 32:2:407-8   R: Adam Bromke

1465.   Morrison, James F. **The Polish People's Republic.** Baltimore, Johns
         Hopkins Press, 1968. 160p. $6.50cl.; $2.95pa.
Though published as part of a series ("Integration and Community Building
in Eastern Europe," ed. by Jan F. Triska), this short survey of the Polish
People's Republic represents a significant contribution to social scientific
analysis of Communist states in itself. Morrison quite correctly assesses Poland's
future development as being determined equally by its foreign relations as by

its domestic conditions. The book's outstanding value rests in its usefulness in the rapidly increasing number of courses on the comparative study of Communist systems.

PR, 15:3:91-2   R: James A. Kuhlman

1466.   Polonsky, Antony. **Politics in Independent Poland 1921-1939: The Crisis of Constitutional Government.** Oxford, Clarendon Press, 1972. 572p. $27.50.

The study is based on broad reading and research. It conscientiously documents the unsurprising thesis that Polish democracy worked poorly in the early 1920s, and that Pilsudski's effort at guided democracy did no better. Pilsudski himself emerges as a tragic figure illustrating the futility of moral approaches to politics. Without greater industrialization, fuller employment, and the diminution of rural poverty, political activity was inevitably restricted to an elite. The book provides a comprehensive, well-documented survey of political development. The author's criterion for political success is not purely political but lies in the solution of pressing economic, nationality, military, and diplomatic problems as well. A particularly fine chapter on the social and economic background sets the stage.

CSP, 15:4:595-6   R: Daniel Stone

1467.   Rothschild, Joseph. **Pilsudski's Coup d'Etat.** New York, Columbia University Press, 1966. 435p. (East Central European Studies of Columbia University). $10.00.

Pilsudski's coup d'état marks a turning point in the interwar history not only of Poland but also of East Central Europe, for it initiated a trend toward dictatorship in that region. This is a masterful study. The author cites hundreds of studies, articles, published and unpublished Polish documents, and memoirs; he used some Polish archival materials and interviewed several men who had been close to Pilsudski. Rothschild is at his best in describing the execution of the coup: both the military operations and the political activities of the antagonists during the fighting. Pilsudski resorted to "armed demonstration" to force the resignation of the newly formed Right-Center coalition government of Witos. It is evident that Rothschild is fascinated by Pilsudski's personality and that he has little sympathy for Pilsudski's opponents.

SR, 27:1:143-5   R: Zygmunt J. Gasiorowski

1468.   Wagner, Wenceslas J., ed. **Polish Law throughout the Ages.** Stanford, Hoover Institution Press, 1970. 476p. (Hoover Institution Publications, 91). $14.00.

The book consists of three groups of essays: historical ones, those dealing with the modern law of Poland, mainly enacted between the wars, and those dealing with Polish contributions to legal theory. This volume is a valuable contribution to the history of Polish legal institutions. An extensive list of Polish books recommends this volume as an important bibliographical tool for scholars and librarians.

SR, 30:2:429-30   R: Kazimierz Grzybowski

1469.   Wynot, Edward D., Jr. **Polish Politics in Transition: The Camp of National Unity and the Struggle for Power 1935-1939**. Athens, University of Georgia Press, 1974. 294p. $12.50.

Extensive research in Warsaw and London provided the background for this book. The study examines the political problems encountered by the men who governed Poland on the eve of World War II—problems complicated by the nation's difficult transition from a traditional agrarian to a modern industrial society in post-Pilsudski Poland. Against a background of increasing international tension and the steady erosion of Poland's diplomatic position, Wynot describes the events of 1935 to 1939 and provides a case study of the political, social, and economic experimentation inherent in the history of a developing country. An extensive bibliography and index make this study a valuable contribution to the existing literature on interwar Poland.   S. M. H.

Foreign Policy

1470.   Bromke, Adam. **Poland's Politics: Idealism or Realism**. Cambridge, Harvard University Press, 1967. 316p. (Russian Research Center Studies, 51). $9.95.

The book is compact, well-written, perceptive, and richly detailed without being pedestrian. It stimulates thought and probably for years to come will shape the understanding of the topic by interested scholars and, perhaps, the consciousness of the Poles themselves. It discusses Polish foreign policy in the context of two basic attitudes which have existed since the eighteenth century—political idealism and political realism. The chapters on contemporary Poland contain a careful analysis not only of the views nurtured within the Communist Party, but also of those marginal political groups that were permitted to exist by the grace of the Communists in post-war Poland. Unfortunately, Bromke failed to take into account the Catholic Church, a highly significant domestic variable influencing the behavior of Polish policy-makers.
　　　　CSP, 11:1:137-40　　　　　　　R: Vincent Chrypinski

1471.   Cienciala, Anna M. **Poland and the Western Powers, 1938-1939: A Study in the Interdependence of Eastern and Western Europe**. Toronto, University of Toronto Press, 1968. 310p. $9.00.

The author points out that, among the post-Versailles states of East Central Europe, Poland was in a uniquely disadvantageous position because she was the neighbor of two dynamic powers who were both dissatisfied with the post-World War I settlement. Poland not only had to strive to avert German menace, but she also had to consider the possibility of Soviet encroachment and expansion. Thus, Poland had to navigate between two dangers. The Western Powers regarded East Central Europe as a nuisance and extended little help to the countries of the area. France, after having signed a treaty of defensive alliance with Poland in 1921, persistently tried to disengage herself from the affairs of East Central Europe. This study is the best defense of Colonel Beck's policy to be published so far.
　　　　SR, 29:1:118-9　　　　　　　R: M. K. Dziewanowski

1472.   **Documents on Polish-Soviet Relations, 1939-1945.** General Sikorski
         Historical Institute. Preface by Count Edward Raczynski. Vol. I:
         1939-1942; Vol. II: *1943-1945*. London, Heinemann, 1941-1967.
         Vol. I. 625p. £3.50. Vol. II. 866p. £5.25.
The purpose of this two-volume work was to make available documentary
evidence relating to the policies of the Polish and Soviet governments during
the Second World War. The Soviet documents are only partially available;
some of them were published in Volume VII of the *Dokumenty i materialy po
istorii Sovetsko-polskikh otnoshenii* (Moscow: Izdatelstvo "Nauka," 1973). The
size as well as the scope of the collection is impressive. It includes texts of
treaties, official documents, letters, statements, and various other pertinent
material. This colossal collection has become indispensable in the study of
Polish-Soviet relations and Soviet political action in the area of foreign relations.
Each volume is complete with appendixes, notes, and index.
S. M. H.

1473.   Gromada, Thaddeus V., ed. **Essays on Poland's Foreign Policy, 1918-
         1939.** New York, Jozef Pilsudski Institute of America, 1970. 71p.
         Paper.
The fiftieth anniversary of Poland's independence was celebrated in New York
in November 1968 with an academic conference, and this book contains papers
presented there on Polish interwar diplomacy. Its main value lies in giving the
reader a quick taste of some of the current scholarship on Polish interwar
diplomatic history.
S. M. H.

1474.   Horak, Stephan. **Poland's International Affairs, 1919-1960: A Calendar
         of Treaties, Agreements, Conventions, and Other International Acts,
         with Annotations, References, and Selections from Documents and
         Text of Treaties.** Bloomington, Indiana University, 1964. 248p.
         (Russian and East European Series, vol. 31). $6.50.
This volume attempts to furnish valuable reference material of modern Polish
history by listing almost all bilateral treaties to which Poland was a signatory
between 1919 and 1960, including selected multilateral treaties and documents
related to Poland in the same period.
SEEJ, 9:3:356   R: Josef Korbel

1475.   Jedrzejewicz, Waclaw, ed. **Diplomat in Paris, 1936-1939: Papers and
         Memoirs of Juliusz Lakasiewicz, Ambassador of Poland.** New York,
         Columbia University Press, 1970. 408p. $12.50.
This is a companion volume to *Diplomat in Berlin, 1933-1939: Papers and
Memoirs of Jozef Lipski* (1968). Skillfully edited, these two volumes constitute
the most important publication in English on Polish foreign policy in the crucial
years leading to the Second World War. The editor has expanded the memoirs,
published first in the form of articles for Polish émigré periodicals, by incorporating 64 documents (mostly Lukasiewicz's reports to the Foreign Minister
Josef Beck) into the text. These documents are by far the most important and
valuable part of the book. The editor also provided excellent introductory and

connecting notes and bibliography, though the notes are sometimes marred by
a strong pro-Polish bias.

SR, 30:2:411   R: Zygmunt J. Gasiorowski

1476.   Lipski, Jozef. **Diplomat in Berlin, 1933-1939: Papers and Memoirs of
         Jozef Lipski, Ambassador of Poland.** Ed. by Waclaw Jedrzejewicz.
         New York, Columbia University Press, 1968. 679p. $17.50.
According to the editor of this volume, Lipski was the "main author and
architect" of the Polish-German Declaration of Nonaggression of September
26, 1934, which—it is today generally recognized—opened the road to Nazi
expansion and the collapse of the French system of security in Europe. Five
years later he was the crown witness to the ruins of his own architectural structure when his policy of "neighborliness' with Germany ended in her invasion
of Poland. The book is an indispensable source for students of the diplomatic
history of the interwar period.

SR, 29:1:118   R: Josef Korbel

1477.   Riekhoff, Harald von. **German-Polish Relations, 1918-1933.** Baltimore,
         Johns Hopkins Press, 1971. 421p. $15.00.
Riekhoff has combined the substantial body of secondary studies and published
primary sources with new unpublished materials from the German Foreign
Ministry files and, to a lesser extent, from the Polish archives, in order to produce
a definitive study of German-Polish relations in the Weimar years. The book's
chief strength is its wealth of consistent, conscientious documentation and its
substantial body of information. Furthermore, the author skillfully relates foreign
affairs to domestic developments in each country, thereby revealing the intimate
connection between international relations and internal political considerations.
Riekhoff also frequently points out the role played by German-Polish affairs in
Soviet, British, and French diplomatic calculations. The book will serve as a
veritable encyclopedia of information for any scholar dealing with the diplomacy
of interwar Europe, not merely Poland or Germany.

SR, 31:4:917-8   R: Edward D. Wynot, Jr.

1478.   Wandycz, Piotr S. **Soviet-Polish Relations, 1917-1921.** Cambridge,
         Harvard University Press, 1969. 403p. (Russian Research Center
         Studies, 59). $10.00.
Basing his work on much hitherto unpublished archival material, Polish, Russian,
and to some extent British, as well as extensive published sources, Wandycz
has produced the most significant study of his subject to date. He demonstrates
that the Soviet version of self-determination was a farce—in reality an attempt
at the federation and then unification with Soviet Russia of all her borderlands,
including Poland. However, while Lenin succeeded in imposing his policy on
the Communist leaders of Belorussia, Lithuania, and the Ukraine, Pilsudski failed
to get strong backing for his aims from the Polish parliament and public opinion,
which were dominated by the National Democratic Party. It is hoped that this
book will be read not only by historians of Eastern Europe but by historians of
Western Europe as well.

SR, 29:3:533-4   R: Anna M. Cienciala

History

1479. Belch, Stanislaus F. **Paulus Vladimiri and His Doctrine Concerning International Law and Politics.** Vols. I and II. The Hague, Mouton, 1965. 1292p. 225Dglds.

These two imposing volumes occupy a truly outstanding place among the numerous scholarly publications that are appearing on the occasion of the millenium of Poland's Christianization. The author compared contributions of the first rectors of the University of Krakow to that of Nicolaus Copernicus. His excellent painstaking method became apparent when he edited, with introductory commentaries, an entirely unknown treatise of Vladimiri in Volume II (1955) and another treatise, previously edited satisfactorily, in Volume II (1956) of the series *Sacrum Poloniae Millennium*, in Rome. After a few more years of exhaustive study in Europe, he has now issued simultaneously one volume of almost 800 pages, which comprises a biography of Vladimiri and a detailed discussion of his political ideas on international relations, and a second (pages 771-1292), which, in addition to a bibliography and helpful indexes for both volumes, contains the text of twelve typical works of Vladimiri himself and two works written against him. The editorial method is perfect.

SR, 25:3:539-42   R: Oscar Halecki

1480. Bethell, Nicholas. **Gomulka: His Poland, His Communism.** New York, Holt, Rinehart and Winston, 1969. 296p. $5.95.

Bethell concentrates on Gomulka's wartime and post-war activities and on his re-emergence during the Polish "October" of 1956. Gomulka's very early socialization, why and how he came to identify with Communism, are, according to the author, too sparely documented to permit thorough investigation, and the years of leadership (1956-1967)—are given only one chapter. The last chapter, "His Darkest Year," describes the events of 1968 and concludes that "he [Gomulka] is a victim of East European politics."

SR, 30:1:182   R: Ellen Mickiewicz

1481. Bethell, Nicholas. **The War Hitler Won: The Fall of Poland, September 1939.** New York, Holt, Rinehart and Winston, 1973. 472p. $10.00.

The English historian and journalist Bethell has utilized the recently opened British archives together with a variety of published materials—including Polish ones—to prepare an account of the first portion of World War II. The author combines a considerable use of quotations with the passing out of evaluations.

SR, 33:2:361   R: Gerhard L. Weinberg

1482. Brock, Peter. **Nationalism and Populism in Partitioned Poland: Selected Essays.** London, Orbis Books, 1974. 219p. £5.00.

This volume is a collection of essays published earlier by Brock in various scholarly journals. The seven essays selected blend together, resulting in a solid review of Polish nationalism and populism in the partitioned era. A useful index of persons has been compiled for this collection. The book is recommended reading for all students of Polish history.

CSP, 16:4:682   R: J. W. S.

1482a. Chmielewski, Edward. **The Polish Question in the Russian State Duma.** Knoxville, University of Tennessee Press, 1970. 188p. $7.50.

This book is a study of an important problem in both Polish and Russian history. The author examines in detail the stenographic reports not only of the four Dumas but also of the State Council, and he makes broad use of contemporary newspaper accounts, memoirs written by participants and witnesses, and the existing literature, both Russian and Polish, on different aspects of the problem. It is a conscientious work and a worthy contribution. The Duma, the author says, "did not change substantially" Russia's "policies toward its Polish subjects."

SR, 31:1:161-3   R: Marc Szeftel

1483.   Ciechanowski, Jan M. **The Warsaw Rising of 1944**. New York, Cambridge University Press, 1974. 332p. $19.50.

This work, a revised version of the author's Polish edition (1971), is an excellent piece of research, richly informative and timely. The author is preoccupied with why the Polish underground Home Army took it upon itself to liberate Warsaw shortly before the Russians entered the capital, even though it was so lacking in troops and ammunition. He examines in detail the political, diplomatic, ideological, and military background of the rising, and the events and decisions which preceded it, in the first three chapters. Then he traces Polish politics, strategy, and diplomacy during the whole of the Second World War, to show the activities of the exiled government in London and the underground movement at home. The last three chapters discuss in detail insurrectionary operations. The book is well annotated with a detailed index.

SR, 34:2:416-7   R: Ludwik Nemec

1484.   Cieplak, Tadeusz N., ed. **Poland since 1956**. New York, Twayne Publishers, 1972. 482p. $9.00.

The book is significant for many reasons, one of which is its correction of certain preconceptions. Cieplak's collection of essays and readings, prefaced by his own brief introductions to each section, helps to explain that "monumental" event of 1956. It is hoped that the book, revised and updated, will have further editions in the future.

PR, 19:3-4:214-6   R: Mieczyslaw Maneli

1485.   Cynk, Jerzy B. **History of the Polish Air Force 1918-1968**. Reading, Engl., Osprey Publishing, 1972. 307p. 244 photographs. £7.50.

This book might very well and more appropriately be called a photographic or illustrated history of Polish military aviation. The photographs are superbly chosen and give an excellent overview of the development of the Polish Air Force in its fifty years of history. However, the author does not attempt to deal with issues of doctrine, strategic or tactical, or the general question of policy. He does not document his sources. Cynk is the first author in English to give an excellent account of the development and current state of the Polish People's Republic Air Force.

PR, 19:1:93-6   R: Michael Alfred Peszke

1486.   Davies, Norman. **White Eagle, Red Star: The Polish-Soviet War, 1919-20**. New York, St. Martin's Press, 1972. 318p. $10.00.

One of the main contributions of the monograph is the final destruction of the myth that General Weygand had anything to do with the Battle of Warsaw. Weygand repeatedly and explicitly denied that he had contributed to the Polish victory. Another merit of the book is that it views the war of 1920 not as an isolated and exotic event but as part of a wider scene of action and as a crucial event which determined the fate of Eastern Europe for some twenty years.

SR, 33:3:566   R: M. K. Dziewanowski

1487.   Dziewanowski, M. K. **Joseph Pilsudski: A European Federalist, 1918-1922.** Stanford, Hoover Institution Press, 1969. 379p. $8.70.
Pilsudski's eastern policy, from his assumption of power as head of the new Polish state in November 1918 to the final incorporation of the Wilno area in March 1922, forms the subject of this study. The author is aware of many of Pilsudski's shortcomings and critical of his policies in some respects. Indeed, it remains unclear if Pilsudski really had any clear-cut federalist policy beyond the romantic notions he imbibed as a member of the prewar Polish Socialist Party. The book, although by no means the last word on the subject, represents a valuable contribution to a continuing debate.
        SR, 29:4:724-5   R: Peter Brock

1488.   Fitzgibbon, Louis. **Katyn.** Intro. by Constantine Fitzgibbon. New York, Charles Scribner's Sons, 1971. 285p. $10.00.
This book on an already well-known subject consists mostly of extensive quotations from the testimonies of the former Polish prisoners of war and other documents. It also contains twenty pages of most gruesome photographs and the list of the 4,143 victims identified at Katyn. This is a thorough and well-written book.
        AHR, 77:5:1486-7   R: Zygmunt J. Gasiorowski

1489.   Kieniewicz, Stefan. **The Emancipation of the Polish Peasantry.** Chicago, University of Chicago Press, 1969. 285p. $11.75.
The book is in fact a history of the Polish peasantry from the end of the eighteenth century to the restoration of Poland at the close of World War I. Legally, the Polish peasant gained his freedom as early as 1794 when Kosciuszko issued the Polaniec Manifesto. Napoleon granted freedom to the peasant again when he established the Duchy of Warsaw in 1807. In reality, however, it was only as a result of the revolutions of 1848 that serfdom was abolished in Prussian and Austrian Poland, and not until 1864, following the January Uprising, in Russian Poland. In addition to the extensive bibliography of primary and secondary sources, almost exclusively in Polish, the most valuable feature of the book is the appendix of legislative documents.
        SR, 30:2:409-10   R: Charles Morley

1490.   Kimmich, Christoph M. **The Free City: Danzig and German Foreign Policy, 1919-1934.** New Haven, Yale University Press, 1968. 196p. $6.50.
The book is based on thorough research in the Politisches Archiv in Bonn, Bundesarchiv in Koblenz, and the Archives of the Secretariat of the League of Nations in Geneva. The main objective of German foreign policy was the revision of the Treaty of Versailles and the recovery of the eastern territories: West Prussia, Upper Silesia, and Danzig. Berlin subsidized the Free City heavily to make it economically independent of Poland and to maintain its irredentism, the aim being to turn it into a thorn in Poland's side. The policy of revisionism proved ineffective because Poland would not give in to pressure. Attempts to take advantage of Poland's economic difficulties failed. Balanced in judgment, well organized, thoroughly documented, and lucidly written, this is an excellent study.
        SR, 28:3:496-7   R: Zygmunt J. Gasiorowski

1491.   Knoll, Paul W. **The Rise of the Polish Monarchy: Piast Poland in East Central Europe, 1320-1370.** Chicago, University of Chicago Press, 1972. 276p. $11.00.

The author in his introduction shows a genuine understanding of what he calls the "context of Polish history," including its past glories and the achievements of Polish historiography old and new. The first two chapters deal with the reign of Wladyslaw Lokietek and explain the background of his "Restauratio Regni" in 1320 and his cooperation during the next thirteen years with his son Casimir, whose much longer reign is treated in the remaining six chapters with well-justified admiration but without uncritical idealization. Casimir's policy relied more on diplomacy than on the military means mainly used by his father, yet he did not hesitate to prosecute wars when they served a just cause and promised success.

SR, 32:3:635-6   R: Oscar Halecki

1492.   Pilsudski, Jozef. **Year 1920 and Its Climax Battle of Warsaw during the Polish-Soviet War, 1919-1920.** Including "March Beyond the Vistula," by M. Tukhachevski. New York, Pilsudski Institute, 1972. 283p. 27 maps in cover pocket. $10.00.

The myth that the plans of Lord d'Abernon and General Weygand "saved" Poland has been considerably weakened by Pilsudski's account of the events leading to the defeat of the Soviet Russian army in August 1920. The over-extended Russian front began to crumble rapidly as a result of Pilsudski's offensive from the northern flank. The victory at the gates of Warsaw in fact saved not only Poland but also Germany, the ultimate target of Soviet advancement to the west. Tukhachevski, who led the Soviet forces in the battle, corroborated Pilsudski's version in his own recollection. The publication of Pilsudski's notes and memoirs presents a valuable contribution to a most crucial period in Polish history.   S. M. H.

1493.   Pounds, Norman J. G. **Poland between East and West.** New York, Van Nostrand, 1964. 132p. (Van Nostrand Searchlight Book, no. 22). $1.45pa.

The theme of this highly readable and provocative book is that the periods of Poland's disappearance as an independent state were due not to Poland's exposed geographical location on the north European lowland plain with open frontiers to west and east, but rather to the weakness of its internal structure, both social and political. Pounds sums up the past thousand years of Polish history as a traditional conflict between the Piast concept of expanding westward to create a bulwark against the Germans and the Jagiellonian desire for expansion eastward. His thought-provoking views will give rise to considerable discussion between those who share them and those who do not.

SR, 24:3:554-5   R: Huey Louis Kostanick

1494.   Rousseau, Jean-Jacques. **The Government of Poland.** Trans. and notes by Willmoore Kendall. Indianapolis, Bobbs-Merrill, 1972. 116p. (Library of Liberal Arts, no. 165). $6.00cl.; $1.95pa.

Although not claiming a thorough expertise in Polish history, the author of *The Social Contract* has nevertheless produced in *The Government of Poland* an incisive work criticizing the institutions of the Polish Commonwealth. The Polish inability to govern such a huge state led Rousseau to pessimistic conclusions about the Commonwealth's survival opposite large and internally well-organized states encircling her. With this in mind, Rousseau prepared a draft for a Polish constitution; however, neither his criticism nor his advice could save Poland from being partitioned. In the absence of a hereditary monarchy, the anarchistic and destructive system of *liberum veto*, combined with the nobility's unwillingness to accept a political reform, aided the disappearance of Poland from the political map of Europe.

1495.   Wandycz, Damian S., ed. **Studies in Polish Civilization.** Institute
         on East Central Europe, Columbia University, and the Polish
         Institute of Arts and Sciences in America, n.d. 552p. $7.50.
The book represents a partial outcome of the first congress of scholars and scientists convened by the Polish Institute of Arts and Sciences in America in November, 1966, in celebration of Poland's Millenium. The collection includes only papers dealing with East Central Europe and with Poland in particular. Yet it offers an absorbing variety of topics and demonstrates a wide range of interests of those participating in the Congress. Some papers are of a general nature, while others refer to particular events. On the whole, this is a very valuable book and István Deák's enthusiasm in his foreword is fully justified.
         CSP, 14:3:552-4   R: V. C. Chrypinski

Language and Literature

1496.   Birkenmayer, Sigmund S., and Jerzy R. Krzyzanowski, eds. **A Modern
         Polish Reader.** University Park, Pa., Pennsylvania State University,
         1970. 187p. $3.00.
This Polish reader for advanced students presents a selection of Polish prose, a dictionary, and a set of exercises. The vocabularies that follow each reading are exhaustive, but their organization is not uniform. The vocabularies for the first two readings are in alphabetical order, but thereafter, they are arranged according to the order of occurrence in the text. The readings selected for the volume are interesting and well chosen, sufficiently complex for advanced students.
         SEEJ, 16:1:119-20   R: Maria Zagorska-Brooks

1497.   Coleman, Arthur Prudden, and Marion Moore Coleman. **Wanderers
         Twain, Modjeska and Sienkiewicz: A View from California.** Cheshire,
         Conn., Cherry Hill Books, 1964. 111p. $5.00.
The late Manfred Kridl wrote in his *Survey of Polish Literature*: "Teaching at American colleges and in various Polish-American centers, I learned that a literature presented against a broad historical and cultural background raises more interest than a literature treated as a field enclosed in itself." This seems to be particularly true as far as Polish matters are concerned, and Mr. and Mrs. Coleman in their story of the life and triumphs of the famous actress Helena Modjeska (Modrzejewska) follow that line. Tracing her path, which crossed

that of another famous Pole, Henryk Sienkiewicz, they did not limit their account to merely biographical and anecdotal material, but placed it against a panorama of Polish life and culture.

SR, 24:4:745   R: Jerzy R. Kryzyzanowski

1498.   Folejewski, Zbigniew. **Maria Dabrowska**. New York, Twayne Publishers, 1967. 123p. $3.95.

The literary fate of Maria Dabrowska (1889-1965) may appear singular, but it is characteristic of many Polish writers of the older generation. Generally recognized as a major author in her own country, abroad her name has only recently begun to achieve the recognition long due. Thus it seemed proper to present Dabrowska in a study intended for English-speaking readers. Folejewski limited his study to a discussion of Dabrowska's fiction, thus focusing on her most valuable accomplishment. Closely related to the Polish literary tradition on the one hand, a close affinity with the best writings of European realism of the turn of the century. And this is precisely the goal Folejewski is seeking to achieve.

SR, 29:1:147-9   R: Jerzy R. Krzyzanowski

1499.   Fredro, Alexander. **The Major Comedies of Alexander Fredro**. Trans. with an introduction and commentaries, by Harold B. Segel. Princeton, Princeton University Press, 1969. 405p. $12.00.

The book offers the largest existing choice of translations from Fredro's works, with the exception of the Russian edition (Moscow, 1956). Fredero was a wizard of the comic poetic idiom, unsurpassed in fluency, raciness, lightness, transparency, in verbal and prosodic invention, in wit and humor. Segel's selection contains the best, artistically most perfect, and most lively of Fredro's plays. He has mastered the entire literature concerning the author. In addition to the useful "Guide to Polish Pronunciation," he has provided his volume with a general introduction and a separate preface for each play.

SR, 29:2:349-50   R: Tymon Terlecki

1500.   Giergielewicz, Mieczyslaw. **Introduction to Polish Versification**. Philadelphia, University of Pennsylvania Press, 1970. 209p. $10.00.

This well-planned introduction to the intricacies of Polish prosody, the first of its kind to appear in English, is based on the practical experiences encountered during the author's many years of university teaching. The monograph was designed to meet the actual needs of American students. Whenever feasible, the author wisely employs the comparative approach in order to make the work more meaningful to the uninitiated reader.

PR, 15:4:116-7   R: Walter Kornel Kondy

1501.   Gillon, Adam, ed. **Poems of the Ghetto: A Testament of Lost Men**. Illus. by Si Lewen. New York, Twayne Publishers, 1969. 96p. $5.00.

Gillon's collection of verse written by Jewish inmates of Poland's wartime ghettos as well as by Poles on the other side of the barbed wire, appeared, through a macabre coincidence, just as the remaining survivors of these ghettos were being expelled from Poland by the country's Communist government. Translations are, for the most part, good, although there is an occasional tendency to multiply the understandably tragic gandiloquence of the Polish.

SR, 30:1:220-1   R: Maurice Friedberg

1502.   Gillon, Adam, and Ludwik Krzyzanowski, eds. **Introduction to Modern Polish Literature: An Anthology of Fiction and Poetry.** New York, Twayne Publishers, 1964. 480p. $6.95.

This anthology includes the work of 47 authors, divided between prose and poetry from the roster of acknowledged major Polish classics of the last century, with a sprinkling of contemporary authors. Among the latter are powerful stories by Brandys and Rozewicz. Female writers are represented, too. In addition to Orzeszkowa, Konopnicka, Illakowicz's controlled passion, and Nalkowska's forcefully vibrant voice, there is the unforgettably solid impact of the work of Maria Pawlikowska, and a sampling of Kossak's psychological historical fiction.

SR, 28:2:360-1   R: Irene Nagurski

1503.   Konwicki, Tadeusz. **A Dreambook for Our Time.** Trans. by David Welsh. Cambridge, MIT Press, 1970. 282p. $5.95.

This book is motivated by a different psychological and philosophical attitude. Set up in the 1960s, it is not only contemporary but also a much sophisticated novelistic technique. Without any doubt one can name it as perhaps the most symbolic novel in contemporary Polish fiction, its symbolism fraught with hidden meanings in a manner resembling Boris Pasternak's *Doctor Zhivago*.

PR, 15:4:110-2   R: Jerzy R. Krzyzanowski

1504.   Krzyzanowski, Jerzy. **Wladyslaw Stanislaw Reymont.** New York, Twayne Publishers, 1972. 169p. (Twayne's World Author Series, no. 248). $5.95.

W. S. Reymont (1876-1925) won the Nobel Prize for literature in 1924 (the second Polish writer to do so) for his peasant epic in novel form, *Chlopi* (The Peasants). This fair, balanced, and very readable account of Reymont's life and work argues well for a new look at other works of Reymont, such as *Ziemia obiecana* (The Promised Land) and *Rok 1794* (The Year 1794).

SR, 33:3:615   R: H. B. Segel

1505.   Lednicki, Wacław, ed. **Zygmunt Krasinski, Romantic Universalist: An International Tribute.** New York, Polish Institute of Arts and Sciences in America, 1964. 228p. $3.00.

Lednicki has assembled and edited a collection of eleven essays in English by various hands, ranging from Backvis to Z. L. Zaleski. He includes an essay of his own on the *Un-divine Comedy*, which provides him with the occasion for a dazzling display of erudition and for making a number of apt comments. Weintraub's contribution, "Krasinski and Reeve," belies its ostensibly biographical title and provides an illuminating study of the *Un-divine Comedy* in the light of their correspondence. Western readers will no doubt be duly impressed by the apparatus of scholarship brought to bear on Krasinski.

SR, 24:3:565   R: David J. Welsh

1506.   Milosz, Czesław. **The History of Polish Literature**. London, Collier-
         Macmillan, 1969. 570p. $14.95.
This is the only book in English covering the history of Polish literature from
its beginnings to the present time, for Manfred Kridl's *Survey of Polish Literature
and Culture* makes no reference to the last thirty years of development. *The
History* is a scholarly work by the leading Polish poet, who, also defining himself
as a Lithuanian, includes discussions of the Eastern Slavic languages (Belorussian
and Ukrainian) and Lithuanisn literature. This work, not subject to the limitations
of censorship imposed upon the literary historian writing in Poland, is able to
pay full tribute to writers and works that are taboo there; it also avoids the
factional pettiness of the so-called literature-in-exile and pays tribute as well
to the writers living in Poland who are ignored in the exile press. One of the
strongest aspects of Milosz's book is his analysis of poetry. His aesthetic sensitivity and experience as a translator lead him to a refined treatment of literary
samples.
         SR, 29:3:561-3   R: Andrzej Wirth

1507.   Milosz, Czesław, ed. **Postwar Polish Poetry: An Anthology**. Selected
         and trans. by C. Milosz. Garden City, N.Y., Doubleday, 1965. 149p.
         $4.95.
Milosz presents 90 poems by 21 poets. He stresses living poets and works written
since 1956, but Staff, Slonimski, Iwaszkiewicz, and other older poets are
included. The editor's remakrs (he is also for the most part the translator)
about the poets are partly biographical, partly critical, and always pertinent
though brief. Since he views the Polish poets as a kind of intellectual community,
he also includes some living outside Poland, among them himself.
         SR, 28:2:360-1   R: Irene Nagurski

1508.   Milosz, Czesław. **Selected Poems**. Intro. by Kenneth Rexroth. New York,
         Seabury Press, 1973. 128p. $5.95.
Milosz's poems represent his own autobiographic explanations and explorations,
stressing his life in Poland until World War II, and then in the United States.
The translations capture a great deal of his Polish feeling and form of the
originals. The quality, however, varies from obscure to a high poetic expression.
Students as well as admirers of Polish literature will read Milosz's poems with joy.
         S. M. H.

1509.   Prus, Bolesław. **The Doll (a novel)**. Trans. by David Welsh. New York,
         Twayne Publishers, 1972. 702p. $8.50.
The Doll can be read as an end-of-the-century view of social decay, a psychological
study of certain human types, a positivist rebuttal of Polish romantic idealism,
and an artistic analysis of the public mask, its tragic forms and consequences.
Prus's novel ranks as one of the few very good Polish novels, and Welsh should
be commended for providing us with the first English translation. The translation
is more than adequate; it succeeds in conveying the overall mood and message
of the novel.
         SEEJ, 16:3:360-1   R: Gerald Darring

1510.   Schenker, Alexander M. **Beginning Polish: Revised Edition**. Vol. 1:
        Lessons, Polish-English Glossary. Vol. 2: *Drills, Survey of Grammar,
        Index*. New Haven, Yale University Press, 1973. Vol. 1. 491p. Vol. 2.
        452p. (Yale Linguistic Series). $10.00cl.; $7.00pa./vol.

This grammar is designed as a first-year introduction to the language, with 25
lessons in the first volume and 25 corresponding drills in the second. Tapes for
materials in both volumes are available from the Yale University Language
Laboratory. Schenker has done an excellent job in preparing the grammar. The
pronunciation and spelling exercises are clear and concise; the Polish grammatical
structure is presented neatly and quite scientifically, for this level.
        SR, 33:3:616-7   R: Lawrence L. Thomas

1511.   Schenker, Alexander M., ed. **Fifteen Modern Polish Short Stories:
        An Annotated Reader and a Glossary**. New Haven, Yale University
        Press, 1970. 186p. $8.50cl.; $3.75pa.

Schenker's selection of Polish short stories is intended as a supplement to his
two-volume textbook, *Beginning Polish*. The book consists of fifteen short
stories, each by a different author, published in the last fifteen years. Thus
he presents a very recent selection of Polish prose, which should make the book
more attractive to its readers. The selection itself is excellent; all the stories
are of good artistic quality and are representative of the main trends and attitudes
in contemporary Polish prose. Each short story included in the *Reader* is
preceded by a concise introduction providing the most important biographical
data on the author and a critical commentary on the nature of his work.
        CSP, 13:4:450-1   R: Yvonne Grabowski

1512.   Tuwim, Julian. **The Dancing Socrates and Other Poems**. Selected and
        trans. by Adam Gillon. New York, Twayne Publishers, 1968. 63p.
        $4.00.

Tuwim (1894-1953), left his most distinguished mark as a poet during the
period between the two world wars. Gillon's selection is comprehensive, representing all of Tuwim's poetry, arranged in four parts. The collection is well
balanced and gives an excellent cross-section of Tuwim's poetry.
        SEEJ, 15:1:126-7   R: Jerzy J. Maciuszko

1513.   Tyrmand, Leopold, ed. **Explorations in Freedom: Prose, Narrative
        and Poetry from** *Kultura*. Trans. by Rulka Langer, M. Czajkowska,
        et al. New York, The Free Press, 1970. 442p. $8.95.

The editor of the anthologies, L. Tyrmand, himself a writer and a recent émigré
from Poland, had a great variety of material, published originally in *Kultura*,
to choose from. He performed his difficult task well. Among other things,
Explorations in Freedom contains excerpts from Witold Gambrowicz's *Diaries*,
a fragment from Czesław Milosz's novel *The Valley of Issa*, sketches by Jozef
Wittlin, and several short stories written by Nowakowski, Lobodowski, and
others. It is good to be reminded of shocking things which in the whirl of
current events and cares one tends all too easily to forget.
        SEEJ, 16:1:112   R: Xenia Gasiorowska

1514.   Welsh, David J. **Ignacy Krasicki.** New York, Twayne Publishers, 1969.
150p. (Twayne's World Authors Series, no. 78). $5.95.
In his presentation of Krasicki's works, Welsh combines chronology with an
arrangement by genre: mock epic, fable, satire, novel, comedy, epistolary form,
and so forth. His analyses of Krasicki's main works are brief and illuminating.
Since these works are unavailable in English, he has to resort to summaries. The
background chapter, "Poland's Augustan Age," gives the reader a good idea of
the atmosphere of that time.
SR, 30:2:445-6   R: Zbigniew Folejewski

1515.   Witkiewicz, Stanisław Ignacy. **The Madman and the Nun and Other
Plays.** Trans. and ed. by Daniel C. Gerould and C. S. Durer. With a
foreword by Jan Kott. Seattle, University of Washington Press, 1968.
303p. $12.50cl.; $3.95pa.
But for the all-pervading anguish and the lack of formal finish of his works,
Witkiewicz (1885-1939) could have been called a Renaissance man, so many
fields did he enter: philosophy, aesthetics, painting, fiction, drama. The twenty-
odd plays which he dashed off mostly in the twenties seem today to be the most
original and the most lasting part of his varied *oeuvre.* Witkiewicz propounded
the theory of pure form in drama. His dramas are written in a peculiar idiom.
The volume contains six plays. The most interesting is the last of them, *The
Shoemakers,* a political parable remarkable for its insight and emotional impact.
SR, 28:4:687-8   R: Wiktor Weintraub

1516.   Yurieff, Zoya. **Joseph Wittlin.** New York, Twayne Publishers, 1973.
175p. (Twayne's World Authors Series, no. 224). $5.95.
Scholars in Slavic literatures will generally be familiar with Wittlin's *The Salt
of the Earth* (1935). This monograph is the first comprehensive study of
Wittlin's work to appear in any language. It demonstrates again the wealth of
artistic genius which exists in Polish literature and which remains to be explored
and to be made accessible to the English-speaking reader. It includes a selected
bibliography of books and articles by Wittlin, of the translations of his works
into other languages, and of the slightly more than one score of articles about
him.
PR, 19:3-4:209-10   R: Joachim T. Baer

National Minorities

1517.   Bartoszewski, Wladyslaw, and Zofia Lewin. **The Samaritans: Heroes
of the Holocaust.** [American ed. edited by Alexander T. Jordan.]
New York, Twayne Publishers, 1970. 442p. $7.50.
The book presents a series of documents which are as important as they are
moving. The Catholic Church in occupied Poland has to be singled out as one
organized body which took part in aiding the Jews. Deserving of the highest
praise is the Ukrainian Metropolitan of the Greek Catholic Church, Szeptycki,
the only Prince of the Church who officially protested in a letter to Hitler the

persecution of the Jews, and who called semi-officially upon convents and monasteries in his diocese to take in Jewish children. The book can be highly recommended to make a self-proclaimed expert in the Western world.

PR, 15:4:108-10 R: Jadwiga Maurer

1518.   Bartoszewski, Wladyslaw, and Zofia Lewin, eds. **Righteous among Nations: How Poles Helped the Jews, 1939-1945**. London, Earlscourt Publications, 1969 834p. £4.25.

This volume is a compilation of documents describing, often in poignant terms, the assistance rendered by Poles from various walks of life and under the most difficult circumstances of the Nazi occupation to a doomed Jewish community. Those Jews who survived the holocaust—estimates range from 50,000 to 100,000 of a total of 3,500,000—were indebted to Poles, for whom a quotation from the Talmud is appropriately dedicated on the flyleaf: "Whoever saves one life is as though he has preserved the existence of the entire world." The documents, mostly narratives written by the rescued, are not intended to be exhaustive. Neither in the documents nor in the introductory essay is there any meaningful discussion of Polish anti-Semitism, a factor bearing upon the indifference or even the collaboration of various segments of the population with the Nazi persecutors. Such tendentiousness can in no way minimize the heroism and humanism of those Polish rescuers whose exploits fill the pages of this work.

SR, 30:1:181 R: William Korey

1519.   Katz, Alfred. **Poland's Ghettos at War**. New York, Twayne Publishers, 1970. 175p. $6.00.

The author's aim is to present a picture of Jewish life in wartime Poland, and to give special emphasis to Jewish resistance. He begins with a succinct description of Jewish parties and politics in pre-war Poland, and in subsequent chapters covers the establishment of ghettos in Poland, their internal organization, the resistance they offered to the Germans, and relations between Jews and Poles during the war. This is a short book, but it embodies a wealth of material and makes a really useful contribution to both Polish and Jewish wartime history.

SR, 31:2:447-9 R: Lionel Kochan

1520.   Weinryb, Bernard D. **The Jews of Poland: A Social and Economic History of the Jewish Community in Poland from 1100 to 1800**. Philadelphia, Jewish Publication Society of America, 1973. 424p. $10.00.

This remarkable survey of the Jewish saga in prepartitioned Poland updates the first volume of Dubnow's *History of the Jews in Russia and Poland* (1916). The author's goal of "humanizing Jewish history in Poland" is brilliantly accomplished within the tri-dimensional task of relating the history of Poland to that of world Jewry and Polish Jewry. In his thoroughly researched twelve chapters, supplemented by 66 pages of elucidating notes and four appendixes, Weinryb covers the seven hundred years of what was to become by 1500 the "largest single group in world Jewry." The author's main emphasis seems to be on the legal status of Polish Jewry, which was "that of freemen, apparently resembling that of the knights and gentry, and in certain respects that of the burghers."

SR, 34:1:169-71 R: George J. Lerski

The Society

1521. Kruszewski, Anthony Z. **The Oder-Neisse Boundary and Poland's Modernization: The Socioeconomic and Political Impact.** Foreword by Morton Kaplan. New York, Praeger, 1972. 246p. (Praeger Special Studies in International Politics and Public Affairs). $16.50.

The author, in a clear and well-organized presentation, tells how the seven million Poles, resettled into the former German territories, molded into the new society effected by the Communist party and the Catholic Church. He illustrates his honestly written book with excellent statistical tables, and he supplies a fine and extensive bibliography. Indeed, the book is a very useful contribution to East European area studies.

    SR, 33:1:159-60   R: Feliks Gross

1522. Lane, David, and George Kolankiewicz, eds. **Social Groups in Polish Society.** New York, Columbia University Press, 1973. 380p. $24.75.

This book, though basically a secondary analysis of earlier Polish research findings, presents a lucid and in-depth description of the main social groups in postwar Poland. The organization of the book follows the division of Poland's population into its most important social groups: the peasantry, the working class, and the intelligentsia, composed of writers and technicians. In addition, there is a part discussing the interaction of social groups in local communities. The volume is a most welcome addition to Szczepanski's *The Polish Society*, and it offers rich material for more comparative studies of social change.

    CSP, 16:3:494-7   R: V. C. Chrypinski

1523. Matejko, Alexander. **Social Change and Stratification in Eastern Europe: An Interpretive Analysis of Poland and her Neighbors.** New York, Praeger, 1974. 272p. $18.50.

The title of the book is slightly misleading. Although there are references to other East European countries, the author almost exclusively analyzes Polish society. The chief merit of the book is that it has been written by a Polish sociologist who has had considerable practical knowledge of the problems he discusses. This is unique. And we have before us an objective and sober study of contemporary Polish society. Matejko ably discusses the impact of industrialization on the Polish social structure, compares pre- and post-war Polish society, and analyzes the resulting classes: the peasants, the bluecollar workers, the managerial establishment, and, of course, the intelligentsia.

    CSP, 17:4:679-80   R: Peter Raina

1524. Pirages, Dennis Clark. **Modernization and Political-Tension Management: A Socialist Society in Perspective: Case Study of Poland.** Foreword by Jan F. Triska. New York, Praeger, 1972. 261p. $16.50.

The book is a useful, informative, and well-documented study of some of the major political, economic, and social institutions and problems of contemporary Poland. It deals with significant issues such as economic development, political stability, participation, and the current techniques of governing a "monist" or socialist society. The author argues that expectations rise in all industrial societies, including Poland. On the other hand, he knows enough of the facts of life of contemporary Poland to recognize the limitations of modernization theory. Hence, the book has its own tension between the attempt to apply the theory and the author's knowledge of existing political-historical realities.

CSP, 15:4:598-9   R: Paul Hollander

1525.   Szczepański, Jan. **Polish Society.** New York, Random House, 1970. 214p. (Studies in Modern Societies). $2.25pa.

This modest book "written primarily for American undergraduate students . . . interested in sociology and political science," must be recognized as the first sociological monograph on modern Polish society. The author is a director of the Sociological Institute of the Polish Academy of Sciences and a member of the Polish Sejm. "The main objective of this book," explains the author in his introduction, "is to show the process of the transformation of Polish society from a capitalist society in the interwar period into a socialist society." The book achieves this task, but it accomplishes much more than this—it presents an informed and objective picture of contemporary Poland set up against the background of its past.

PR, 16:3:95-100   R: Konstantin Symmons-Symonolewicz

RUMANIA

General Reference Works

1526.   Fischer-Galati, Stephen A. **Rumania: A Bibliographic Guide.** Washington, D.C., Slavic and Central European Division, Reference Department, Library of Congress, 1963. 75p. $0.45.

The first in a projected series of concise bibliographical surveys, this guide incorporates a number of excellent features: a balanced coverage of the major categories of knowledge, a helpful cross-reference between its two major divisions, an evaluative survey and a detailed bibliographic listing, and the critical comments of the author, which, though necessarily brief, are knowledgeable and fair.

SR, 23:4:792-3   R: Glenn Torrey

1527.   Matley, Ian M. **Romania: A Profile.** New York, Praeger, 1970. 292p. $8.50.

This is a handy and generally reliable book of data and insights on Rumania's past and present. It is not a piece of original scholarship, but rather a penetrating description and evaluation of Rumanian geography, culture, ethnic groups, and history. The general reader, including undergraduate students, should feel indebted to Matley for a lucid synopsis of Rumanian affairs.

SR, 30:3:691   R: Frederick Kellogg

Economics

1528.   Montias, John Michael. **Economic Development in Communist Rumania.** Cambridge, Mass., MIT Press, 1967. 327p. $15.00.

The book represents the first full-scale scholarly treatment of the economy of "new Rumania." The picture which emerges from this study is that of a rapidly industrializing and modernizing economy. According to Montias, the Rumanian policy makers and planners have been able to raise significantly the investment level, particularly in the late 1950s; expand substantially the per capita outputs, especially for basic industrial products; and more than double total industrial output in the decade between 1953 and 1963. The author has carefully gone through the official statistics with a fine comb and determined what is usable, what is doubtful, and what must be rejected outright. Second, he has rightfully stressed the identity of certain pre-war and post-war policies and concepts concerning the industrialization of the country and its foreign trade.

SR, 27:1:162-3   R: Nicolas Spulber

1529.   Morariu, Tiberiu, Vasile Cucu, and Ion Velcea. **The Geography of Romania**. Bucharest, Meridiane, 1966. 133p., maps, photographs.
The three authors present a detailed picture of the major factors of Rumania's geography under two broad headings, physical and economic geography. A little more than half of the book is devoted to a descriptive economic geography, including such headings as "Administrative Division of Romania's Territory," "Population and the Towns," and "Ways of Communication." This book is a real gold mine of information.

EEQ, 1:4:401-3   R: George W. Hoffman

1530.   Spigler, Iancu. **Economic Reform in Rumanian Industry**. Foreword by Michael Kaser. New York, Oxford University Press, 1973. 176p. Fold-out map. (Institute of Soviet and East European Studies, University of Glasgow. Economic Reforms in East European Industry Series). $12.50.
This study complements and goes beyond Montias' earlier work on Rumania's economy. It is crammed with information on the changes that have taken place since mid-1967 in Rumanian macro-, branch-, and micro-planning, the industrial management mechanism, budgetary procedures, and banking. It is generally assumed that the Rumanian economy is the most conservatively Stalinist in the bloc. Compared with the previous system, the Rumanian reforms do indeed devolve some decision-making power to industrial associations and enterprises. But the system remains centralized, directive, and physical.

SR, 33:4:813-4   R: Jan S. Prybyla

Government and Politics

1531.   Fischer-Galati, Stephen. **The New Rumania: From People's Democracy to Socialist Republic**. Cambridge, Mass., MIT Press, 1967. 126p. (Center for International Studies, Massachusetts Institute of Technology, Studies in International Communism, 10). $6.00.
This informative study traces Rumania's evolution since 1944, with emphasis on the strategies and tactics adopted by the Communist Party in the transformation of the country first into a "people's democracy" and then into a full-fledged "socialist republic." The author relies to a large extent on primary source materials

and firsthand information received from Rumanian officials. His aim is to demonstrate, *inter alia*, that the current "independence" of Communist Rumania that was first cautiously asserted at the Second Party Congress of 1955 is in fact the result of the policies originally formulated by Gheorghiu-Dej in 1945. The book contains many interesting interpretive insights into the dynamics of post-war Rumanian society.

    SR, 28:4:505-7   R: Randolph L. Braham

1532. Jowitt, Kenneth. **Revolutionary Breakthrough and National Develop-ment: The Case of Romania, 1944-1965.** Berkeley, University of California Press, 1971. 317p. $12.00.

Jowitt's is the first book to approach contemporary Rumania through the medium of political science. Presented as a "theoretical case study" in the tradition of comparative analysis, his work consists of the elaboration of a theory about "the process of nation building" and its application to the experience of Rumania between 1944 and 1965. Though Jowitt's reappraisal cannot be endorsed without qualification, he can be applauded for forcing a reconsideration of Rumania's independent course, still one of Eastern Europe's more baffling and abstruse phenomena.

    SEER, 53:130:139-42   R: J. Michael Kitch

Foreign Policy

1533. Oprea, I. M. **Nicolae Titulescu's Diplomatic Activity.** Bucharest, Publishing House of the Academy of the Socialist Republic of Romania, 1968. 188p. (Bibliotheca Historica Romaniae, Studies, no. 22). Lei 7.75.

Titulescu was the most distinguished Rumanian diplomat of the interwar period. He advocated international reconciliation and normalization of European relations with the Soviet Union. He is also known for his opposition to German and Italian totalitarianism and for his proposals to establish a system of collec-tive security in Europe. The revival of interest in the activities of Titulescu is directly connected with the emulation of the policies identified with him by the current leaders of Rumania. The book is remarkably objective.

    AHR, 75:2:544-5   R: Stephen Fischer-Galati

History

1534. Bodea, Cornelia. **The Romanians' Struggle for Unification, 1834-1849.** Trans. by Liliana Teodoreanu. Bucharest, Publishing House of the Academy of the Socialist Republic of Romania, 1970. 295p. (Bibliotheca Historica Romaniae, Studies, no. 25). Lei 15.50.

This book, an English translation of a work published in 1967, is a painstaking piece of research. Its object is to present "the common path pursued by the Romanian national movement both in the period of preparation for revolutionary actions and during their development in the years 1848-1849." Bodea has discovered, assembled, and analyzed carefully and intelligently a great many sources from several countries. The study, apart from some uncritical nationalistic tones, will doubtless be useful to scholars of nineteenth-century revolutionary and national movements.

SR, 30:2:418-9 R: Victoria F. Brown

1535. Boia, Lucian. **Eugene Brote (1850-1912).** Bucharest, Editura Litera, 1974. 211p. Lei 13.50.

This book is a valuable addition to the historical literature on the Rumanians of Transylvania during the dualist period. The many-sidedness of Brote's career imposes a broad treatment of the political, economic, and cultural development of the Rumanians. Boia also sheds considerable light on both the involvement of the National-Liberal Party of Rumania in political affairs of the Transylvanian Rumanians and the economic orientation of the Tribunists—matters which stand at the very heart of the national movement. The author has made an exhaustive investigation of unpublished documents and newspapers dealing with Brote's life and public career. His use of them is judicious and reveals both a deep understanding of the period and a sense of history.

SR, 34:2:422-3 R: Keith Hitchins

1536. Constantinescu, Miron, and Stefan Pascu, eds. **Unification of the Romanian National State: The Union of Transylvania with Old Romania.** Bucharest, Publishing House of the Academy of the Socialist Republic of Romania, 1971. 367p. Lei 30.

The book is a translation of a collective work initially issued in connection with the fiftieth anniversary of the Union of Transylvania with the Romanian Kingdom in 1918. Relying heavily on newly organized Romanian archival sources, this study aims to provide a comprehensive examination of this event in its complex historical context. It covers a variety of subjects, ranging from "The Romanian People's Concept, Tendencies, and Fight for Unity" to "The Position of the Nationalities Toward Union," in an attempt to cover all facets of the Union of 1918 as well as the actual event itself. The organizational scheme is, in general, plausible, coherent, and concise.

CASS, 9:3:400-2 R: Paul E. Michelson

1537. Eidelberg, Philip Gabriel. **The Great Rumanian Peasant Revolt of 1907: Origins of a Modern Jacquerie.** Leiden, E. J. Brill, 1974. 259p. (Studies of the Institute on East Central Europe, Columbia University). 64Dglds.

Eidelberg meshes the immediate causes of the revolt into the long-range trends in a detailed analysis of the issue of agricultural reform (1903-1907). This discussion forms the heart of his book. Existing accounts agree that the peasants were encouraged to revolt by outside influences, variously attributed to the "village bourgeoisie," the "urban bougeoisie," or the political radicals. The exact nature of this influence, however, had never been described in detail, much less satisfactorily explained. Eidelberg explains and documents this influence. According to his argument, the Liberal Party, in order to create an internal market for its sheltered industrialization program, began to press for the creation of village land-renting cooperatives, whose purpose was to transfer control of the great private estates to a minority of well-to-do peasants.

SR, 34:1:178 R: Glenn E. Torrey

1538. Fischer-Galati, Stephen. **Twentieth Century Rumania**. New York,
Columbia University Press, 1970. 248p. $7.95.

The author has chosen historical change and continuity as his main theme. His
purpose is to examine the validity of the present regime's claim that the Socialist
Republic of Rumania represents the fulfillment of the Rumanian people's age-
old aspirations. Three chapters deal with the period before 1914 and six with
installation and evolution of the Communist system. Throughout, the author
confines himself mainly to political history. Perhaps the most important single
ingredient in the Rumanian historical tradition is nationalism—specifically, the
idea of the essential oneness of the Rumanian people. In describing Rumania's
development under Communism, the author gives particular attention to the
national current in the Rumanian Communist movement and demonstrates
that the policies pursued by Gheorghiu-Dej and Ceauçescu in the sixties had
their origins in the preceding decade.

    SR, 30:1:187-8   R: Keith Hitchins

1539. Georgescu, Vlad. **Political Ideas and the Enlightenment in the Romanian
Principalities (1750-1831)**. Boulder, *East European Quarterly*, 1971;
distr. by Columbia University Press, New York. 232p. (East European
Monographs, 1). $7.50.

The author, a researcher at the Institute of Southeast European Studies in
Bucharest who has also taught at UCLA, aims to give a history of political
ideas in the Rumanian Principalities during the Enlightenment. By delineating
the main coordinates of this political thought, he wishes to define the role it
played in the history of Rumanian political ideology and development as well
as to place it in the general movement of Enlightenment thought. The book's
comprehensive analysis of the political ideas of the Phanariot era is both much
needed and usefully done.

    SR, 32:2:417-8   R: Paul E. Michelson

1540. Hitchins, Keith. **The Rumanian National Movement in Transylvania,
1780-1849**. Cambridge, Harvard University Press, 1969. 316p. (Harvard
Historical Monographs, 61). $8.00.

Hitchins's book is a careful survey of the evolution of the Rumanian national
movement in Transylvania from its inception until its arrest during the reaction
of 1848. The methodology is that of the conventional historians of the national
awakening in Rumania, stressing biographical and bibliographical details. The
book is scholarly, informative, and impartial.

    SR, 29:2:318   R: Stephen Fischer-Galati

1541. Ionescu, Ghita. **Communism in Rumania 1944-1962**. London, Oxford
University Press, for Royal Institute of International Affairs, 1964.
378p. $7.20.

Ionescu's analysis of the Rumanian Communist Party since its foundation in
1921 and of its post-war administration is a study not so much in historiography
as in history: he examines not only events, but also the national interpretation
of events when "the Party has become its own historian." As history, the book
modestly claims only "a strictly chronological basis" as opposed to "the
customary method of synoptical treatment under subjects." In the result, the

synopsis—of political moves, economic development, and international relations—
is achieved within well-chosen time-spans.

SEER, 44:102:250-2   R: M. C. Kaser

1542.   Matei, Horia C., et al. **Chronological History of Romania.** 2nd rev.
and enl. ed. Bucharest, Editura Enciclopedica Romana, 1974 (1972).
608p. Lei 38.

This is a revision of the original Rumanian edition published under the title
Istoria Romaniei in date. Chronological History is arranged by periods and dates,
beginning with the Paleolithic age and ending with the year 1971. Under each
date there is a short description of events. The book is a closely detailed calendar,
useful to both the specialist and general reader in search of quick chronological
references. An extensive selected bibliography and a useful name and subject
index round out this handy reference tool.   S. M. H.

1543.   Mitrany, David. **The Land and the Peasant in Rumania: The War and
Agrarian Reform (1917-21).** New York, Greenwood Press, 1969. 627p.
(Publication of the Carnegie Endowment for International Peace,
1930). $20.75.

The author offers in this study a detailed account of the agrarian reform carried
out in Rumania after World War I. Against a broad historical background,
Mitrany discusses the conditions of the Rumanian peasantry and the new land
reforms. The applications of the reforms and their effect on the Rumanian
economy are given much space. This is still the most comprehensive study on
the subject to date. Its extensive bibliography will be appreciated by scholars
of Rumanian economic and general history.   S. M. H.

1544.   Oldson, William O. **The Historical and Nationalistic Thought of Nicolae
Iorga.** Boulder, Colo., *East European Quarterly*, 1973; distr. by Columbia
University Press, New York. 135p. (East European Monographs, no. 5).
$10.00.

1545.   Bulgaru, Maria Matilda Alexandrescu-Dersca. **Nicolae Iorga: A Romanian
Historian of the Ottoman Empire.** Trans. by Mary Lăzărescu. Bucharest,
Publishing House of the Academy of the Socialist Republic of Romania,
1972. 190p. (Bibliotheca Historica Romaniae, Studies, no. 40). Lei 10.
Paper.

These two studies present a tantalizing peek at the tip of the proverbial iceberg.
The first is an analysis of Iorga's primarily nationalistic histories of his countrymen,
whereas the second is a recounting of Iorga's four-volume history of the Ottoman
Empire (originally published in German in 1908-1939) and other works treating
the Turkish occupation. Although Iorga was virtually ignored by Rumania's
Marxist historians before 1964, he has now emerged to take his rightful place
as that nation's most distinguished savant. Oldson's book boldly suggests that
Iorga's distortions, admittedly for didactic purpose, resemble the intricate
gyrations of Rumanian historiography under the present regime. The force of
nationalism is probably stronger than that of Marxism, or even truth.

SR, 33:4:812   R: Sherman D. Spector

1546. Prodan, D. **Supplex Libellus Valachorum, or the Political Struggle of the Romanians in Transylvania during the 18th Century**. Trans. by Mary Lăzărescu. Bucharest, Publishing House of the Academy of the Socialist Republic of Romania, 1971. 476p. Lei 33.

Here is a brilliant and cogent explanation of the Transylvanian Rumanians' petition *Supplex Libellus Valachorum*, which was submitted to Emperor Leopold II in 1791. Prodan's monograph is a translation of the second Rumanian edition of 1967; the first edition appeared in 1948. The *Supplex* demanded the political emancipation of the Rumanians in Transylvania and was, according to Prodan, the Rumanians' "most important political act" in the eighteenth century. It may be read with profit in conjunction with Keith Hitchins' *Rumanian National Movement in Transylvania, 1780-1849* (1969).

SR, 32:3:650-1   R: Frederick Kellogg

Language and Literature

1547. Augerot, James E., and Florin D. Popescu. **Modern Romanian**. Seattle, University of Washington Press, 1971. 329p. $12.00.

This is the best up-to-date Rumanian textbook for English speakers. The book is divided into two parts of sixteen lessons each. There is a useful appendix in two parts ("Pronunciation" and "Inflection") and a Rumanian-English glossary.

SR, 31:2:488-9   R: Kostas Kazaris

1548. Cioranescu, Alexandre. **Vasile Alecsandri**. Trans. by Maria Golescu and rev. by E. D. Tappe. New York, Twayne Publishers, 1973. 179p. (Twayne's World Authors Series, no. 204). $5.95.

V. Alecsandri (1821-90) served the cause of Rumanian nationalism with great distinction, especially in his self-appointed role of cultural propagandist. As the first major national poet and the first collector and interpreter of Rumanian folk poetry, the immense influence he exercised in his own time and on succeeding generations is thus undeniable; what is still open to question, however, is the intrinsic as opposed to the extrinsic merit of his work.

SR, 33:3:586-8   R: Michael H. Impey

1549. Steinberg, Jacob, ed. **Introduction to Rumanian Literature**. Foreword by Demostene Botez. New York, Twayne Publishers, 1966. 411p. $6.95.

The editor has succeeded in choosing some of the most representative prose works of modern Rumanian literature, and his anthology is a first step toward the understanding of an original literary phenomenon. All the writers included in the anthology are pre-eminent personalities of the Rumanian literature of the last hundred years; they were the ones who determined the new currents of the new aesthetic approaches, and their names are synonymous with the most important moments in the intellectual history of Rumania. The introductory notes to each short story draw convincing portraits of these writers, revealing the main characteristics of their work.

SR, 30:1:218-9   R: Dan Grigorescu

1550. Tappe, Eric D. **Ion Luca Caragiale.** New York, Twayne Publishers, 1974. 117p. (Twayne's World Authors Series, no. 276). $5.95.
The author is intimately familiar with Rumanian culture, Anglo-Rumanian relations, and the classical Rumanian writers. His anthologies, *Romanian Prose and Verse* (1956) and *Fantastic Tales* (1969), amply prove his knowledge of Rumanian literature. This most recent work, dedicated to one of the most important Rumanian writers, I. L. Caragiale (1852-1912), is characterized by the limited emphasis on information that is generally found in this series of biographies. Tappe's work is a dense monographic sketch, useful for the foreign reader's rapid initiation into the subject. The final chapters consist of a portrait of Caragiale the man, drawing on the memoirs of his contemporaries, and Caragiale the artist, which is rather sketchy. Tappe's book is a good source of information.
       SR, 34:3:658-9   R: Mircea Zaciu

YUGOSLAVIA

General Reference Works

1551. Eterovich, Francis H., and Christopher Spalatin, eds. **Croatia: Land, People, Culture.** Toronto, University of Toronto Press, 1970. 568p. $17.50.
This volume, like the first one (1964), contains independent monographic studies on Croatian history, language, literature, and culture, whose common denominator is the extended region of Croatia, including Bosnia and Hercegovina, as well as Croatians living abroad. The book is a major effort of Crotian émigré scholars to affirm the Croatian presence in the contemporary world and to document their own scholarly activity abroad. Although one would question many details of fact and interpretation, the general tone of the volume makes it a welcome addition to the body of literature on Croatian existence.
       SR, 33:4:816-7   R: Joseph Velikonja

1552. Petrovich, Michael B. **Yugoslavia: A Bibliographic Guide.** Washington, D.C., Slavic and Central European Division, Library of Congress, 1974. 270p. $2.60pa. [Order from Superintendent of Documents, G. P. O., Washington, D.C. 20402.]
This compilation, organized in two parts, covers more than 2,500 bibliographical items published in the Yugoslav and other East European languages. The first part of the *Guide* is a collection of essays, discussing literature relating to thirteen specific topics in the social sciences and the humanities. Part II is the alphabetical listing, by author, of the items covered in Part I. The *Guide* covers publications up to 1970. It emphasizes standard works and is designed to serve three types of users: the general reader, the research specialist, and the librarian.
       CSP, 16:4:683   R: Teresa Rakovska-Harmstone

1553.   Prpic, George J., comp. **Croatian Publications Abroad after 1939:**
        A Bibliography. Cleveland, Institute for Soviet and East European
        Studies, John Carroll University, 1969. 66p. $5.00pa.
This is the first bibliography on Croatia covering books and articles published
abroad, each entry briefly annotated. Though marred by typographical errors,
the mimeographed compilation is a useful guide, as it is the most complete
collection on the various aspects of Croatia.   S. M. H.

Fine Arts

1554.   Kečkemet, Duško. **Ivan Meštrovič.** New York, McGraw-Hill (1971).
        39p. 42 col. pl. and 168 black and white illus. $17.95.
This monograph offers a full description of the life and work of the artist whom
Rodin called "the greatest phenomenon among sculptors." In his commentary
Kečkemet traces Meštrovič's life (1883-1962) from his childhood as a poor
Croatian shepherd to his adult years of work in his own country and in the
United States.
        SR, 32:2:434-5   R: Vojeslav Molé

Economics

1555.   Adizes, Ichak. **Industrial Democracy: Yugoslav Style: The Effect of**
        Decentralization on Organizational Behavior. New York, The Free
        Press; London, Collier-Macmillan, 1971. 297p. $9.95.
Adizes's book is a major contribution, since few studies based on research within
the enterprise have appeared in English. His goals are dual: 1) to analyze the
decision-making structure in Yugoslavia and the suitability of that system,
designed in the fifties, for the new economic environment of competition and
market pressures, and 2) on the basis of the Yugoslav experience, to enrich the
theory of participative organization generally. The subjects of his study were
two enterprises similar in several respects but different in one key independent
variable: the leadership pattern. The two companies were studies in 1967.
Adizes concludes that the Yugoslav system of decision-making does not give
anyone in the enterprise sufficient authority to react adequately (i.e., efficiently)
in the competitive, post-reform economy.
        SR, 31:3:726-8   R: Deborah Duff Milenkovitch

1556.   Bicanic, Rudolf. **Economic Policy in Socialist Yugoslavia.** London,
        Cambridge University Press, 1973. 254p. $15.50.
Bicanic begins with a description of the creation of the Yugoslav state and
formation of the Socialist sector. He demonstrates that the manner of political
formation of a country profoundly affects the pattern of socialization. Thus,
the political security of the regime determines the speed and direction of
socialization. In Chapter 3 Bicanic describes the models of Yugoslav planning:
the centralized (1957-1951), decentralized (1952-1964), and polycentric (1965)
models. He then traces the evolution of the administrative bureaucracy that
that controls the planning mechanism. Chapters 5-8 deal more specifically with

patterns of industrialization, income policy, economic growth, and foreign trade. This book should be placed on the top of one's reading list.

EEQ, 8:4:515-6   R: Ryan C. Amacher

1557.   Dimitrijević, Dimitrije, and George Marcesich. **Money and Finance in Contemporary Yugoslavia**. New York, Praeger, 1973. 261p. $17.50.
The authors set out to test a monetarist hypothesis in Yugoslavia. This is of interest because of the unique conditions of the Yugoslav economy. The study is broken into four parts. Part I develops the institutional background of the financial system, breaking it into four stages of development. Part II examines the basic questions of monetary theory in the Yugoslav framework and especially the determinants of the changes in the money supply. In Part III the authors put the first two sections together to deal with monetary policy and the problems associated with policy formation and implementation. Part IV summarizes the study and offers some observations concerning future developments in Yugoslav monetary policy. The book has a valuable seventy-page statistical appendix, but suffers from the lack of an index.

EEQ, 9:1:120-1   R: Ryan C. Amacher

1558.   Dirlam, Joel, and James L. Plummer. **An Introduction to the Yugoslav Economy**. Columbus, Ohio, Charles E. Merrill, 1973. 259p. (Merrill's Economics Systems Series). $5.50pa.
The authors conduct their brisk, well-organized inquiry, relying on personal interviews and the Yugoslav press more than traditional academic sources. Frequent parallels and contrasts between the U.S. and Yugoslav economies recommend this paperback to American university courses in comparative economic systems. Balkan historians will appreciate the authors' perception of the increasingly important role that regional conflicts have played in the Yugoslav economy.

SR, 33:3:597-8   R: John R. Lampe

1559.   Hamilton, F. E. Ian. **Yugoslavia: Patterns of Economic Activity**. New York, Praeger, 1968. 384p. $8.00.
The prime object of the study "is to present the aims and methods of planning in this socialist state, and to assess its achievements in the distribution and location of economic activity." To achieve this task, Hamilton begins the study with a description of the historical, demographic, and physical environment of Yugoslavia. Parts 2 and 3 of the book contain a careful analysis of the economic policy and development of Yugoslavia since 1945. The various sectors of the economy are minutely described, full attention being given both to actual developments and to potentials for development. The material is treated in a way that makes clear the relations between such factors as resources, population, transportation, facilities, and industrial and agricultural progress. The book is such a masterful display of scholarship, and so well written, that even the footnotes are interesting.

SR, 29:1:129-30   R: Michael Rabbitt

1560.   Horvat, Branko. **Business Cycles in Yugoslavia**. Trans. by Helen M.
          Kramer. White Plains, N.Y., International Arts and Sciences Press,
          1971. 259p. $15.00.
Branko believes that much of the country's apparent economic instability can
be directly attributed to mistaken intervention by the government. The problems
are compounded because the Yugoslav economy is being opened up just when
the world finds itself on the downward phase of a secular Kondratiev cycle. The
five cycles discussed in the study present the following picture: Cycle I, New
Economic Policy (1949-1955); Cycle II, Transition to Second Five-Year Plan
(1955-1958); Cycle III, New System of Income Distribution (1958-1960);
Cycle IV, New Economic System, 2 (1960-1965); Cycle V, Economic Reform
(1965– ?).
          SR, 32:2:422-3   R: George Macesich

1561.   Milenkovitch, Deborah D. **Plan and Market in Yugoslav Economic
          Thought**. New Haven, Yale University Press, 1971. 323p. (Yale Russian
          and East European Studies, 9). $10.00.
Milenkovitch's study represents an ambitious piece of research and is a valuable
aid to understanding Yugoslavia's unique approach to economic organization.
It is a review of the doctrinal debates in Yugoslavia which have accompanied
the substitution of a market mechanism for the centrally planned, Soviet-style
system adopted immediately after the war. It is not a study of the Yugoslav
economy in operation. It does serve the important purpose of making the full
range of Yugoslav economic thought available, in a generally sensitive survey
and interpretation, to those not able to read the Yugoslav originals. While the
author's focus is on Yugoslav economic doctrine, she does not lose sight of the
essentially pragmatic nature of Yugoslavia's socioeconomic evolution.
          CSP, 16:1:124-6   R: C. H. McMillan

1562.   Sukijasović, Miodrag. **Foreign Investment in Yugoslavia**. Dobbs Ferry,
          N.Y., Oceana Publications, 1970. 178p. $9.00.
Sukijasović outlines the multiple Yugoslav statutes which cover equity capital
in a socialist economy, the method of joint investment venture, and protection
of the property rights of foreign investors; then he goes on to deal with their
implementation in practice. Because the law breaks new ground for a socialist
society, this book is a valuable addition to a better understanding of the Yugoslav
economic structure, system, and workings.   S. M. H.

1563.   Sukijasović, Miodrag. **Yugoslav Foreign Investment Legislation at
          Work: Experiences So Far.** Belgrade, Institute of International
          Politics and Economics; New York, Oceanea Publications, 1970. 178p.
          $9.00.
To make exports more competitive on world markets by raising the level of
technology, the Yugoslavs decided to permit foreigners to invest in Yugoslav
enterprises. In his book Sukijasović provides the ideological and legislative
background of the July 1967 law permitting foreign equity capital and profit
repatriation. He then examines the fifteen contracts which had been concluded

by the end of 1969, focusing on problems that appeared in the course of contract negotiations and on some loopholes and inconsistencies in the law.

SR, 31:3:726-8   R: Deborah Duff Milenkovitch

1564.   Wachtel, Howard M. **Workers' Management and Workers' Wages in Yugoslavia: The Theory and Practice of Participatory Socialism.**
Ithaca and London, Cornell University Press, 1973. 220p. $14.50.
Wachtel uses regression techniques soundly to test the behavior of industrial wage differentials between skills, between regions, and between industries from 1956 to 1969. Further tests clearly establish that over time wage differentials have widened between industries as a result of increasing labor productivity far more frequently than for any reasons attributable to industrial concentration or regional differences. The author concludes by using these results to support a shaky inference about the operation of workers' self-management.

SR, 33:3:597-9   R: John R. Lampe

Government and Politics

1565.   Chloros, A. G. **Yugoslav Civil Law: History, Family, Property.**
Oxford, Clarendon Press, 1970. 285p. $9.75.
This excellent book does not attempt to treat the whole civil legal system of Yugoslavia. Three fields are chosen for discussion: the history of Yugoslav law, family law, and the law of property. The book is supplemented by four basic statutes and a minutely prepared index. The author's style is simple, the presentation lucid, and the book will be easily understood by persons having no legal background. Chloros discusses the various elements that have blended with and influenced each other to create especially difficult problems: local customary law, Greek-Byzantine thinking (introduced mainly in Serbia), and Hungarian and then Austrian solutions (in force in Croatia). Besides unwritten law, numerous codes and statutes have from early times shaped the legal system of present-day Yugoslavia. This book should be read by everyone interested in Southeastern Europe.

SR, 30:4:921-2   R: W. J. Wagner

1566.   Fisher, Jack C. **Yugoslavia—A Multinational State: Regional Difference and Administrative Response.** San Francisco, Chandler, 1966. 244p. $15.00.
The book is an original and very challenging study. Two approaches are used concurrently: the first, an explanatory description, rests on insight, careful use of non-English sources, and constant references to theoretical postulates pertinent to the Yugoslav scene; the second, the adoption of statistical analyses (primarily multiple correlation and regression with factor analysis) is used to express quantitatively the regional variation of socioeconomic characteristics and to provide significant groupings of the 55 principal cities and 611 communes (1961 status) on the basis of 26 and 63 variables, respectively. The five chapters explore the development of the Yugoslav state, the historical background of

regional differences, regional variation of economic development, and housing policy and conditions; the concluding chapters deal with the communal system.

SR, 27:2:343-5 R: Joseph Velikonja

1567. Hondius, Frits W. **Yugoslav Community of Nations.** The Hague, Mouton, 1968. 375p. 65Dglds.

This book is a historically grounded analytic monograph that focuses on the federal aspect of the Yugoslav constitutional system. Although Hondius relies heavily on an institutional and legalistic data-base, he also locates this within a broader ecological context touching upon both ethnoregional and historical factors. The author has made an important contribution to our knowledge of Yugoslavia and to the literature in the field.

SR, 29:4:735 R: M. George Zaninovich

1568. Rusic, Eugen, and Annmarie Hauck Walsh. **Urban Government for Zagreb, Yugoslavia.** New York, Praeger, 1968. 151p. (The International Urban Studies of the Institute of Public Administration, New York, no. 3). $10.00.

The emphasis of this study is on the institutional and legal arrangements rather than on the functioning of the urban government of Zagreb, a city of half a million population and capital of the republic of Croatia. The book is a very useful outline of an administrative scheme as conceived in a decentralized socialist country; it reflects the philosophy of socialist planners, allowing considerable freedom in the day-to-day operating responsibilities within the legal, financial, and policy framework bodies. The delegation of power to lower-level agencies is therefore severely curtailed.

SR, 28:3:516 R: Joseph Velikonja

1569. Shoup, Paul. **Communism and the Yugoslav National Question.** New York, Columbia University Press, 1968. 308p. $9.50.

After a brief, rather sketchy introduction Shoup surveys the CPY's positions on the nationalities question from 1919 through 1966, making a side trip into domestic and international politics known as the Macedonian question. He considers, extensively, the important relationship between economics and the central goal: national unity. This study is a highly satisfactory start that will frequently be consulted by students of East European history and politics.

SR, 29:1:128-9 R: J. B. Hoptner

Foreign Policy

1570. Campbell, John C. **Tito's Separate Road: America and Yugoslavia in World Politics.** New York, Harper & Row, 1967. 180p. (Published for the Council on Foreign Relations). $3.95.

In this book the author reviews and assesses United States policy concerning Tito's Yugoslavia. He notes at the outset that American policy toward Yugoslavia goes "far beyond the pattern of bilateral relations with a single country; it has involved, simultaneously, issues connected with policy toward the Soviet Union, Eastern Europe, China, the Third World, and the Western community."

Surprised by the Cominform action against Yugoslavia, the United States waited until the beginning of 1949 before concluding that it was in the interest of the United States to see the Yugoslav-Soviet break continue. The United States chose "a course of helping a Communist country to maintain its independence" of the Soviet bloc and ultimately to strengthen its ties with the West. Campbell's analysis of American-Yugoslav relations and their impact on world politics is both authoritative and scholarly.

SR, 27:2:331-2　　　　　　　R: Wayne S. Vucinich

1571.　　Roberts, Walter R. **Tito, Mihailović and the Allies, 1941-1945.** New
　　　　Brunswick, N.J., Rutgers University Press, 1973. 406p. $15.00.
This book is an extremely useful compilation of a great many facts relevant to the Mihailović-Tito question, based on a wide range of sources, both official and unofficial. The author had available new and fresh documents, notably the Kasche-Ribbentrop correspondence of March 1943. All is set out in clear, neat, and digestible form, and also with objectivity. The serious gap is that the author was obviously unable, at the time of writing, to go through the British Foreign Office and other files now available in the Public Record Office. Nevertheless, for any serious student of war-time Yugoslavia, Robert's book is an essential work of reference.

　　　　SEER, 53:130:135-6　　　　　　R: Elisabeth Barker

1572.　　Rubinstein, Alvin Z. **Yugoslavia and the Nonaligned World.** Princeton,
　　　　Princeton University Press, 1970. 353p. $11.00.
Rubinstein argues that Yugoslav leaders first initiated a policy that aimed at the creation of a group of nonaligned states for pragmatic reasons—to break out of their diplomatic isolation, to find markets for Yugoslavia's goods (especially the products of the new industries), and to develop a policy that appealed to various factions within the Yugoslav Community Party. The author has produced a study valuable for students of Yugoslav foreign policy; but interest in his work should extend beyond this audience. He has skillfully analyzed both the role of personalities in Yugoslavia's foreign policy and the ways in which the instruments of twentieth-century diplomacy have been fashioned and employed to achieve foreign policy goals.

　　　　SR, 30:2:416-7　　　　　　R: Roger E. Kanet

Communist Party

1573.　　Avakumovic, Ivan. **History of the Communist Party of Yugoslavia.**
　　　　Aberdeen, Aberdeen University Press, 1967. 207p. (Vol. I). 60s.
This study is instructive not only for the history of the CPY but also for that of Communist parties elsewhere. The author has come up with a most useful, readable, and enlightening work. The study is copiously documented and replete with unusually valuable social statistics.

　　　　AHR, 71:1:254-5　　　　　　R: Ivo J. Lederer

1574.　　Dedijer, Vladimir. **The Battle Stalin Lost: Memoirs of Yugoslavia,
　　　　1948-1953.** New York, Viking Press, 1971. 341p. $8.50.

Ironically, the first fissure in the Soviet bloc monolith after World War II occurred in Yugoslavia, where partisan zealots had died with Stalin's name on their lips. In exploiting the revolutionary idealism of "honest fools," as he termed his Yugoslav followers, Stalin provoked the most calamitous and consequential schism in the Communist world since Trotsky. Dedijer, journalist, biographer of Tito, and erstwhile high Communist functionary, presents us with his lucid recollections of those dramatic days after Yugoslavia's expulsion from the bloc in June 1948, when many expected the Tito regime to fold under Stalin's relentless pressure. Dedijer's work goes over much old ground. Nevertheless, this is an important account by an influential insider, and it reminds us of the often underestimated influence of small countries on world affairs.

SR, 30:4:921 R: Paul N. Hehn

1575. Djilas, Milovan. **Memoir of a Revolutionary**. Trans. by Drenka Willen. New York, Harcourt Brace Jovanovich, 1973. 402p. $12.00.

This is the second volume of Djilas's autobiography, recounting events of the thirties in Yugoslavia. Djilas rose from poverty to become one of the most powerful men in the successful European revolution since 1917. In this volume Djilas offers descriptions of the personal relations and political disputes among Yugoslav Communists in the period before World War II.

SR, 33:3:595-6 R: Gale Stokes

1576. Johnson, A. Ross. **The Transformation of Communist Ideology: The Yugoslav Case, 1945-1953**. Cambridge, Mass., MIT Press, 1972. 269p.

This is an important book which makes a major contribution to our knowledge of post-war Yugoslavia and international Communism. It is the first systematic effort to analyze in depth the emergence and evolution of the ideological underpinnings of what is commonly known as "Titoism" or the "Yugoslav road to socialism." The most valuable aspect of the study is the in-depth analysis of "the six most important tenets of the post-1948 doctrine: the critique of the Soviet system, the re-examination of the nature of the epoch, the withering away of the state, worker self-management, the renunciation of collectivization of agriculture, and the new conception of the leading role of the Party."

SR, 33:3596-7 R: Andrzej Korbonski

History

1577. Alexander, John T. **Yugoslavia: Before the Roman Conquest**. New York, Praeger, 1972. 175p. (Ancient Peoples and Places, no. 77). $12.50.

This book presents a summary of the archaeological data on Yugoslavia from the earliest human occupation to the Roman Conquest. The five chapters of the book deal successively with the Paleolithic and Mesolithic periods, the Neolithic, the Early Bronze Age, the Middle and Late Bronze Age, and the pre-Roman Iron Age. Each of the chapters presents essentially a catalog of the known data for that period and contains a map and a list of sites.

SR, 33:3:593-4 R: Robert K. Evans

1578. Bjelovučic, Harriet. **The Ragusan Republic: Victim of Napoleon and Its Own Conservatism**. Leiden, E. J. Brill, 1970. 184p. 32Dglds. Paper.

This study attempts to show how, between 1750 or 1760 and 1813, the history of Ragusa (Dubrovnik) fits into the pattern of R. R. Palmer's well-known thesis of a

Western and Central Europe. In particular, the author sees a close analogy between the Ragusan and Genevan revolutionary patterns, which she explains by the similarity of the political and social institutions of the two republics. The book contains a useful bibliographical essay.

SR, 31:1:224-5 R: Traian Stoianovich

1579. Darby, H. C., et al. **A Short History of Yugoslavia: From Early Times to 1966.** Ed. by Stephen Clissold. New York, Cambridge University Press, 1966. 279p. $5.95.

This revision and continuation of the historical sections of the restricted three-volume handbook on Yugoslavia published by the Naval Intelligence Division of the British Admiralty during the Second World War should be useful to general readers and students and may have value for specialists. The introduction, an essay in interpretation, is especially rewarding. The region-by-region approach results in good encyclopedic articles on each region written by H. C. Darby, R. W. Seton-Watson, R. G. D. Laffan, S. Clissold and P. Auty. This is a valuable handbook.

AHR, 72:3:1031-2 R: Traian Stoianovich

1580. Deakin, F. W. D. **The Embattled Mountain.** New York, Oxford University Press, 1971. 284p. $9.50.

In May 1943, Deakin, Oxford historian and literary secretary to Winston Churchill, parachuted into Tito's headquarters in the midst of the fierce battle of the Sutjeska River. Wounded by the same bomb that struck Tito, he survived to report that Tito was indeed "killing Germans," as Churchill put it. Deakin became convinced that Mihailović was collaborating with the Axis, and his reports to that effect were influential in turning English support away from the Chetniks and toward the Partisans. This book is half personal memoir and half scholarly history.

SR, 31:3:725-6 R: Gale Stokes

1581. Dragnich, Alex N. **Servia, Nikola Pašič, and Yugoslavia.** New Brunswick, N.J., Rutgers University Press, 1974. 266p. $15.00.

Dragnich offers the first scholarly biography of Pašič in any language. His book is a welcome contribution and somewhat of a disappointment. Dragnich has given his readers a conscientious synthesis of the political activities of an important figure. Yet he tells little that is new and too little of what is already known. Nevertheless he presents a point of view that is not without merit and which may offer a useful corrective to the more extravagant charges of Pašič's earlier critics.

SR, 34:3:639-40 R: Michael B. Petrovich

1582. Edwards, Lovett F., ed. and trans. **The Memoirs of Prota Matija Nenadović.** Oxford, Clarendon Press, 1969. 227p. $7.00.

Nenadović (Archpriest) is known mainly as the diplomat of the First Serb Revolt (1804-13); he visited Russia in 1804-1805 and was a steadfast admirer of Russia during the rest of his long life. He served Serbia as a statesman and administrator from 1807, when he became the first president of his country's first Legislative Council, until he retired from politics for the third and final time in 1852. During the First Serb Revolt, Nenadović was one of the most important military field commanders, and during the second revolt (1814) he occupied himself with smuggling arms before he returned to serve again as a diplomat. Students of East European history and literature will appreciate this well-done translation from the Serbian.

SR, 30:1:188-9   R: Peter F. Sugar

1583.   Gazi, Stephen. **A History of Croatia.** New York, Philosophical Library, 1973. 362p. $11.95.
This is the first major survey in English to take the reader across the whole span of Croatian history, from the earliest times down to the present. The author writes from a strongly pro-Croatian and anti-Serbian viewpoint. Unlike many Croat-oriented writers, however, Gazi tries to be restrained and to speak without anger. Although he favors the concept of Croatian independence, he has some critical comments to make about Croatia's first venture into independence, the period of the Ustasha regime during World War II. He also favours the preservation of the Habsburg Monarchy. He envisages a reorganized monarchy in which the Croats would be on a par with Germans and Magyars, and in which Croatia would incorporate all territories to which he believes her to be historically entitled, including Bosnia-Hercegovina.

CSP, 16:3:485-6   R: Stanley Z. Pech

1584.   Guldescu, Stanko. **The Croatian-Slavonian Kingdom, 1526-1792.**
The Hague, Mouton, 1970. 318p. (Studies in European History, 21). 54Dglds.
In this volume Guldescu continues his work on the history of the ancient Triune Kingdom. His previous study, *History of Medieval Croatia* (The Hague, 1964), covered developments up to the fall of the Hungarian-Croatian state at Mohács. In the present volume he carries the story to 1792, when, in the wake of the Hungarian feudal revolt against Habsburg centralism, the Croatian magnates entered into a closer relationship with Hungary. As in his previous work, the author has tried to cover not only the political and military developments but also the economic, cultural, and social life of the country. In keeping with the moderate approach, his treatment concentrates on Habsburg Croatia-Slavonia and excludes Bosnia and Dalmatia, then under Turkish and Venetian rule. And because there is so little in English on the subject, the author has performed a useful service to students of this area and this period in history.

SR, 30:3:689-90   R: Gunther E. Rothenberg

1585.   Hammond, N. G. L. **A History of Macedonia. Vol. 1: Historical Geography and Prehistory.** Oxford, Clarendon Press, 1972. 493p. $38.50.
In Part 1 the author describes the physical features of the province of Macedonia and her neighbors—the territory drained by the two great rivers, the Haliacmon and the Vardar, and the surrounding area. He regards Macedonia as a geographic entity, different from Greece and related to the continental land mass of the Balkans. Part 2 is dedicated to the prehistory of Macedonia, from Paleolithic times to 550 B.C. This work is an essential volume in the library of every linguist, historian, and archaeologist whose concern is the area in question.

SR, 33:3:599-600   R: Marija Gimbutas

1586. Jukić, Ilija. **The Fall of Yugoslavia.** Trans. by Dorian Cooke. New York, Harcourt Brace Jovanovich, 1974. 315p. $8.50.
In this book Jukić gives a political history of the last months of Prince Paul's regime in Yugoslavia; the *coup d'état* which brought the Simović government to power in March 1941; the intrigues and bickering within the Yugoslav government in exile; and the switch of Allied support from Mihailović to Tito, with all that it implied for the course of the civil war, as well as the war against the Germans and Italians in Yugoslavia, and for the future of the Yugoslav nation of nations. Being a participant in the pre-war government, his story is thus largely a first-hand and eye-witness account. His story is at best a sad one, but it deserves to be read and pondered.
        SEER, 53:132:456   R: Duncan Wilson

1587. MacKenzie, David. **The Serbs and Russian Pan-Slavism, 1875-1878.** Ithaca, Cornell University Press, 1967. 365p. $10.00.
The author has focused his attention upon a single Balkan people, the Serbs—those of the Voivodina, Bosnia-Hercegovina, and Montenegro as well as of the Principality of Serbia—and has traced the vicissitudes of their relations with official and unofficial Russia. Based largely upon unpublished Serbian, Russian, and Austrian sources and the Serbian and Russian newspaper press, it is the most comprehensive account of Serbian-Russian relations for the period in any language. An introductory chapter on Serbian-Russian relations from the beginnings down to the revolts in Bosnia and Hercegovina in 1875 prepares the reader for the stresses and open conflicts which were to follow. The author makes it clear that throughout the crisis Serbia, Montenegro, and Russia were primarily concerned with the attainment of their own selfish ends.
        SR, 27:3:489-90   R: Keith Hitchins

1588. Maček, Vladko. **In the Struggle for Freedom.** Trans. by Elizabeth Gazi and Stjepan Gazi. University Park, Pennsylvania State University Press, 1968. 280p. $7.95.
Maček's autobiographical story of the twentieth-century struggle for Croatian autonomy was written in the late 1940s and first published in English in 1968. Maček's major topic is the struggle for Croatian independence led by the Croatian Peasant Party, which was founded in 1905 by Ante Radić and his brother Stjepan. Most of Maček's book chronicles—from the Croatian point of view—the political struggles that tore at the existence of a unified South Slav state during a twenty-year period. His memoirs are of value to the student of Yugoslav history, both as a source of information and, probably more importantly, as an indication of the views and motives of one of the most important political figures of inter-war Yugoslavia.
        SR, 30:3:690   R: Roger E. Kanet

1589. Novak, Bogdan. **Trieste, 1941-1954: The Ethnic, Political, and Ideological Struggle.** Chicago, University of Chicago Press, 1970. 526p. $16.50.
The Trieste dispute involved—between the destruction of Austria-Hungary in 1918 and the Italian peace treaty in 1947—the entire region which the Italians call Venezia Giulia and the Yugoslavs the Julian March. From 1947 to 1954

the dispute was confined to the zone of the Free Territory of Trieste, which was created by the treaty but could not be put into operation, for the Allied powers could not agree on the choice of a governor. Finally the most logical solution was reached. In October 1954 Yugoslavia received Zone B, with minor changes; Italy, Zone A. The big dispute (1918-1947) and the little one (1947-1954) were passionate because they involved nationalism. Novak's book should be consulted on the diverse local political factions as well as on ethnographic composition of the area in question.

SR, 30:4:919-20   R: J. B. Duroselle

1590.   Prcela, John, and Stanko Guldescu, eds. **Operation Slaughterhouse**: **Eyewitness Accounts of Postwar Massacres in Yugoslavia.** Philadelphia, Dorrance, 1970. 557p. $10.00.

This book purports to be a factual and documented account of the so-called Bleiburg massacres, perpetrated by the Yugoslav Communists on Croat soldiers who had surrendered to the British in Austria, and were then handed over by the British to the Partisans to be abused, mistreated, and often killed. The book is factual only in part. The Partisans did kill Ustaši and Domobrans by the thousands in southern Austria, and later during so-called death marches across Yugoslavia, long after the guns of war fell silent in Europe. The liquidations were in part the result of deliberate policy, in part the expression of individual bestiality of Partisan commanders and certain units. The murders were motivated by ideological and national hatred.

SR, 30:2:413-5   R: Mathew Mestrovic

1591.   Vucinich, Wayne S., ed. **Contemporary Yugoslavia: Twenty Years of Socialist Experiment.** Berkeley, University of California Press, 1969. 441p. $9.50.

This is a collection of eight research papers attempting to place the twenty years of socialist experiment in perspective. The following topics are discussed: 1) Kingdom of Yugoslavia; 2) Mihailovich-Tito conflict; 3) Establishment of a new political order; 4) Tito's foreign policies; 5) Conflict of nationalities; 6) Economy and industrialization; 7) Modernization of the Yugoslav society. The book is a highly competent work and an important addition to the literature. Of particular value to the reader are the bibliographical notes for each chapter and the excellent index.

SR, 30:2:415-6   R: J. B. Hoptner

Language and Literature

1592.   Benson, Morton, with Biljana Šljivić-Šimšić. **Serbocroatian-English Dictionary.** Philadelphia, University of Pennsylvania Press; Gelgrade, Prosveta, 1971. 807p. $27.50.

This book represents the first attempt to compile a dictionary which reflects both the ekavian and jekavian variants of standard Serbo-Croatian as well as the first attempt to make American rather than British English the target language. This is a useful book.

SEEJ, 16:3:370-5   R: Kenneth E. Naylor

1593. Heiliger, Wilhelm. **Nostalgie bei Ivan Cankar.** London, Slavic Press, 1972. 130p. $4.00pa. [in German].

Ivan Cankar (1876-1918) is probably the greatest of Slovene prosaists. He passed through Decadence and Symbolism, and championed art for art's sake and tendentious literature. But he ultimately discovered his own, completely personal vision. His art is rooted in Slovene national life and in the problems of a small nation. During some twenty years of literary activity, Cankar published novels, plays, and short stories, but the genre most typical of him is the lyrical sketch, often autobiographical in subject matter, realistic in tone, and distinctly poetic in expression. This work is concerned with the recurrent theme of nostalgia in Cankar's works, a preoccupation reflecting the large emigration of peasants at the turn of the century to escape impoverished living conditions in Slovenia. This book is a valuable contribution to the study of Cankar and his works, but it will be useful only to those who know both German and Slovene well.

    SEEJ, 18:4:449-50   R: Joseph Suhadolc

1594. Holton, Milne, ed. and intro. **The Big Horse and Other Stories of Modern Macedonia.** Trans. by Alan McConnell. Columbia, University of Missouri Press, 1974. 232p. $9.50.

This anthology is a welcome addition to the field of Yugoslav literature in English translation. Macedonian is the youngest Slavic literary language, and the short story is the youngest of its art forms. This collection presents one short story by each of twenty writers, including S. Drakul, K. Čašule, V. Uroševik, and V. Kostav. It also contains a general introduction and biographical notes on each of the authors. The selections present a reasonably accurate illustration of the state of the art of the short story in Macedonia today.

    SEEJ, 18:4:448-9   R: Victor A. Friedman

1595. Johnson, Bernard, ed. **New Writing in Yugoslavia.** Baltimore, Penguin Books, 1970. 342p. $2.95pa.

This collection of contemporary Yugoslav prose and poetry is extraordinarily well done. It can be recommended without reservation as an introduction to Yugoslav literature of the past two decades—both for its selection, including works by Slovenian and Macedonian writers as well as by Croats and Serbs, and for the remarkable level of its translations. The editor has provided an interesting and informative introduction that sketches the cultural and political background against which current Yugoslav literature has developed and explains the scope and structure of the anthology. A very useful set of biobibliographical notes on the authors is appended.

    CSP, 14:4:724-7   R: Benjamin A. Stolz

1596. Kadić, Ante. **Contemporary Serbian Literature.** The Hague, Mouton, 1964. 105p. 1250Dglds.

In the absence of a full study of Serbian literature between the two world wars and also of any definitive history of Serbian literature in English, this book is, of necessity, interesting. The period covered is from 1903 to the present day. If, as the author tells us, it is only the precursor of a larger and more carefully prepared monograph, then we may look forward to its successor as a very welcome contribution to the study of Serbian literature.

SEER, 44:102:215-6   R: E. D. Goy

1597.   Kadić, Ante. **From Croatian Renaissance to Yugoslav Socialism: Essays.**
The Hague, Mouton, 1969. 301p. (Slavistic Printings and Reprintings,
90). 48Dglds.
Kadić has collected in this book a number of his articles on Yugoslav history
and literature published during the last thirteen years. Among the most interesting
of the historical pieces is his article on the Croatian Renaissance. In another
study he examines the contributions of Jurai Kiržanić not only to Croatian
literature but also to the development of a common South Slavic language. In
an essay entitled "Vladimir Solovev and Bishop Strossmayer," Kadić examines
the strong personal and intellectual ties that bound the Russian philosopher and
the Croatian bishop. For the student of Yugoslav culture and history, Kadić
has produced a volume which provides insights into a number of areas important
for a better understanding of literature in Yugoslavia—particularly in Croatia—
since the sixteenth century.

SR, 30:2:412   R: Roger E. Kanet

1598.   Lenček, Rado L. **The Verb Patterns of Contemporary Standard Slovene,
with an Attempt at a Generative Description of the Slovene Verb by
Horace G. Lunt.** Wiesbaden, Otto Harrassowitz, 1966. 194p. DM34pa.
Lenček's study is probably the last and certainly the most thorough description
of a Slavic verbal system in the well-known chain of such events that rest directly
on Roman Jakobson's original and stimulating article on the Russian conjugation.
Since that time, however, some very significant strides have been made in phonological theory, in particular, and in grammatical theory, in general. Lenček's
work is adequately characterized by Lunt, who underlines its absolutely exhaustive
coverage of all verbal forms in Slovene. The study should remain for years the
primary point of departure for any scientific discussion of the Slovene verbal
system.

SR, 38:4:692-3   R: Lew R. Micklesen

1599.   Lukić, Sveta. **Contemporary Yugoslav Literature: A Sociopolitical
Approach.** Ed. by Gertrude Joch Robinson. Trans. by Pola Triandis.
Urbana, University of Illinois Press, 1972. 280p. $11.95.
This book, written by an erudite young Serbian literary critic, poet, and editor
of *Delo* (1956-1961), is also the first post-war study on the subject written by a
Yugoslav; since the war, the only other surveys of Yugoslav literature have been
written by foreigners, such as Zoltan Czuka and Giovanni Mayer. Lukić's
volume focuses on just those aspects of literature which would usually be regarded
as secondary, and which a reader would normally "prefer to skip": it traces,
sketches, and analyzes the interrelationship of socio-political and historical
forces and literary activity in Yugoslavia in the last 25 years. There is an excellent biographical list of contemporary Yugoslav writers and their works from 1945
to 1965, an extensive chronology of Yugoslav literary events, and a very useful
index.

CSP, 15:1-2:241-2   R: Želimir B. Juričić

1600.   Magner, Thomas F. **Introduction to the Croatian and Serbian Language.**
        State College, Pa., Singidunum Press, 1972. 351p. $12.50.
This book is a thoroughly revised version of the author's *Introduction to the
Serbo-Croatian Language* of 1956 (2nd ed. 1962). The glossary, containing a
large number of additional words and usable for other purposes as well, was
published by the same press in 1970 as *The Student's Dictionary of Serbo-
Croatian.* The Croatian and Serbian versions of the dialogues are separated right
from the start and given in that order throughout, which obviously involves a
lot of repetition.
        SEEJ, 16:3:368-70   R: Ranko Bugarski

1601.   Magner, Thomas F. **The Student's Dictionary of Serbo-Croatian**:
        Serbo-Croatian-English, English-Serbo-Croatian. State College, Pa.,
        Singidunum Press, 1970. 201p. $5.50.
This is an enlarged version of the glossary to the author's *Introduction to the
Serbo-Croatian Language*; it contains about 7,000 entries in each of its two
sections.
        SEEJ, 15:2:245   R: Thomas J. Butler

1602.   Magner, Thomas F., and Ladislav Matejka. **Word Accent in Modern
        Serbo-Croatian.** University Park, Pennsylvania State University Press,
        1971. 210p. $10.00.
The work describes experimental investigations into the status of prosodic
features in modern Serbo-Croatian. It concludes that the accents and lengths
which Vuk and Daničić codified in the last century are well preserved only
in rural areas and among accentologists; city speakers as a rule distinguish nothing
more than place of accent and length of the accented vowel. But these conclusions
are not entirely justified.
        SEEJ, 16:4:503-8   R: Wayles Browne

1603.   Mikasinovich, Branko, et al., eds. **Introduction to Yugoslav Literature:
        An Anthology of Fiction and Poetry.** New York, Twayne Publishers,
        1973. 647p. $8.95.
This book contains samples from the works of important Serbian, Croatian,
Slovenian, and Macedonian authors since the beginnings of each modern literature. Especially valuable are the nineteenth-century writings which have not
been readily available in English. The introductions to the volume's four sections periodize and characterize the respective national literatures. Generally,
they are factual and informative. The anthology provides a useful general view
of the literary history of the peoples of Yugoslavia.
        SEEJ, 17:3:346-7   R: Mary P. Coote

1604.   Popa, Vasko. **Selected Poems.** Trans. by Anne Pennington. Intro. by
        Ted Hughes. Baltimore, Penguin Books, 1969. 128p. $1.95pa.
This is a notable addition to the Penguin series of Modern European Poets. Popa
is one of the most significant among contemporary Yugoslav (Serbian) writers.
Miss Pennington's translation accurately represents Popa's concise, elliptical
style. Hughes's introduction places Popa in the context of his generation of

European poets and gives a general picture of the fantastic, absurd, often terrifying world of his poetry. The work is aimed at the general reader rather than at the student of Serbo-Croatian literature.

SEEJ, 16:1:112-3   R: Mary P. Coote

1605.   Wilson, Duncan. **The Life and Times of Vuk Stafanović Karadžić, 1787-1864: Literacy, Literature, and National Independence in Serbia**. Oxford, Clarendon Press, 1970. 415p. $12.50.
The book offers a wealth of information about Vuk in various forms. It opens with a chapter surveying all of Vuk's life and work and attempting to suggest his overall importance as an introduction to the detailed chronological account that follows. This study fills a need for a solid reference work on one of the most important figures in Balkan cultural history.

SEEJ, 15:3:396   R: Mary P. Coote

The Society

1606.   Barton, Allen H., Bogdan Denitch, and Charles Kadushin, eds. **Opinion-Making Elites in Yugoslavia**. New York, Praeger, 1973. 344p. $18.50.
These articles on opinion-making elites in Yugoslavia, written by four Yugoslavs, four Americans, and one Yugoslav-American, make a number of positive reflections on the state of social science research both in and on contemporary Yugoslavia. The inter-disciplinary composition of the research team has ensured a well-rounded research effort on an exciting and important topic of inquiry. For the most part, the contributors show a firm methodological grounding and approach without losing sight of the sensitive human and social dimensions underlying the problem they study.

EEQ, 9:1:115-7   R: Gary K. Bertch

1607.   Halpern, Joel M. **A Serbian Village**. Illus. by Barbara Kerewsky Halpern. Rev. ed. New York, Harper & Row, 1967. 359p. $2.75pa.
The greater part of the book, which was first published in 1958, is based on field research in 1953-1954 in the village of Orašac, in the Šumadija region of central Serbia. In the historical and demographic information used, the author shows a close acquaintance with the relevant Yugoslav and Serbian sources, which supplements his own first-hand knowledge. In the field work itself, he had remarkable success in gathering data and he shows that he established meaningful contact and rapport with the residents of Orašac.

SR, 28:3:514-6   R: Bette S. Denitch

1608.   Halpern, Joel M., and Barbara K. Halpern. **A Serbian Village in Historical Perspective**. New York, Holt, Rinehart and Winston, 1972. 152p. (Case Studies in Cultural Anthropology).
This case study of the Serbian village of Orašac from the standpoint of cultural anthropology is intended as a supplementary text for beginning and intermediate courses in the social sciences. The authors cover a period of over a century during which Serbia and the village of Orašac have undergone tremendous political,

socioeconomic, and psychological changes, and they touch upon all aspects of village life.

SR, 33:3:595   R: Jozo Tomasevich

1609.   Hammel, Eugene A. **Alternative Social Structures and Ritual Relations in the Balkans.** Englewood Cliffs, N.J., Prentice-Hall, 1968. 110p. $6.95cl.; $2.95pa.

In this study of marriage, baptismal, and haircutting sponsorship in southwestern and eastern Yugoslavia, Hammel makes an important contribution to structural anthropology by his development of the thesis that the ritual, affinal, and agnastic institutions of this region are allomorphs and form in fact part of a more general system of exchange or communication of goods, services, women, information, and values.

SR, 28:3:513-4   R: Traian Stoianovich

1610.   Horvat, Branko. **An Essay on Yugoslav Society.** Trans. by Henry F. Mins. New York, International Arts and Sciences Press, 1969. 245p. $12.00.

In six chapters, Horvat covers everything which is relevant for a scholarly analysis of the self-managing socialism in his country. He distinguishes two basic interpretations of the Marxist doctrine: the first is based on state socialism; the second on associationist socialism. In a sense, the very term "state socialism" is a *contradictio in adjecto* since, according to the original Marxian concept, the state should be withering away immediately after the completion of the socialist revolution. The author carefully provides the reader with a frank and objective confrontation of two concepts which are present in the original Marxist doctrine. He suggests his own resolution to the inner contradiction of authentic Marxism with its tension between the hierarchical economic command system and the democratic political organization of socialist society; the state socialism should be replaced, as soon as possible, by a higher associationist socialism based on self-management both in economic units and communities.

CSP, 17:1:173-4   R: Radoslav Selucky

1611.   Winner, Irene. **A Slovenian Village: Žerovnica.** Providence, R.I., Brown University Press, 1971. 267p. $14.00.

This book, the first professional ethnographic account of a Slovenian community (in the English language), fills a serious gap in the literature. It is also a beautifully produced book, with good photographs and charming drawings. Most of the book is about peasant economics and the relationship between social organization, everyday interaction, and economic factors. It is particularly helpful in its emphasis on the internal stratification of a peasant community.

SR, 31:3:724-5   R: E. A. Hammel

Author/Title Index

A. K. Tolstoy, 793
Ablin, Fred, 263
Abouchar, Alan, 222
Academic Writer's Guide to Periodicals, 2
Aczel, Tamas, 1421, 1438
Adams, Arthur E., 20, 42, 320, 629, 1145
Adams, Charles Francis, 139
Adams, Jan S., 20
Adizes, Ichak, 1555
Adolescent, 897
Ady, Endre, 1439
Against the Current, 919
Aid to Russia, 1941-1946, 481
Aitken, Gillon, 950
Albanian National Awakening, 1878-1912, 1299
Aleksandr Solzhenitsyn: Critical Essays and Documentary Materials, 798
Alexander, Alex E., 157
Alexander Blok: A Study in Rhythm and Metre, 816
Alexander Herzen and the Birth of Russian Socialism, 1812-1855, 1014
Alexander, John T., 590, 594, 595, 1577
Alexander Pushkin, 875
Alexander Solzhenitsyn: An International Bibliography of Writings by and about Him, 1962-1972, 804
Alexander, Tania, 1245
Alexandrov, Victor, 673
Allan, Richard, 1412
Allard, Sven, 312
Allen, W. E. D., 446
Allied Intervention in Russia, (1917-1920), 631
Alliluyeva, Svetlana, 127
Allworth, Edward, 1083, 1192, 1193, 1201
Alston, Patrick L., 269
Alternative Social Structures and Ritual Relations in the Balkans, 1609
Altshuler, Mordechai, 1206
Amalrik, Andrei, 395, 649, 879
Ambassador's Memoirs, 310
Ambler, Effie, 1078

Ambroz, Oton, 502
Amens in Amber, 1123
America and Russia in a Changing World, 480
America in Contemporary Soviet Literature, 494
America, Russia, Hemp and Napoleon, 252
American and Soviet Aid, 498
American and Soviet Society, 1055
American-Baltic Relations 1918-1922, 1118
American Bibliography of Slavic and East European Studies, 1
American Images of Soviet Foreign Policy, 500
American Liberals and the Russian Revolution, 487
American Policy toward Communist Eastern Europe, 1269
American Views of Soviet Russia, 1917-1965, 477
Americans and the Soviet Experiment, 1917-1933, 476
Amosoff, N., 775
Amphoux, Nancy, 854
An, Tai Sung, 503
Anabaptists and the Czech Brethren in Moravia, 1526-1628, 1383
Anarchists in the Russian Revolution, 630
Anatoli, A., 880
Ancient Civilization of Southern Siberia, 567
Anderson, M. S., 47
Anderson, Roger B., 776
Andrei Siniavskii and Julii Daniel, 794
Andres, Karl, 374
Andreyev, Nikolay, 1010
Andriekus, Leonardas, 1123
Anglo-Soviet Relations, 1917-1921, 543
Anna Akhmatova, 797
Annotated Bibliography of Writings on Judaism Published in the Soviet Union, 1960-1965, 1207

SUBJECT INDEX

This index lists topical subjects, primarily, with geographic subdivisions. For compound subjects, the uninverted form is preferred—e.g., "Intellectual history," instead of "History, Intellectual"—therefore, historical topics are scattered. The term "Russia" is used to refer to the country prior to 1917; "USSR" is used to designate the country after that time. In this index, "Russia" does *not* refer to the republic within the present-day USSR.